D0502908

inches	mm
Sixteenths	1cm
	2cm
1in.	3cm
	4cm
2in.	5cm
	6cm
	7cm
3in.	8cm
	9cm
4in.	10cm
	11cm
	12cm
5in.	13cm
	14cm
	15cm
6in.	16cm
	17cm
7in.	18cm
	19cm
	20cm

inches	mm
8in.	21cm
	22cm
9in.	23cm
	24cm
10in.	25cm
	26cm
	27cm
11in.	28cm
	29cm
	30cm
12in.	31cm
	32cm
1ft 1in.	33cm
	34cm
	35cm
1ft 2in.	36cm
	37cm
1ft 3in.	38cm
	39cm
	40cm

inches	mm
1ft 4in.	41cm
	42cm
1ft 5in.	43cm
	44cm
	45cm
1ft 6in.	46cm
	47cm
1ft 7in.	48cm
	49cm
	50cm
1ft 8in.	51cm
	52cm
1ft 9in.	53cm
	54cm
	55cm
1ft 10in.	56cm
	57cm
1ft 11in.	58cm
	59cm
	60cm

inches	mm
2ft	61cm
	62cm
2ft 1in.	63cm
	64cm
	65cm
2ft 2in.	66cm
	67cm
2ft 3in.	68cm
	69cm
	70cm
2ft 4in.	71cm
	72cm
2ft 5in.	73cm
	74cm
	75cm
2ft 6in.	76cm
	77cm
	78cm
2ft 7in.	79cm
	80cm

inches	mm
2ft 8in.	81cm
	82cm
	83cm
2ft 9in.	84cm
	85cm
	86cm
2ft 10in.	87cm
	88cm
2ft 11in.	89cm
	90cm
	91cm
3ft	92cm
	93cm
3ft 1in.	94cm
	95cm
	96cm
3ft 2in.	97cm
	98cm
3ft 3in.	99cm
	100cm

inches	es
1ft	30·5cm
2ft	61·0cm
3ft	91·4cm
3ft 3¼in.	1 metre (100cm)
4ft	121·9cm
5ft	152·4cm
6ft	182·9cm
6ft 6¾in.	2 metres (200cm)
7ft	213·4cm
8ft	243·8cm
9ft	274·3cm
9ft 10¹⁄₁₆in.	3 metres (300cm)

Reader's Digest

Crafts & Hobbies

Reader's Digest

CRAFTS & HOBBIES

The Reader's Digest Association, Inc.
Pleasantville, New York / Montreal

Staff

Project Director
John Speicher

Project Art Director
Judy Skorpil

Associate Editors
Valentin Chu
Sally French
James Forsht
Robert V. Huber
Ian Walker

Designers
Morris Karol
Edward R. Lipinski
Joel Musler

Art Production Associate
Nina Kowaloff

Picture Researcher
Margaret Mathews

Copy Editor
Susan Parker

Art Assistant
Ken Chaya

Editorial Assistants
Marguerite Anderson
Caroline Miller

Photography
Ernest Coppolino
Morris Karol
W. A. Sonntag

Group Art Director
David Trooper

Special Illustrations
Nicholas Calabrese
pages 232, 234, 235
Larissa Lawrynenko
pages 227, 228, 229, 230, 231

Contributors

Contributing Editor
Daniel Weiss

Contributing Writers
Susan Chace
Lilla Pennant
John Maury Warde
David Wright

Contributing Artists
John A. Lind Corporation
Ken Rice
Jim Silks/Randall Lieu
Ray Skibinski
Vicki Vebell
Mary Wilshire

Chief Photographer
Joseph Barnell

Technical Adviser
Sandra Cruickshank

Consultants
See pages 6–7

Photo Credits
See page 456

Special Credits
See page 456

The editors are grateful for the assistance provided by the following organizations:

Allcraft Tool & Supply Co., Inc.
The American Crafts Council
Associated American Artists, Inc.
Baldwin Pottery, Inc.
S.A. Bendheim
Brooklyn Botanic Garden
Charles Brand Etching
    and Litho Presses
Cooper-Hewitt Museum,
    Smithsonian Institution's
    National Museum of Design
Craft Students League,
    YWCA of the City of New York
Editorial Photocolor Archives, Inc.
Excalibur Bronze Sculpture Corp.
Florence Duhl Gallery
Garrett Wade Co., Inc.
General Electric Co.
Glass Masters Guild
Joseph Dross Woodworking
The Max Corp.
Metropolitan Museum of Art
Milan Labs
Origami Center of America
Robert Brent Corp.
Rockwell International,
    Power Tool Division
School Products Co., Inc.
Sculpture House
Sears, Roebuck and Co.
Simon's Hardware, Inc.
The Stanley Works
Talas, Division of Technical
    Library Service, Inc.
Tehnicraft Lapidaries Corp.
Wetzler Clamp Co., Inc.

The credits that appear on page 456 are hereby made a part of this copyright page.

ISBN 0-88850-089-0

Contents

Consultants' biographies

Carolyn Bell—*Macramé.* Miss Bell is a distinguished macramé artist whose work has been shown in New York galleries. As consultant for the macramé chapter, she made a major contribution to this book by translating her expertise into directions that can easily be understood and followed by laymen. She also designed the projects for the chapter—a simple but beautiful plant hanger and a wall hanging, the design for which can be reduced and used to make a necklace.

Anthony Bianchi—*Woodworking: small box project.* Mr. Bianchi is a free-lance industrial designer and craftsman. He received a bachelor of fine arts degree in dimensional design from the Philadelphia College of Art and did graduate work at the School for American Craftsmen at the Rochester Institute of Technology. While still an undergraduate, he was awarded a National Merit Award for Young Americans from the American Crafts Council. His work has been exhibited at the Museum of Contemporary Crafts in New York City.

Nancy Bullard—*Basketry: splint and wicker baskets.* Mrs. Bullard teaches basketry at the New Canaan YMCA and at the Ridgefield Community House (both in Connecticut). She studied preschool education at Alfred and Wayne State universities. But after participating in a one-day crafts workshop in 1974, she became entranced with basketry and went on to amass more than 90 hours of study in the subject at the Brookfield (Connecticut) Craft Center and to do independent research in the history of basketry. Mrs. Bullard has exhibited her work in art shows and crafts fairs throughout the northeastern United States and at various historic preservation sites. She is a specialist in wickerwork and in American Indian basketry techniques.

Victoria Chess—*Drawing; Painting; Printmaking: silk screen.* Interested in the fine arts since her childhood, Victoria Chess attended the Boston Museum School for specialized study after completing high school. Today she is a prominent illustrator of both books and magazine articles. She is widely known for her award-winning children's books.

Robert Conover—*Printmaking: etching.* Mr. Conover, an artist who has won renown for his abstract paintings and woodcuts, teaches painting, drawing, woodcutting, and graphics at The New School for Social Research, the Brooklyn Museum Art School, and the Newark School of Fine and Industrial Art. He studied art at the Philadelphia Museum School, the Barnes Foundation (Merion, Pennsylvania), the Art Students League of New York, and the Brooklyn Museum School—thus receiving a thorough grounding in all the techniques of painting, drawing, and printmaking. Mr. Conover has had several one-man shows and has been represented in group shows at many major art museums throughout the world. His work is in the permanent collections of many individuals and museums, including the Smithsonian Institution, the Library of Congress, the New Jersey State Museum, the Brooklyn Museum, the Baltimore Museum, the Philadelphia Museum of Art, the National Gallery of Art, the Whitney Museum of American Art, the Museum of Art in Skopje, Yugoslavia, and the Tokyo Museum of Modern Art.

Barbara Montgomery Danneman—*Quiltmaking.* Mrs. Danneman is the author of *Step-by-Step Quiltmaking.* She currently teaches quiltmaking at four different schools in New York City, including Barnard College and the Craft Students League. After receiving a bachelor of arts degree from Bowling Green State University in Ohio and a master's degree in painting from Teacher's College of Columbia University, she successfully pursued a painting career. Then, in the mid-1960's, she turned almost exclusively to weaving and quiltmaking, devoting most of her time to demonstrating, teaching, and working in those crafts. Her work has been shown in various exhibits throughout the nation.

Doris R. Davis—*Decoupage.* Mrs. Davis is the founder and owner of Adventures in Crafts, a decoupage specialty shop and instruction center, and coauthor of *Step-by-Step Decoupage.* She has a bachelor of arts degree from Sarah Lawrence College. After seeing her first piece of decoupage (a glass lamp in an antique-store window in Virginia), she was not satisfied until she had learned the craft herself. Mrs. Davis taught herself decoupage, then took advanced seminars in the craft. Since she founded Adventures in Crafts in 1971, she has devoted herself to decoupage and its "endless varieties of materials, styles, and techniques."

Randi Feldman—*Pottery: techniques* (in part) *and projects.* Miss Feldman is a ceramics instructor and a cooperative partner in the Ceramics Retail Shop and Gallery in New York City. Her work has won awards at shows in New York and New Jersey. Miss Feldman earned a bachelor's degree in philosophy (with a minor in art) at the City College of the City University of New York and studied pottery techniques at various New York workshops. She was the principal consultant for the pottery chapter and created most of the pottery projects in this book.

Kathleen Finneran—*Printmaking: woodcut.* Mrs. Finneran is a commercial illustrator. She has a master's degree in art from the University of Michigan and has taught two-dimensional design at Wisconsin State University. Besides doing illustrations, she constructs three-dimensional models for advertising displays.

William J. Finneran, Jr.—*Wood sculpture; Modeling, moldmaking, and casting sculpture.* Mr. Finneran is an associate professor and chairman of the Department of Art and Art History at the William Paterson College of New Jersey and a consultant to the Brookhaven National Laboratories Division of Applied Science for testing new sculpture materials. He has a master of fine arts degree from the University of Michigan. Mr. Finneran has had his sculpture shown at more than a dozen galleries around the United States, and he has served as visiting artist at several U.S. and Canadian universities.

Maurice Fraser—*Woodworking.* Mr. Fraser is a cabinetmaker and a harpsicord builder. After acquiring a bachelor's degree in musicology from Temple University, he did graduate work in music at Hunter College and New York University. He also studied art at the Queen Street Settlement House in Philadelphia and at the Philadelphia Museum of Art. In order to learn to build harpsichords, he studied woodworking at the Craft Students League in New York City and became so adept that he was asked to teach woodworking at the school. In addition to building harpsichords, Mr. Fraser also repairs and tunes them for Columbia Artists and Hunter College. Most of the projects in the woodworking chapter were designed and built by him.

Jennie French—*Stained glass: copper foil technique.* Miss French is the author of *Glass Works,* a widely read introduction to working in the copper foil technique of stained glass. Her latest book, *Design for Stained Glass,* was published in 1979. Miss French has worked in various arts and crafts from an early age, but now she devotes all her time to glass. After being introduced to stained glass by friends, she taught herself the essentials of the craft, then studied advanced techniques at the Philadelphia Museum College of Art. Between books, she does free-lance stained glass work and frequently gives lectures and demonstrations. She created the stained glass box, terrarium, and lamp that appear as projects in the stained glass chapter.

Allan Geschwind—*Woodworking: Shaker sewing table.* Mr. Geschwind is a lawyer who devotes much of his free time to woodworking. He studied woodworking at the Craft Students League in New York City, where he now occasionally teaches. His special interest is Shaker furniture.

Jack Grossman—*Woodworking: jewelry chest.* Mr. Grossman is a structural draftsman who discovered the joys of woodworking in mid-life. He studied woodworking at the Craft Students League in New York City, where he later taught courses in making working drawings for woodcraft. All his work is of his own design. It ranges from jewelry boxes and birdcages to worktables and beds.

Fay Halpern—*Batik and tie-dyeing.* Mrs. Halpern is a textile artist and an educator. After graduating with honors from Indiana University (M.F.A. in painting), she advanced to batik and tie-dyeing as an art form. She has taught art, art history, batik, and fabric dyeing at major universities in the United States and England. Her work is in the Metropolitan Museum of Art and in many private collections. Aware of the health hazards associated with many chemical dyes, Mrs. Halpern has been among the pioneers in developing techniques for working in contemporary ways with natural plant dyes. She has provided her own dye recipes for this book.

Helen Hosking—*Enameling.* Mrs. Hosking is an artist and a teacher. After receiving a bachelor's degree in painting and sculpture from The Cooper Union, she took graduate courses in working with gold and silver at New Paltz University, where she learned enameling techniques. She has taught enameling in a number of schools in New York and North Carolina, and her work has been shown in galleries throughout the United States and in Mexico. Mrs. Hosking specializes in the painting techniques of enameling, often putting her work on large pieces of metal she has salvaged from old stoves. She created the cloisonné and Limoges pieces shown on page 349 and all the projects in the enameling chapter.

Frank E. Johnson—*Winemaking.* Mr. Johnson is vice president of Bonsal Seggerman and Co., Inc. (wine importers), East Coast editor of *Wine World* magazine, and coauthor of the *World Catalogue of Wine Labels.* He has a master's degree in history from the University of Massachusetts. While studying European history and traveling extensively in Europe, he became actively interested in wines and began writing on the subject. As wine editor for *Beverage Media,* he created the *Professional Wine Reference,* a wine dictionary.

Kathleen Adelmann Koch—*Quiltmaking: quilting frame.* Mrs. Koch is a self-taught quilter. Feeling the need for a more efficient quilting frame, she spent three years developing the frame shown in this book.

Michelle Lester—*Weaving.* Mrs. Lester heads her own textiles studio, which produces tapestries to decorate the offices of many of the nation's major corporations. After studying at the Penland School of Crafts and earning a master's degree in design from Syracuse University, Mrs. Lester taught courses in textiles, weaving, and dyeing fabrics at colleges, museums, and craft schools throughout the northeastern United States. Her work has been shown at numerous galleries and she has had one-woman shows in New York City and Los Angeles.

Sandra Newman—*Basketry: coiling and twining.* Mrs. Newman is an anthropologist, teacher, poet, basket weaver, and author of *Indian Basket Weaving,* published in 1974. She was born in Calcutta, India, on Christmas Day, received a bachelor of arts degree from Wilson College, and studied anthropology at London School of Anthropology and Arizona State University. For nine years she worked with American Indian weavers on reservations in California and the Southwest. She has also taught at numerous universities and workshops throughout the United States. Her work includes a wide range of contemporary forms as well as traditional basketry.

Richard Rapaport—*Pottery: techniques* (in part). Mr. Rapaport is the founder and director of Studio Workshop, a pottery school in New York City. He earned a master of fine arts degree at Yale University. Then, after visiting the Hayatack Mountain School of Crafts in 1968, he became interested in pottery and taught himself the craft. Mr. Rapaport has developed a method of teaching the basics of pottery in a short time. He also founded Center Line Arts, a corporation devoted to teaching the creative arts to the elderly, handicapped, and disadvantaged.

Joe Rothstein—*Lapidary.* Mr. Rothstein, a retired industrial engineer and an associate in mineral sciences with the American Museum of Natural History, teaches lapidary and mineralogy at the museum, at Baruch College of the City University of New York, and at the Craft Students League. He began studying gemology at the American Museum in 1930 and went on to study lapidary and mineralogy in the United States and England. He is a charter member and past president of the Lapidary and Gem Society of New York and past president of the New York Mineralogical Club. The *Lapidary Journal* lists him as one of the writers who have contributed greatly to the increasing American interest in lapidary since World War II. Mr. Rothstein has crisscrossed the United States twice on field trips and has also collected extensively in Canada. He claims that in the 50 years he has been working with gemstones he has "turned over enough rock in the field looking for minerals to build a tower higher than the Empire State Building."

Thomas Venturella—*Stained glass: lead came technique.* Mr. Venturella designs and builds stained glass windows, lamps, and other pieces for churches, commercial establishments, and private collections. His work often incorporates intricate, detailed designs calling for tiny pieces of glass. He is associated with the New York studio of artist Benoît Gilsoul, where he restores and repairs the works of leading glaziers of all eras, including pieces by Louis Comfort Tiffany. Mr. Venturella has a bachelor's degree in painting from the Art Institute of Chicago and the University of Chicago. After experimenting with glass, he fell in love with the medium and abandoned painting for it. He apprenticed in glasswork with Greenland Studios in New York and has been working in glass ever since. Mr. Venturella designed and built the leaded glass panel used as a project for the stained glass chapter.

Joan Berg Victor—*Papier-mâché.* Mrs. Victor is an artist, craftsman, and writer with a master's degree in art from Yale University. She has worked in a wide variety of crafts and art forms, including papier-mâché, jewelry design, dough sculpture, and painting. Books play as large a part in her life as art. She has written and illustrated many works, including children's books on the family, shells, and tarantulas as well as adult fiction and poetry. Mrs. Victor also works with handicapped children as an art therapist.

John Warde—*Metalworking.* Mr. Warde is a free-lance writer and a self-taught craftsman in metal and wood. He was educated at Middlebury College and the University of Virginia. His interest in metalworking grew out of watching a tinsmith make lanterns and chandeliers using only the simplest traditional hand tools. Mr. Warde designed and made the projects in the metalworking chapter.

Carol Westfall—*Basketry: plaiting.* Miss Westfall, a leading authority on fibers and fabrics, is assistant professor of fine arts at Montclair State College and author of *Plaiting, Step-by-Step,* published in 1976. After receiving a master of fine arts degree from the Maryland Institute College of Art, she studied weaving at the Instituto Allende in Mexico. Her work has been exhibited throughout North America and Europe, often in one-woman shows, and her pieces are in the permanent collections of the Delaware Art Museum, the New Jersey State Museum, and various private collections.

John Westinghouse—*Leatherworking.* Mr. Westinghouse has established a reputation for his modern sandal and shoulder-bag designs with simple, unobtrusive lines and has exhibited his leatherware at the prestigious International Craft Show. Most recently, he has been associated with Mad Brook Design and the Sandal Shop in Hartford, Connecticut.

Catherine Wood—*Jewelry.* Miss Wood is a professional jeweler who designs and makes jewelry for many fine stores throughout the country. She studied painting and environmental design at the Philadelphia College of Art, and then, seeking a way to use her artistic talents to supplement her income, she took some craft courses and became drawn to jewelry. Miss Wood studied jewelrymaking at the Abbey School of Jewelry and Art Metal Design and has been devoting herself to the craft ever since. She has shown her jewelry at crafts fairs throughout the country, including the prestigious Rhinebeck Crafts Fair. Miss Wood designed and made the silver jewelry projects in this book.

About this book

We live in an age when the flick of a dial on a television set brings us immediate diversion—enough to fill all our evenings and weekends year in and year out. A quick trip to a department store or shopping center provides us with an endless choice of manufactured comforts—machine-made wearing apparel, veneer furniture, plastic toys, vinyl fabrics, precooked foods, and even reproductions of famous works of art. While we have grown accustomed to these conveniences and rely upon some of them as necessities of everyday life, many of us have begun looking back to a less commercial, more individually creative time. To a time when people enjoyed the pleasures of the quilting bee and savored the aroma of bread baking in their own kitchens. To a time when they knew the feel of natural woven fabrics and the unalloyed honesty of handcrafted furniture.

All over North America people are once again doing things with their own hands. Hundreds of thousands are forsaking their television sets and heading for the sewing room or basement workshop for a few hours of stimulating creative activity. Some of them concentrate on handcrafting home furnishings that they cannot afford to buy or that are just not available any longer. Others create gifts for friends and relatives or work simply to enjoy the satisfaction of personal creation. In response to this new surge of interest in crafts, schools and community centers are giving classes in crafts of every description. In addition, crafts fairs, where home craftsmen can display—and market—their creations, are springing up in almost every county of every province and state.

Some observers of current trends have gone so far as to call this phenomenal new interest in crafts a crafts revival. We at Reader's Digest agree with this assessment. More and more people who have never before attempted to build or stitch or weave or carve or shape or paint with their own hands are now eager to learn how. We have designed this book to provide basic help for such enthusiasts.

There is much in this book for the newcomer to the world of crafts. More than 40 crafts are treated in these pages. Each chapter provides a brief history of a craft and photographs of one or two of its finest examples. Then the tools, materials, and techniques of the craft are illustrated and discussed in detail. Finally, specific projects are suggested for most of the crafts, complete with plans and illustrated instructions for making them.

You can use this book in many ways. You can browse through it for your reading pleasure or to satisfy your curiosity about the way certain things are done—how a loom works, for example, or how a stained glass window is put together or how a dovetail joint is cut for a wooden cabinet. You can also use it as a textbook and teach yourself crafts you have always wanted to learn. If you are considering working in a craft but cannot decide which craft you would best like to work in, you can use this book as a giant menu. Read through it or dip first into one chapter, then into another, and find out exactly what is involved in the crafts you think might interest you, paying particular attention to the variety of tools and materials needed and the ease or difficulty of the techniques.

Crafts & Hobbies contains more than 4,000 drawings and photographs, detailing just about everything there is to know about each craft. The chapters on the more complex crafts present a variety of possible do-it-yourself projects, ranging from the easy to the difficult. If you are new to a craft, you can begin with the easy projects and then, if you wish, proceed to the difficult ones. But one word of warning: before you do any work on a project from this book, read through the entire chapter it appears in. Do not plunge right into the project, as there is much pertinent information in the techniques section of the chapter that you will need to know, but which is not repeated in the directions for making the project.

In consideration of the part-time craftsman who does not wish to spend a lot of money on a craft, many of the chapters offer choices as to investment in equipment and supplies. For example, the chapter on pottery provides instructions for creating pots on a potter's wheel and firing them in an electric kiln. But you do not have to buy either a wheel or an electric kiln to work with pottery, for the chapter also contains pages on hand-building pottery and on firing earthenware pots in a charcoal-burning kiln you can build yourself with rocks or bricks.

But *Crafts & Hobbies* is not for beginners only. Far from it. The consultants who worked with us in creating these pages (see *Consultants' biographies,* pp. 6–7) are among the leading craftsmen and craftswomen working today. In conjunction with the editors, these experts have striven to make this volume a veritable encyclopedia of major crafts techniques. Thus, the experienced artisan or hobbyist will find *Crafts & Hobbies* a helpful reference volume, not only to check himself on key steps in his own craft activities but to familiarize himself with the work of others.

Although the consultants and editors pride themselves on the wealth of high-level technical information in this volume, the book also contains many activities and projects that make simple and enjoyable pastimes for youngsters. Turn, for instance, to Decoupage, Candlemaking, Papier-mâché, Batik and tie-dyeing, Origami, Painting, Printing on fabric, Stenciling, or Collage. Similarly, an adult can find inspiration for activities on a rainy afternoon or an evening at home in almost any chapter. It costs very little, for example, to make a fashionable and attractive jump-ring bracelet (see the jewelry chapter) or to bake one of the exotic or traditional breads from another part of the world (see Breads from around the world) or to dry flowers for your own arrangements (see the chapter on drying and preserving flowers).

Best of all, this is a book that may introduce you to talents you never realized you had. It may bring you face to face for the first time with that wonderful instinct, your own creative urge.

—The Editors

Creating a home workshop

A room of one's own—or a garage or basement workshop

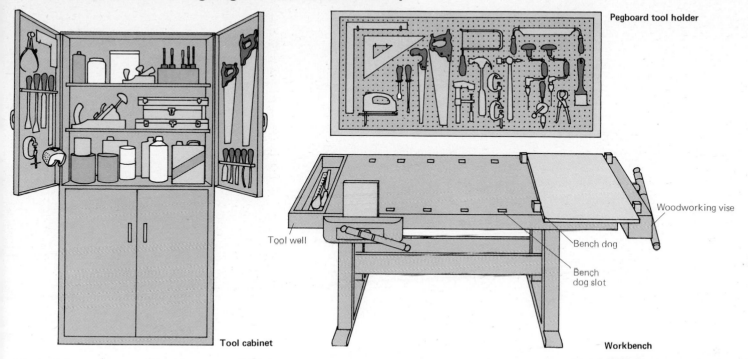

Pegboard tool holder

Tool well

Tool cabinet

Bench dog

Bench dog slot

Woodworking vise

Workbench

A good workbench is a necessity in such crafts as woodworking and wood sculpting. A bench provides a stable, level work surface; its vises and adjustable bench dogs act as a system to hold almost any piece firmly in a variety of positions, as suggested by the illustration at left. Benches come in a range of prices. They are often sold as kits that can be assembled at home. Choose one of a sturdy hardwood, with a tool well.

Tool storage is an important consideration in any workroom. Wall-mounted pegboard offers the simplest way to hold light tools. If you build or purchase a cabinet, provide a holder for long tools, such as the inner door areas of the cabinet illustrated at left.

Many of the crafts covered in this volume do not require a workshop.

Macramé, origami (paper folding), string art, and flower drying can be done in almost any location in your house or apartment. Likewise, batik, tie-dyeing, collage, printing on cloth, bookbinding, papier-mâché, decoupage, basket weaving, stenciling, candlemaking, and watercolor can be done in the kitchen, the laundry room, the den, or any convenient room you can temporarily take over. Few flammable or toxic materials are involved—only the wax used in making candles and dyes for batik and tie-dyeing—and these are easily controlled and contained. Cleanup time is not long. The necessary storage space for tools and materials is small—a shelf or two or a drawer in a cabinet. A small table or a kitchen counter makes an adequate work surface, which can be covered with newspaper or a drop cloth to catch drippings and waste.

But certain crafts either require or are more conveniently carried on in a permanent workshop, workroom, or studio. Some of these crafts, such as pottery and woodworking, involve large numbers of tools and materials or heavy equipment that cannot easily be stored in a closet or cupboard. Other crafts require techniques that can be a bit messy, such as cutting glass and soldering for stained glass construction, or grinding and polishing for lapidary and jewelrymaking. Still other crafts take long periods of time, and unfinished projects must be left undisturbed between work sessions, as in quilting and weaving. A separate studio is also advisable for enameling, oil painting, printmaking, wood sculpture, modeling, moldmaking and casting, metalworking, and other artistic crafts that you plan to do on a sustained basis.

As suggested, for crafts such as quilting and weaving the workshop may be no more than a separate room within your house. For woodworking and pottery, for which the equipment and tools are numerous, often heavy, and may require special wiring, the workshop should be located outside the living area of the house—in the basement, in the garage, or in an outbuilding. And where fumes or dusts must be ventilated or contained, or where toxic or flammable chemicals are employed, it is always wise to locate the shop well away from the house.

This chapter covers such aspects of the home workshop as ventilation, tool storage, workbenches, flammables, and workshop housekeeping. Attention is directed in particular to the health hazards associated with the procedures and materials used in certain crafts.

The chapters that follow—*Leatherworking, Stained glass, Woodworking, Pottery,* etc.—detail each craft's tools and materials. By consulting these pages, and by drawing on your own growing experience in a new craft, you will eventually decide whether you want your own individual workshop, where to locate it, and how you want to furnish and equip it.

Many schools and community centers offer crafts classes. Enrolling in classes is one of the best ways to experience firsthand the essentials of a good workshop. If you become deeply involved in any craft, no matter how light the equipment used, you may find it best to set aside a room of your own within your residence. Why? Simply so that you will not always have to pick up after yourself, and to keep your family and friends from disturbing you in moments of creation.

Creating a home workshop

Ventilation

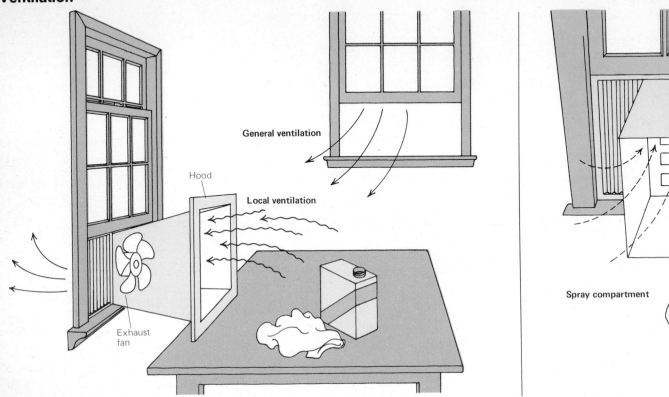

General ventilation

Local ventilation

Hood

Exhaust fan

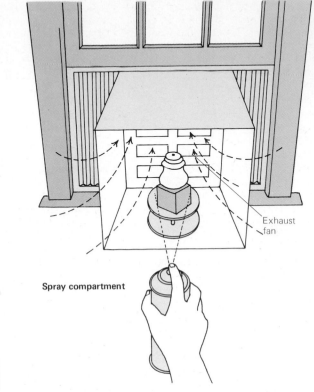

Exhaust fan

Spray compartment

Good ventilation is among the most important considerations in designing a home workshop. Many crafts procedures and materials raise dust or emit toxic fumes. Anyone breathing the air in such an environment risks serious injury to his or her health, as explained in *Health hazards of crafts materials,* beginning on page 11. In combination with good housekeeping habits, proper ventilation can eliminate or greatly reduce any threat to your health.

The meaning of the term "ventilation" is often misunderstood. In fact, there are two types of ventilation: local, or exhaust, ventilation, and general ventilation. Local ventilation systems capture contaminants at or near their point of origin and remove them

from the workshop environment before they can pollute it. General ventilation systems—open windows, a window fan, or an air conditioner—that bring fresh air into the room simply dilute the pollutants, lowering their concentrations in the air.

General ventilation, therefore, cannot make the air safe to breathe, particularly when concentrations of certain substances as low as a few parts per million are dangerous to human health. General ventilation is used primarily to cool the air and to make it more comfortable. Local ventilation is necessary to remove harmful substances from the air.

Local ventilation. The diagram above shows a typical local ventilation

setup. General ventilation is used with it to bring in outside air to replace that exhausted by the local system.

A local system usually employs a hood to trap fumes and dust. The hood is attached to a duct leading to an exhaust fan, which draws the contaminants through the duct, expelling them to the outside. Such a system can be fitted with a filtering device to clean the contaminated air before it is expelled into the environment. A connecting duct may not be necessary where the work surface can be located directly before a window exhaust fan.

The most important consideration is the location of the hood. It should be as close as possible to the source of the contaminant. The hood should be po-

sitioned so that it draws the contaminated air away from you; in other words, the work area should be in front of you with the hood behind the work area—either at the same level as the work or slightly higher. Contaminated air should not pass through your breathing zone or the breathing zones of anyone else moving about the workshop before it is captured by the hood.

To trap the pollutants and to pull them into the hood, the exhaust velocity must be greater than the normal velocity of the air in the work area (as caused by drafts or mechanical agitation). Since exhaust velocity decreases sharply with distance, the farther away the hood is located from the work area, the stronger the exhaust fan must be.

Health hazards of crafts materials

In recent years medical researchers have turned their attention to so-called occupational diseases. These are illnesses that afflict people who are exposed by the nature of their jobs to toxic substances, often over long periods of time. Largely as a result of this recent research, new information has come to light concerning materials and substances that are used in a number of popular crafts.

A few of the substances traditionally employed by craftsmen are now known to be so hazardous that no one should risk even brief exposure to them. But this is not true for the majority of crafts materials; with these, the danger is directly related to the frequency and quantity of exposure. Moreover, there are many means by which you can protect yourself against the ill effects of toxic materials—means that are often as simple as good studio housekeeping or wearing a dust mask. Ventilation is a primary consideration for a healthy working environment, and an article on the subject appears on page 10.

The purpose of this section is not to detract from your pleasure in your craft. Rather, the purpose is to help ensure you years of excellent health in pursuing your art or craft. The first subject discussed below is volatile and caustic chemicals. Various crafts are then discussed, with the emphasis on protecting against specific hazards involved in each craft.

In addition to the information given in these paragraphs, there are a few rules that you should always follow. First, never use any substance before reading the instructions and warnings on the manufacturer's label. Second, consult your physician at the first sign of any infirmity—such as a skin rash, headache, dizziness, difficulty in breathing, or nausea—that you feel may be caused by toxic substances. Finally, always suspect exposure to toxic substances if a symptom goes away or improves when you take a few days off from working at your craft, then returns or worsens when you begin working again.

Remember that if your workshop is located within your home, both you and your family may be subject to continuing exposure to a toxic agent. For this reason, the workshop housekeeping procedures recommended in the ensuing paragraphs are doubly important in a home workshop.

Solvents and other chemicals. The threat from volatile chemicals is threefold: disease or poisoning that results from breathing toxic fumes or from accidentally swallowing a substance; burns and injuries resulting from contact between a substance and skin or eyes or with the mouth, nose, and throat passages; and the danger of fire or explosion where volatile vapors are present near a source of ignition.

The hazards of breathing the air in a workshop where volatile chemicals are used can be greatly reduced and even eliminated with proper ventilation (see *Ventilation*, p. 10). Good housekeeping habits are also important—containers of volatile fluids should be capped or corked immediately after use, spills should be wiped up at once, and soaked rags and paper towels should be kept in a closed container until you can dispose of them.

Never eat or drink in an area where you are working with toxic fluids. You risk picking up the wrong container or accidentally getting poison into the food or drink.

Never smoke in a workshop where volatile fluids are present. Many solvents are flammable at room temperatures. Flammability is determined by the fluid's flash point. This is the lowest temperature at which a liquid emits enough vapor to form an ignitable mixture with the surrounding air.

Combustion can be triggered by any ignition source, such as a lit cigarette, a pilot flame, or an electrical spark.

The National Fire Code of Canada classifies any liquid as flammable if its flash point is below 37.8°C. And as the table at right shows, many common solvents are flammable at ordinary room temperatures. The fluids that appear in the table should be stored only in the approved safety containers in which they are sold.

The best way to protect your hands from contact with caustic chemicals is by wearing gloves. Polyvinyl gloves—including the inexpensive disposable "surgeons'" type—will protect against most solvents except those containing heavy concentrations of ketones such as acetone. Butyl and natural rubber protect against acetone and other ketones but not against aromatic solvents, such as polyester resin, chlorinated hydrocarbons, petroleum distillates, and acids. Polyvinyl chloride or neoprene rubber is the best choice for working with acids and caustics.

In lieu of gloves, silicone barrier creams, available in many drugstores, may provide an effective protective coating for your hands. Follow the instructions on the packages.

In general, the hazard posed by a toxic substance depends on its potency, on the amount to which you are exposed, and on the length of time of the exposure. A person working with toxic solvents eight hours a day every day is generally more vulnerable than someone using them a few hours a week.

With this in mind, we will examine what is known about the toxicity of the most common solvents. They may be present as ingredients in brand-name products, or they may be sold under their generic names. Check manufacturers' labels to determine which are present in any product.

(continued on next page)

Flash points of solvents

Under 22.8°C	acetone
	benzine (VM&P naphtha)
	benzol
	ethyl acetate
	ethyl alcohol
	ethyl ether
	gasoline
	methanol
	methyl ethyl ketone
	petroleum ether
	(petroleum naphtha)
	toluene
22.8°C–37.8°C	isopropyl alcohol
	methyl isobutyl ketone
	propyl alcohol
	styrene
	trichlorethylene
	turpentine
	xylene
37.8°C–60°C	acetic acid
	kerosene
	mineral spirits
	Stoddard solvent

Safety goggles

Respirator

Polyvinyl gloves

Creating a home workshop

Health hazards of crafts materials (continued)

Alcohols. Almost all solvents are poisonous if breathed in or swallowed in sufficient amounts. Alcohols are no exception. They are both anesthetics and irritants. Breathing high concentrations of methanol (wood or methyl alcohol) can cause fatigue, headache, dizziness, blurred vision, and permanent damage to body organs. If swallowed, methanol can cause blindness and sometimes death. Amyl alcohol acts on the nervous system to produce symptoms similar to those caused by methanol. Denatured alcohol—ethanol (potable alcohol) containing some methanol—is the safest of the alcohols for the workshop. It is used as a shellac thinner, as a varnish and paint remover, and as a lacquer thinner.

Aromatic hydrocarbons. These and chlorinated hydrocarbons are the most lethal solvents. Benzene (or benzol) is an aromatic hydrocarbon that is so dangerous that you should never use it, even for brief periods. Long-term exposure to small amounts has a cumulative effect that may include the destruction of bone marrow and blood cells. It is a known cause of leukemia. Xylene is also highly toxic. A somewhat safer substitute for benzene and xylene is toluol; however, it should be used only sparingly and where there is excellent local ventilation (see *Ventilation*, p. 10). Aromatic hydrocarbons are used as resin solvents, as paint and varnish removers, as dye solvents, and for silk-screen washup. Other solvents perform many of these functions adequately enough for crafts purposes, and they are not as dangerous.

(Note: the less powerful solvent called benzine, an aliphatic hydrocarbon, is not the same as benzene. See *Aliphatic hydrocarbons*.)

Chlorinated hydrocarbons. All of these chemicals are very dangerous. They dissolve the fatty layer in the skin, causing severe dermatitis. They can cause cancer in such body organs as the kidneys and liver.

The most potent of these solvents is carbon tetrachloride. It can be absorbed through the skin. Exposure to high concentrations in the air results in unconsciousness and may cause death. Related chemicals include chloroform, acetylene tetrachloride (tetrachloroethane), ethylene dichloride, perchloroethylene, and trichloroethylene. All are used as solvents for waxes, oils, resins, and greases. Always substitute a safer solvent.

Aliphatic hydrocarbons. When used in a well-ventilated workshop (see *Ventilation*, p. 10), these are fairly safe solvents. All are derived from petroleum. The most volatile is naptha (petroleum ether). It is followed in order of volatility by gasoline, benzine (VM & P naptha), mineral spirits, and kerosene. Kerosene poses the most serious threat to health, as it is a strong lung and skin irritant. All of these solvents are highly flammable, and strong precautions should be taken regarding their safe storage. Use them only away from possible ignition sources. They serve as paint thinners, varnish thinners, and solvents for rubber cement and for some cleanup tasks.

Ketones and other odorous solvents. These solvents have strong odors that warn of heavy concentrations in the air. Acetone (nail polish remover), a ketone, is among the safest of solvents, although its flammability dictates that it be used cautiously. Ketones such as methyl butyl (MBK) should be avoided because they cause paralysis of the extremities. Acetone is a solvent for lacquers, oils, waxes, and plastics. Turpentine, among the most commonly used solvents, is a paint and varnish thinner. For many, however, it is a skin irritant, and its vapors will irritate the eyes, sinuses, and throat after protracted exposure. Turpentine can cause headache, anxiety, mental confusion, and gastritis, and it should be used only in a well-ventilated area (see *Ventilation*, p. 10). Containers should be capped immediately after use.

Aerosols, acids, and alkalies. Aerosol sprays should be used only in conjunction with local ventilation (see *Ventilation*, p. 10). Good general ventilation is not adequate to protect your health. Airbrushes and spray guns should also be used only with the very best local ventilation arrangements.

Acids are used primarily for etching designs in metal—either on metalware or on printmaking plates. Wear PVC or neoprene rubber protective gloves when handling acids. Should you get any on your skin, wash immediately with cool water. When you are diluting an acid, always pour the acid into the water—never the other way around.

The fumes that are produced when metal is etched with nitric acid burn lung tissue. Protracted exposure to the fumes can cause death. Therefore, etching with nitric acid and other strong acids should be done only in conjunction with local ventilation (see *Ventilation*, p. 10). Most etching processes can be carried out with relatively weak acids, such as ferric chloride; their use is advocated for the beginner.

Alkalies will burn and ulcerate the skin. Wear protective gloves when handling them. The most dangerous are caustic potash (potassium hydroxide) and caustic soda (sodium hydroxide). Quicklime (calcium oxide), slaked lime (calcium hydroxide), ammonia, and sodium silicate and metasilicate can also burn the skin.

Both quicklime dust and ammonia vapors can harm the lungs. If you use these substances frequently, do so only in conjunction with local ventilation.

Dyeing fabric and yarn. Because they are sold under manufacturers' trade names and are not always identified chemically, it is difficult to single out any dye that can be considered perfectly safe. Researchers suspect that the ingredients in some chemical dyes cause such diseases as asthma, dermatitis, and bladder cancer.

Exposure occurs as the result of inhaling dye powders when mixing dyes and by absorption of the liquid dyes through the skin. The latter is a hazard even when using premixed dyes.

People who become engaged full time in a craft involving powdered dyes may want to acquire an air-purifying respirator to wear when handling the powders. Anyone who works with dyes even infrequently should observe the following precautions:

1. To minimize the amount of dust in the air, use scissors to snip open dye packets. Do not tear them open.

2. Add the powder carefully to the water to avoid stirring up dust. If the powder comes in jars, transfer it to the water using a long-handled spoon.

3. Wear heavy-duty rubber gloves when handling dye solutions and freshly dyed fabrics. If you get some dye onto your skin or hair, wash it off with soap and water or shampoo. Do not use bleach or solvents to remove dye, as these may break the dye down into more dangerous components.

4. Do not sweep up spilled dye powders. Pick them up with a disposable paper towel.

5. Store solutions and powders in sealed containers.

6. Do not eat, drink, or smoke in your work area.

7. Do not prepare dye solutions in utensils that will later be used for cooking. Wash soiled work clothes separately from other clothes.

8. Do not allow young children to work with any chemical dyes. If children work with natural dyes, the mordanting and preparation of the dyebaths should be done by an adult.

The consultants who advised in preparing the *Spinning and dyeing* and *Batik and tie-dyeing* chapters of this book advocate the use of natural dyes over chemical dyes. The former are believed to be much less toxic than their chemical counterparts; moreover, no powders need be handled in mixing natural dyes. Recipes for natural dyes are given with the projects in the chapters mentioned above.

Woodworking. Obvious hazards are associated with the operation of power tools and the use of certain hand tools. Some people develop allergies to certain woods. Both subjects are discussed in detail in the *Woodworking* chapter.

To control the spread of sawdust from stationary power tools, some professional woodworkers install dust-collection systems. Plastic hoses lead from each power tool to an industrial-type collector containing an exhaust fan. A damper is fitted to each pipe and is opened only when the tool is in operation. An excellent design for such a system has been published by *Fine Woodworking* magazine. The magazine is headquartered at Newtown, Connecticut 06470. Woodworkers may want to write *Fine Woodworking* to buy the back issue (September 1978) explaining this system.

The inhalation of wood dust can cause serious injury to the lungs. Good exhaust ventilation is not sufficient protection against the inhaling of dust when running such tools as power sanders. During stints of power sanding wear either a dust mask or an air-purifying respirator.

Ceramics. Potters should routinely take certain precautions. A dust mask or an air-purifying respirator should be worn when handling clay in dry form; inhaling the free silica present in clays can lead to silicosis ("potter's rot"). To avoid this problem entirely, buy only wet—already prepared—clay.

The raw materials used for colors and glazes—including such metals as cadmium, barium, nickel, cobalt, and chromium—are highly toxic. Wear a dust mask or respirator when grinding and handling large quantities of these materials; store the powders in sealed containers when not in use; mix glazes with disposable stirrers, not with your hands or a kitchen utensil. Lead is so dangerous even after the glaze has been fired that we recommend you never use it.

To catch spills, put the pot to be glazed on a drop cloth of newspaper, paper towels, or plastic that can be thrown away after use. Wear a mask if you are spraying the glaze, and work in an area with good local ventilation (see *Ventilation,* p. 10). Kiln firing of ceramic materials produces toxic fumes; therefore, kilns should be vented to the outside, either by chimneys and flues (in gas-, wood-, or charcoal-burning kilns) or through an overhead fume-hood exhaust ventilation system (in an electric kiln).

Finally, a potter's hands are prone to chapping and cracking because of the skin's constant exposure to clay and moisture. Clays often contain molds that can cause fungus infections of the skin or fingernails. You should clean your nails and wash your hands after each working session. At the end of the day apply a hand lotion to replace depleted body oils.

Painting and printmaking. Most artists are aware that lead pigments are extremely hazardous and, to avoid breathing in the dust, never handle lead pigments in powdered form. Ready-to-use lead pigments are also hazardous. After using them always clean your fingernails and wash your hands thoroughly.

Like precautions should be followed in using any paint. Many of the most common pigments are made from

metals that are almost as dangerous as lead. Metallic pigments include emerald green and cobalt violet, which contain arsenic compounds; all cadmium pigments; chromium oxide green, zinc yellow, strontium yellow, and viridian, all containing chromium; true Naples yellow, flake white, and mixed white, all with lead; burnt umber, raw umber, Mars brown, manganese blue, and manganese violet, all containing manganese; and vermilion, containing mercury.

In addition to the dangers associated with the metals in the pigments, the vehicles, binders, and solvents employed in modern synthetic acrylic paints may pose health hazards. These include mineral spirits, turpentine, and toluol, as well as ammonia, which is used in acrylic media. To protect yourself against these hazards, follow the same careful housekeeping and ventilation procedures recommended earlier for the use of solvents.

In printmaking the greatest hazards are those associated with breathing in the fumes from solvents used mainly in cleaning up. The precautions suggested earlier for the use of solvents should be followed. Similar precautions should govern your use of inks; in particular, prints should be put to dry in a well-ventilated place. Try to avoid skin contact with the inks, and wash up thoroughly if you do get ink on your skin.

Definite hazards are associated with the acids used in etching. Refer to the discussion of acids that appears earlier.

Sculpting, modeling, and casting. Stone is not a good medium for the beginning sculptor, and no projects in stone are included in this book. If you do work in stone, wear protective goggles to shield your eyes from flying chips and a dust mask to prevent the inhalation of dust, which can cause silicosis. Any workshop where stone is cut or ground on a continuing basis

should have an exhaust ventilation system (see *Ventilation*, p. 10).

As noted earlier in this article, woods can cause allergic reactions in some people, including dermatitis. Among the toxic woods most likely to be encountered by a wood sculptor are East Indian satinwood, South American boxwood, mahogany, rosewood, ebony, teak, and cocobolo. You should not continue to work with a wood to which you have an allergic reaction.

Modeling clay presents no dust problems if it is kept wet. After working in clay or plasticine, wash your hands thoroughly and apply a hand lotion to replace depleted skin oils.

The *Modeling, moldmaking, and casting sculpture* chapter recommends plaster of paris (calcium sulfate) as one of a number of casting mediums. Plaster of paris dust is irritating, and you should wear a dust mask or respirator if you are exposed to it in quantity. Because of the difficulty and the hazards involved in casting metals, the chapter advocates that pieces be sent to a commercial foundry for casting.

Plastics. The industrial processes used to formulate plastics can be extremely hazardous. This is also true for anyone employing laminating, casting, and foam processes in a workshop. The solvents, catalysts, hardeners, etc., can cause serious diseases, as can the dusts thrown off in sawing, sanding, and polishing plastics. Largely for these reasons, no projects in plastics are included in this book.

Anyone interested in a more complete analysis of the health hazards associated with crafts materials will find excellent information in Dr. Michael McCann's *Health Hazards Manual for Artists.* The pamphlet is available for a small fee from The Foundation for the Community of Artists, 220 Fifth Avenue, New York, New York 10001.

Leatherworking

Man's most ancient fabric

Leather has long been one of the most important and useful materials known to mankind. It is the oldest form of permanent clothing that we know of; our Stone Age ancestors probably made garments of animal hides and skins at least 25,000 years ago. Leather has been made into wine and water casks, boats, tents, saddles, whips, luggage, bows and quivers, slings, sheaths, helmets and shields, powder horns, upholstery, and book covers.

Tanning. Leather by definition is a hide or skin that has been preserved by a chemical process known as tanning. Tanning arrests decomposition. It prevents leather from drying out and from rotting when exposed to water, and it keeps the leather porous.

We do not know exactly how prehistoric man first tanned leather, but very probably it was similar to a process developed by North American Indians. Fresh hides and skins were either stacked or buried in the ground until a partial decomposition had loosened the hair. They were then soaked in a lye solution of wood ashes and water and afterward scraped with bone or flint knives until the hair was removed and both sides of the hide were clean.

At that point the actual tanning began. First the hides were sprinkled with a wood powder. (Wood contains tannic acid, or tannin, the preservative that gives the tanning process its name.) The hides were then rubbed with an oily compound consisting of animal fats and brains. After a period of time the hides were further softened by hand, and sometimes they were chewed to make them even softer. Finally, they were smoked over a smoldering wood fire for several days, in a process not unlike curing bacon.

Tanning did not follow a uniform evolution around the world, and the North American Indian method really incorporated two different tanning methods—vegetable, or wood, tanning and oil tanning. Inuit, for example, relied on oil tanning because of the availability of fish oils. The ancient Chinese, among others, used yet a third method of tanning, which was to cure skins and hides in a mixture of mud and alum salts.

The Hebrews first used oak bark to tan leather several thousand years before Christ, and vegetable tanning remained the predominant tanning technique in the western world until the 19th century. Oak bark was the main source of tannic acid, though North American and European tanning also relied upon spruce, chestnut, and hemlock. The process was a long one. After the hair was loosened by a limewater bath, it was scraped off with knives. Then the hides were soaked in vats of oak bark and water for several months.

Only in the 19th century did the preparation of leather undergo any significant change. The invention of a splitting machine made it possible to split hides and skins to different thicknesses. Another invention made possible the removal of hair by mechanical means. Finally, and more importantly, it was discovered that leather could be tanned by using certain chromium salts, and chrome tanning is now the most often used method. Chrome tanning is quick, reducing the tanning process from many months to several days. Also, it has made possible a far greater variety of leathers.

The more traditional tanning methods have not disappeared, however, and retain certain advantages. Vegetable-tanned leather is firm, heavy, and more water resistant than chrome-tanned leather, which by comparison is softer and more supple.

This 19th-century Japanese tooled-leather panel was painted with colored lacquers.

How leather is sold

Leather is sold by the square foot and the ounce. For example, 1-ounce leather weighs 1 ounce per square foot, 2-ounce leather, 2 ounces per square foot, etc. The weight of the leather is related to its thickness: 1-ounce leather is 1/64 inch thick. Thus, 4-ounce leather would be 4/64, or 1/16, inch thick; 8-ounce, 1/8 inch thick.

While some suppliers sell whole skins, others sell only half hides or half skins, or parts only—such as backs, bends, and shoulders. It is not always possible to buy leather cut exactly to size; thus, you may have to purchase more than you immediately need.

The project you intend to make will determine what sort of leather you should buy, as suggested below.

Belts. Thick leather, 7–9 ounce weight; cowhide, pigskin, calfskin.

Briefcases. Cowhide, 4–6 ounce.

Garments (including hats). Buckskin, chamois, garment suede (lambskin), split cowhide, doeskin, kidskin, pigskin, 2–3 ounce weight.

Handbags. Garment suede (lambskin) and split cowhide, 4–10 ounce.

Sandals, top sole. Hydraulic bend leather (an oil-tanned cowhide), 8–10 ounce weight. **Bottom sole.** Heavy-weight cowhide, 12 ounce weight.

Upholstery. Top-grain, prestretched cowhide, 1–4 ounce weight.

Wallets, keycases, bookbindings. Calfskin, cowhide, goatskin, pigskin, 2–4 ounce weight.

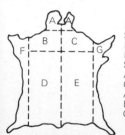

Head—A
Shoulder—B or C
Bend—D or E
Belly—F or G
Side—A+B+D+F or
A+C+E+G
Crops—A+B+D or
A+C+E
Back—B+D or C+E
Croupon—D+E

Diagram of hide shows cuts of leather.

Leatherworking tools

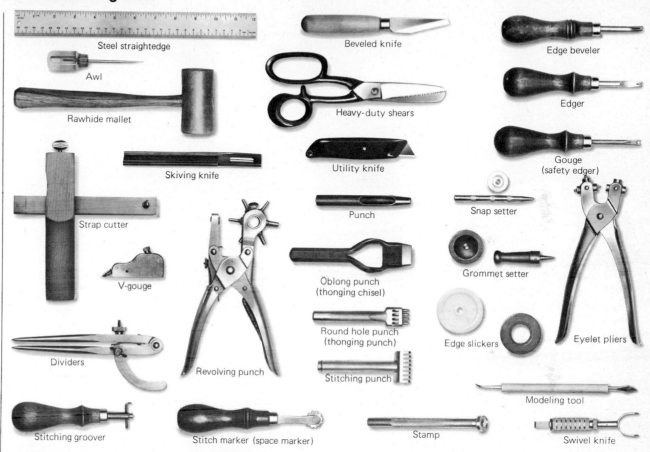

Steel straightedge

Awl

Rawhide mallet

Beveled knife

Heavy-duty shears

Edge beveler

Edger

Skiving knife

Utility knife

Gouge (safety edger)

Strap cutter

Punch

Snap setter

V-gouge

Oblong punch (thonging chisel)

Grommet setter

Round hole punch (thonging punch)

Edge slickers

Eyelet pliers

Dividers

Revolving punch

Stitching punch

Modeling tool

Stitching groover

Stitch marker (space marker)

Stamp

Swivel knife

A glossary of leatherworking terms

Back. Cut of leather: one shoulder plus one bend; two such cuts per animal, left and right sides
Belly. Underpart of hide; usually 3–5 sq ft
Bend. Cut of leather: back minus shoulder; two such cuts per animal, left and right sides
Buckskin. From deer or elk; grain removed
Calfskin. From young bovine
Cattlehide. From fully grown bovine
Chamois. Oil-tanned sheepskin from which the grain side has been split away
Cordovan. Special cut of horsehide
Cowhide. From fully grown bovine
Crop. Cut of leather: side section (head, one shoulder, and one bend), belly removed
Croupon. Cut of leather: both bends. This is the best part of the hide
Deerskin. Skin of deer or elk, grain intact

Doeskin. Skin of lamb or sheep, grain removed
Flesh side. Soft underside of hide
Glove leather. Skin of sheep, pig, deer, or kid tanned to produce a soft, supple leather
Goatskin. Skin of a fully grown goat
Grain side. Outer side of the hide, from which the hair has been removed
Hide. As a cut of leather the hide is the entire usable skin. Hides are further defined as leathers obtained from horses, colts, or fully grown bovines. A cowhide generally ranges from 44 to 55 sq ft in size
Horsehide. Hide of a horse or a colt
Kidskin. Skin of a young goat
Kipskin. Leather from a bovine older than a calf but not fully matured
Lambskin. Skin of a lamb

Latigo. A supple leather produced from cowhide by tanning with alum, oil, and plant extracts
Live oak. Type of leather; a clear-grained, vegetable-tanned cowhide
Moroccan. Leather from a goat tanned with either hard or soft grains; commonly used in bags, wallets, and belts
Pigskin. Skin of a pig or a hog
Sheepskin. Skin of a sheep
Shoulder. Cut of leather between head and bend
Side. Half of a whole skin or hide; 22–27 sq ft
Single bend. A bend; half a croupon; 8–12 sq ft
Split. A hide with the soft flesh side mechanically split from the grain side
Suede. A cut of leather in which the flesh side is split from the grain side and buffed by machine to produce a soft nap

Leatherworking

Cutting leather

The most difficult part of cutting leather is making an accurate cut along the intended lines. Knives tend to take their own paths. To prevent this, trace the pattern on the leather with an awl before cutting (or first use a pencil, then retrace this line with the awl). The awl makes a slight indentation, giving the knife a path to follow.

It is best to make two cuts when working with thick leather. First trace the cut line with an awl, then make the initial cut only partway through the leather. This further establishes the cut line. After the cut line is established, make the final cut.

Since you want a line of consistent width to cut along, trace the pattern and do the cutting on the smooth, grain side of the leather rather than on the rougher flesh side. Hold the pencil perpendicular to the leather when tracing the pattern. Make the cut through the middle of the line. Because the width of the pencil point determines the width of the cutting line, don't let the pencil point get too dull.

Avoid cutting on hard metal or formica surfaces, as these will damage the edge of the cutting tool. Place a piece of linoleum, fiberboard, wood block, or hard rubber under the leather to serve as a cutting surface.

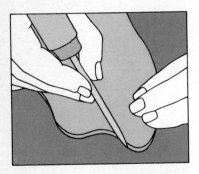

Before any cutting is done, the pattern must be traced on the leather. Thin cardboard makes better templates than paper. You can trace the pattern with a pencil, an awl, or a combination of the two (see text above). Here an awl is drawn along the edge of a round template, providing an indented line for the knife blade to follow.

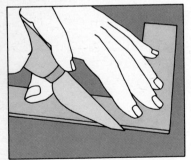

Steel rules or squares are often used as guides when cutting straight lines. Press down firmly on the rule so that it does not slip as you make the cut. Leather and utility knives are by and large interchangeable, but leather knives are more solidly constructed and tend to work better than utility knives when cutting thick leather.

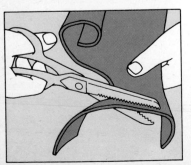

Leather knives and shears both have advantages. Because shears have serrated edges, they grip the leather and prevent slipping. They are thus ideal for cutting curved or irregular lines, as shown at left. Shears are generally best for cutting lighter weight leather. Knives work best with very thick leather.

Wooden strap cutters consist of two ruled crossbars that slide through a handle. The bars house a replaceable blade at one end. A thumb screw on the handle is used to set the cutting width. The leather is inserted between the crossbars, flush against the handle. The cutter is pulled to cut a strap of uniform width.

To save leather, lay out patterns close together, leaving just enough space to perform the cutting. Do not cut past a corner. Instead, cut toward the corner to within 1/4 in. of it. Then place the blade directly at the corner and complete the cut in the opposite directions, as shown at left.

Experienced leatherworkers will cut heavy leather as shown at left. Begin the cut on a flat surface. Then hold the leather in one hand and pull the knife toward you along the marked line. When cutting curved or circular forms, slowly rotate the leather piece with one hand while you cut with the other. Use a leather knife, not a utility knife.

Skiving

Skiving is the process of thinning leather. It may be done for any of several reasons. Most often the purpose is to thin the edges of two pieces that are to be joined, so that the resulting joint thickness matches the original thickness of the leather.

Skiving is also done when thick leather is being folded. The leather is then skived along the flesh side to make it bend more easily.

Skiving can be done with a skiving knife (left) or a leather knife (right). Pulled along the leather like a peeler, the skiving knife makes a uniformly thinned edge. Leather knife is held at an angle to shave leather to the desired thickness.

Edging

In edging leather, the top or bottom edges, and often both, are either beveled or rounded to produce a finished edge. A beveled edge is an angled edge. It is created by using one of the specialized tools discussed in the caption below. Specialized tools are also used in the rounding of edges, as discussed and illustrated below.

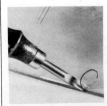

The edge beveler (left) and the common edge tool (see p. 15) are pushed along the edge of the leather. The safety edger (p. 15) is pushed or pulled to make a rounded edge. The edge slicker (right) is rubbed along the edge to round it.

Stitching tools

For a series of uniformly spaced stitching holes along a straight line, use the stitching punch for holes that are to be sewn with thread and the thonging punch for lacing. You can also use an awl or drive punches: first mark the leather with the stitch marker or a pencil and straightedge, then punch the holes individually. Mark curved lines with dividers or a stitch marker; make holes with a punch or an awl.

Stitches are usually set 1/8–1/4 in. from edges. For straight lines push marker (left) along a steel straightedge. For curves, draw guidelines with compass. Then use stitch marker or divider points to mark holes (right).

Push the awl (left) through the leather to make individual holes—part way for sewing holes and all the way for lacing holes. Use the thonging punch (right) for a uniformly spaced series of lacing holes; strike punch with a mallet.

Use the stitch groover (left) to cut a narrow stitch line where thread must lie flush with surface. Set the stitching punch within the groove and strike it with a mallet to make a series of uniformly spaced sewing slits (right).

Sewing and lacing

Two kinds of needles are used in hand sewing leather. Thin leather is sewn with glover's needles, which have sharp points. Harness needles, which have blunt points, are used for thick leather. Both types come in different diameters, as does the thread. Buy needles and

Thread is fastened to glover's needle.

thread of the same diameter; match them precisely to the diameter of the holes punched to accept the stitches.

Thread can be either nylon or waxed linen. Do not knot it. One common means of fastening thread to a needle is to pass the needle through the thread near one end. Next, pass the short end through the end of the needle, then pull the thread back.

In lacing, narrow strips of leather are used in place of thread. Two kinds of lacing are commonly employed—thong lacing and flat lacing.

Thongs are made from square cuts of cowhide, 5/32–3/16 inch wide. The thong is screwed into the hollow end of a special brass lacing needle.

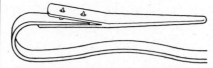

Two-prong lacing needle holds lacing.

Flat lacing may be either calf or Florentine. Calf lacing is about 1/8 inch wide. Florentine lacing is made from kidskin and is 1/4–3/8 inch wide.

Flat lacing requires a special two-prong lacing needle. The lacing is inserted between two separable metal strips that wedge it in place against the prongs. Common sewing and lacing stitches are illustrated at right.

Sewing and lacing stitches

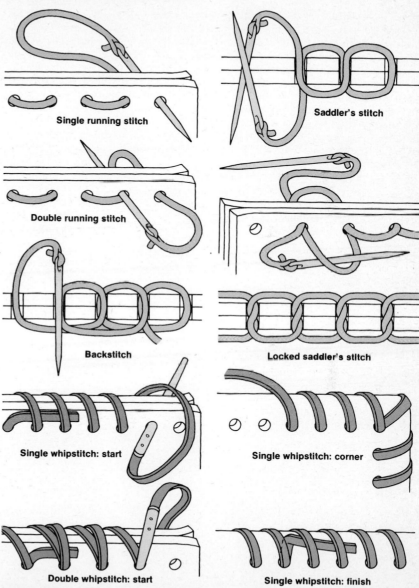

Single running stitch

Saddler's stitch

Double running stitch

Backstitch

Locked saddler's stitch

Single whipstitch: start

Single whipstitch: corner

Double whipstitch: start

Single whipstitch: finish

Sewing stitches. Of the commonly used sewing stitches illustrated above, the saddler's stitch is the strongest. It is often finished with a locked stitch: one or both needles are pulled back through the last loop or loops, and the ends are pulled tight and cut flush with the leather. The single running stitch is knotted at both start and finish. The double running stitch is sewn back to the start where the ends are knotted together. The backstitch is finished by knotting the ends flush against the leather.
Lacing stitches. Whipstitches are begun and finished by tucking the ends under several stitches. When lacing around corners, the single whipstitch is doubled.

Leatherworking

Punching holes

Before most hardware can be set, it is necessary to make holes in the leather to receive the hardware. This is done with either individual drive punches or a revolving punch consisting of six tubes of different diameters. Certain revolving punches are made with threaded and replaceable tubes. In others the tubes are permanently fixed.

Tube sizes vary with model but normally run from 5/64 to 1/4 inch. Holes larger than 1/4 inch require drive punches. The jaws of revolving punches can reach only about 1¼ inches across the leather. Holes farther from the edge are made with single punches or an awl.

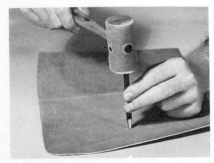

To use the drive punch, hold it vertically over the point that you have marked for a hole. Then strike the punch squarely and sharply with a mallet to cut through the leather.

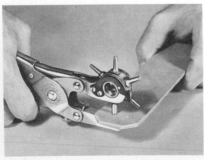

To use the revolving punch, first rotate the tube of the desired diameter into the punch position. Then place the tube on the leather and squeeze the handles to cut the hole.

Setting hardware

Grommets. Grommets, which consist of eyelets and washers, are set with an anvil and a grommet setter. The washer reinforces the hole. Grommets are generally used for heavy drawstring articles. Washer diameters range from 3/16 to 13/16 inch. Grommet kits, including the anvil and grommet setter, are available at hardware stores.

Eyelets. Eyelets are set with one-unit eyelet setters or revolving eyelet pliers. Eyelets are used to reinforce small holes and as fasteners—for example, to attach the metal plate of a key holder to the leather. Grommets are stronger and will not loosen as individual eyelets sometimes do. The most common eyelet diameters are 5/32 and 3/16 inch. Grommets are generally used for holes larger than 3/16 inch.

Snap fasteners. These are used instead of buttons on a wide range of leather articles—handbags, briefcases, purses, jackets. Each snap fastener consists of two two-piece units, or four pieces in all. Two types of snap fasteners are generally available at notions counters:
Spring-type: (1) Cap; (2) Eyelet; (3) Spring; (4) Post
Stud-type: (1) Button; (2) Socket; (3) Stud; (4) Eyelet
Each works exactly the same way: units 1 and 2 are fastened together on one piece of leather, units 3 and 4 on the other. When the snap is fastened, unit 3 is snapped into and held by unit 2. The spring-type fastener is shown in the illustrations below. Snap fasteners are set with a two-piece snap setter consisting of an anvil and a setter.

Rivets. Rivets are used to permanently fasten thick pieces of leather together, to reinforce stress points, and to lock folds of leather (such as the end of a belt around a buckle). Rivets consist of a cap and a shaft. The two parts are tapped together with a mallet.

Spots. These are pronged, ornamental caps used as decoration on jackets, belts, dog collars, and other items.

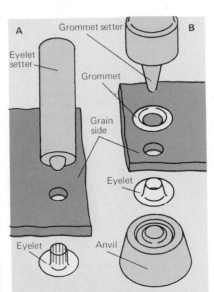

To set eyelets (A), punch a hole the diameter of the eyelet in the leather. Insert the eyelet through the hole. Place the eyelet setter over the top rim of the eyelet. Tap the eyelet setter sharply with a mallet until the eyelet grips the leather. To set grommets (B), place the eyelet in the hollow end of the anvil. Insert the top of the eyelet through the hole. Place the grommet washer around the eyelet top, convex side up. Place the grommet setter over the rim of the eyelet top. Tap the setter sharply with a mallet until the eyelet is bent down and grips the washer.

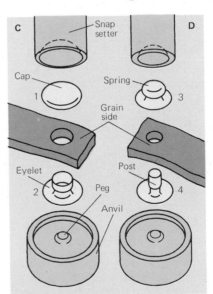

To set the caps on snap fasteners (C), place eyelet on pegged eyelet seat of anvil. Insert eyelet through hole. Place the cap on the eyelet and the hollow end of the snap setter over the cap. Tap the setter sharply with a mallet until the cap locks onto the eyelet. To set the springs (D), place post on eyelet seat of anvil. Insert the post through the hole. Place the spring on the post and the hollow end of the snap setter over it. Tap the setter sharply with a mallet until the spring locks onto the post. Follow the same sequence for setting the stud-type fastener.

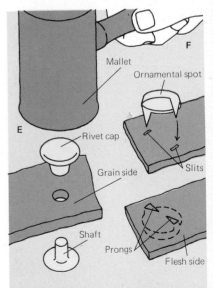

To set rivets (E), insert shaft of rivet through hole in leather. Then place cap of rivet on top of shaft and tap the cap sharply with a mallet until the cap locks solidly onto the shaft. To set single-unit ornamental spots (F), first press the spot against the leather so that the two prongs make two indented marks. Using a leather or utility knife, cut two slits through the leather where the marks were made. Place the spot on the leather so that the two prongs pass through the pair of slits. Then turn the leather over and sharply tap down the prongs with a mallet.

Dyeing, cementing, and folding leather

Modern suede and chrome-tanned leathers are dyed at the tannery. If you want a natural color or a leather that can be dyed to your own preference, buy oak-tanned cowhide or latigo (oil-tanned) cowhide. Oak-tanned leather is a natural, neutral tan, while latigo is a light yellow.

Leather dyes are available in a wide range of colors. Undiluted they tend to be dark, so they are often thinned with a dye solvent. Before actually dyeing leather, run color tests by mixing dyes and solvents and applying them to scrap pieces of the kind of leather you plan to dye.

Leather articles can be lined with cloth or a soft, supple lining leather: suede and chrome-tanned calf are most often used. When cloth is used as a lining, it is sewn. Lining leather can be either sewn or cemented. It is cemented when you want the lining to conform perfectly to the outer piece. An all-purpose contact cement or a rubber cement is applied to the flesh sides of the leather. Because these cements bind on contact, aligning the pieces can be tricky. You should therefore leave yourself a margin of error and cut the lining a little larger than necessary. After the pieces are cemented together, trim away the excess lining.

Cement is also used to attach zippers to such pieces as briefcases. First the zipper is cemented to a leather strip (see illustration below), then the strip is sewn in place on the briefcase.

Leather must be folded to make many articles. Lightweight or supple leathers can be folded with no special preparation. Heavier leathers are folded after cutting a groove on the flesh side with an adjustable V-gouge. The grain side is then moistened and worked with a mallet.

Edges are frequently folded for appearance's sake, as in pockets. Edges are skived so that they will lie closer to the leather. Skiving also makes leather easier to fold.

Apply dye with the grain. Use a piece of lamb's wool or cloth. Experiment with colors by mixing dyes and solvents together in separate containers.

Dye edges with a wool dauber. All cutting, hole punching, edging, and tooling (see following page) should be done before any dye is applied.

Cementing leather

To cement a lining to leather, use applicator that comes with cement. Spread an even coat on flesh side of both pieces. When cement becomes tacky, press the two pieces together.

To cement lining to leather when the pieces are to be folded, brush cement on flesh side of both pieces. Join pieces on one side of fold; smooth the lining down in this area.

Next, fold the unjoined half of the lining back on itself and bend the outer piece of leather carefully over the fold to meet it. Smooth the two pieces of leather together with your hand.

To attach zippers to leather, brush cement on the flesh side of the leather and the cloth of the zipper. Place the leather on the zipper side of the cloth and smooth the pieces together.

Folding leather

To fold edges, first skive the leather along the edge of the flesh side, as shown. Then score the fold line on the flesh side by firmly drawing an awl along a straightedge.

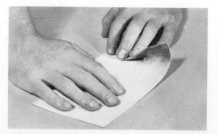

Using a damp sponge, moisten the leather along the fold line on the grain side. The edge is then folded flesh side to flesh side. It can be either stitched or cemented in place.

To fold heavy leather, mark the fold line on the flesh side with an awl and straightedge. Adjust V-gouge to half the thickness of the leather. Push it along the line made with the awl to cut a groove.

Using a damp sponge, moisten the leather along the fold line on the grain side. Place the piece on a flat surface, and firmly tap along the folded grain side with a mallet.

Leatherworking

Decorating leather

The grain side of leather is often decorated by flat modeling (below), stamping (right), or painting (far right). In flat modeling a design is transferred to the moistened leather by tracing its outline with a modeling tool. Most such tools have a blunt-pointed stylus at one end. The other end may be shaped like a narrow spoon (see Step 6), a triangle, or a ball. Each of these shapes produces its own distinct modeling effect.

Stamps are also commonly used for decorating leather. Most stamping tools make textured impressions, but some have smooth and slightly rounded ends (see Step 5).

Leather can be painted with regular leather dye (see p. 19) or with special leather acrylic paints, the colors of which are more brilliant than dyes.

Stamping

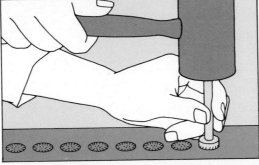

Stamping is an easy means of decorating leather. Some of the many available stamp designs are shown above. The leather is first moistened, then the stamp is tapped with a mallet.

Painting

To transfer a design to leather without making an indentation, draw design on tracing paper. Turn paper over. Hold it in place and on the back side retrace the design with a pencil (1). This will transfer the original leaded line to the leather (2). Using a camel's hair brush, paint the areas you want to color (3 and 4).

Flat Modeling

1. With a damp sponge, thoroughly moisten the section of the grain side you want to model.

2. Place the design on the leather. Trace its lines with the stylus end of a modeling tool.

3. Tracing the design should produce a clearly indented outline. Retrace any weak lines.

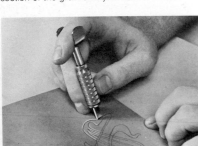

4. Put the design into relief by scoring the traced outline with a swivel knife (see p. 15).

5. Areas between scored lines are modeled using a smooth stamp and a mallet.

6. Use the spoon end of the modeling tool to depress any areas too narrow for the stamp.

Leatherworking/project

Belt

Belts are ordinarily made from a single strip of heavy leather thick enough to require no backing. The belt shown below is made from 8-ounce French back, a strong but supple vegetable-tanned cowhide that can be tooled and dyed. The belt is cut so that its length runs with, rather than across, the grain. This minimizes stretching.

Begin by measuring the waist of the person for whom the belt is intended. Cut a strip of leather 12 inches longer than the waist size. The width of the belt is cut to fit the inside width of the

buckle. The dimensions given on this page are for a buckle with an inside width of 1¾ inches. A slot for the tongue of the buckle is punched 1⅜ inches from the buckle end of the belt; it should be just wide enough for the tongue to move unimpaired. This slot is cut with an oblong punch. Use a punch that exactly matches the width of the tongue.

The width and thickness of the belt determine the size and placement of rivets, Since rivets are cheap, it is a good idea to have several sizes on hand.

After Step 11 (see illustrations below) the belt is given a final fitting and a hole is punched for the exact waist length. Additional holes are then punched on either side to allow for weight fluctuation.

The final step (not shown) is to repeat Step 2 with the unfinished end: the belt is cut about 5 inches from the hole nearest the end, the corners are trimmed and beveled, and the edges are dyed. Enough leather should be left for the belt end to pass through the first belt loop on the trousers.

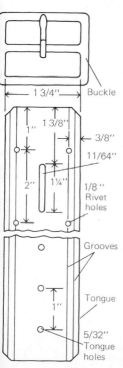

Placement of rivet holes, decorative grooves, and tongue slot is indicated on diagram. Use rivets ¼ in. long and ⅛ in. in diameter. The holes for the buckle tongue are 5/32 in. in diameter.

1. Set the strap cutter to the inner width of the buckle. Cut a strap about 12 in. longer than the waist length.

2. Use a straightedge and a knife to cut the belt square at the buckle end. Then trim the corners to 45° angles.

3. Cut two decorative grooves with the stitch groover, 3/16 and 3/8 in. respectively from the top edge of the belt.

4. Pencil in the slot for the buckle tongue. To make the slot, sharply strike the oblong punch with a mallet.

5. Mark four rivet holes (see drawing, far left). Punch the holes with a drive punch or a rotary punch.

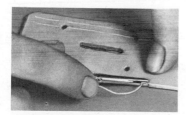

6. Using an edge beveler, neatly bevel all edges on both sides of the belt except the unfinished end.

7. Dye all edges except the unfinished end with a dauber. Use a pipe cleaner to dye the buckle slot, as shown here.

8. Dye the grain side of the belt by rubbing it with a piece of lamb's wool dipped in the desired color dye.

9. With a cloth, apply neat's-foot oil to outer side of belt. Rub it into the belt by hand, then polish with newspaper.

10. To insert rivets, first mount the buckle. Then bend back the strap end and insert the rivets from beneath.

11. Place the belt on an anvil, grain side up. Place the rivet caps on the rivets. Tap them sharply with a mallet.

12. Fit belt, then punch first hole. Punch holes at 1-in. intervals to each side. Finish end as described in text.

Leatherworking/project

Shoulder bag

To make this handsome shoulder bag, you will need 15 square feet of 4½-ounce naked-grain crust cowhide, a sturdy but supple chrome-tanned leather that is predyed various colors at the tannery. These many different colors include tan, rust, black, burgundy, and shades of brown and blue.

All pieces are sewn together with a running stitch, but stress points are reinforced with backstitching. (The stitches are illustrated on page 17.) The stress points are the top side edges of all pockets, the top inside edges where the gusset is stitched to the front and back pieces, and the top stitching that connects the straps to the gussets.

Use a waxed linen thread. Experiment on scraps of the same leather with different stitching punches and needles to find a combination of needle and hole size you feel comfortable working with. Use an extra-long-point stitching punch to punch the holes that pass through the strap ends and the gusset.

You will note from the specifications on the pattern (below) that when any two pieces are glued together, the backing will be larger than the facing. This permits leeway in the gluing process. After such pieces are glued, the backing is trimmed to the size of its matching piece.

Bevel and dye all exposed edges be-fore they are permanently assembled. For example, after the front pocket is glued and stitched to its backing, the excess backing is trimmed away. The edges should then be carefully beveled and dyed before the pocket is stitched to the front piece.

The final stitching of the gussets to the front and back pieces illustrated in Steps 10–12 (p. 23) is done with the bag turned inside out. After the bag is finished, turn it right-side out.

The final step (not illustrated) is to measure and punch the buckle tongue holes on the long strap end so that the bag hangs at a comfortable length from the shoulder.

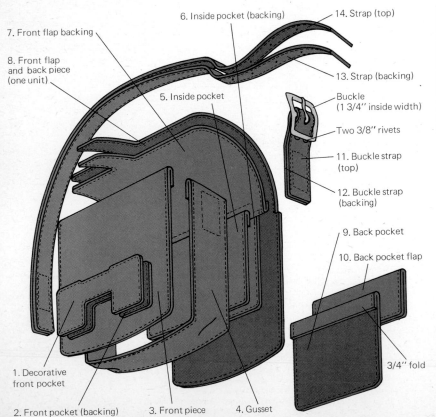

- 6. Inside pocket (backing)
- 7. Front flap backing
- 8. Front flap and back piece (one unit)
- 5. Inside pocket
- 14. Strap (top)
- 13. Strap (backing)
- Buckle (1 3/4" inside width)
- Two 3/8" rivets
- 11. Buckle strap (top)
- 12. Buckle strap (backing)
- 9. Back pocket
- 10. Back pocket flap
- 3/4" fold
- 1. Decorative front pocket
- 2. Front pocket (backing)
- 3. Front piece
- 4. Gusset

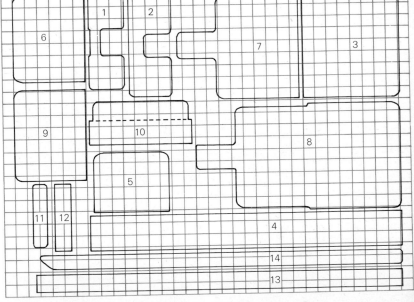

In this drawing each square equals 1½ sq in. on the leather. Begin by transferring each of the above patterns to template paper. Use either cross-section paper or graph paper, which can be purchased at art stores; or, using a ruler and a right angle, draw a grid with 1½-in. squares on brown paper. In transferring patterns you will actually be enlarging them from their size on the above grid to the true size of the bag. For example, to transfer the pattern for the back pocket, begin by counting the squares along its length and width on the grid. This will give you 6 squares by 7⅔ squares. This translates to 9 by 11½ in. when these figures are transferred to the 1½-in. grid. Use a straightedge to draw straight lines in transferring the pattern.

Shoulder bag assembly

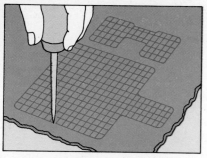

1. After you have transferred the pattern design to the cross section paper, cut out the templates. Lay them on the grain side of the leather, close together so that you do not waste leather. Trace the template outlines with an awl.

2. Cut out the traced pieces with a knife. Use a straightedge as an aid in cutting straight lines. Cut the rounded corners by first indenting the line with an awl, then cutting all the way through the indented line with a knife.

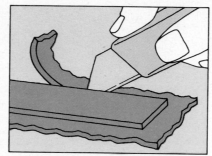

3. Glue straps to their backings, flesh side to flesh side. Trim excess. Punch stitching holes along strap edges with a stitching punch. Mark and punch corner holes with an awl. Backstitch pieces together (p. 17).

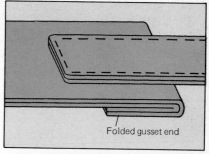

4. Fold back the gusset ends 2 in. and glue them down with rubber cement, flesh side to flesh side. Center each strap as shown on the outside of the gusset at the folded gusset ends, with the strap grain sides against the gusset end grain sides.

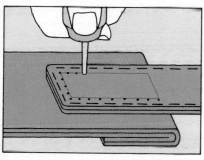

5. Glue the strap ends to the gusset. Punch stitching holes through the straps and gusset with a stitching punch or awl. Punch the inner stitch line near the outer one. Stitch the strap ends and gusset together.

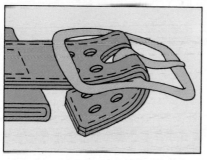

6. Punch a buckle slot in the center of the short strap, 1½ in. from end. Mount buckle and fold the strap end. Punch four rivet holes so that the buckle will be held tightly by the rivets. Set rivets as shown on page 21.

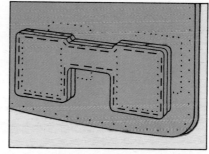

7. Glue front pocket to its backing. Trim excess. Punch holes along edges and stitch pocket to backing. Punch two U-shaped stitch lines inside outer stitching. Punch corresponding holes in front piece. Stitch pocket to front piece.

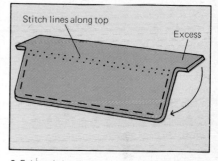

8. Fold and glue the back pocket flap, flesh side to flesh side. Trim off the excess. Punch stitch lines along the sides and bottom, then stitch the piece together. Punch two more stitch lines along the top for use in the next step.

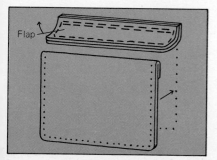

9. Punch corresponding stitch lines on back piece and sew flap to back. Fold and glue top edge of back pocket. Punch stitch line along sides and bottom of pocket; punch matching line on back piece. Stitch pocket to back.

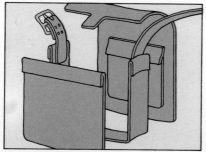

10. Turn bag inside out. Glue gusset to front and back, grain side to grain side, one piece at a time, one edge at a time. Glue bottom edge first. Make glue line and punch stitch line 1/4 in. from edges. Stitch the pieces together.

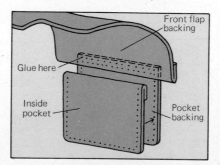

11. Next assemble inside pocket and front flap backing. Fold over and glue top edge of pocket front and bottom edge of flap backing. Stitch pocket to its backing on sides and bottom. Glue pocket backing under flap backing.

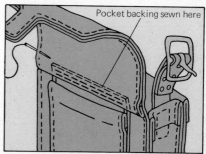

12. Stitch top of pocket backing to flap backing. Glue flap backing into place on flap. Trim away excess leather, punch stitch lines, and sew flap backing and flap together along outside edges. Turn finished bag right-side out.

Leatherworking/project

Sandals

No definite dimensions can be given for sandals. Those you make will depend on the size of the feet they are intended for. For small feet you can cut narrower straps, and therefore punch narrower strap slits. The drawings at right show where strap slits should be made in proportion to the foot and how straps should fit the foot.

The first step is to make paper templates. (See drawings A and B, right, and the explanation beneath.) Trace the template outlines on the grain side of the top sole leather. Then proceed with Step 1 on the opposite page.

After Step 2 place the bottom soles in a pail of water until they are saturated (20–30 minutes). The straps are cut in Step 5 and skived in Step 6. After Step 6 bevel and dye all strap edges. Apply neat's-foot oil to the straps with a piece of sheepskin and work it into the leather by hand. Then cut both of the 40-inch straps 11 inches from one end. The shorter pieces become the buckle straps. The longer, 29-inch straps are the main straps.

After removing the bottom soles from the water, let them stand 5–10 minutes before forming the arches in Step 8. Forming the arches requires a mold. (See explanation beneath the assembly drawing.) After you form the arches, let the bottom soles dry before proceeding further. They will dry naturally overnight or in front of a fan in approximately 2–3 hours. After Step 19 bevel the top edges of the top soles. Then dye the sole edges. (Although not shown here, a third, flat sole can easily be cobbled onto the sandal as a bottom sole, with a rubber arch support inserted above it.)

The leathers required are listed beneath the assembly drawing. Large, rough-cut bottom soles are sometimes available from shoe repairmen. Otherwise, each of the leathers is normally sold in pieces larger than necessary.

Sandal assembly

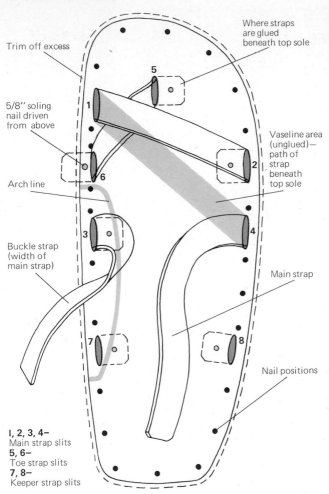

Trim off excess

Where straps are glued beneath top sole

5/8" soling nail driven from above

Vaseline area (unglued)—path of strap beneath top sole

Arch line

Buckle strap (width of main strap)

Main strap

Nail positions

I, 2, 3, 4– Main strap slits
5, 6– Toe strap slits
7, 8– Keeper strap slits

Assembly drawing shows all strap and strap slit positions. Gray area between slits 1 and 4 shows path of the main strap beneath the top sole and the area to which petroleum jelly is applied in Step 10. No rubber cement is applied to bottom of top sole in this area. Exterior dotted line shows the excess on the bottom sole that is trimmed in Step 18. Dotted lines at slits show where strap ends are glued to bottom of top sole (Step 12) and where toe strap protrudes between the two soles. Dots show nail positions. Use 5/8-in. soling nails in Step 16; use 4/8 extra-iron clinching nails for all other cobbling. To make mold for arch (Step 8), use a piece of 2 by 4. Hollow out one side with a jigsaw until it approximates the curve of an arch. Then sand the curve smooth. You will need the following kinds of leather: top soles, 10–12 oz hydraulic-bend leather; bottom soles, 13-iron soling leather, "prime" (grades marked "prime X" and "C–D prime" are inferior; the thickness of soling leather is measured in irons rather than ounces—one iron is 1/48 in. thick); straps, 6-oz ski-grain leather. Always cut leather with the grain.

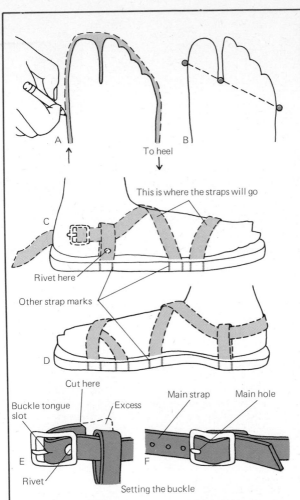

Where the straps will go

Rivet here

Other strap marks

To heel

Cut here

Buckle tongue slot

Excess

Main strap

Main hole

Rivet

Setting the buckle

To make templates, have the subject stand on a sheet of paper. Trace the outline of the feet as in drawing A. Make three strap marks on template as in drawing B. Drawings C and D show where other strap marks are made on template. To fit straps (Step 15), place sandal on foot. Fold down keeper straps to form loops for main strap and buckle strap. Trim keeper strap excess. Cut strap corners, and skive ends on flesh side. Rivet keeper straps as in drawing C. Slip buckle strap through outer keeper strap as shown in drawing C. Punch buckle tongue slot in the position shown in drawing E. Trim buckle strap excess. Skive its end on flesh side. Mount the buckle. Rivet the buckle strap. Slip main strap through buckle. Pull it tightly about foot. Punch one main hole and several others, 1/4 in. apart (drawing F). Proceed to Step 16.

1. Holding the leather firmly in one hand, cut out the top soles by drawing the knife toward you, along the template outline.

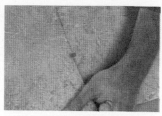

2. Trace top sole outline on flesh side of bottom sole leather. Cut out bottom soles, but leave 1/4 in. excess. Put soles in water (see text).

3. Place template on top sole. With pencil, transfer template strap marks to sides of sole. Pierce toe strap mark with pencil to mark top sole.

4. Punch the main strap slits numbered 1–4 with a 7/8- by 1/8-in. oblong punch. Punch all other slits with a 5/8-in. chisel.

5. Use strap cutter to cut two main straps, each 3/4 by 40 in. Also cut two toe straps and four keeper straps, each 5/8 by 6 in.

6. Cut the corners on one end of each strap to 45° angles. Skive the same ends on the flesh side, as above. See text for next steps.

7. To mount straps, follow assembly drawing (opposite). With pliers, pull skived ends through slits to protrude 3/4 in. from bottom of top soles.

8. Remove bottom soles from water (see text, opposite page). Put them on a mold, grain side up. Pound with a ball peen hammer to form arch.

9. Place top sole, flesh side up, on an iron anvil or any hard surface. With flat end of a ball peen hammer pound ball and heel until firm.

10. Working with bottom of top sole, rub petroleum jelly on both sides of main strap and on the bottom of the top sole just beneath this strap.

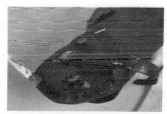

11. Coat bottom of top sole with rubber cement, except petroleum jelly area beneath main strap. Coat entire top of bottom sole with cement.

12. Coat flesh side of strap ends with rubber cement except toe strap end running through slit 6. Press glued strap ends against the sole.

13. Allow strap ends to set several seconds. Press top and bottom soles together. Let unglued toe strap protrude between the two soles.

14. Place sandal on anvil, bottom side up. With flat end of ball peen hammer, drive clinching nails into sole on both sides of strap slit 6.

15. Put sandal on foot. With pliers, pull out unglued toe strap to fit snugly over toe. To fit straps and buckle, see caption, drawings A–E.

16. Remove sandal. Trim main strap excess. Bevel and dye strap end. Then drive soling nail through the top sole, as seen above.

17. Drive a clinching nail through bottom sole to secure toe strap at toe strap slit 5. Then cobble the bottom sole (see assembly drawing).

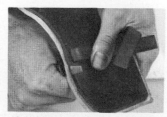

18. Hold leather knife flush with edge of top sole to trim bottom sole excess. Also cut the protruding toe strap flush with side of sole.

19. Sand sole edges. Seal them with beeswax. Then rub neat's-foot oil over the edges, first with sheepskin, then by hand.

Leatherworking/project

Briefcase

NO.	PIECE	LENGTH	WIDTH
I	Body	38″	16″
2	Gusset	12¼″	3¾″
3	Handle	11½″	1″
4	Handle cover	4½″	2½″
5	Flap stiffener	11½″	1″
6	Strap	24″	1″
7	Strap stiffener	6″	1″
8	Strap keeper	3¾″	5/8″

To make this briefcase, first complete the initial steps described beneath the pattern drawing (below right). Then skive the squared ends of the strap stiffeners on the flesh side. Glue them to the straps, flesh side to flesh side. Rivet the straps to the body piece. Set rivets with mallet and anvil, rivet caps facing outward.

Skive 1/2 inch of each strap keeper end on the flesh side. Insert the strap keeper ends through the slits. Glue the skived ends to the flesh side of the case so that they fit flush together, meeting behind the slits.

Next fold and glue the handle as shown in the drawing (below left).

Leave unglued loops at each end for the D-rings. Punch stitch holes along the long sides of the handle cover, 1/8 inch from each edge. Stitch the handle cover with a running stitch. Slip the handle cover over the handle, with the stitching on the underside. Mount the D-rings on the handle by slipping the handle loops through the gaps in the D-rings. Then insert the D-ring ends through the D-ring holes in the case. The flap stiffener will help to hold the D-rings firmly in place.

Skive the flap stiffener. Glue it to the inside of the case, flesh side to flesh side, so that it is centered and covers the gapped ends of the D-rings.

Cut out three pieces of lining leather to match the body and the gussets. Then glue the lining to these pieces, flesh side to flesh side.

The following three types of lining leather are most commonly used to line leather objects: Italian kipskin, English kipskin, and garment cowhide. Italian kipskin and garment cowhide are available in a wide variety of predyed colors, but if you wish to dye the lining yourself, purchase English kipskin.

The final steps in assembling the briefcase are to punch stitch holes 1/4 inch in from the edges where the gussets meet the body of the case and to stitch the gussets to the body.

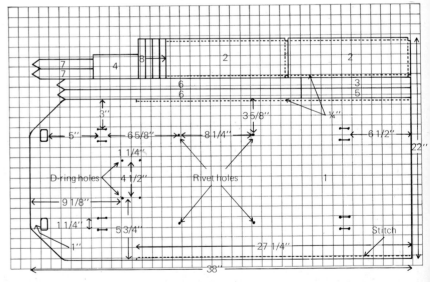

This briefcase requires a piece of 5-oz double-bend cowhide, at least 38 by 22 in., and a piece of 2-oz lining leather (see text). Since the lining is glued to the body piece and the two gussets, its size should be slightly larger than these pieces to give you leeway when gluing. Use D-rings 1¼ in. wide and rivets numbered 410-D. Buy solid brass, rather than "brassed," hardware, which is steel with a brass coating. D-ring and rivet widths vary with manufacturers. Use drive punch sizes to match the widths of the rings and rivets you purchase.

Initial steps. Dye the grain side of the main leather any color you wish. Then make enlarged paper templates from the above patterns (see p. 22). Each square above equals 1 sq in. on the leather. Trace template outlines on the leather with pencil and straightedge. Cut out the pieces, then cut out the two slots. Round the slot corners to soften the square effect. Punch the eight strap keeper slits with a 5/8- by 1/8-in. oblong punch. Punch the four D-ring holes and the four rivet holes on the body piece. Punch the two rivet holes on each strap. Then dye all edges.

Leatherworking/project

Envelope carrying case

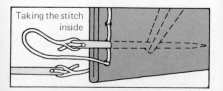

The first step in constructing this envelope carrying case is to make a paper template following the dimensions given in the pattern drawing on this page. Use a very sharp pencil to trace its outline on the grain side of the leather, then cut out the piece.

With a damp sponge, moisten the piece on both flesh and grain sides along the fold line between the front and back sides. Fold the piece along the line, grain side outward. Firmly tap along the grain side fold with a mallet (see *Folding leather*, p.19).

Next use a stitching groover to make a stitching groove along all the leather except the top edge of the front side.

Bevel the grain side edges and dye them. Then dye the entire grain side. Be sure to dye the flesh side of the flap—though you may, if you wish, dye the entire flesh side for appearance sake. Dye the stitching groove by tracing it with a black felt-tipped pen. Then follow the steps illustrated below.

The side stitching (see Steps 7–8) is done with two needles. It is completed by taking the stitch inside (see drawing, bottom left) after the last hole is stitched. Insert one needle through the second-to-last hole on that needle's side. Push it halfway through the hole so that its point emerges on the inside of the case between the two stitched

sides. After you stitch the first side, you may be able to pull the needle through by hand, but after the second side is stitched, it is harder to grip the needle since there is less room in which to maneuver. It is therefore easiest to push the needle halfway through the hole, then pull it through with needle-nose pliers. Pull the needle and thread completely through. Then do the same with the other needle on the other side. Cut and knot the thread.

The last step (not shown) is to rub the stitched edges with a cake of beeswax, which acts as a sealer. This procedure is shown in Step 19 on page 25 of the sandalmaking project.

This case requires a single piece of 7-oz French-back cowhide cut to the above dimensions. The brass cap and eyelet form one unit. Buy brass caps with a 9/16-in. diameter, which come with heavy-duty snaps. Use eyelets and posts 3/16 in. long and 5/32 in. in diameter.

1. Starting at top edge of front side, punch stitching holes along one side with a stitching punch to within 1/4 in. of fold line.

2. Punch matching holes on back side by folding the front side into place. Punch through holes made in Step 1 and through back side.

3. Pin the punched side to the work surface with an awl. Punch stitching holes through front and back sides along the other edge.

4. Eyelet holes can be made with a rotary punch. The post holes being made here require a drive punch. All holes are 5/32 in. in diameter.

5. To set flap snaps, seat cap on anvil. Insert eyelet through hole. Mount snap on flesh side. Set with eyelet setter and mallet.

6. To set front side snaps, seat post on anvil. Insert post through hole. Mount the snap on the grain side. Set as in Step 5.

7. To stitch the sides, start stitching at the top. Use a saddler's stitch (see illustrations, p. 17) and a waxed linen thread.

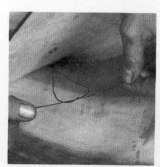

8. Finish stitching on both sides by taking needles inside. See explanation in text and drawing at left. Tie and cut the thread.

Taking the stitch inside

Macramé

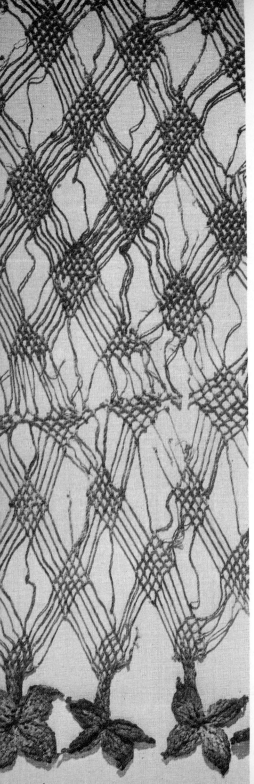

From sailors and royal courts

Macramé, the modern art of decorating with knots, is believed to have originated with 13th-century Arabian weavers. They knotted the excess thread and yarn along the edges of hand-loomed fabrics into decorative fringes on bath towels, shawls, and veils. The original meaning of the Arabic *Migramah*, from which the word macramé is derived, is variously rendered as "striped towel," "ornamental fringe," and "embroidered veil."

As a result of the Moorish conquest the art of macramé was taken to Spain, and from there it spread throughout Europe. It was first introduced into England at the court of Queen Mary, the wife of William of Orange, in the late 17th century.

Sailors played an important part in keeping alive and spreading this exported Arab art. From China to the New World they sold or bartered their own novel macramé objects made during the long months at sea. Macramé remained a popular pastime with 19th-century British and American seamen, who called it square knotting after the knot they most preferred in making their hammocks, bell fringes, and belts.

Macramé reached its zenith during the Victorian era. *Sylvia's Book of Macramé Lace,* a favorite at that time, urged its readers "to work rich trimmings for black and coloured costumes, both for home wear, garden parties, seaside ramblings, and balls—fairylike adornments for household and underlinens ..." Few Victorian homes went unadorned.

While the craze for macramé waned in subsequent years, it is now enjoying a renewed and widespread popularity as a technique for making wall hangings, articles of clothing, bedspreads, tablecloths, draperies, plant hangers, and other furnishings.

This ancient Egyptian macramé netting is in the collection of the Museum of Fine Arts, Boston.

Tools and materials

It is not unusual to do macramé with as few tools and materials as a pair of scissors, pins, cords, and something to support the cords while you knot them.

Mounting cords, rods, and rings. The vertical cords are called the knotting cords. They are often mounted simply by attaching them to another horizontal cord, called the mounting cord. But you will have occasion to use other types of mounting. Knotting cords can be mounted on wooden rods or on wooden or metal rings. When rings or rods are used, it is usually because they will form an integral part of the finished project (see *Wall hanging,* p. 31, and *Plant hanger,* p. 34).

Knotting board. Generally the work is begun on a knotting board. The knotting board should be light and fairly stiff, but it should give enough to hold pins. You can make your own boards of heavy cardboard or of insulating material. Cork is not recommended, as it crumbles. You may want to make several knotting boards for projects of different sizes. Standard board sizes are 12 by 24 inches, 20 by 36 inches, and 24 by 48 inches.

The mounting cord, ring, or rod is pinned to the knotting board with U-pins. The cords themselves are then knotted onto the mounting cord, ring, or rod. At various stages of the work you may temporarily need to pin the cords to the board. T-pins or ordinary straight pins are customarily used for this purpose.

For smaller objects (see *Necklace,* p. 31) you may prefer to work with the board propped in your lap or lying on a table. For larger projects using longer lengths of cord you will probably find it convenient to devise some means of mounting the knotting board itself on a wall or on some other vertical surface. Another useful and common technique is to begin a large project on the knotting board and then to transfer the

Lightweight jute

Heavyweight jute

Clothesline

Lightweight clothesline

Rayon-covered cotton

Mason's line

Twine

Macramé cords. The cords shown are ideal for macramé. They are available at hardware stores and department store notions counters.

work to another type of support when it becomes too unwieldy for the knotting board, as is done with the plant hanger project, illustrated on page 34.

Improvising. You need not work on a knotting board. You can, for example, use a padded ironing board. As you become more adept, you may find or improvise other means of mounting large projects. You can hang mounting rings on elevated doorknobs, such as those on kitchen cabinets. You may want to make a permanent arrangement by fastening a peg to a wall.

Macramé

Basic techniques

The two most basic knots used in macramé are the half-knot and the half-hitch. Most other macramé knots are derived from these two. The two derivations you will use most often are the square knot, which consists of two half-knots, and the clove hitch, which is made of two half-hitches.

Great variety in texture and design can result from just these few knots, since each knot can be tied in two different ways—regular and reverse. As seen in the illustrations on this page, these directions are left to right (the regular knot) and right to left (the reverse knot). A series of regular (left-to-right) half-knots will create a spiral chain twisting to the right; a series of reverse (right-to-left) half-knots, conversely, will result in a spiral chain twisting to the left.

The same is true for half-hitches, though they are not as commonly used for macramé spiral effects. However, diagonal rows of half-hitches and clove hitches are quite commonly employed (see illustrations of samplers, below left, and the wall hanging, pp. 31–33).

Sennits and samplers. Generally, people will tie knots more easily in one direction than in the other. Practice *(Continued on next page)*

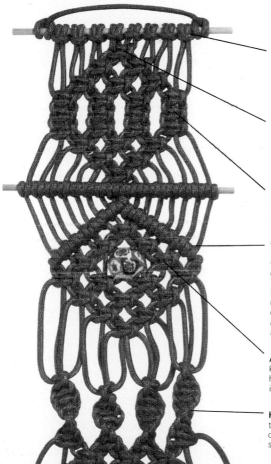

This sampler employs a variety of basic macramé knots. Its purpose is to illustrate ways in which you can use simple knotting patterns to create designs.

Lark's head knot: most commonly used to mount cords on a rod or ring to support the project. Cords are doubled and mounted using this knot. Each cord mounted in this fashion produces two working cords. Cords may be mounted using a reverse lark's head if so desired.

Square knot: consists of two half-knots, one to the left and one to the right. Usually tied with four working cords, two used as holding cords and two as knotting cords.

Square knot chain: square knots tied in succession on the same two holding cords.

Clove hitches: usually tied around a common holding cord, which runs horizontally or diagonally to the left or right. Therefore, they must be learned in both directions. They are used to produce linear effects or often to add a new piece to a project, such as a rod or a dowel, as in this sampler.

Alternating square knots: square knots tied on alternating pairs of holding cords produce this intricate pattern.

Half-knot twists: half-knots tied repeatedly in the same direction produce a twist or spiral as shown.

Inside-out square knot: by exchanging holding cords for the knotting cords after each knot, this variation occurs. Butterfly effect is produced by tying a square knot about 1½" below the preceding knot and sliding it upward.

Lark's head   **Reverse lark's head**

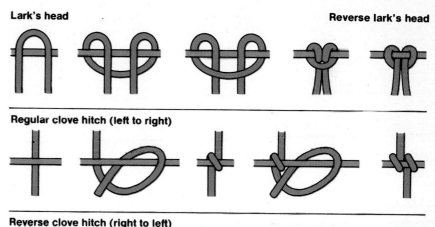

Regular clove hitch (left to right)

Reverse clove hitch (right to left)

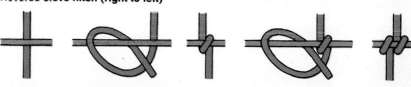

Square knot (two half-knots)

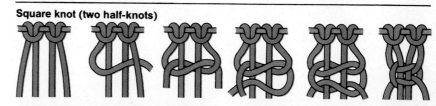

Alternating square knots   **Inside-out square knot** **Butterfly effect**

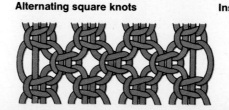

Macramé

Basic techniques (continued)

until you can tie knots equally well in both directions. Be sure to tie all knots with the same degree of tension, otherwise your work will lack symmetry.

The best way to learn knots is by repetition. Practice your knotting on sample cords, called *sennits*. A sennit is one or more cords that have been doubled in mounting to make two or more strands of equal length. From sennits you can move on to samplers. Samplers are composed of more than one sennit and employ a variety of knots.

As a beginner you should not try to make complicated projects from your own designs, since it is difficult to anticipate what kinds of knots will best complete a design. It is better to work from patterns that have already been planned, such as those in the projects on the following pages. In time, you will be experienced enough to realize your own designs, particularly if you practice making samplers, experimenting with different knots to see what kinds of designs naturally arise from certain knotting patterns. This will teach you to visualize how different knots and patterns will look in a finished project.

Cords and fibers. Practice with different kinds of cords to learn their qualities and textures. Knitting yarn, for example, is too elastic for most macramé work. Cotton, sisal, and jute are good all-around fibers, and each has its own distinctive properties. Nylon and rayon have an attractive, silky texture, but they are slippery and do not hold knots well. If you choose to work with such synthetic fibers, wet them before you begin so that they will hold the knots. Ordinary clothesline is good cord to use for practice sennits.

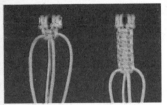
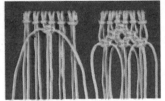
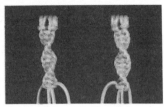
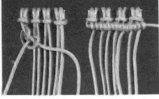
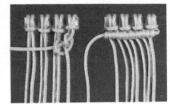

Practice exercises. 1. Mount four cords. Tie two chains of square knots. Start is shown, left; finish, right.

2. Mount four cords. Use them all to tie one chain of alternating square knots, as shown in the pattern above.

3. Mount four cords. Tie spiral square knots to the left (left chain above) and to the right (right chain above.)

4. Mount four cords. Run far left cord to right as holding cord. Tie clove hitches about it with remaining cords.

5. Mount four cords. Run far right cord to left. Tie reverse clove hitches about it with the remaining cords.

Estimating, measuring, and cutting cords

There is no exact formula for estimating the length to which cords should be cut in preparing for a macramé project. A standard rule of thumb is to work with individual strands that, before they are doubled in mounting, are seven to eight times longer than the length of the finished project. The mounted cords will then be three and a half to four times longer than the finished piece.

Factors in estimating. This rule is a sound one for many macramé objects, but there will be times when you will need either more or less cord. Such predominantly vertical designs as plant hangers, which have few horizontal or diagonal lines, may not require strands as long as those suggested above. However, elaborate designs having many knots and many horizontal or diagonal lines may call for strands that are longer than seven to eight times the finished length.

Cord thickness is another factor that you should consider in estimating cord length. Thicker cords mean thicker knots, which could mean that strands of greater length than those estimated by the above rule will be needed.

It is always preferable to have extra cord left over rather than to be faced with the sudden necessity of having to add cord to a work in progress. So while the formula is reasonably accurate, allow a margin of error when you estimate material needs for your own designs. As you become more experienced and learn to work with cords of different thicknesses, you will become better at estimating necessary cord lengths. You may arrive at certain formulas of your own, depending on the designs you work from, the knots you use, and the thickness of the cord you employ.

Measuring and cutting. Some macramé artists use a weaver's warping board to help them measure and cut cord to the needed lengths. The warping board is a large wooden frame with projecting pegs around which cords are wound and measured for cutting. However, such boards are not always readily available, and other methods of measuring work as well.

For instance, you can work with C-clamps. Attach them to the opposite ends of a table, to the tops of chairs, or to any objects that can be set up a measured distance apart. If you want five lengths of 20 feet, for example, begin by placing the C-clamps 10 feet apart. Tie one end of the cord to one of the clamps. Wind the cord around the other clamp, and bring it back, winding it around the first clamp. Repeat this five times. Cut the cords at the clamp where you began.

The simplest method is to measure out one strand, cut it, and use this to measure and cut the other strands.

Bobbins. Working with very long lengths of cord can be confusing and unwieldy, which is why bobbins are sometimes used. A bobbin is a device around which cord is wound to make it shorter and easier to handle. Yarn bobbins are made for this purpose and are available in needlework shops. But you can easily make your own by winding the cord in a figure 8 around your thumb and little finger and fastening the coil with a rubber band.

Bobbins can be clumsy. They are generally useful only when working with a great many long cords. Then they may be used temporarily to tie up cords to keep them out of the way of those cords you are knotting. Sometimes you will find a bobbin helpful when you have one or a few long cords that are used almost exclusively for a certain part of the design. In such cases simplify your handling of these cords by making bobbins of them.

Macramé/project

Wall hanging

The wall hanging (right) and the necklace (below) were made from the same design, as illustrated beginning at right. The necklace requires thinner cord than the hanging, and its loose bottom strands are not unraveled; beads mounted on these strands are held with an overhand knot. The wall hanging measures 4½ by 1½ ft, the necklace, 11 by 5 in. Since nails are used in adding new cords to the hanging, you will need a knotting board both larger and thicker than that required for the necklace, to which cords are added using pins.

Materials, wall hanging:
You will need 423 ft of 7/16-in., 5-ply jute; cut it into 12 strands 34 ft in length, leaving a 15-ft strand for the ring. Ten large ceramic beads; eight of these are 1¼ in. long; two (the outer two) are 7/8 in. long. One mounting ring, 6 in. in diameter.

Necklace: Use 125 ft of 1/8 in. cotton-filled rayon cord, cut into 12 10-ft strands, leaving 5 ft for the ring. Ten hollow beads 3/16 in. high. One metal neck ring.

1. Mount a cord on the mounting ring using a reverse lark's head knot, as shown above (see p. 29).

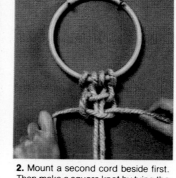

2. Mount a second cord beside first. Then make a square knot by tying the outer two strands about the inner two.

3. Run second cord from left as a holding cord to left. Tie right-to-left (reverse) clove hitch (p. 29) around it.

4. Add a new cord on the left. Drive a nail into knotting board where shown and drape the cord over it.

5. With right-hand strand of new cord tie a right-to-left (reverse) clove hitch around holding cord.

6. Repeat Step 5 with left strand. Always use reverse clove hitch when moving to left, regular to right.

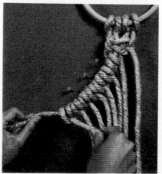

7. After adding two more new cords continue the series of right-to-left clove hitches along holding cord.

8. Tie a series of left-to-right (regular) clove hitches (p. 29) along right holding cord, repeating Steps 3–7.

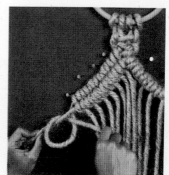

9. Run right middle cord to left. Tie vertical cords on left side about it with reverse clove hitches. *(Continued)*

Macramé/project

Wall hanging (continued)

10. Run eighth cord from right to right side as holding cord. Repeat Step 9 on right with regular clove hitches.

11. After tying two more diagonal rows, tie a square knot with middle four cords, outer two about inner two.

12. Tie two alternating square knots (Steps 7–8, p. 34) under knot from Step 11. Tie square knot in middle.

13. Through Step 19 you will work with and count only the eight middle cords. Slip bead on second from left.

14. Tie a square knot beneath the bead, using the first and fourth of the left middle cords.

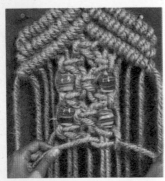

15. Fill the middle of the hanging with a total of four beads, following Steps 12, 13, and 14.

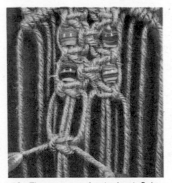

16. Tie a square knot about 3 in. beneath the knot under the left bead. Push this knot up under bead.

17. The knot tied in Step 16 creates two loops as shown above. Tie an identical knot beneath it.

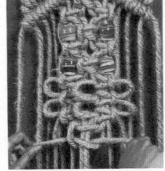

18. Repeat Steps 16 and 17 on right side. Then tie a square knot using four middle cords.

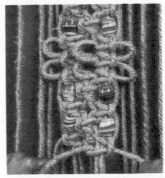

19. Add four more beads by repeating Steps 13–15. Then tie a square knot with the four middle cords.

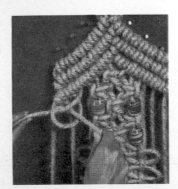

20. With center complete, take fourth cord from far left to left. Tie reverse clove hitches over it, as shown.

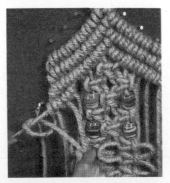

21. Tie reverse clove hitches with remaining cords on left. Then add two new cords as in Steps 4–6.

22. Make two more rows of reverse clove hitches, using two innermost left middle cords as holding cords.

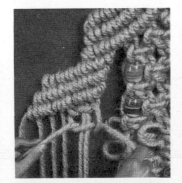

23. Working with the four inner left middle cords, tie a square knot with two outer cords around inner two.

24. Tie three square knots as in Steps 16–17. Take fourth cord from left to left; tie reverse clove hitches on it.

25. Slip bead on far left cord; run cord right. Tie regular clove hitches on it with three cords to its right.

26. Run outer left cord to right. Tie regular clove hitches on it with seven cords to its right.

27. Repeat Step 26 two more times to make a total of three full rows of diagonal clove hitches.

28. Run fifth cord from left to right. Tie regular clove hitches about it with next seven cords to its right.

29. Repeat Steps 20–28 on the right side, filling out the last knotted section with reverse clove hitches.

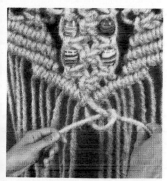

30. Run the middle left cord to the right. Tie a regular clove hitch around it with the middle right cord.

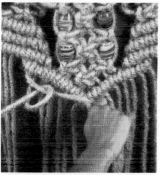

31. Repeat Step 28 twice again on left and right sides to make two final rows of diagonal clove hitches.

32. After cutting the free strands to a length of about 2 ft, unravel them to form a decorative fringe.

33. Trim the fringe, leaving the center section cords a little longer than those to either side.

34. Cut 15 ft of cord. Make it into a hand bobbin (see text, p. 30) and fasten it with a rubber band.

35. Begin a chain of lark's head knots by tying the free end of the cord to the ring with a half-hitch.

36. Complete the lark's head by holding the free end, then tying a reverse half-hitch, as shown.

37. Fill out the entire mounting ring with a tight chain of lark's head knots, repeating Steps 35 and 36.

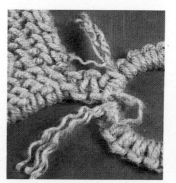

38. Unravel the leftover cord. Use a large tapestry needle to tuck these strands beneath the rear square knot.

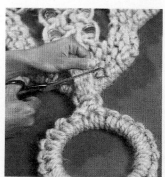

39. Weave these strands under and out through the horizontal cords at back. Trim strands as shown.

Macramé/project

Plant hanger

1. Secure mounting ring to board with U-pins (see text, p. 28). Tie cords to ring using a reverse lark's head knot.

2. The 8 mounted cords create 16 strands; make a hand bobbin of each, using rubber bands (see text, p. 30).

3. Run right middle cord to left as holding cord. Tie right-to-left clove hitches about it with cords to its left.

4. Repeat Step 3 on right, using eighth cord from right as holding cord and left-to-right clove hitches.

5. Repeat Steps 3 and 4 to make two more rows of clove hitches, one running left, the other, right.

6. Take the four middle cords. Using the outer two of these, tie a square knot around the inner two cords.

7. Begin alternating square knots: use two left-hand strands from knot in Step 6 and two free strands to left.

8. Advance the sequence by tying another square knot, using the two left-hand strands from knot in Step 7.

This simple but striking plant hanger is almost 5 ft long. Steps 1–16 are done on a knotting board, and hand bobbins are used. At Step 17 the work is taken from the board, and the mounting ring is suspended from a cord fastened to a peg on a wall. The use of hand bobbins for the main work is discontinued at this point, though a bobbin is used to finish the mounting ring. The ring is finished in the same way as the ring in the wall hanging (see p. 33).

You may want to refer back to page 29 to review the following knots: alternating square knots (Steps 6–14 and 33-34); a spiral chain of regular (left-to-right) half-knots (Steps 20 and 25–26); a spiral chain of reverse (right-to-left) half-knots (Steps 20 and 29); inside-out square knots (26–28).
Materials. 170 ft of 3/16-in., 6-ply jute, cut into eight 20-ft strands, leaving a 10-ft strand for the ring; wooden bead, 1¼ in. long; mounting ring, 3½ in. in diameter.

9. Complete the alternating sequence by tying two square knots with the last four cords on the left.

10. Repeat Steps 7–9 on the right side. Then tie a square knot with the four middle cords.

11. Undo bobbins holding the two middle cords. Thread cords through a bead. Push bead up tight.

12. Make a square knot by tying the two cords above the bead around the two cords beneath it.

13. Drop off two outer cords on left. Working from left, tie two alternating square knots, using cords 3–8.

14. Tie alternating square knots on right side as done on left. Then tie a square knot with middle four cords.

15. Using the outermost cords on each side as holding cords, make diagonal rows of clove hitches.

16. Again using outermost cords, repeat Step 15 to make a second row of diagonal clove hitches on each side.

17. Hang the ring from a wall peg and undo all of the bobbins. Tie a square knot with the middle four cords.

18. Using the next two cords closest to the center, tie another square knot beneath the one tied in Step 17.

19. Repeat Step 18 with next two cords closest to center, for a total of three square knots in middle.

20. With four outer cords on left, tie six regular half-knots. Repeat on right with reverse half-knots.

21. Tie the two inside cords on the right and left in a square knot around the two middle cords.

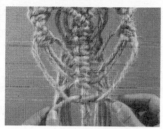

22. Repeat Step 21, working outward with each successive pair of free cords from the right and left sides.

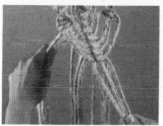

23. You will now begin working with four groups of four cords each: front, back, right, and left groups.

24. The back, left, and right cord groups are tied with square knots to align with knots tied in front (Step 22).

25. Tie front group into spiral chain of 10 regular half-knots, outer two about inner two. Finish with square knot.

26. Repeat Step 25 on all groups. Begin inside-out square knots, using inner two cords as knotting cords.

27. Complete the first of the inside-out square knots. Seven such knots are tied in each cord group.

28. Shown here is the beginning of the second knot in the series of seven inside-out square knots.

29. Under inside-out square knots make spiral chains of 16 reverse half-knots. Finish with square knot.

30. Repeat Step 29 on all groups. Begin square-knot chains with outer two cords of adjacent groups.

31. A chain of nine square knots extends for about 5 in. beneath each pair of spiral chains.

32. The completed four groups of square-knot chains form the pot holder of the plant hanger.

33. Tie the cord groups securely together at the base with one row of alternating square knots.

34. Repeat Step 33 twice more to make a total of three rows of alternating square knots, four per row.

35. Cut the bottom strands off about a foot beneath the last knots, or at any length that you desire.

36. Strands may be left as they are or unraveled. Finish ring as in Steps 34–39 on page 33.

Decoupage

A high art of humble origins

Although we now call it by its French name, *découpage* ("cutting out"), the art of decorating wood, glass, and ceramic surfaces with paper cutouts first flourished in 18th-century Italy. In Venice, the early center of the craft, decoupage was initially called *l'arte povero* ("the poor man's art"), because it began as an inexpensive way of imitating the ornately hand-painted and lacquered furniture then being imported from China and Japan. Venetian artisans soon attained a level of intricacy in the new technique that rivaled the artistry of Oriental lacquers.

From Venice decoupage spread to France, Germany, Belgium, Poland, Spain, Britain, colonial America, and Mexico. By the mid-19th century the development of new engraving, printing, embossing, and die-cutting processes had made available to the public a wide variety of colored scrapbook pictures, prints, gold leaf, and the like—all of a quality formerly known only in original works of art. Decoupage became a family pastime. It was used to decorate all sorts of furniture, screens, and music and jewelry boxes, as well as china and ceramic urns and vases.

Britain's Queen Victoria became the most famous collector of decoupage. Among the finest practitioners of the craft was an English invalid, Amelia Blackburn. She took up the art as a hobby, but her exquisitely colored paper birds and garlands of flowers set the style for the beautiful "Amelias" her contemporaries were soon attempting to imitate.

Without question, decoupage is a time-consuming and exacting craft. Yet it is basically very simple, and these techniques can transform ordinary furnishings into prized possessions.

The prints on this Victorian decoupage cabinet were cut from newspapers and magazines.

Tools and materials

Decoupage can be used to beautify wood, porcelain, or glass. Wooden objects are first sanded (see below) and then usually painted or stained before the decoupage is applied (see p. 40). Sealers are used to prepare wooden surfaces for paint and to prevent the running, or "bleeding," of color in the prints.

Plastic-based putty adhesive, a removable substance, permits the temporary arrangement of the cutout prints on the object; it is a great aid to arriving at a pleasing design before the final gluing. The cutouts are glued to wood with white glue (PVA adhesive), to glass or porcelain with acrylic adhesive. A tool called a brayer is used to flatten the cutouts and to expel excess glue and air bubbles. Finally, the burnisher is used to press down the edges.

Varnish is applied to wooden surfaces over the cutouts and, after the 10th coat of varnish, is wet-sanded. Steel wool, oil and pumice, and white wax are used in the finishing stage. The tack cloth is used to wipe the surface clean after each sanding.

All the above tools but the brayer, burnisher, and decoupage scissors are available from most hardware or paint stores. You can substitute cuticle scissors for decoupage scissors, a rolling pin or round pencil for a brayer, and the back of a spoon for a burnisher. Commercial spray-can sealers are easy to use and readily available. You can make your own brush-on sealer, however, by mixing 3 parts shellac to 1 part alcohol. A tack cloth is made by soaking cheesecloth in varnish and then wringing it out.

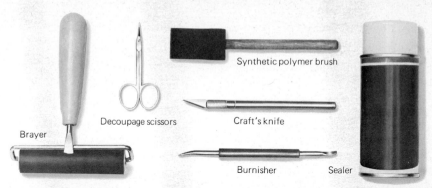

The only specialized tools required for the decoupage projects shown on these pages are the brayer, burnisher, and decoupage scissors illustrated above. You may want to prepare the surface with gesso, metallic wax, paint, or stains. You will also need sponges, turpentine, sealer, varnish, brushes, sandpaper, garnet (finishing) paper, steel wool, a tack cloth, oil and pumice, a sanding block, art coloring pencils, white glue, and acrylic adhesive (which comes in two parts, liquid and powder, mixed just before use). Two kinds of spray sealer are employed—an acrylic sealer and a vinyl (plastic) sealer. Brushes made of synthetic polymer sponge leave no brush marks. You will also need small three-ply synthetic sponges (cut any synthetic sponge into small pieces). Use a felt-covered sanding block. If you cannot find one, it is easily made by gluing a piece of felt to the sanding side of a sanding block and wrapping the sandpaper over the felt.

Preparing wood for the application of sealers and paints

Smoothly sanded boxes and plaques suitable for decoupaging are available in crafts shops, but you can always make your own. If you are decoupaging old wood, strip it of its finish, using a chemical stripper or paint remover, and then sand it smooth.

Even presanded boxes bought from a crafts shop should be given a final sanding before applying the background paint or stain. Seal the wood *before* painting it. If you are staining the wood, seal it *after* the stain has been applied and has dried. Use a fine garnet sandpaper—No. 220 or No. 240. If the wood feels particularly rough, begin with a coarser grade of sandpaper—No. 100 or No. 120—then finish with the garnet paper. To test for smoothness, rub the wood with an old stocking.

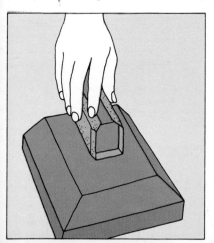

Wrap sandpaper around a felt-padded sanding block. Sand the wood lightly with the grain.

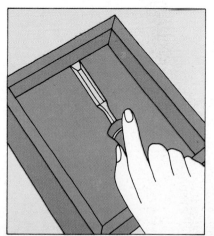

Inner edges and corners of boxes often contain lumps of dried glue. Remove them with a chisel.

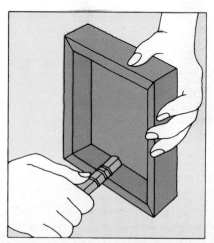

To sand inner edges, wrap sandpaper about a thin, solid piece of wood like an ice-cream stick.

After each sanding wipe the surface absolutely clean of fine dust with a tack cloth.

Decoupage

Selection and preparation of prints

Prints are sold by crafts shops. But you can as easily find your own designs in a variety of printed materials, such as children's and art books, gift paper, photos, postcards, and greeting cards.

Thick prints such as photos and postcards should be thinned as shown in the illustrations at right. Although raised edges may be used for their sculptured effect, a smooth surface is generally desired. This is why the print edges are pressed down with the burnisher after the prints have been glued. It is also why, when cutting borders, scissors are held at a slant to produce a finely beveled edge. A beveled edge will lie closer to the wood than an ordinary straight edge. You may also singe or serrate the edge. Serration of the edge produces an attractive three-dimensional effect.

Ladders and sealers. After you have selected your print, first determine which parts of the design you plan to use. If there are any delicate sections that might tear in handling, draw ladders between them as illustrated in Step 1 at right. Also thicken stems and other thin lines with a pencil of the appropriate color, as seen in Step 2. Seal the colored areas with a spray sealer or thinned shellac.

Seal the whole print before you begin to cut it. If you have done any hand coloring on the print, seal it with a vinyl (plastic) sealer. If not, use acrylic sealer. After sealing, cut away the extra paper around the print, then make rough cuts outlining the sections you will use. Next cut away interior sections, including those enclosed by ladders. Then cut the border. Since you want to leave ladders intact as long as possible, they should not be cut off until after you apply glue just before placing the cutout on the object.

When cutting, hold the scissors with the thumb and middle finger. Use the index finger as a guide.

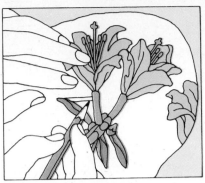

1. Draw ladders between any long, thin sections of the print that might tear due to their fragility. Cut off these ladders just before the actual gluing.

2. Widen any stems, tendrils, or other thin lines by thickening them with colored pencils. This will make them somewhat easier to cut.

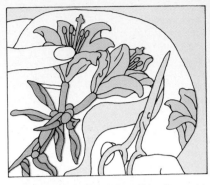

3. Begin making rough cuts outlining those sections or details of the print that you have decided to use in your design.

4. To make interior cuts, first poke a hole with the scissor tips through the paper from above. Then insert scissors from beneath to cut.

5. Cut the outside edges of the pattern next. Bevel the edges by angling the scissors inward as you cut, as shown.

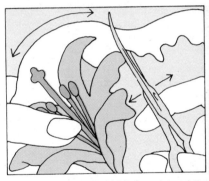

6. To serrate an edge, both the print and the scissors are rotated toward and away from each other in short, quick movements.

7. To make a singed edge for soft, burnt effects, cut the print to shape, then singe the edges by touching them with a burning cigarette.

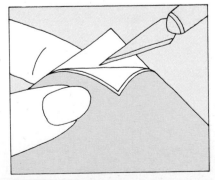

Thinning prints. Before doing any cutting, apply white glue to the back of the paper. Let it dry. Then peel back a corner edge with a thin knife.

Roll the peeled edge around a pencil. Peel off the entire layer by rolling the pencil. Sand the back lightly with No. 220 or No. 240 garnet paper.

Decoupage/project

Decorating a glass plate

The process of decoupaging glass differs significantly from that of decoupaging wood (as illustrated on pages 40 and 41). Since the print is seen "under glass," the translucent effect is obtained by means of the glass itself rather than by many coats of varnish.

Begin by spraying the backs of prints with acrylic sealer. Cut your designs from the prints and arrange them (see Steps 1–3 below). Glue the cutouts face up to the bottom of the glass plate with an acrylic adhesive. This is white when it is wet, but it dries clear.

Next press out any air bubbles between the cutouts and the glass with a damp cloth. This is of crucial importance in all decoupage. Seen under glass, these bubbles will appear as shiny white spots. Keep checking the front of the plate for any remaining bubbles. Wipe off any large lumps of adhesive.

After the cutouts are dry, use a small synthetic sponge to pat the entire bottom of the plate with emulsion. After this coat dries, pat on a background film of acrylic water-base paint. Wait 24 hours for the acrylic to dry, then apply a second coat. Finally, apply two coats of protective varnish, allowing 24 hours drying time between coats.

Decorating a glass lamp

1. Place the glass plate on a piece of paper and trace its circumference accurately with a pencil.

2. Arrange the composition by placing the cutouts face up on the paper inside the circumference line.

3. Place the plate on top of the cutouts. Outline the cutouts on the plate with a grease pencil.

4. With a synthetic sponge, pat a full coat of acrylic adhesive on the bottom of the plate.

Decoupaging a lamp presents a special problem because of the difficulty of applying the cutouts to the inside of the glass base. Work on a lamp big enough to permit free movement of your hand inside the base during the gluing and painting stages. Using putty adhesive (see text, p. 37), first arrange composition on the outside of the base as shown here.

5. Ladders were drawn (see p. 38) and were left on in initial cutting. They are cut off just before gluing.

6. Lay cutout on adhesive. Turn plate over to check its position within lines made in Step 3.

7. Press out bubbles with damp cloth. When all the cutouts are dry, pat adhesive over entire back.

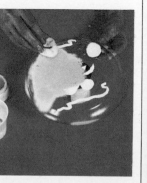

8. Pat on a thin coat of acrylic paint. Apply second coat in 24 hr. After it dries, varnish twice.

Mark the outlines of the cutouts on the outside of the glass with grease pencil. Number the back of each cutout to indicate the exact section of glass to which it will be glued. Place papers inside the glass to simulate a painted background, as shown here. Then glue the cutouts to the inside of the base, face outward, using acrylic adhesive. Finally, paint background.

Decoupage/project

Decorating a wooden jewelry box

After the box is sanded smooth and clean, it is given a background—in this case, wax containing a metallic ruby-colored stain. Wax is best applied with small, three-ply synthetic sponges, but any synthetic sponge will do. After the box is waxed, spray it with vinyl sealer.

Apply a thin, even coat of glue to the back of each cutout. The less you use, the less you will have to remove. You can apply glue with a brush, but a finger is easiest. Glue the largest cutouts first. Clean your fingers before placing the cutouts on the box.

The traditional finish is varnish. This alone gives the mellow glow desired in decoupage. Use the clearest varnish you can find. You should apply a minimum of 20 coats. After each coat, allow a day's drying time before sanding and applying the next coat. Work in a dust-free room and never varnish on a humid day. Wet-sand after the 10th coat of varnish and every 3rd coat thereafter. Use No. 400 wet-and-dry sandpaper, and dip it into soapy water.

When gluing braid, first measure it against the side of the box. Initially apply glue only to within 1 inch of where the lengths of braid meet at the box corners. The unglued ends are pasted down after the braid is mitered to meet at a neat 45° angle (Step 9, this page). The final step (not shown in the illustrations) is to polish the box with white wax.

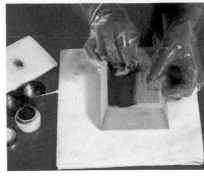

1. Begin by applying metallic wax. First dip sponge into turpentine, blotting on paper towel. Then rub sponge in wax and apply.

2. Let wax dry 20 min. Wipe off excess with soft, dry cloth. Rub till metal in wax begins to shine. (Gloves will keep stain off your hands.)

3. Place waxed box inside cardboard carton. Spray with vinyl sealer. Reverse the box to seal the inside area, then repeat with the lid.

4. Put box aside and prepare print. Spray front with a thin coat of acrylic sealer. Hold can 1 ft away. Apply second coat after 2 min.

5. Cut prints into sections. Make detailed cuts with decoupage scissors, angled to produce a beveled edge (see p. 38).

6. Tape lid to box. Press pieces of putty adhesive (see p. 37) to bottoms of cutouts, then arrange them on box according to your own design.

7. With pencil, mark box where cutouts will be glued. Do not make a complete outline. Just mark some opposite points to permit positioning.

8. Remove the putty adhesive. Cover the backs of the cutouts with thin, even coats of white glue. Work on cellophane or aluminum foil.

9. Glue cutouts one at a time. With clean finger, press outward on cutout from center to edge to squeeze out excess glue and air bubbles.

10. Use tweezers to hold very fine cutouts such as this leaf. Apply glue with a toothpick, then position with tweezers. Gently press with finger.

11. After all the cutouts are glued onto the box, carefully wipe away any excess glue with a damp cloth or a damp sponge.

12. Place clean, damp cloth over cutouts. Roll brayer firmly in one direction, then in opposite direction. Begin in center and work outward.

13. After the glue has dried (2–3 hr) use the rounded, paddle end of the burnisher to press down the edges of the cutouts.

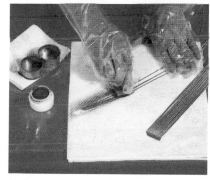

14. This cutout has been glued over the line where the lid meets the box. Cut through this line with a crafts knife or single-edged razor blade.

15. Stain the gold braid in the same manner as the box. Place it on a paper towel when staining so that the paper absorbs any superfluous stain.

16. Using toothpick, apply glue to braid to within 1 in. of corners. Position; wipe away excess glue. Press braid with burnisher as shown.

17. Cut a neat mitered joint. Finish gluing braid ends with toothpick. Press down ends with burnisher. Wipe clean. Finish other corners.

18. Apply first coat of varnish and allow 24 hr for it to dry. Wipe box with the tack cloth before applying next coat.

19. Wet-sand after 10th coat of varnish. Wrap paper about sponge, dip in soapy water. Sand surface smooth and matte (a dull, cloudy finish).

20. Wet-sand after every successive third coat and again after last. Lightly rub with steel wool till smooth. Use No. 0000 steel wool.

21. Mix 1 part pumice to 2 parts lemon or linseed oil. Apply with soft cloth. Rub vigorously. Dry with clean cloth. Polish with white wax.

Candlemaking

The basics of the craft

Tallow (rendered cattle or sheep fat) and beeswax have been used in candlemaking since Roman times. Paraffin—a distillate of wood, coal, or petroleum—was developed in the 19th century and soon became the main form of candle wax. Despite the advent of electric lighting, more candles are produced today than ever before. Candlemaking is now enjoying a burgeoning popularity both as a fine craft and as an amateur's hobby.

Only a few simple materials and tools are required to make your own handsome candles.

Paraffin wax. Paraffin is usually sold at crafts shops in 10- or 11-pound slabs, one of which will make about four quarts of liquid wax when melted. Paraffin is graded low, medium, or high according to its melting point: low, 51.7–57.2°C; medium, 61.7–65.6°C; high, 71.1–73.9°C. Different grades are required for different kinds of molds. Melting points can be raised by adding stearine (see below).

Beeswax makes lovely candles, but it is expensive. However, a small percentage (5–10 percent) of beeswax added to paraffin will raise the melting point, which makes candles burn longer, and will add a pleasant aroma. Wax does not boil or evaporate except under special laboratory conditions, but above 100°C it smokes and turns brown and should therefore not be raised to that temperature. Prolonged exposure to paraffin fumes can be dangerous, so always work in an open and well-ventilated area.

Before pouring wax into metal molds, warm the molds in an oven to about 38°C. This helps give the candles a smooth finish. After the wax is poured, cooling can be hastened by weighting down the mold in a pail filled with water (see Step 9, right).

Candles are poured upside down, and the candle end nearest the mold opening is actually the bottom. Wax contracts as it cools, causing a well, or cavity, to form beneath the crust around the wick. You must periodically puncture this crust and fill the well with melted wax until the candle has solidified and the cavity has been completely eliminated.

Double boiler and candy thermometer. If you work with a very shallow pot over a flame, there is a danger that the flame may leap up the sides and ignite the wax. It is thus safer to melt paraffin in a double boiler. First bring the water to a boil. Use an ice pick or a hammer to break up the paraffin slab into manageable chunks. A candy thermometer allows you to measure the temperature of the wax precisely.

Stearine (stearic acid). Stearine raises the melting point of wax, thereby making the candle harder. Stearine also makes candles more opaque, and some candlemakers prefer not to use it because of this associated loss of translucency. When used in conjunction with dyes, stearine darkens colors. A standard formula for candles is 90 percent paraffin to 10 percent stearine, or about 3 tablespoons of stearine per pound of wax. Stearine is sold as a powder, which is stirred into the melted wax. Experiment by making variously colored candles with and without stearine.

Dyes. Dye is added after the stearine has dissolved. Use only commercial dyes made for candlemaking. They are available as liquids or as solid cakes or pellets. To control the density of the color, add a little dye at a time—either by drops or by shaving off slivers of the cake or pellet. To test for color, pour a little of the dyed wax onto a white surface. The finished candle will be

A Spanish candlemaker is depicted in this 18th century Catalan tile design, which is in the collection of Barcelona's Museo de Bellas Artes de Cataluña.

slightly darker than is this test wax.

Molds. Molds can be purchased, made, or found. Wax is poured at different temperatures depending on the material used for the mold. For molds made of cardboard, glass, plastic, and rubber, use a low- or medium-grade wax and pour at a temperature between 65°C and 74°C. For metal molds, use the same grades, but pour the wax between 88°C and 93°C.

Silicone spray. This is sprayed into the mold before the wax is poured so that the candle will slide out easily.

Wicks. Wicks are made of braided cotton and come in three diameters: small, large, and extra-large. If the wick is too large for the candle, it will smoke. If it is too small, the melted wax will eventually extinguish the flame. Normally candles less than 2 inches in diameter take small wicks, those 2–4 inches in diameter take large wicks, and those with diameters over 4 inches take extra-large wicks. The wick is usually placed in the mold before the wax is poured. A wick several inches longer than the candle is inserted through the wick hole in the bottom of the mold and is pushed through until only about an inch protrudes from the bottom. This wick end is then secured by placing a piece of mold sealer over the hole and the wick end. (Mold sealer is a puttylike adhesive substance that is available in crafts shops).

The wick at the open end of the mold is wrapped around a thin rod longer than the width of the mold, such as a pencil. The wick must be fairly taut and centered before the wax is poured. Metal candle molds come with gaskets and metal bars for securing the wick.

Certain candles require that the wick be inserted after the candle is made. This is done by piercing a wick hole in the candle with a hot ice pick. A wire-core wick is inserted, and the area around the wick is filled with wax.

Casting a candle

1. Bring water to boil in double boiler. Add chunks of wax, a few at a time, to top of boiler.

2. Measure wax temperature by clipping a candy thermometer to the top part of the boiler.

3. When paraffin has completely melted, slowly stir in 3 tbsp of stearine per pound of wax.

4. After stearine has dissolved, slice in slivers of dye. To test for dye color, refer to text at left.

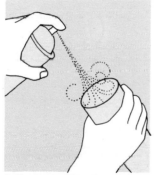

5. Prepare mold to release candle by spraying the inside with a light coat of silicone spray.

6. Slip most of the wick through the wick hole. Secure bottom with a screw, gasket, or mold sealer.

7. Wrap free wick end about metal bar, pencil, or piece of wood. Center wick and make it taut.

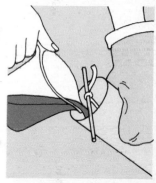

8. Hold mold with oven mit. Pour wax from pot into measuring cup, then from cup slowly into mold.

9. Place mold in pail filled with cool water to level of wax. Hold down with heavy object.

10. After 30 min, remove weight; puncture crust about wick. Pour wax into cavity beneath crust.

11. After wax has set, remove mold from water. Hold mold as shown. To release candle, pull wick gently.

12. Most metal molds have a slight seam, which leaves a seam line on candle. Pare line away with knife.

Candlemaking

Found molds

A surprising variety of household items can serve as candle molds. Milk cartons, for instance, come in various sizes and can be cut to any height. Puncture a wick hole in the bottom of the carton and attach the wick to a rod at the top, as illustrated on page 43.

Molds can also be made from glass Christmas tree balls. First remove the metal cap. Using an oven mit, hold the ball and fill it with wax. After the wax has set and you have filled the cavity (Step 10, p. 43), break the ball by tapping it against a table. Cut off the tubular top to form a round candle.

Aluminum foil can be used to create candles with crinkled, free-form shapes. Fill a container with sand or potting soil and make a depression in it. Push the foil into the depression, shaping it with your hands. Pour in wax, allow it to set, and peel off foil.

Aspic, jelly, and cupcake molds can double as candle molds. For all of the above except milk cartons, use wire-core wicks and insert them after the wax has hardened by using an ice pick as described in the text on page 43.

Hurricane candles

A hurricane candle consists of a wax shell with translucent walls within which sits a small candle. The candle glows through the wax shell, which protects the flame from wind. Although there is some distance between the candle flame and the surrounding walls, the shell must be made from a wax grade that will not melt easily.

You can use a saucepan as a mold for the hurricane shell. Each shell requires about 2 quarts of wax, though much of this is reusable, as it is poured out of the mold before it solidifies.

Add dye when the wax reaches 93°C, but do not add stearine, which would darken the wax and make it opaque. The shell must remain translucent so that the candle flame will shine through.

Fill the mold with wax and place it in a cool water bath (Step 9, p. 43) until the walls and base have solidified to a thickness of about 1 inch. Then remove the crust from the top and pour out the liquid wax from the center. The shell can be reused indefinitely by adding new candles.

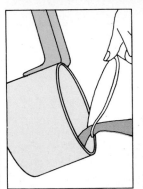

1. Spray interior of saucepan with silicone so that shell can be easily removed. Fill can with lightly dyed wax to within about 1 in. of top.

2. As the top crust forms during cooling, test its thickness. When crust is 1/4 in. thick, insert knife into wax 1/2 in. from wall. Cut out a circle.

3. Remove mold from water. Lift off the top crust with a knife, then pour out the liquid wax from the center. Allow shell to cool 24 hr in mold.

Dipped candles

Dipping a wick into hot melted wax is the oldest and simplest means of making candles. Begin by cutting the wick(s) several inches longer than the desired candle length. If you want to dip several candles at the same time, tie the wicks 2 to 3 inches apart on a rod or a hoop. Have the melted wax of desired grade ready in a container that is deep enough for the candle length you want to make. Tall metal candle molds are good containers for dipping one candle at a time, and kettles are good for dipping multiple wicks.

In Step 1, illustrated below, after the candle is first dipped into the wax, the end of the waxed wick is gripped and held taut for a few seconds while the wax hardens. This serves to produce a straight wick for subsequent dippings.

You can make dipped candles of any color wax, or plain white candles can later be glazed with dyed wax. A striped glaze is obtained by dipping white candles into successively shallower wax baths of different colors. This process is best done with gradations of the same color. For example, prepare several shades of blue wax baths. First dip the white candle all the way down into the lightest dye bath. Then, after allowing this glaze to dry, dip the candle into the next darkest shade—but only three-quarters of the way or less. Follow this procedure with successive dye baths to produce a candle with subtly differentiated horizontal stripes along its full length.

To make the bottoms of your dipped candles flat and smooth, heat a metal spatula over a gas flame or an electric burner. Rub the candle bottom against the hot metal surface, melting away wax until the bottom is flat.

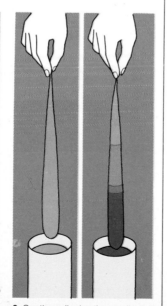

1. Holding the wick by one end, dip it into the hot wax. Withdraw the wick and pull on the other end to make it taut. Dip the wick again after the first wax hardens.

2. Continue dipping the candle until it reaches the thickness you desire. Be sure to allow each layer of wax to harden thoroughly before the next dipping.

Layered candles

In layered candles each color is poured after the previous one has hardened, which produces either horizontal or angled layers, as illustrated at right. Prepare a batch of each color wax your design calls for and let them all harden in trays. As they are needed, break them into chunks and remelt them to pour the various layers.

The time allowed between pouring successive layers is crucial. If a new layer is poured before the previous one has thoroughly set, the colors will blend together where they meet—an effect you may or may not desire. But if each layer is allowed to set for 3 to 5 hours, the lines between them will be clearly demarcated. This leaves ample time to melt your dyed wax, pour it, then empty and clean the boiler before melting wax of a different color for the candle's next layer.

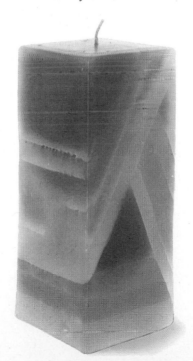

1. Use a medium-grade wax, stearine, and dyes to make batches of each color wax needed. Pour into individual trays. Let harden.

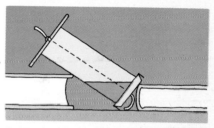

2. Mount wick in mold and spray inside with silicone mold release. Place mold on support to hold it at desired angle for first layer.

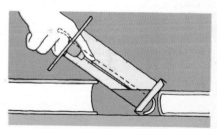

3. Outer edges of the wax will set before the area around the wick. Test wick area to be sure it is firm before adding a new layer.

4. After one layer of wax has set completely, pour a different color. Change the angle of the mold between pourings as desired.

45

Candlemaking

Egg candles

Empty eggshells make unique and appealing found molds. The key to success with an egg candle is to let the shell dry thoroughly—about 24 hours—after emptying and rinsing it as described in Step 1 below. Use a low- or medium-grade wax and heat it to 82°C before pouring it into the eggshell.

There are two ways of coloring the candle. You can make a white egg, then glaze it by dipping it into a hot (55°C) dyed wax bath (Step 4). In following this procedure do not add stearine to the white wax used for the candle, but make the color bath for the glaze with both stearine and dye.

If you prefer to make the colored candle out of dyed wax, add stearine and dye to the candle wax, and in Step 4 dip the colored candle into a hot water bath instead of a dye bath. Fill the area around the wick with melted wax the same color as the candle.

Vertically striped candles

To make a vertically striped candle, begin with a regular solid-color candle, then follow the two steps illustrated below. When the tape is removed, stripes the color of the original candle are revealed. The base candle can be white or colored wax, and you can roll it in a darker shade of the same color or in a contrasting color. Other simple patterns can be made the same way.

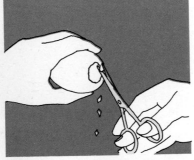
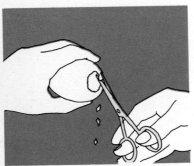

1. Make hole in large end of a raw egg by puncturing shell with a pin, then cutting out a neat disk with cuticle scissors. Empty the egg into a bowl. Rinse out the inside with water. Be sure to let the shell dry very thoroughly.

2. Holding the eggshell in an egg carton, carefully pour melted wax into the hole from a small measuring cup. Fill shell to brim. Wax should be low or medium grade.

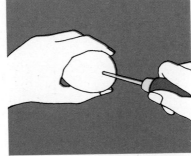

3. Allow the wax to set in shell overnight; then chip the shell away. Be careful not to mar the candle as you remove the shell. Make a wick hole straight through the center, using the heated prong of an ice pick.

4. After inserting a wire-core wick into the candle and filling in the area around it with hot wax, let the candle sit until the wax around the wick hardens. Then glaze the candle by dipping it into a hot dye bath. When glaze dries, trim wick.

Apply masking tape to the sides of a candle from top to bottom over those areas you want to remain the original color of the base candle.

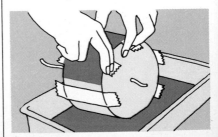

Pour about 1/2 in. of hot, dyed wax into a pan. Roll candle in wax, covering sides evenly but leaving top unglazed. Remove tape when wax sets.

Whipped wax

Whipping wax is much like whipping cream. Hot wax of high grade, or medium grade with stearine added, is allowed to cool to the point where a fine scum forms on the surface. Then the wax is whipped into a lather with an eggbeater or a mixer. Before this lather hardens, it is applied to a candle. Clean wax from instruments by placing them on a foil sheet in a warm oven.

Allow a scum to form on the melted wax. Whip the wax until it froths up to form a heavy lather with a creamy consistency.

Before the whipped wax has time to harden, apply it to the candle with a spoon or a flat knife blade. Any ordinary candle can be decorated this way.

Chunk candles

Chunk candles contain embedded pieces of varicolored wax that are visible through the translucent walls of the candle. Make the chunks as shown at right. Then, when they have hardened, arrange them in the mold, leaving spaces in between. Wax of a contrasting or complementary color—usually a lighter color—is poured over them.

Use a low-grade wax, stearine, and dye for the chunks. Make them dark enough so that they will be visible through the background wax. This should be made of the same grade wax as the chunks, but leave out the stearine to preserve translucency. Pour it at a temperature slightly below the melting point of the wax used for the chunks.

A milk carton makes an ideal mold. Puncture a wick hole in the bottom of the carton. Before positioning the chunks, mount the wick and seal the hole with mold sealer.

Ice candles

Ice candles are created by taking advantage of the principle that water and wax do not naturally mix. Pieces of ice are placed in a mold; when the hot wax is poured over them, it sets instantaneously where it comes in contact with the ice. At the same time, the ice is melted by the heat of the wax. The result is a delicate, lacey candle.

Use an ordinary taper candle as a core to hold the fragile lacework together. Put it into the mold first, anchoring it with a base layer of melted wax as illustrated at right. When the core candle is secure in the base, add the ice and pour the wax.

A wide mold, such as a milk carton, will provide stability in the finished candle. Use a medium-grade wax, adding stearine and dye when it reaches 82°C. Allow the candle to set overnight before removing it from the mold. Be sure all the water drains out.

Prepare the wax for the chunks in a double boiler, then pour it into a metal tray to set. When the wax reaches the taffy stage, cut it into squares, triangles, or rectangles. Let them stand until they harden completely.

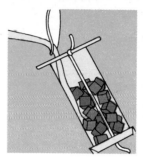

Spray the mold with silicone mold release. Mount wick; arrange chunks inside mold. Finally, pour in wax, covering all the chunks. When the candle has hardened, remove it from mold. Chunk candles may not burn as evenly as ordinary candles.

Center the core candle in the mold, and pour in a base layer of wax about 1½ in. thick. Hold the core candle steady until the base wax sets. When the base wax has hardened completely, pack the mold with pieces of ice, then pour hot wax into the mold.

Remember that the mold contains water from the melted ice. Remove the candle from its mold over a sink in order to catch the spilling water. Dry the candle on a paper towel.

47

These elegant Tibetan papier-mâché masks are from the American Museum of Natural History.

A simple and appealing art

Until almost 2,000 years ago man wrote and drew pictures on such materials as papyrus, parchment, vellum, cloth, and tree bark. About A.D. 100 the Chinese invented paper—a combination of bark, hemp, old cloth, and fishnet.

The Chinese explored both the esthetic and the functional possibilities of paper, finding that it combined well with natural glues and could be fashioned into objects that were not only elegant but durable. Paper-based trays, decorative boxes, and figures graced many Chinese households.

The French gave the craft the name *papier-mâché* ("chewed paper"). Papier-mâché reached its zenith as a popular craft in Europe in the 18th century. Since paper was then still handmade, it was a precious commodity, and papier-mâché became a creative means of recycling broadsides, posters, and newspapers into a variety of useful objects.

As a functional craft, papier-mâché was eclipsed at the dawn of the Industrial Revolution. Yet many papier-mâché objects made 200 and more years ago remain as sound and attractive today as when they were made.

Armatures. The skeleton on which the papier-mâché is molded is called the armature. On subsequent pages different types of armatures are shown as the basis for papier-mâché animals. However, armatures for a wide variety of delightful objects can be made by following the same principles and methods as those illustrated for the animal armatures.

Making armatures will spur both your imagination and your sense of improvisation. Since papier-mâché is light, armatures also can be lightweight. Ordinary cardboard, easily cut into any shape, is an excellent structural material for armatures. A number of basic shapes can be obtained from containers made of plastic or aluminum foil. Tin cans may be right for cylindrical shapes. Wire mesh and single-strand wire of various gauges are also commonly used. Since wire is easily bent, it is ideal for sculptural forms. For round objects you can work with armatures made simply of balled-up newspaper—or even inflated balloons.

Busts and masks. Complex objects can be formed on armatures that are made of combinations of materials. Cardboard and a balloon, for example, can be combined as the framework for a bust. Cut corrugated cardboard for the neck and shoulders, then flesh it out by covering it with strips of glued

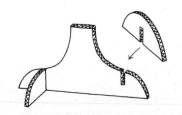

Cardboard armature for a bust

paper. To make the head, glue strips of paper over an inflated balloon, leaving a small uncovered opening at the base.

Balloon armature for a head or a mask

After the paper has dried, puncture the balloon and pull it out through the hole. Attach the head to the neck by means of glued paper strips. Mash (see illustrations, facing page) is then applied to the surface of the form, modeled to form features, and sanded after it dries. The bust may then be painted or simply finished with lacquer. A mask, too, can be made on a balloon armature, but only half of the balloon should be covered.

Papier-mâché

Basic techniques

Two basic methods are used in papier-mâché—one employing paper strips, the other, mash. In the first method paper is torn into strips and the strips are coated with paste before applying them to an armature. The second method entails cooking shredded paper in a solution of water and glue to form a mash of a doughy consistency, which can be applied to the armature and sculpted almost like clay. The paper strip method produces surfaces and textures more suggestive of the natural qualities of paper, while mash surfaces, especially when sanded and painted, are more like wood, enameled metal, or glazed pottery.

The two methods can be combined (as they were in the bust on page 48). First paper strips are used to build up the basic form on the armature, then mash is applied for a smooth finished surface.

Glues and gluing. The two most commonly used adhesives are liquid white glue (PVA) and wallpaper paste. If you choose to work with white glue, thin it by mixing 1 part glue to 1 part water. Wallpaper paste, available at hardware stores, comes in powder form and is mixed with water. Slowly stir 1 part powder to 10 parts water.

Do not cut strips with scissors. Tear them using a straightedge, or along the edge of a table. The rough edges of torn strips will mesh to make a smoother surface. The length and width of the strips you tear will depend on the size of the object you plan to make.

There are two ways to coat the strips with glue or paste: either put a handful of the strips into the water-thinned adhesive and let them soak for a few minutes before applying them to the armature, or soak a sponge in the adhesive solution and coat the strips with the sponge. Be careful not to saturate the strips to the point where they begin to fall apart. As you apply the strips, use your hand or a sponge to wipe away excessive adhesive.

Both newspaper and paper toweling are good for building up the form on an armature before applying finer paper to the exterior. Tissue paper is difficult to work with because it may pull apart when the excess glue or paste is removed. Still, it is ideal for imparting a soft texture to an object (as seen in the finishing touches being applied to the papier-mâché rabbit on page 52).

Mash is easily made by following the steps illustrated at right. Boiling the water hastens the breakdown of paper fiber and makes it easier to whisk. Crafts shops carry commercial mash, a powder to which water is added.

Drying and finishing. Most papier-mâché objects will dry overnight. Drying time can be hastened by using an oven preheated to a low or medium temperature. Dried objects can then be finished by sanding and painting their surfaces. A mash surface is usually sanded smooth. Paper strip surfaces, on the other hand, are best left with the texture of the paper itself. Sanded or not, papier-mâché objects may be painted with any water-base paint.

Waterproofing and fireproofing. To waterproof surfaces and make them more durable, spray the finished object with a clear vinyl sealer (see *Decoupage,* p. 37) or give it at least three coats of lacquer. To fireproof an object, stir in 1 teaspoon of sodium phosphate (available at drugstores) to each cup of paste for strips or to each cup of water when making mash.

Both the strip and the mash techniques are illustrated in the step-by-step photo sequences on pages 50–53. In the creation of the papier-mâché box (p. 53) the strip method is illustrated. If you use mash instead of strips, the surface can be sanded smooth, decorated with hand-painted designs, and finished with clear lacquer.

Making mash

1. To make 1 qt of mash, tear four large newspaper sheets into small pieces. Place in container with 2 qt water and let soak overnight.

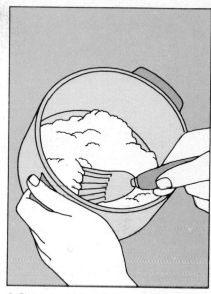

2. Place the above mixture in a cooking vessel. Boil it for 20 min. Using a whisk, whip the paper until it is soft and pulpy.

3. Place the pulp in a strainer. Tap it several times to shake out water, then squeeze it gently until the pulp is a soft, moist lump.

4. Put the pulp into a bowl. Stir in 2 tbsp of liquid white glue (PVA), then 2 tbsp of wallpaper paste. Stir until mixture is not lumpy.

Papier-mâché/projects

Wire armatures

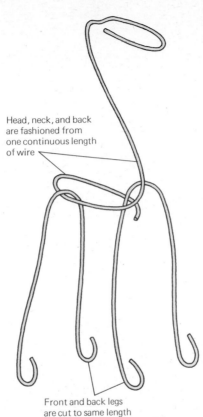

Head, neck, and back are fashioned from one continuous length of wire

Front and back legs are cut to same length

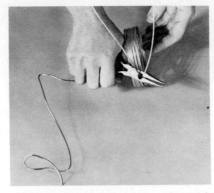

1. Bend wire into the configurations shown at left and cut the wire with wire snips.

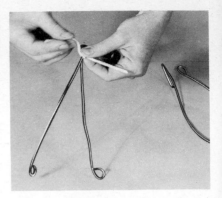

2. Bind front and back legs tightly to the main body with pipe cleaners or thin florist's wire.

5. Make another ball of strips for head. Use wrapping of strips to bind it to frame.

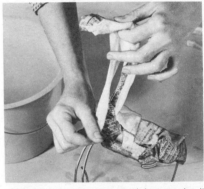

6. Continue to build up the neck by wrapping it with glue-soaked strips of paper towel.

9. For mane fringe and tail tassel snip strips of brown tissue paper.

10. Paste mane and tail tassel carefully into place. Ruffle mane's cut edge.

A wire armature is ideal for this giraffe or for any other papier-mâché form—such as the human figure—with slender sections or members. The wire used for this armature is galvanized single strand, 1/16 inch in diameter.

Wire comes in spools of various lengths and gauges (diameters) and is available at hardware stores. The gauge required will depend on the size and weight of the form you are creating. You should be able to bend the wire with relative ease, and it should be sturdy enough to support the amount of paper you plan to use without sagging. You can try using a coat hanger as

a substitute, but generally coat hangers are too rigid for intricate manipulation.

For this giraffe, cut the wire, using wire snips, into the three basic armature components shown above. Round the feet, head, and back into their proper curvatures by carefully bending the wire with pliers.

Two kinds of paper are used to make the figure: newspaper strips to build up the basic form and paper towels to finish it. Paper toweling provides a better background for paint than does newspaper, which would require two or more coats of paint just to cover the ink of the newsprint.

Cylindrical and aluminum-foil armatures

3. With legs attached, the form should stand on its own. Correct any defects by bending wire.

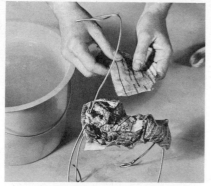

4. Make ball of glue-soaked strips (see p. 49) for body. Bind to frame using wrapping of strips.

Build up the leg forms by wrapping them with glue-soaked strips of paper towel.

7. Build up the leg forms by wrapping them with glue-soaked strips of paper towel.

8. Mold paper ears. Secure with soaked strips. Do same for horns and tail. Dry figure.

11. Paint giraffe a golden color. Let paint dry. Then cover the animal with brown dots.

12. Finish by painting hooves, nostrils, mouth, eyes, and tops of horns brown.

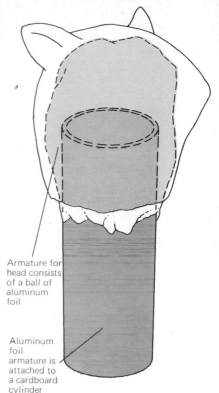

Gerbil's head is made of papier-mâché applied over the aluminum foil armature

Armature for head consists of a ball of aluminum foil

Aluminum foil armature is attached to a cardboard cylinder

Roll aluminum foil into oval ball. Anchor it to cardboard cylinder with another strip of foil (left). Then cover foil with mash. Shape and hollow out ears with thumb (right).

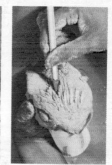

With thumb and fingers pinch out mash to form a nose. Then shape the eyes with a pencil (left). Next use pencil point to mark hair lines on all but very front of face (right).

The armature for this gerbil's head is a ball of aluminum foil attached to a cardboard tube. First the foil is molded into a ball with the oval shape of a gerbil's head. The foil is anchored to the tube by covering the tube with a strip of foil and crimping this foil where the head joins the cardboard neck. Next, papier-mâché mash (see *Making mash*, p. 49) is rolled on a foil sheet with a rolling pin until it becomes a slab about 1/4-inch thick. The mash is then wrapped around the foil head and pressed into a firm sphere with the desired oval shape. Mash is also applied to the neck.

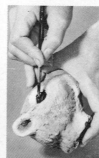

After the mash has completely dried, paint in the gerbil's hair (left) with an almost dry brush. For solid color areas such as the eyes, cheeks, and nose, paint with a very wet brush.

51

Papier-mâché/projects

Combination box and paper armature

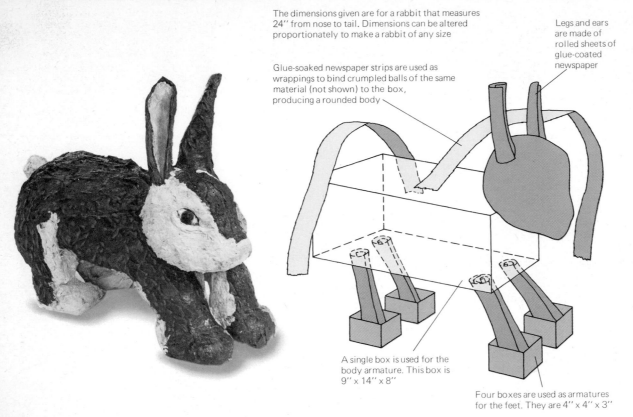

The dimensions given are for a rabbit that measures 24" from nose to tail. Dimensions can be altered proportionately to make a rabbit of any size

Glue-soaked newspaper strips are used as wrappings to bind crumpled balls of the same material (not shown) to the box, producing a rounded body

Legs and ears are made of rolled sheets of glue-coated newspaper

A single box is used for the body armature. This box is 9" x 14" x 8"

Four boxes are used as armatures for the feet. They are 4" x 4" x 3"

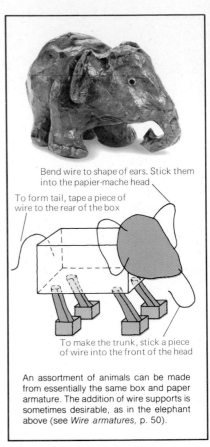

Bend wire to shape of ears. Stick them into the papier-mache head

To form tail, tape a piece of wire to the rear of the box

To make the trunk, stick a piece of wire into the front of the head

An assortment of animals can be made from essentially the same box and paper armature. The addition of wire supports is sometimes desirable, as in the elephant above (see *Wire armatures*, p. 50).

The armature for the rabbit illustrated here is made from rolled sheets of newspaper and cardboard boxes of the sort that cakes and pastries often come in. The dimensions for a 24-inch-long finished rabbit are given in the drawing above, but if you choose to make a different size rabbit or a combination armature for a different figure, say a lion or an elephant, then your box sizes should vary proportionately.

The legs and ears of the rabbit are made with loosely rolled sheets of glue-coated newspaper. The head is a single ball of glue-soaked strips of newspaper (see text, p. 49), molded to

shape. The body is filled out with loosely rolled glue-soaked paper balls. As with the giraffe (see pp. 50–51), glue-coated strips of paper act as wrappings to secure these paper balls and sheets to the armature.

All four legs of the rabbit are attached and then wedged apart with paper cups (Step 3) to prevent their sticking together while drying. Alternatively, two legs can be attached on the same side of the rabbit and be allowed to dry before the other two legs are added on the second side. The rabbit is finished with colored tissue paper rather than with paint.

1. Dip sponge into thinned paste (see p. 49) and coat four sheets of newspaper. Roll each sheet as shown to form the armatures for the legs.

2. Attach two of the legs to the box that serves as the rabbit's body and then to those that form its feet, using glue-coated strips of newspaper.

Making a papier-mâché box

3. Form head and round out body with balls of glue-soaked strips of newspaper. Attach third and fourth legs, wedging the legs apart until dry.

4. To make an ear, roll a glue-coated sheet of newspaper and wrap it around the head as shown. Let one ear dry before adding the other.

5. Neatly finish the figure with layers of glue-coated newspaper strips. Tear white tissue paper into furlike tufts and glue them to belly.

6. Repeat Step 5 for brown areas, using brown tissue paper. Apply the paste sparingly to the tissue paper so that it does not tear.

7. Make round wads of glue-coated red tissue paper for the eyes. Cover with a layer of pink tissue paper. Use ball of white tissue for the tail.

8. Use pink tissue paper for the insides of the ears. Coat paper with paste, apply to ears, and tear off any excess.

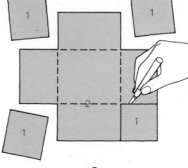

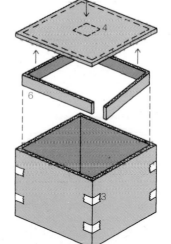

A simple cardboard box armature is one of the most useful in papier-mâché. Mark off desired dimensions on a piece of cardboard. Cut out unnecessary corners (1). Score dotted lines (2) with a crafts knife. Fold the sides up along scored edges and secure corner joints (3) with masking tape. Cut lid (4) to size. Cut and fold cardboard for handle (5) in the same manner as box (above). Cut the flange (6) 1/8 in. smaller than the top all around. Score flange at corners and tape to form closed rectangle. Glue handle and flange to lid with white (PVA) glue.

To cover the box, tear paper towels into small strips. Dip them in paste. Apply to box, inside and out. Cover lid and handle in same way.

Braid is made of three narrow rolled strips of paper toweling. Use a sponge to coat them with paste. Entwine them as shown to make the braid.

Apply braid to top of lid after box has dried. Cut neat ends with scissors. Wipe off excess paste. Finish other three sides in same way.

Place the box and lid inside a large protective box. Spray all sides with an acrylic spray paint or use a brush and poster paint.

Basketry

Man's most ancient craft

Basket making survives in many parts of the world today in forms, techniques, and materials similar to those used in past ages. While continuing as a living tradition, it has undergone a revival of interest among craftspeople, leading to new forms of expression. Just as weavers make pictures with tapestry, basket makers now use basketry techniques to create sculptures.

Archeologists tell us that the oldest known baskets presently appear to be some unearthed in Faiyum in upper Egypt; radiocarbon dating tests have shown them to be between 10,000 and 12,000 years old. Other Middle Eastern sites, notably in Mesopotamia and Palestine, have produced baskets up to 7,000 years old. A cave in Utah yielded baskets 9,000 years old. The earliest dates are older than any yet established by archeologists for pottery.

Basketry is the weaving of unspun vegetable fibers, usually to form a container, although basketry techniques have been and still are used to make clothing, hats, shoes, boats, furniture, traps for fish and game, cooking utensils, and houses.

Varieties of basketry. There are five types of basketry (see opposite page); the one that predominates in an area depends largely upon the native materials. *Coiled* basketry tends to use grasses and rushes. *Plaiting* flourishes where materials are wide and ribbon-like—the palms of the tropics or the yucca of the deserts. *Twining* occurs where roots and tree bark are the most readily available materials. *Wicker* and *splint* baskets are made where reed, cane, willow, oak, and ash grow.

Traditionally, basket makers gather and prepare their own materials. Until you have grasped the medium, you may prefer to purchase materials (see chart, opposite page), but eventually you may decide to gather your own. A chart and illustrations on page 56 describe those that are widespread and easily prepared.

The main tools of basketry are your own fingers. Beyond that, the implements are few and simple, most of them already in your tool kit or sewing basket. They include an awl—6 inches is a good size—a utility knife, a jack-knife, 5-inch side-cutting pliers, 5-inch needle-nose pliers, a cloth or plastic measuring tape, a No. 4 or No. 5 metal knitting needle, heavy scissors, a crochet hook, a short needle with a big eye such as a tapestry needle, and clip clothespins. Not all of these tools are required for every basket; those needed are indicated with each project. You will also need a large pan for soaking materials; some materials are so bulky that you may prefer to use the bathtub or kitchen sink.

A basket maker does not always know ahead of time how a basket will turn out, since its final shape and size may be governed by the pliability of the materials. The base is the experimental stage and is usually worked until the basket maker gets the feel of the materials. By the time the sides are turned up—the point at which problems tend to arise—the materials should be under control.

Whether you make or collect baskets, take care of them by wetting them briefly once a year to restore moisture to the fibers. Dry them quickly in the shade. If a basket is dirty, wash it gently with a very soft brush dipped in mild soapsuds. Old baskets may need a restorative coat made of 1 part boiled linseed oil to 3 parts pure turpentine. Use the same solution if you want to darken new baskets slightly. You can dye basket materials with vegetable dyes (see *Spinning and dyeing*, p. 73).

Pacific Coast and Southwestern American Indians wove these coiled baskets with native plant fibers in age-old designs.

Materials and structure

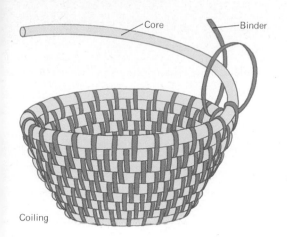

Core

Binder

Coiling

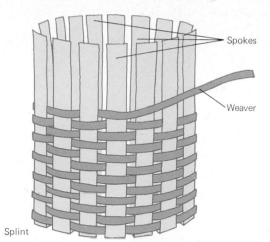

Spokes

Weaver

Splint

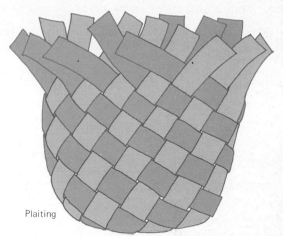

Plaiting

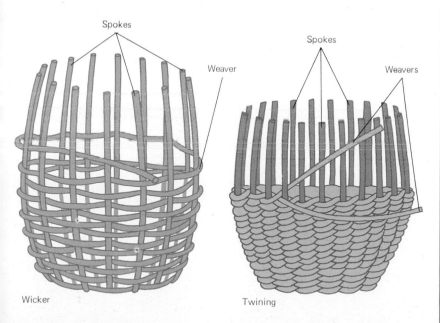

Spokes

Weaver

Wicker

Spokes

Weavers

Twining

Materials that can be bought

MATERIAL	BASKET—ELEMENT	SIZES; HOW SOLD
Round reed	Coiled—core Wicker—spoke, weaver Twined—spoke, weaver	No. 0-10, 3/8″, 1/2″, 5/8″ 3/4″; by the lb. No. 2 and No. 4 best to use
Flat reed	Splint—spoke, weaver Wicker—weaver Plaited—warp, weft	1/4″, 3/8″, 1/2″, 5/8″; by the lb
Flat oval reed	Splint—weaver	1/4″, 3/8″; by the lb
Cane, natural strand	Splint—weaver Wicker—weaver	Superfine, fine fine, fine, narrow medium, medium, common; by the bunch—1,000′
White ash	Splint—spoke, weaver	5/8″; 15 strands to a bundle, 6′ or 8′ long
White oak	Splint—spoke, weaver	5/8″; 15 strands to a bundle, 6′ long
Fiber rush	Coiled—core Twined—weaver	3/32″, 4/32″, 5/32″, 6/32″; by the lb—about 250′
Sea grass or Hong Kong grass	Coiled—core Twined—spoke, weaver	3/16″; 3-lb coil—600′
Raffia, natural or dyed	Coiled—core (bundled), binder Twined—weaver	Varies; by the lb or 1/2 lb
Corn husks	Coiled—core (bundled) Twined—spokes	Varies
Cord, rope, yarn, jute, sisal, linen	Coiled—core, weaver Wicker—weaver Twined—spoke, weaver	Varies

Basket anatomy. Wicker, twined, and splint baskets have similar parts: spokes that form the supporting framework and weavers that hold the spokes together. In plaiting the elements are usually equal in size and strength and can be likened to the warp and weft of weaving. Coiled baskets are composed of a core, which may be a single rod or a bundle of material, and a binder, which wraps and stitches the spiraling rows of core together.

Basketry

Materials that can be found in the wild

MATERIAL	BASKET—ELEMENT	WHEN GATHERED	PREPARATION
Willow shoots *(Salix)* (except pussy willow)	Coiled—binder, core Wicker—spoke, weaver Twined—spoke, weaver	Spring	Use whole with or without bark; for weavers, split and remove core
Weeping willow branches *(Salix babylonica)*	Coiled—core (bundled) Wicker—spoke, weaver Twined—spoke, weaver	Fall	Boil 6 hr; peel bark. Wrap in wet newspaper 24 hr. Use whole
Honeysuckle vine *(Lonicera japonica)*	Wicker—spoke (thick) Twined—weaver (thin)	Anytime; best between September and April	Use fresh, or coil and dry. Use whole
Wisteria runners	Wicker—spoke, weaver Twined—spoke, weaver	Fall or early spring	Remove leaves, coil, and dry 1 wk
Cattail stalks *(Typha latifolia)*	Coiled—core	Fall, before seed sets	Split stalks in half, dry. Moisten in wet towel
Cattail leaves *(Typha latifolia)*	Coiled—binder Wicker—decorative Twined—weaver Plaited—warp, weft	Winter, when brown and dry	Dry and store in bundles. If thin, twist two together
Rush, bulrush *(Juncus; Scirpus)*	Twined—weaver	Anytime when green	Dry and store in bundles, use whole
Virginia creeper *(Parthenocissus quinquefolia)*	Wicker—weaver Twined—weaver	Anytime	Remove leaves, coil, and dry 1 wk
Iris leaves	Coiled—core (bundled), binder	Fall, after first frost	Dry on newspaper, store in cool place
Day lily leaves *(Hemerocallis)*	Coiled—core (bundled), binder	Fall, after first frost	Dry on newspaper, store in cool place
Yucca leaves	Coiled—core (bundled), binder Plaited—warp, weft	Spring, summer, fall Anytime	Split lengthwise, dry
Broom sedge *(Andropogon virginicus)*	Coiled—core (bundled) Wicker—weaver, decorative only	Anytime	Pick brown stems, store bundled. Moisten in towel
Corn husks	Coiled—core (bundled) Twined—spokes	When corn is ripe	Dry spread out, store in bags in dry place

Willows, cattails, rushes, and bulrushes grow in or near swamps. Grasses, honeysuckle, and Virginia creeper inhabit fields; the vines often climb stone walls. While the wisteria, the iris, and the day lily are garden plants, the latter sometimes grows in profusion on roadsides. Yucca likes hot climates. Generally, soak materials until they are pliable just before working with them. If there is a tradition of basket making where you live, inquire of a local museum what native materials are used. You may be able to locate a wealth of materials not far from your backyard.

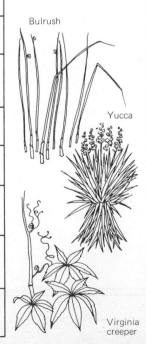

Bulrush

Yucca

Virginia creeper

Coiled baskets

A coiled basket is a *tour de force*: from such insubstantial materials as corn husks, grass, pine needles, raffia, or yarn emerges a basket of considerable solidity. Or such unyielding materials as reeds, vines, roots, or cane are bent and stitched into a tight spiral. Because the radius of the spiral increases continuously, a coiled basket is dynamic, constantly swirling outward.

Coiling is basically a process of wrapping a binder around a core and stitching rows of core together (see illustrations on facing page). The core may be a single rod, such as reed or thick rope; it may be two or three rods or a bundle of grass, pine needles, or corn husks. The binder may be raffia, cane, or some other supple material. The core may be exposed by spacing the stitches widely; more often it is covered by the binder.

A soft binder, such as raffia or yarn, is wrapped and stitched using a heavy needle with a large eye. For stiff binder a hole is made through the core with an awl, and the binder is pushed through.

The most difficult part of a coiled basket is the start (see facing page). The wrapped start is used when the core material can be bent into a tight circle. The knot start is used with very soft core materials or, conversely, when the core is too stiff to bend into a circle. In the latter case the start is made with the binder material; the core is added later.

Mark the starting point of the first row of stitching with a piece of colored thread or raffia. Always begin a change in stitch or pattern opposite that point.

The row currently being incorporated into the basket is called the working row; the row before, into which it is stitched, is the previous row. Turning the basket walls upward from the base is accomplished by placing the working row slightly higher than the previous row. The turn may be either abrupt or gradual.

Coiling starts

Knot start with raffia. Double a piece of raffia and twist it, leaving a loop at one end. Tie an overhand knot 8 in. from the looped end.

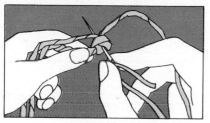

Thread one loose end of raffia in a needle; hold the knot, the loop, and the other loose end in left hand. Stitch through knot's center front to back.

Stitch counterclockwise around knot, putting needle through center front to back. Keep knot flat. Mark starting point with colored thread.

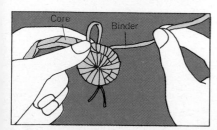

For the second round, raffia in left hand, including loop, becomes core. Stitch core to top of previous row, twisting core before each stitch.

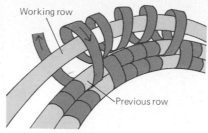

Wrapped start. Lay one end of binder along core; wrap binder over core toward the end of the core, getting as close to the end as possible.

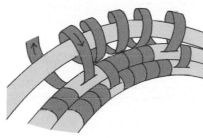

Wrap in the opposite direction, completely covering the core material, until enough core is covered to bend it into a tight circle.

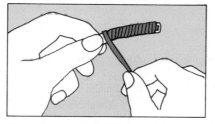

Thread needle with binder. Hold wrapped core in a tight circle. Make the first few stitches around the working core and through the center.

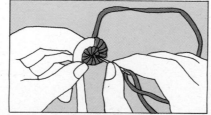

Working counterclockwise, stitch the working row to the circle through center hole for one full round. Mark starting point with a thread.

A sampling of coiling stitches

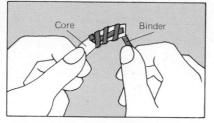

Lazy stitch variant 1

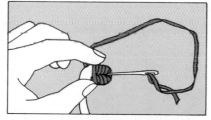

Lazy stitch variant 2

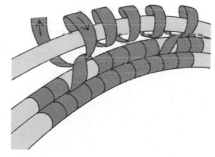

Lazy stitch variant 3

Open stitch

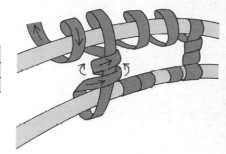

Lace stitch

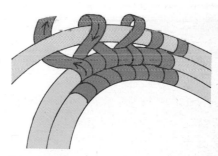

Figure 8 stitch

Coiling stitches usually involve two motions: one is the wrapping, done prior to the stitch. The binder is held in the hand and wound around the working row. The other motion is the actual stitching. This is done with a short, thick needle if the binder is soft. If the binder is stiff, an awl is used to make a hole in the core through which the binder (trimmed to a point) is poked. In the lazy stitch the binder may pass around the previous row (variant 1) or through it (variant 2), or it may just catch the binder of the previous row (variant 3). The working row may be wrapped once, twice, or three times, according to the materials and the basket maker's inclination. The open stitch is a simple coiling stitch spread apart to leave the core showing. The binder can either go through the core of the previous row or simply catch the binder of the previous row, as shown. The lace stitch is an embellishment of the lazy stitch; the binder may be wrapped once or twice around itself. The figure 8 can have an extra wrap of the binder around the working row between stitches.

Basketry/project

A basket for fruit

Raw sisal and cane from a crafts store make this light-colored container to grace a summer table. It is 9 inches across at the base and 2½ inches high. Stop the coiling before turning up the sides (Step 9), and you have a perfect hot mat. Finish it as in Step 12.

Materials and equipment. Purchase one bundle of flat cane (narrow medium size) for binder, one bundle of light-colored raw sisal for the core, and one of darker color for the rim. The equipment is a small awl, scissors, a measuring tape, and a bowl for soaking the cane. Soak the cane 10 minutes and keep it wrapped in a damp towel. Work with 3-foot lengths of cane, except for the first, which should be 4 feet.

Begin the basket with a wrapped start and use the open stitch (see p. 57). In the first few rows, where the stitches are close together, be careful not to pierce the binder with the awl. As the spiral increases in diameter, the spaces between stitches grow. It is then necessary to increase the number of stitches in the working row until the sides are turned up. Distribute the increases evenly (see Step 6).

1. Make a wrapped start (see p. 57). When enough core is wrapped to make the first circle, trim end of core; cut binder to a point.

2. While binding in the first round of core, hold the circle tightly and stitch through the center. Note that the sisal core is twisted.

3. With second round begin open stitch, sewing it through the core of previous row. Use awl to open holes straight through the core.

4. When the binder runs short, bring it between the rows. Snip off the end, leaving just enough to be enclosed by the next stitch.

5. Run new binder through core, leaving its end between the rows of core. Reopen the hole and take a second stitch in same place.

6. When the exposed core between stitches lengthens, place two stitches in the working row where previously there was one.

7. When the core material begins to feel thin, cut off its end on a slant. Do the same with the new core material to be added.

8. Lay the old and new core material against each other and work them together by gently rolling them between the fingers.

9. When the base is 9 in. across, begin to turn up the sides. Lift the working row above the previous row; insert the awl at a 45° angle.

10. The sides of the basket gradually spiral upward. Wrap and stitch five more rows, placing working row directly above previous row.

11. Work the final row with a contrasting darker sisal for core material. Join it to the lighter core as in Steps 7 and 8.

12. Taper the core and anchor it by crisscrossing the binder. Run binder inside core and cut it off. Trim loose bits of sisal.

Basketry/project

House of the Whirlwind basket

The Pima Indians of Arizona call this pattern House of the Whirlwind. It is a universal design that emphasizes the spiral form of the coiling technique.

Materials. The core is dried corn husk; dry your own or buy 8 ounces from a crafts store. The binder is raffia in two colors—natural and dyed brown or any combination of light and dark. Buy 1 pound of light, 1/2 pound of dark.

Equipment. You need a needle with a large eye, scissors, a measuring tape, a pin, and a bowl for soaking husks. Soak them 5 to 10 minutes, blot on a towel, and split into 1/2-inch strips. Use raffia dry, two at a time if pieces are thin.

This basket is 9½ inches across and 5 inches high. Since its shape and size result from how tightly it is stitched and how much the working row is raised above the previous row, every basket will be slightly different.

The basket is worked mainly in the figure 8 stitch. The pattern is achieved by advancing the dark color beyond the light a little more in each succeeding row (see Step 9).

1. Make knot start (p. 57) of six husk strips; knot one-third of way from end. Hold all ends while stitching around knot with dark raffia.

2. Keeping the core twisted, use lazy stitch (p. 57) for second round. Wrap the working row twice and stitch into top of previous row.

3. When corn husks are down to 1 in., spread out ends and insert three strips. Take a few stitches before adding three more strips.

4. When the binder becomes thin, put it into core bundle. Sew a new binder through top of previous row. Hold its end along with core.

5. For third row bring binder to front beneath previous row. Begin figure 8 stitch (p. 57) but wrap working row one extra time, as shown.

6. Do three full rounds of figure 8. Measure basket; place pin one-third of way around base from last stitch. Continue dark binder to pin.

7. Thread a light-colored binder and add it as in Step 4. Finish remaining two-thirds of row. Light binder will cover previous row too.

8. As you begin the next row, do the lazy stitch (p. 57) to move the light color 1/4 in. farther along; catch only the top of the previous row.

9. With the next round place the working row a little higher than the previous row. Move the dark color past the light as in Step 8.

10. Continue sloping basket. Keep dark color a constant one-third of each row. Use lazy stitch where dark is above light or vice versa.

11. When last passage of dark is above start of dark pattern in base, decrease the core by cutting off corn husk every few stitches.

12. When the core tapers to nothing, crisscross the binder over its end. Run binder behind the last few stitches and cut it off.

Basketry/project

Plaiting: the fastest baskets

Plaiting is used all over the world to make everything from sandals to houses as well as baskets. Because materials are likely to be wide, plaiting is usually a fast way of making a basket. However, preparation of the materials is frequently long and arduous.

In Mexico many people are born, sleep, and die on a *petate,* a mat plaited from yucca or palm leaves. In warm climates the natural materials suitable for plaiting are readily available. These include pandanus and coconut leaves, split bamboo, and cane.

But many natural plaiting materials are unavailable commercially, and their distribution in nature is limited. Consequently, modern-day plaiters have turned to manufactured and "found" materials, such as cloth, plastic, leather, wallpaper, and even discarded film and magnetic tape. The basket pictured below is of plain and striped ribbon that is no farther away than a variety store. But the design is adaptable to natural materials.

Plaiting's basic technique is the over one, under one of plain weave. The two elements may be thought of as the warp and weft of woven fabrics; they are usually of equal size and strength. The typical natural materials are flat and thin, and the resulting basket is light and flexible.

Two-element plaiting is either parallel, as in the bottom of the ribbon basket illustrated below, or diagonal, as in its sides. In both cases the elements are at right angles to each other; the difference lies in how they are worked. In parallel plaiting one element at a time is added and woven, whereas in diagonal plaiting all elements are in motion simultaneously and could be woven all at once—if the weaver had enough hands. More difficult but more varied in design possibilities is hexagonal plaiting (opposite).

Before plaiting with the actual materials, it is a good idea to practice by making a mock-up of strips of paper. In designing your own basket, a mock-up lets you work out the length and number of elements in advance. Where color is desired, mark the paper strips. Then take the mock-up apart; the marked strips indicate the number of colored strips needed. You can now cut materials for the basket to the exact size and number with no waste.

A ribbon basket

A basket 5 inches tall and 5 inches across might hold hair ribbons or jewelry. It is made of two kinds of ribbon—plain grosgrain and taffeta that is striped in the same color as the grosgrain.

Materials and equipment. Buy 36 feet of each kind of ribbon in 1-inch width. Cut the ribbon into 3-foot lengths. The necessary equipment comes from the sewing basket: needle, thread, scissors, measuring tape, and pins. Round-headed pins are more visible than plain straight pins.

As with all plaiting, the elements must be pushed close together, leaving no holes where they intersect.

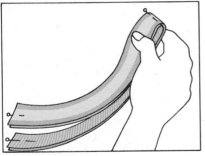

1. Pair off 3-ft pieces of grosgrain and striped ribbon. Pin them together back to back to make 12 double-ribbon elements. Fold in half first two to be used; mark center points with pins.

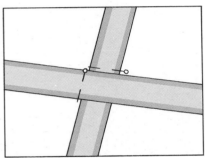

2. On a flat surface lay vertically one element made in Step 1. Place the second element horizontally across the first. Line up the center pins with the edges of the ribbons.

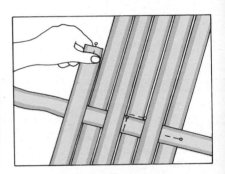

3. Lay other five vertical elements alternately over and under the horizontal element. The pin in the horizontal element should remain centered. Pin the verticals to horizontal element as shown.

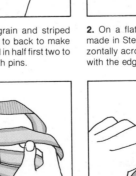

8. Continue to weave over one, under one toward the top of the basket one row at a time until the basket is 5 in. high. Pin the elements wherever necessary to hold them in place.

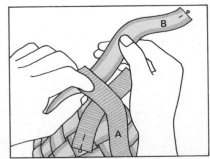

9. To make the sawtoothed top edge of the basket, begin doubling the elements back on one another as seen here. The loose ends will hang out until trimmed in Step 13.

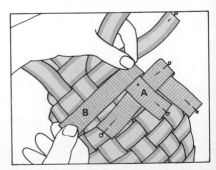

10. To complete each sawtoothed edge at the top of the basket (begun as illustrated in Step 9), make the fold shown here. Do this all the way around the top of the basket.

A variety of plaiting weaves

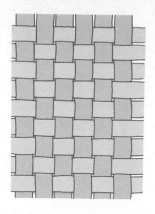

Plain weave. A simple over one, under one weave, plain weave can be varied by the addition of color in one direction.

Twill weave. Elements are woven over two, under two, or over three, under three, but the longer "float" over other elements weakens the basket's structure.

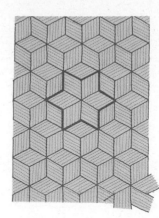

Hexagonal plaiting. Sometimes called mad weave because its execution is fiendishly difficult, the three elements appear to form a six-pointed star.

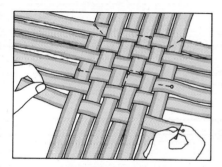

4. Weave other five horizontal elements alternately over and under the verticals. The pins in the first vertical element should remain centered. Pin horizontal elements as shown.

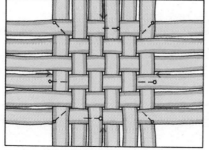

5. Pin the elements at the four right angles to secure them. The corners of the basket will be formed at the center of each set of six elements where the arrows point.

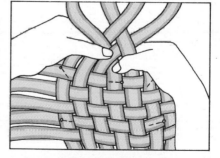

6. Pick up the side of the basket away from you and, with three elements in each hand, force a corner by bending the elements toward each other at right angles.

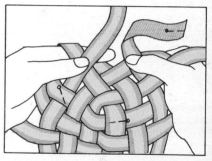

7. Weave each of the six elements over and under once. Secure the elements with pins. Rotate the basket and create the other three corners in the same way. Pin to secure.

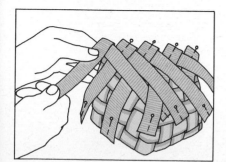

11. Work clockwise around the edge of basket, carefully repeating the motions of Steps 9 and 10 until all the ribbon elements have been folded and pinned in place.

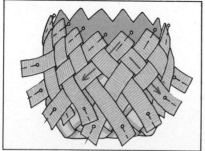

12. Continue to work clockwise. Take each loose end formed in Steps 9 and 10 and slide it under the next ribbon element below it. Pull the ends all the way through.

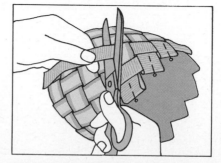

13. Cut off all the ends facing one way, then those facing the other way. Before cutting, pull ends of ribbon slightly so that when cut, the ends will slide back and be hidden.

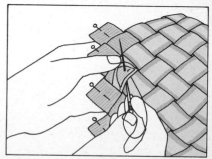

14. Push back the elements that cross the hidden ends, and with needle and thread tack each of them with an overhand stitch. Remove all pins remaining in the basket.

Basketry/project

Working with splint

Splint baskets are the workhorses of basketry. They are the baskets in which farmers transport produce to market. They are laundry baskets. They are the pack baskets favored by guides.

The Passamaquoddy Indians of Maine, the Mohawks of New York, and the Cherokees of the Great Smoky Mountains are famed for their splint baskets. The Shakers made splint baskets of delicate refinement.

The materials of splint basketry are flat, thin strips of wood, usually ash or oak. Spokes and weavers may be the same material, or the weavers may be finer strands of another material. The weaves are uncomplicated: plain weave—over one, under one—or twill weave—over two, under two (see pp. 64–65). If the basket has an even number of spokes, a new weaver is usually used for each round. With an uneven number of spokes, one weaver is worked in continuous rounds.

Splints from black and white ash trees are traditionally made by pounding a log that has soaked over the winter to loosen the annual rings of growth. Today splints of white ash and oak are cut by machine and are available from firms that sell materials for chair-seat weaving (see chart, p. 55).

All splints must be thoroughly soaked—at least 20 minutes—before working with them. Machine-cut splints have a right and a wrong side; to find the right side, bend the soaked splint. Small splinters will be raised on the wrong side. The smooth side should be on the outside of the basket; work the base with the rough side facing up.

Designing your own splint basket is easy. Since the weavers hold the spokes slightly apart, allow about 1/4 inch between spokes. To determine the length to cut spokes, add the desired dimension of the base, plus twice the height of the sides, plus 8 inches for each spoke to be turned down.

A splint and cane basket

This basket makes a fine receptacle for mail or other objects that collect on desk or bureau. It is 7 inches wide, 8½ inches long, and 5 inches high.

Materials. Buy one bundle of 5/8-inch oak splint (or substitute easier-to-work-with ash) and a bunch of natural strand cane, medium size. For spokes cut seven pieces of splint 26 inches long and nine pieces 24 inches. Cut splint in half lengthwise with scissors for half-width splints; you need eight pieces 36 inches long for weavers and others as indicated in the instructions.

Equipment. Assemble a utility knife, jackknife, clip clothespins, scissors, measuring tape, awl, side-cutting pliers, and a tub for soaking materials.

Soak splints in lukewarm water about 20 minutes. Before soaking cane, make a coil of each strand and tie it in the middle so the strands do not become tangled. You will need 12 to 15 strands. Soak the cane 5 to 10 minutes. Wrap the splint and cane in a towel to keep them damp until needed, but do not leave wet overnight.

The weave throughout is plain weave. As there is an even number of spokes, a new weaver is used for each round. Before beginning the border, dry the basket overnight. The weaving will become loose. Starting with the bottom weaver, push each row toward the base to pack the weaving firmly.

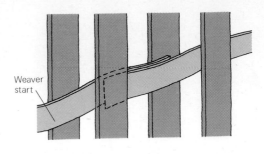

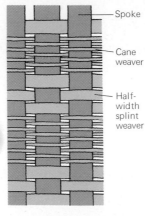

In the diagram for basket sides (left), wide weavers are half-width splint, narrow weavers are cane. To hide ends of weavers (above), place starting end in front of a spoke, weave around clockwise, cover starting end, and cut off weaver behind next spoke. Begin weavers three spokes in from corner, except first (Step 4). Rotate basket one-quarter from start of last weaver for each new row.

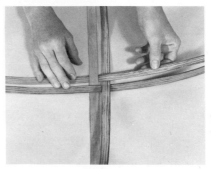

1. Making the base. All splints should be well soaked. Lay two 24-in. spokes side by side with their ends even. Weave in two 26-in. spokes at right angles. Leave 1/4 in. between spokes.

2. Continue laying 24-in. and 26-in. spokes alternately until there are nine in one direction and seven in the other with all their ends even. First four spokes should remain near center.

7. Making border. Pack down weaving. Soak basket upside down until spokes are pliable. Cut off spokes inside top weaver so they are flush with it. Cut spokes outside top weaver to 3 in. tall.

8. With side-cutting pliers cut halfway across protruding spokes along the line of the top weaver and strip the splints upward—splitting them in half lengthwise. Trim the ends almost to points.

Making the handles

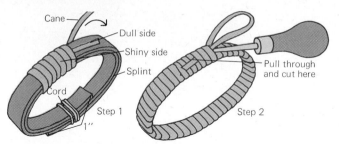

Cane
Dull side
Shiny side
Splint
Cord
Step 1
1"
Pull through and cut here
Step 2

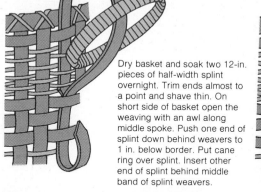

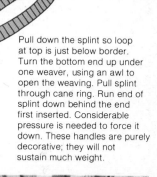

Each of the two handles is made of a 19-in. piece of half-width splint wrapped with cane. Soak splint overnight. **Step 1.** With each piece make a double circle with a 1-in. overlap. Tie overlap with thin cord. Lay a strand of cane, dull side out, along outside of splint circle. Fold cane back on itself at a right angle, so that shiny side faces up. Begin to wrap around circle. Cut cord as wrapping passes it. **Step 2.** When wrapping is complete, open first few wraps with an awl. Tuck cane underneath, pull it through, and cut off the end.

Dry basket and soak two 12-in. pieces of half-width splint overnight. Trim ends almost to a point and shave thin. On short side of basket open the weaving with an awl along middle spoke. Push one end of splint down behind weavers to 1 in. below border. Put cane ring over splint. Insert other end of splint behind middle band of splint weavers.

Pull down the splint so loop at top is just below border. Turn the bottom end up under one weaver, using an awl to open the weaving. Pull splint through cane ring. Run end of splint down behind the end first inserted. Considerable pressure is needed to force it down. These handles are purely decorative; they will not sustain much weight.

3. Using a utility knife, score each spoke close to the woven base, using the crossing spoke as a visual guide. Turn the base over; the inside of the basket's base now faces up.

4. Turning up the sides. Insert a cane weaver through hole near a corner; tuck its end between splints. Weave around base clockwise; pull firmly to raise the spokes upright.

5. Continue weaver past its starting point to third spoke from corner. Cut it and hold temporarily with a clothespin. Start second weaver one-quarter turn around base.

6. At the third corner begin a half-width splint weaver. Straighten the spokes with arm and hand. Hold the ends of weaver with a clothespin until the next round is done.

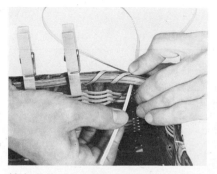

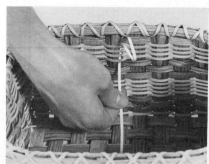

9. With an awl open the weaving inside the basket below the protruding, split spokes. Push each spoke down behind weavers. If the spokes splinter when bent, trim them with pliers.

10. Cut three half-width splints the perimeter of basket's top plus 4 in. Midway on long side, attach two inside and one outside with a clothespin. Insert cane 2 in. down behind splint.

11. Lash the oak splints to the basket with the cane weaver, passing it over the top and then through the holes between spokes from the outside to the inside of the basket.

12. When the starting point is reached, weave once around in opposite direction to make a crisscross pattern. Tuck end of cane down inside the basket's weavers and cut it off.

Basketry/project

A gathering basket

Resembling a traditional berry basket, this white ash splint basket could be used for gathering or displaying fruits, vegetables, or flowers. It is 8¼ inches in diameter and 5¼ inches tall.

Materials and equipment. You need a bundle of 5/8-inch ash splint and one bunch each of fine size and common size natural strand cane. The handle is a limb from a hickory sapling, but a substitute can be made of No. 12 round reed. Assemble an awl, scissors, side-cutting pliers, utility knife, jackknife, clothespins, measuring tape, and a large tub to soak the materials.

The basket begins with two separate bases that are placed one over the other and woven together. Cut 16 pieces of splint 36 inches long and soak them at least 20 minutes. Soak the cane 10 minutes. The twill weave of the basket's sides requires an uneven number of spokes, so one spoke is split in half lengthwise to make the odd number. The cane weavers are worked continuously around the basket until they run out. When that happens, end the old weaver on top of a spoke on the outside of the basket, and start the new weaver three spokes back on top of the old weaver and in back of a spoke. Both ends will be hidden.

1. Making the base. Lay eight spokes in a circle, placing two at a time at right angles to each other. The spokes must be equidistant with their ends even. Hold them in the center.

2. Use scissors to cut one spoke in half lengthwise but no closer than 1½ in. to the center. This creates the odd number of spokes that will be needed for the twill weave.

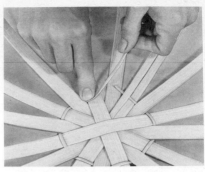

3. Start a fine cane weaver, shiny side up, at split spoke. Weave over one, under one twice around; pull weaver close to center. Cut it off beneath third spoke past starting point.

8. Weave a second round of over one, under one; this serves to hold up the alternate spokes. Remove clothespin as weaver passes it. Push weavers down firmly with fingers.

9. Weaving the sides. Starting with the third round, continue the same weaver but weave over two, under two. This is twill weave (see p. 61), done for 22 rounds to the basket's top.

10. To add a new weaver, slide it behind a spoke and weave with it over the end of the old weaver. Cut the old weaver so its end rests atop a spoke and is hidden.

15. Making the border. Soak basket upside down until spokes are pliant. Cut off the pairs of spokes inside top weaver so they are flush with it. Cut outside spokes 2½ in. above top weaver.

16. Trim the spokes with side-cutting pliers as in Step 8 on page 62. Bend the spokes over the top weaver and push them down behind the other weavers as shown.

17. Insert the handle between a spoke and weavers on inside of basket. Align the top of the notch with basket top so the rim will fit into it. Fit in other end of handle on opposite side.

4. Lay the eight spokes for second base as in Step 1. Hold them with one hand and place first base on top. Make sure that all of the spokes in both bases are equidistant, with the ends even.

5. Weave three rounds of over one, under one with a fine cane weaver to bind the two bases together. Pull the weaver tight and push it as close to the center as possible.

6. With a utility knife score the spokes very lightly close to the last round of cane to aid in turning up the sides. Turn the base over so that the scoring is on the underside of the base.

7. Turning the sides up. Use a clothespin to clip a common size cane weaver, shiny side out, to any spoke. Bend the spokes up; weave over one, under one, pulling cane firmly.

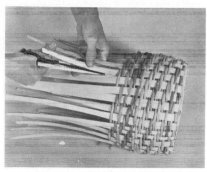
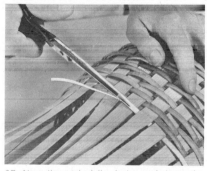
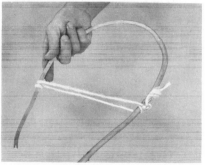

11. Halfway to the top begin to push the spokes toward the center. If they become crowded, taper them slightly, but cut no closer to the base than 6 in. Work carefully.

12. Near the end of the last round, taper the weaver to a point so the basket will be the same height all around. Dry basket overnight; push down the weaving until it is firmly packed.

13. Making the handle. Cut a 3/8-in. by 24-in. piece from a hickory sapling limb. Soak it for four days, strip off bark with a knife, and tie it in a U-shape. As a substitute use a No. 12 round reed.

14. Dry the handle for two days. Remove the string, and with a jackknife whittle the ends to flat-sided points. Make 1/2-in. notches starting 2 in. above the points on the inside of the U.

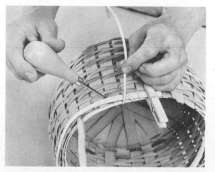

18. Cut two ash splints to encircle the basket top plus 3 in.; split them in half lengthwise. Clip one to outside of basket with clothespin. Check length and trim so there is a 2-in. overlap.

19. Place two other pieces of half-width splint along inside of the basket's top with a fine cane weaver between them, shiny side facing toward inside of basket. Discard fourth piece of splint.

20. Open a hole below second weaver from top. Wrap cane over top and through hole to inside counterclockwise around basket. Overlap three wraps and tuck end down as in Step 12, page 63.

21. Strengthen binding at handle with an extra piece of cane. Cross it back and forth on both sides of handle, inside and outside of border. Tuck end down between spokes and weavers.

65

Basketry

Wickerwork and twining

Experts usually classify wicker and twining as two distinct types of basketry. But the practicing basket maker finds much overlap between the two; it is impossible to learn one without becoming acquainted with some materials and techniques of the other.

Spokes and weavers. Both wicker and twining are composed of spokes that create a framework and weavers that hold the spokes in shape. Strictly speaking, a wicker basket is woven with one weaver in motion, whereas twining always involves two or more

weavers that are twisted between spokes. In practice, twining is often used in wicker baskets, particularly for strength at stress points.

A wicker basket has a hard, twiggy look. Its spokes and weavers are usually stiff rods of willow, reed, or cane. Wicker baskets bring to mind traditional European and American forms—the market basket, the picnic hamper, the fishing creel, the Irish potato basket, for example—but wicker baskets are found in a multitude of forms from the Orient to South

America. Twined baskets occasionally have reed or willow spokes, but more often the spokes are a softer material, and the weavers are always more flexible than those in wickerwork. The basket gets its firmness from the twisting of the weavers between the spokes. A twined basket may be so finely woven that it looks like fabric.

Soaking materials. The secret to working stiff material into a round form is in soaking it until it is pliable. The thicker the material, the longer the soaking required. If the material begins

to dry while you are working, give it another soaking until its pliability returns. But never leave an unfinished basket wrapped in wet towels or plastic overnight because it may become mildewed. Let it dry and resoak it.

Before breaking open a bundle of reed, soak it (otherwise the strands become tangled and break easily). Then make a coil of each separated strand, tie it in the middle, and leave it in the tub. When you need a new reed, you will not have to disentangle it.

Every basket maker weaves dif-

Wicker and twining weaves

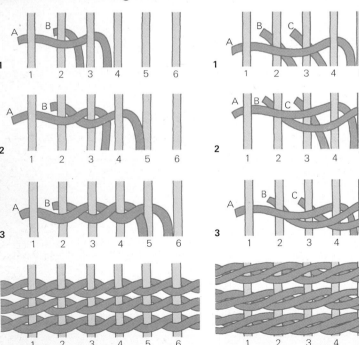

Two-ply twining. Step 1. Insert two weavers, one behind the initial spoke and the other behind the spoke to its right. Carry weaver A in front of spoke to its right, over weaver B, behind third spoke and to the front. Step 2. Repeat same motions with weaver B. Step 3. Continue motion to the right, alternating weavers.

Three-ply twining. Step 1. Beginning at the initial spoke, place three weavers behind three consecutive spokes. Pick up weaver A, bring it in front of two spokes, over the other two weavers, and behind the next spoke to the front. Step 2. Repeat these same motions with weaver B. Step 3. Repeat motions with weaver C.

Wicker weaves

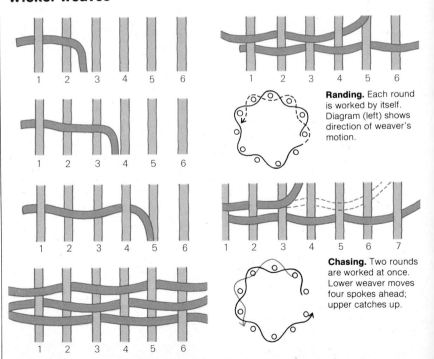

Randing. Each round is worked by itself. Diagram (left) shows direction of weaver's motion.

Chasing. Two rounds are worked at once. Lower weaver moves four spokes ahead; upper catches up.

Japanese weave. This is done with one weaver passing alternately behind one spoke and in front of two in continuous rounds. It cannot be done on a number of spokes that is divisible by three because the same spokes would be passed in the rear and in the front with each round. The weave has a diagonal look.

Randing and chasing. These wicker weaves look alike—a simple over one spoke, under the next. Randing is done with one weaver continuously circling an uneven number of spokes. Chasing is done with two weavers on an even number of spokes. Second weaver always stops just short of first, hence the name chasing.

Basketry/project

Twined basket of corn husk and raffia

ferently; some work tightly, others loosely. Therefore, the directions for the wicker basket and much of the twined basket are given in inches rather than number of rows.

The initial spoke. Always mark the initial spoke—where you begin weaving the first round—with a piece of thread or raffia. Begin any changes in weave at that spoke.

The weaves used in both twining and wicker and those exclusive to wicker are pictured on page 66. Twill weave (below) appears in the twined basket.

Twining weave

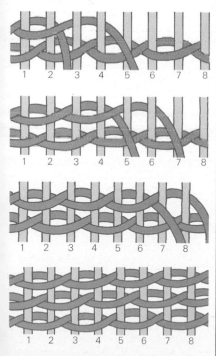

Twill weave. This weave is similar to two-ply twining (see diagrams opposite) except that the weavers pass in front of and behind two spokes at a time. Twill weave has a diagonal look. It must be done on an uneven number of spokes so that alternate spokes are paired in each round, as seen in this schematic drawing.

This small basket—4½ inches tall and 5½ inches across at its widest—resembles the twined baskets of the Yurok Indians of northern California. Basic techniques are shown below, step-by-step procedures on page 68.

Materials and equipment. Spokes are corn husk; weavers are raffia in two colors, natural and black. Gather your own corn husks, or buy 8 ounces in a crafts shop. One bundle of each color raffia is sufficient. If the raffia is thin, use two pieces as one weaver. You will need scissors and a bowl for soaking materials.

Soak corn husks for 10 minutes, raffia 1 minute. Blot them on a towel. Tear the husks into 3/4-inch strips. If they dry out while you are working or are left overnight, wet them briefly. Never leave materials soaking overnight.

Adding spokes. Sometimes the pattern calls for multiplying spokes. Make those additions as shown in the two steps below, left. If a corn husk becomes shorter than 1 inch or feels thin, replenish it as in Step 1 only. Then twine old and new spokes together until the old one runs out. Six rows from the top of the basket, check that husks are 3 inches long so there will be enough for the finish. If not, add more.

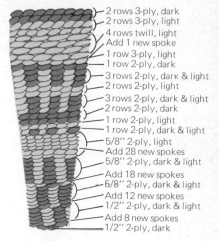

- 2 rows 3-ply, dark
- 2 rows 3-ply, light
- 4 rows twill, light
- Add 1 new spoke
- 1 row 3-ply, light
- 1 row 2-ply, dark
- 3 rows 2-ply, dark & light
- 2 rows 2-ply, light
- 3 rows 2-ply, dark & light
- 2 rows 2-ply, dark
- 1 row 2-ply, light
- 1 row 2-ply, dark & light
- 5/8" 2-ply, light
- Add 28 new spokes
- 5/8" 2-ply, dark & light
- Add 18 new spokes
- 5/8" 2-ply, dark & light
- Add 12 new spokes
- 1/2" 2-ply, dark & light
- Add 8 new spokes
- 1/2" 2-ply, dark

Read pattern diagram from bottom up. It indicates the rows or inches of each weave, what color weaver to use (dark or light or both), and where to increase the number of spokes. After the fourth addition (see below), there should be 82.

Adding new spokes

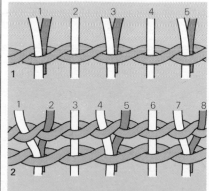

The basket attains its rounded shape by the addition of spokes—usually half the number of existing spokes. The original 16 spokes (see p. 68) are the white ones here. (Step 1). Twine the required number of new spokes to every other existing spoke. Step 2. In the next round separate spokes as you twine. When spokes grow short, lengthen them by following Step 1.

Changing weavers

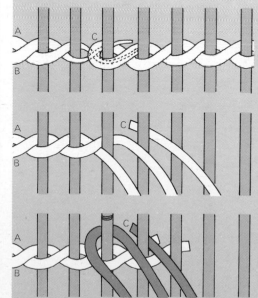

When raffia weavers begin to thin, cut both ends to 2 in. Loop a new weaver around a spoke and twine it once with old ends. Let old ends hang inside. Change color of weavers the same way, but only at initial spoke.

To switch from two to three weavers, add weaver C to the right of weavers A and B at initial spoke. To do the reverse—switch from three to two weavers—drop one inside the basket, cut it off, and twine past it.

To change color of weavers at the same time as changing the weave, loop the new color behind initial spoke, twine the two colors once together, and then drop the old color inside the basket.

Basketry/project

Twined basket of corn husk and raffia (continued)

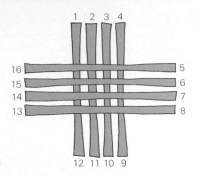

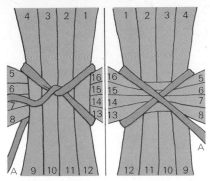

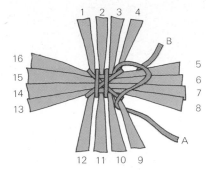

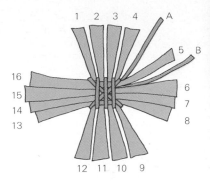

Making the start. 1. Use stiff pieces of corn husk. Lay four side by side and four more on top at right angles. The ends of each piece of corn husk become spokes, numbered clockwise.

2. Bind the spokes corner-to-corner with a piece of dark raffia. At the back (left), twist strands together and bring one, weaver A, around to complete the X in front (right).

3. Spread spokes 1–4 and 9–12 evenly. Pass weaver A (tinted) from back to front between spokes 1–2 and to back between 11–12. Pass it between 2–3 and 10–11, then 3–4 and 9–10.

4. Bring weavers to front, A between spokes 4 and 5 and B between spokes 5 and 6. Mark 5 as initial spoke, and begin two-ply twining, spreading other spokes apart. Follow pattern on page 67.

Progress of the basket. As spokes are added, the basket curves outward and the pattern automatically shifts. After third addition, as seen here, the basket has 54 spokes.

After fourth addition of spokes, the basket should have 82 spokes. When the light-colored band in progress above is finished, turn the basket inside out and clip off loose ends.

A single row of three-ply twining above the patterned band begins to pull the spokes inward. At the end of this row, drop one of the three weavers inside the basket and cut it short.

Before beginning twill weave (see p. 67), add one spoke to make an uneven number—83. The four rows of twill weave, in progress above, serve to further pull the basket inward toward border.

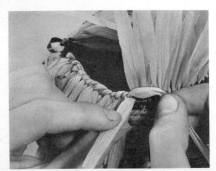

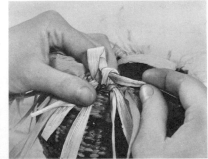

Finish. 1. After the final row of three-ply twining, drop the weavers inside the basket. Weave each spoke behind the next one to its right and pull it to the front. Work counterclockwise around basket.

2. For the critical final step of this round, carefully pull up the initial spoke in the weave; then run the end of the last spoke through it and pull tight to lock the border firmly in place.

3. Cut off corn husks to within 3/4 in. of the edge to make a decorative fringe around the border. Neatly trim away any loose ends of raffia or corn husk that remain inside the basket.

4. Wet the basket and indent the bottom to provide a stable base for the basket to rest on. If the basket is irregularly shaped, stuff it with paper to round it out while it dries.

Basketry/project

Wicker basket with lid

Bold enough to accent a fireplace hearth, this basket measures 12 inches across, 9 inches tall without the lid, and 10 inches with it. Without a lid it might serve as a wastebasket or hold magazines; with the lid it could store yarns.

Materials. The basket requires one bundle each of No. 4 reed (for spokes) and Nos. 2 and 1 reed (for weavers). The dark bands are of Virginia creeper (see chart, p. 56). If this is unavailable, substitute some other natural material, such as native grasses, or dye some reed for contrast (see *Spinning and dyeing*, p. 73). The handle is a piece of cholla cactus held on with jute cord.

Equipment. Assemble a No. 4 metal knitting needle, 5-inch side-cutting pliers, needle-nose pliers, scissors, measuring tape, an awl, and a large tub for soaking the reeds. Soak them 20 minutes. Wear old clothes because you will get wet.

Upside down and minus its handle, the lid could be a tray. In fact, the basket and lid demonstrate two methods of making a base. In the lid the spokes that form the base continue up the sides. In the basket the spokes are cut off at the edge of the base, and new spokes are inserted for the body of the basket. This is called a separate base and is a stronger construction.

The shape of the basket is adjusted by exerting pressure on the spokes. Considerable pressure is required to bring the spokes inward, especially near the top. If the spokes dry out, soak them again to make them pliable.

Once you have tried a wicker basket, you may want to create your own design. It is not difficult. Make a scale drawing on graph paper and figure the length for the spokes by adding the desired height, plus 2 inches for insertion into the base (if using a separate base), plus 9 inches for the border, plus 1 inch for the curve. Spokes must be larger than weavers—two sizes larger is usual. Nos. 2 and 4 are the most commonly used reed sizes.

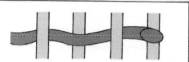

Trimming ends of reeds. Miter the ends of reed weavers so that the cut surfaces lie flush with the side of the basket. Use side-cutting pliers.

New weaver

Starting a new weaver. When a weaver runs out, clip it off so that it rests on top of a spoke. Start new weaver behind preceding spoke.

Old weaver

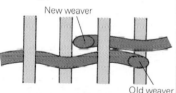

Initial spoke

Changing weaves. Clip off old weaver(s) at initial spoke. Begin one new weaver behind that spoke and others (if any) behind preceding one or two.

Border
2-ply twining 1"
3-ply twining 3½"
Chasing 1"
2-ply twining 1"
Chasing 1"
3-ply twining ¾"
Japanese weave 1"
3-ply twining 4"
Start

Pattern for the basket. For start and first half of Japanese weave (p. 66) at base of basket, use No. 1 reed. Complete body of basket with No. 2 reed, except for dark band of two-ply twining.

1. A separate base. Take eight 10-in. pieces of No. 4 reed; lay four one way, four at right angle. Pass a No. 1 reed diagonally beneath; bring it to front at corner and across four top spokes.

2. Weave around the cross-shaped start, going over the top four spokes and under the bottom four spokes. Pull the reed firmly as you weave. Make three rounds in this manner.

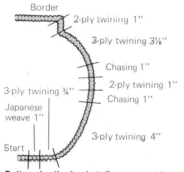

3. Spread spokes evenly and begin Japanese weave (p. 66), marking spoke where it starts with thread. This is the initial spoke. Continue for 1/2 in., then switch to No. 2 reed for another 1/2 in.

4. As you make the first round of three-ply twining, hold the beginning ends of the reeds with left hand. After two rounds turn the base over and cut these ends so they each lie against a spoke.

5. When the base is 5 in. across, cut the three weavers to points, leaving them an extra inch long. With knitting needle open weaving next to a spoke; tuck the weavers inside. *(Continued)*

Basketry/project

Wicker basket with lid (continued)

6. Adding spokes. Cut 32 24-in. spokes to points. With a knitting needle open weaving to right of each of the existing 16 spokes and insert 16 new spokes. Push them in close to center.

7. Cut off the old spokes flush with the base. Again using the knitting needle to open the weaving, insert the remaining 16 spokes to the left of each old spoke.

8. Turning up the spokes. Soak base thoroughly to soften the reeds. Pick up base and press it against your body so that the spokes bend downward. Begin three-ply twining with No. 2 reed.

9. As the weaving begins to hold the curve in the spokes, continue to press the basket against your body and exert firm downward pressure with your left hand on opposite side of basket.

10. Working the sides. After band of chasing (see p. 66), begin two-ply band of Virginia creeper by looping a piece—two together if vines are thin—around initial spoke to create two weavers.

11. Chase with reed after twining with Virginia creeper (see diagram, p. 69). As you begin three-ply twining near top, push spokes inward firmly to round basket. Untangle ends as you weave.

12. Making the collar. Pinch the spokes with needle-nose pliers. This aids in bending them straight up. If no lid is desired, at this point make a border as in Steps 14–17 below.

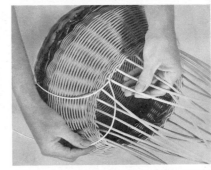

13. As you work the collar with two-ply twining, make sure that you hold the spokes straight upward. After twining until the collar is 1 in. high, trim the spoke tips to points.

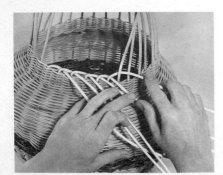

14. Weaving the border. Turn basket upside down in tub to soak spokes. Starting with any spoke, bend it behind the next spoke to its right and bring it to outside. Work from left to right.

15. When you have gone around the basket and reached the last upright spoke, raise the loop made by the first spoke slightly; pull the last spoke through this loop.

16. Go around a second time, carrying each spoke across two spokes to the right, then through to the inside. Use an awl to open the weaving. Pull the spokes tight.

17. The last two spokes are somewhat tricky. Count very carefully across two spokes to find the loop where the spokes should be inserted. Cut off the ends close to the weaving.

The lid: another basket form

The lid is begun like the wicker basket (see p. 69), but since randing requires an uneven number of spokes, a single spoke is added after the start. Unlike the basket, the same spokes that form the base are turned up for the sides. Therefore, they must be long enough from the start—24 inches—to form the base, sides, and border.

As the lid's diameter grows, the spokes become too widely spaced for the weaving. At that point additional spokes are poked into the weaving.

The handle here is a piece of cholla cactus from a crafts store, but you may prefer some other decorative bead or knob—or you can make a braided loop of jute cord to serve as a handle.

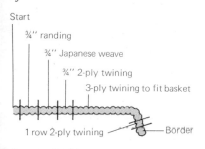

Pattern for the lid. Use a No. 1 reed as weaver for the start and for 3/4 in. of randing. The rest is worked with No. 2 reed for weavers, except for the decorative band of Virginia creeper.

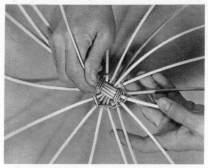

1. Base. Begin as in Steps 1 and 2, page 69, but use eight 24-in. No. 4 reeds. Open starting corner with knitting needle; insert 12-in. No. 4 reed for 17th spoke. Run diagonally through to front.

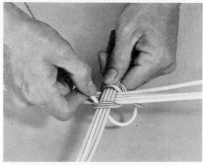

2. Soak start until spokes are very pliable. Do 3/4 in. of randing, spreading the spokes evenly. Push the weaver toward the center with a knitting needle after each round.

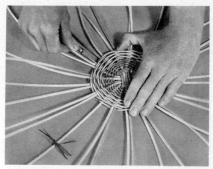

3. After 3/4 in. of Japanese weave, sharpen 16 12-in. No. 4 reeds. Open weaving with awl, and insert a spoke next to each existing spoke except the initial spoke (tied with raffia here).

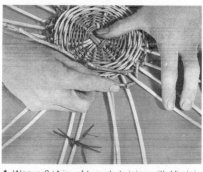

4. Weave 3/4 in. of two-ply twining with Virginia creeper, beginning weavers as in Step 10, page 70. Separate spokes and spread them evenly. Follow with three-ply twining.

5. Turning up the spokes. Try lid for size during three-ply twining. When it is two rounds wider than basket's border, pinch spokes with needle-nose pliers at the edge of the weaving.

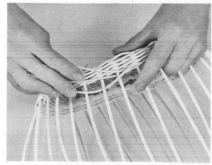

6. Bend the spokes and force them sharply upward. Press the lid against a table or your body as you continue three-ply twining. Exert pressure against spokes with left hand.

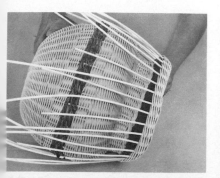

7. Try lid for size occasionally. Stop weaving when there is 1/2 in. clearance between lid and basket for border. Lid will then sit snugly on basket, as border will pull spokes inward.

8. Weaving the border. Cut off three weavers and start two new ones (see p. 69) for single round of two-ply twining. Soak lid. Make border as in Steps 14–17, page 70, but do not cut spokes.

9. Pass each spoke behind one spoke to its left. Open the weaving with an awl and push the spoke through to the outside. Miter the ends as shown on page 69.

10. Handle. Knot two pieces of jute cord together; run both ends through center of cholla cactus. Open weaving with awl, pull jute through with crochet hook, and tie ends inside lid.

71

Spinning and Dyeing

From wool fiber to yarn

A woman spins; 6th-century B.C. Greek vase.

Today hand spinning—the drawing out and twisting of fiber—is still done in the way it was thousands of years ago.

Material. Fleece is sold by the pound in three forms: unscoured, or "in the grease;" scoured, or washed; and carded, or "wool top." Fleece that is not too dirty can be spun in the grease, but usually it requires washing. Lay it in a bath of mild soap and tepid water, rinse in cool water, and hang to dry. Because washing removes the natural oils, add a few drops of vegetable oil before teasing.

Next the wool is carded and spun as shown below. Buy medium cards (also called medium cloth) and, if possible, a spindle with a removable whorl.

Plying yarn. The product of spinning is called a single of yarn; for most weaving you will want to ply the yarn—that is, twist together two singles. Plying is done exactly like spinning, using the spindle, but usually in the opposite direction from which the singles were spun. Place the cones of yarn on pegs and run the yarns between the fingers while plying. Wind the plied yarn from the cone into a skein around two upright pegs. The pegs should be 18 inches apart. Tie the start of the yarn to one peg. When wound, untie the start and tie the plied yarn end to end.

Washing the yarn. To keep the skein organized during washing, tie several figure 8's (p. 77) of string around it. Wash the yarn as you did the fleece. Run a rod through the center of the skein and hang it up to dry. Tie a weight to a string and suspend it from the skein. When the top of the skein is dry, revolve it and change the position of the weight. Wind skeins into balls.

It takes a bit of practice to acquire the smooth, rhythmic motions that produce an even yarn and to feel confident that the diaphanous rolls of wool will actually turn into a solid strand.

Teasing and carding

Teasing. Take a small handful of fleece and pull it apart lightly with your fingers. Work from one end of fleece to the other. Repeat until it looks cloudlike and has no dense spots.

Carding. 1. Holding card in left hand, distribute a fistful of teased wool evenly across it. Catch fiber on wire hooks near edge and draw it down. Do not overload the card.

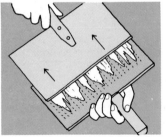

2. Rest one card, held with left hand, on left knee. Draw the second card across it very lightly with an upward motion at the end of stroke. Repeat until all wool is transferred to the second card.

3. Transfer wool back to first card with wiping motion of second. Keep wool in a sheetlike shape. Repeat Step 2 and this step until all fiber looks uniform across the sheet.

4. Hold cards at right angles and brush them briskly but lightly against each other several times to work the wool into a light roll. Brush upward in the direction of the handles.

5. Using your hands, gently work wool into an even roll, called a *rolag*. Make about 24 rolags before beginning to spin, so that spinning can continue without interruption.

Spinning the yarn

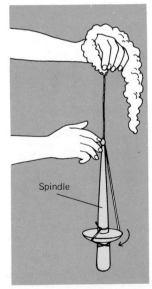

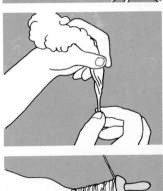

Whorl

Spindle

Tie a piece of finished yarn to spindle above whorl. Bring it beneath whorl, wind it around spindle shaft 1½ times (top right), and loop it around notch at top of shaft (detail). Cut yarn to leave 10-in. tail. Fray its end. Hold rolag (see Step 5) and yarn gently together between fingers and thumb. Begin spinning by twirling spindle with your free hand; then with same hand draw out the fiber (center right); release it and spin the spindle again. Note triangular shape of fiber. Keep spindle rotating. Repeat rhythmic process of drawing out yarn and spinning. When spindle is near floor, unfasten yarn from notch and from beneath whorl. Wind yarn around spindle shaft, building it into a cone shape (lower right). Before resuming spinning, attach yarn again as in top right drawing. Spin clockwise for Z twist, counterclockwise for S (see text, p. 76).

Dyeing with natural materials

While chemical dyes (p. 95) are easy to use and produce bright, predictable colors, the colors from natural plant and animal materials have a subtlety seldom achieved with chemicals. Because of the variables in natural materials the results are seldom twice alike. Therefore, dye all material of the same color in one dyebath. Most synthetic fibers do not absorb natural dyes.

Equipment. You need stainless steel or enamel pots, a wooden dowel for each color or one glass rod, rubber gloves, a fine strainer or cheesecloth, a postage scale, measuring cup and spoons. Use these only for dyeing.

Mordants. Natural dyes require a chemical substance called a mordant to make the dye "bite." Some weaving shops carry mordants, or you can buy them from a chemical supplier. The same dyestuffs used with different mordants produce different colors.

Caution: Keep mordants and dyes out of children's reach. Wear rubber gloves to protect your hands, and work in a well ventilated room. Chrome in particular is corrosive and produces noxious fumes. Never use cooking utensils, as the residues of mordants and dyes are generally toxic.

Common mordants, their chemical names, and amounts to use per ounce of yarn or cloth are given in the chart.

MORDANT	CHEMICAL	AMOUNT
Alum*	Potassium aluminum sulfate	3/4 tsp per oz
Chrome	Potassium dichromate	1/16 tsp per oz
Iron (copperas)	Ferrous sulfate	1/16 tsp per oz
Tin	Stannous chloride	1/16 tsp per oz

* Do not use ammonium aluminum sulfate, commonly sold for pickling.

Plant materials. Gather flowers when first in bloom, leaves and bark in spring, berries when ripe. Materials such as coffee and tea are in your kitchen; cochineal, madder, and logwood can be bought from weaving shops or botanical gardens. If not used right away, air dry materials and store in paper bags. Berries can be frozen.

Making the dyebath. For each ounce of yarn or cloth use 1 ounce of leaves, berries, or flowers; 2–3 ounces of bark; 1/2 ounce of spices, coffee, or tea. If your tap water is hard, add water softener or vinegar. Place crushed dyestuff, loose or tied in cheesecloth, in a pan, and barely cover with water. Soak flowers and berries overnight, stems and leaves three days, woody parts a week, walnut hulls a month.

Bring soaked materials to a rolling boil. Boil 30 minutes or more, until you obtain the desired color. Remember that it looks deeper in the liquid than it will in the yarn. Remove dyestuff or, if loose, strain through a fine strainer. Measure the concentrate, and add enough water to make 1 quart for each ounce of yarn. Dissolve mordant in 1/2 cup water, and add it to the dyebath.

Dyeing. Yarn for dyeing should be in a skein. If dyeing wool yarn, prewash and rinse it in successively warmer baths until it is the temperature of the dyebath. Squeeze out excess water, and put the yarn in the dyebath all at once. Slowly increase the water temperature until it is just barely simmering; do not boil. Simmer for 30 minutes or more— until the color in the bath is exhausted or the yarn has reached the desired depth of color. Remove the yarn and rinse it in successively cooler water until the rinse water is clean. Hang the skein to dry out of the sun and direct heat, rotating it occasionally. Keep a record of every dye project: include a sample; note the dyestuff, mordant, and quantities of all substances used.

Hues from nature

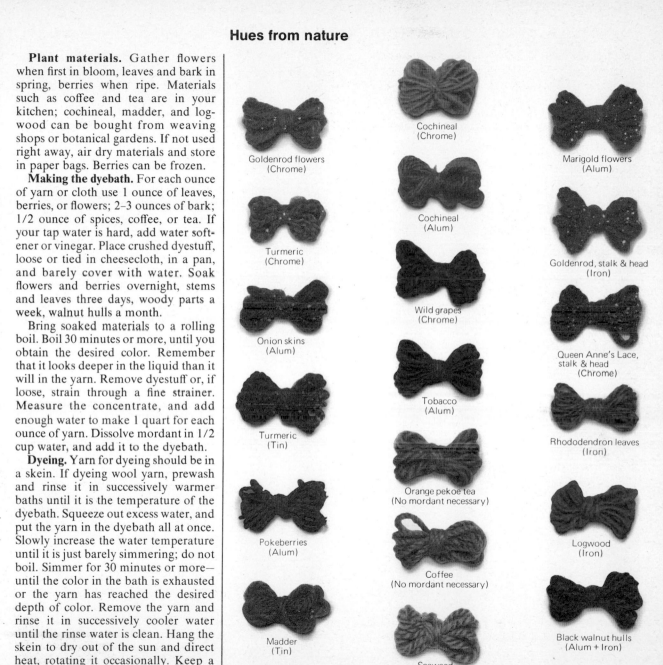

Goldenrod flowers (Chrome)

Turmeric (Chrome)

Onion skins (Alum)

Turmeric (Tin)

Pokeberries (Alum)

Madder (Tin)

Cochineal (Chrome)

Cochineal (Alum)

Wild grapes (Chrome)

Tobacco (Alum)

Orange pekoe tea (No mordant necessary)

Coffee (No mordant necessary)

Seaweed (Alum)

Marigold flowers (Alum)

Goldenrod, stalk & head (Iron)

Queen Anne's Lace, stalk & head (Chrome)

Rhododendron leaves (Iron)

Logwood (Iron)

Black walnut hulls (Alum + Iron)

The top line of each label indicates the dyestuff; the bottom line, the mordant.

73

Weaving

The craft that clothed man

Weaving has its roots in basketry; the essential difference lies in the mechanism of the loom to hold taut the lengthwise strands, called the warp, while crosswise strands, the weft, are woven in.

Where basket weaving requires stiff fibers, the development of a loom mechanism permitted the use of flexible fibers—linen, silk, cotton, and wool. Except for silk, all required, in addition to a loom, a method of spinning fibers into yarn (see p. 72).

The oldest depiction of a loom is on a pottery dish dated c. 4400 B.C. that was found in a tomb at El Badari, Egypt. The elements of the modern loom are already there. The warp is stretched horizontally between two rods that resemble today's warp beam and cloth beam (see looms, opposite page). Four pegs driven into the ground at the corners hold the rods. At right angles to the warp are three rods, presumably to separate alternate warp threads. With these devices the weaver probably raised warp threads to pass the weft through, lowered them, and raised other warp threads for the weft to pass in the opposite direction. The opening thus created is called a shed. A row of weft is called a pick, and putting it in the shed is called picking.

Beside this ancient loom are two devices, one of which may have been a comb to beat in the weft, that is, to pack it down against the previous row of weft. Thus this loom had all the elements needed to carry out the three basic movements of weaving: making the shed, picking, and beating.

The heddle rod, which may or may not be represented on the El Badari dish, was a significant advance in the ability to manipulate the shed. It is placed at a right angle to the warp threads, called warp ends, and every other warp end is tied to it. Raising the rod lifts the warp ends to form the shed, allowing the weft pick to be made.

A loom not unlike today's tapestry loom appeared in Egypt during the 18th Dynasty (1567–1320 B.C.). Today the Navajo Indians use a similar loom.

Between 1766 B.C. and 1122 B.C. the Chinese developed a more complex loom for the weaving of silk in intricate patterns impossible to produce on a loom that could make only two sheds. Probably these looms had foot-controlled treadles to operate harnesses to which the warp ends were tied.

A horizontal loom with treadle-operated harnesses appeared in Europe in the 13th century. Concurrent with the development of the loom with multiple harnesses came the warping board (see opposite and p. 77). It provided a method for keeping the many warp threads in order while measuring them out before dressing the loom.

The Industrial Revolution. Looms changed very little until the 18th century. Beginning then and on into the 19th century, inventions, mostly by Englishmen, increasingly mechanized weaving. During the 19th century handweaving very nearly became a lost art in the industrialized world. But it continued as a living tradition in the Scandinavian and other European countries, the mountains of Tennessee and Kentucky, and the rural districts of the British Isles. With the revival of interest in handcrafts in this century, craftspeople sought out weavers in those places to learn their ancient art.

Today handweaving is pursued less for profit than for pleasure—the joy of working with color and design, the fascination with the web of threads, the relaxing rhythm of weaving, and, of course, the pride in creating a unique fabric for clothing or wall hangings.

Woven coverlet of the Wise and Foolish Virgins, 18th century, The Oslo Museum of Applied Art.

Looms and other equipment

Some factors to consider in deciding on a loom are size, portability, expense, and the kind of weaving you intend to do. While there is some flexibility in what can be woven on a specific loom (see equipment suggestions in the projects), generally, a four-harness loom is best for weaving yardage, a tapestry loom for rugs or tapestries. A rigid heddle loom operates with ease and simplicity, but the warp threads must always be the same number per inch, usually six or eight depending on the heddle. A homemade frame loom

will be the least expensive, but you must take care to tension the warp evenly (see p.85).

Once the type of loom is determined, look at the available models with these factors in mind: sturdiness, smoothness and ease of operation of all moving parts, quality of wood (close-grained hardwood is best), weaving width, and weaving space (the working area between beater and breast beam on a four-harness loom). Other preferences, such as whether you like string or metal heddles better, come with experience.

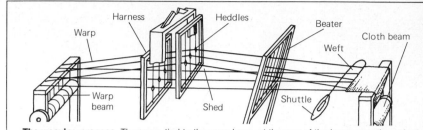

The weaving process. The warp, tied to the warp beam at the rear of the loom, runs through heddles held by harnesses and is tied to the cloth beam. The latter holds the woven cloth. The harnesses move up and down to open the sheds. The shuttle carrying the weft passes across the warp each time the shed is changed. The beater packs down each pick of weft.

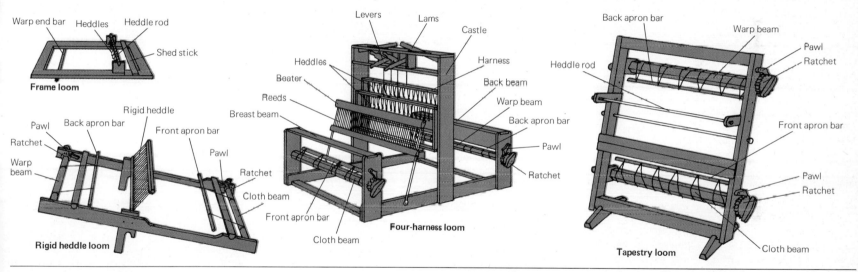

Frame loom

Rigid heddle loom

Four-harness loom

Tapestry loom

Warping equipment

Warping board

Warping pegs

Above: Warping pegs are for preparing a short warp; a long warp requires a warping board. At right: Lease sticks and raddle are used in dressing the loom (see pp. 78–79). The raddle is easy to make of a 1- by 1-in. piece of wood the length of the warp beam with nails at 1-in. intervals. Bobbin winder winds bobbins for boat shuttle. The ball winder is faster than hand winding of balls of yarn. Use boat shuttle for inserting weft on a four-harness loom; otherwise use a stick shuttle. The tapestry beater packs the weft. The sleying hook pulls yarn through the beater.

Loom accessories

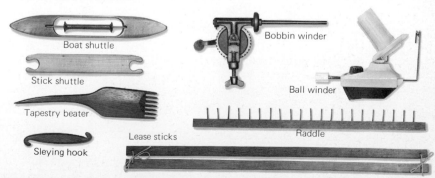

Boat shuttle

Stick shuttle

Tapestry beater

Sleying hook

Bobbin winder

Ball winder

Lease sticks

Raddle

Weaving

Fibers and yarns

The design of a fabric starts with the choice of fiber. Although there is much to recommend synthetics—strength, washability, and wrinkle resistance—most handweavers choose natural fibers—wool, cotton, linen, or silk.

Before they can be woven, fibers must be spun into yarn (see p. 72). A yarn spun once is called a single, or single-ply, yarn. If spun clockwise, it has a Z twist; if counterclockwise, an S twist. Singles are plied together, usually in the opposite direction of their spin, to make 2-ply, 3-ply, or even 10-ply yarn. Two or more plied yarns twisted together make a cord.

Wool fiber is prepared and spun in several ways. So-called woolen yarn is soft, loosely twisted, and suitable for apparel and blankets. Worsted yarn is a hard, smooth yarn, used for suiting and decorative fabrics. Knitting yarns are loosely twisted; they are unsuitable for warp but can be used for weft. Weave a sample with the yarns you choose.

Yarn labels do not always state the number of yards in a skein or spool; instead they give its weight and two numbers, such as 10/2. The first number is called the count. It indicates the size of the yarn. Size 1 is the thickest and the standard by which all yarn of that fiber is measured. Size 2 is half as thick as 1; 10 is one-tenth as thick. In the system most commonly used in Canada, a pound of size 1 yarn produces the following yardages: woolen, 1,600 yards; worsted, 560 yards; cotton, 840 yards; linen, 300 yards; and spun silk, 840 yards.

The second number in the example 10/2 is the number of plies in the yarn. To find the yardage per pound of a plied yarn, multiply the count by the standard for that fiber and divide the result by the number of plies. Thus the formula for a pound of woolen yarn marked 10/2 would be $10 \times 1{,}600 \div 2$, or 8,000 yards.

Choosing the weft

Color, size, and yarn construction enter into the choice of weft. To see how the colors you want to use interact with each other, it is a good idea to weave a sample. This is easily done. Cut slits at opposite edges of a small rectangle of cardboard at the intended ends per inch (epi) of the warp (see facing page). Wind the cardboard with a 2-inch width of the warp yarn you have chosen. Then thread a needle with the weft and weave for an inch or so. Beat the weaving with a fork.

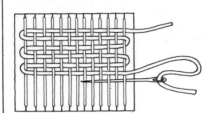

To create a weft-faced fabric (where the weft shows and the warp is covered), choose a weft yarn that is thicker than the warp, and space the warp widely in relation to the weft's thickness. Tapestries and rugs are usually weft-faced. For a balanced weave (where the warp and weft show equally) choose a weft yarn the same size as the warp. If you desire a warp-faced fabric (where the warp predominates), choose a weft yarn thinner than the warp, and space the warp closely.

Weft yarn need not be as strong as warp because it is not under tension. Therefore, you can choose from a wider variety of yarns. Mix different kinds of yarn, but not of such disparate sizes that the weaving stretches out at one place and pulls in at another. You can use other materials as well, such as grasses, feathers, and plastics. But until you have mastered basic weaving techniques, the best choice is a yarn designed for handweaving.

So that you can buy all yarn for a project at one time and thus ensure getting the same dye lot, you will need to calculate how much weft yarn is required. Here again the cardboard sample comes in handy. Count the number of weft picks in an inch of weaving. Figure the length of each pick by adding the width of your fabric plus 25 percent for shrinkage. Then multiply the picks per inch times the length of one pick times the length of the cloth in inches. Divide by 36 to get the number of yards.

Different ways of preparing the weft for weaving are illustrated below. If the yarn is in a skein, wind it into a ball first, either around your hand or using the ball winder shown on page 75.

Preparing the weft

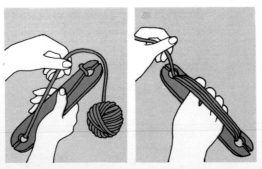

Making a butterfly. Wind the yarn first around the thumb, then around the second and third fingers, making a crisscross of yarn in between. When butterfly is 1 in. thick, slip it off the hand, wrap yarn tightly around the crisscross a few times, and tie a half-hitch, as shown. Pull on the loose end of yarn for weaving. Butterflies are used in tapestry, rug, and inlay weaving wherever the picks of weft are too short for the stick shuttle.

Winding a stick shuttle. Loop the yarn around one protruding end of the shuttle. Wind yarn around the shuttle and over end of yarn. Hold fingers across one side of shuttle and wind yarn over them so that it will not be too tight. The hand that holds yarn should be still; rotate the shuttle back and forth—it is faster and the yarn does not become twisted. Do not build up the yarn so high that the shuttle cannot pass easily through the sheds in the warp.

Loading a shuttle

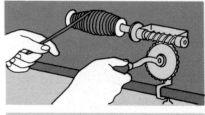

Winding bobbins for boat shuttle. Hold yarn in one hand and feed it evenly back and forth while turning crank with other hand. Do not tie at beginning; winding over end of yarn holds it. When yarn is height of bobbin end pieces, build it up in the center a bit more, but no thicker than depth of shuttle. Raise metal bar in shuttle and slide bobbin over it. Drop metal bar and thread yarn through hole in shuttle.

Preparing the warp

Navajo Indian women never prepare a warp or put it on the loom near mealtime or when children are about. They wait for a quiet time when they will not be interrupted or distracted. It is a wise custom to follow. Preparing the warp is an orderly way of measuring out the length and breadth of the warp. The process requires undivided attention.

Choosing the warp. Linen, cotton, wool, silk, or synthetics are all suitable for warp. Since the warp is under tension and must take considerable beating in the weaving process, it should be strong. Test the yarn of your choice by holding it with hands 6 inches apart. Yank on it; if it snaps readily, it is not strong enough. It must not fray easily and should be smooth—a fuzzy yarn will stick to itself, making the sheds difficult to clear. Generally, a plied yarn is better than a single.

Calculating the warp. Warp has two dimensions: width and length. The former is the desired width of the finished cloth plus 10 percent for pulling in at the selvedges—the nonraveling edges created by the turn of the weft around the outside warp ends. For example, the warp for a piece of cloth 20 inches wide should be 22 inches. Then you must decide on the number of warp ends per inch (epi), also called the warp sett. Experience will teach you how to space the warp for the fabric effect you want. If you are uncertain, wrap the warp around a ruler, laying the threads next to each other. Count the threads per inch and divide by two.

Other factors influence warp sett. If you want a loose, open weave or if the warp is to be covered by weft, use fewer epi. If you want a warp-faced fabric, use more epi. Once the sett is established—8 epi, for example—multiply that by the width of the warp—say, 22 inches. The result: 176 warp threads.

To calculate the warp length, add together the length of the finished cloth plus 10 percent for shrinkage plus 8 inches for tying onto the front apron bar (more if you want fringe), plus an amount for loom waste. This last figure will vary from loom to loom; it is the amount of warp between the back apron bar and the point where the weaving stops. For most tapestry or rigid heddle looms, loom waste is 8 inches; for a table loom allow 4 inches per harness.

For a piece of cloth 60 inches long woven on a four-harnesss loom, the calculation would be: $60 + 6 + 8 + 16 = 90$ inches. Multiply that by the epi—176—and you have the total amount of warp: 15,840 inches, or 440 yards.

For a short warp, warping pegs are adequate. Place them so that the distance between end pegs equals the warp length. For a warp of several yards or more a warping board is preferable. The distance across the board between pegs is 36 inches.

The cross. The purpose of the cross is to keep the warp ends in sequence, as they were placed on the pegs. It ensures that while threading them onto the loom, the warp ends will not jump over each other and become tangled.

If the yarn is in a ball or spool, place it on the floor in a box or bowl as you wind off it. Place a cone on an upright peg. If the yarn is in a skein, ball it first. Keep even and very slight tension on the yarn; do not allow slack in it. Stack the yarn up in sequence on the end pegs until it reaches the top. Then push it down without disturbing the sequence. There must be no knots in the part of the warp that will be woven. If you come to one, cut the yarn, unwind it to the nearest end peg, make a knot there, and resume winding. If the warp is striped, begin the new color at the nearest end peg.

Chaining. If the warp is long or if it is not to be put on the loom right away, chain it to preserve its order.

Warping on pegs or board

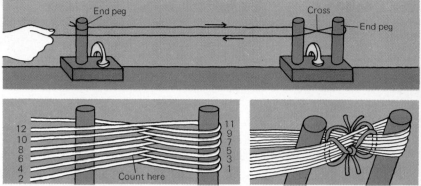

Clamp warping pegs to a table with end pegs spaced the warp's length apart. Tie warp to single end peg. Follow path of arrows, making the cross as indicated. Count warp ends at cross by dropping one thread alternately from each hand. Tie last warp thread to an end peg. Tie both sides of cross with cord. Tie cord around warp at other end peg and at 36-in. intervals.

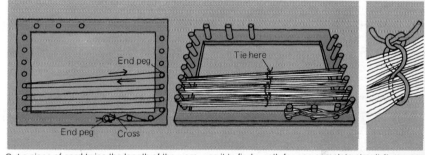

Cut a piece of cord twice the length of the warp; use it to find a path for one complete circuit (two warp ends) on warping board. Make cross between end peg and adjacent peg. Count as above; tie warp at 36-in. intervals to keep it organized (center). If number of warp ends is large, tie figure-8 knots (right) around equal groups to avoid recounting all the warps.

Chaining the warp off pegs

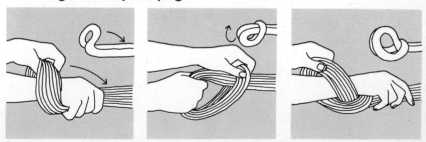

Step 1. Slide warp off peg away from cross, keeping light tension on it. With right hand reach through loop and grasp warp. **Step 2.** Pull loop over hand and let it drop on warp ahead of hand. Grasp newly made loop with left hand. **Step 3.** Put right hand through new loop and grasp warp ahead of previous loop. Drop end loop over hand as in Step 2. Continue to the cross.

Weaving

Putting the warp on the loom

Dressing the loom is the second stage in weaving. Like warping (see previous page), it is best done without distractions. At first, spreading those closely bunched threads across the loom in correct sequence may seem like a hopeless chore. But after a few times it becomes clear that with care, patience, and the device of the cross illustrated below, a well-dressed loom happens almost automatically.

In dressing the loom, one end of the warp is first attached to the back apron bar and then rolled onto the warp beam (see illustrations below). When enough warp has been rolled on so that the other end reaches just to the breast beam, the warp is threaded through the

heddles (see opposite page). Then it is passed through the beater's reeds, a process called sleying. Finally, the warp is attached to the front apron bar, its tension is adjusted, and you are ready to weave. As weaving progresses, the finished cloth is rolled forward onto the cloth beam.

Shown on these pages is the step-by-step procedure for warping a four-harness loom. Whatever the kind of loom you use, the steps are the same with only minor variations. For example, the tapestry loom differs in that the warp is strung vertically instead of horizontally; thus the warp beam is at the top, the cloth beam at the bottom. In addition, the lease sticks are sus-

pended in front of the loom while the warp is being rolled on (see p. 86). There is no beater, so sleying is not necessary, and the loom may or may not have one set of heddles to thread.

On the rigid heddle loom, the heddles serve as beater too, so there is only one threading to do. The lease sticks with the warp on them are suspended in front of the heddle frame, and the warp is first threaded through the alternating holes and slots of the heddles. Next the warp is tied to the back apron bar in groups of four threads, rolled onto the warp beam, and then tied to the front apron bar in groups according to the epi (see text, p. 77). The setting up of the warp on a rigid heddle loom

is shown on page 90, Steps 1 and 2.

On any loom always center the warp. As it is rolled onto the warp beam, insert sheets of newspaper or dowels to separate the layers of warp and to maintain even tension. Use newspaper if the warp is short and of fairly soft wool or cotton; use dowels if the warp is strong and hard—linen, for instance—or longer than a few yards.

When you are ready to thread the heddles, position all harnesses at the same level, whatever is comfortable for working. Push heddles you will not need equally to either side, and group those you plan to use at the right. Removing the beater may make threading the heddles easier.

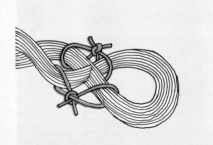

Locating the cross. Find the knots of the two strings you tied in the cross (see illustrations, p. 77). Pull them in opposite directions, and the cross will reappear.

Tying lease sticks. Insert lease sticks either side of cross. Run cord through holes in their ends, leaving a 1-in. space between sticks. Wrap cord around itself and knot, as shown.

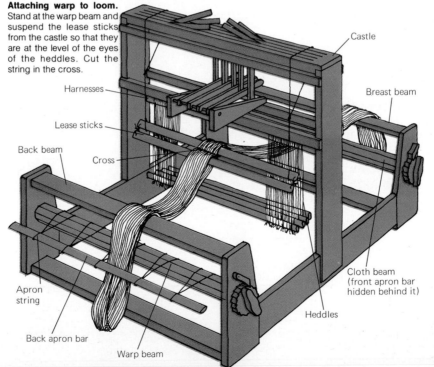

Attaching warp to loom. Stand at the warp beam and suspend the lease sticks from the castle so that they are at the level of the eyes of the heddles. Cut the string in the cross.

- Castle
- Harnesses
- Lease sticks
- Back beam
- Cross
- Apron string
- Back apron bar
- Warp beam
- Breast beam
- Cloth beam (front apron bar hidden behind it)
- Heddles

Adjusting back apron bar. The apron string runs continuously through bar and warp beam. With apron bar extended as shown, adjust string so that bar is parallel to warp beam. In preparation for next step, spread warp evenly on lease sticks.

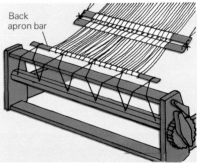

Back apron bar

Back apron bar. Center warp; spread full width on loom. Slip strings from one side of apron bar. Distribute half the warp evenly between strings; replace strings. Repeat on other side.

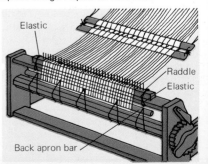

- Elastic
- Raddle
- Elastic
- Back apron bar

Raddle. Roll apron bar to back of warp beam. Attach raddle (p. 75) to back beam with heavy elastics. Roll apron bar to front of warp beam. Arrange warp between nails by ends per inch.

Rolling warp onto the beam.
1. Have a helper hold the warp at breast beam with even tension, fingers between threads. Slowly turn the warp beam, inserting sheets of newspaper. Gradually cut the ties as the chain unravels. As lease sticks move toward back beam, keep pushing them toward castle; turn them on edge for easier passage of warp. If warp becomes stuck, look for a knot or bunching. **2.** Helper shakes out warp to organize it. **3.** When end loop reaches breast beam, cut string, then cut through loop in groups approximating the epi (see text, p. 77). If there are many knots at loop, cut off 1 in. of warp to get rid of them. **4.** As you cut, tie each group of threads in a slipknot to prevent losing the cross while threading the heddles.

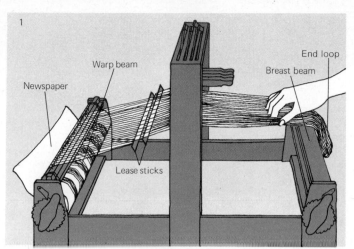

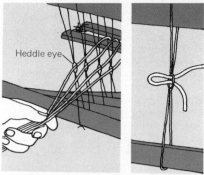

Threading heddles. Starting at left, take each warp in order it comes through lease sticks. Double it and thread through heddle eye (detail, right). After each repeat of threading order (p. 83), check that warps are on correct harnesses. Tie slipknot in groups the same as epi.

1. Sleying the reed. Replace beater if you took it out earlier. Center the reed in beater. From the center of the beater measure half of the warp's width in each direction. Mark the outside limits of the warp with string tied around the top of the beater. Starting at left, untie slipknots one at a time. With a sleying hook reach through the reed and pull each warp end through in the same sequence as their threading in heddles. Make sure none are crossed. If reed has fewer openings, called dents, than the epi (see text, p. 77), double threads at regular intervals; if more openings, leave empty dents at regular intervals. **2. Tying to front apron bar.** Remove raddle and lease sticks. Adjust front apron bar in same manner as back apron bar (p. 78). Turn cloth beam until front apron bar extends 1½ in. toward harnesses. Starting at outside and working on alternate sides toward center, tie warp ends to front apron bar in inch-wide groups. Tie with double half-hitch, threads divided equally.

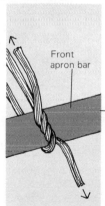
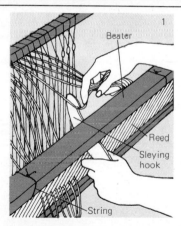
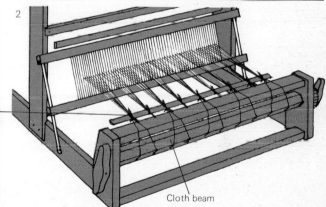

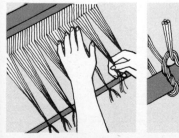

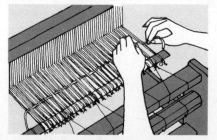
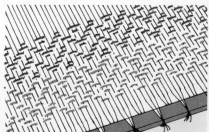

Checking warp tension. When all ends are tied to front apron bar, check for even tension by patting warp with hand. Tighten or loosen warp as necessary, then tie another half-hitch (detail).

Adjusting harnesses. Manipulate the cords that run continuously through one pair of lams to the castle until harnesses are parallel. Note: some looms adjust automatically.

Leveling the warp. Weave a cord tied to one end of the apron bar over the warp ends that cross the top of the apron bar, under the others. Tie to other end of apron bar and beat with beater.

Heading. Use scrap yarn of same type and size as weft. Go through one repeat of pattern (p. 83), and check to see that weave is correct. Do enough heading to even the warp ends.

Weaving

Putting in the weft

The actual weaving process consists of three movements repeated rhythmically: opening the shed, passing the weft through, and beating the weft.

Opening the shed. On most two-shed looms, one shed is made by turning the shed stick on its edge. The second shed is made by raising the heddle rod, if the loom has one, so that the string heddles (pp. 84–85) pull up alternate warp ends. If the loom lacks heddles, the weaver's fingers hold up every other warp, a few threads at a time, while the shuttle passes through. On a four-harness table loom the sheds are made by pulling levers (p. 93). The drawings below illustrate three ways of making a shed on a two-shed loom.

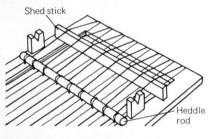

Shed stick

Heddle rod

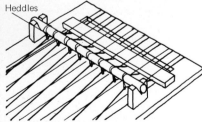

Heddles

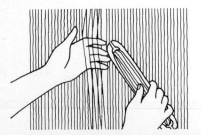

Sheds in the warp are opened for the weft.

Bubbling and slanting. The weft is bubbled or slanted, giving the pick extra weft that is taken up as the weft is packed down into the warp. To make the edge flat, pinch the yarn where it turns around the selvedge. Bubble the weft for a weft-faced fabric such as a tapestry. Poke the weft down with your fingers, making small arches, as you pass the weft through the warp. Slant weft for a fabric in which both warp and weft are to show.

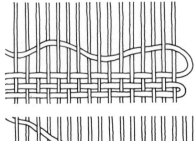

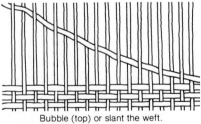

Bubble (top) or slant the weft.

Beating the weft. Fit the beat as well as the beater to the fabric. On a delicate weave use a gentle beat with fingers, table fork, or a comb. A dense, weft-faced fabric such as a tapestry or a rug calls for heavy beating with a tapestry beater. Beaters come in different weights, and some have metal inserts for added weight. Use wrist motion with a tapestry beater, or your arm will tire. On a four-harness loom place one hand in the center of the built-in beater, and move it forward and back crisply after each pick. For a delicate fabric a gentle tap will do; for heavy yarns and close weave, beat firmly. Methods of beating are shown at the top of the next column.

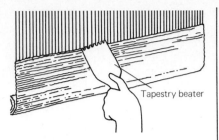

Tapestry beater

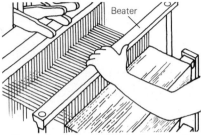

Beater

Two methods are used for beating the weft.

When the weaving gets too close to the beater or heddles or the shed no longer opens wide enough to accept the shuttle easily, roll some of the fabric onto the cloth beam. To do this, relax the tension on the warp beam by releasing the pawl that holds the ratchet (p. 75); take up the slack by slowly rotating the cloth beam. Make sure the beater still reaches the edge of the weaving. Recheck that the tension is even across the warp by patting the warp as shown on page 79. If it is not, remedy the problem by one of the methods listed in the chart opposite.

You can leave tension on the warp overnight, but if you are not going to weave for several days, relax the tension so that the warp will not stretch.

Keep track of the length of your weaving by tying a small piece of yarn to one selvedge every foot; then as it is rolled onto the cloth beam, you need only count pieces of yarn.

When the shuttle runs out or the weft yarn changes, start new weft in one of the three ways shown at right.

Starting new weft

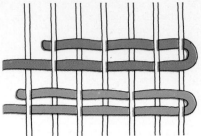

At the selvedge. Cut old weft, leaving a 2-in. tail. Loop it around outside warp; put it in above last pick in the same shed. Beat and change shed. Pass new weft through, leaving a 2-in. tail. Loop it around outside warp, and weave it back in above the pick just made. Beat. Next time start new weft at opposite selvedge.

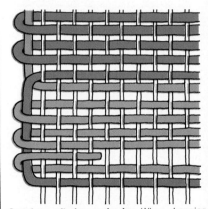

Carrying weft along selvedge. When changing weft every few picks, as in narrow stripes or checks, carry it along selvedge as shown. Include it in the same shed as outside warp.

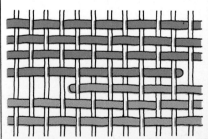

Starting new weft in body of cloth. Weft can begin and end in middle of some fabrics without showing. Overlap ends 2 in. If ends stick out, cut them when cloth is finished.

Finishing the fabric

At the end of the cloth weave a heading like the one at the start (see illustration, p. 79). If you are weaving another piece on the same warp, leave enough warp in between for the finish of both pieces. Weave a heading for the second piece. Remove the piece or pieces from the loom by cutting the warp or untying it from the front and back apron bars. Be sure to remove headings before finishing the cloth.

Choose the finish according to the function of the weaving. An overcast stitch may be sufficient for cloth that will be made into apparel. You may want to do a temporary overcast to hold weft in place while cutting out the heading and tying a fringe (p. 85). For a scarf, a wall hanging, or a rug, the warp ends may be tied with an overhand knot and left as a fringe. Or they may be twisted into plied fringe (p. 90) or a braid (p. 87). When only one side of the weaving is seen, the best finish may be to stitch down the ends of the warps and to cover them with seam tape (p. 89). Never machine stitch a handwoven article. If you make a rolled hem, take the time to stitch it by hand.

Apparel fabric need only be washed in mild soap and lukewarm water—cold water for wool—then steam pressed. Weavings that are not washable articles (such as wall hangings and tapestries) or weavings that are distorted must be blocked to the correct size and shape. Draw the planned dimensions of the weaving on a flat board. Tack or staple the weaving to the board with nonrusting tacks or staples. If the weaving needs stretching, wet it by blotting it all over with a damp cloth. If shrinking is required, press it with a steam iron or cover it with a damp cotton cloth and press it with the iron set for cotton. Dry the weaving in place. While it is tacked down, make the finishing stitches or the decorative fringe shown at right.

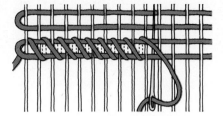

Overcast stitch. Use weft yarn to stitch over the last two rows of weft across each warp end, as shown. If overcast stitches are to be removed later, you can use a wider stitch.

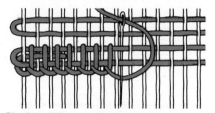

Blanket stitch. A sturdier finish than the overcast stitch, the blanket stitch forms a row of loops that enclose the last picks of weft. Use weft yarn, and make the stitch as shown.

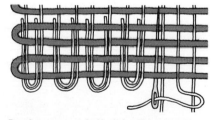

Darning warp ends back in. This looks like a selvedge. Thread each warp end on a needle and weave it alongside the adjacent warp end. Pairs of warp ends turn toward each other, as shown.

Overhand knot for fringe. If warp is fine, tie 4 to 10 ends together, as shown; if thick, 2 or 3. Overhand knot may also precede a braid (p. 87) or secure plied fringe (p. 90).

Solving weaving problems

PROBLEM	CAUSE	SOLUTION
On 2-shed loom, 2 adjacent warps in same shed	Incorrect threading	Cut out one warp end, or tie new warp end into other shed
Pattern of weave deviates	Incorrect threading	Make new heddle (see below)
Warp end breaks	Tension is too tight, or yarn is weak	Tie new warp end in place of broken one (see drawing below)
Warp end breaks often	Tension is uneven Warp is twisted in heddle	See below for correcting warp that is too loose or too tight Make sure warp has a clear path through heddle
Warp ends break often at selvedge	Weft is too tight; reed is abrading outside warps	Leave more slack weft in each pick
Bumps in weaving; weft will not pack down	Warp ends in that section are looser than other warps	Put thin strip of wood or layers of cardboard beneath loose warp ends on back beam
Depression in weaving; weaving packs down too much in one section	Warp ends in that section are tighter than rest of warp	If knots reachable, loosen those warps; otherwise, tighten rest of warp (see above)
Shed does not open enough for shuttle to pass through easily	Weaving is too close to heddles Harnesses not dropping or rising enough Warp yarn is fuzzy Tension on warp is too loose	Roll weaving onto cloth beam Adjust cords from lams to castle (see *Adjusting harnesses,* p. 79) Beat after changing shed Tighten tension on warp, but not so much that warp breaks

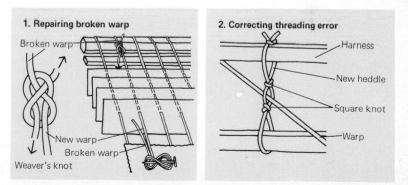

1. Cut piece of warp length of remaining unwoven warp plus 6 in. Anchor 3 in. from weaving's edge; thread through heddle. Tie to broken warp with weaver's knot (detail) at warp beam. Continue weaving; when knot reaches heddle, untie it and retie at warp beam. Repeat until end of weaving; then tie new warp to back apron bar and discard broken warp. When cloth is done, remove T-pin and darn loose ends into cloth so that they overlap 3 in. Cut off ends. **2.** If warp is threaded on wrong harness, make a new heddle and tie it to correct harness in proper position. Form the eye of heddle by tying two square knots. Rethread warp in the new heddle, and leave the other heddle hanging loose on its harness.

Weaving

The structure of fabrics

All weaving patterns derive from three basic weaves: plain, twill, and satin. The last is complex, requires a loom with at least five harnesses, and is used frequently for machine-woven fabrics.

Plain weave requires only two sheds (although it can be done on a four-harness loom) and is simply the weft passing over one, under one warp thread in alternating rows. Strong and durable, plain weave is probably the oldest structure and is often a good choice for items that will get hard wear. When plain weave is balanced so that there are the same number of warp ends per inch (epi) as there are weft picks per inch, it is called tabby weave.

Although plain weave seems simple in construction, it has so many possible variations that some weavers devote a lifetime to experimenting with it. Consider stripes: they can be in the warp or weft; they can be of two or more colors; they can be different yarn types; or they can be made by varying the density of warp ends. These variations can be intermixed, with the possibilities for combinations almost endless. Illustrated below are plain weaves in stripes, checks, and plaids.

Basket weave is a variation of plain weave that is done with two wefts passing over two, under two warps at a time, or even over three, under three. On a two-shed loom the two warp ends are threaded through the same heddle; on a four-harness loom, they are threaded through adjacent harnesses that are operated together. The double weft is accomplished several ways: by winding two threads on a bobbin; by making two passes of the shuttle in one shed and wrapping the yarn around the selvedge warp between passes; or by using two shuttles simultaneously. Because of the long floats of the weft across the warp, basket weave makes a warm cloth that is especially good for scarves and blankets.

In twill weaves (opposite page) the exposure of warp and weft is staggered diagonally across the fabric instead of being aligned in the alternating, squared-off rows of plain weave. Twill weave must be done on at least three harnesses and is usually done on four. Twill fabrics are softer and more drapeable than most others, and the long float makes them warm.

Twills can be over two, under two; over three, under one; or over one, under three. Those that are arranged in a diagonal running from the left or right selvedge to the opposite selvedge are called straight twills. In a reverse twill the diagonal switches back and forth, going first in one direction, then the other. Herringbone twill is similar to reverse twill, but the zigzag goes across the width of the fabric rather than the length of it. Offset twill, a variation on herringbone, is used in the project on pages 92–93. Other twill weaves are shown on the opposite page along with the required pattern drafts for their execution.

Plain weave. A balanced plain weave, such as the one at far left, has the same number of warp ends per inch (epi) as weft picks per inch.
Basket weave (left) is a variant of plain weave in which the warp ends are paired and the weft is woven two strands at a time, resulting in an over two, under two weave.

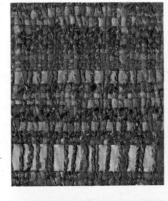

Novelty yarn weft (far left) includes silk, silk knitting ribbons, and rayon grosgrain woven into rayon warp.
Spaced and crammed warp (left) is arranged at three intervals. Although easier to control on a four-harness loom, it can be set up on a frame loom.

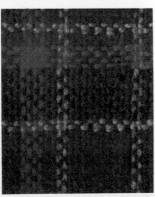

Checks (far left) are formed by a two-color striped warp and a weft that repeats the same stripe.
Plaids (left) are much like checks—the weft exactly repeats the warp pattern—but the stripes vary in width, and more colors are used.

Striped warp. Four colors of wool yarn and a metallic thread make up this striped warp. Weft in the example at far left is 12-ply linen yarn. At left the same warp produces a different look when woven with a brown wool weft.

Reading weaver's drafts

Pattern drafts are like musical notation: they tell the weaver how to thread and manipulate the loom to achieve the desired composition. Drafts may be written several ways—for instance, numbers may appear in place of X's in the threading order. The one constant is that a dark square represents a warp thread exposed on the fabric's surface; a white square, a weft thread. The method shown at right is the one most commonly used.

There are five elements to a pattern draft. The *basic pattern* is one complete repeat of the fabric's pattern. The *multiplied pattern* is the basic pattern expanded to give an idea of the weave's look. The *threading order* tells how the warp is to be threaded through the harnesses. Read it from bottom to top; the bottom row stands for the first harness going from front to back of the loom, the next line up for the second, and so on. (Note: in the Scandinavian countries loom harnesses are tradition-

ally numbered back to front, 1 to 4.)

The square to the right of the threading order, called the *tie-up,* tells which harnesses to operate together. Read the bottom line as harness 1, the next line up as harness 2, and so on, as in the threading order.

Below the tie-up, the *chain draft* indicates the order in which to operate the harness combinations of the tie-up. Start at the line beneath the tie-up and move down the column. By looking to the left in the same line as the X, you can see which warp ends should be raised and which lowered for that pick. Remember that black squares represent raised warp ends; white squares are lowered warp ends that will be covered by weft.

The drafts on this page are for a loom with rising harnesses. If your loom has sinking harnesses—harnesses that drop when the levers are operated—reverse the tie-up, making black squares white and vice versa.

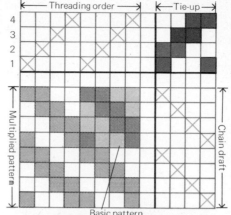

Basic pattern

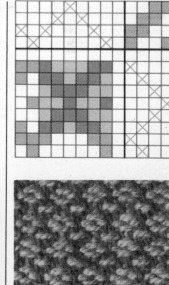
Straight twill may slant to left or right.

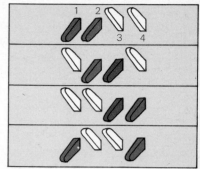

Weaving to the draft. To thread the loom, begin at the left side of the threading order and the loom. Thread the first warp through a heddle on harness 1, the second on harness 2, the third on harness 3, and the fourth on harness 4; then, starting over, the fifth warp on harness 1, and so on. This threading pattern is known as a straight draw. To weave, follow the chain draft from top to bottom. From the X in the chain draft look up the column to the tie-up, and raise the harnesses indicated in that column by black squares. Each column is color-keyed to the drawing at right, above, to show which levers operate the correct harness combinations.

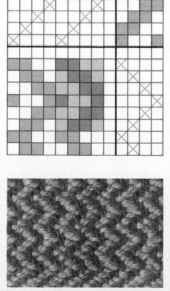
Reverse twill has a zigzag look.

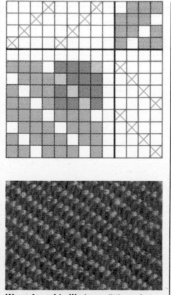
Warp-faced twill shows little weft.

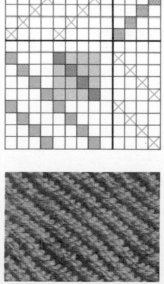
Weft-faced twill features the weft.

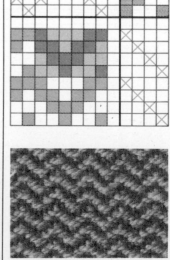
Herringbone zigzags horizontally.

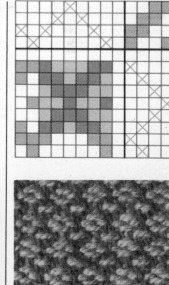
Bird's eye is type of diamond twill.

Weaving/project

Table mats from a homemade loom

The table mat in the photograph above is one of a pair woven on a simple frame loom. The warp is wound continuously around the loom, as seen on the facing page, so that two mats are woven on one warp.

It is easy to make a frame loom of canvas stretcher strips by following the diagram at right. You will learn about a loom's structure, and should you decide to weave on more complex looms, you can use the frame loom for trying out ideas. One shed is created by a shed stick; the other, by a heddle rod on which you make string heddles. The rod rests on the warp while the shed stick opens one shed (see text, p. 80). Flatten the stick and place rod in supports' notches for the second shed.

Materials and tools for loom. From an art supply store buy two canvas stretcher strips 26 inches long and two 22 inches long. The stretchers have fin-and-slot corners ready to be joined. The supports that hold the heddle rod are 3/4 inch plywood 3 by 4 inches with

a 1-inch-deep notch cut in one short end. The warp-end bar and heddle rod are 1/2 inch dowels the width of the loom—22 inches. Four L-shaped corner irons secure the corners. For a shed stick (p. 80) use a strip of wood several inches longer than the loom's outside width, 1½ inches wide, and 1/4 inch thick. Smooth it well with fine sandpaper and steel wool. Tension sticks can be strips of thick corrugated cardboard or several layers of thin cardboard. Tape them to the ends of the loom, and remove them as the warp tension becomes too tight. You will need a drill, screwdriver, carpenter's square, small C-clamps, and hammer.

Materials for table mats. The warp requires four 175-yard balls of crochet cotton: two light gold, one bright gold, and one variegated. The weft is rayon rug yarn; buy one 2-ounce skein of light gold that matches the main warp color and one 2-ounce skein of cream color. You also need 1-inch-wide rag strips (old sheets are fine) and white cotton string similar in size to the warp. Colors can be changed to suit your decorating scheme. The border weft color should be the same as the main warp; the outside warp (see below) is a deeper tone of the same color.

Warp. Mark the end pieces of the loom at 1/2-inch intervals as guidelines for the warp. The warp sett is 10 ends per inch, so there should be 5 warp ends per mark, evenly spaced. Warp width on the loom is 15 inches. The warp pattern is 1 inch bright gold, 1 inch variegated, 11 inches light gold, 1 inch variegated, 1 inch bright gold.

Weft. There are 8 picks per inch of weft. The weft pattern is 3 inches light gold, 12 inches cream, 3 inches light gold. Wind the weft onto a shuttle (p. 76). Use plain weave throughout. Because the tension cannot be great, the weaving will pull in, reducing the width of the mat to about 12 inches.

Constructing the loom

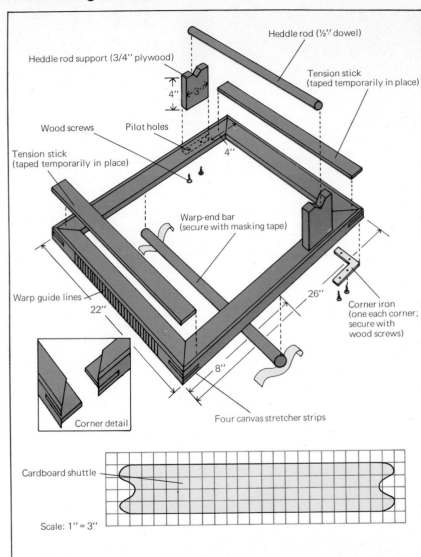

A frame loom. Put the canvas stretcher strips together. Use a carpenter's square, and with light hammer blows square the frame. Hold three corners with C-clamps while fastening the fourth with a corner iron. One by one, remove the C-clamps and screw on the corner irons. Drill pilot holes for screws to hold the heddle rod supports. Mount the supports 4 in. from the top of the frame. Starting 2 in. from a corner of the frame, mark lines at 1/2-in. intervals across top and bottom as guides for warp. Tape warp-end bar to back of loom 8 in. from end, as indicated.
Shuttle. From heavy cardboard cut out a shuttle with a utility knife. Or use hardwood 1/8 in. thick; round the edges and smooth surface with sandpaper.

Weaving the mats

Warping the loom. 1. Tape tension sticks to loom ends, placing tape so that it marks outer limits of warp width (15 in.). Tie warp yarn to warp-end bar and pass yarn around near end of loom.

2. Lead the yarn straight across front of loom to other end, over that end, and return it to warp-end bar. Circle the bar with yarn, and repeat procedure. Keep tension firm and even.

3. After 10 passes with gold, switch to variegated yarn. Tie the yarns together at the warp-end bar as shown. See the text (opposite page) for the rest of the warp pattern.

Creating the first shed. Place a sheet of white paper between layers of warp ends. Pick up every other warp end—1, 3, 5, etc.—on top of paper, and insert a shed stick beneath them.

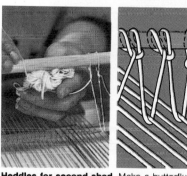

Heddles for second shed. Make a butterfly (p. 76) of white string. Tie it to heddle rod, pass it beneath warp end 2, and knot it to heddle rod (detail). Pick up even warp ends across loom.

Adjusting heddles. Prop up loom. Start at one end of heddle rod and manipulate knots until heddles are of uniform length. Make sure the shed opens wide enough for passage of shuttle.

Warp-end bar. Turn loom over. Remove tape from warp-end bar. Wiggle bar toward the closer end of loom until it is over frame. Keep pushing shed stick back to its original position.

Putting in weft. Make heading of string (p. 79), and begin mat over end of loom so that no warp is wasted. Slant the weft, and beat each pick with a table fork, as shown.

New weft. Change color following first method on page 80. The weft pattern is 3 in. gold, 12 in. cream, and 3 in. gold. When shed becomes too narrow for shuttle, move warp-end bar.

Headings. At the end of the first mat, put in a heading of two picks of 1-in. strips of rags. Rotate mat to back of loom. Start the second mat with another rag heading.

Ending second mat. Whipstitch end with doubled cotton string. Then cut the warp halfway between ends of two mats. Cut rapidly so that tension on warp is released all at once.

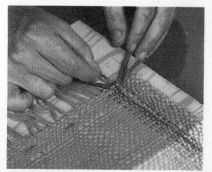

Finish. Let mats rest overnight. Block by dampening (see text, p. 81). When dry and still tacked to board, tie fringe, four warp ends at a time, into overhand knots (p. 81).

Weaving/project

The opulence of rya

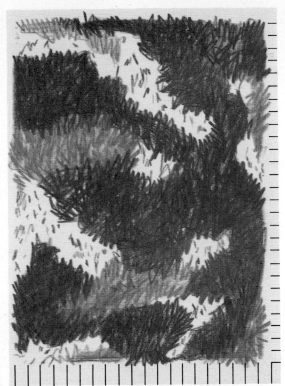

The cartoon. With pencil and ruler, use tick marks along cartoon's edges to draw the lines for a grid of squares on a piece of tracing paper taped over this cartoon. Draw a dark line down the middle to indicate the two halves, which are woven separately on a continuous warp. Each square in your grid represents 4 sq in. on the rug; thus, when transferring the design to the warp (opposite page), measure 2 in. vertically and 2 in. horizontally for each square.

Scandinavian rya (pronounced ree-eh) rugs were originally substitutes for fur bedcovers. With long knotted pile on both sides, they were very warm. Later, without the pile on the back, they became wall hangings and table covers; still later they migrated to the floor. Rya combines bands of plain weave (p. 82) with single rows of Ghiordes knots, the ends of which are left long to form a dense, high pile that hides the weave.

The rug pictured is 40 by 54 inches, made in two sections sewn together lengthwise. You can interpret the de-

sign freely from the cartoon appearing beside the photograph. The large areas of color—brown, tan, and white—are drawn on the warp threads (see opposite), while smaller areas of color are improvised by the weaver. Thus each rug is a unique interpretation.

If your decorating scheme calls for other colors, you can still use this design, substituting for the brown and tan dark and light tones of the same color, for the rust and medium brown two medium colors—one of which can be a contrast—and leaving the white as is.

Equipment. You will need a tapestry loom, used here, or a four-harness loom with at least a 20-inch weaving width; a warping board; a raddle (p. 75); a stick shuttle (see p. 84 for a homemade one); and a tapestry beater.

Materials. For warp buy one tube of 10/6 rug linen, natural color. For the plain weave of the weft you need 2¼ pounds of brown 2-ply wool rug yarn. Double it when weaving. For the knots use wool rug yarns as follows: 3-ply tan, 3/4 pound; 4-ply white, 1¼ pounds; 2-ply rust, 2 pounds; 2-ply

medium brown, 1¼ pounds; 2- and 4-ply dark brown, 1 pound each. Use four strands of 2-ply and two strands of 3- and 4-ply yarn for the knots. In addition, you need heavy-duty thread, cotton cord for headings, and 3 yards of 1⅜-inch cotton twill rug binding tape.

The warp. The warp sett is 6 epi (p. 77), the width 20 inches, the length 162 inches. Tie warp into four groups of 30 ends each on the warping board.

Dressing the loom. Although a tapestry loom is vertical and lacks harnesses and beater, it is dressed the same way as the four-harness loom shown on pages 78–79. Spread and center the warp on the raddle six threads to each space between nails; tie onto the front apron bar six threads at a time. Before removing the lease sticks, insert a shed stick above them. Check the shed by turning the stick to make sure all warp ends are straight and in the correct sheds. Tie the shed stick to back beam.

Some tapestry looms have a heddle bar; if yours does, make the second shed by tying string heddles as on page 85. Otherwise, make the second shed by hand, as shown opposite.

If you are using a four-harness loom, thread it with a straight draw (see *Reading weaver's drafts*, p. 83). Operate harnesses 1 and 3 together for one shed, 2 and 4 for the other. Beat each pick with the loom's beater, then go over it with the tapestry beater.

Headings. Follow the instructions on page 79 for leveling the warp and making headings at the beginning and end of each half of the rug.

Finishing. After cutting the second half from the loom, lay the halves side by side, back up. Match the rows of knots, and tie the halves together every 10 inches with yarn. Then whipstitch a seam with doubled brown weft. Fluff the pile by kicking the rug's back. Clean it by vacuuming with an extension tool. Dry clean if necessary.

Weaving the rya rug

Two ways to tie a Ghiordes knot

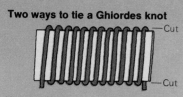

Method A. Use for a few knots of one color or for mixing yarn colors in one knot. **1.** Wrap yarn on 5½-in.-wide piece of cardboard—yarn will relax to 5 in. Cut the yarn as indicated here.

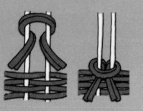

2. Use two or four yarn pieces. Lay them across two warp threads, wrap around them, and bring ends to front between warps (left). Pull yarn down firmly but not too tight (right).

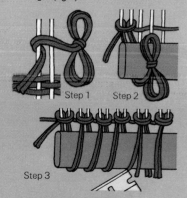

Method B. Use when doing a number of knots of same color. Make a butterfly of doubled yarn (p. 76). Wrap it around left warp, across in front of two warps, and around right warp (Step 1). Bring butterfly to front between two warps; pull knot down. Wrap yarn around a cardboard or wooden gauge the height of pile (Step 2). Repeat knot and wrap gauge between each knot for rest of color area. Cut loops with a razor blade or scissors (Step 3).

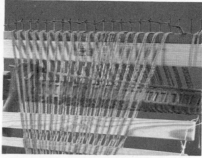

Rolling warp onto warp beam. Insert 1/4-in. dowels, spaced so that they are not atop each other, to separate layers of warp. String is wound around raddle nails to keep warp in place.

Making a pick. One shed is made with a shed stick; the other, by raising warp ends by hand, six at a time, as shown. Bubble weft (p. 80), punching it down with fingers every 2 in.

Transferring the design. After 1 in. of plain weave, mark key points of design on warp with permanent felt-tip pen. Connect dots; steady warp with back of hand while drawing.

Design emerges. Bands of plain weave are 3/4 in. wide, alternating with single rows of knots. After 54 in. of weaving, cut the warp as shown in the next picture.

Cutting between rug halves. Weave 1 in. of heading, leave 12 in. of warp, and weave a second heading. Cut warp halfway between. Remove finished half from cloth beam. Retie warp.

Matching the rug halves. While making second half, have the first beside loom so that you can watch design and blend colors. Rows of knots on back of first half are a helpful guide.

Finishing the edges: Swedish braid

1. Cut heading in 6-in. sections and remove. Tie warp ends in pairs with overhand knot (p. 81). Tighten knots to even rug's edge.

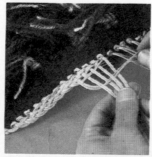

2. Using five pairs of warp ends, weave left pair as shown. Tuck it under rug. Push up on weaving. Repeat, adding next pair of ends.

3. At corner continue weaving with last five pairs, always using left one as weaver. Make a tail 2 in. long; turn under and stitch down.

4. Whipstitch across warp threads, tacking down two pairs at a time. Cut warp 1/2 in. above stitching. Sew twill tape over the warp.

Weaving/project

Tapestry: art in plain weave

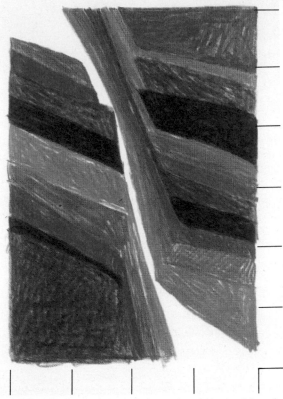

Cartoon. Lay tracing paper over design; make a grid using tick marks along edges as guides; trace outlines. On 20- by 32-in. paper that will not tear when pinned to weaving, draw a grid of 5-in. squares. Following method explained in *Drawing*, p. 212, redraw design. Leave 2-in. space at bottom of paper. Pin behind warp.

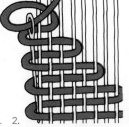

Tapestry techniques. 1. Correct a depression in weaving as explained in chart on page 81; add some extra weft picks to fill the depression. **2.** Begin and end weft at selvedge as shown on page 80, but where color is narrow at selvedge, thread a needle with the weft end and run it parallel to the outside warp. **3.** Sew slits on back of tapestry. Make small stitches paralleling the warp. Cross the slit with one stitch if it is short, several stitches if it is long, and pull the slit together.

Materials. For this 20- by 30-inch tapestry buy 4 ounces of white 8-ply cotton twine of the hardware store variety for warp. For weft buy 2- and 4-ply rug wools in the following quantities: 4 ounces of maroon and 2 ounces each of black, white, gold, orange, bright red, and deep red. In addition, you need 2 yards of 1/2-inch seam tape, 1 yard of 1-inch ribbon, a 1/8-inch-thick strip of metal or wood 20 by 1/2 inches, and a few feet of colorless monofilament—fishing line will do. For headings use scrap yarn of weight similar to the weft.

Equipment. Here the tapestry is woven on an upright tapestry loom, but any other loom with a 20-inch weaving width can be substituted. Warping pegs or board, raddle, stick shuttle, and tapestry needle complete the list.

Preparing to weave. The warp length is 49 inches; the sett, 6 epi; and the width on the loom, 20 inches. Dress the loom as on pages 78 and 79, omitting threading and sleying. Because the picks are short, both sheds are made by hand (p. 80). For the same reason, wind the weft into butterflies (p. 76), although you can use a stick shuttle for wide color areas.

Adding weft. When using 2-ply yarn, double it; use 4-ply yarn single. Bubble the weft (p. 80), and do not allow it to pull in the selvedges or individual color areas. Beat the weft until the warp is visible only as slight ridges in the texture. Weave all or most of a major color area at one time; if it does pull in, it is easily removed and rewoven.

Finish. Block and steam press the tapestry (see text, p. 81). While it is still on the blocking board, finish the edges with knots and seam binding.

Designing a tapestry. Use broad color areas with diagonal and curved outlines; avoid verticals. Strong cotton, linen, or Navajo wool-rug warp make the best warp; wool, the best weft.

Tapestries are made with the simplest weave—plain weave. The art lies in the design, to which famous artists over the centuries have devoted their talents.

Tapestry weaving requires unique techniques and tricks. The weaver fills in color areas one at a time, with no attempt to align picks across the warp. Color areas abut several ways (see opposite), slits being most common. Vertical slits may be left open or stitched if the tapestry is hung vertically. If hung the traditional way, with the warp horizontal, all slits must be stitched.

Joining color areas

Vertical slit. Weft turns around adjacent warp threads. Every 5 to 10 picks weft can interlock (top and bottom). Slit can be sewn later if desired (see opposite page).

Dovetailing. The weft picks from adjoining color areas turn around the same warp thread. This creates a raised ridge and should be done for a short distance only.

Diagonal weave. Weft moves across the warp regularly, one or more threads at a time, depending on angle of line. For a steeper angle combine vertical slits and diagonals.

Curves. Weft moves across warp irregularly, e.g., by 2, 1, 1, 1, 2 warps, forming curve. First two picks of next color are made right up against curve, then lower area is filled.

Weaving the tapestry

Attaching the cartoon. The weaver positions the cartoon behind the warp prior to pinning it with T-pins to the heading. Watercolor sketch serves as guide to colors.

Beating the weft. Beat individual picks with fingers. After 1/2 in. of weaving has built up, use the tapestry beater. It need not be as heavy as the one used for rugs.

Making an interlock. Wrap two yarns around each other where they meet. Vertical slits should interlock every inch or so. Where the color moves to right or left, they interlock naturally.

Moving color diagonally. Step the color across the warp one or more threads at a time, depending on the angle. Work a number of picks in one color area before going to another.

Filling in a curve. The curve has been outlined with two picks (see drawing, top right). Weaver then does regular picks back and forth to fill area. T-pins hold cartoon to tapestry.

Advancing the weaving. As weaving area moves up, roll tapestry onto cloth beam to keep it at a comfortable working level. One at a time weave color areas up to about same level.

Finish. Remove headings. Tie the warp in half-knots (inset), joining warps 1 and 2, then 2 and 3, and so on, across each edge. Trim warp as shown. Sew or iron 1/2-in. seam tape over it.

Hanging. At top of tapestry sew 1-in. ribbon on three sides. Insert metal or wood strip, and hem fourth side of ribbon. Run monofilament behind bar in two places and knot. Hang tapestry.

Weaving/project

A wall hanging with leno and inlay

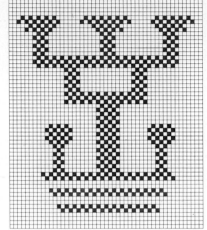

27 warps →

Weft pattern. Beginning at bottom of hanging, weave each pick with color indicated. All picks are plain weave unless otherwise stated: 8 beige; 2 black; 2 beige; 1 beige leno; 7 beige; 2 black; 3 beige; 1 beige leno; 8 beige. Tree design: 49 beige for background; for inlay count 27 warps from right selvedge and follow tree design above, with beige background picks extending across warp's width. Following the tree design: 9 beige; 1 beige leno; 6 beige; 2 black; 5 beige; 1 black; 1 beige; 1 black; 1 beige; 1 beige leno; 1 beige; 1 black; 1 beige; 1 black; 9 beige; 1 beige leno; 10 beige; dowel; 6 beige.

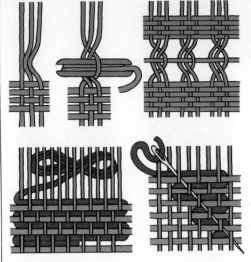

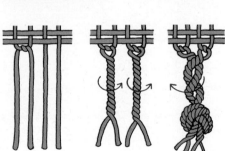

Leno weave. Change shed after left-to-right pick of plain weave. With fingers pick up two warps at right selvedge. Pull them across next warp, and pick it up. Place stick shuttle beneath the single warp and over the two. Make several more twists, and pull shuttle through. Repeat across to left selvedge, then beat very firmly. Insert next few picks of plain weave with care to restore correct width. Adjust openings in leno (see opposite).

Inlay. Make a pick of background weft and beat it, but do not change shed. Count the required number of warp ends in from each selvedge (see diagram). Double back end of black thread as when starting weft (p. 80); lay in black thread according to the diagram. Change to other shed, do a pick of background weft, and beat it. Pick up butterfly and weave across the indicated warps. Later, weave loose ends under beige warp on reverse side.

Plied fringe. Tie every two warp ends in a half-hitch, as in illustration at extreme left. Align all knots with the line on the blocking board (p. 81). Twist each pair of warp ends to the right between thumb and fingers. Then cross right ply over left, wrapping the two plies around one another. Keep the two plies twisted. Finally, when the fringe is 2½ in. long, secure it with an overhand knot, allowing the loose ends to dangle.

Leno and inlay are decorative, hand-controlled weaves that are always done in combination with plain weave. This 8½- by 17-inch wall hanging, woven on a rigid heddle loom, illustrates both.

Leno involves the twisting of warp threads by hand to produce an open-work design. It can either extend from selvedge to selvedge or occur in the body of the fabric. It adds texture to table mats, curtains, handbag fabrics, and apparel trimmings. The twisting of warp threads may be one over one, two over two, or even three over three. Here the warp threads are twisted two over one, except the last two threads in

a leno pick, which are one over one.

Leno tends to pull in the selvedges, so be sure to slant the weft and not to pull it too tight. With the next pick of plain weave the warp ends revert to their former position.

Inlay is a weft yarn of contrasting texture or color laid in by hand along with picks of background weft. The tree design is done in this technique.

The contrasting weft is made into a butterfly (p. 76). It dangles below the weaving between rows if inlaid sections are close. Where sections of the design are separated by 1/2 inch or more, as in the tree branches, use separate butter-

flies of the weft yarn for each section.

Materials. An example of the artistry that can be accomplished with simple, inexpensive materials, the wall hanging is made of beige 8-ply cotton twine for warp and weft. Buy 4½ ounces of it. For the inlay and the black picks you need a small amount of black cotton twine—embroidery floss will do. Use white cotton twine for headings and heavy-duty beige sewing thread for finishing the top. Buy 1 foot of 1/4-inch dowel to hang the weaving.

Equipment. A rigid heddle loom is used here, but the hanging could be woven on the homemade frame loom

(p. 84), taking extra care to tension the warp well and evenly. You also need warping pegs, a stick shuttle, and a tapestry needle.

Fabric structure. Prepare a warp (p. 77) 40 inches long with 80 warp ends. The warp sett is 8 epi, its width, 10 inches. There should be 8 picks of weft per inch of the balanced plain weave.

Finish. Block the weaving as described in the text on page 81. After finishing the top and bottom (see opposite), remove tape from the dowel and glue the outside warp threads to the dowel. Cut the dowel to 3/8 inch wider than the cloth on each side.

Making the wall hanging

Dressing the loom. See pages 78–79 for general procedure. Lease sticks are being tied to heddle on front, or weaving, side. Strings around heddle frame are for centering the warp.

Warp ends are threaded through heddle from front to back and tied to back apron bar. Weaver is rolling warp onto warp beam. Place newspaper between layers of warp on warp beam.

Weaving on the rigid heddle loom. The first pick of background weft is beaten in with the heddle. Place hands on heddle either side of weaving to keep heddle parallel with the weft.

For one shed (above) the heddle is positioned in notches atop the loom's frame. Second shed is made by placing top of heddle frame in notches at bottom of loom rests (arrow).

Leno weave. Shuttle is pulled through the last warp threads at end of row of leno. Note that weft is slanted; this helps diminish the pulling in at selvedges from twisted warps.

After the row of leno, weave several picks of plain weave. Then stop and take the time to adjust the weft in the leno with fingertips so that all of the openings will be equal in size.

Inlay. Weaver is making the second pick of inlay. Note background weft between first and second picks of inlay. The loose end of black thread will be woven in later on back side.

The dowel. Insert dowel in place of one pick of weft (see weft pattern, opposite), changing sheds before and after. Put tape temporarily around ends of dowel to hold it in place.

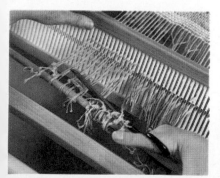

Removing weaving from loom. Cut warp from back apron bar as close to knots as possible. Unroll weaving from cloth beam, and untie the knots that hold it to front apron bar.

Cables. Cut out heading at bottom of hanging. Make cables of warp ends (see opposite) while weaving is still tacked to blocking board. Cut ends below knots so that they are uniform length.

Weaving in ends of black yarn. On reverse side run needle underneath beige twine where black shows on front. Thread black yarn in needle's eye and pull needle through.

Finishing the top. With beige thread, overcast the last two rows of weft (p. 81). Remove heading; cut warp 1/4 in. from overcasting. Fold back the fabric, and hem as shown.

Weaving/project

A ruana woven on a four-harness loom

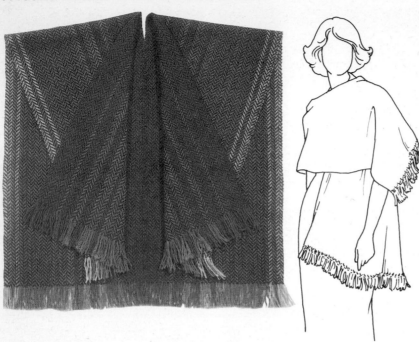

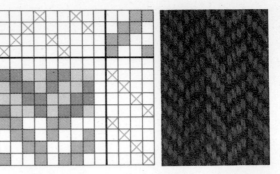

Offset twill weave. See page 83 for an explanation of how to read the pattern draft (far left). The close-up of the weave (left) shows the correct angle for the twill—about a 45° angle. Control this angle by the firmness with which you beat the weaving.

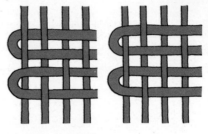

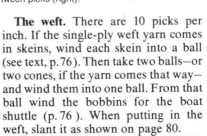

Correcting a selvedge problem. In an unbalanced twill weave such as this one, frequently the warp at the selvedge is not caught by the weft (left). Check both edges of the weaving for this fault. Correct the problem by passing the shuttle around the selvedge after changing sheds between picks (right).

Seaming the ruana. Lay halves side by side lengthwise with bronze-gold warps abutting. Thread tapestry needle with same yarn, take one stitch at fringe, and tie overhand knot (p. 81). Run yarn between halves, picking up weft from each side as shown. The yarn straightens and looks like another warp. Knot yarn at top.

Traditionally the ruana is worn with the ends crossed in front. A more stylish way might be to flip one side across the opposite shoulder, as in the drawing at right. The wearer should try on the ruana when the back seam has been sewn to not quite half the length of the strips. Make sure that the front and back hang to the same length; then finish the seam with a knot.

The shawl-like ruana, of South American origin, is an ideal outer garment for cool fall and spring days and adds a welcome layer of warmth indoors in winter. Unlike a shawl, it stays in place on the shoulders, leaving hands free. It is simple to make: two identical pieces of woven wool cloth are seamed lengthwise up the back. The pieces are made on one continuous warp; each is 16 inches wide and 60 inches long with the warp in between and on the ends used for a simple decorative fringe.

Equipment. The offset twill weave requires a four-harness loom; it must have an 18-inch weaving width. In addition, you need a warping board, a raddle, a boat shuttle with bobbins, and a tapestry needle.

Materials. The weft is dark olive-green single-ply homespun wool, doubled to give the look of two lines. Buy 14 ounces of it. The four-color warp requires 2 ounces of pale gold, 8 ounces of bright gold, and 6 ounces of bronze-gold, all 4-ply rug yarn, and 3 ounces of light olive-green single-ply homespun. Use the last doubled. Scrap yarn the size of the weft will do for heading.

The warp is 164 inches long, 18 inches wide, with a sett of 8 epi. There are 144 warp ends, arranged as follows: 8 pale gold, 4 bright gold, 4 pale gold, 48 bright gold, 8 light olive-green, 4 bronze-gold, 4 bright gold, 8 light olive-green, 8 bronze-gold, 4 light olive-green, 4 bright gold, 12 bronze-gold, 4 bright gold, 24 bronze-gold.

The weft. There are 10 picks per inch. If the single-ply weft yarn comes in skeins, wind each skein into a ball (see text, p. 76). Then take two balls—or two cones, if the yarn comes that way—and wind them into one ball. From that ball wind the bobbins for the boat shuttle (p. 76). When putting in the weft, slant it as shown on page 80.

Weaving hints. Shown opposite are some steps in preparing the warp and dressing the loom; for detailed directions see pages 77–79. In rolling fabric onto the cloth beam, first release tension on warp beam, then roll cloth beam until slack is taken up. Do not roll so far that the edge of weaving is out of reach of the beater. Check the warp tension with the palm of your hand each time you roll onto the cloth beam. Whenever you leave the loom for a time, stop at the end of a repeat, so that when you resume, you will know where to start.

Finish. Whipstitch the last two rows of weft (p. 81), and leave the warp as a plain fringe. After removing the heading (see opposite), wash the ruana in tepid water with mild soap and fabric softener. Steam press it when dry.

Because of the long float of the weft, the offset twill weave makes a warm blanket. The same two pieces, woven with soft yarns in light colors, could make a baby blanket. Woven with thicker, fuzzier yarns, a blanket or throw could be made by sewing four or five sections together.

Weaving a ruana

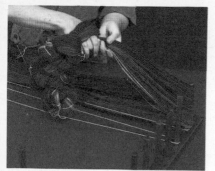

1. Weaver chains the warp off warping board (p. 77). Since the warp is long, it has been tied every yard to keep it organized. Note different color warps neatly stacked at the peg.

2. The lease sticks, inserted into the cross and tied at the ends (p. 78), are suspended from the back of the castle. Next the weaver will cut the strings holding the cross.

3. Having centered the warp on the back apron bar and rolled the apron bar to the warp beam, the weaver distributes warp in the raddle, eight ends between each pair of nails.

4. With a helper to hold the warp in front of the loom, the weaver rolls warp onto warp beam. Newspaper is placed between layers. Roll until end loop of warp meets breast beam (p. 79).

5. Threading heddles. One at a time untie slipknots made as warp's loop was cut. Thread heddles following pattern draft (opposite). Tie every eight warps in a slipknot.

6. One at a time untie slipknots and sley warp in the reed (p. 79). After each group of eight warp ends, check that threading of heddles is correct. If it is not, redo the threading.

7. Weaver changes shed while making heading. After one repeat, check pattern and correct threading if necessary (p. 81). Also check whether outside warp is caught (see opposite).

8. Before beginning to weave with green weft, move apron bar to breast beam. Weaver is about to throw shuttle with left hand; the right hand waits to catch it.

9. As the weaving progresses, the weaver measures occasionally and ties pieces of white yarn onto the selvedge at 12-in. intervals. To calculate footage, count these pieces of yarn.

10. At end of first half of ruana, weave 1½ in. of heading, leave 5 in. of warp, and weave 1½ in. of heading for second half. Always end headings with last shed of weft pattern.

11. At end of second half, release tension on warp and cut the warp. Unroll cloth from cloth beam; untie warp from front apron bar. Cut warp midway between the two sections.

12. After seaming back of ruana (opposite), whipstitch (p. 81) across both ends with doubled weft yarn, catching two rows of weft. Cut headings every 5 in. and remove them.

Batik and tie-dyeing

Resist dyeing

Batik and tie-dyeing both developed in the Orient about the sixth century A.D. as methods of decorating fabric. Although the origins of batik are attributed to several countries, it is justifiably associated with Java: the Javanese have elevated batik from an ancient craft to a contemporary art form that enjoys universal appeal. No less an art in its own right, tie-dyeing is generally associated with the cultures of India, China, and Japan.

Common to both of these crafts is a technique known as resist dyeing. In batik, wax is applied to those areas of the fabric that are not to be dyed. When the fabric is immersed in the dye-bath, the waxed areas resist the dye, permitting only the unwaxed areas to absorb the color. The wax is often applied with a traditional Javanese tool called a *tjanting* (pronounced janting). When the tjanting is trailed or drawn over the fabric, a thin line of wax is leaked onto the cloth. In Javanese, *batik* means, roughly, "writing with wax," and the tjanting provides a means of delicate control not unlike a pen. The tjanting has its limitations, though, and a brush is used to apply wax to larger areas of the design.

In tie-dyeing, the fabric can be knotted, tied with twine, or sewn, according to the planned design. When the fabric is dyed, these tied areas resist the dye, while the rest of the fabric absorbs it. *Tritik* ("sewing" in Javanese) is the most intricate of these methods, and with practice, astonishingly minute circles can be sewn. In India separate grains of rice and nail points are used to form the circles in the fabric. Thread is then sewn around these tiny points to create tied-off circles. After dyeing, the thread is removed. Some Indian examples contain as many as 30 sewn circles to each square inch of fabric.

Fabrics, waxes, and dyes

Fabrics are classified according to their constituent fibers as either natural or synthetic. In turn, natural fibers are further defined as either cellulose (plant fibers) or protein (animal fibers).

Cellulose fibers include cotton, linen, and viscose rayon. Protein fibers include silk and wool. All of these natural fibers are good for batik work. The differences among them relate primarily to the dyeing process. Certain dyes will produce more vivid colors with cellulose fibers than with protein fibers, and vice versa.

Synthetic fibers are not recommended. They generally do not bind well with dyes. Very thin silk and thick wool also present special problems. The wax used to resist the dyes tends to run through thin silk without adhering to the material. With thick wool the problem is the reverse: it is difficult for the wax to penetrate the fiber. Corduroy, velvet, and other pile fabrics are also hard to work with.

Beginners should practice dyeing techniques first on soft cotton, such as old, frequently washed bed sheeting. It is smooth, closely woven, absorbs wax easily, and can be evenly dyed with commonly available chemical dyes.

Removing sizing. New fabric often contains a stiffening agent called sizing. Before such fabric can be used in batik, the sizing must be removed by washing the material in hot, soapy water. The fabric is then rinsed and dried (ironing is optional). Several such washings may be needed to remove all sizing.

Frames. After the fabric is dry, it is stretched tautly over a frame. Canvas stretchers of various sizes are available at art supply houses, but you can also use an old picture frame or build your own framework. The fabric is attached to the frame with tacks in the order indicated in the accompanying dia-

The rich and subtle colors that distinguish fine batik are evident in this detail from a Javanese wall hanging. Java has long been the center of this art.

gram. If more tacks are used than appear in the diagram, continue placing them in the same alternating pattern in order to maintain even tension.

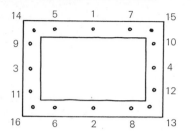

Fabric is tacked to frame in this order.

Drawing the design. After the stretching is completed, a design is drawn on the fabric with a charcoal pencil or stick. If the fabric is light enough to see through, draw a design on paper with very heavy outlines; then place it beneath the frame and trace the design on the fabric. With heavier fabric draw the design on cardboard, cut it out, place it on top of the fabric, and trace its outline.

Waxing. After the design has been transferred to the fabric, the piece is ready for waxing. The wax is applied before the first dyeing to those areas of the design that you want to remain undyed by that color (see p. 96).

When the first dye has taken, the first wax is removed by boiling the fabric or by pressing it with a hot iron. A second waxing is then applied to other areas of the design before the second dyeing, and the whole process is repeated until the final dyeing is completed.

This is a traditional batik method that gives very sharply delineated color contrasts. However, the removal of the wax after every dyeing is a tedious process. The method described on the following pages is less time-consuming and easier. The waxes applied between dyeings are removed all at the same time when the piece is finished. Al-

though also traditional, this method produces more muted colors.

The so-called crackle effect traditional to batik is obtained by applying wax to the fabric, letting it harden, then manipulating it to produce random cracks. The cracks can also be created by using a metal stylus to remove the wax exactly where you wish. The fabric will absorb dye that seeps through the cracks in the wax. If you plan to dye a fabric several times using different colors, you will have to apply wax to all the delicate lines to preserve the crackle effect of the first dyeing.

Wax formulas. Batik wax consists of a mixture of paraffin and beeswax. Batik artists all have their own favorite proportions. In general, however, the higher the percentage of beeswax, the softer the wax. This means less crackle effect (which you may desire). Conversely, the higher the percentage of paraffin, the harder the wax, which means a greater crackle effect.

Some beeswax is always necessary. Pure paraffin will crumble rather than crack. Adding 5 tablespoons of bees-

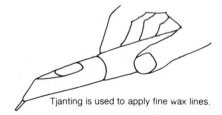

Tjanting is used to apply fine wax lines.

wax per pound of paraffin is a good working formula, but if you want more crackle, use no more than 2 to 3 tablespoons of the beeswax.

Wax temperature. The temperature of the melted wax should be about 77°C, but a few degrees either way is not critical. However, if the wax is too cool, it may not completely soak through the fabric. If it is too hot, it may run through the fabric without adhering to it.

Application of wax. Wax can be applied with a tjanting, *tjaps* (stamps), or brushes, or with a combination of all three of these tools.

The tjanting, the traditional Javanese tool, consists of a small, hollow metal container with a spout attached to a wooden handle. It is filled by dipping it into the hot liquid wax. With the tjanting it is possible to apply extremely thin lines of wax, but brushes must be used to wax larger areas. The brushes most commonly used are Japanese calligraphy brushes or sable brushes. Both are equally effective. While the sable brushes last longer, they are also more expensive. After you have finished using a brush, gently squeeze the bristles together and let them dry naturally. The wax in the bristles will remelt the next time the brush is used.

Wax cools more quickly on a brush than in a tjanting. The wax should therefore be a little hotter when working with brushes.

Tjaps (pronounced chops) are traditional Indonesian stamping tools. These stamps, which are actually printing blocks, are made of metal and have wooden handles. Tjaps of different designs are available at crafts shops. The stamp face of the tjap is immersed in hot melted wax, then stamped on the fabric. Traditionally, one pattern is repeated over the entire fabric, but equally pleasing designs can be obtained by using several tjaps.

Interesting stamps can be made from such common household articles as nails, nuts, bolts, screws, coins, thimbles, and cookie cutters.

Dyeing. The colors you achieve are affected by the type and the amount of dye you use, the type of fabric and its thickness, and the amount of time the fabric remains in the dye. Chemical dyes are discussed below. For a discussion of natural dyes, see *Spinning and*

dyeing, p. 73, and text accompanying the projects later in this chapter.

There are several types of commonly available chemical dyes. Of these, the fiber-reactive types are ideal for batik work. They are cold-water dyes, which will not melt the wax when the fabric is immersed. For this reason cold-water dyes are often called batik dyes.

Cold-water dyes produce vivid colors that will not run. However, they cannot be used on synthetic fibers. Always follow the instructions that come with the chemical dyes you use. The instructions will tell you the amount of dye to use per yard or per pound of fabric. Generally, a little more dye than called for will result in a darker color; a little less, in a lighter color. But there are limits to this simple approach. If you use too much dye, the resulting color will be darker, but it may also be streaked.

Overdyeing—dyeing a fabric several colors—also presents problems. You should always work from lighter to darker colors, choosing only those that will combine well. For example, you could start with yellow; then, if the second dye bath were blue, the overdyed areas would become green. A final dyebath of red would produce overdyed fabric areas of the colors orange, purple, and brown (see *Color and design,* pp. 220–221).

Since dyeing is an art rather than a science, you will need to experiment with different fabrics and dyes before you can consistently produce the colors you want. Natural dyes require the addition of special mordants, as described on pages 73 and 97.

Dye temperatures. When using dyes that must be dissolved in hot water, let the dyebath temperature cool to 43°C or less before dyeing your waxed fabrics; temperatures higher than this level may very well melt the wax from the fabric during the dyeing.

Batik and tie-dyeing

Waxing, dyeing, and ironing batik

The drawings on this page illustrate the techniques and stages in waxing and overdyeing a typical batik piece. The finished work is shown in the color-keyed design (below left).

First, the fabric is washed and rinsed to remove the sizing. After the fabric has dried, it is tacked to a frame as illustrated on page 95. The design is drawn on a piece of paper and transferred to the fabric as described in the text on page 95.

Lighter colors are dyed before darker colors. The flowerpot, which is to remain the color of the undyed fabric, is waxed first. Traditional batik fabrics are unbleached and come in various shades of off-white. This off-white will be the color of the flowerpot in the finished piece. When cotton is used with natural dyes, a special mordanting process must be followed, as described on the opposite page.

The last step (not shown) is to iron out the wax. The fabric is allowed to dry, then it is placed between layers of paper towels or old newspaper sheets for ironing. Colored newspaper, such as comic strips, and recent newspaper are never used, as the ink would be ironed onto the fabric.

A dry iron—not a steam iron—is set at the next lower setting to the one normally used for the particular fabric. (For muslin, use a wool setting.) As the fabric is ironed, the wax melts and is absorbed by the layers of paper. The paper sheets should be changed frequently to keep them absorbent. You will not be able to remove all the wax, but a little residual wax is often desirable, especially for such projects as curtains and wall hangings. Dry cleaning will remove the wax remaining in scarves, blouses, or other garments.

After you finish ironing, there may be some dark rings, or halos, on the fabric. They are caused by the ironed wax spreading into the areas that were left unwaxed. If you do not want the halo effect, you can cover the entire piece with wax before ironing so that the ironing will produce a uniform, if darker, background color. Or you can have the piece dry-cleaned to remove the halo.

This simplified batik design results from the waxing and dyeing procedures illustrated at right. The same basic steps should be followed in all of the batik projects.

1. Melt wax and brush onto flowerpot area (labeled 1 at left).

2. Remove fabric from frame and immerse in gray dyebath.

3. Dry fabric and put back on frame. Apply wax to background (2).

4. Remove fabric from frame and immerse in light blue dyebath.

5. Dry fabric and put back on frame. Apply wax to alternate petals (3).

6. Immerse fabric in dark blue dye. Dry. Iron out all wax.

Batik and tie-dyeing/project

Batik with onion-skin and cochineal dyes

Unbleached muslin is the fabric used in this batik project. The dyes are natural—onion skins for the yellow and cochineal, a red dyestuff made from cochineal insects, for the maroon.

Mordanting. Cottons, including muslins, require a special mordanting process before they can be used with natural dyes. (You can substitute household chemical dyes, for which no mordanting is needed. Simply follow the instructions on the container.) Two mordanting processes can be used, a long one or a short one. The long process is time-consuming, but the dye colors will be weaker if the short process is used. For the long mordanting process follow the complete instructions below. For the short process follow Steps 1–3 only.

1. Wash and rinse the muslin several times to remove the sizing.

2. For every pound of cotton make a solution of 4 ounces alum, 1 ounce washing soda, and enough water to permit the fabric to circulate freely.

3. Simmer the fabric in this solution for 1 hour, then let it cool in the solution for 12 to 24 hours. Remove the fabric and rinse it.

4. Make a new solution of 1 ounce tannic acid per pound of fabric and the same amount of water used in Step 2.

5. Repeat Step 3 with this solution.

6. Repeat Steps 2 and 3 with the alum and washing soda solution. Rinse the fabric thoroughly and allow it to dry before batiking.

Dyes. To make the dyes, use a double handful of onion skins per quart of water and enough water to permit free circulation of the fabric. Cochineal is a highly concentrated dye; use 1 teaspoon per quart of water. (For specific instructions on preparing the dyes, see *Spinning and dyeing*, p. 73.) Before each dyeing, rinse the dry fabric.

This design can be enlarged to any size you want (see *Drawing*, p. 212).

Design can be enlarged to any size as described in Drawing, p. 212.

1. After muslin is mordanted, prepare yellow dye as described in text. Immerse fabric in dyebath and let it simmer for 1 hr.

2. Rinse fabric; let dry. Mount on frame. Draw design with charcoal stick. For circles, tie string about stick to act as a compass.

3. Using sable or calligraphy brushes, apply hot liquid wax to the circles, the diamonds, and the four outer triangles.

4. Prepare 2 qt of maroon dye as described in text. Stir and let stand before immersing fabric. Let fabric soak about 12 hr.

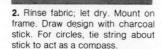

5. Rinse fabric; let dry. Mount on frame. Rewax areas waxed in Step 3 to seal cracks, which will remain a lighter maroon.

6. Fill tjanting by dipping it into hot wax. Using paper towel to cut off unwanted drippings, carefully wax fine lines.

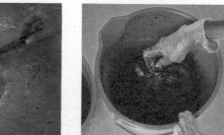

7. Immerse the fabric in the same maroon dyebath as used in Step 4. Let it soak about 12 hr. Remove fabric. Rinse it well.

8. After the fabric has dried, place it between sheets of paper towels or old newspaper sheets. Iron out wax (see text, p. 96).

97

Batik and tie-dyeing/project

Batik with logwood, turmeric, and cochineal dyes

While the flower design of this wall hanging appears intricate, it is not really difficult. You may, if you like, regard the design as a general outline to alter freely in form and color.

Don't worry if you accidentally drip wax onto the fabric from your brush or tjanting. This kind of random accident can imbue your work with an appealing air of spontaneity.

Here again, the dyes used are natural dyes, but you can substitute household dyes, but you can substitute household chemical dyes. The natural dyes, in the order in which they are used, are derived from turmeric (shades of yellow), an East Indian herb; cochineal (shades of red), an insect; and logwood (shades of blue). The cochineal dye-bath is prepared as for the previous project. Instructions for preparing the turmeric and logwood are given below.

Place 8 ounces of each dyestuff into separate cheesecloth bags. Turmeric expands; use a large bag.

The large photo is of the finished wall hanging. The three panels at right show how the project appears when held against the light at key stages. Holding the panel against the light permits you to check the thoroughness of the waxing and the effectiveness of the dyeing. Specifically, Panel 1 shows the project after the first waxing. Panel 2 shows the results of the second waxing and dyeing. The areas waxed in the third waxing appear pinkish in Panel 3.

Design can be enlarged to any size as described in Drawing, p. 212.

Soak each bag in 2 gallons of warm water for 12 hours.

After soaking, boil the turmeric bath for about 2 hours and the logwood bath for about 1 hour. When the baths have cooled, the dye bags are removed. The remaining dyebaths are each sufficient for about a pound of cotton.

Unbleached muslin fabric is suggested for this project. If you use the natural dyes, mordant the muslin following the instructions given on page 97. (Household chemical dyes do not require that the fabric be mordanted.) When dyeing the fabric, immerse it in the appropriate dyebath for about 12 hours. Just before using the logwood dyebath (the third dyeing), dissolve 1/4 teaspoon of copper sulfate in it. This additive produces a darker blue.

The design on page 98 can be enlarged to any size needed by following the procedures illustrated and described in *Drawing*, p. 212.

1. Mount the mordanted muslin fabric on the frame. Sketch in the design with a charcoal stick.

2. Use the tjanting to wax in the stem and petal outlines. The paper towel stops the flow of the wax.

3. Remove the fabric from the frame. Thoroughly soak it in a pail of cool water to prepare it for dyeing.

4. Immerse fabric in yellow dyebath (turmeric). Let it soak 12 hr. Remove and rinse fabric.

5. Mount dry fabric on the frame. Use a brush to wax in petals that are to remain yellow.

6. Soak fabric in water. Immerse it in red bath (cochineal) for 12 hr. Remove and rinse fabric.

7. Mount dry fabric. Apply third waxing to areas that remain orange. Remove fabric. Soak in cool water.

8. Immerse in blue dyebath (logwood and copper sulfate) for 12 hr. Remove and rinse fabric. Let dry.

9. To iron, place dry fabric between paper towels, old newspaper sheets, or a combination of both, as here.

10. Wax melted by the iron will soak through and adhere to both layers of paper. Change them frequently.

Batik and tie-dyeing

Tie-dyeing techniques

Tie-dyeing is a simple process. Areas of the fabric are tied off in accordance with your design. ("Tying" is a general term that includes knotting and sewing.) The fabric is then dyed and rinsed, and the ties are removed. The tied areas resist the dye and remain the color of the original fabric. The fabric can then be retied and redyed as described in subsequent paragraphs.

Which areas you tie off and the kind of ties you use depend on the design you have in mind, but a tie-dye design need not be as carefully planned as a batik design. Tying off areas at random often produces results as interesting as tying the fabric according to a specific prepared plan.

In fact, the unpredictability of tie-dyeing is perhaps its most exciting aspect. Although two different pieces of fabric may ostensibly be tied the same way, they will never look quite the same after they have been dyed. One reason is that there are bound to be slightly different folds in the two fabrics. It is also virtually impossible to tie off areas with exactly the same degree of tension.

Nevertheless, there are certain standard methods of tying that will produce approximately the same results every time you use them. Some of these methods are shown at right. However, there is no end to the number of possible ways a piece of fabric can be tied or the ways in which different kinds of ties can be combined. With the exception of tritik (see p. 102), improvisation is an integral part of tie-dyeing.

Fine fabrics are most commonly used in tie-dyeing. These include unbleached silk, linen, and various types of cotton. As with batik, the fabric should first be washed to remove the sizing. When using cotton with natural dyes, follow the mordanting process described on page 97; with silk chiffon, use the process given on page 102.

You need not limit yourself to cold-water batik dyes for tie-dyeing. There is no wax to melt, and the use of hot dyes greatly reduces the dyeing time. When using chemical dyes, follow the instructions on the package. In the case of natural dyes, immerse the fabric in a simmering dyebath. Although the total time of immersion will vary according to the dye, the process often requires no more than a half hour to an hour.

Like batik fabrics, tie-dyed articles are commonly overdyed (see text, p. 95). After the first dyeing the fabric is rinsed thoroughly. The first set of ties is then removed or left on, depending on your design, and new ties are applied. Then the fabric is dyed for the second time. The whole process, including rinsing, is repeated for each dyeing.

The photos and drawings at right illustrate some of the many ways that fabrics can be folded, knotted, tied, and sewn to produce a variety of geometric designs. The top illustration in each panel shows how the fabric is folded, and the middle one shows how it is tied, knotted, or sewn. The photos at bottom show the finished result, after the ties have been removed.

Note that each finished project contains shades of color, rather than uniform color. This is because the fabric has not resisted the dye uniformly.

Note also that the number of folds in the fabric determines the number of forms produced by a single tie. In panel 2, for example, each of the three ties produces many more shapes because the fabric is folded twice before the ties are made. Panel 1 shows how ties can be made by knotting the fabric itself. Panel 4 shows a typical design created by sewing. The drawings to the right of panel 4 show how the ties are sewn.

Ties can be made using any thickness of twine, string, or thread. Generally, finer string or thread is used for smaller, more intricate shapes.

Panel 1

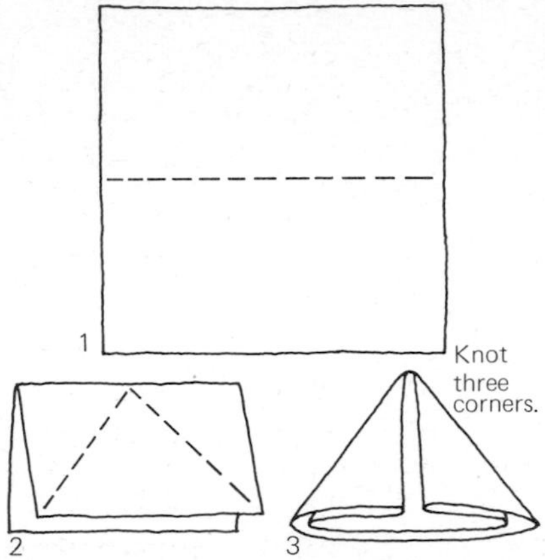

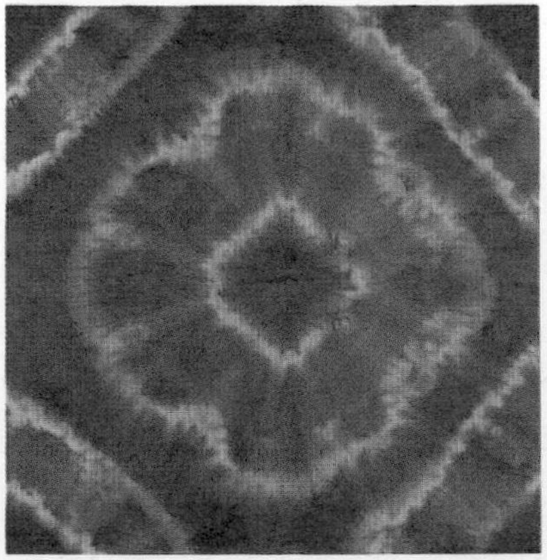

Knot three corners.

Panel 2

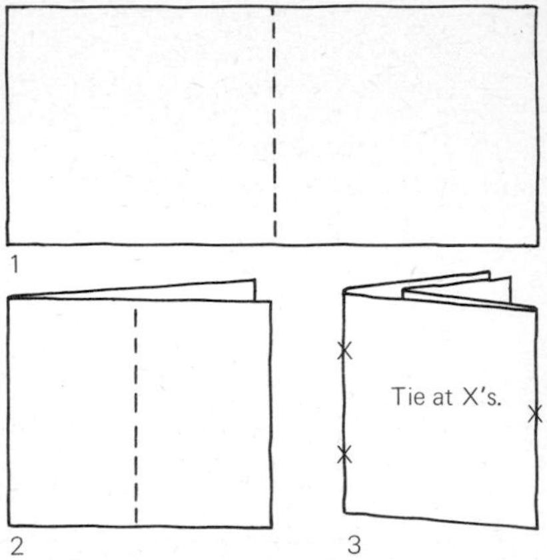

Tie at X's.

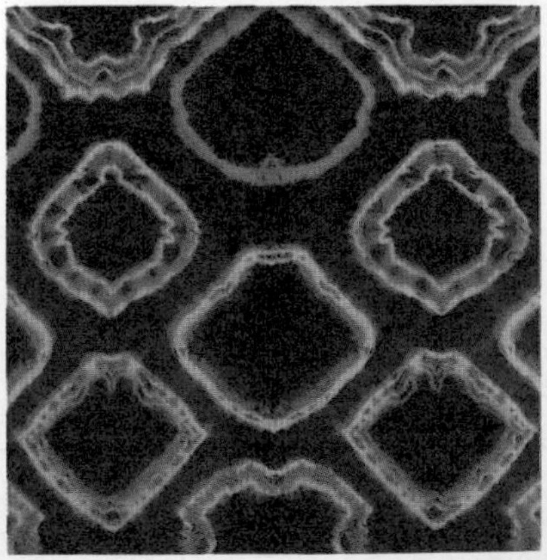

Panel 3

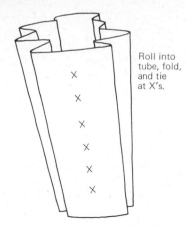

Roll into tube, fold, and tie at X's.

Panel 4

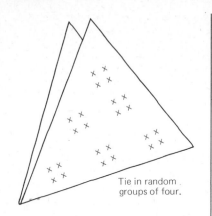

Tie in random groups of four.

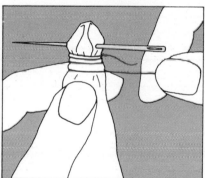

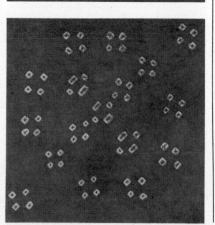

How to make ties

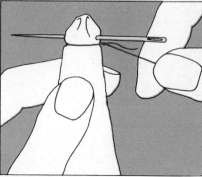

Needle used to hold fabric point.

1. Pinch fabric into a 1/8-in.-thick bunch. Hold between thumb and index finger about 1/4 in. from top. Insert needle through top.

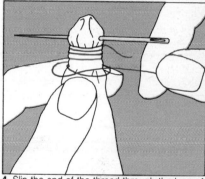

2. Cut a piece of thread 4–5 in. long. Using one of the thread ends, make a slipknot around the fabric Pull the knot tight.

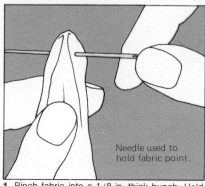

3. Hold fabric as in Step 2. Wrap long end of thread tightly about bunch. Length of wrapping determines diameter of form.

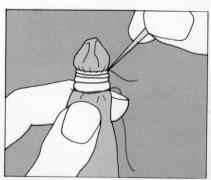

4. Slip the end of the thread through the loop of the last winding. Pull thread tightly through loop to firmly secure this last winding.

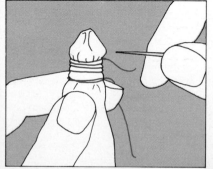

5. Remove the needle and trim excess thread with scissors. All ties are made before the fabric is soaked in the dye bath.

6. After the fabric has been dyed and rinsed, pick apart the last slipknot with a needle point. Remove thread. Let fabric dry, then iron.

101

Batik and tie-dyeing/projects

Tritik butterfly

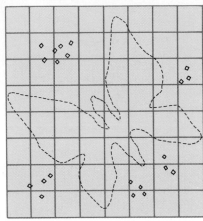

Design can be enlarged as described on p. 212.

This butterfly design illustrates the technique of tritik, a stitching method commonly used in tying fabric. In tritik a pattern outline is first drawn on the fabric with a charcoal stick. The fabric is then stitched along the outline with a needle and thread, using a simple running stitch. When the stitching is complete, the fabric is gathered along the stitch line by pulling both ends of the thread as shown in Step 4 in the illustrations at right.

In tritik the sewing is done with a single strand of thread that is doubled back and held during the stitching so that it does not slip from the needle's eye. The long end is knotted so that it will not pass through the stitch holes. The short end is knotted when the stitching is finished and the needle has been removed.

Tritik is generally most effective with simple and fairly large outlines. It can also be used in combination with other methods of tying, as in this project. The tritik butterfly forms the main design, while the outer areas of the fabric are decorated with groups of small squares created by using the sewing method shown on page 101.

The fabric used in this project is silk chiffon, perfect for a light scarf. When used with natural dyes, silk requires a special mordanting process. Put enough water into a container to allow the fabric to circulate freely—at least 6 quarts (1½ gallons) for each yard of silk fabric. Dissolve 3 tablespoons of alum and 1 tablespoon of cream of tartar for each 1½ gallons of water, and simmer the silk in this mixture for 1 hour.

After mordanting, the dyeing time required is only 5 minutes. Some of the dye bath may evaporate when it is simmered; add water after Step 9 to bring the bath back to its original level. The dyes used here are natural ones, but you can substitute chemical dyes, which require no mordanting.

Do not expect your finished piece to look exactly like the one depicted above, even though you have carefully followed all the instructions for the project. Variations are bound to occur in the sewing, tying, and folding, and in the strength and quality of natural dyestuffs. So your object will be not to make an exact copy of the design shown on this page but to create a piece of like freedom and attractiveness. The spontaneity of the form is one of its most appealing charms.

1. Fold fabric in half. With charcoal stick, draw outline of butterfly on one side of folded fabric. Then pin the fabric together on both sides of the outline. Turn the fabric over. Trace the same outline on the other side of the fabric.

2. Thread a needle with medium-weight thread and knot it. Start stitching at one end of design. Stitch the outline, using very small stitches. Pull each stitch tight. When finished, knot the thread. Remove the pins.

3. With a needle and thread, tie off the outer groups of small squares. (For their placement, see the pattern at left.) Use the method of sewing ties that is shown on page 101.

4. Pull on the two thread ends used to stitch the butterfly outline. Gather them, like drawstrings, to form pleats. Make certain that the butterfly body is on just one side of the pleat line.

5. Tie the thread ends together. Then use a slipknot to tie a length of light cord around the thread line. Pull the knot tight. Then wrap the cord around the line several times. In Step 6 hold the free end of the cord in place.

6. Make a cochineal dyebath. Use enough water for the fabric to circulate freely and 1 tsp cochineal per qt of water. Bring dyebath to a simmer. Wear plastic gloves. Dip the "puff" (the butterfly body) into the dye. Hold it there 5 min. Then rinse in cool water.

7. Wind the free end of the cord tied in Step 5 about the dyed puff in parallel lines, getting as close as possible to the end of the puff. Secure the last winding with a tight slipknot. Cut off excess cord.

8. Separate the groups of squares sewn in Step 3 from the rest of the fabric by bunching them together. Tie off the base of this bunch with a cord, using a slipknot.

9. Dye just this bunched fabric in the simmering dye-bath for 5 min. During this step hold the puff dyed in Step 6 out of the dyebath. Remove the bunch and rinse it in cool water.

10. Add 1 tsp of alum to dyebath to make it purple. Hold the bunch dyed in Step 9 out of the dyebath. Immerse all of remaining fabric in dyebath long enough to make a sufficient color contrast between this fabric and the withheld bunch.

11. Rinse the fabric in cool water. Then remove all the slipknotted cords. Use a needle point to pick apart the slipknots made in Step 3 (refer to the illustrations on p. 101).

12. Iron the fabric after it has dried. As some of the dye may not be quite fixed, cover the fabric with paper towels or old newspaper sheets, after first sprinkling fabric with water. Then iron, using the appropriate setting.

Combination tie-dyeing and batik

When used in combination, batik and tie-dyeing provide a variety of colorful and creative design possibilities whose full range can only be hinted at in the example shown below. In the project on this page the dye is resisted both by the waxed areas in the fabric and by the ways in which the fabric is folded. In effect, these folds serve the general purpose of ties.

The fabric used is cotton muslin. If dyed with natural dyes, it should be mordanted following the procedure given on page 97 and allowed to dry before it is folded. After the waxing it is important to open the fabric immediately so that the wax permeates only the sides of the folded fabric.

The natural dyebath used is logwood with a copper sulfate additive. To make this bath, follow the instructions on page 98. Thoroughly rinse the fabric after removing it from the dyebath, and let it dry before ironing it.

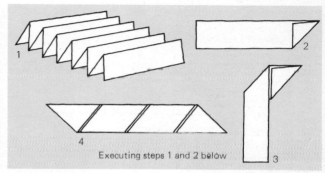

Executing steps 1 and 2 below

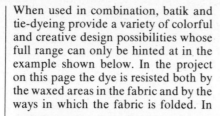

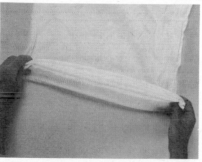

1. Fold the fabric into accordion pleats.

2. Fold pleated fabric into diagonal spirals.

3. Dip each folded side into hot liquid wax.

4. Open fabric immediately. Soak it in water.

5. Soak the fabric in the dyebath for 12 hr.

6. Iron, following instructions on page 96.

103

Stained glass

Mosaics of colored light

Glass in some form has been used for decorative purposes for the past 6,000 years, but it was not widely used until the technique of glass blowing was developed by the Syrians in the first century B.C. The Romans were the first to make glass windows—transparent windows were installed in their baths to let in the light without letting out the heated air. Colored glass windows were used in the church of Hagia Sophia, Constantinople, in the sixth century. The oldest surviving pictorial windows were installed in the cathedral at Augsburg, Germany, in 1095. But it was a new architectural style that brought stained glass to its peak.

Gothic lead came windows. In Romanesque and Byzantine churches and cathedrals massive walls of solid masonry were needed to support the weight of the roof, so windows were small and limited in number. The large expanses of blank walls were often covered with mosaics that illustrated sacred stories, thus decorating the building and instructing the largely illiterate congregation at the same time. In the 12th century Gothic architecture was introduced, making possible the building of cathedrals and churches in which rib-vaulted roofs were supported by skeletons of piers and buttresses. Such construction allowed large numbers of windows, which were filled in with panels of small pieces of colored glass. These were held together by grooved lead rods, called cames.

Some of the medieval stained glass windows were painted with enamel and fired to fuse the enamel and the glass, but the term stained glass is used for all colored glass. Color is added to glass when it is manufactured, by mixing in metal oxides while the raw materials are in a molten state. Properly used, this colored glass can be arranged to create pictures of great detail without the addition of enamel.

Some of the early stained glass windows were merely decorative, but most of them illustrated sacred stories. These fragmented glass pictures transformed the sunlight into jewellike particles that arranged themselves into mosaics of colored light.

Stained glass windows soon took the place of mosaics in the churches, both as art and as an educational tool. Glaziers quickly developed a style that was perfectly suited to glass and lead. The most beautiful of all stained glass windows are those in the Gothic cathedrals of Europe.

During the Reformation, Protestant leaders discouraged the use of pictorial aids to faith. At the same time, the invention of printing made books accessible to more people, raising the literacy rate. As a consequence, stained glass was little used in new churches, although windows depicting coats of arms and secular scenes were sometimes installed in other public buildings and in homes.

Copper foil technique. Stained glass regained its popularity with the Gothic revival of the 19th century. In the late 19th or early 20th century a new technique was developed. Copper foil coated with solder was used in place of lead cames. The art nouveau designer Louis Comfort Tiffany worked extensively in the copper foil technique, attempting in all his work to capture the essence of oil painting in glass. His stained glass lamps became very popular and widely imitated.

Many of the finest artists of the 20th century have designed for glass. The windows of Marc Chagall and Henri Matisse are particularly noteworthy. And today stained glass is winning wide popularity among hobbyists.

Early 13th-century decorative window is from choir of Abbey of Saint-Remi in Rheims.

The copper foil technique

Although the lead came technique of stained glass is far older and more widely used, the copper foil technique is much less complicated and is therefore better suited to a beginner. But that is not to say that copper foil is an inferior technique. It is used by many master glaziers, who find it especially good for projects that include small pieces of glass that would be difficult to surround with the more cumbersome lead cames. It is also easier to handle in making curved glass projects, such as lamps or terrariums. Some glaziers mix the techniques. Copper foil is used to wrap very small pieces of glass that are inserted into a large lead came work.

Making a simple panel. Begin by tracing two carbon copies of your original design. Cut one of the copies into glass patterns—templates for the individual pieces of glass in the panel. Using these patterns as guides, cut all the glass and lay it in place on the other copy of the design.

Wrap all the edges of each piece of glass with copper foil and crimp the protruding sides of the foil down against the front and back of the glass. Tack the pieces of glass together in their proper positions by soldering adjacent sections of copper foil together. Then float a coat of solder over all the foil and round off (raise a bead on) these solder lines. Repeat the soldering on the back and edges of the panel.

When all the foil is covered with a rounded bead of solder, clean the panel and rub it down with an antiquing solution of copper sulfate or cupric nitrate. This will discolor the solder and give it the appearance of antique copper. Wash the finished panel with detergent and water and dry it.

More complete directions are given in the next few pages. Once you have practiced cutting glass and soldering, you will be ready to work on the three copper foil projects.

Types of glass

Glass is made by bringing a mixture of sand, soda, ash, and metal oxides to a molten state. The molten glass is either rolled into sheets by machines or blown into long balloon shapes that are split open and flattened by reheating. Machine-made glass is of uniform thickness. Blown glass—called antique glass because it is made by the centuries-old method—may be uneven in thickness and contain bubbles or reams (undulations), which increase its beauty and reflective properties.

Antique glass may also be flashed. Flashed glass has a thin layer of bright color added to its surface while it is still in the molten state.

Machine-made glass comes in a large variety of types, including cathedral glass and opalescent, or opal, glass. Textures resembling the accidental faults in antique glass are deliberately rolled into cathedral glass, resulting in pebbled, granite, satin, and hammered glass. Opalescent glass is semi-opaque and semi-iridescent. Catspaw is a glass with spotted patterns that resemble the paw prints of a cat.

In your work use whatever types and colors of glass please you. There is no "right" glass for a particular project. Choose complementary colors and textures that suit your design and appeal to your eye.

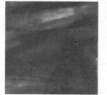 

Streaky antique glass   Streaky opalescent glass

Cathedral glass   Catspaw

Tools and materials

Aside from the glass and copper foil, the special tools and materials needed for working in the copper foil technique fall into two categories: glass cutting tools and soldering equipment. You will also need a few common household items, such as masking tape and kerosene. Glass is discussed above. Copper foil with adhesive backing is sold in rolls of various widths. The most common are 1/4 and 3/16 inch.

Glass cutting tools. Buy several single-edged steel-wheel glass cutters and a small-wheel carbide glass cutter. Use the steel-wheel cutters for most glass, but if you must use a lot of pressure to cut a piece of glass, switch to the carbide cutter.

Three types of special pliers will help you cut glass exactly and evenly. *Grozing pliers* are made of soft metal and have rough jaws for trimming edges. The type with arched jaws (shown at right) work best. If you cannot find grozers, use needle-nose pliers instead. *Breaking pliers* have wide, straight, parallel jaws that help you break off narrow strips of glass. If necessary, use slip-joint pliers. *Cut-running pliers*

have curved jaws that exert even pressure on both sides of a score, making it easier to cut curves.

Soldering equipment. Get a good, heavy-duty soldering iron with a plug-type tip 3/8 inch in diameter. This will be your most important tool; do not hesitate to buy an expensive one. A lightweight iron or soldering gun will not do the job. You will also need something on which to rest the hot soldering iron while you are working. Buy an iron rest or make one by securing a bent length of metal to the table.

Use 60/40 solid wire solder (60 percent tin and 40 percent lead). Do not use rosin-core solder (solder with flux in the center). You must apply the flux separately before soldering.

Flux cleans the foil or metal, prevents oxidation, and allows molten solder to flow and adhere properly. Zinc chloride or oleic acid are the most widely used fluxes, but water soluble fluxes are best if you can find them.

Finally, you will need an antiquing solution to give the solder the look of antique copper. Use either copper sulfate or cupric nitrate.

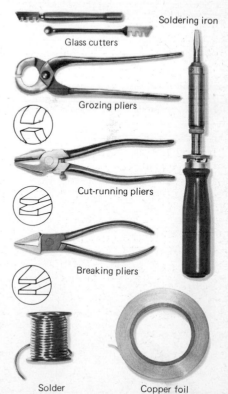

Glass cutters

Soldering iron

Grozing pliers

Cut-running pliers

Breaking pliers

Solder

Copper foil

Stained glass

Cutting glass

The process of cutting glass is basically a simple one, but cutting curved pieces to an exact shape and size can be very tricky and requires practice. If you have never cut glass before, practice cutting some inexpensive window glass into various shapes before attempting to cut the glass for a project.

Glass cutters must be kept lubricated, or they will not work properly. Put a bit of soft cloth in the bottom of a small jar and add a thin layer of kerosene or light machine oil. Keep your cutters in this jar while you are working and dip the wheel of the cutter into the lubricant before making each cut. You can cut freehand if you do not care about the exact size and shape of the piece, but when you are cutting glass that must fit into a project, always use a pattern or straightedge to guide the cutter along the glass.

Hold the glass cutter between your index and middle fingers and brace it in back with your thumb. Stand up and lean over the glass so that you will have more freedom of movement. Press the wheel of the cutter down at the farthest edge of the glass and move the cutter toward you along the cut line, applying firm, even pressure as you proceed. If you are applying the correct amount of pressure, you will usually hear a sound that is akin to light static on a radio. This is the sound of the glass being scored by the cutter.

Complete the scoring in one continuous motion, ending only after the cutter has come off the near end of the glass. If you try to go over a score, you will not only get a bad cut, you will also dull the cutter. If the glass you are using is rough or uneven on one side, score the smooth side.

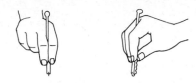

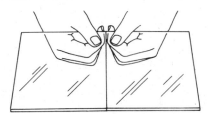

Position hands as shown to cut and break glass.

Once the glass has been scored, pick it up at one end of the score and break it along the score line. Hold the scored glass in both hands. Make loose fists and place the backs of your fingers nearly together under the glass on either side of the score line. Place your thumbs together on top of the glass with the score line between them. Do not be afraid of the glass, as it is unlikely to cut you when held this way.

Apply even pressure to both sides of the glass—press down and outward with your thumbs and up and outward with your bent fingers. The glass will snap in two along the score line. When you are breaking a curved piece, hold your hands in the same position, but point them in the same direction as the line of the curve.

1. To cut straight line, run lubricated glass cutter along side of straightedge, applying firm pressure. Move cutter toward you from edge to edge in one movement.

2. Hold scored glass in both hands, as shown above. Exert equal pressure on both sides of score line, but do not jerk. Increase pressure gradually until glass snaps in two.

3. Narrow strip is difficult to break off with hands. Hold narrow side with breaking pliers near score line. Use hand on wide side. Apply pressure. Strip will snap off.

4. To cut glass for project, make patterns from copy of cartoon and draw outline of piece on glass with grease pencil. Cut one side at a time from edge to edge of glass.

5. When scoring a curve, swing your arm and body to assure unimpaired movement of cutter. Score just inside line drawn from pattern, or cut piece will be too large.

6. To break curve, apply cut-running pliers across score. Line etched on jaw of pliers must run in same direction as score. Squeeze handles until you hear snap.

7. Snap indicates beginning of break. Take glass in hands and complete break in usual way. Hands should point in same direction as beginning of curve.

8. Remove rough edges or tiny sections by nibbling them away with grozing pliers. **Caution: Wear protective glasses or goggles; bits of glass may fly into eyes.**

Cutting a complex curve

Glass is basically brittle and inflexible. To cut sharp curves into it, you must remove the excess glass in sections, following the steps shown above. **1.** Make score. To keep glass from breaking wild, rap score gently on back with ball end of cutter. This will cause a partial break, but glass will not separate. **2.** Score and break off as much excess glass as possible with a straight cut. **3.** Divide remaining area to be cut away with series of scores. **4.** Remove sections in sequence shown, using breaking pliers. Groze away remaining bits of glass.

Wrapping with copper foil

After all the glass has been cut, each piece must be wrapped in copper foil and the edges of the foil crimped down over the front and back surfaces of the glass. The foil hugs the edges of the glass on all sides in a U-shape, making it possible to solder the pieces of glass together. When the foil has been

Crimp foil around edge of glass in a U-shape.

coated with solder, it will resemble the lead cames used in the older technique.

Be sure to get the foil on straight. Wrapping is easy, and the tendency to work automatically is strong. Auto-matic wrapping results in an uneven application, which will make the finished project unattractive and structurally weak. Wrap carefully and always watch what you are doing.

Copper foil comes in rolls and has a paper backing that must be peeled off as you wrap. Begin wrapping each piece of glass about 1/4 inch from one corner and end at the same corner, overlapping the beginning. The end of the foil should not be on a side of the glass that will be on the perimeter of the finished project, or it might pull away in time. If the end of the foil overlaps the beginning at a slight angle, trim off the protruding piece with a razor blade to get a straight line. If it is very crooked, remove it and put on fresh foil.

1. Hold piece of glass in one hand and foil in other. Begin wrapping about 1/4 in. from a corner of glass. Center end of foil on edge of glass and pull foil tautly around corner.

2. Be careful to keep foil centered on edge of glass. Keep your eye on it at all times. Wrap one side of glass, then crimp down foil with your fingers. Wrap other sides in same way.

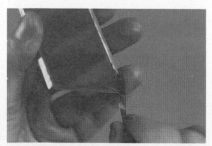

3. End wrapping at corner where you began. There will be an overlap. Tear off foil by twisting it back and forth a few times. Crimp down the foil on all sides of glass and at corners.

4. Go around perimeter of glass on each side, carefully pressing foil against glass. Be especially sure the corners are snug. Foil should be even on all edges of glass.

Working with a soldering iron

A lot of soldering is required for working in stained glass, particularly if you use the copper foil technique. If you have not handled a soldering iron before, you may be apprehensive, but you shouldn't be. With a little practice you can master its use.

Never pick up the iron by the shaft or cord, even if it is unplugged, or a serious burn could result. Always brush a generous amount of flux onto the foil or lead before applying the solder, or the solder will not adhere. Keep a damp cellulose sponge nearby and wipe the tip of the iron clean with it from time to time as you work.

Maintenance. Your soldering iron must be carefully maintained. Its tip must be kept clean and well tinned, as shown at right, and the tip should be replaced if it becomes too corroded.

Occasionally remove the tip of the iron and clean the inside of the shaft into which it fits; otherwise the tip may become frozen into place. Loosen the single screw that holds in the tip and remove it. Scrape away any corrosion in the shaft with a narrow circular file and shake out the filings. Clean the base of the tip with a flat file, then replace the tip, making sure it is seated all the way down into the shaft. Tighten the screw securely.

Heat control. Unfortunately, soldering irons are not equipped with thermostats, and they can become too hot while you are working with them. Consequently, you must keep unplugging them and plugging them back in again to maintain the proper temperature for soldering. There is no way to gauge the temperature, but after you have done a bit of soldering, you will be able to tell whether the iron is too hot or too cool by the way the solder behaves. If the solder does not melt freely, the iron is too cool. If the iron smokes or if the solder is runny, the iron is too hot.

All soldering iron tips must be tinned before use. Copper tips should be filed down before tinning, but iron-coated tips should be filed only if they become corroded and pitted like the one at left. Tin iron as often as needed; tip should always be covered with an even coat of solder.

Unplug iron and let it cool before filing. With a rasp or bastard file, file across and down length of tip with a gentle, circular motion. Shape end of tip to give maximum amount of contact with work. Tip should be smooth and rounded, with a bright metallic shine.

Plug in iron and let it get hot. Nail a jar lid to a block of wood and put a little flux into it. Use soldering iron to melt some solder into flux, then dip tip of iron into mixture of molten solder and flux. Turn tip slowly to coat it with solder.

Tip of iron should be evenly coated with solder all the way around. If you keep your iron well tinned, soldering will be easier. Tin your iron whenever necessary. If iron works sluggishly after several hours of use, try re-tinning it to restore its efficiency.

Stained glass

Soldering a small panel

Soldering is done in three stages. First all the pieces of wrapped glass are tacked together with drops of solder. Then a thin coat of solder is run along all visible lines of copper foil. Finally, more solder is added on top of the first coat, and a bead is raised—that is, the solder is rounded off on top. The interior lines of the front of the panel are soldered first, the interior lines of the back are done next, and the perimeters are done last. The perimeters have three surfaces: the actual outer edge and its two adjacent sides on the front and back of the panel. Both sides are soldered before the outer edge.

Beading can be tricky and will require practice to master. Be patient and work slowly, but do not hold the soldering iron in one spot for too long, or the heat may crack the glass. Solder solidifies almost instantly, but it cools slowly, so be careful not to touch a newly soldered surface. If some solder flashes through (drips through to the underside of the panel), let it cool before reworking the area. If solder lumps in one spot, apply flux to the spot, heat it with the iron, and push away the excess solder. If solder drips or runs onto the glass, simply flick it off with your fingers when it is cool.

1. Arrange wrapped glass in correct pattern. Hold pieces in place by nailing a frame of laths around them. Generously brush flux over all visible foil.

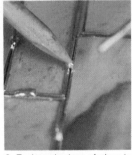

2. Tack each piece of glass to its neighbor by holding end of wire solder over place where strips of foil join and touching hot iron to solder.

3. When all pieces are joined, float coat of solder over all visible foil except perimeters. If solder lumps, spread it along line with hot iron. Remove laths.

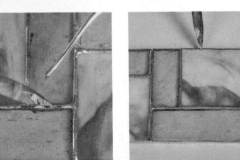

4. Slowly add more solder over top of first coat, and raise a rounded bead of solder along all front interior lines of panel. Do not solder perimeters.

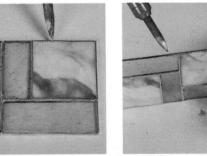

5. When all but perimeters are completely soldered, turn panel over and repeat Steps 3 and 4 on back. Then raise bead on back side of perimeter.

6. Turn panel over and raise bead on front side of perimeter, then hold panel on end and raise bead on edges that also covers two side beads.

Stained glass / project

Copper foil box

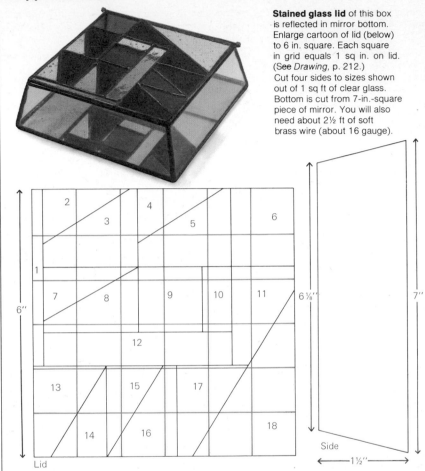

Stained glass lid of this box is reflected in mirror bottom. Enlarge cartoon of lid (below) to 6 in. square. Each square in grid equals 1 sq in. on lid. (See *Drawing,* p. 212.) Cut four sides to sizes shown out of 1 sq ft of clear glass. Bottom is cut from 7-in.-square piece of mirror. You will also need about 2½ ft of soft brass wire (about 16 gauge).

The pieces of glass in this decorative box are all made up of straight lines and are easy to cut, but take care to cut them to the exact sizes and shapes indicated. Otherwise the box may be lopsided or the lid may not fit. If your cutting is just a bit off and small gaps appear between some pieces, fill in the gaps with a little extra solder.

If you prefer, you can make just the box lid as a decorative panel. Simply follow the directions through Step 5, then solder soft brass wire around the perimeter on the bottom and both sides to reinforce the panel. Along the top edge solder a length of wire that has two loops in it for hanging the panel. (Bend the loops into the wire with needle-nose pliers.) Raise a bead of solder around the entire perimeter and antique and wash the panel as described in Step 15.

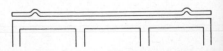

Solder looped wire to edge of panel to hang it.

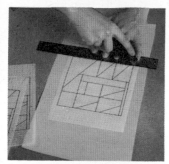

1. Make two copies of cartoon and number all sections of each copy. Carefully cut one copy of the cartoon into individual pieces to serve as patterns for cutting the glass.

2. Trace outlines of patterns on glass with grease pencil. Cut glass carefully and groze off any rough edges (p. 106). Put cut glass in place on other copy of cartoon.

3. Pick up one piece of cut glass, wrap it carefully with copper foil, and crimp foil down flat (p. 107). Place glass back on cartoon. Repeat until all glass for lid is wrapped.

4. Arrange glass for lid on worktable or on sheet of plywood. Nail a frame of laths around glass to keep pieces from moving. Use a square to make sure you get perfect right angles.

5. Tack pieces with solder, then run a coat of solder over all interior pieces of foil and raise a bead on them. Pull up laths and solder the interior of the other side of the lid.

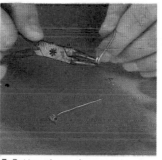

6. Reinforce perimeter of lid by soldering brass wire to side and front edges. Trim wire to fit. Repeat on back edge but let wire protrude at both ends to form hinge pin.

7. Cut two pieces of copper wire a few inches long. With needle-nose pliers twist one end of each piece into two congruent circles. Put them aside. These will be hinges.

8. Cut clear glass for four sides of box. All pieces should be identical. Wrap them with copper foil and place them end to end on work surface. Tape them together.

9. Pull side pieces up and around to form square. Tack them together with solder at top and bottom of each corner. Remove tape, being careful not to pull off foil.

10. Using connected sides as pattern, cut mirror glass for bottom of box. (Score mirror on reflecting side.) Wrap mirror with foil and solder it to the sides from inside.

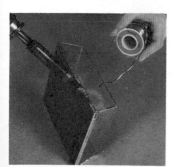

11. Turn box on one end and solder over all foil between sides and mirror bottom. Repeat on other three sides. Be sure to raise a good rounded bead all the way around.

12. Tape one hinge (made in Step 7) to one of back corners of box. Trim end to fit, if necessary. Tack hinge into place with solder, remove tape, and complete soldering.

13. Put lid onto box, inserting hinge pin on lid into attached hinge. Place second hinge over other end of hinge pin, tape it into place on side of box, and tack it with solder.

14. Solder over all foil still visible. Keep bead small on back edges where lid and back wall of box meet. Snip off protruding ends of hinge pins with wire clippers.

15. Wearing a rubber glove, soak rag with antiquing solution and rub down all solder on box until it takes on color of antique copper. Wash box with detergent and water.

Stained glass/project

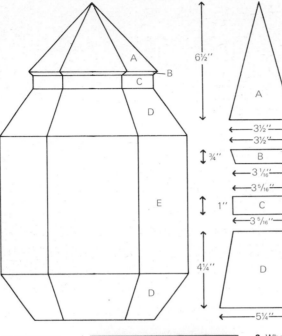

Draw the cartoon to the measurements indicated. Section D is used for both lower section (in opalescent glass) and upper section (in clear glass) You will need about 7 sq ft of clear glass and 3 sq ft of opalescent glass.

A

B

C

D

E

D

6½''

¾''

1''

4¼''

3½''
3½''
3 1/16''
3 5/16''
3 5/16''
5¼''

5¼''

10''

Copper foil terrarium

The terrarium illustrated at left is put together in much the same way as the box on the preceding two pages. Like the box, the terrarium is made up of pieces of glass that have no curves. However, the octagonal shape of the terrarium will make soldering the outside seams more difficult. Work patiently and use a cooler iron on these seams. Imperfect soldering can be reworked with a hot iron and small amounts of solder until smooth.

Opalescent glass is used for the bottom and for the lower section of the terrarium to keep the soil from showing through. Clear glass is used in the midsection, upper section (except the neck), and lid to allow light to reach the plants. If you prefer, use mirrors in place of the opalescent glass or stagger a few stained glass panels around the upper sections.

For instructions on planting a terrarium, see *Indoor gardening*, p. 297.

1. Make glass patterns from copy of cartoon drawn to size. Using them as guides, cut eight pieces of opalescent glass for section C of cartoon and eight for section D. Then cut eight pieces of clear glass for section D and for each of remaining sections—A, B, and E. Wrap all glass with foil.

2. Lay the eight pieces of glass for the lid side by side and tape all the sections together with masking tape.

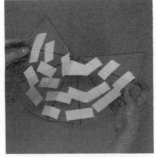

3. When all the sections of the lid are securely taped together, carefully lift the lid, turn it over, and pull its free edges together to form a standing cone. Secure with one piece of tape.

4. Tack all the sections together with solder on the outside, then float a coat of solder along each of the vertical lines of copper foil. When all the vertical lines of foil are covered with solder, raise a good, rounded bead on all these lines.

5. Turn lid over and solder inside vertical lines, removing tape as you proceed. Be careful when removing tape not to lift up the copper foil. Raise bead on inside lines.

6. Hold first section of skirt of lid in place at a slight inward angle and tack it into place with a few drops of solder.

7. Hold second section of skirt in place and tack it with solder both to lid and to first section of skirt. Continue adding sections of skirt until all eight are in place. Float a coat of solder along all visible foil and raise a bead. Solder and bead inside of skirt.

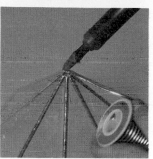

8. Add a large, well rounded ball of solder to the point of the lid. If the solder runs, add it a little at a time and use a cooler iron.

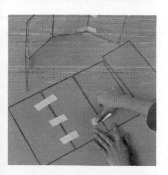

9. Arrange the panels of the midsection on the work surface and tape them together. Lift the taped sections and pull them together to form an octagon.

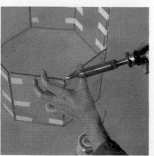

10. Tack the panels of the midsection together with solder. Tack in several spots along each line to be sure they will hold together while you work.

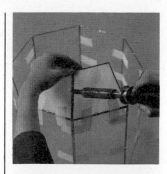

11. Add the opalescent lower section to the mid-section one panel at a time, as you did with the skirt of the lid. Use tape to help hold the panels to the midsection, as the panels of the lower section are heavier than those of the skirt of the lid.

12. Solder and bead all outside vertical lines. Solder may run, making it difficult to work with. Use a cooler iron to prevent solder from flashing through to the other side. Flick spilled solder off the glass with your finger. Solder and bead line between lower section and midsection.

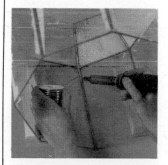

13. Solder and bead all inside vertical lines. Prop up the terrarium on blocks of wood so that the line you are working on is perfectly flat. This will make the soldering much easier, as gravity will pull the molten solder down into a neat line.

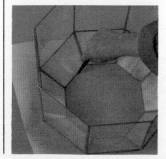

14. Place the bottom of the terrarium on a sheet of opalescent glass and trace a line around the inside perimeter with a grease pencil. Cut the opalescent glass along the line marked to form the bottom of the terrarium. Wrap edges of bottom.

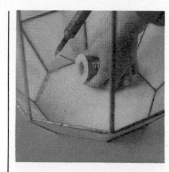

15. Tack the bottom into place on the inside with solder, then complete soldering and beading of bottom on both the inside and the outside.

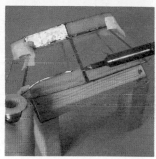

16. Assemble, solder, and bead upper section and neck in the same way you did lower section (Steps 11-13). Use wood props to hold lines level for soldering. Tape the upper section in place on the body of the terrarium and solder over all the copper foil still visible inside and out, including the edges.

17. When soldering the outside corners, be sure the solder comes into contact with all four pieces of foil that form the corner. If the solder does not cover all the foil on first attempt, let solder cool slightly and rework it. All joints should look like the one pictured here.

18. Wearing a glove, rub down all the solder with antiquing solution. Wash terrarium with detergent and water, dry it, and apply clear silicone glue and seal to inside seams to waterproof them.

Stained glass/project

Copper foil lamp

The stained glass lamp shown above is a challenging but rewarding project. The lamp has 12 sides, each of which is made up of one large panel and three successive skirts. Each of the skirts turns slightly inward to give the bottom of the lamp a curved look. There are three different patterns for the main panels and upper skirts. Each pattern is used four times.

To reproduce the lamp as shown, you will need a maximum of 12 square feet of opalescent glass in six shades. This will allow extra glass for bad cuts that have to be repeated. Get 3½ square feet of brown glass for the background, 2½ square feet of orange glass for the flowers, 1 square foot of brown glass for the centers of the flowers, 1½ square feet of each shade of green for the leaves, and 2 square feet of gray glass for the borders.

To wire the lamp, you will need a socket with a threaded nipple, two locknuts, a brace bar (which may have to be cut down to size), a vase cap that is the same size as the upper opening of the lamp or slightly larger, and a finial. Attach a length of chain to the finial and hang the lamp from the ceiling. With the electricity turned off, wire the socket to the ceiling fixture and run the wire alongside the chain. Screw in a light bulb and the lamp is ready.

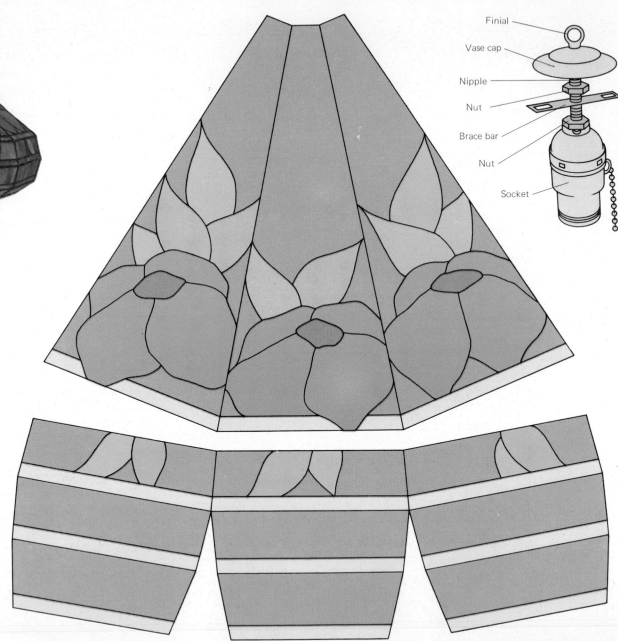

Above cartoon is half size; double all measurements (p. 212). Cut one copy of enlarged cartoon into patterns. Cut four pieces of glass for each pattern. Before wrapping, stack like pieces of glass together to be sure they are same size. Hardware for wiring is shown in insert.

112

  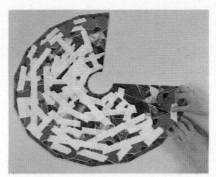 

1. Cut all glass and wrap it with foil. Position glass for one panel on work surface and frame it with laths. Use two laths at bottom. Solder and raise bead on all of panel but edges.

2. Pull up inside bottom lath and slide out panel. Solder and raise bead on back of panel. Position glass for second panel into lath frame and replace pulled-up lath. Solder second panel.

3. Repeat Steps 1 and 2 for other 10 panels and 36 skirts. If any solder drips onto edges, remove it with soldering iron. Wash soldered pieces with detergent and water. Tape main panels together.

4. Lift the sides of the outermost panels and turn lamp over on work surface. Pull free edges together to form a standing cone and fasten with a single piece of masking tape.

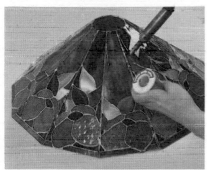   

5. Tack all the panels together with dabs of solder on the outside. Remove outside piece of tape and float a coat of solder over upper rim and all the outside vertical lines of copper foil.

6. Turn lamp over. Add light coat of solder to bottom rim. Pull tape off one joint at a time and float coat of solder over it. Turn lamp over and raise bead of solder on all outside vertical lines.

7. Raise a bead on inside vertical lines. With soldering iron, clear bottom rim of lamp of any lumps of solder. Tack first skirt of any panel onto rim of lamp with one spot of solder.

8. Tack first skirts of other panels to rim and each other. Complete soldering of outside of skirt, then inside. Wash lamp. Add other skirts in same way. Raise bead on rim of last skirt. Wash lamp.

9. With a drill and 1/8-in. bit, make eight holes in vase cap to allow heat from light bulb to escape. Coat vase cap and finial with solder to make them match rest of metal on lamp.

10. With a hacksaw, trim brace bar to make it fit snugly across top of lamp on inside. Bar must touch solder on both sides. Solder the trimmed brace bar into place on bottom and top.

11. Solder the vase cap into place on top of the lamp and solder the finial onto the top of the vase cap. Be careful not to get solder into hole in finial, as the wire must fit through it.

12. Wearing gloves, rub down all metal on lamp with antiquing solution until it attains uniform antique copper color. Wash lamp carefully in detergent and water, dry it, and install it.

Stained glass

The lead came technique

The lead came technique is nearly a thousand years old. It was first described in an early 12-century manuscript by the monk Theophilus. This same method, unchanged in its essentials, is still the best way to put together a large panel or window. It is a bit more complicated than the copper foil technique presented in previous pages and can be more time consuming, but it will give you the added satisfaction of knowing you are working in the same way as the master glaziers who created the gothic windows in the great medieval cathedrals.

The lead came technique is more complicated only in that it requires more steps. But none of these steps is difficult once mastered, and the soldering is simpler. Instead of floating a bead of solder along all the metal, as you must do with copper foil, you need only apply a dab of solder at each of the places where pieces of lead came are joined.

The basic technique. Patterns are made and the glass is cut for the entire project. A copy of the cartoon, called the leading guide, is fastened to the work surface, and laths are nailed down along the guide's edges. Pieces of lead came are laid along two of the edges and glass is fitted into the grooves, or channels, along their sides. More lead came and more glass are added, following the leading guide beneath, until the panel is filled.

This process is called *glazing*. The lead cames take the place of the copper foil. Instead of wrapping each piece of glass with foil, the edges of the glass are fitted into the channels of the lead cames. Since the cames are sturdy enough to hold the glass in place, unlike the flimsy foil, they need not be covered with solder, but are merely tacked together with solder at the joints. Putty is then forced into the grooves, and the panel is cleaned.

Tools and materials

You will need most of the tools and materials used for the copper foil technique (p. 105) plus a few others.

Materials. The new materials are putty, plaster of Paris, and lead came.

Lead came is sold in long strips of various thicknesses, ranging from 3/8 inch to 1½ inches. The thickness you use depends on the amount of lead you want to show in the finished project, the size of the pieces of glass it will hold, and the overall size of the project.

The most commonly used cames are H-leads, so called because in cross section they resemble the letter H. Glass is slipped into the channels of the H to fit snugly against the heart (the connecting central piece) of the lead. The flanges (outside wings) on the standard H-lead are flat, but H-leads with rounded flanges are used for a different visual effect. Special U-leads are occasionally used for the outside edges of a panel, but standard H-leads can easily be adapted to the same use.

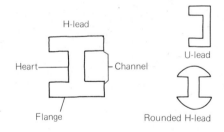

Tools. To prepare the lead, you will need a lead stretcher. This tool has jaws that clamp down on one end of a length of lead came to hold it steady while you pull the other end in order to straighten

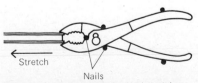
Pliers and nails substitute for lead stretcher.

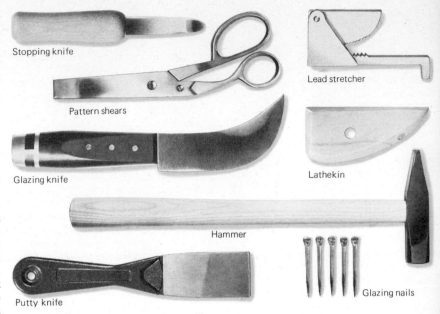

Stopping knife

Pattern shears

Glazing knife

Lead stretcher

Lathekin

Hammer

Putty knife

Glazing nails

the lead and make it taut. If you cannot get a lead stretcher, improvise by driving three nails into your work surface around a pair of pliers as shown at left.

Pattern shears are needed to cut the paper patterns for the glass. As they cut, they remove a strip of paper 1/16 inch wide—the width of the hearts of most leads. This allows you to cut complicated patterns without having the leads throw off your measurements, which could result in a misshapen panel. Get a good pair of pattern shears, even though they are expensive. If you absolutely cannot get them, try using a utility knife with two blades in it and a 1/16-inch-thick piece of cardboard between them or two single-edged razor blades taped together with the cardboard between them. But use these makeshift devices only as a last resort. They will be hard to work with, and the resulting measurements of the cut glass may still be incorrect.

A glazing knife is used to cut lead

cames. The saber type shown above is best, and it has the added advantage of a metal weight in its handle, which can be used as a hammer while you are glazing. If you cannot get one, make one by filing down a stiff-bladed putty knife on a grinding wheel, then honing it further with a sharpening stone.

A stopping knife is a great help in straightening and aligning lead cames. It is a flat, dull-bladed knife with a slight curve in the end of its blade. Buy one or make one from an oyster knife. You can use a glazing knife in its place, but if you do, exercise extreme caution, as the glazing knife is very sharp.

You will also need a lathekin—a small, flat piece of wood or bone for opening the channels of the leads. Buy one or make one out of hardwood.

Finally, you will need a putty knife and some glazing nails—special flat-sided nails used to hold the glass and lead in place during glazing. Horseshoe nails can be substituted.

Working with lead came

Lead cames tend to become slightly twisted and misshapen when in transit or in storage. Whether they are misshapen or not, they must be stretched before use.

Stretch and straighten the lead as shown at right until all the kinks, waves, and twists are out of it. Then open its channels with a lathekin. First wet the lathekin, then place a length of lead on the work surface with one of its channels facing up. Slide the lathekin through the channel, using firm, even pressure. Repeat on the opposite side.

When you are ready to cut the lead cames for glazing, follow the directions illustrated at right. Most lead cames have tiny lines running across the insides of their channels. These are handy guides for cutting a came straight across.

Installing a window. If you want to install a leaded glass panel in a window frame, be sure your measurements are precise (see below). When the panel is ready for installation, prepare the frame. Pull off the molding and the glazier's points or nails, scrape away all the old putty, and remove the old glass. Clean the frame and seal it with a coat of half shellac and half alcohol to make the new putty adhere better.

Apply a thin bead of putty around the frame, carefully fit the panel into the frame, and tack it in at its joints with glazier's points or small brads. Apply more putty, replace the molding, and cut away any excess putty. If you prefer to install the stained glass panel without the molding, fill in with putty, cutting it so that it slopes from the inner edge of the peripheral leads to the outside of the frame.

Caution: When handling a leaded glass panel, hold it carefully only at the soldered joints along the edges.

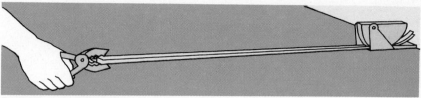

To stretch lead came, insert one end of a length of came into jaws of lead stretcher. Hold other end with pliers and pull. Jaws of lead stretcher will tighten and hold lead securely. Exert steady tension on lead, turning it slightly to untwist it if necessary. Lead will stretch visibly.

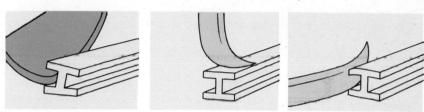

To open channels of stretched lead, wet lathekin and run it through channels on both sides (left). To cut lead came, place it with one flange facing up. Position blade of glazing knife on top of flange at right angle (center). Press down on knife, centering pressure on heart of lead rather than on edges of flange, or flange will collapse. Apply pressure evenly, and wiggle knife slightly by twisting your wrist to distribute weight evenly as you cut. Trim off any bits that protrude from cut end. Flanges may be bent at cutting point. Straighten with blade of glazing knife (right).

Preparing patterns

When drawing a design for a leaded glass panel, include three peripheral lines, as shown at right. The inside, or sight, line indicates the outermost edges of the glass that will be visible in the finished panel. The center, or cut, line represents the actual cut edge of the glass. The outside, or full-size, line shows the size of the entire panel. The distances between the lines should be equal to the distances between the heart of the peripheral lead and the edges of its flanges.

These lines are important if a new panel is to fit securely in an old window. The cut line must be followed exactly: if the outside pieces were cut to the sight line or to the full-size line, they would not fit. In order to mount the panel in a window frame, the full-size line must have the same dimensions as the outer channels of the frame and the sight line should follow the outermost visible edges of the old glass.

Making copies. Make two copies of the original design, or cartoon (including the three peripheral lines). On the work surface make a paper sandwich: first a piece of stiff paper, then a piece of carbon paper (carbon side down), then a piece of brown paper, then a second carbon, and finally the cartoon on top. Staple everything down and trace the design carefully. Number all the sections of the cartoon.

Keep the original cartoon on file for future reference. It will come in handy if you ever decide to make a second panel of the same design. The stiff paper copy is the project pattern, which is cut up to make individual patterns for cutting each piece of glass. The brown paper copy is the leading guide, which is stapled to the work surface and used to place the lead cames and pieces of glass correctly during glazing.

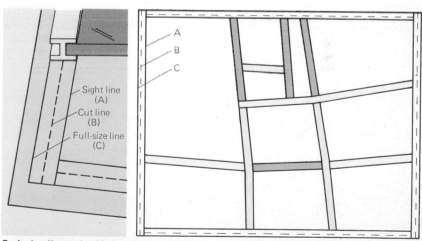

Project patterns should show three peripheral lines to indicate sight line, cut line, and full-size line. Heart of outside lead should fall directly over cut line. Glass will fit into channel of lead and butt against heart at cutline (left). Portion of glass between cut line and sight line will be invisible in finished panel. Portion of lead between sight line and full-size line will form lead border around panel. In pattern shown here (right), colored lines indicate pieces of lead came in panel. No inside piece of lead should stretch across panel, or structure will be weak. Different colored lines in pattern indicate separate pieces of lead. Actual lead cames will all be dull gray.

Sight line (A)
Cut line (B)
Full-size line (C)

115

Stained glass

Glazing a small panel

1. Prepare the cartoon, pattern, and leading guide (p. 115). Using pattern shears, cut the stiff paper pattern into small patterns for each piece of glass that will go into the panel. Cut the outside edges with scissors, following the cut lines.

2. Following the small patterns, carefully cut all the glass (see p. 106). Leave patterns in place on pieces of glass and keep them nearby. (When working on a large panel, put patterns and glass in place on cartoon.)

3. Position laths along full-size (outside) lines of left vertical and bottom horizontal sides of leading guide. Use a square to get a perfect right angle and nail the laths down.

4. Stretch lead. Cut a piece and place it along vertical lath. Cut lead for horizontal side. For best support, vertical lead should run entire length of panel and horizontal lead should butt against it. You can leave these leads a bit long and trim them later.

5. Hammer in glazing nails at ends of leads to keep leads in place. Push corner glass into lead channels. Position next vertical lead and second piece of glass. Measure distance from heart to edge of lead. Mark off this space below top of glass on vertical lead.

6. Remove and cut vertical lead at mark. Reposition it and tap glass securely into place with butt of glazing knife. Measure, cut, and position next horizontal lead. It should cross tops of first two pieces of glass. Position layer of glass and vertical leads above it.

7. Wedge in top pieces of glass with glazing nails. Continue fitting together pieces of lead and glass in the same manner, moving up and to your right. As you proceed, make sure that the edges of the glass always line up with the lines on the leading guide.

8. When the last piece of glass is in place, remove all glazing nails, trim edges of first two outside leads, and fit in remaining two outside leads. Then nail down two more laths to frame panel. Use a square to make sure frame is perfectly straight.

9. Straighten and align leads with stopping knife. Tap knife with hammer if necessary. Short adjacent pieces of lead should line up so that they will look like long, single lengths of lead after they are soldered, giving panel clean, even lines.

10. Hammer down all the joints in the leads, but be careful not to hit the glass. Apply flux to the joints. (With lead came technique, only the joints between the leads are soldered. It is not necessary to float solder over all the metal as in copper foil technique.)

11. Solder all lead joints, using only enough solder to completely cover joint. Solder should not spill over and get under leads. Solder corners first. Be careful not to hold iron too long in one spot, or came will melt and cave in. If it does, fill in hole with solder.

12. Pull up laths and turn panel over. Nail laths back down again to hold panel steady. Then hammer down joints on back of panel and flux and solder them as you did on front of panel.

13. Push putty into all open spaces between glass and lead cames. Using putty knife, force putty in and push all leads down, being careful not to apply pressure directly to glass, or it will break. Remove excess putty with point of a nail or other sharp object.

14. Lightly sprinkle dry plaster of Paris over the surface of the panel and wipe it off with a soft cloth. This will remove any excess oil deposits from glass. Rub leads with burlap to remove excess putty and to give the leads an even patina.

15. Clean panel with a dry scrub brush, tipping brush slightly to get into grooves. Get up last bits with a vacuum cleaner. If you wish, add hooks for hanging panel (see p. 118). Press sides of cames closed with putty knife and gently hammer corners closed.

Stained glass/project

Making a leaded window

Once you have mastered the techniques illustrated on the facing page, you will be ready to make a full-size leaded glass window or a large leaded panel to hang in a window. Below, at left, is a pattern for a floral window. Step-by-step directions on how to make this window are given on the following two pages.

To make the panel exactly as illustrated on page 118, enlarge the pattern to 16 by 20 inches. If you want the panel to fit into an existing window, you will have to carefully adjust pattern to fit. To make the panel, you will need a maximum of 1 square foot of dark blue glass, 2 square feet of turquoise glass, 2 square feet of green glass, 1 square foot of orange glass, and 2 square feet of light beige glass. Three types of H-leads are needed: about 75 feet of standard, flat 1/4-inch leads for the four edges of the window, about 24 feet of rounded 1/4-inch leads for the other pieces in the border, and about 30 feet of 1/8-inch rounded leads for the floral part of the window.

If you feel that the pattern at left is too difficult for you to cut without more practice, substitute the one at right. The steps for making both windows are the same—only the shapes and number of pieces involved are different. Once you have made the simpler window, you will surely be ready to tackle the more difficult one. *(continued on page 118)*

Enlarge cartoon (see *Drawing*, p. 212). Each square on grid equals 1 sq in. on panel.

Border and flowers in this design are easier to cut and glaze. You can substitute either or both.

Stained glass/project

Making a leaded window *(continued)*

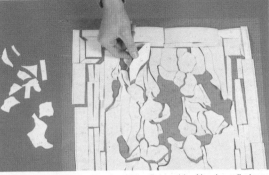

1. Prepare cartoon, pattern, and leading guide. Number all pieces on pattern and leading guide. Cut panel pattern into individual patterns for glass and put them in place on leading guide.

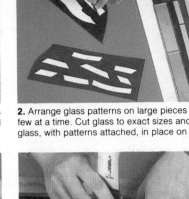

2. Arrange glass patterns on large pieces of the right color glass a few at a time. Cut glass to exact sizes and shapes of patterns. Put glass, with patterns attached, in place on cartoon.

6. Put in full border on two sides, then begin floral pattern. Before putting the lead cames down, bend them roughly to fit the pieces of glass, then press them firmly into glass.

7. Hammer each piece of glass into channels of leads with butt of glazing knife or with a hammer buffered with a piece of wood, or glass will not line up properly with lines of leading guide.

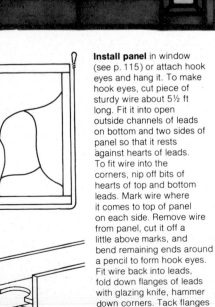

Install panel in window (see p. 115) or attach hook eyes and hang it. To make hook eyes, cut piece of sturdy wire about 5½ ft long. Fit it into open outside channels of leads on bottom and two sides of panel so that it rests against hearts of leads. To fit wire into the corners, nip off bits of hearts of top and bottom leads. Mark wire where it comes to top of panel on each side. Remove wire from panel, cut it off a little above marks, and bend remaining ends around a pencil to form hook eyes. Fit wire back into leads, fold down flanges of leads with glazing knife, hammer down corners. Tack flanges together with solder at every joint to hold wire in. Solder hook eyes in place.

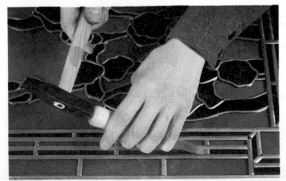

11. If flanges are stubborn, tap butt of stopping knife with a hammer to get the leads straight. When all leads connect evenly, hammer down joints, being careful not to hit or break glass.

12. Lead sometimes corrodes, in which case it is difficult or impossible to solder. If this happens, rub down the lead with steel wool before fluxing and soldering it.

3. Cut pieces with complex curves in stages to prevent glass from shattering or breaking in wrong direction. Use breaking pliers, cut-running pliers, or grozing pliers as needed.

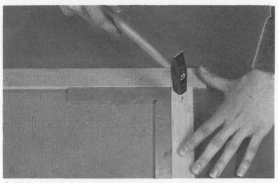

4. Nail down left vertical and bottom horizontal laths along the full-size lines of leading guide. Be sure to line up laths with a square, or the finished window may be lopsided.

5. Begin glazing. Remember to put in full-length vertical lead first, then butt bottom horizontal lead against it. Wedge glass in with glazing nails. Glass must line up with leading guide.

8. Proceed to glaze upward and to the right. Work carefully. If a piece of glass has been cut wrong and will not fit properly, take it out and groze it or cut it over.

9. When all glass is in place, carefully put in last two outside pieces of lead and trim off any protruding ends. Square off and nail down other two laths to fully frame window.

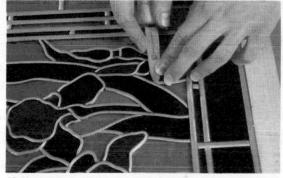

10. Use a stopping knife to straighten and align all the lead cames on the window. Use the curved end of the blade of the knife to pry up any bent down flanges.

13. Flux all joints in leading and heat and tin soldering iron (p. 107). First tack all corners with solder. Then solder joints in border. Finally, tack all inside joints with solder.

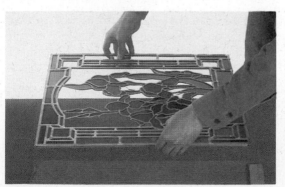

14. Pull up laths and slide panel toward you so that half of it remains on table and half is off. Carefully turn panel over. Straighten leads, hammer down joints, and flux and solder joints.

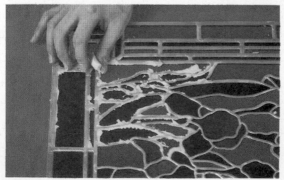

15. Apply putty and clean panel (Steps 13–15, p. 116). Install in window (p. 115), or add hooks and close outside cames with glazing knife and corners with hammer (facing page).

String art utilizes basic geometric forms.

The symmetrical art

String art makes circles out of straight lines—and this is probably as close as we will ever get to squaring the circle. The art form originated early in the 20th century, when drawings were used in mathematics books to show how to draw curves from straight lines. Later these pictures were re-created with string stretched across nails, and artists soon adapted the technique, adding color and combining textures, to create string pictures and sculptures that transcended their instructional value.

True to its orgins, string art is highly dependent on geometric forms. Its great order and symmetry are the basis of its appeal.

Tools and materials

To make a string picture, only a few common tools and materials are required. For designing the picture you need a pencil (or several colored pencils), paper, and a compass and a protractor to draw and measure circles.

To form the background surface, choose a board into which you can drive nails easily. A piece of 1/2-inch plywood is ideal, but any kind of wood can be used. The length and width of the board are determined by the size of the picture. The board may be painted, shellacked, varnished, or covered with fabric (which is attached to the board with a good stapler or staple gun). You will also need a supply of masking tape

with which to temporarily attach the pattern to the board.

The most important tool used for string art is a hammer. Get one that is comfortable for you to work with, as you will be driving a lot of nails. You may also want to keep a pair of pliers handy for straightening nails that get driven in at an angle by mistake.

The key materials are nails and string. Any type of nail can be used, but 16-gauge brads are ideal. Gilt- or nickle-plated nails look better. If your picture will be fairly flat, use 1/2-inch brads. If you want to create depth, or if certain nails will have to support many windings of string, use 1-inch or even

1½-inch brads. If you design a picture with layers of different designs, use nails of different heights.

Any type of string, thread, yarn, or fine wire can be used to form the design. Your only considerations are how it will suit your pattern and how it will look against the background. If you prefer to use wire, get fine (28- or 32-gauge) copper, brass, or galvanized wire at a hardware store. Use a variety of different colors, types, and thicknesses of string in a picture to create an interplay of colors and textures. It is a good idea to create the design for your picture first, and let the design rule the materials you will use.

String art

Designing a string picture

You can make a string picture of almost anything under the sun (and of the sun itself, if you wish). Generally, abstract forms work best in string art, but representational pictures can also be effective and beautiful. Among the most popular subjects are sunbursts, owls, butterflies, and bridges.

String art relies greatly on geometric shapes. Designs made up of straight lines are easy to deal with. You simply stretch string across the board to form the shape as your eye sees it. But circles and other curves are different.

Illusion of a curve. There is no way to make a string stay curved in midair. You must create what looks like a curve by using straight lines.

Circles are formed by arranging points in a circle and by connecting these points with straight lines in such a way as to fill in the area enclosed by the points. The area may be filled completely, or it may be filled partially, with a circular opening suspended in midair at the center. Any number of points can be used. The more points you use, the more closely knit the circle will be. Instructions for drawing an 18-point circle are given below.

Other curved figures are simpler than the circle. Any two lines can be connected with crisscrossing lines to produce a curved, weblike figure.

Learn to draw the figures shown at right and on the following two pages, and experiment with shapes of your own devising. Then design a string picture with pencil and paper, combining and altering these basic figures.

Rules of designing. When designing for string, keep in mind two important rules: (1) the distance between adjacent points on the line the nails will follow must be exactly the same; (2) when two lines are connected, the number of points on each line must be the same. These will assure the symmetry that is so important to string art.

Drawing open and closed circles

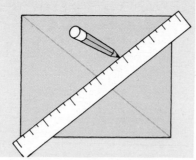

1. To find the center for the circle, draw diagonal lines against a straightedge from the upper left corner of the paper to the lower right corner and from the upper right corner to the lower left.

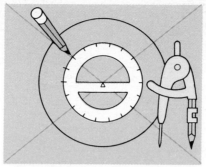

2. Place point of compass where lines intersect and draw circle. Place protractor on drawing, with its center on center of circle, and draw dots every 20 degrees around circumference of protractor.

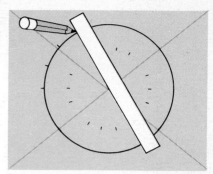

3. If circle is to be larger than protractor, run straightedge through the center of the circle and two of the dots drawn in Step 2. Mark dots on the circle drawn in Step 1.

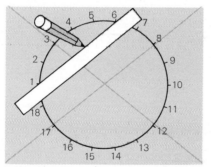

4. Open circle. Continue marking off dots all around the circle, then number the dots. Using a straightedge as guide, draw a line from point 1 to point 6, and another from point 6 to point 2.

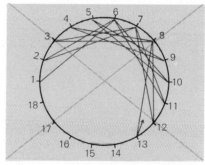

5. Continue drawing lines against straightedge, moving in a clockwise direction. Draw a line from point 2 to point 7, then from 7 to 3, 3 to 8, 8 to 4, 4 to 9, 9 to 5, 5 to 10, and so on.

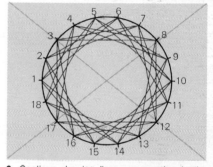

6. Continue drawing lines, progressing in the same clockwise manner, until you have come full circle. A line stretching from point 5 to point 1 should be the last.

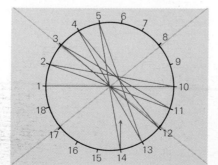

7. Closed circle. Begin by drawing the line between points 1 and 10 (directly opposite). Progress clockwise, as with the open circle: 10 to 2, 2 to 11, 11 to 3, 3 to 12, 12 to 4, and so on.

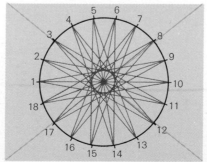

8. Line from point 9 to point 1 completes circle. If you prefer a slightly open circle, begin lines between 1 and 9 or 1 and 8. The fewer points you skip, the wider the inner opening will be.

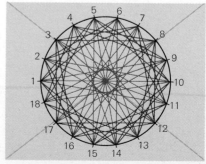

9. To superimpose one circle on another, draw the points and fill in the lines across the circle with the smaller inside opening first. Then, using the same points, fill in the other circle.

121

String art

Drawing an oval

Although it is not as basic to the art as the circle, the oval can be used to great effect in a string picture. As with a circle, the oval can be filled completely or in such a way as to leave an open center. Use a circular protractor to mark off equidistant points on the circumference of the oval.

Although the oval is filled in the same way as the circle, it is more difficult to draw. If you have something the right size and shape, trace it onto your design. If you do not, follow the instructions below. Do the drawing on a board or worktable, as you will have to drive two nails into it in Step 3.

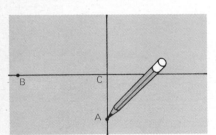

1. Put paper on a board. Divide it into four equal parts with two intersecting lines. Using the intersection of the lines (C) as a center, mark desired width (A) and length (B) of oval on the lines.

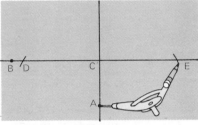

2. Set a compass to reach from B to C (half the length of the oval). Position the point of the compass on A and make a mark on each end of the intersecting line: D and E.

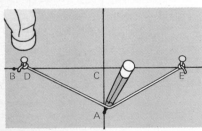

3. Hammer a nail into drawing at D and another at E. Tie one end of a piece of string to nail at D; tie other end to nail at E. Adjust string so that it is taut when pulled to A.

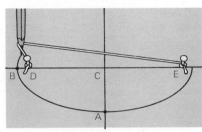

4. Place a pencil against the string and pull the slack taut so that the pencil moves behind one of the nails. Draw the oval, letting the restraint of the string guide the pencil.

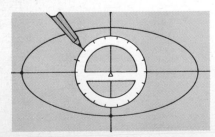

5. Center a protractor on C and draw dots every 20 degrees around it. Run a straightedge through center of circle; copy corresponding dots onto perimeter of oval as with circle (p. 121, Step 3).

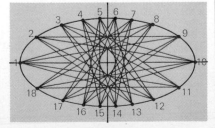

6. Fill in the oval as you would a circle. The oval shown here was filled by drawing the first line from point 1 to point 9, then proceeding clockwise all around the figure.

Curves from straight lines

The basic curved figure is the most important and versatile of all. Draw two lines at right angles to each other and mark off points every 1/4 inch on both lines. Number the points from top to bottom on the vertical line and from left to right on the horizontal line, as in Fig. 1. Then simply draw lines between points of the same number: 1 to 1, 2 to 2, and so on. The curve shown in Fig. 2 will result. If you prefer a figure that is shorter on one side, use a shorter distance between the points of that line, say 1/8 inch. But remember that the distance between points on any one line must be the same. Two parallel lines with the points numbered in opposite directions can be connected in the same way to produce the shape seen in Fig. 3. The shape can be greatly changed by using semicircles or free-form curves in place of one or both straight lines or by placing the straight lines at different angles, as seen in Figs. 4, 5, and 6. (If you use a semicircle, draw it and mark it off with a compass and protractor. The basic curved figure and its variations can be combined to form innumerable string pictures.

Combining basic curved forms

Various designs can be made by combining two or more basic curved forms in different positions. Wherever two forms touch, they can share a common point. If they share a common side, all points on it can serve both forms. Thus two basic curved forms (Fig. 2, p.122) can be drawn with sides together, but only one vertical need be drawn and pointed off. These points will be used to draw lines up to the left and right, resulting in the design seen in Fig. 1. Draw two of the shapes in Fig. 1 with one common base to get the design in Fig. 2. Draw Fig. 1 four times, tips together, to get Fig. 3. Two basic curved forms are connected to form an M on its side, and the space between the forms is filled to get Fig. 4. In Fig. 5 two basic curved forms are joined at one end to form a crescent, and the form in Fig. 1 is superimposed on it. The superimposed form shares points on one side with the crescent. An interlacing of lines results on that side. The box in Fig. 6 is made of four basic curved forms. The forms are drawn normally, but the vertical side of each one shares points with the horizontal side of the adjacent one.

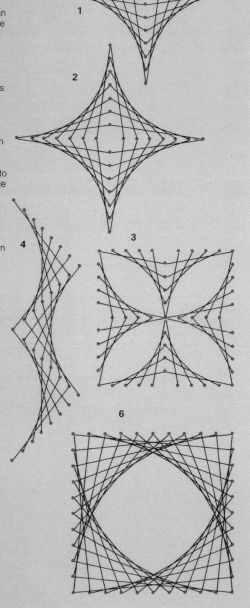

1

2

3

4

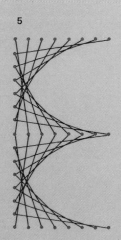
5

6

Preparing the board

Once you have completed your design, draw it to the exact size you want the picture to be. This will serve as a pattern. Then choose a background and appropriate string. You can use heavy fiberboard or wood of any kind, preferably about 1/2 inch thick. Leave the board as is, paint it, stain and varnish it, or cover it with fabric (as shown below). Use the background that will best show up the string you will be using. If you plan to frame the picture, do so after it is finished (see *Picture framing*, pp. 404–408). Otherwise, put a hanging hook on the back before you begin the picture.

1. Place board on wrong side of fabric, pull fabric tightly around sides, and staple it to back.

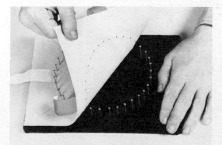

2. Unless you plan to frame the finished piece, nail a picture-hanging hook on back at this point.

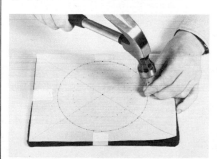

3. Tape pattern to front of covered board. Hammer a nail into each point on the pattern.

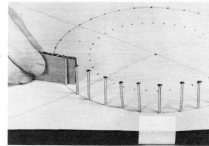

4. To keep all nails at the same height, use a piece of cardboard cut to size as a gauge.

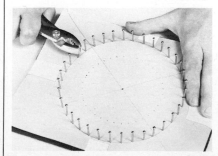

5. If you accidentally hammer a nail in at an angle, straighten it with a pair of pliers.

6. When all the nails are in place, pull off the pattern. The board will then be ready for stringing.

String art

Stringing a three-layered circle

Stringing is the last and most exciting step in string art. Basically, the strings follow the lines drawn in the designs. Instructions for stringing a circle are given below. The circle shown, however, has 36 points—one every 10 degrees. This is twice the number of points used in the drawings on page 121, demonstrating the versatility of the circle design. This circle is more closely knit than the one on page 121. If you want an even tighter texture, use 72 points (one every 5 degrees). The pattern of stringing remains the same, even though the actual numbers change. Ovals are strung in the same way. Other stringing methods are shown on the facing page.

Begin the stringing by tying the end of the string for the first layer onto the beginning nail. Use a simple overhand knot of the type used in tying a shoe-

Tying on: Use simple overhand knot

lace. Bring the string across the board to the nail it must connect with, pass the string around the nail in a clockwise direction, and go to the next nail. Always keep the string taut, but do not pull too hard or you may break it. Keep the layers of string even. Depending on your design, you may want to push the string all the way down, keep it just under the head of the nail, or place it somewhere in between.

The more layers you have, the more depth will be created in the final picture. Always string the lowest sections and sections that will be more thickly filled first—you may not be able to reach the nails to string them later. When you finish with each color of string, tie it off at the last nail it was brought around. To tie off, wrap the string around the nail twice, make a

loop in the string, twist the loop around your finger twice, and slip the loop over the top of the nail. When you pull the

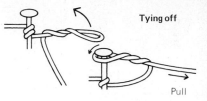

Tying off

Pull

string, the loop will tighten around the nail and hold there. Cut the end off short and tuck it out of sight. If the loose end will not stay in place, fasten it down with a bit of glue.

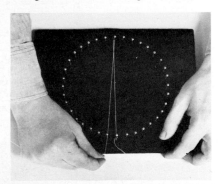

1. Tie end of string to any nail. Call it point 1. Pull string across board, around nail that is 19th down from point 1, and across to point 2.

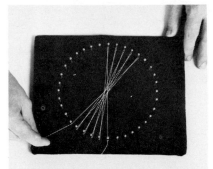

2. Proceed as when drawing circle. Pull string from point 2 to 20, 20 to 3, and so on. Always wrap clockwise. Keep string flat against board.

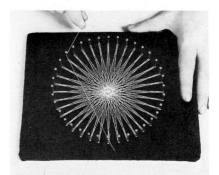

3. When you have completed circle, tie off (see above) at point 1. Tie string of a different color to point 1 and wrap it around point 14.

4. Wrap clockwise, as in first layer, proceeding from point 14 to 2, 2 to 15, and so on. Keep string midway between top and bottom of nail.

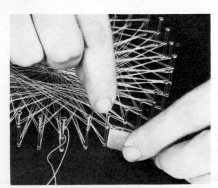

5. Use a piece of cardboard half the height of the exposed nail as a gauge to make sure the string is the same height all around.

6. Upon completion of the second layer, tie off at point 1. Tie string of a third color to point 1 and stretch it to point 9.

7. Continue wrapping clockwise, as before. Keep string just under nail heads. Three layers should be evenly spaced all around circle.

8. Again tie off at point 1. Make any adjustments needed and tuck all the short ends out of sight. If they will not stay, secure them with a bit of glue.

Stringing noncircular forms

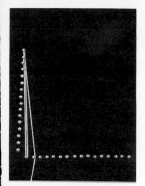

Basic curved forms. Tie onto top nail, wrap string around first horizontal nail.

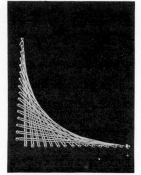

Wrap from point to point, as illustrated on page 122. Tie off when finished and tuck in ends.

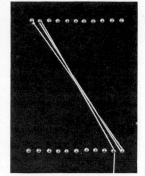

Twist. Tie onto nail at far left on top row, wrap around nail at far right on bottom row.

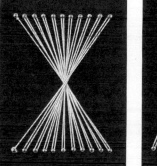

Continue wrapping to right on top and to left on bottom, all across. Tie off, tuck in ends.

Triangle. Tie string to top nail, pull it around lower left nail and back around top nail.

Pull string around each lower nail in turn, moving to right and always returning to top. Tie off.

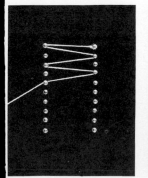

Zigzag. Wrap string across two top nails. Zigzag down, skipping every other nail.

At bottom, pull string straight across as at top, and either tie off or zigzag up again.

If you zigzag up again, tie off on top nail, tuck in ends. This is the double zigzag.

Outlining a figure

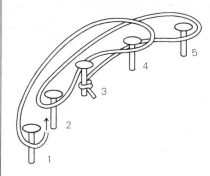

Use woven edging to accentuate a shape. Following pattern, tie onto point 3, pass string around outside of point 4, in and around 5, and down around 2. Proceed around outside of 3, inside of 4, and back around 1. Pull tight. Repeat pattern as needed.

Three-dimensional string art

String art need not be flat. Designs can be lifted away from the board to create free-form sculpture, stabiles, or mobiles by winding the string over or around wooden hoops, standing cylinders, picture frames, plexiglass, or anything else that will accept slots or nails.

This stabile is based on three wooden embroidery hoops that are notched from top to bottom with a saw every 10 degrees around their outside edges. Each hoop is strung with wire in the same way as a circle on a board, except that the wire is wound around the edges of the hoops and fitted into the notches instead of being wound around nails. Deep X-shaped notches are then cut into the ends of a wooden dowel. Wire is fixed into the top notch of the dowel and brought down through one notch in each of the three hoops, through the notch in the bottom of the dowel, up through notches in the opposite sides of the hoops, and back to the top of the dowel. This stringing process is repeated, moving over one notch in the hoops each time, until all the notches are filled. Adapt these general principles to design your own string sculpture.

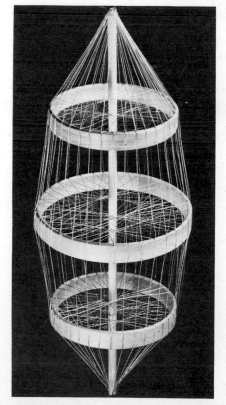

Origami

The art of folding paper

Origami is the ancient Japanese art of folding paper into models that represent people, animals, and plants, or into delicate abstract forms. Most traditional models are made without cutting or gluing: the Japanese word *origami* means "paper folding."

No one knows when or how origami was developed, but it has been a tradition in Japan for many centuries. It was brought to Europe in the Middle Ages. Some drawings by Leonardo da Vinci seem to be of folded paper—one is remarkably like a modern paper airplane. In our own century origami has been used to teach architects how to deal with flat surfaces and to teach math students solid geometry. It is also still practiced as an art throughout the world, and it never fails to delight and entertain children.

Tools and materials. All you really need for origami are paper and your two hands, although some models call for a drop of glue and perhaps a pair of scissors or a razor blade. Any foldable paper of any size will do, but it is best to use special origami paper, which is colored on one side and white on the other. It is available at Japanese novelty stores and hobby shops. The best size is about 6 inches square.

Going beyond. Once you have mastered the models in these pages, you can find other models in pamphlets and books. But better still, you can add a little imagination to your scant store of tools and materials and create your own models. Who knows? If you use enough imagination, your name may one day be revered in the Orient as that of a fine origami artist.

Winged dragon is a complex origami model that begins with the simple bird base.

Some basics of folding

When making a model from this book, follow the sketches and read the captions step by step. Broken lines in a sketch show you where to fold, and the completed fold is shown in the next sketch. A line made up entirely of dashes indicates that you should fold up, toward you. This is called a valley fold. A line made up of dots and dashes indicates that you should fold down, away from you. This is called a mountain fold. These folds will be shown like this:

| Valley fold | Fold up | Mountain fold | Fold down |

The reverse fold is often used for animal legs, necks, and tails. Begin with doubled paper. **1.** Make a valley fold where indicated. **2.** Unfold to beginning position in preceding step. **3.** Open paper slightly and push corner to be folded inside. **4.** Smooth down folds.

1   2   3   4

The preliminary fold is used to begin many origami figures. Start it by folding a square piece of paper in half diagonally to form a triangle. Fold the triangle in half to form a second triangle, then follow drawings below. **1.** Lift top triangle until it is perpendicular to bottom one. **2.** Push down upper tip, squashing it to form model shown in next drawing. **3.** Turn model over and repeat Steps 1 and 2 on back. **4.** The result is the preliminary fold.

1   2   3   4

Baby frog, a beginner's project

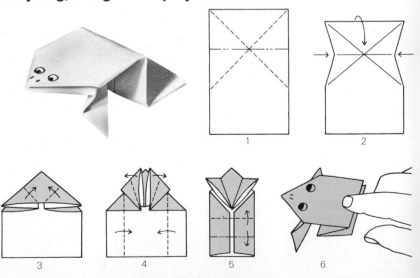

1   2

3   4   5   6

If you are new to origami, try this baby frog first. Use a 3- by 5-in. index card. **1.** Remembering to distinguish between mountain and valley folds (see *Some basics of folding*, left), make folds indicated one at a time and unfold each immediately. **2.** Push in sides of card at crease and smooth down resulting triangular form. **3–5.** Make all folds indicated, turn figure over, and draw a face on it. **6.** To make the frog jump, push down gently on its back with your finger, then slide your finger off.

Origami/projects

Working with the frog base

A large number of origami models share certain initial folds. The incomplete models resulting from these folds are called bases. There are some half dozen common bases, the most versatile of which are the bird base (treated on pages 128–129) and the frog base (shown below). From the frog base you can make a wide variety of marvelous models, including the jumping frog and the lily at right.

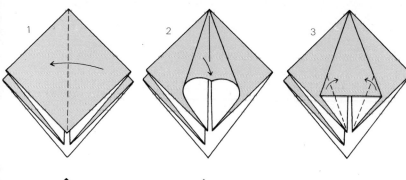

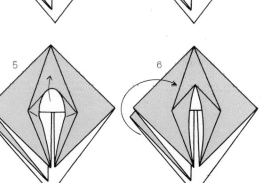

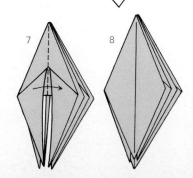

Frog base. 1. Make a preliminary fold and raise one flap until it is perpendicular to the whole. **2.** Squash it down to center line and smooth down fold. **3.** Make folds indicated meet at center. **4.** Make valley fold and undo it. Reach in and pull the edge toward the top. **5.** Continue to pull until sides meet at center. **6.** Smooth down folds. Repeat Steps 1–6 on back and both sides. **7.** Turn left flap of model like a book page to give a smooth surface on top. Repeat on back. **8.** Completed frog base should have four flaps on each side. Continue with directions at right to make frog (symbol of love and fertility in Japan) or lily.

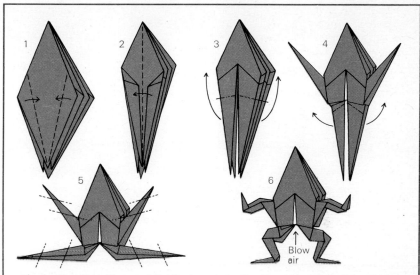

Jumping frog. Use stiff paper. **1.** Fold in sides of a frog base to middle crease. Repeat on back and sides. **2.** Fold top right flap to left; repeat on back. **3.** Bring up two top points in reverse folds. **4.** Bring remaining points out in reverse folds. **5.** Fold legs. **6.** Blow into opening at bottom to inflate frog, draw face if you wish. Frog will jump in same manner as baby frog on facing page.

Lily. 1. Fold in top layer of sides of a frog base to meet at center. **2.** Repeat on the back and sides. **3.** Roll down tips to form petals. **4.** Make stamens from thin strips of paper and tuck them into flower. **5.** Roll long strip of green paper into a stem and glue it to blossom. Wrap another strip or two of green paper around stem, letting ends stick out to form leaves.

Origami/projects

Working with the bird base

The crane, the flapping bird, and the dog are three of the many models made from the bird base. The crane is considered lucky by the Japanese, and an ancient legend holds that a magician made one that was so realistic it came to life and flew away. The dog is made from two pieces of paper.

Making a mobile. You can display your origami models on a mobile. Make the crane mobile pictured at right with wire coat hangers, thread, and any number of cranes.

Clip off the tops of the hangers with wire cutters. Straighten out the rest of the wire and cut it to different lengths. Thread a needle and slip the thread through the back of the crane. Knot the end of the thread so that it does not pull through the paper. Cut the other end of the thread and tie it to one end of a length of wire. Tie a second crane to the opposite end of the wire. Others can be hung in between.

Make a second section in the same way. Tie thread to the middle of each section and tie the other end of the thread to a longer piece of wire hanging above it. Move the threads along the wires to balance the mobile. Make as many sections as you wish, varying the lengths of the threads and wires and the number of models.

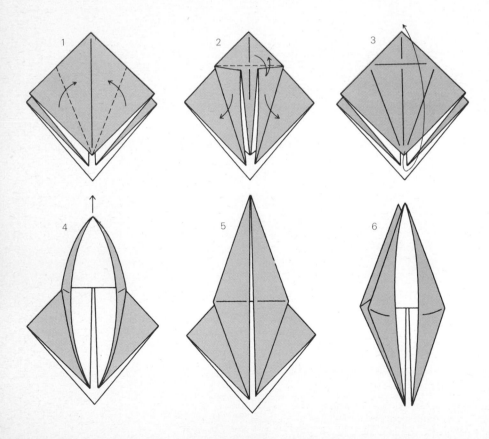

Bird base. 1. Make a preliminary fold (p. 126) and turn its top flaps in to center. **2.** Unfold flaps; fold down top, then unfold it. **3.** With one hand grasp bottom corner of top layer of paper and gently pull it toward top of model, while holding bottom layers down with other hand. **4.** Continue to pull corner up until edges come together at center—you may have to nudge creases with a finger or pull sides in if fold is stubborn. Smooth down the fold. **5.** Turn model over and repeat Steps 1–4 on back. **6.** Bird base is complete.

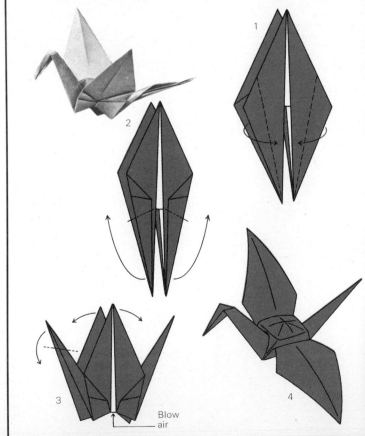

Lucky crane. 1. Fold in sides of a bird base, front and back. **2.** Pull up bottom pieces in reverse folds (see p. 126). **3.** Make reverse fold to form head, then gently pull wings apart and blow through bottom to inflate. **4.** Crane is complete.

Blow air

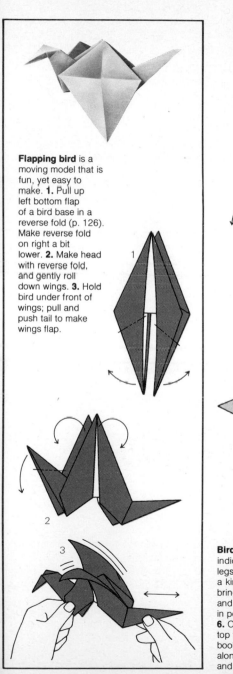

Flapping bird is a moving model that is fun, yet easy to make. **1.** Pull up left bottom flap of a bird base in a reverse fold (p. 126). Make reverse fold on right a bit lower. **2.** Make head with reverse fold, and gently roll down wings. **3.** Hold bird under front of wings; pull and push tail to make wings flap.

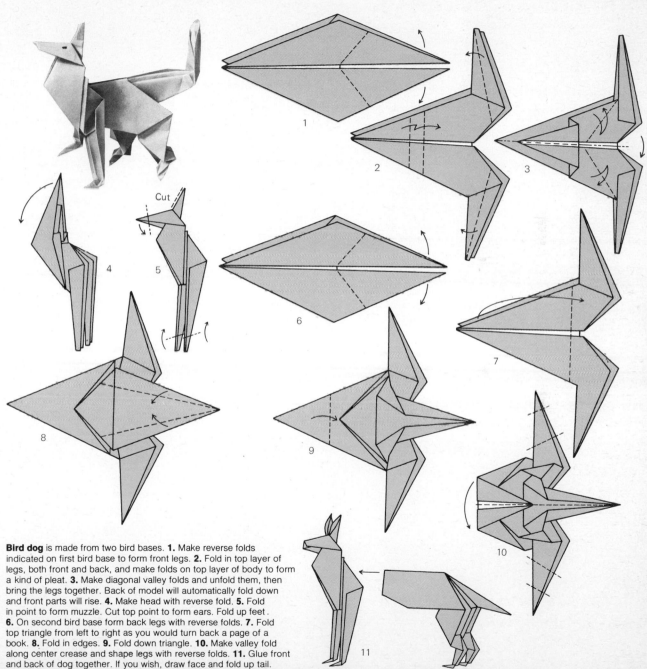

Cut

Bird dog is made from two bird bases. **1.** Make reverse folds indicated on first bird base to form front legs. **2.** Fold in top layer of legs, both front and back, and make folds on top layer of body to form a kind of pleat. **3.** Make diagonal valley folds and unfold them, then bring the legs together. Back of model will automatically fold down and front parts will rise. **4.** Make head with reverse fold. **5.** Fold in point to form muzzle. Cut top point to form ears. Fold up feet . **6.** On second bird base form back legs with reverse folds. **7.** Fold top triangle from left to right as you would turn back a page of a book. **8.** Fold in edges. **9.** Fold down triangle. **10.** Make valley fold along center crease and shape legs with reverse folds. **11.** Glue front and back of dog together. If you wish, draw face and fold up tail.

129

Pottery

Clay in the life of man

Pottery is among man's oldest and most universal crafts. It is important both in its role in the evolution of civilization and as an invaluable source of archeological information.

The earliest surviving pottery often has a corded, basketlike design on its surface. To some scholars this suggests that clay was first used to line baskets so that they would better hold water or small fruits and grains; thereafter, accidental baking in the sun may have led to the discovery that fired clay, on its own, can be used to create nonporous, rigid vessels.

Production of pottery was essential to the development of the first human settlements, as the vessels permitted food to be stored over long periods of time and facilitated cooking and the containment of liquids. Most societies have had distinct pottery forms. Since many early civilizations buried pottery with the dead, graves are the best sources of undamaged pieces. But fragments of pottery (potsherds) are found at almost every archeological site, and these often provide information about both the chronology and character of early human cultures.

Early Pottery. Although the earliest known fired clay, dating from 8000 to 7000 B.C., comes from Mesopotamia, the oldest known pottery vessels, dating from 7000 B.C., were found on the Anatolian Plain of what is now Turkey. These are a crude earthenware, a slightly porous form of pottery fired at a relatively low temperature. Harder pieces, fired at higher temperature, were made 500 years later. By 5000 B.C. pottery was being made in Egypt and throughout the Near East. Decorations were usually simple geometric patterns that were either impressed into the pot or painted on the surface in colored liquid clays, called slips.

This porcelain storage jar was made in China during the Ming Dynasty (15th century A.D.).

The Babylonians and Assyrians used a writing system known as cuneiform, after the wedge shape of its characters. These were impressed into wet clay tablets, which were baked or dried.

The potter's wheel, a rotating disk that enables the potter to make perfectly symmetrical forms, was probably invented in the Near East about 4000 B.C. and was in common use three 1,000 years later. It changed pottery from a domestic chore generally done by women into a man's trade.

Glaze, a substance that is applied to a pot and becomes glassy when fired, is believed to have been invented by the Egyptians about 3500 B.C.

The Far East. Chinese pottery has been the world's standard for technical and artistic excellence since ancient times. The first Chinese pottery may have been made later than in the Middle East, perhaps around 3000 B.C. But fine white stoneware, a hard, nonporous pottery fired at high temperature, was made in China at least by 1400 B.C.—a feat not accomplished in Europe until the 16th century A.D. Glazes were produced by the Chinese by the third century B.C. By the time of the T'ang Dynasty (A.D. 618–906) the Chinese had a full palette of colored glazes. The first true porcelain was also made during the T'ang Dynasty.

The work of the Sung Dynasty (A.D. 960–1279), considered by many to represent a high point in Oriental pottery, is characterized by simple stoneware forms covered by subtle glazes.

During the Ming Dynasty (A.D. 1368–1644) potters rarely bothered to smooth over incidental imperfections in their pots. This practice changed in the Ch'ing Dynasty (A.D. 1644–1912), when many men worked on the same pot. The resulting smooth perfection came at the cost of spontaneity.

The excellence of Chinese pottery is a reflection of its importance in Chinese culture. Spectacular evidence of this was discovered in 1975, when a lifesize army of 6,000 men made of pottery, with armor, weapons, and pottery horses and chariots, dating from 200 B.C., was unearthed near the tomb of an emperor in northwest China.

Korean pottery has always been strongly influenced by the Chinese and has in turn influenced the Japanese. The Koreans introduced a decorative style using inlays of colored clays, called *mishima*. The Japanese have always valued Korean pottery. The prize booty of their invasion of Korea in 1592 is often said to have been the potters they brought back to Japan. Since the 15th century Japanese potters have been greatly influenced by the tea ceremony, for which they devised their most famous wares, a distinctive pottery called *raku*, which is fired at relatively low temperature.

The Aegean and Greece. The first great Aegean pottery was made by the Minoan civilization on Crete during the Cretan Bronze Age (2800–1100 B.C.). It is characterized by colorful abstract and realistic patterns derived from plant and marine life. The vestiges of Minoan motifs can be seen in early Athenian pottery. The Greeks later invented beautiful orange-red and lustrous black slips, which were used in the great Attic black-figure and red-figure pottery painting styles that flourished from 1000 B.C. to 400 B.C.

Islam. Islamic pottery is second only to Chinese in its influence on European pottery, as well as in its technical and artistic excellence. In the ninth century A.D. the Moslems rediscovered tin glaze, which may have been invented by the Assyrians in 1100 B.C., but which was then lost. Tin glazing was later to play a major role in European pottery. The Moslems also popularized, and probably invented, luster, a metallic pigment containing copper, gold, or silver, which is applied over an already fired glaze. Islamic potters concentrated far more on elaborate decoration than on form in their work.

Europe. Because Christians do not bury pottery with their dead, undamaged examples of early Christian pottery are few. The history of European pottery is only well documented from the late Middle Ages.

By the 13th century the use of tin glaze had spread from Moslem Spain into Italy. The Italians painted excellent, elaborate decorations over the plain white tin glaze, a technique called majolica. The French and Dutch later developed their own variations of majolica, called respectively faience and delft. Production of stoneware began in Germany in the 15th century. Italy and France, in the 17th and 18th centuries, developed a form of porcelain called soft-paste porcelain, but the first true European porcelain was made in Germany in 1710. Molds made from plaster of paris came into use in England in 1745, making possible the mass production of intricate pottery shapes. In the late 18th century the English potter Josiah Wedgwood invented jasperware, usually an unglazed pale blue stoneware frequently decorated with white Grecian figures. Around 1800 Josiah Spode II added bone ash to porcelain to make bone china.

The Americas. Native American pottery is fundamentally different from anything in the Old World. The potter's wheel was never invented, and most pottery was made by building coils of clay by hand. The great American civilizations, such as the Aztecs, Mayas, and Incas, produced fine pottery. Some Central American cultures developed a technique of decorating pots similar to batik (see pp. 94–103).

Hacilar, Anatolia
c. 6000 B.C.

Egypt, predynastic
before 3200 B.C.

Minos-Mycenae
1500-1425 B.C.

Greece, black figure
c. 530 B.C.

China, Sung Dynasty
11th-12th centuries A.D.

Islam
16th-17th centuries A.D.

England, Jasperware
18th century A.D.

Pottery

The geologic origins of clay

All pottery is made of clay, an abundant material with remarkable qualities. Clay can be molded into almost any shape. When it is fired, it can become as hard as rock. Clays are found that fire to a full palette of colors, as well as to pure white and jet black. They can be homogenous in color or spotted, streaked, or speckled; as smooth as ivory or as rough as coarse sandpaper. They can be close to glass in translucence or as opaque as stone.

Understanding something of the origins and of the chemical and physical properties of clay can be an invaluable aid in exploiting the full potential of this remarkable medium.

In early geological time, billions of years ago, the earth was a mass of molten material. Over a long period the molten materials in the earth settled into layers; heavier elements, such as metals, sank to deeper levels, while the lighter elements rose to the surface.

This geological settling resulted in a surface layer of relatively light material of nearly uniform composition.

As the surface of the earth cooled into a solid, the molten elements combined to form minerals—natural, inorganic, homogenous substances that have definite chemical compositions. Feldspars are by far the most common minerals, composing almost 60 percent of the earth's crust. Clay is largely the result of the decomposition of feldspar.

About 3.5 billion years ago the earth's surface cooled sufficiently to allow the water vapor in the atmosphere to condense. The resulting torrential downpour, which probably lasted millions of years, began the erosion of the earth's surface that is still going on. Over the ages water, along with wind and glaciers, has reduced mountains to silt, eroding away an incalculable quantity of rock. One of the products of this weathering is clay.

The chemical and physical properties of clay

Because clay is eroded from the earth's surface, its chemical composition is similar to that of the crust as a whole. Below is a comparison of the percentages of oxides in the earth's crust and in common red clay. You can see that there is a preponderance of silicon and aluminum in both. The oxides of these very light elements, called silica and alumina, are, along with water, the essential components of clay. Other compounds found in a clay can be thought of as impurities.

The relative concentrations of alumina, silica, and other elements vary from clay to clay. For example, clays that are fired at a high temperature tend to have a higher concentration of alumina and a lower concentration of iron oxide (Fe_2O_3) than do those clays

that are fired at lower temperatures.

Feldspar, believed the mineral source of most clay, is a generic name for a family of substances. All feldspars contain alumina, silica, and one or more other oxides of an alkaline nature. When a feldspar is broken down by geological erosion, the alkaline part dissolves into the water and is carried away. In a reaction that takes millions of years, the remaining alumina and silica become chemically combined with water, or hydrated. The formula for this reaction is shown below.

Alumina and silica, when hydrated, produce a clay mineral called kaolinite ($Al_2O_3 \cdot 2SiO_2 \cdot 2H_2O$). In nature clay is never found as pure kaolinite. It always contains impurities. However, alumina, silica, and water are the only

compounds that are present in significant quantities in *all* clays.

Primary and secondary clays. Clays can be divided into two broad classifications: primary, or residual, clays and secondary, or sedimentary, clays. Primary clays are made of weathered particles that remain close to their parent rock; they are not carried away by water, wind, or glaciers. Primary clays have relatively large particles, therefore, and are largely free of impurities.

Secondary clays are carried away from their source by eroding forces. As the clay is transported, especially by running water, some of the larger particles settle out of the current. The remaining particles are carried farther and are ground finer by the water. The resulting particles of secondary clays

are smaller than those of primary clays. During their transport secondary clays tend to become mixed with other substances, such as iron, quartz, mica, and organic residue.

Plasticity. The size and surface area of the clay particles are important to the potter because they bear directly on the plasticity of the clay. Plasticity is the quality of clay that allows it to be molded and to hold different shapes without breaking or cracking. (See facing page.)

Clay particles are microscopic in size. When magnified by powerful electron microscopes, they appear thin, flat, and platelike in shape (see electron micrograph on facing page.) Even in primary clays, which have relatively large particles, many are less than 1 micron (.001 millimeter, or .00004 inch) in diameter. When wet, they cling to each other. The smaller the particles are, the more water the clay holds, the tighter the particles cling, and the more plastic the clay is. Because of their particle sizes, sedimentary clays are more plastic than residual clays.

Plasticity is also affected by electrical attraction between the clay particles and by the presence of certain impurities. Aging improves plasticity, probably because of excretions of bacteria that live in the clay.

CHEMICAL	EARTH AS A WHOLE	COMMON RED CLAY
Silicon dioxide (silica)—SiO_2	59.14%	57.64%
Aluminum oxide (alumina)—Al_2O_3	15.34	18.66
Ferric oxide—Fe_2O_3	6.88	6.20
Magnesium oxide (magnesia)—MgO	3.49	2.68
Calcium oxide (lime)—CaO	5.08	5.78
Sodium oxide—Na_2O	3.84	2.35
Potassium oxide—K_2O	3.13	2.10
Water—H_2O	1.15	3.45
Titanium dioxide (titania)—TiO_2	1.05	0.94

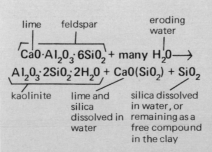

$$\underset{\text{lime}}{\underset{|}{Ca}}O \cdot \underset{\text{feldspar}}{Al_2O_3 \cdot 6SiO_2} + \text{many } \underset{\underset{\text{eroding water}}{|}}{H_2O} \longrightarrow$$

$$\underset{\text{kaolinite}}{Al_2O_3 \cdot 2SiO_2 \cdot 2H_2O} + \underset{\substack{\text{lime and}\\\text{silica}\\\text{dissolved in}\\\text{water}}}{CaO(SiO_2)} + \underset{\substack{\text{silica dissolved}\\\text{in water, or}\\\text{remaining as a}\\\text{free compound}\\\text{in the clay}}}{SiO_2}$$

The geological decomposition of feldspar. Feldspar is broken down by exposure to water over millions of years. The alkaline component of the feldspar, in this case lime, is dissolved away, leaving kaolinite (the clay mineral) and several compounds in solution. This reaction cannot be duplicated in a laboratory.

Drying and shrinking of clay

As clay dries, the water between the particles evaporates and the particles compact to fill the vacated space. The resulting shrinkage of a piece of clay is significant, up to about 8 percent of its wet size. Clay shrinks further when it is fired, as seen in the photographs of five clay slabs at right.

The more water clay holds, the more it shrinks as it dries. Clays with fine particles, which are quite plastic, also hold a lot of water. Therefore, in general, the more plastic a clay is, the more it shrinks as it dries. This is important to remember, because excessive shrinkage can easily result in warping and cracking of the pot.

One way the potter can prevent this is by adding nonplastic materials to the clay. They do not absorb much water, so they promote rapid drying. They also form pores in the clay that facilitate the escape of moisture to the surface. Grog, clay that has been fired and then ground up, is commonly used for this purpose, as are flint and feldspar.

The photographs at right show how clay loses moisture by evaporation during five distinct phases of drying and firing, each resulting in shrinking.

Small rings

Large rings

One measure of plasticity of a clay is its ability to be rolled into a small ring. The three different clays shown at the left are rolled into coils about as thick as a pencil. They can all be made into large rings. However, the degree of cracking and crumbling of the small rings shows that the first clay is the most plastic and the third clay is the least plastic of the group.

Electron micrograph shows particles of kaolin (a type of clay) enlarged 40,000 times. The particles are thin, flat, hexagonal shapes. When they are wet, they stick together, not unlike the way a wet deck of cards sticks together. This is in large part responsible for the plasticity of clay. The particles of most clays are even smaller than the particles of kaolin.

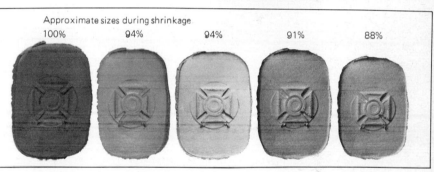

These photographs of five slabs of clay illustrate shrinkage of clay during five stages of drying and firing. The first slab is made of wet, plastic clay. After clay dries for about 12 hours, it becomes rigid but is still wet. This state, called leather hard, is shown by the second slab. Several days later most of the water has evaporated, and the clay is called bone dry (third slab). The fourth slab shows the clay after the first, or bisque, firing. The fifth slab has been fired to maturation temperature. The shrinkage rate will vary with different types of clay.

Approximate sizes during shrinkage
100% 94% 94% 91% 88%

Types of clay

Clays come from different geological sources and vary in the extent of the weathering of particles. In the course of erosion they become mixed with each other, as well as with impurities. Because of these variables in their composition, clays cannot be classified precisely. Potters grade clays according to general type:

Kaolin. Kaolin is a very pure, white, primary clay. Because it has coarse particles, it is not very plastic and shrinks only slightly. It is very refractory—that is, when fired it matures at a very high temperature (1800°C). Because of its low plasticity and high refractoriness, kaolin is rarely used alone. Other materials are mixed with it to enhance its workability and to lower its maturation temperature.

Ball clays. These are fine-grained, highly plastic secondary clays. They are largely free of impurities, and they mature at a high temperature (1300°C). Because of their great shrinkage, up to 20 percent when fired, they cannot be used alone. Ball clays are often mixed with kaolin.

Fire clays. These clays are very refractory, resistant to heat up to a high temperature (1500°C). Some fire clays are quite plastic; others lack plasticity.

Coarse-particled fire clay is sometimes added to stoneware clay to give it more "tooth"—to roughen the texture of the clay and help it hold its shape when wet.

Stoneware. These are plastic clays that are fired to a fairly high temperature (1200°C–1300°C). Sometimes they are used just as they are found in the earth, but more often they are mixed with different clays and other additives.

Earthenware. These are the most common natural clays. They contain significant amounts of iron and other impurities, which act as fluxes—that is, they reduce the maturation temperature of the clay (950°C–1100°C). Unlike stoneware and other higher firing clays, earthenware is somewhat soft and porous after it is fired. Earthenwares vary in their plasticity and color in accordance with the presence of different impurities.

Porcelain. Porcelain is made of kaolin, ball clay, feldspar, and flint (a form of silica). It is the highest firing (1300°C) workable clay, and it fires to a translucent white color. Its low plasticity makes it difficult to use.

Bentonite. This is added to other clays to increase their plasticity.

Pottery

Clay bodies

Clay is rarely used just as it is found in the ground. Usually a blend of clays and other materials can give the potter a combination of qualities more closely suited to his or her needs. A specific mixture of clays and other substances is called a *clay body.*

There are three basic adjustments that can be made to clay to enhance its value to the potter. By adding clays and other materials of varying plasticity and particle size, the plasticity and shrinkage properties of the clay can be altered. By adding clays and other materials of varying maturing or melting temperatures, the maturing temperature of the clay can be altered. By adding clays and other materials of different colors and textures, the color and texture of the clay can be altered.

The common mixing formulas, or recipes, for seven different clay bodies are given at right. The compositions of clay bodies vary greatly with their intended use. The mixing formulas suggested here are especially good for hand building and for use on the potter's wheel.

Firing temperatures in pottery are measured in units called cones, usually ranging from about cone 020 to cone 14. A table of cones and their corresponding kiln temperatures can be found on page 167.

Earthenware. Earthenware bodies are fired to low temperatures, usually below cone 1 but sometimes up to cone 5. Porous when fired, they come in a range of beautiful colors that are unattainable in higher firing clays.

Most of the clays found in the earth are earthenware clays, which can sometimes be used almost in their natural state (see *Digging and preparing your own clay* on facing page). Clay companies also sell earthenware, or common red, clays.

In the ingredients list for earthenware clay body 1, at right, the fire clay and grog add "tooth" to the clay. This reduces its shrinkage, makes its texture rougher, and helps it hold its shape when it is wet. The ball clay increases its plasticity.

In earthenware clay body 2, ball clay is needed to increase the plasticity of the relatively unplastic fire clay. Because fire clay is also very refractory (very high firing), soda feldspar and talc are added as fluxes to lower the maturing temperature. Flint helps prevent the clay from warping.

Earthenwares that are fired between cone 1 and cone 5 approach the hardness of stoneware, yet remain porous and retain color possibilities not available at high temperatures. In earthenware clay body 3 the stoneware clay and the fire clay raise the common red clay's maturation temperature.

Stoneware. These clay bodies fire to a hard, nonporous texture, between cone 6 and cone 14. Stoneware formulas tend to be simpler than those for earthenware, because the higher firing temperatures make less flux necessary.

The atmosphere in the kiln during firing at high temperatures is sometimes altered to affect the color and texture of the glaze. A reducing atmosphere removes oxygen from the glaze; an oxidizing atmosphere adds oxygen. (This process is discussed in detail on pp. 167–168). The change in atmosphere affects the color of the clay as well as of the glaze. Stoneware clay bodies 4, 5, and 6 can be fired in either reducing or oxidizing atmospheres but will look best if fired as suggested.

Porcelain. These bodies are fired above cone 9. Bentonite is added to porcelain body 7 to increase plasticity.

All of the clays and chemicals listed in the clay body formulas can be purchased at a ceramic supply house. Most potters have favorite formulas. After you try these, you can make minor alterations to suit your taste.

EARTHENWARE CLAY BODIES	FORMULAS (parts per hundred)
1. Fires to a reddish color and matures between cone 08 and cone 1	59 common red clay 23 red fire clay 9 ball clay 9 grog
2. Fires white and matures between cone 08 and cone 1	50 fire clay 26 ball clay 8 flint 8 soda feldspar 8 talc
3. Fires red and matures between cone 1 and cone 5	45 fire clay 30 common red clay 15 stoneware clay 10 feldspar

STONEWARE CLAY BODIES	
4. Fires toasty brown in an oxidizing atmosphere and matures between cone 6 and cone 9	45 fire clay 23 stoneware clay 23 common red clay 9 soda feldspar
5. Fires dark orange-brown in a reducing atmosphere and matures at cone 9 or 10	35 stoneware clay 35 fire clay 10 common red clay 10 flint 10 grog
6. Fires white in an oxidizing atmosphere and matures at cone 6	38 kaolin 21 potash feldspar 20 flint 9 silica sand 9 nepheline syenite 3 bentonite

PORCELAIN CLAY BODY	
7. Fires creamy white in an oxidizing atmosphere, fires white with a bluish tint in a reducing atmosphere, and matures at cone 9 or cone 10	54 kaolin (china clay) 22 potash feldspar 22 flint 2 bentonite

Earthenware

Stoneware

Porcelain

Colors and textures of clay

In general, a reducing atmosphere in a kiln will bring out cooler tones in clay than will an oxidizing atmosphere. The color of the clay body can also be affected by adding chemicals.

A light-colored clay will fire red or brown if 2 to 4 parts per hundred of red iron oxide are added. Similar amounts of iron oxide plus 2 parts manganese dioxide will turn a clay gray-brown. Manufacturers make stains that will dye light-colored clay bodies different colors, such as blue, green, or ocher.

Clays can be speckled by adding granular manganese dioxide, colored grog, or bits of iron, such as iron filings or flakes of rust.

Two clays of different colors can be mixed to give a marbled or mottled appearance. Be sure the clays have similar shrinkage properties, or the pot will warp or crack as it dries.

The physical texture of clay can be roughened by the addition of coarse grog or rough fire clay, up to 40 percent of the clay body.

The correct percentage of additives for a specific effect can be found only by experimentation. As you mix in chemicals, remember that some additives have more than one effect on the clay. For example, iron oxide is a powerful flux as well as a colorant, grog reduces plasticity as it adds "tooth" (roughens texture), and clay reacts with the glaze that covers it.

Buying, preparing, and storing clay

Clay can be bought wet or dry. Wet clay comes in batches of 25 pounds or more. If there is a specific clay body formula you want, some clay companies will mix it for you.

Buying dry clays saves you the trouble of transporting all the water in wet clay, but more work is required to prepare it. Weigh out the dry components of your clay body (p. 134) and thoroughly mix them in a large container. Gradually sprinkle on water, mixing the clay constantly until it becomes workable. Before using the clay, let it sit, wrapped in plastic or in a covered container, for a few days.

If you are mixing clay bodies using wet clay, you must first add a lot of water in order to break down the lumps. This solution of clay is called a *slip*. Mix the slip thoroughly, either mechanically with a blunger (a vat with stirrers) or by hand, until the lumps are gone. Let the slip sit for several days and siphon the excess water off the top. Put the remaining slip on a porous wooden or plaster surface (for example, a wedging board, see p. 140) until it is firm enough to use.

Clay can be stored in any airtight container, such as a trash can or plastic bag. Place a damp towel in the container to keep the clay moist.

If clay becomes too hard, slice it up, sprinkle water on it, and put it back into the container. If a piece gets very hard, put it in a bucket of water and it will eventually turn into slip. Until it is fired, clay can be used, dried, wetted, and reused indefinitely.

You may find fresh clay difficult to work. Clay becomes more plastic as it ages. The aging process can be expedited by adding a mild acid to the clay, such as vinegar or a carbonated beverage. Use about 8 fluid ounces per 100 pounds. In a month or two the clay will become noticeably more plastic.

Digging and preparing your own clay

Digging your own clay saves the cost of buying and shipping commercial clay, but it requires time and hard work. Nevertheless, there is an unmistakable lure to making a pot out of clay that you find and dig up yourself.

Because clay generally lies several feet beneath surface soil, the easiest place to gain access to it is where the earth has been cut away, such as beside a building foundation, road, or stream. Frequently it has a dry, crumbly texture. If you find earth that might be clay, take a handful and wet it. If it becomes plastic, not muddy, it is clay.

Avoid clay that is covered with white scum or stain or that is black and very sticky. Such clay is mixed with impurities that will cause problems when you try to use it. If you are going to need a lot of clay, try to find an area where the color of the clay is uniform.

Dig up the clay and spread it out on boards to dry hard in the sun. Drying may take several days. Cover the clay if it rains. When the clay is dry, break up the lumps with a mallet and pick out the rocks, twigs, and other debris. Then mix it with water to make slip. After several hours screen it through a 40-mesh sieve and put it on boards or a plaster surface to dry indoors.

Clay can sometimes be used as it is found, but more often additives are needed to enhance or correct certain qualities. Several tests can be made to determine which additives are needed.

To test for plasticity, try out the clay in the same way you will use it later. If it breaks or cracks, its plasticity must be increased. If it is too sticky, its plasticity must be decreased. See the chart at right for suggested additives.

Test for maturation temperature by trial firings. Make four slabs of clay, 6 inches by 2 inches by ½ inch, and lay them across two supports inside the kiln. Fire one each to cones 08, 04, 1, and 4. The clay will become denser and harder the higher it is fired, until it reaches its maturation temperature. Above that it will sag, then melt. Because most of the clay you are likely to find will be earthenware, your clay may deform above cone 1. You can raise or lower the maturation temperature of your clay, or change the density it achieves at any given temperature, by altering it as suggested in the chart.

Shrinkage can be tested by scratching two marks 4 inches apart on a slab of wet clay and then firing it to maturation temperature. The shrinkage can be calculated by the formula:

(4 – the number of inches between marks after firing) × 25 = % shrinkage

If shrinkage is above 16 percent, the clay will probably warp or crack when you fire your pots. Consider using the proper additives to reduce shrinking, as suggested in the chart.

TO ACHIEVE:	ADD:
Greater plasticity	Ball clay (up to 25%)
	Bentonite (up to 3%)
Less plasticity or lower shrinkage	Grog (up to 20%)
	Flint (up to 15%)
	Fire clay (up to 25%)
Lower maturation temperature or greater density	Iron oxide (up to 25%)
	Talc (up to 40%)
	Frits (up to 15%)
Higher maturation temperature	Kaolin (up to 25%)
	Fire clay (up to 25%)
	Stoneware clay (up to 50%)
	Ball clay (up to 25%)
	Flint (up to 15%)

Pottery

Tools

Most of the work in creating pottery can be accomplished with the hands alone. However, there are some tools that you will find necessary, as well as some others that you will find useful. None of them is expensive, and all can be purchased at a ceramic supply house. Perfectly acceptable substitutes for most of the tools can be easily improvised.

A potter's, or fettling, knife has many uses. However, any household or paring knife will do as well.

A pin or needle mounted on a handle is used for scoring and cutting clay.

Wire and ribbon tools, in various sizes and shapes, are used for cutting and trimming pots.

Wooden modeling tools come in different sizes, shapes, and textures. They are used to smooth, shape, and texture pots as well as to reach their difficult interior recesses.

Sponges are used to wet, smooth, and then remove the excess water from pots made on the potter's wheel. A natural sponge, called an elephant's ear, is more durable than most artificial sponges. A sponge attached to the end of a stick will be needed for work on deep, narrow-necked pots.

A piece of fishing line or wire attached to two small handles should be used to cut finished pieces off the potter's wheel.

Wooden or rubber ribs are used to shape pieces on the wheel.

Calipers are used to measure pots so that they can be duplicated, or so that a top can be made to fit precisely.

A rolling pin or dowel is used to make clay slabs of even thickness.

Brushes are used to apply slips and glazes to pots. Fine Japanese brushes are good for intricate work, and larger flat brushes are good for uniform application on large surfaces.

An extruder with a changeable head makes strands of clay in various shapes.

Removable plaster bats can be placed on the head of the potter's wheel. They make it much easier to remove finished pots from the wheel.

A ruler can be used for measuring and as a paddle to change the texture on wet pots.

A banding wheel is a small turntable that can be rotated by hand. It is used in hand building projects and sometimes for applying slips and glazes.

A syringe is used to apply lines of slips and glazes to pots.

Screens of various meshes are used to sieve slips and glazes.

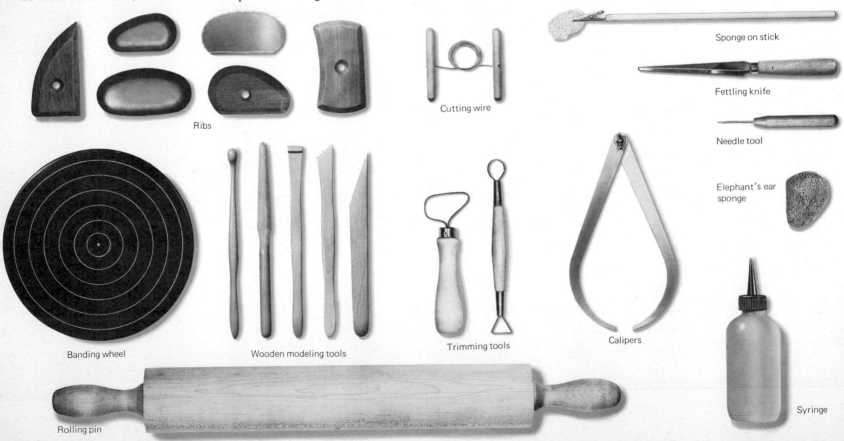

Ribs

Cutting wire

Sponge on stick

Fettling knife

Needle tool

Elephant's ear sponge

Banding wheel

Wooden modeling tools

Trimming tools

Calipers

Rolling pin

Syringe

The potter's wheel

Making pottery on the potter's wheel, called throwing, is the most popular and most difficult of the pottery techniques. You can get an idea of the range of possibilities of things you can make on the wheel by looking at *Throwing on the wheel,* pages 146–161.

There are basically two types of potter's wheels. The first is the kick wheel, which is powered by the potter, who kicks a heavy flywheel attached by a shaft to the wheelhead. The second is the electric wheel, which is powered by a variable speed electric motor.

The kick wheel. The design of the kick wheel has changed little in the 6,000 years since its invention. Some potters like the kick wheel because of this tradition. They also think the kick wheel is more sensitive than the electric wheel, because its speed can be controlled more precisely. Perhaps the greatest advantage of the kick wheel is its cost, which is a small fraction of that of an electric wheel.

Plans for building a kick wheel are given on this page. The flywheel in this model is a thin, heavy disk. Two possibilities are a manhole cover or similar cast-iron disk, which you can purchase from a foundry, or a concrete well cover, which you can get from a masonry supplier for very little money. The flywheel must be an evenly balanced disk that weighs at least 100 pounds. As an inexpensive alternative to a metal disk or a well cover, you can use bricks or cinder blocks sandwiched between disks cut from plywood.

The bearings are available at bearing distributors (listed in your telephone book Yellow Pages). The flanges can be bought at an engineering supply store or made out of pieces of iron or steel from a plumbing supply store or a junkyard. Pipe for a shaft is available at a plumbing or hardware store; the wood comes from a lumberyard.

(continued on page 138)

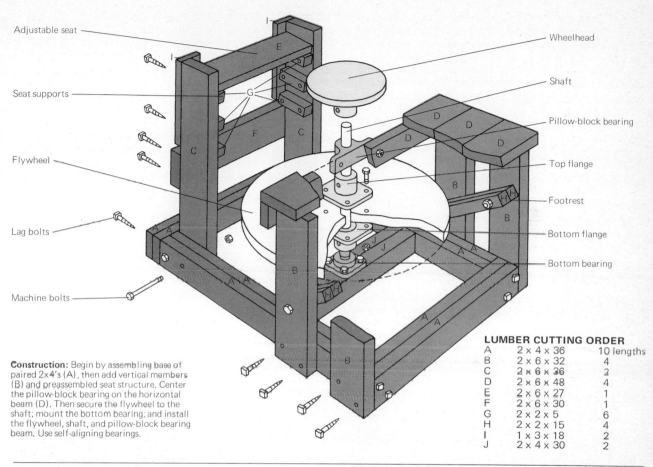

Construction: Begin by assembling base of paired 2x4's (A), then add vertical members (B) and preassembled seat structure. Center the pillow-block bearing on the horizontal beam (D). Then secure the flywheel to the shaft; mount the bottom bearing; and install the flywheel, shaft, and pillow-block bearing beam. Use self-aligning bearings.

LUMBER CUTTING ORDER

A	2 x 4 x 36	10 lengths
B	2 x 6 x 32	4
C	2 x 6 x 36	2
D	2 x 6 x 48	4
E	2 x 6 x 27	1
F	2 x 6 x 30	1
G	2 x 2 x 5	6
H	2 x 2 x 15	4
I	1 x 3 x 18	2
J	2 x 4 x 30	2

Securing the flywheel to the shaft

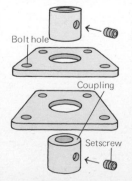

Bolt hole

Coupling

Setscrew

The flywheel is held by two flanges, one of which rests on the bottom bearing. Each flange is a steel plate with a hole cut to take a pipe coupling, which is welded in place. Holes are drilled in the couplings for setscrews and in the plates for connecting bolts.

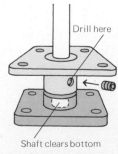

Drill here

Shaft clears bottom

Put shaft through bottom flange and into bearing, but not quite all the way through. Drill through setscrew hole in coupling into shaft to depth of 3/16 in. Turn in setscrew. This secures flange to shaft and prevents shaft from slipping through bearing.

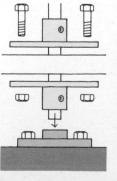

Attach the bottom bearing to the frame. With bottom flange attached to shaft, set shaft into bottom bearing. Put flywheel onto shaft and add the top flange. Bolt two flanges, flywheel together. Drill into shaft for setscrews on top flange. Tighten screw.

Pottery

The potter's wheel (continued)

You can also form a concrete flywheel right on your kick wheel by making a round plywood mold supported in place on the wheel frame, laying in a few iron rods for reinforcement, and pouring in wet concrete. Bearings and flanges can usually be improvised. If you rummage around a junkyard, you can find the materials to build a wheel for almost nothing.

Because the parts you use may vary from those shown in the plans, you may have to compensate by adjusting the size of the frame. There are, however, three dimensions that you should maintain in your design: the distance from the middle of the wheel to the middle of the seat should be about 18 inches; the distance from the wheelhead to the top of the flywheel should be about 25 inches; and the seat should be about as high as the wheelhead (see drawing below).

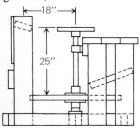

Kick wheels can be bought already constructed or in a kit form. Constructed wheels can cost over $300, plus the cost of shipping them. Some kits contain only the metal parts and plans for the wooden frame. Others also include the wood. This makes building the wheel easier, but it is also more expensive than building a kick wheel from scratch.

The electric wheel. The electric wheel is lighter and more transportable than the kick wheel. It is also smaller, so it requires less floor space. Because it is powered by a motor, it saves the potter from the fatigue caused by kick-ing a heavy flywheel. Electric wheels generally have greater torque than kick wheels, enabling the potter to make larger pots. The motor also frees the potter to concentrate solely on hand techniques. For this reason it is easier to learn to throw on an electric wheel than on a kick wheel.

The great liability of the electric wheel is its price—most good ones cost over $400. If you decide to invest in an electric wheel, look around carefully before you make your choice. There are many electric wheels on the market, and some of them are not as good as others. Below are some things you should look for in an electric wheel:
—The wheel should have a speed range of 0–200 rpm. The pedal should let you change speeds perfectly smoothly and stop at any speed you desire.
—The pedal should change the speed of the wheel gradually. That is, the wheel should not go from 0 to 200 rpm as you move the pedal 1/4 inch, then remain at that speed as the pedal uselessly moves farther.
—The motor and wheelhead should turn smoothly, without vibration.
—Press your fists on the wheelhead as hard as you can while the wheel is turning. If you can stop it, the motor is too weak.
—The wheelhead must be made of smooth metal.
—The wheel should be designed so that it is easy to clean. The surfaces should be resistant to corrosion.
—Be sure service and spare parts are readily available.

There is also a wheel that combines the features of the electric wheel and the kick wheel, called a motorized kick wheel. The motorized kick wheel can be driven by a motor that turns the flywheel with a rubber friction wheel; or the motor can be disengaged at will so that the wheel can be driven by the potter's foot.

The kiln

After a pot is constructed and left to dry, it is fired at high temperature (usually more than 1100°C) in a special oven called a kiln. A kiln is made of a refractory material (usually brick) that holds the heat within a chamber. The volume of kiln chambers can range from 1/2 cubic foot to 30,000 times that size. Kilns can be heated by anything from burning dung to solar energy, though electricity, gas, coal, and wood are the most common heat sources.

Electric kilns. An electric kiln consists of a chamber of refractory brick lined with rows of coiled electric heating elements. The elements heat the pots in the chamber by radiation, unlike fuel-burning kilns, which heat by the convection of hot air and gases through the chamber.

Electric kilns have some distinct advantages over fuel-burning kilns. Because they are clean-firing, safe, relatively portable, and often run on household current, they can be used almost anywhere. They are easy to operate. The heat in electric kilns is very evenly distributed, which makes for predictable results in firing. They are relatively inexpensive—you can get small used ones for well under $100.

Electric kilns also have their drawbacks. The elements burn out and have to be replaced. The kiln cannot be much more than 24 inches in width; otherwise the heat from standard coils will not reach the center of the chamber. The upper firing limit of electric kilns is usually cone 10 (see p. 167) or lower, unless special elements and insulation are used. Reduction firing cannot be done without causing damage to the elements.

If you decide to buy an electric kiln, keep the following factors in mind:
—The heating elements should be made by a reliable manufacturer.
—The elements should be set into deep grooves in the kiln wall. This prevents the elements from being broken. The

Electric Kiln

This inexpensive electric kiln is called a sectional kiln because rings of refractory brick can be added or removed to alter its height. The elements are recessed into the walls to prevent breaking. Other types of electric kilns have additional elements in the top and bottom. The automatic shutoff is built into the kiln wall.

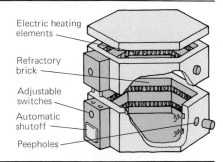

Electric heating elements
Refractory brick
Adjustable switches
Automatic shutoff
Peepholes

Updraft Kiln

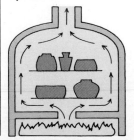

In an updraft kiln heat enters the chamber from the firebox below and exits through a flue at the top. In the primitive kiln on the facing page the firebox is inside the brick chamber.

Downdraft kiln

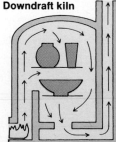

A downdraft kiln is more efficient than the updraft. It utilizes a chimney to create a draft that sucks the hot gases into the chamber from the firebox and out the exit flues in the bottom of the chamber.

grooves should be big enough to make replacing the elements easy.

—The kiln should have switches for the elements that adjust for low, medium, and high heat. No more than two rows of elements should connect to each switch.

—An automatic kiln shutoff, which is activated when the kiln reaches a certain temperature, saves the potter from having to sit and watch the kiln all day. They are available on most kilns. You should also get a timer that will shut the kiln off in case the automatic temperature shutoff fails. This will prevent the kiln from overfiring and burning out.

—Be sure the voltage and amperage demands of the kiln are compatible with the capacity of the socket you plan to use.

—Buy from a company where service and parts are readily available.

Fuel-burning kilns. Fuel-burning kilns come in a great variety of sizes and designs. They are classified by the type of fuel they use and by the direction of convection the hot gases take inside the kiln chamber.

Many fuels can be used to fire a kiln, but some are impractical and others can have a deleterious effect on the ware in the kiln. The most common fuel in urban areas is natural gas, which burns cleanly, without smoke. Rural potters also use coal and wood. Wood is particularly valued for the effect its residue has on the finish of the pots.

The fuel is burned in a part of the bottom of the kiln called the firebox. The hot gases either enter the kiln chamber from the bottom and go out the top or enter the kiln chamber from the bottom, circulate through the kiln, and exit out a flue in the bottom, drawn out by a draft created by a chimney. The first of these, called an updraft kiln, is cheaper and easier to build but is less efficient with fuel than the second. The second, called a downdraft kiln, is expensive and complex, but it is efficient with fuel and heats the kiln chamber more evenly. These two kiln types appear on the preceding page.

Fuel-burning kilns are usually quite large because about half of their inside space is used up by the firebox and by the area that must be left free for the circulation of gases. They are constructed of heavy refractory brick, which is fairly expensive. Thus the cost of a fuel-burning kiln, even if you build it yourself, is quite high. Kilns can be built out of nonrefractory brick (see below), but they are of limited versatility. If you do not wish to invest in a fuel-burning kiln, there are usually gas kilns at schools, Y's, and crafts centers that you can use for a small fee.

The reason for the popularity of fuel-burning kilns, in spite of their cost, is that they can fire either with an oxidizing or a reducing atmosphere. This allows the potter to achieve a much greater range of glaze colors and textures than by oxidation alone. Fuel-burning kilns also can fire higher than electric kilns, permitting the use of a greater range of clays.

As with the kick wheel, some potters prefer fuel-burning kilns because of their tradition, which goes back thousands of years. You can make a primitive kiln, using common red bricks, by following the directions below. This is a simple updraft kiln, which will reach temperatures high enough for firing earthenware or raku. Because of the many air intake flues in the kiln, the fuel (wood or charcoal) burns efficiently, with very little smoke. But because there is no top to the kiln, much of the heat is lost. Therefore, the kiln will consume a great deal of fuel to reach temperature.

Pots are not put right into the kiln, but are first put into a container, called a sagger, which protects them from flames and soot. Sagger construction, and the entire firing process, are discussed in detail on pages 167–168.

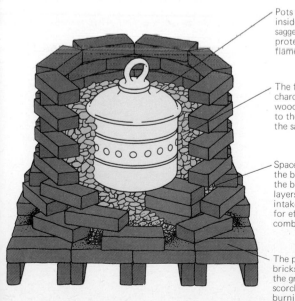

Pots are placed inside the sagger for protection from flames and soot.

The fuel, charcoal or wood, is stacked to the top of the sagger.

Spaces between the bricks in the bottom three layers allow the intake of air for efficient combustion.

The platform of bricks prevents the ground from scorching or burning during firing.

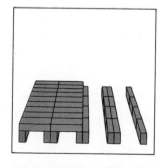

1. Arrange eight rows of four bricks, on their sides, to act as runners. Lay a 4-by-9 layer of bricks flat on top of the runners, as shown. This base prevents the ground from scorching or melting when the kiln is fired.

2. Place eight bricks in the shape of a regular octagon on top of the base. Leave a 2-in. gap between each pair of bricks for air intake flues. Put two stacks of three bricks each in the center, to support the sagger.

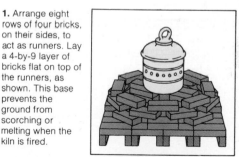

3. Place a second layer of eight bricks on top of the first, staggering them as shown. Leave a 1½-in. gap between the bricks. Stagger a third layer of eight on top of the second, leaving a 1-in. gap between every two bricks.

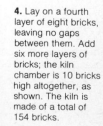

4. Lay on a fourth layer of eight bricks, leaving no gaps between them. Add six more layers of bricks; the kiln chamber is 10 bricks high altogether, as shown. The kiln is made of a total of 154 bricks.

Pottery

Wedging

Screw eye

Turnbuckle

Fishing line

Plaster

Nails

Nails

Screw eye

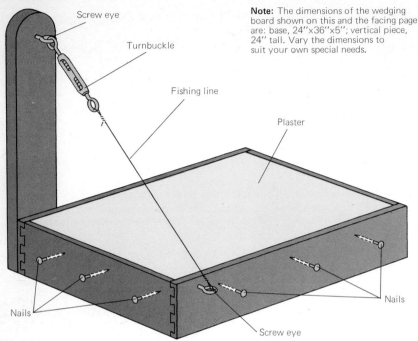

Note: The dimensions of the wedging board shown on this and the facing page are: base, 24"x36"x5"; vertical piece, 24" tall. Vary the dimensions to suit your own special needs.

Before clay is used to make pottery, it is kneaded into a homogeneous mass by a process called *wedging*. It is best to do wedging on a special plaster-filled wedging board, for which the plans are shown above.

After you construct the wooden frame, you should varnish it to protect it from the water in the plaster. Mix the plaster with water in the proportions recommended by the manufacturer, and pour it into the frame, as shown in Steps 1 to 6. The nails projecting from the sides of the frame help to support the plaster. Plain wood or a slab of concrete can be used instead of plaster.

Wedging evenly distributes moisture throughout the clay. It removes lumps and irregularities, eliminates air pockets, and compacts and aligns the clay particles. This makes the clay easier to work with and helps prevent it

from warping, cracking, or exploding during firing.

Wedging can be done in several ways. You can follow the methods shown in Steps 1 to 10 on the next page or invent your own method of kneading. All that matters is that you end up with a homogeneous mass, as shown in Step 9. Whatever method you use, be careful not to make deep finger impressions in the clay or to fold the clay over so that air becomes trapped in it. Plaster absorbs water, so the longer you wedge, the drier and harder the clay becomes. Several minutes of wedging are usually sufficient—do not wedge for too long.

Oxides and stains are sometimes added to the clay to change its color (see *Colors and textures of clay*, p. 135). These can be mixed in during wedging, as shown in Steps 11 and 12.

Making the board

1. Slowly sprinkle plaster into a bucket of water. When plaster is no longer absorbed into water, but sits on surface, you have added enough.

2. Stir plaster thoroughly with your hand or a stick. Let the plaster sit for a few minutes, then pour it into the wooden frame.

3. When the frame is filled to a little over the top edge, strike the side of the frame with a hammer. This eliminates air bubbles.

4. Smooth the surface by pulling a piece of wood over the top of the frame. You will feel heat from the plaster as it starts to set.

5. Fill any small depressions on the surface with more plaster, then smooth them over. Work quickly—the plaster hardens rapidly.

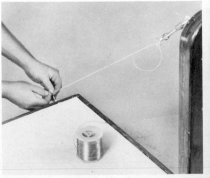

6. Tie a piece of fishing line from the turnbuckle to the screw eye. Let the board sit for several weeks before you use it.

Using the board

1. Tear off a piece of clay about the size of a small grapefruit. It should be moist and firm—not soft and sticky or hard and dry.

2. Place the clay on the wedging board. Push the clay firmly downward and forward with the heels of your hands, as shown.

3. Push with your hands until the clay flattens against the wedging board. If you lift your hands, the clay will look something like a "bull's face."

4. Pull the far edge of the clay up until the slab is vertical. Push the top of the clay down again, as shown in Steps 2 and 3.

5. Repeat Steps 2–4 for several minutes. Cut clay open by pushing it against fishing line. If there are air pockets (as shown), more wedging is needed.

6. Throw the two halves of the clay on the wedging board hard, one half on top of the other. This action helps to break up air pockets.

7. Steps 7 and 8 show a variation of the conventional wedging process. First push the clay down with your hands, as illustrated in Step 2.

8. As you lift the clay, rotate the edge toward you. Then push down and continue wedging. This is called the spiral method.

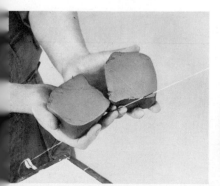

9. Test the clay. Slice it open on the fishing line. If the clay is homogeneous, without air holes, as shown, it is ready to be used.

10. When you are done wedging the clay, slap it into a spherical shape. It is easiest to start most pottery projects from this shape.

11. In order to add coloring oxides or stains to the clay, make an indentation in the clay and sprinkle in the correct amount.

12. After adding color, wedge the clay thoroughly, as shown in the steps above. The color will spread evenly throughout the clay.

Pottery

Hand building: pinch method

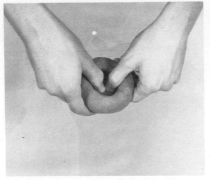

1. Sink your thumbs into the ball of clay, leaving a base of 1/4–1/2 in. Start to open the hole by lightly squeezing the clay from the inside.

There are several ways of forming a finished shape from a lump of clay. The hand-building techniques, unlike throwing on the potter's wheel, do not involve the use of any special equipment. Because of this, they are easier to master and far cheaper than work on the wheel. Hand-building methods can be combined, and they easily lend themselves to improvisation.

There are three basic hand-building methods. The pinch method, in which clay is simply squeezed into its finished shape, is shown on this page. In the coil method (shown on this and the facing page) clay is rolled into ropes (called coils), which are then assembled. The slab method, in which clay is flattened into slabs and then assembled, is shown on page 144. Three hand-built projects are shown on page 145.

The pinch method. The pinch method is the simplest hand-building technique, involving only the use of the hands. Wedge a ball of clay about the size of an orange, and shape it as shown in the steps at right. Do not make the lip too thin, or it will dry out and crumble. If cracks do develop, repair them by slightly dampening the clay.

Pinch pots, and all hand-built pots, can be textured, decorated, and glazed, as illustrated in subsequent sections.

2. As you rotate the pot, move your pinching fingers slowly up the side of the pot. Make the walls an even thickness, but not too thin.

3. Make the rim a bit thicker than the walls. Smooth out any lumps in the walls. Set the pot on a flat surface to give it a flat base.

Hand building: coil method

In the coil method pieces of clay are rolled into long thin coils, as shown in Step 1. It is a good idea to make several coils before you start to build, so that you do not have to stop building to roll more. Keep the extra coils under a damp cloth to prevent them from drying out while you work.

It is easiest to construct a coil pot on a small turntable, called a banding wheel (shown in Steps 2–10). This allows you to turn the pot as you build, but it is not necessary.

As you build, the joints between the coils are made secure by scoring and brushing on slip, shown in Step 3. Make the slip ahead of time by repeatedly squeezing a piece of clay submerged in a little water.

If you are making a large pot, as shown in the left box on the facing page, you should periodically let the pot dry for a few minutes. This lets it stiffen and prevents it from sagging under its own weight. The large pot is shown being paddled to give it a rough texture. The adjacent illustrations demonstrate how a coiled pot can be given a very smooth finish.

When your pot is finished, put it under a piece of plastic for a week. This retards drying and prevents the pot from pulling apart at the joints.

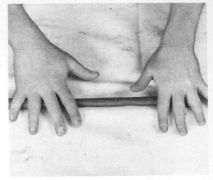

1. Roll your palms gently over a piece of clay. Move your hands apart slowly as you roll, making a long coil of even thickness.

6. Score and apply slip to the top of each coil before the next coil is put on top of it, as shown. Continue adding coils to build up the pot.

Three coil pots

2. Flatten a piece of clay with your hands and put it on the banding wheel. With a pointed tool, score shallow grooves around the perimeter.

3. Make some thick slip by thoroughly mixing clay and a little water in a bowl. Brush slip over the scores, as shown.

4. Press a coil down firmly on the base, over the scores. Wrap the coil around the perimeter, pressing where it overlaps itself to prevent gaps.

5. With a wooden tool, smooth down coil so that it fuses with the base, as shown. Repeat this procedure to fuse each coil to the one below it.

7. You can alter the shape of the pot by pushing from the inside with the handle of a tool. Hold a hand outside the pot to prevent it from tearing.

8. Attach two coils on the top that are slightly longer than those below them. Shape them to a point at one spot to form a spout.

9. To attach a handle, score the pot near the top, opposite the spout. Press the end of a coil onto the score so that it adheres firmly.

10. Score and attach the other end of the handle, as shown. Instructions for making other types of handles can be found on page 162.

Large coil pot with rough texture

If you are making a large pot, you should build with thicker coils than those used for a small pot. When the pot is completed, it can be textured in many different ways. This large pot is being paddled with a stick to give it a rough texture.

Coil pot with smooth texture

Coiled pots can be textured so that they are as smooth as pots thrown on the wheel. As you build your pot, roll very thin coils and attach them in the seams between the larger coils, as shown at left. With your hand and a wooden tool, smooth clay as shown at right.

Pottery

Hand building: slab method

In the slab method clay is rolled into flat, even slabs, which are then cut up and assembled. A lump of clay can be dropped sideways onto a table, as shown in Step 1 (below), to flatten it out. This makes it easier to roll the clay with a rolling pin into its final thickness (Step 2). Sticks of wood serve as guides for the rolling and ensure that the clay will be perfectly even in thickness.

It is important to make the joints of any slab project very sturdy and secure, or they will pull apart during drying or firing. Do not make any unnecessary joints. When you dry your project, put it under a piece of plastic for at least a week to prevent too rapid and uneven evaporation of moisture.

If you let your slabs sit for a while, they will stiffen. You may find that this makes them easier to assemble.

Because of their flat surfaces, slab projects make excellent vehicles for texturing and decoration. This is discussed on pages 163–166.

The pictures below show the construction of the box photographed in a finished state at left. The mug appearing next to the slab box is an easier project, made simply by rolling a slab into a cylinder and attaching a base and a handle to the cylinder.

1. Throw the clay nearly parallel to table; do not drop it straight down. Repeat throwing until clay flattens into nearly uniform thickness.

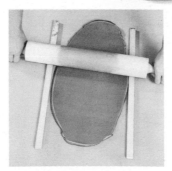

2. Place two sticks, 1/4-1/2 in. thick, on either side of the clay. Roll a rolling pin over the clay and sticks to make a flat, even slab.

3. With a piece of wood as a guide, use the fettling knife to cut the clay into five sections that will fit together as the base and walls of a box.

4. Score perimeter of section that will serve as base of box. Brush slip over the scores. Slip should be made in advance (see p. 142).

5. Roll a thin coil (see p. 142). Holding wall on top of base, smooth coil into seam between them with wooden tool so that they fuse, as shown.

6. Hold the second wall in place. Put coils in the seams between it and the base and the other wall. Smooth them so that the joints fuse.

7. Attach the other two walls in the same way as shown in Step 6. With a wooden tool, smooth over all the joints on the outside of the box.

8. Push a piece of wood against the box to make the sides straight and the corners square, as shown. Also level off the top edges of the box.

9. Cut a slab for the lid. Attach two long, thin slabs of clay as shown, leaving 1/2 in. clearance all around. These small slabs are the flanges.

10. Turn the lid over. Cut a small slab for the handle and attach it to the lid as shown. Other types of handles are shown on page 162.

Hand building: three forms

Free-form coiled cylinder

1. Roll 15 or 20 coils of clay (p. 142). Lay them close together on a piece of cloth so that together they cover an area that is approximately rectangular, as shown.

2. Smear the coils together with your finger until they fuse into one flat slab. Add clay between the coils where needed. Add extra clay to thicken the slab. Roll the slab with a rolling pin to make it smooth.

3. With a wooden stick as a guide, use the fettling knife to trim the edges of the slab. Keep in mind that when you roll it to form a cylinder, the diameter of the cylinder will be about one-third the length of the slab.

4. Very carefully lift the slab off of the piece of cloth. If the slab feels like it will break as you lift it, let it dry for about 15 min and then try again. Turn the slab upright and shape to form cylinder.

5. Score vertical edges of cylinder and brush on slip, as shown. Then push two edges together firmly. Smooth over the joint with your finger from both the inside and the outside of the cylinder to make a secure connection.

6. Roll a slab. Place cylinder on this slab. Cut slab around the cylinder, as shown. Attach as shown on p. 144, Step 5. Wrap the cylinder in plastic, and leave it there for about a month to dry very slowly.

Woven basket

1. Roll a slab on a piece of burlap, to give it texture. Cut about 10 long, thin strips from the slab. With the texture to the outside, weave the strips together, under and over, as shown.

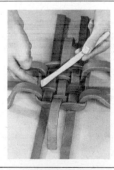

2. Lift the tails of the woven strips, and weave another strip in and out of them to start the walls of the basket, as shown. Press the tails to this lateral strip so that they stick together. Join two ends of lateral strip inside one of the tails.

3. Continue weaving up the sides of the basket. Do not weave the last lateral strip in and out— wrap it around the outside of the tails. Attach another strip inside tails, so that the ends of the tails are sandwiched, as shown. Squeeze them to make the connection secure.

Bowl

1. Make a mold by pouring plaster into a bowl and letting it harden. Turn it upside down. Cut many small pieces of clay from a slab and lay them together on the plaster, as shown. Cover the entire surface of the plaster with the clay pieces.

2. With your thumb, smear extra clay over the entire layer of small pieces of clay already on the mold. Smooth the surface until the small pieces can no longer be seen, as shown.

3. In a few hours the clay will shrink a bit, and it can be pulled off of the mold. Gently remove it and put it in a bowl for support, as shown. Put it under a piece of plastic to dry slowly.

Pottery

Throwing on the wheel

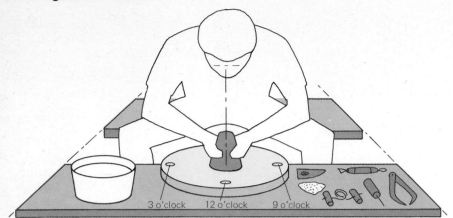

3 o'clock   12 o'clock   9 o'clock

This diagram shows a potter sitting in the proper position at the wheel, equipped with all the necessary tools. The seat is level with the wheelhead, and the potter leans forward in a comfortable but stable posture so that his nose is over the center of the wheel. The tools—a bucket of water, a sponge, a sponge on the end of a stick, wooden tools, metal trimming tools, ribs, a needle tool, and a cutting wire—are all discussed on page 136. The clock system of describing locations on the wheel is also shown.

The art of making pots on the potter's wheel, called throwing, is shown on the following 15 pages. Throwing is difficult to master; nevertheless, it is sufficiently rewarding to have become the most popular pottery technique of potters throughout the world.

The circular motion of the wheel allows the potter to apply pressure at only one point to alter the shape of a pot while retaining its perfect symmetry. It is essential to hold the pressure points very steady to preserve symmetry; the potter sits in a position that allows him to brace his arms against his body so that he can hold his hands absolutely still. This basic position—the potter's seat level with the wheelhead, the body leaning forward so that the nose is over the center of the wheel—is shown above. Learning to throw is basically learning how to apply a constant but subtle pressure to the clay. The right pressure will differ according to the condition of the clay—when it is a big lump, a fair amount of force is required, while a light touch is sufficient to shape a thin wall. All motions in throwing must be made gradually. Pressures must be applied and changed gradually—even the removal of the hands from the rotating clay

must be gradual—or the symmetry of the pot will be ruined.

To prevent this constant pressure from drying and tearing the clay, a lubricating layer of water is repeatedly applied to the clay and/or to the hands. Unfortunately, this water also softens the clay, and if too much is applied to a pot, the walls will sag. Therefore, a pot cannot be worked indefinitely; the best results are achieved when the pot is thrown quickly and decisively.

Because throwing is mastery of a touch, there is no one correct way to do it. For several of the procedures shown in the following 15 pages, alternative methods are shown or discussed. It is a good idea to try all of the options, then either pick the one that suits you or combine them to synthesize a personal technique. As you become more adept at throwing, you will improvise techniques spontaneously.

Since touch and pressure are all-important, it is easiest to learn throwing from someone who pushes your hands on the clay and gives you direct experience of the proper pressures. If you can receive such personal attention, use these pages to complement the instruction, for alternative techniques, and for project suggestions. You can learn to

throw without such instruction simply by practicing until your results match those in the pictures. The first instance of this will probably happen quite dramatically, when you finally find the correct pressure for centering the clay. After that it becomes easier. Throwing is a difficult and delicate process, so do not be deterred by early failures. It is also a good idea to throw only a pot or two at a time when you first start; after that mental and physical fatigue contribute to poor results.

Several of the basic instructions on the next 15 pages are intended to familiarize you with the wheel, and probably you will need to consider them only once. The speed of the wheel, which is given in revolutions per minute (rpm's), can be measured by placing a piece of adhesive tape on the wheel and counting the revolutions. The rpm's given in the instructions are approximate; you should adjust them to suit your work. For locating positions on the wheel, imagine the wheelhead as a clockface with 6 o'clock nearest the potter and 12 o'clock opposite (see above). Cross sections of pots are shown throughout this section to give a clearer view of the procedures. It is a good idea to cut your own pots in

half periodically to check your progress. You should always have an assortment of tools on hand when you throw (see left).

If you are using a kick wheel, you must kick the flywheel to speed, rather than merely depress the pedal, as with an electric wheel. Always remove your hands from the clay before you kick—never kick and throw simultaneously.

About this section. Centering, the process that makes the clay perfectly symmetrical and on center, is shown on pages 147–148. The clay is shaped into its final form after being worked into an intermediate form, either a cylinder (pp. 148–152) or a lower, open shape (pp. 153–154). Several pots can be made in succession from one big lump of clay, a process called throwing off the mound (p. 155). The pot is cut from the wheel (p. 156), then the base is trimmed (pp. 156–157). Lids too can be thrown on the wheel (pp. 158–159). Four more difficult throwing projects are shown on pages 160–161.

Centering. Centering is the first, most important, and most difficult step to learn in throwing. The irregular lump of clay is forced, by firm, constant pressure of the hands, into a perfectly symmetrical mound, from which the pot is made. It is essential to brace your arms securely against your body and never to let your hands ride with the bumps in the clay. You must make the clay mold to your hands, not the other way around. The centering process must be repeated until the clay is perfectly on center—it is very difficult to make a symmetrical pot from an asymmetrical lump of clay. Once you learn the proper touch for centering, the rest of throwing becomes easier.

Alternative methods for centering, especially for large balls of clay, are shown on page 148. Some common problems in centering, along with their remedies, are also shown on page 148.

Centering

1. Wedge a ball of clay about the size of a grapefruit. Using the rings on the wheelhead as guides, throw the clay down on the wheelhead as close to center as possible. If you miss badly, pick up the clay and throw it down again.

2. Slap the clay hard with your hand to make it stick fast to the wheel. If any of the clay projects asymmetrically, push it in toward the center. Turn on the wheel and press down the pedal until it is turning at nearly top speed.

3. Wet the sponge and squeeze it over the clay. The interface between the clay and your hands must be kept wet at all times—wet the clay and/or your hands whenever you feel that the clay is drying or pulling.

4. Scratch the center of your left palm with the fingers of your right hand, as shown, and do the same for your right palm. These are the areas of your hands that should contact the clay as you squeeze it in the following three steps.

5. Lean forward with your nose over center of clay. Place your hands opposite each other, at 3 o'clock and 9 o'clock, 1/4 in. above wheelhead. Brace your arms firmly against your legs. For variation of this posture, see page 148, Step 1.

6. Squeeze the clay with your palms by pushing your hands together as if you were clapping. Establish a diameter with your hands and make the clay conform to it. Push firmly—do not let your hands ride with the bumps in the clay.

7. As you squeeze, move your hands slowly up the clay and tilt them slightly inward to bring the clay into a cone shape, as shown. Keep the clay wet. Always lift your hands off the clay slowly, or you will throw it off center.

8. Your left and right hands have different functions in bringing the cone of clay down. The outside of the heel of the right hand (shown above) is placed on top of the cone and is used to push the clay downward.

9. The palm of the left hand collects the clay that is pushed down by the right and gives it a fixed diameter. It is very important that you push firmly with your left hand: do not allow it to follow the irregularities of the clay.

10. Place your hands as shown, wrapping your right thumb around your left thumb to hold your hands together. Brace your left elbow against your leg or ribs. Slowly push down with your right hand as you push toward 12 o'clock with left.

11. Push clay down 1–2 in. at a time. Keep it wet. As you push with your left hand, you will feel the clay move to fit its contour. Stop pushing when clay is about as high as it is wide. For a variation, see page 148, Step 3.

12. If there are any lumps still in the clay, repeat Steps 6–11 until the clay is perfectly smooth and symmetrical. Push your thumb in at the base of the clay to remove any excess clay from the wheelhead whenever it appears, as shown.

Pottery

Centering a large ball of clay

1. To bring up the cone of a large ball of clay, lock your elbows into your sides. Instead of using the hand position shown on page 147, Steps 5–7, use the heels and palms of both hands to push straight into the clay at 6 o'clock. Move both hands up slowly to make the cone.

2. Another way of raising the cone is to use your wrist as a source of pressure. Wet your right wrist, and brace your right elbow against your leg. With your left hand push the clay in, against your right wrist. Slowly raise them together to make the cone. Keep the clay wet.

3. To bring the cone down, you need to apply more downward pressure than you can by using the hand position shown in Steps 8–11, page 147. Hold your left hand as shown in Step 9, but turn your right hand so that you can push the clay down hard with the heel and palm of the hand.

Common problems in centering

If you ever take your hands off the clay and see that it is distorted and off center, as shown above, it means that you are taking your hands off too quickly. All motions in throwing must be made smoothly and gradually.

If you move your hands too quickly as you bring up the cone, you will make a spiral in the clay. Once the spiral is made, your hands tend to follow it, making it worse. Move your hands up slowly, and do not let them ride with bumps in the clay.

If you leave any off-center clay at the base of the cone, your hands will ride on it and it will throw them off center. Remove any extra clay from the wheelhead by holding your thumb firmly on the wheel, as shown on page 147, Step 12.

If the top of the cone tears off while you are raising it, you are pushing too hard. You may also have let the surface of the clay get too dry. Another possibility is that you have worked the clay too long, and it has become too soft.

If you let your hands separate, or if you do not exert enough pressure with your left hand while you are bringing the cone down, your cone will flare into a mushroom shape. Avoid this—it will cause problems when you try to raise the walls.

If the entire ball of clay ever becomes significantly off center, brace your left elbow on your leg, support your left hand with your right, and push hard at 7 or 8 o'clock toward the center of the clay. The clay will recenter.

Making a cylinder

The centered lump of clay is not formed directly into its final shape. It is first made into a basic intermediate form, which is then altered to give the final shape. The intermediate step for many pottery shapes is the cylinder, which is shown on the next two pages. The other basic shape, the low bowl or plate, is shown on pages 153–154.

The formation of the cylinder is accomplished in two stages. First a hole is sunk into the lump of clay to open it up and to form a flat base. After this step the walls are raised and thinned to make the cylinder.

Opening the clay. Reduce the speed of the wheel slightly from the speed used for centering. Hold your hands on the clay and sink in your thumbs, as shown in Steps 1–3, page 149. Check the thickness of the base with the needle tool. If you have sunk the hole too deep, do not attempt to fill it with more clay. Take the lump of clay off the wheel, clean the wheel, and start again with new clay.

After the hole is sunk, it is widened to the full width of the base of the finished piece. Be sure you draw your fingers straight across the base (Steps 5–7 p. 149) to prevent it from curving. Some potters prefer to switch hands for Steps 5–9, using the left hand on the outside and the right hand inside.

Raising the walls. The walls of the cylinder are raised by squeezing up clay from the short thick walls of the opened lump of clay. The clay is raised by holding the hands (the left on the inside and the right on the outside) at a fixed point on the circumference of the clay and bringing them up the wall slowly, pushing a roll of clay above them. Each movement of the hands from the bottom to the top is called a pull. The raising of the walls is usually completed in three pulls.

The centrifugal force created by the spinning wheel will tend to make the top of the cylinder flare out. To counteract this, it is important to keep the cylinder tapered in at the top. Step 21 on page 150 shows how to restore the taper if it is lost. It is also important to keep the rim centered at all times. Steps 10 and 18 on page 150 show how this is done.

To start the first pull, reduce the speed of the wheel to about 100 rpm. The first pull straightens and evens the walls, raises them a little, and establishes the taper (Steps 11–13, p. 150). In the second pull most of the raising of the clay is accomplished (Steps 15–17, p. 150). When you start the second pull, squeeze your hands together at the base of the cylinder until you feel a large roll of clay start to move up. A common error is to leave too much clay at the base. The third pull (Steps 19–20) eliminates irregularities in the walls and gives the cylinder its final shape.

Raising the walls requires a good amount of dexterity and sensitivity to the clay. You must push the clay firmly, or it will not move; but if you push too hard, the cylinder will tear. You must always make the clay shape to your hands—never let your hands be moved by irregularities in the clay. To do this, brace your hands against each other whenever possible, and lock your arms in against your body. Always bring your hands off the clay slowly, or you will throw it off center. Keep the clay wet (Step 14).

It is a good idea to cut your cylinders in half periodically to see how the walls look. If you have moved your hands up too quickly, or if you have applied inconstant pressure, the walls will be uneven. Short thick walls mean you are not pushing the clay hard enough. Torn rims are an indication that you are not easing up on the pressure as you reach the top. If your cylinder flares, you are pushing too hard with your left hand and not hard enough with your right.

1. Place both hands on the clay as shown, with your fingers resting on, but not pushing, the clay and your thumbs together at the center. Slowly push your thumbs down into the clay.

2. Keep your thumbs dead center in the clay, and gradually push them straight down. Keep your elbows braced against your body. When the clay gets dry, remove your hands and wet the clay.

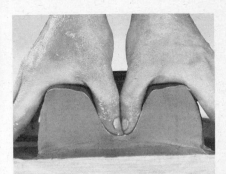

3. This cutaway shows the hands resting on the clay while the thumbs are sunk in. Stop pushing your thumbs when you are between 1/2 and 1/4 in. from the surface of the wheelhead.

4. Stop the wheel. Push the needle tool through the base of the clay to measure its thickness. If it is more than 1/2 in., sink the hole deeper. If it is less than 1/8 in., start again with new clay.

5. After the hole is sunk, hold your right hand on the side of the clay. Anchoring your left thumb on your right hand, pull the hole open by pulling the clay with the fingers of your left hand.

6. Pull your left fingers toward the heel of your right hand. Be sure they move straight across the bottom of the clay: do not let them rise, or the base will be curved.

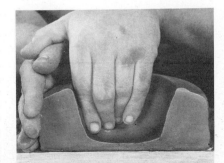

7. This cutaway shows the fingers of the left hand pulling the hole open. In this step the hole is opened up as wide as it will be in the finished shape of the cylinder.

8. After the hole is opened up all the way, straighten the index finger of your left hand and push it sideways against the inside of the wall, toward the heel of your right hand.

9. In this cutaway you can see how the left index finger is pushed against the right hand to straighten the wall. Also notice that the base of the cylinder is perfectly flat.

Pottery

Making a cylinder (continued)

10. To correct irregularities in the rim, lay your left hand on the clay at 6 o'clock so that the clay runs between the thumb and index finger. Lean your right hand against your left, and push the clay down with the outside of the right hand until the rim becomes thicker and is on center.

11. To start the first pull, hold your right hand flat against the clay at 3 o'clock. Put your left hand inside and brace the thumb against your right hand. Push the clay at the base of the cylinder walls with your left fingertips until you feel some of it start to rise up the walls.

12. This cutaway shows the cylinder about halfway through the first pull. Notice how the left fingers are curved so that the fingertips push directly against the right palm. The walls are thick, even, and tilt slightly toward the center of the cylinder.

13. Keeping your hands locked together with your left thumb, slowly move them up the wall, squeezing the clay up between them. Push with your left hand until you get halfway up the wall, then apply more pressure with your right. This will taper the top of the cylinder.

14. You must keep both the inside and outside of the wall wet while you are pulling, or the clay will tear. Put your hand over the wall, as shown, and let water run down your hand to wet both sides. Do not let water accumulate in the bottom of the cylinder; absorb and remove it with the sponge.

15. For second pull hold thumb and first three fingers of right hand together on outside. Hold left hand as in Steps 11–13. With left fingers, push the base of the clay firmly against your right hand (more firmly than in first pull) until a bulge of clay forms and starts to rise.

16. Move your hands slowly up the clay. Gradually increase the pressure with your right hand and reduce it with your left. Move both hands gradually from 3 o'clock to 5 or 6 o'clock to help make the taper. The walls should rise dramatically between your hands.

17. Reduce the pressure of your hands at the top of the cylinder so that the walls do not get too thin. This cutaway shows the proper evenness of the walls. Uneven walls are the result of inconstant pressure. If your cylinder does not rise, you are not pushing the clay hard enough.

18. Recenter the rim after each pull. After the cylinder has been raised, this can be done by firmly holding your left forefinger and thumb on either side of the rim and pushing down with the right forefinger until the rim thickens and becomes perfectly even and centered.

19. The third, and final, pull is done with the hands in the same position as in the second pull. It is done to correct any irregularities in the walls and to bring the cylinder to its final shape. The pressure of your hands should be light because the walls are now thin.

20. Keep your hands locked together with your left thumb whenever possible. If the height of the cylinder prevents this, guide your left hand by riding your thumb lightly against the wall and bracing your arm against your ribs. Lock your hands together as they approach the rim.

21. If your cylinder ever flares out at the top, the taper must be restored. Hold your hands around the cylinder, as shown. Slowly bring them up, applying a gentle constant pressure inward around the entire circumference of the cylinder, bringing the top to a taper.

Shaping the cylinder

After the walls of the cylinder are raised, the cylinder is shaped into its final form. Shaping basically consists of widening and narrowing the walls at different points; the height of the cylinder and the diameter of the base remain virtually unchanged.

The hand position for most shaping is shown in the first two pictures at right. Start at the bottom of the cylinder and work your way up, pushing with your left fingertips to widen the wall, with your right fingertips to narrow it. Push lightly and keep your hands very steady. Decide on your shape and make it quickly; do not overwork the clay, or it will collapse. Watch the clay from the outside as you shape so that you can see the line of the pot. You may find it easier to give the shoulder and the top of the pot an attractive shape by moving your hands downward from the rim of the cylinder after you have shaped the bottom.

When you widen the walls, they become thinner. Therefore you cannot widen them too much, or they will collapse. Clay cannot be raised from other parts of the wall during shaping; if you are going to make a very wide shape, leave the walls thicker when you first raise the cylinder (pp. 149–150).

Do not make any part of the wall extend horizontally in a cantilever, or it will collapse. Avoid abrupt changes in shape—keep the line of the wall rounded and gradual.

The cylinder can be given a narrow neck by a process called collaring, shown in the illustrations at right. A vase collared to a long thin neck appears among the illustrations on the following page.

If the rim becomes uneven during shaping, it should be trimmed, as shown at right. Examples of three standard shapes derived from the cylinder—the mug, the pitcher, and the vase—are shown on the following page.

To shape the cylinder, hold the fingers of your right hand outside the wall as shown. Hold the fingers of your left hand inside the wall as seen in the photo below. Keep the fingers of the two hands directly opposite each other. Brace your left thumb on your right hand whenever possible.

To collar the cylinder, first bring in the top as shown in Step 21, page 150. You will then contact the clay at three points on each hand: the tip of the thumb, the tip of the forefinger, and the bent first knuckle of the middle finger. The proper hand position is shown here.

To cut off an uneven rim, reduce the speed of the wheel to about 60 rpm. Hold the needle tool with your right hand and support the point with your left thumb. Keeping both arms braced on your body, slowly push the point of the tool into the side of the cylinder.

To bring the wall out, push with the fingertips of your left hand. Use the right hand to support the left hand and the clay, but do not squeeze the clay. To bring the wall in, push with the fingertips of your right hand and support the clay lightly with your left fingertips. Keep your fingers wet.

Narrow the neck by pushing the cylinder at the six contact points and raising both hands slowly. Do not push too hard, or the clay will ripple. Because the clay thickens as it is collared, it must be periodically thinned (see the photos on the shaping of the vase, p. 152).

Push the tool until it goes through the wall of the cylinder. A ring of clay will separate from the rest of the cylinder; carefully remove it. Thicken the rim, as shown in Step 18, page 150. It is structurally necessary to keep the rim even and on center at all times.

Pottery

Three shapes made from a cylinder

Mug

1. To make a mug, throw cylinder with dimensions similar to those of the desired finished shape. Bring your hands up the walls, shaping as you go, as shown on page 151.

2. When you get to the top, thicken the rim as shown in Step 18, page 150. Do not flare the rim out, or the mug will be difficult to drink from.

3. After the mug is cut from the wheel (see p.156), the base is trimmed (see p.157), and a handle is attached (see p.162).

Pitcher

1. To make a pitcher, throw a cylinder and shape it so that it tapers inward just below the rim and then flares slightly outward.

2. Hold two fingers against the cylinder at the rim. With a finger of the other hand, gently stroke the rim outward between them to make a spout. Keep the stroking finger wet.

3. The pitcher is then cut from the wheel and trimmed, and a handle is attached.

Vase

1. To make a vase, throw a cylinder and shape bottom to its desired form. Once the top is collared, no further shaping of the bottom is possible.

2. Bring the top of the cylinder in to a taper to begin the collaring. Be careful never to push down on the shoulder of the pot, or it will collapse.

3. Water used to lubricate the walls has to be removed from the bottom of the cylinder. Once the top has been narrowed, this can be done with a sponge attached to the end of a stick.

4. To collar the neck, place your hands as shown on preceding page. Move your hands up the neck as you move them together and contract them. The clay will thicken.

5. To thin the clay in the neck, put your hands as shown and pull the clay up the neck as if you were raising the walls of a cylinder (p.150). Keep the neck as thick as the rest of the walls.

6. Alternate between collaring and thinning until the neck is the desired height and thickness. Then carefully finish the rim.

The three illustrations above are of three standard shapes derived from a cylinder. Raising a cylinder is shown on pages 149–150. Techniques for shaping the cylinder are shown on page 151.

Throwing open shapes

The techniques used in throwing open shapes, such as plates, low bowls, and casseroles, vary from those used to make shapes derived from a cylinder (pp. 148–152). Basically, the clay is centered and flattened to a shape that roughly corresponds to the desired final shape. Then the clay is opened and the walls are raised.

Open shapes are rarely thrown directly on the wheelhead because it is almost impossible to lift them off when they are still wet. Instead, a removable disk, usually made of plaster or wood, called a bat, is placed on the wheelhead. The open shape is then thrown on the bat, and afterward the bat is pried from the wheel. With the use of the bat, the pot does not have to be disturbed before it dries. When the bat is attached to the wheel (Step 1, this page) it should adhere so firmly that you cannot move it with your hands.

The clay is centered and flattened out (Steps 2 and 3). When the hole is dropped (Step 4), the base is left almost twice as thick as in a cylinder. The extra thickness of the base helps prevent the walls from sagging. Much of this extra thickness is trimmed away later, when the clay has hardened somewhat.

The hole is opened (Steps 4–6) with the hands in a position similar to that used in opening the cylinder, but here the hole is opened up wider. The fingers lift up as they draw across the bottom, making a gentle curve in the base (Step 7). This establishes the final shape of the base.

The method of raising and shaping the walls varies according to the type of pot being thrown. For a low bowl the walls are raised straight up and then shaped outward. In a plate the walls are made to flare outward as they are raised so that the rim does not elevate. Shaping a low bowl and a plate are shown on page 154. Some bowls can be shaped from a cylinder (p. 154).

1. To attach the bat, put some thick slip on the wheelhead. Put the bat down and move it back and forth several times as you push down hard to seal the bat to the wheel. Let it sit for a few minutes—it should stick fast.

2. Center the clay (see p. 147). Then flatten it further by pressing down with your right hand as you press inward with your left hand to keep the clay on center. Flatten the clay gradually, keeping it wet at all times.

3. Make the mound of clay about as flat and wide as you want your final shape to be. You can adjust the diameter of the clay and correct irregularities by pushing in with your right fingers, supported by your left hand.

4. Drop the hole by gradually sinking your thumbs into the center. Your other fingers should rest lightly on the clay for support. Leave the base almost twice as thick as in a cylinder—much of it will later be trimmed to make a foot (p. 157).

5. The hole is opened by pulling the clay with the fingers of the left hand toward the left thumb, which is on the outside of the clay. The right hand, resting against the left, pushes down to prevent the clay from rising.

6. As your fingers are pulled to the outside of the clay, they should rise slightly, giving the bottom of the shape a gentle, even curve. Fold the fingers of your right hand over the fingers of your left hand to help pull the hole open.

7. After opening the hole, move the fingertips of your right hand, supported by your left hand, slowly across the bottom of the clay. Move from the outside inward, pushing down firmly to compact the clay and to smooth the shape.

8. This cutaway shows the shape of the clay after opening and smoothing. Notice the gradual curve of the base and the short, thick walls that taper slightly outward. The base undergoes no further changes during shaping.

9. Clean excess clay off the bat (Step 12, p. 147). The hand position for raising the walls (shown above) is very similar to that for the cylinder. As you raise the walls, do not disrupt the continuity of the curve of the base.

153

Pottery

Three open shapes

Low bowl

To make a low bowl, use several gentle pulls (see p. 150) to bring the walls straight up to their final height. Keep the wheel at a slow speed to prevent the walls from flaring out.

Bring the rim out to its final position. Then shape the walls with your left hand, supporting the outside with your right (p. 151). Shape quickly—do not overwork the clay.

Shaping and smoothing, especially of open shapes, is frequently done with a tool called a rib. Gently move the rib across the bowl—do not push down hard, or the walls will collapse.

Plate

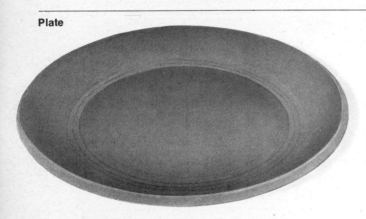

To make a plate, push harder with your left hand as you raise the walls so that the sides flare outward. Turn the wheel slowly and be very gentle, or the cantilevered walls will collapse.

The plate can be shaped or smoothed with a rib or a sponge held tightly between the fingers (above). Always support the underside with your right hand as you shape with your left.

Whenever you are throwing on a bat, push the needle tool into the base of the pot after you are done shaping, as shown. This breaks the seal with the bat and promotes even drying.

Bowl from a cylinder

To make a bowl from a cylinder, throw a cylinder to about the desired height of the finished shape. The base of the cylinder should be curved, and the taper of the walls should be slight.

Bring the rim out to its final diameter. The first shaping should be done with your hands, to alter the form and to compress and strengthen the clay. Work quickly, with a light touch.

Final shaping can be done with the rib. Remember that when you pull the clay out, it becomes thinner, and thus weaker—do not overextend the clay. Avoid abrupt changes in the shape.

Throwing off the mound

The production of small pots can be accelerated by throwing several from one large lump of clay, a process called throwing off the mound. The top of the mound is centered, made into a pot, and cut off. Then more of the mound is centered and made into a pot. The process can continue until all the clay in the mound is used up.

Throwing off the mound saves the potter from having to clean the wheel-head after throwing each pot. Because the mound is approximately on center, the centering for each pot is faster than it is for separate throws. The mound is also very useful for small shapes that would be difficult to cut directly from the wheelhead.

Because only the top of the mound is centered for each pot, you cannot rest your hands on the wheelhead for a guide. Therefore you must master the feel for centering before you attempt to throw off the mound.

After the clay is centered (Steps 2 and 3), an indentation is made to mark the bottom of the clay that will be used to make the pot. When the hole is sunk (Step 4), use this indentation as a guide for the correct depth—you do not want the base of the pot to be less than 1/4 inch or more than 1/2 inch thick. Re-establish this indentation if it ever becomes blurred during the throwing.

Opening the hole, raising the walls, and shaping the pot are done just as for pieces thrown directly on the wheel-head. Because the pots are small, you probably will not need three pulls to raise the walls. The only constraint on the size and shape of the pots you throw off the mound is that you must be able to lift them off the mound (Step 7) without distorting them.

1. Throw a large lump of clay down firmly on the wheelhead. Push it into a thick cone shape. Start the wheel and bring your hands up the clay, roughly centering it.

2. Center the top of the cone by pushing down with your right hand and in with your left, as shown in Steps 9 and 10, page 147. Center only as much clay as you will use for your pot.

3. Cup the centered clay between your hands to perfect the centering and to separate it from the rest of the clay. Indent the bottom of this clay with your finger to mark the base of the pot.

4. To open the clay, sink in your thumbs, using the indentation made in Step 3 as the guide for where to stop. The hole should be sunk to 1/4–1/2 in. above the indentation.

5. Opening the hole, raising the walls, and shaping the pot are done just as shown on pages 149–151. The pieces must be small enough to be removed from the mound without distorting.

6. With a rib, make a narrow mark where you will cut the pot off. Wrap a piece of fishing line or wire around the pot in this groove. Pull the wire until it cuts through the pot.

7. Be sure you pull the wire so that it cuts horizontally through the pot. With the thumb and forefinger of each hand, hold base of pot, twist it a little, and lift the pot off.

8. Push the remaining clay up into a cone shape. Repeat Steps 2–7 to make the next pot. Continue the process until you run out of clay or have as many pots as you want.

Pottery

Removing a pot from the wheel

After a pot is thrown on the wheel, it is cut off with a wire and placed on a piece of wood to dry. Pots that are well thrown, with thin, even walls, are usually fairly easy to remove from the wheel right after they are thrown. Pots that have been worked until their walls are wet and soft, or that have either very thick, very thin, or uneven walls, should sit on the wheel to harden for a while before they are removed.

Two methods of cutting a pot from the wheel are shown below. In both methods the wheel can be stationary as the wire is pulled across or it can rotate very slowly. The force of the rotating wheel aids in the cutting, so less force is needed as you pull the wire. In either case it is essential to push the wire firmly against the wheelhead with your thumbs as you cut, or the wire will rise and cut the bottom off the pot. In both methods the only part of the pot that is touched is the base. Never touch the rim of a wet pot. If the pot distorts as it is removed from the wheel, it can usually be corrected by pushing in at the base on the elongated side when the pot is on a piece of wood. The pot is then left to dry until it is ready to trim.

Stretch the wire, holding your thumbs slightly farther apart than the width of the pot. Pull the wire through the bottom of the pot, pushing down to prevent the wire from rising.

Hold the base of the pot firmly with your fingertips. Twist the pot slightly, lift it off the wheel, and put it on a piece of wood to dry. Clean the wheel carefully before you use it again.

Hold the wire as shown above. Wet the wheelhead thoroughly. Pull the wire through the bottom of the pot. Repeat procedure, drawing the wire from different directions.

Gently push the pot across the wet wheelhead with your fingers. Hold a piece of wood level with the wheelhead, and carefully push the pot onto it. Put the pot aside to dry.

Trimming

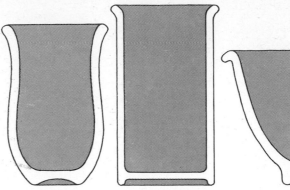

The pot is given its final shape when excess clay at the bottom is trimmed away. There are many possible shapes for bases; in some pots only the rough edges are trimmed off the bottom, while in others the bottom is carved to make a prominent foot. A base that is well-shaped should make a pot more stable and structurally secure. It can also enhance the form and make the pot look more graceful.

With the exception of wet trimming (discussed below), pots are trimmed when they are leather hard. A pot becomes leather hard—that is, still damp but stiff enough to be handled without deforming—when it dries overnight after being thrown. It may take longer on humid days. Pots that are too wet will warp when they are being trimmed; pots that are too dry will chip, if they can be trimmed at all.

Trimming tools are shown on page 136. The cutting ends should be stiff, not flexible. It is good to have several trimming tools of different sizes and shapes on hand.

Before you start to trim, look at your pot and decide on the basic shape for the base. Just as one hallmark of a well-thrown pot is walls of even thickness, one objective of trimming is to make the thickness of the base equal to that of the walls. Make a mark on the outside of the pot level with the top of the base on the inside—this mark is your guide for the upper limit of the trimming. You can also make a mark on the bottom as a guide for the final diameter of the base.

Any pot can have any type of base. In general, however, open shapes are usually given distinct, raised feet, while cylindrical shapes have less pronounced bases (see diagram). This is one reason the bases are left thicker in open shapes than in cylinders.

Pronounced raised bases can only be made if the pot is trimmed upside down. Simpler bases can be trimmed this way, though they are often trimmed with the pot right-side up. Pots that are tapered at the top or that have frail rims that cannot support the pot must be trimmed either right-side up or in a chuck. You can make a chuck by throwing a cylinder, cutting out the base when it is leather hard, and bisque firing it (see pp. 167–168).

After the pot is centered and secured to the wheel, trimming is begun. Pots to be trimmed right-side up can be done immediately after throwing, when the clay is still wet. This technique, called wet trimming, is usually used for making simple bases on cylinders.

1. For upside-down trimming, put the pot on the center of the wheel. As the wheel turns slowly, hold a needle tool so that it scratches the pot at one point. Stop the wheel and move the pot in the direction opposite the mark.

2. Repeat Step 1 until the tool touches the pot evenly all around. Take three pieces of clay and push them firmly onto the wheelhead around the pot. Then push the clay inward until the centered pot is locked firmly on the wheel.

3. Hold the tool with your right hand, as shown. Brace it with your left, which rests on the pot. Gradually shave the sides with the tool by holding it against the pot as the pot turns at centering speed. Tilt the tool to curve the sides.

4. Mark the inside diameter of the foot with the edge of a tool. Remove the clay inside the mark by moving the tip of the tool from the center to the mark, as shown. The bottom can be given several different shapes (see diagrams at left).

5. Finish shaping the side walls to give the final form to the foot, as shown. Be careful not to make the foot too narrow. Level the foot by holding the tool very steady on top of it and shaving it evenly all the way around.

6. If there is grog in your clay, it will make marks during trimming that will later affect the glaze. To prevent this, smooth the clay with a wooden tool, as shown. You can also smooth the foot with your moistened fingers.

1. To trim right-side up, wet the wheelhead, put the pot down, and center it as shown in Step 1, above. While the wheel is turning very slowly, press the edge of the base down with a tool to seal the pot to the wheelhead.

2. Use the trimming tool to shape the bottom of the pot. You can undercut the pot with the tip of the tool. Stop the shaping 1/8 in. above the wheelhead—if you cut any lower, you will break the seal with the wheelhead.

3. Cut the pot off the wheel by breaking the seal with a knife as the wheel turns very slowly, as shown. Smooth the foot with your fingers. Tap in the center of the bottom with your fingers so that the pot will sit on the rim of the base.

To trim in a chuck, center chuck and attach it to wheel, as shown above. Place the pot in the chuck upside down and seal it to the chuck with pieces of clay. When pot is level and on center, trim it as shown in Steps 3–6.

Wet trimming is done immediately after the pot is shaped. Use a wooden tool, tilted back at a 45° angle, to trim excess clay off the bottom walls of the pot by pushing the clay down as the wheel turns at about 100 rpm.

When the trimming is complete, use a needle tool to cut under the clay that has been trimmed; remove this excess clay. Cut the pot from the wheel (p. 156). This process is very similar to trimming right-side up (above).

Pottery

Lids

Lids can be thrown on the wheel. Because the shrinkage of clay is variable, the greatest difficulty in throwing a lid is to get it to fit its intended pot.

There are several things you can do to increase your chances for a good fit. First, the pot and the lid should be thrown from the same wedged lump of clay so that shrinkage will be uniform. Second, you should throw several lids for each pot—one is bound to fit. Third, measure the necessary diameter(s) of the pot immediately after it is thrown, before it starts to dry and shrink. And last, drying and firing should be done with the lid in place.

A lid can either sit on top of a pot (see diagrams 2, 3, 5, 6, 8, 9), or the pot can be given an inside lip or seat, on which the lid will sit (see diagrams 1, 4, 7). This inside seat (Steps 1 and 2) generally makes the connection between the lid and the pot more secure.

Lids made on the wheel can be thrown right-side up—that is, thrown so that they sit on the wheel the way they will sit on the pot—or they can be thrown upside down. The simplest lid, which is thrown right-side up, is the flat lid, shown in Steps 3–5. A flat lid can also be given a flange (Steps 6 and 7). Although flat lids are usually thrown right on the wheelhead or off the mound (Steps 8 and 9), a large lid should be thrown on a bat.

The simplest type of lid thrown upside down is a plate or shallow bowl, called an Oriental cover (Step 10). When this type of lid is small, it needs no handle or knob. Larger lids can have knobs attached when the lids are leather hard (Steps 11–13). The other standard lid that is thrown upside down is the traditional flanged teapot lid, shown in Steps 14 and 15. Lids that are thrown upside down are usually trimmed, either on the wheelhead or set in place in the pot, which functions as a chuck (see p. 157).

1. To make a pot with an inside seat for the lid, leave the top of the walls thicker than you normally would as you raise the walls. Hold your hands as shown to form the seat.

6. To make a flat lid with a flange (diagrams 2,3,4), flatten some clay (Step 3) but leave a wall of clay for the flange. Bring the wall out to the appropriate diameter of the pot.

11. Knobs can be made on lids thrown upside down in two ways. If excess clay is left in the base when the lid is thrown, make a knob by trimming when the lid is leather hard (see diagram 6).

2. Use a wooden tool with a square end to flatten the seat and to create a right angle with the rim. This makes the seat more stable and easier to measure for the lid.

3. To make a flat lid (diagram 1), center some clay and flatten it, leaving a lump in the center for the handle. Push the clay until it is slightly thicker and wider than the final shape.

4. The knob can be shaped from the solid lump of clay, or the lump can be opened, raised, and shaped like a small pot, as shown. You can finish the lid with a rib or sponge.

5. Hold the calipers, which are set to the inside diameter of the wet pot, above the rim. Cut the lid to that diameter with a needle tool. Carefully cut the lid from the wheel.

7. Shape the wall to make a flange of the correct diameter to fit the pot. Shape the knob as shown in Step 4. Very carefully cut the lid from the wheel—try not to touch the wet flange.

8. To throw a flat lid off the mound, center the top, make an indentation to separate it from the rest of the mound, and push the clay down (Step 3). Support the lid from underneath.

9. Shape the knob as in Step 4. You can finish both the top and part of the bottom of the lid with a sponge. A flange can be made by shaping the outside of the lid.

10. To make an Oriental cover, (diagram 5) simply throw a straight-sided bowl or plate to the appropriate diameter. A small Oriental lid does not need a knob or handle.

12. The other way to make a knob is to throw one from wet clay attached to the lid when it is leather hard. Center the lid on the wheel and put a piece of wet clay in the middle of it.

13. Press the wet clay down to seal it to the lid. Then shape it to form a knob (see diagram 7). This procedure can be used to make a knob on any lid that is thrown upside down.

14. To make a flanged lid, flatten a piece of clay to the appropriate diameter, then raise a short wall for the flange so that the flange will fit inside the pot (diagram 8).

15. A knob is either trimmed (Step 11) or thrown (Steps 12 and 13) when the lid is leather hard. A curved flanged lid can be thrown from a bowl with thick rims (diagram 9).

Pottery

Combining more than one shape

Goblet

1. For the stem of the goblet throw a tall, thin cylinder off the mound. Shape the stem so that it tapers gradually inward from the base and flares outward a bit at the top. Rings and lines can be added as decoration.

2. Push a rib down into the bottom of the stem to spread and flatten base. Finish shaping the stem and cut it from the mound.

3. Throw a cup with a diameter roughly equal to the diameter of the base of the stem. Wet trim the cup so that it tapers in sharply at the base. Cut the cup from the mound.

4. When the stem becomes leather hard, cut underside out with a fettling knife. Smooth the bottom with your finger so that it will sit level on a flat surface.

5. When the cup is leather hard, finish trimming its bottom with a fettling knife. Then score and apply slip to the top of the stem and the bottom of the cup.

6. Place the cup on top of the stem and press down firmly. Seal them together by smoothing the clay at the interface with your finger. Dry the goblet slowly.

Teapot

1. To make a teapot, first throw a cylinder that tapers in somewhat at the top. The traditional teapot lid, the flanged lid, can be made by following the directions given on page 159.

2. To make the spout, throw a small cylinder that tapers in sharply at the top. This taper will help the teapot to pour well.

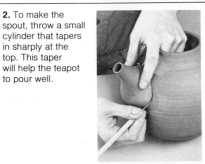

3. When the spout is leather hard, cut it at an angle, as shown above. Place it against the leather-hard body of the teapot so that the top of the spout is above the top of the pot. Trace the perimeter of the spout on the body with a needle tool.

The goblet and the teapot shown above are assembled from components that are made using the techniques shown on the preceding 14 pages. Throwing a cylinder, the basic component for both the goblet and the teapot, is shown on pages 148–151. Handles (for the teapot) are shown on page 162. Lids (also for the teapot) are shown on pages 158–159.

4. With a fettling knife, cut 7 to 10 small holes through the pot within the line traced in Step 3. Then score over the traced line with a needle tool.

5. Apply slip over the scores, and press the spout firmly against the pot. The connection should be made secure by carefully fusing the clay at the joint.

6. Attach a handle to the pot on the side opposite the spout. Pulled handles are usually used on teapots. Pulled handles and other types are shown on page 162. Dry the teapot slowly.

Coffee filter holder

1. To make a coffee filter holder, first throw a mug that the holder will sit on. Measure the inside diameter of the top of the mug when it is wet—the bottom of the holder must be smaller than this diameter.

2. Throw the filter holder off the mound. Center the top of the mound and make the indentation that separates the top from the rest of the mound. Drop a hole all the way through the top until it is deeper than the base of the holder will be.

3. Raise the walls and flare them outward with several gentle pulls. The top should be wide enough for the coffee filter to sit securely inside it.

4. Push your finger into the mound slightly below the bottom of the walls raised in Step 3. Push until a roll of clay forms above your finger, but do not push all the way through the mound.

5. Squeeze the roll of clay formed in Step 4 gently between your fingers to form a wide, thin disk. Shape this disk until it is wide enough to support the holder on top of the mug.

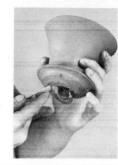

6. When the holder stiffens, push In and trim the bottom below the supporting disk so that it fits inside the mug. If the hole has closed, open it with a cutting tool or a pencil.

Bowl with thrown base

The coffee filter holder and the bowl with a thrown base, shown above, also employ the techniques shown in the preceding 14 pages. The filter is thrown from the mound, a technique shown on page 155. The major shape for the bowl with the thrown base is the low bowl, shown on pages 153–154. All pieces assembled from separately made components should be dried very slowly to prevent them from cracking and splitting apart.

1. To make a bowl with a thrown base, first throw a low bowl of any shape you want. The rim cannot be very thin, or it will crumble in a later step. Put the bowl aside to dry.

2. Throw a thick-walled cylinder that has a diameter at the top equal to the diameter of the base of the bowl made in Step 1. Cut off the top of the cylinder with a needle tool.

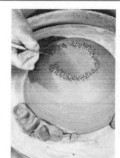

3. When the bowl is leather hard, center it upside down on the wheel and attach it with pieces of clay. Trim any excess clay off the base. Then score the perimeter.

4. Take the wet ring of clay cut from the top of the cylinder and center it over the score marks. Push the clay down, but not too hard or the bowl will collapse.

5. Seal the outside of the ring of clay to the base of the bowl by pushing the edges down with your fingertips. Repeat this to seal the inside of the wet clay to the bowl.

6. Raise and shape the wet clay to form a foot, as if you were shaping the walls of a low bowl. Leave the foot thick enough to support the weight of the bowl.

Pottery

Handles

Handles can be esthetic as well as functional additions to both thrown and hand-built pots. Handles can be made in a variety of ways; some standard handles fashioned from coils, slabs, and thrown cylinders are shown below. The most common type is the pulled handle, so named because it is shaped by repeated pullings of a lump of clay. Pulled handles can be formed, cut, and then attached to the pot (Steps 1–5), or clay can be fused to the pot and the handle pulled right in place (Steps 6–9). The basic motion in pulling handles is a gentle tugging, with the wet hand wrapped lightly around the clay, somewhat like milking a cow.

Once the handle is attached, the pot should be dried very slowly under a piece of plastic.

Handles made from coils and slabs can be shaped in many ways—some typical examples are shown above. Coils can also be twisted or braided together. Regular rounded handles, such as those for a casserole dish, can be cut from a thick-walled cylinder. Handles made from coils, slabs, and thrown cylinders are attached to pots in the same way as the pulled handle, which is illustrated in Steps 4 and 5.

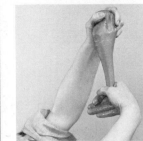

1. Wedge a lump of clay, a bit harder than the clay used for throwing, and shape it into an upside-down elongated pear. Hold it with your left hand and gently pull down with your right.

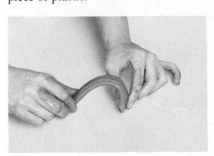

2. Keeping your right hand wet, continue pulling with gentle, even strokes, bringing down more clay from the top with each pull. Pull until the clay is the desired length and thickness.

3. Cut off a section of the clay for the handle. Bend it into the shape it will have on the pot. Place it on a table so that it holds this shape and let it stiffen for a while.

4. Using a needle tool, score the leather-hard pot on the wall opposite the spout, where the handle will be attached. Then apply some water or slip over the score marks.

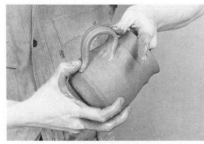

5. Attach the top of the handle of the pot at the scores, and smooth the clay so that it adheres firmly. Bend the handle to its final shape, and fuse the bottom of the handle to the pot.

6. To make a more natural looking handle, hold some clay as in Steps 1 and 2, but pull only three or four times, so that clay is still round and thick. Cut off a piece about 3 or 4 in. long.

7. Bang the thick end of the handle on a table to thicken it further. Score and apply slip to the point of attachment on the pot. Then push the handle firmly against the pot until it fuses.

8. Hold the pot up with your left hand and gently pull the handle with your right, as in Step 2, until it is the desired length and thickness. Keep your right hand wet.

9. Bend the handle to give it its final shape. Attach the other end to the pot by smoothing it against the wall. A little extra clay can be added to make this connection more secure.

Decoration

Though the most popular way to decorate pots is to glaze them after they are bisque fired (p. 168), there are many interesting and attractive ways to decorate unfired pots, or greenware.

Altering the shape of a wet pot. When a pot is freshly thrown or hand-built and is still wet, you can modify its shape with your hands. A finger can be drawn up the side of the pot to make ridges; these can be slight indentations or deep enough to create pronounced lobes in the pot. The rim can be given a square shape by pushing it out from the inside at four points. The pot can be basically reshaped by pushing in the sides with the palms of your hands.

Impressed

Impressed decoration and texture. When clay is firm enough to be handled but still too soft to be trimmed, it is said to be soft leather-hard, the optimal state for impressed decoration. Almost anything that can be held can be pushed into clay; the possibilities of impressed decoration and texture are limitless. Stamps for impressing decoration can be carved from clay, plaster, or linoleum. Repeating patterns can be impressed with household items that rotate, such as furniture casters. Rolling stamps can also be made out of plaster or clay. Clay can be paddled into various textures with wood.

Impressed decoration is so easy to create that there is a tendency for beginners to overuse the techniques and to clutter pots with overworked and ponderously redundant designs. Exercise moderation in decoration.

Fluted   Faceted

Altering a leather-hard pot. When a pot becomes leather hard, its shape can be modified by cutting away portions of the wall. Long parallel ridges can be made by pulling a special tool down the sides of the pot, a process called fluting. The walls can be shaved down to make a polygon, with several or many flat sides, by a process called faceting. Pots have to be prepared for these techniques by being thrown or built with thick walls.

Carving a leather-hard pot. Decorative incisions can be scratched into clay when the pot is soft leather-hard or leather hard. Incisions that are barely visible on greenware can be accentuated with certain glazes that dramatically change color when they pool and thicken in a depression (pp. 170–171, glaze 22). Oxide washes can be used to accentuate a relief incised design (p. 176). Designs can be cut right through the pot (pierced) when the clay is dry enough so that the cut edge is sharp but not so hard that the clay cracks as it is cut. Be careful not to cut away too much clay, or the walls will collapse.

Carved   Pierced

Adding clay decorations. Pieces of clay that are attached to pots as decorations are called sprigs. Sprigs should be made from the same clay used to make the pot so that the shrinkage rate of sprig and pot is the same. Sprigs can be colored by wedging oxides into the clay (p. 141). They are attached to the wetted surface of a leather-hard pot. Sprigs of fluid design can be made by trailing slip on newspaper, waiting for it to dry, then pressing it onto the pot.

Slip   Sprigged

Decorating with slip. Slips can be applied directly to greenware or to bisque-fired pots. Because greenware will shrink more than bisque-fired ware during firing, the slips used for greenware must have a greater shrinkage rate than those used on bisque-fired ware. Formulas for slips for greenware are given on page 166, and those for use on bisque-fired ware are on page 175.

The constituents of the slip should be mixed thoroughly, and the slip should be screened through an 80-mesh sieve before being used. Normally the best working consistency for slip is that of heavy cream, but this will vary somewhat according to its use. Experiment with various slips before using them on a finished pot.

Slip can be applied to a pot with a syringe or with a plastic bag with a small hole cut in the bottom, a technique called slip trailing. Slip trailing can be done on the wheel to make concentric patterns or on a stationary pot to make textures or designs.

Marbled

Feather combing and marbling. Feather combing and marbling are two techniques used to create interesting interplay between slips of contrasting colors. A layer of slip is applied to a slab or plate, and slip of contrasting color(s) is trailed across it. In feather combing, a flexible point, such as the tip of a feather, a thin wire, or a broom straw, is drawn across the slip so that the colors run into each other. In marbling, the clay is jarred so that the slips swirl together. Both techniques require that the slip be just the right consistency; practice on newspaper or on slabs that you don't need before you try these techniques on your finished ware.

Sgraffito. Sgraffito is the art of incising a layer of colored slip to expose a clay of contrasting color below it. The pot should be leather hard and the slip moist but firm enough to cut cleanly.

Sgraffito   Mishima

Mishima. Mishima is the art of inlaying colored slip into decorative depressed designs in a pot. (In the pictures on page 166 the design was made by rolling a plant into a soft slab of clay.) Mishima can be done with slips of several colors on the same pot.

Pottery

Altering the shape of a wet pot

To alter a wet pot from the outside, hold finger of your right hand against the wall and support the clay with the thumb and forefinger of your left hand on the inside. Bring both hands up the pot, pushing in gently to form an indentation.

To alter a pot from the inside, bring your finger up the inside of the pot. No support on the outside is needed. Because the clay is wet, it will stretch as you push—be careful not to push too hard, or the clay will tear.

To give the rim of a pot a square shape, push against opposite sides of the inside of the pot with two fingers. Then repeat to make the other two corners of the square. Push firmly, but be careful not to tear the clay.

A wet pot can be distorted into various forms by simply pushing on the walls. A common alteration is an elongated shape (shown above). It is made by pushing opposite sides of the pot with the palms of the hands.

Impressed decoration and texture

The simplest way to impress a decoration in clay is to push something into it when it is near leatherhard. Fingers can give a great variety of textures. Common household items can make very interesting impressions.

Thin objects with interesting textures, such as coarse cloth or plant leaves, can be impressed into clay with a rolling pin. Usually this is done on a slab. Thick rope can be delicately pushed into the sides of soft pots.

A lump of clay can be shaped to make a stamp for impressed decoration. Clay is easiest to carve when it is leather hard. To prevent sticking or eroding, you should bisque fire it (pp. 167–168) before you use it for stamping.

Stamps can also be made of wood, linoleum, or plaster. It is easiest to carve plaster several hours after it sets, when it is still damp. Refractory brick, used to make kiln walls, can be carved to make stamps with an interesting rough texture.

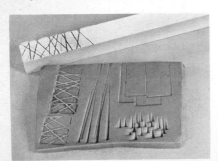

Various textures can be made by paddling the clay with a piece of wood. Paddling textures can be varied by altering the angle, frequency, and intensity of the blows. The paddles themselves can be given designs or textures with a saw or file.

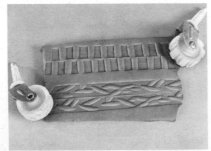

Continuous repeating patterns can be made with rolling stamps. Some household items, such as furniture casters, are good for this purpose. The patterns on the rollers can be embellished, clarified, or otherwise altered with a knife, saw, or file.

Rolling stamps can be made of plaster, as shown here and right. Carve or impress the pattern you want on your pots on a thin slab of clay. Bend the slab into a circle with the pattern on the inside and fuse the ends together.

Pour wet plaster into the clay. Hold a straw in the center to form a hole for an axle the stamp can rotate about. When the plaster dries, remove the clay and mount the stamp on a handle with a nail or wire running through the center hole.

Altering a leather-hard pot

Fluting tool

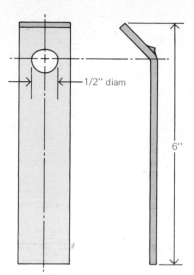

1/2" diam

6"

The tool that is usually used for fluting was introduced to America from the Orient by the eminent American potter Bernard Leach. You can easily make one at home. Cut a piece of soft metal (e.g., iron or aluminum) about 6 in. long and 1 in. wide. Drill a hole 1/2 in. in diameter 1 in. from the end of the strip. Hit the perimeter of the hole with a ball peen hammer to raise a sharp edge on the other side. Put the short end into a vise, with about half of the hole showing, and bend the strip to a 45° angle with the sharp edge out.

To flute a pot, pull the tool down the walls with the raised edge against the clay. Use long, steady strokes to cut even grooves in the clay. Repeat, forming ridges around the pot.

To facet a pot, pull a wire down the sides of it to cut flat faces. You can either hold wire taut between your hands or use a cheese slicer that has a wire cutter, as shown.

Carving a leather-hard pot

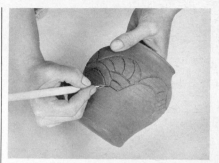

To incise a pot, scratch the walls with a needle tool. Areas can be carved away with trimming or sgraffito (p. 166) tools to form relief decoration. Incisions can be accentuated with glazes.

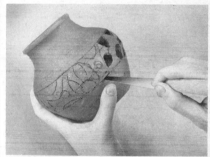

To make a pierced decoration, first lightly incise a design in the pot. Cut away the clay with a fettling knife; a needle tool is good for fine detail. Dry the pot very slowly.

Adding clay decorations

To attach a sprig to a pot, first shape the sprig. Wet the leather-hard pot at the point of attachment and press or lightly paddle the sprig against the pot until the connection is secure.

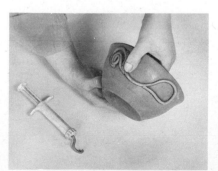

A tool called an extruder has interchangeable heads that produce strands of clay with different shapes. Strands from an extruder can be used to make interesting sprigs.

To transfer slip to a pot, make the slip from the same clay as was used to make the pot. Using a syringe or other applicator, lay down a pattern of slip on a piece of newspaper.

When the slip dries somewhat, wet the pot at the point of attachment. Pick up the newspaper and press it against the pot firmly until the slip adheres. Carefully pull off the newspaper.

Pottery

Decorating with slip

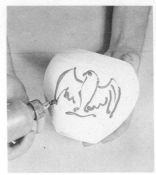

To slip trail on the wheel, hold the syringe over the pot and squeeze out a steady line of slip as the wheel turns very slowly.

You can leave the concentric trails as they are or lightly run your finger over them, as shown, to form a starlike slip pattern.

You can create a rough texture on a pot by applying a densely packed group of small cones of slip. This is easiest with thick slip.

Graceful drawings can be made with trailed slip. This takes practice; hesitations make blobs, and mistakes are difficult to remove.

Slip formulas

SLIP FOR GREENWARE			
White slip (parts)	To color	Add (parts)	
Ball clay 20	Blue	Cobalt carbonate	5
Kaolin 20		Yellow ocher	2
Nepheline syenite 10		Manganese dioxide	1
Borax 5	Green	Copper carbonate	10
Whiting 5	Yellow	Vanadium stain	10
Flint 25	Black	Manganese dioxide	10
Soda		Red iron oxide	8
feldspar 15		Cobalt carbonate	5
	Pearly yellow	Rutile	10
	Blue-green	Chromium oxide	4
		Cobalt carbonate	3

Feather combing and marbling

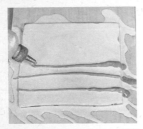

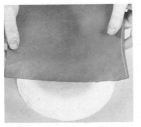

To feather comb, pour thick slip on a wet slab or plate. Trail lines of slip of a different color over the surface.

Jar the clay to make the slip level. Draw a flexible point across the slip to make the colors run together.

Interesting concentric patterns can be made by applying slip to a plate and feather combing on a slowly rotating wheel.

To marble, apply slips as shown at left. Jar plate or slab sharply in several directions so that colors swirl together.

A decorated slab can be made into a bowl using a plaster mold. When the slab is nearly leather-hard, put it over the mold.

Trim away excess clay. Attach several small pieces of clay to the slab to form feet. Dry the bowl slowly.

Sgraffito

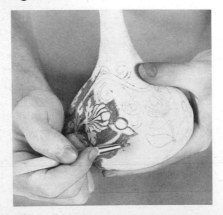

To make sgraffito decoration, coat the leather-hard pot with slip (brushing is usually easiest). When the slip is dry enough to be cut cleanly, incise the design with a needle tool or a sgraffito tool (a tool with a small, stiff, metal loop, shown at left). Areas of slip can be removed with a sgraffito tool or a trimming tool.

Sgraffito tools

Mishima

To make mishima decoration, incise, stamp, or roll a depressed design into a clay surface. Cover the surface and fill the depressions with thick slip of a contrasting color.

When the slip becomes leather hard, gently scrape the surface of the clay with a trimming tool, removing the surface slip but leaving the slip in the depressions. Dry the clay slowly.

Firing

After clay has been shaped and decorated, it is still a fragile substance that will reduce to slip if soaked in water. When the clay is placed in a kiln and fired to several thousand degrees Celsius, it becomes pottery, a durable, rock-hard, inert substance.

Firing is usually done in two steps. In the first, or bisque, firing the clay is fired to a relatively low temperature, leaving it stiff and porous. This makes the ware safer to handle when glaze is applied (p. 169) and also ensures that the surface will absorb the correct amount of glaze. The ware is then fired again, to the full maturation temperature, in the second, or glaze, firing.

Chemistry of firing. The plasticity of clay is due to the presence of water between the platelike clay particles (p. 132). When this water, called the water of plasticity, evaporates, the clay particles compact and the clay shrinks. When clay sits for a week or two, it attains the stiff, brittle state called bone dry, containing little water of plasticity. This drying does not entail any chemical change in the clay—if a bone-dry pot is put into water, it will eventually dissolve into slip.

In the early stages of firing the temperature is brought up slowly to allow the remaining water of plasticity to vaporize. If the temperature reaches 100°C too quickly, any small pockets of water remaining in the clay will turn to steam and blow the pot apart.

The first change in the chemical composition of the clay begins to occur at about 350°C, when the water that is chemically combined with silica and alumina (p. 132) begins to be driven off. By about 500°C this dehydration process is complete, and the chemical composition of the clay is permanently altered; if you place a pot that has been fired to 500°C in water, it will sit, unchanged, indefinitely, though it is still very fragile.

When the kiln reaches 555°C, quartz crystals (which are present in all clay) undergo a change in structure that increases the total volume of the clay by about 2 percent. After the clay is fired to its highest temperature and descends back to 555°C, the crystals revert to their original structure, with an attendant decrease in volume of about 2 percent. It is essential that both the heating and the cooling of the clay at this critical temperature be very gradual and very even, or the ware will be damaged.

Carbon and other impurities in the clay that are not already in oxide form are either oxidized or decomposed by the time the kiln reaches 900°C. If the firing proceeds too rapidly or if there is insufficient oxygen in the kiln, some carbon will remain in the clay and blacken the surface.

Vitrification. As the temperature increases, certain impurities in the clay, such as iron oxide, begin to melt. The melted impurities are absorbed by the surrounding clay and bind the particles together like glue. They also promote the melting and fusion of other constituents of the clay (certain combinations of chemicals have lower melting points than any one of the chemicals alone). This melting and fusing at very high temperatures, which makes the clay hard, glassy, and nonporous, is called vitrification.

Different clays vitrify at different temperatures. Earthenware clays, which contain many impurities, harden at low temperatures; they melt to liquid at temperatures at which high-firing clays, such as kaolin, do not approach vitrification. It is important to fire a clay to the temperature at which it attains maximum hardness and density without melting or sagging. This is called the *maturation temperature.*

In addition to the partial melting and fusion of the particles, fired clay gains hardness because of the growth of mullite $(3Al_2O_3 \cdot 2SiO_2)$ crystals. These long, thin crystals begin to grow at 955°C and interlock to form a lattice of considerable strength.

Because of the melting, absorption, and other changes that occur, clay shrinks further during firing, as much as 10 percent (see diagram, p. 133).

Pyrometric cones. Temperatures inside the kiln are measured in units

Cones before firing   Cones fired to cone 9

CONE	TEMPERATURE (rising 150°C/hr) °C
020	635
019	683
018	717
017	747
016	792
015	804
014	838
013	852
012	884
011	894
010	894
09	923
08	955
07	984
06	999
05	1046
04	1060
03	1101
02	1120
01	1137
1	1154
2	1162
3	1168
4	1186
5	1196
6	1222
7	1240
8	1263
9	1280
10	1305
11	1315
12	1326

called cones. This name is derived from small pyramid-shaped pieces of clay and flux called pyrometric cones. Pyrometric cones are formulated to soften and bend at specific temperatures; they are placed inside the kiln, in front of a peephole, so that the potter can see when they bend.

Actually, cones measure work heat rather than temperature—if the temperature of a kiln rises very slowly, more heat will be absorbed and some chemical reactions will be completed at a lower temperature than if the kiln temperature rises quickly. Because it takes the cone time to absorb enough heat to melt, the cone provides a more accurate indicator of the heat being absorbed by the ware than a device such as a thermometer, which measures only temperature.

Pyrometric cones are set in a pat of clay mixed with vermiculite. Three cones of consecutive numbers are usually used for one firing. For example, if you want to fire to cone 9, place cones 8, 9, and 10 into the pat, as shown in the schematic diagram on this page. When cone 8 bends over, it serves notice that the kiln is approaching temperature. When the tip of cone 9 touches the base, temperature has been reached. If cone 10 starts to bend, you are overfiring.

A smaller version of the pyrometric cone is used in kiln automatic shutoff devices. When the cone bends, a small piece of metal that rests on the cone descends, shutting off the kiln.

Loading the kiln. It is a good idea to let your pots dry for at least a week (longer for pots with very thick walls) before firing. If you are not sure that a pot is dry enough to fire, touch it to your cheek—if you feel any coolness from the pot, it still contains too much moisture to be fired. To accelerate drying once a pot is almost ready to fire,

(Continued on next page)

Pottery

Firing (continued)

Kiln stacking

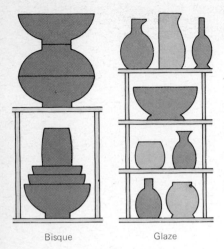

Bisque   Glaze

In a bisque firing (left) pots can be stacked on top of one another, foot-to-foot, rim-to-rim, or one inside of the other. Clay softens as it is fired, so do not stack too high or place fragile pieces on the bottom of the stack. In a glaze firing (right) pieces cannot touch and should be 1/4 in. apart. Refractory shelves are used to distribute the ware evenly throughout the kiln.

place it on top of the kiln while another load is being fired. The low heat radiated from the kiln will complete the drying process.

Posts and shelves of refractory material can be purchased from kiln dealers. Called kiln furniture, they are used to load the kiln in several layers (see diagram, above). Small balls of plastic fire clay can be stuck onto the ends of the posts to make the shelves level and stable. The kiln should be loaded evenly to prevent the shelves from toppling and to promote even firing. In an electric kiln leave at least 1 inch between the pots and the heating elements. In fuel-burning kilns space also has to be left between the ware and the walls to allow for the convection of the hot gases.

The kiln is loaded differently for bisque and glaze firings. Pots can be stacked on top of each other in the bisque firing, while in the glaze firing pots must not touch and should be at least 1/4 inch apart.

Kiln wash. Before the kiln is loaded for a glaze firing, the bottom of the kiln and the shelves should be brushed with several coats of kiln wash. Kiln wash is made of equal parts of kaolin and flint, mixed with water to the consistency of cream. It prevents the kiln and the shelves from sticking to the pots when glaze accidentally runs during firing.

In some fuel-burning kilns pots are placed in containers made out of fire clay, called saggers, which protect the pots from the flames and soot. A sagger for the primitive kiln shown on pages 138–139 is illustrated at right.

Firing the kiln. Once the kiln is loaded and the cone pats are put in place in front of the peepholes, the kiln is fired. The single most important thing to remember about firing is that it must be done slowly; rapid firing can cause explosions, bloating and blackening of the clay, or defects in the glaze. A typical bisque-firing schedule for an electric kiln would be to leave the kiln cracked open and on low heat for 1 to 2 hours; then close the kiln and leave it on low heat for 1 hour; turn it up to medium heat for 1 hour; turn it to high until the kiln reaches temperature.

For a glaze firing the temperature can be brought up faster in the beginning, but it should be slowed as maturation temperature is reached; there should be at least a 30-minute interval between the bending of the final two cones, or else the kiln should be held at constant temperature for at least 30 minutes after the final cone goes down. Bisque temperatures are usually reached in 4–10 hours, and glaze firing takes longer. The firing procedure will vary with fuel-burning kilns, depending on their size, fuel, and design.

Saggers

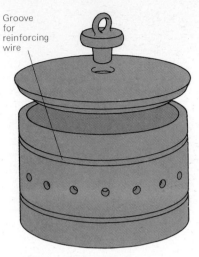

Groove for reinforcing wire

Saggers are used to protect ware from flames and soot in some fuel-burning kilns. The shape of the sagger will vary with the shape of the kiln. For the primitive kiln on page 139 the sagger should be round. It has three parts—the body, the lid, and a plug that can be removed from a distance with a poker so that you can see inside during firing. Throw or hand build the sagger out of fire clay.

When the firing of an electric kiln is finished, it is simply shut off. In fuel-burning kilns the damper and other openings must be sealed to prevent cold air from being sucked in. The kiln can be opened a crack after about 10 hours. Do not remove the ware until the kiln is cool enough to put your bare hand in. It usually takes a kiln at least as long to cool as it does to heat up.

Kiln safety. Before you fire your kiln, make a commonsense inspection of its surroundings: the kiln should be away from combustible materials; there must be adequate ventilation to dispel heat and vapors; electric kilns should be well grounded. Do not leave your kiln untended during firing.

Reduction firing. In fuel-burning kilns the chamber can be filled with smoke, which will chemically alter both the clay and the glazes inside. This is done by cutting back the air supply and partially closing the damper of the kiln, so that the combustion of the fuel is incomplete. The result is that the carbon in the fuel does not completely oxidize to carbon dioxide (CO_2), but instead becomes carbon monoxide (CO). Carbon monoxide is an unstable compound; it absorbs oxygen from the oxides in the clay and glaze, altering their color and texture. For example, most iron oxide in clay is ferric, or red, iron oxide (Fe_2O_3). In a reducing atmosphere some of this changes to ferrous, or black, iron oxide (FeO). As a result, all red clay that is not covered with a glaze will darken if fired in a reducing atmosphere. Reduction glazes are shown on pages 170–171.

A reducing atmosphere is created in a gas kiln by partially closing the damper and cutting back the primary air intake to about one-quarter of normal, so that the flame turns a dirty orange. If you look through the peephole and see dusty, murky air, you have created a reducing atmosphere. Do not make your kiln belch thick clouds of heavy smoke—this can ruin the ware by overreduction. Some types of fuel-burning kilns naturally burn with an orange flame, making it easy to produce a reducing atmosphere.

A typical reduction schedule for cones 9–10 would be to fire in an oxidizing atmosphere until cone 08; reduce the atmosphere for 30–60 minutes to reduce the clay body; fire with a neutral (neither oxidizing nor reducing) atmosphere (the flame should have some green in it) until cone 7 or 8; reduce the kiln for 30–60 minutes, bringing the kiln up slowly to maturation temperature. A brief period of oxidizing firing sometimes follows before the kiln is sealed and shut off to cool. Note: reduction firing should not be attempted with an electric kiln.

Glazing

A glaze is a glassy coating that is melted onto a piece of clay during firing. It adds strength and beauty to the clay, while usually making it nonporous.

Silica. There are three main ingredients in a glaze. The most important is silica, the chief component of glass. Silica alone could serve as a glaze if not for its melting point, which is far higher than that of clay. The more silica in a glaze, the harder the glaze is; the high proportion of silica in high-firing glazes makes them more durable than low-firing glazes.

Flux. To lower the melting point of the silica, fluxes are added. Different fluxes are active at different temperatures; a chart of common fluxes and their firing ranges appears on page 172.

Alumina. The third constituent of a glaze is alumina, which gives greater viscosity to the glaze to prevent it from running off vertical surfaces during firing. Alumina also adds strength to the glaze and prevents other chemicals from crystallizing during cooling, which can disturb the smoothness and homogeneity of the glaze.

Low-firing glazes. Low-firing glazes contain more fluxes and less alumina and silica than high-firing glazes. As a result, low-firing glazes are softer, more easily scratched, and more soluble in mild acids (such as those contained in fruit juices) than high-firing glazes. Low-firing glazes come in a great variety of colors, many of which are not attainable at high temperatures. The most versatile of the low-firing fluxes is lead. However, lead can be a deadly poison, both to the potter who uses the raw material and to anyone who eats from a lead-glazed dish, as the lead can be dissolved and absorbed by certain foods. Though there are ways to neutralize the toxicity of lead, it is a good idea to avoid lead glazes altogether; other fluxes and combinations of fluxes can be used instead.

High-firing glazes. High-firing glazes, like high-firing clays, are simpler to formulate than those for low temperatures because the high temperatures make less flux necessary. For example, in the stoneware firing range, feldspar—which contains silica, alumina, and at least one alkaline oxide (which acts as a flux)—can be used as a glaze with few if any additives. At cones 9–10 colors become soft, but the glazes themselves are rock hard.

Colors. Colors are created in glazes by the addition of certain metallic oxides (see chart, p. 172). Ingredients can also be added to affect the opacity and the texture of the glaze (p. 173).

Glazes in almost every color for every firing range are available at ceramic supply stores. If you buy a low-firing glaze for use on dinnerware, be sure there is no lead in it.

Mixing glazes. You may tire of commercial glazes and want to mix your own. Besides those depicted on the following pages, formulas for glazes can be found in many other crafts books and magazines.

Glazing results depend on the clay body and the firing atmosphere and schedule as well as on the glaze, so there will always be some differences between pictures in books and your own glaze results. A variety of popular glazes is shown on the following two pages; information for altering these glazes and for creating new formulas from scratch is given on pages 172–174.

Working with dry ingredients. To prepare a glaze, carefully weigh out and mix the dry ingredients and add water until the mixture is the consistency of heavy cream. To achieve consistent results in glazing, note the amount of water you add; the thickness of the glaze can radically affect its appearance (see p. 174). Screen the glaze through an 80-mesh sieve. Stir the glaze thoroughly before you apply it.

Applying glazes. You should handle your bisque-fired ware as little as possible and keep it away from dirt and dust. Before you apply the glaze, wipe each piece with a damp sponge. Glaze can then be applied to the dampened clay by brushing, pouring, or dipping, as shown below. Pouring and dipping require more glaze but give more even results than brushing. Glaze can also be sprayed using special equipment.

There should be no glaze on the underside or the bottom ¼ inch of a piece, or the glaze might run and stick to the shelf during firing. An easy way to achieve this is to dip the base in melted wax before glazing.

Once the glaze is applied, it should not be touched, either to be sponged off, retouched, or redipped, until it has dried. Glazed pieces must be completely dry before they are fired.

To brush on a glaze, use a thick, wide brush. Apply glaze thickly and evenly, or the finish will be splotchy. About three brushings of glaze give the thickness of one dipping.

To apply a glaze by pouring, pour the glaze into the pot and rotate it until all areas are covered. Pour out the excess glaze immediately, and shake any extra droplets from the rim.

The undersides of pots, especially of plates, can also be glazed by pouring. Place plate on sticks that rest on rim of a large bowl; pour glaze over plate so that excess runs into bowl.

To apply a glaze by dipping, hold the pot by the foot and immerse it in the bowl of glaze. Pull the pot out, shake off the excess glaze, and touch up any finger marks with a brush.

Dipping can be used to create interesting effects. For example, the pot can be dipped into the glaze sideways. After the glaze dries, the pot can be redipped at another angle.

Pottery

Glazes and glaze formulas

1 2 3 4 5 6 7

8 9 10 11 12 13 14

There are 28 glazes and their formulas shown on these two pages. The ingredients in the formulas are given approximately in parts per hundred (because of the small amounts of certain ingredients, especially colorants, the total is not always exactly 100). The ingredients are mixed and applied as discussed on page 169.

The clay body numbers, indicating the constitution of the clays under the glazes, refer to the formulas given on page 134.

The glazes should be fired to the temperatures indicated by the cone numbers. Firing should be in an oxidizing atmosphere, except as noted. The firing procedure is discussed on pages 167–168.

1. Clear
Clay body 1, cone 04
Frit #3195	75
Ball clay	24
Magnesium carbonate	1

2. Spotted green
Clay body 1, cone 04
Frit #3195	69.0
Ball clay	23.0
Tin oxide	7.0
Magnesium carbonate	1.0
Chrome oxide	0.5

3. Blue
Clay body 1, cone 04
Frit #3195	69
Ball clay	23
Tin oxide	7
Magnesium carbonate	1
Cobalt carbonate	1

4. Red
Clay body 1, cone 04
Frit #3195	75
Ball clay	25
Red stain	10

5. Speckled blue matte
Clay body 4, cone 6
Soda feldspar	34.0
Nepheline syenite	17.0
Whiting	12.6
Barium carbonate	1.6
Zinc oxide	6.0
Gerstley borate	3.3
Dolomite	2.6
Talc	3.3
Kaolin	12.3
Flint	7.3
Tin oxide	1.3
Cobalt carbonate	0.6
Manganese dioxide	2.0
Copper carbonate	1.3
Ilmenite	1.3

6. Red
Clay body 4, cone 6
Flint	30
Kaolin	5
Soda feldspar	20
Talc	14
Gerstley borate	32
Red iron oxide	15

7. Albany slip
Clay body 4, cone 6
Albany clay	90
Lithium carbonate	10

8. Black
Clay body 4, cone 6
Albany clay	75
Nepheline syenite	15
Barium carbonate	10
Cobalt carbonate	5
Manganese dioxide	1
Bentonite	1

9. Lavender
Clay body 4, cone 6
Nepheline syenite	30
Gerstley borate	15
Barium carbonate	10
Whiting	10
Flint	20
Kaolin	5
Lithium carbonate	5
Talc	5

10. Speckled beige
Clay body 4, cone 6
Gerstley borate	14
Spodumene	30
Kaolin	3
Dolomite	7
Talc	13
Flint	28
Rutile	5
Manganese dioxide	1

11. Purple opalescence
Clay body 4, cone 6
Gerstley borate	14
Spodumene	30
Kaolin	5
Dolomite	7
Talc	13
Flint	20
Rutile	6
Granular manganese dioxide	1

12. Speckled white matte
Clay body 4, cone 6
Nepheline syenite	5.0
Whiting	12.0
Zinc oxide	10.0
Kaolin	18.0
Flint	1.5
Lithium carbonate	5.0
Barnard clay	1.2
Bentonite	2.0

13. Cream-breaking red
Clay body 4, cone 6
Gerstley borate	35
Soda feldspar	15
Whiting	10
Barium carbonate	5
Flint	10
Tin oxide	13
Red iron oxide	2

14. Purple opalescence
Clay body 6, cone 6
Same formula as glaze 11

15   16   17   18   19   20   21

22   23   24   25   26   27   28

15. Robin's-egg blue
Clay body 6, cone 6

Potash feldspar	32.0
Flint	24.0
Kaolin	12.0
Zinc oxide	8.0
Whiting	24.0
Rutile	7.0
Cobalt carbonate	0.5
Tin oxide	7.5

16. Clear
Clay body 6, cone 6

Gerstley borate	49
Kaolin	17
Flint	34

17. Pearly
Clay body 6, cone 6

Dolomite	15.4
Nepheline syenite	15.4
Frit #3195	30.8
Zinc oxide	9.2
Ball clay	15.4
Tin oxide	3.5
Rutile	9.6
Borax	4.8
Red iron oxide	2.0

18. Pale blue-gray celadon
Clay body 6, cone 6

Spodumene	50.000
Flint	25.000
Gerstley borate	25.000
Chrome oxide	0.009
Cobalt oxide	0.038
Red iron oxide	0.046
Manganese dioxide	0.015
Nickel oxide	0.016

19. Red-green
Clay body 5,
cones 9–10, reduction

Soda feldspar	49
Talc	4
Kaolin	23
Bone ash	4
Whiting	20
Red iron oxide	4

20. Cream
Clay body 5,
cones 9–10, reduction

Soda feldspar	26
Dolomite	30
Whiting	5
Kaolin	33
Flint	6

21. Yellow-brown
Clay body 5,
cones 9–10, reduction

Dolomite	31.0
Whiting	4.0
Potash feldspar	25.0
Kaolin	32.0
Flint	7.0
Red iron oxide	1.0
Cobalt carbonate	0.5

22. Grassy celadon
Clay body 5,
cones 9–10, reduction

Ball clay	11.0
Whiting	16.5
Flint	30.5
Soda feldspar	41.0
Red iron oxide	1.0

23. Temmoku
Clay body 7,
cones 9–10, reduction

Albany clay	59
Flint	13
Whiting	10
Soda feldspar	12
Tin oxide	2
Red iron oxide	5

24. Mottled blue
Clay body 7,
cones 9–10, reduction

Soda feldspar	42.0
Kaolin	3.3
Flint	26.0
Whiting	2.6
Gerstley borate	9.0
Dolomite	9.0
Zinc oxide	1.7
Barium carbonate	4.3
Tin oxide	2.6
Rutile	5.9
Copper carbonate	0.5

25. Lung chun green
Clay body 7,
cones 9–10, reduction

Soda feldspar	35
Dolomite	15
Whiting	5
Kaolin	9
Flint	35
Red iron oxide	2

26. Clear
Clay body 7,
cones 9–10, reduction

Soda feldspar	44
Whiting	18
Flint	28
Kaolin	10

27. Green celadon
Clay body 7,
cones 9–10, reduction

Soda feldspar	44.0
Whiting	18.0
Flint	28.0
Kaolin	10.0
Black iron oxide	1.5

28. Blue celadon
Clay body 7,
cones 9–10, reduction

Potash feldspar	50.6
Whiting	6.2
Kaolin	4.0
Flint	20.5
Barium carbonate	16.5
Red iron oxide	2.1

Pottery

Glazes: advanced formulations and special effects

The formulation of glazes is a tricky and somewhat unpredictable business, as it is rarely possible to add an ingredient to a glaze to achieve one effect without its having other effects as well.

Not only does each glaze ingredient have its own individual nature; each combination of ingredients also has peculiarities. The challenge of making glazes is to master these idiosyncracies.

Do not let this deter you from making your own glazes, but do not have the expectation that you can pick any source of silica, any source of alumina, any flux, and a colorant, and then be able to accurately predict the appearance of the glaze.

An easy way to make new glazes is to add colorants to a clear glaze, such as glazes 1, 16, and 26, on pages 170–171. Common metallic oxides used as colorants are shown in Chart 3 at right.

Major alterations in the glazes shown on pages 170–171 or formulation of glazes from scratch require more information about fluxes and other glaze chemicals. Chart 2 (right) shows the firing ranges of the common fluxes used in glazes.

Raw ingredients. Fluxes and the other glaze components are rarely used in their pure forms, which can be quite expensive and difficult to obtain. Sometimes cheaper chemicals that yield the desired glaze chemical during firing are used; for example, common whiting ($CaCO_3$) becomes calcium oxide (CaO) at high temperature. Some chemicals contribute more than one of the desired components (kaolin, for instance, gives both silica and alumina to a glaze).

Chart 1 on this page shows the raw materials of common glazes and their derivatives during firing. This table is useful for formulating glazes because it tells which raw ingredients are the sources of the desired glaze chemicals. Also, the chemical formulas of the raw

CHART 1: GLAZE MATERIALS AND THEIR DERIVATIVES

Raw glaze material	Formula	Result in firing
Soda feldspar	$Na_2O \cdot Al_2O_3 \cdot 6SiO_2$	Na_2O, Al_2O_3, SiO_2
Potash feldspar	$K_2O \cdot Al_2O_3 \cdot 6SiO_2$	K_2O, Al_2O_3, SiO_2
Spodumene	$Li_2O \cdot Al_2O_3 \cdot 4SiO_2$	Li_2O, Al_2O_3, SiO_2
Nepheline syenite		K_2O, Na_2O, Al_2O_3, SiO_2
Clay	$Al_2O_3 \cdot 2SiO_2 \cdot 2H_2O$	Al_2O_3, SiO_2
Talc	$3MgO \cdot 4SiO_2 \cdot H_2O$	MgO, SiO_2
Flint	SiO_2	SiO_2
Wollastonite	$CaO \cdot SiO_2$	CaO, SiO_2
Magnesium carbonate	$MgCO_3$	MgO
Lithium carbonate	Li_2CO_3	Li_2O
Barium carbonate	$BaCO_3$	BaO
Zinc oxide	ZnO	ZnO
Dolomite	$CaCO_3 \cdot MgCO_3$	MgO, CaO
Gerstley borate	$2CaO \cdot 3B_2O_3 \cdot 5H_2O$	CaO, B_2O_3
Whiting	$CaCO_3$	CaO
Soda ash	Na_2CO_3	Na_2O
Kaolin	$Al_2O_3 \cdot 2SiO_2 \cdot 2H_2O$	Al_2O_3, SiO_2
Frit #3195		Na_2O (.311 part)
		CaO (.689 part)
		Al_2O_3 (.405 part)
		B_2O_3 (1.100 parts)
		SiO_2 (2.760 parts)
Frit #P25		Na_2O (.311 part)
		ZnO (.035 part)
		Al_2O_3 (.364 part)
		B_2O_3 (.695 part)
		SiO_2 (2.330 parts)
Borax	$Na_2O \cdot B_2O_3 \cdot 10H_2O$	Na_2O, B_2O_3
Bone ash	$4Ca_3(PO_4) \cdot 2CaCO_3$	CaO

CHART 2: FLUXES

Flux	Formula	Firing range
Sodium oxide (soda)	Na_2O	all temperatures
Potassium oxide (potash)	K_2O	all temperatures
Boric oxide	B_2O_3	all temperatures
Lithium oxide	Li_2O	all temperatures
Zinc oxide	ZnO	cone 03 and up
Calcium oxide	CaO	cone 03 and up
Barium oxide	BaO	cone 3 and up
Magnesium oxide	MgO	cone 3 and up

CHART 3: COLORANTS

To color	Add	Percentage
Medium blue to blue-black	Cobalt carbonate	¼-1½%
Light metallic green	Copper carbonate	1-5
Tan to brown-black	Red iron oxide	1
Medium to dark purple	Manganese carbonate	4-6
Green	Chrome oxide	½-3
Tan	Rutile	5
Gray to brown	Nickel oxide	1-2
Gray	Iron chromate	2
Yellow	Vanadium stain	10
Gray-blue	Cobalt carbonate	¼
	Red iron oxide	2
Blue-green	Cobalt carbonate	¼
	Copper carbonate	2
Yellow-green	Copper carbonate	3
	Vanadium stain	3
Warm blue	Cobalt carbonate	¼
	Rutile	5
Warm ocher	Vanadium stain	8
	Rutile	5

For reduction firing

	Add	Percentage
Light to dark blue	Cobalt carbonate	⅛-1
Turquoise	Cobalt carbonate	¼
	Chrome oxide	1
Warm blue	Cobalt carbonate	¼
	Rutile	5
Gray-blue	Cobalt carbonate	¼
	Nickel oxide	1
Brown	Manganese carbonate	4
Textured brown	Manganese carbonate	4
	Rutile	5
Spotty brown	Ilmenite	2
Celadon	Red iron oxide	1
Dark olive celadon	Red iron oxide	3
Mottled green or brown	Red iron oxide	4
Copper red	Copper carbonate	¼-½
Black	Cobalt carbonate	1
	Red iron oxide	8
	Manganese carbonate	3

Clear glaze 16, pp. 170-171

Clear glaze 16

Clear glaze with 1 percent cobalt carbonate

Clear glaze with 5 percent tin oxide

Ash glaze

Unaccentuated crackle

Crackle accentuated with ink

Crackle glaze accentuated with ink

ingredients in the chart show the proportions of the constituent chemicals.

For example, if you are trying to formulate a glaze that will mature at earthenware temperatures, the glaze must have a fairly high proportion of flux relative to the amount of silica. (The basic proportions of alumina, silica, and flux for any firing range can be found by examining the formulas given on pages 170–171.) If you select soda or potash as your flux, there are several raw chemicals to choose from. Feldspars will yield these fluxes but will also give you six molecules of silica for every molecule of flux. As a result, the glaze with feldspar as the flux will not mature at earthenware temperatures.

Frits. Look at the frits in Chart 1. (A frit is a mixture of chemicals that is heated to a high temperature, cooled, and ground up for the purpose of neutralizing the solubility, toxicity, or some other undesirable quality of one or more of its constituent chemicals before it is added to the glaze mixture.) You will notice that the relative pro-

portion of fluxes to silica in frits is much higher than in feldspar. Therefore the frits would be much better sources for the fluxes of an earthenware glaze. Chart 1 gives the proportions of the chemicals that make up two widely used frits.

Science vs. pure hunch. The chemical proportions of a glaze can be calculated very precisely by taking into consideration the weight of the molecules of the different chemicals; many volumes have been written about this scientific approach to glaze formulation. However, there is also something to be said for mixing glazes by hunch or impulse, and some of the most beautiful glazes you are likely to create will be made this way.

Transparent and opaque glazes. When a glaze is fired to maturity, it is usually transparent. Transparency is frequently desired in a glaze, especially if there is underglaze decoration on the surface of the clay (see pp. 175–176). Glazes can be made opaque by underfiring or by adding opacifiers to the

glaze formula. The addition of 1 to 3 percent tin oxide will make a glaze cloudy, and 5 percent will make it opaque. About 7 percent zirconium oxide will also make a glaze opaque (see illustrations, above).

Matte glazes. Just as glazes are usually transparent when fired to maturity, they are also usually glossy. A glaze can be given a dull, nonreflecting (matte) surface by underfiring or by changing the formulation of the glaze so that is does not reach full maturity at the planned firing temperature. This can be done by adding more silica and/or alumina to the glaze. The addition of calcium oxide or magnesium oxide can have a similar effect (see glaze 5, pp. 170–171).

Ash glazes. Ashes from burned organic matter can be used to make glazes with soft, mottled surfaces (see above). Ashes contain alkaline fluxes, so they can either be substituted for a flux in a stoneware glaze or simply added in increasing amounts to the glaze until the desired appearance is

attained. The ashes should be screened through a 60-mesh sieve before being added to the other chemicals.

Slip glazes. Earthenware clays, which mature at low temperatures, melt to a liquid at stoneware temperatures. They can, therefore, constitute the bodies of attractive glazes for stoneware in a range of earthy colors. The most common of these slip glazes is Albany (glaze 7, pp. 170–171), but other earthenware clays can also be used, either by themselves or with a few additives.

Crackle glazes. Crackle is the network of fine lines that occurs in a glaze for decorative effect. (When this effect is not desired, it is called crazing.) A glaze can be made to crackle by adding fluxes that have high rates of expansion. In high-firing glazes feldspar should be added; in low-firing glazes use potash or soda. Crackle can be accentuated by rubbing ink or some other colorant over the pot (see illustrations, above). A pot may continue to develop crackle months after firing.

Pottery

Glazes: advanced formulations and special effects *(continued)*

Crystalline glazes. The presence of alumina in a glaze prevents crystals from forming as the glaze cools. If there is no alumina, certain chemicals can be made to crystallize in the glaze if the kiln is cooled very slowly. Crystalline glazes are difficult to produce, and much experimentation with the formulation and the cooling schedule is required (see illustration, below).

Salt glazes. An interesting "orange peel" textured glaze can be given to a pot by throwing salt into the kiln when the clay is at maturation temperature (see illustration, below). The salt (NaCl) dissociates into sodium and chlorine; the sodium reacts with the silica in the clay to make the glaze, while the deadly chlorine gas is released into the atmosphere.

Because chlorine gas is so poisonous, salt glazing must only be done where you are absolutely certain that there is adequate ventilation. The salt attacks the walls of the kiln, eventually destroying it. The salt also leaves a residue on the kiln walls that is reactivated each time the kiln is heated, so once a kiln is fired with salt, thereafter it can only be used for salt glazing. Because of these difficulties, salt glazing is not recommended for beginners.

Crystalline glaze

Salt glaze with slip decoration

Glaze 9, thick application

Glaze 9, thin application

Piece dipped in glaze 6, then glaze 5

Piece dipped in glaze 7, then glaze 11

Piece dipped in glaze 14, then glaze 15

Piece dipped in glaze 8, then glaze 11

Glaze flaws

There are several common flaws that can spoil the appearance of a glaze (see illustrations, right). The remedies suggested below cannot always correct the flaws, and sometimes the correction causes a change in the color or texture of the glaze.

Crazing. Crackling that is not wanted can occur during cooling, when the glaze contracts more than the clay body, causing the glaze to split apart and form fine lines. Not only does crazing spoil the appearance of a glaze, it can also make pots unsanitary for use as dinnerware, because food can seep through the cracks and be absorbed by the clay. Crazing can be corrected by doing the opposite of what is suggested to cause crackling (see p. 173) or, more simply, by adding flint to the glaze.

Shivering. The opposite of crazing, this is caused by the cooling clay body shrinking more than the glaze. It can be corrected by making, in moderation, the alterations suggested to cause crackling or by removing some flint from the glaze.

Crawling. The glaze parts during cooling, exposing some of the clay underneath. This can be caused by applying glaze over ware that is dirty or dusty. Glazes that contain a lot of clay sometimes crawl; this can be corrected by bisque firing the powdered clay before you mix it into the glaze.

Pitting and pinholing. The appearance of these small holes in the surface of the glaze most frequently occurs in glazes that have an underfired look, such as matte glazes. If pitting and pinholing can be corrected, it is usually by making the glaze more fluid so that it covers the holes and pits after they form. This can be done by lengthening the firing cycle, by firing slightly higher, or by adding more flux to the glaze. Applying the glaze more thinly and cutting down on the zinc oxide and rutile in the glaze can also help.

Crazing

The glaze on the side of the bowl has formed unattractive crazed lines.

Shivering

The glaze on the rim of the pitcher has shivered and, as frequently happens, has fallen off.

The glaze on the vase has crawled seriously, exposing the white clay body beneath.

Crawling

The glaze on the pot was applied very thickly and shows considerable pitting near the bottom of the pot.

Pitting and pinholing

Underglaze and overglaze decoration

The thickness of glazes adds a dimension to their decorative potential. Different colors and textures can appear at different levels of the glaze, either on the clay body itself as underglaze decoration, as part of the glaze, or on top of the glaze as overglaze decoration.

Underglaze decoration. Slips can be applied to dampened bisque-fired ware if the slips are formulated with low enough shrinkage rates so that they will not pull away from the pot during firing. A formula for slip for use on bisque-fired ware is given below.

WHITE SLIP

Nepheline syenite	20
Kaolin	25
Ball clay	20
Flint	30
Borax	5
Bentonite	3

For use on bisque fire to cones 04-9 (for colorants, see chart, p. 166)

Oxide washes can be used to accentuate textures or carved decoration. Metallic oxide colorants are mixed with water (for example, 2 teaspoons of red iron oxide per cup of water), and then applied (see illustrations, p. 176).

Special underglaze pigments are available from ceramic supply stores. Commercial pigments are more powerful colorants than oxides, and they are available in a complete pallette of colors. They come as powders, which are usually mixed with water and brushed on. Glycerine can be added to the mixture to make it smoother and more viscous. The color of the pigments will vary with the thickness of applications, but underglazes should not be applied too thickly, or they will cause crawling or blistering of the covering glaze. Some pigments are affected by reduction firing, while others are not (see illustration, p. 176).

Overglaze decoration. Overglaze decoration can be applied over an unfired glaze, a technique called majolica, or over a fired glaze, using overglaze colors and/or lusters.

Majolica is usually made by brushing a colored glaze decoration over a layer of white or light-colored raw glaze. The background glaze should be opaque—tin glaze is usually used—and it should be applied evenly, either by dipping or pouring. It is a good idea to brush on the colored decoration when the background is still moist, so that the background does not flake off as you paint. When the piece is fired, the decoration melts and fuses with the background glaze (see illustration, p. 176).

Overglaze colors are applied to a piece over a fired glaze. The piece is then refired to a much lower temperature, usually between cones 018 and 014. The great advantage to overglaze decoration is that the low firing temperatures make a complete spectrum of colors possible. Because the colors are much the same before and after firing, it is possible to paint with accuracy and predictability. Porcelain and china are frequently used as the backgrounds for overglaze painting, as they enhance the brilliance of the colors; this process is called *china painting*.

Because of their low firing temperatures, overglaze colors do not have the durability of glazes that are fired considerably higher. Repeated washings may cause the colors to fade and eventually to disappear.

Lusters. Lusters are shiny, metallic overglaze decorations that are fired between cones 021 and 015. They are usually made of metallic salts mixed with a medium that burns off during firing. Lusters require reduction, and traditionally the kiln atmosphere was

(Continued on next page)

Pottery

Underglaze and overglaze decoration *(continued)*

reduced to achieve the metallic shininess in the lusters. However, many modern commercial lusters are mixed with chemicals that create a very local reduction, allowing the luster-decorated piece itself to be fired in an oxidizing or a neutral atmosphere.

Lusters are usually brushed onto a glazed surface. If they are applied over a large area, they can look gaudy, and the best luster patterns are those that form a counterpoint to an underglaze or another overglaze decoration (see illustration, below).

Wax resist. If a pattern of wax is applied to a pot, glazes, slips, or colorants that are subsequently applied will adhere only to the unwaxed surfaces. The wax burns off during firing.

Wax resist can be used on greenware or on bisque-fired ware, in conjunction with almost any kind of decorative colorant. It can also be used over a layer of colorant to form a resist pattern with the following layer.

Although wax resist can be done with heated paraffin wax, emulsion-type wax sold at ceramic supply stores is easier to use because it can be painted on without heating. It also creates less smoke during firing than does paraffin wax.

Underglaze painting beneath transparent glaze

Majolica

Luster decoration

Painted china

Oxide wash decoration. To accentuate an incised decoration with oxide wash, first mix an oxide or underglaze pigment with water (see text). Then soak a sponge in the solution and wipe it over the incised decoration.

Wipe over the pot with a clean sponge, removing the oxide from the raised areas but leaving it in the depressions of the design. Do not make underglaze decoration too thick, or it may blister a glaze that is applied over it.

Wax-resist decoration. To create a wax-resist decoration on greenware or bisque-fired ware, first paint the wax pattern on the pot with a brush. Then apply a glaze or slip over the surface of the pot, including the waxed areas.

After the glaze or slip dries (usually in a few minutes), dampen a sponge and remove the dried glaze or slip from the waxed areas only, leaving the unwaxed areas covered. The wax will burn off during firing.

Raku

Raku, a rapid, spontaneous method of glazing and firing, was invented in Japan in the 16th century A.D. The word *raku* means "felicity," a title bestowed upon the earliest raku wares by the reigning ruler of Japan.

In raku firing, bisque-fired ware is glazed, placed in a red-hot kiln, then removed from the kiln when the piece itself becomes red-hot and the glaze melts. In order to withstand the thermal shock of the rapid heating and cooling, the raku clay body should contain a high proportion of fire clay and/or stoneware clay and at least 20 percent grog or silica sand.

Traditional Japanese raku forms are small, irregular, hand-built cups used for the tea ceremony. Contemporary potters use all kinds of forms for raku, but the violent nature of the process precludes the use of especially delicate clay pieces.

Raku glazes are formulated to melt at low temperatures. Although traditional raku glazes are soft and subdued, contemporary raku utilizes glazes in a wide color range, including metallic lusters. Four raku glaze formulas are given below, at right.

Raku firing. Glaze your bisque-fired pieces and let them dry thoroughly before firing. Heat the kiln to red heat (cones are not used in raku because heat is lost when the kiln is constantly opened and closed, and because different raku glazes melt at different temperatures). Place the ware in the hot kiln with tongs, positioning some of it in front of a peephole.

Caution: If you are using an electric kiln, never place the tongs inside the kiln when the current is on.

Usually in about 10 or 15 minutes the ware will start to glow red. The glaze will start to melt, then bubble, then become shiny and smooth. When you see this (by looking through the peephole), remove the ware from the

The ware is removed from the kiln with tongs after it has become red-hot and the glazes have melted and become shiny and smooth.

Can filled with leaves or sawdust

Red-hot pot — Bucket of water — Finished piece

The ware is either left to cool or placed in a can full of combustible material with the lid on. After a few minutes pieces are removed from can and either immediately doused in water or partially reoxidized and then doused in water. Rubbing with steel wool brings out colors and lusters.

kiln with the tongs. The red-hot ware can be left to cool in the air or immediately doused in a bucket of water.

Reducing raku. Much modern raku is reduced after it is removed from the kiln. This is done by putting it into a can full of combustible material, such as sawdust, leaves, or straw. The hot ware starts a fire in the can, and when the top is quickly put on, thick, acrid smoke (a reducing atmosphere) is produced. The ware should ordinarily be left in the can with the lid on for 2 minutes or longer. Reduction will darken or blacken all unglazed surfaces, and will produce certain glaze colors, especially lusters (see illustra-

tion, above). If the pot is taken out of the can (using the tongs) when it is still red-hot, it will partially reoxidize. Reoxidation can be prevented by putting the hot pot immediately into a bucket of water. When the pot cools, rubbing it with steel wool will bring out the colors and lusters.

The final look of a raku piece depends on many factors, including the form of the piece, the glaze, the amount of reduction, the texture of the reducing agent in the can, the amount of reoxidation, and the timing and speed of cooling. Thus, raku is a technique with great potential for spontaneity and variation.

RAKU GLAZES

1. Clear	Gerstley borate	80
	Nepheline syenite	20
2. Crackle white	Gerstley borate	80
	Potash feldspar	20
3. Copper penny	Gerstley borate	80
	Potash feldspar	20
	Yellow ocher	7
	Copper carbonate	2
	Cobalt carbonate	1
4. Blue	Gerstley borate	87
	Copper carbonate	9
	Cobalt carbonate	4

Pottery/projects

Nine projects

The projects on this and the facing page can be constructed using the techniques illustrated throughout the chapter. A wide variety of methods, from simple hand construction by the slab technique through difficult pieces thrown on the wheel and covered with multiple glazes, are demonstrated. Use these to understand how different clay bodies and glazes combine, as well as to derive ideas for your own designs, but by all means improvise.

The clay body numbers, indicating the constitution of the clays under the glazes, refer to the formulas given on page 134. The glaze numbers refer to the glazes that are shown, with their chemical recipes, on pages 170–171.

The pots should be fired to the temperatures indicated by the cone numbers (pp.167–168). The firing atmosphere (reduction or oxidation) is determined by the glaze (see directions on pages 167–168, 170–171).

This massive vase was thrown, then embellished with a series of pulled handles, using clay body 7. It was fired to cone 9 (oxidation atmosphere). After mother-of-pearl luster was applied, the vase was fired again to cone 018. Then platinum luster was added for highlights, and the vase was fired once more, to cone 019.

This plate and cannister set was thrown on the wheel, using clay body 4. Flanged lids sit securely in the cannisters. The pieces were dipped in glazes 7 and 8; the third color was created by the overlapping of the other two. Fire to cone 6.

The classic Chinese vase below was thrown from clay body 7, then incised when it dried to leather hard. The celadon glaze, 27, pooled in the incisions during firing. Fire to cone 9.

This thrown pot and the elaborate attached sprigs (p.163) were made from clay body 5. Glazed 27, which covers the body of the pot, does not cover the sprigs because of the wax resist (p.176). Fire to cone 9.

This teapot (p.160) and cup set was thrown from clay body 6. The underglaze decoration, in copper and cobalt oxides, is covered by glaze 18. Fire to cone 6.

This tureen and bowl set was thrown using clay body 4. The tureen was thrown in two sections, the pedestal and the bowl (p.161). The bowl has an inside lip for the lid. The pulled handle of the lid was twisted before being attached. The ladle is a small thrown bowl attached to a long, curved, pulled handle. The glazes are 5 and 6. Fire to cone 6.

This pottery house has a removable roof so that it can be used as a cookie jar or other container. It was constructed from slabs of clay body 5. Roof has manganese dioxide and red iron oxide washes under glaze 26; the rest of the house is covered with glaze 20. Fire to cone 9.

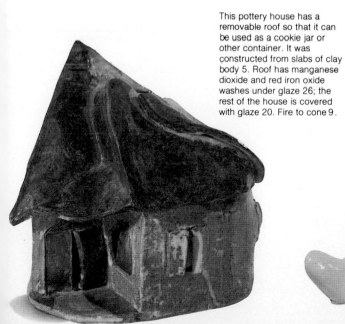

These dolls were carefully constructed from textured slabs of clay body 6. Glaze 16 was used, and highlights were added with gold luster. Fire to cone 6.

This vase was constructed from many slabs of different widths cut out of clay body 5. Underglaze washes of manganese dioxide and red iron oxide covered by varying thicknesses of glaze 20 give it its variegated color. Fire to cone 9.

Quiltmaking

A craft born of frugality

Quilting was carried to Europe in the Middle Ages by the Crusaders, who returned from the Middle East with padded linings for their armor—sandwiches of two layers of fabric with thick filling between, all stitched together.

During the 14th century Europe's climate grew markedly colder, and quilting was seized upon as a way of adding warmth to clothing and bedding. Fabrics were generally of one color, although the stitching was often very elaborate: the oldest known bed quilt, made in Sicily around 1400, depicts the Tristan legend in brown and white thread on natural linen.

In the 15th century fabric cutouts were introduced as a substitute for more expensive embroidery on clothing and household furnishings; thus was born appliqué. In the 18th century ladies at the court of Maria Theresa of Austria appliquéd a satin quilt for Marie Antoinette's wedding. In France appliqué quilts reached a high state of refinement, and American quiltmakers paid tribute to their Revolutionary War allies by imitating elaborate French designs.

Peculiarly North American was the development of patchwork. Pioneer women pieced together scraps from worn clothing to make quilt tops. The earliest were so-called crazy quilts, in which scraps of irregular sizes and shapes were sewn together to form large sheets. Later the pieces used became more regular, and the custom grew of working in lap-size blocks. Quilting bees became social occasions, as ladies gathered around the quilting frame to sew and gossip.

Contemporary quiltmakers still enjoy companionship, as they transform the old patterns or original designs into works of art fit to hang on museum walls.

This detail is from a quilt pieced and appliquéd by Mary Totten of Staten Island, N.Y., in 1810.

Materials and equipment

Fabric. Today's quiltmaker, no longer under the necessity of making do with scraps of worn clothing, usually buys fabrics that carry out a carefully planned color scheme. Fine-textured cotton is the best choice because it does not stretch or fray easily, but cotton-synthetic blends are acceptable too. Extra-warm quilts can be made of corduroy, fancy ones of velvet or silk, but attempt these only when you feel at home with the basic techniques. Avoid fabrics that are stretchy (such as knits), sheer, or coarse. Wash fabrics in hot water to preshrink them and to be sure that dyes are colorfast. Press when dry.

Backing. White muslin is the traditional backing. Many quiltmakers prefer to use sheets because they require no seams, but do not use percale—it is difficult to quilt. Cotton flannel is also appropriate. You can back the quilt with a solid color or with one of the prints in the top, turning the backing over the top as binding (p. 186). Whatever fabric you choose, make sure it will be easy to quilt.

Filling. The best choice is polyester fiberfill batting sold for quiltmaking. About 1/4 inch thick, it comes in rolls wide and long enough for even the largest quilt. If you want a warmer quilt, simply use two layers of batting.

Thread. For quilting only, use a special cotton quilting thread. If it is unavailable, substitute No. 50 mercerized cotton thread. If tangling and knotting become problems, run the thread across beeswax. For joining patches or appliquéing, use No. 50 cotton or polyester thread.

Equipment. For making small, even hand stitches in piecing or quilting, use Nos. 7–10 needles in either "sharps" (1½ inches long) or "betweens" (1¼ inches long). Try both and see which suits you better. If you have a sewing machine, by all means use it for piecing patchwork (p. 183). A zigzag sewing machine can stitch appliqué (p. 185).

You will need two pairs of scissors: one for cutting out patterns and templates, another for cutting fabric (not pinking shears). Pins, a ruler, and a yardstick or a steel tape measure are necessities. Do not rely on a cloth tape measure, as it may stretch. Very helpful for adding seam allowances is a clear plastic ruler with lines running its length at 1/8-inch intervals. Use a pencil or a ballpoint pen for marking light fabrics, a dressmaker's pencil for dark ones. Some quiltmakers wear thimbles; even more helpful is a red rubber finger pad, sold in office supply stores.

Use large-size graph paper with eight squares per inch and large sheets of tracing paper for drawing cartoons and block patterns. Make the templates of cardboard or clear plastic.

Quilting frame. For holding the quilt taut, the traditional quilting frame is preferred by most quiltmakers who have the space, and it is essential if several people are quilting simultaneously. A collapsible, easily made version is shown below. An acceptable substitute is a quilting hoop, a device resembling an oversized embroidery hoop. Some come with stands, or the hoop can be held in the lap. Some quiltmakers use neither hoop nor frame, preferring a flat surface.

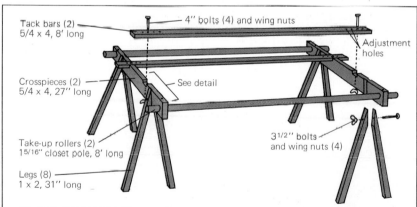

Tack bars (2)
5/4 x 4, 8' long

4" bolts (4) and wing nuts

Adjustment holes

Crosspieces (2)
5/4 x 4, 27" long

See detail

Take-up rollers (2)
1 5/16" closet pole, 8' long

3 1/2" bolts and wing nuts (4)

Legs (8)
1 x 2, 31" long

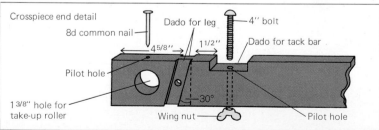

Crosspiece end detail

8d common nail

Dado for leg

4" bolt

4 5/8"   1 1/2"

Dado for tack bar

Pilot hole

1 3/8" hole for take-up roller

30°

Wing nut

Pilot hole

Quilting frame. All wood is clear pine, designated by nominal sizes. Actual sizes will differ, so measure wood for legs and tack bars before cutting dadoes in crosspieces with saw and chisel or router (see *Woodworking*, p. 376). Tack bars are flush with tops of crosspieces. Drill pilot holes for bolts holding legs and tack bars to crosspieces and for eight-penny nails in crosspieces and take-up rollers. Page 187 shows frame in use. This 8-ft tack bar will take quilt up to 90 in.; for smaller quilt use shorter bars and rollers or drill adjustment holes.

Planning and design

Most quilts, whether patchwork or appliqué, are assembled in square or rectangular blocks measuring 8 to 16 inches per side. The blocks are then stitched together to form the quilt's top. For convenience and portability, some quiltmakers prefer to join four to six blocks, quilt them, then sew all the quilted sections together (p. 186).

Sizing a bed quilt. With the bed made up and the pillow in place, measure the length of the bed from head to foot over the pillow, allowing 12–14 inches for tucking under the pillow. Add the number of inches you want the quilt to hang over the foot of the bed; this gives the length of the quilt. Now measure the width of the bed and add twice the number of inches as the overhang at the foot; this gives the width of the quilt.

The size of a quilt can be readily adjusted by altering the size of the blocks, by adding or subtracting blocks, or by using lattice strips, borders, or bindings.

A typical standard double-bed quilt is six blocks across and seven blocks long. If each block is 12 inches square, you might add lattice strips between blocks and binding on all four sides (p. 186) to enlarge the quilt. If, on the other hand, you want the blocks set side by side (p. 186), you can make them larger, say 14 inches square, and use the same number of blocks; or you can make the blocks 10 inches square and use more of them.

Making a cartoon. After choosing a block pattern, draw the whole quilt to scale (1 inch equals 1 foot is convenient) on graph paper. Draw only the outlines of the pattern and blocks, including lattice strips and borders if you plan to use them; do not fill in colors. Next tape a piece of tracing paper over your scale drawing, and with colored pencils fill in the colors you plan to use (see text, p. 182). Experiment with several sheets of tracing paper to discover the scheme you like best.

Calculating fabric requirements. Count the number of pieces of each shape and color in the entire quilt. Make a chart like the one on page 191. For each color cut a piece of shelf or butcher paper 45 inches wide. With the templates (pp. 182 and 184) trace on the paper as many pieces as you need in that color. Now measure the amount of paper you have used. This gives you the yardage requirement for 45-inch-wide fabric. Repeat the procedure for each different color. Figure yardage for lattice strips and borders the same way. Remember to add 1/4-inch seam allowances all around. Quilting suppliers will sell as little as 1/4 yard of fabric; other stores may require a minimum purchase of 1/2 yard of each fabric.

Backing, filling, and binding. Fabric for the backing should be 2 inches larger on all sides than the planned dimensions of the top. If you plan to bind the quilt by making a border of the backing (p. 188), add 2 to 4 inches more on all four sides, depending on how much backing you want to bring around to the front. The filling should be the size of the finished quilt plus 1 inch on each of the four sides to allow for take-up in sewing; remember to include the amount needed to fill the borders (p. 188). Both backing and filling will probably require trimming later. When calculating fabric for straight-cut binding (p. 188), make allowances for seams and for the fact that the binding will be longer than the quilt dimensions.

Seek out a fabric shop that specializes in the diminutive prints typical of quilts, as such a shop will inspire you with the widest possible choice of patterns in a rainbow of hues and subtle shadings. Do not hesitate to shift your color scheme if you find fabrics you prefer to those you planned.

Quiltmaking

Patchwork: a geometric art

Patchwork blocks are composed of rectangles, squares, triangles, diamonds, hexagons, and arcs. These elements are arranged within a superimposed grid of squares—4, 9, 16, 25, or even 36 squares to a block. Patterns are identified by the number of squares per block, hence the designations 4-patch block, 9-patch block, 16-patch block, and so on. In this context the numbers refer not to the block's pieces but to the squares of the imaginary grid.

By analyzing patchwork patterns as shown on this page, you will be able to garner a wealth of ideas from old quilts in museums and books. With pencil, ruler, and graph paper you can then devise your own blocks.

In planning the dimensions of a patchwork block, take into consideration the number of squares per block in your design. A 12-inch square divides easily for a 4-, 9-, or 16-patch block. But a pattern like Grandmother's Choice, a 25-patch block, works better in a 10- or 15-inch square. A pattern with a 4-patch or a 16-patch

block works with a 14- or 16-inch square; a 9-patch block works better with a 12- or 15-inch square.

In designing patchwork consider color, depth of color, and what combinations will make certain elements stand out. A good rule of thumb is to use dark, medium, and light pieces in each block. You can arrange colors and shades to set up strong diagonals, verticals, or horizontals across the quilt's surface. The quilt on page 190, for example, has strongly emphasized diagonals. Varying the scale of prints adds interest to a quilt.

After you have a pleasing color scheme on tracing paper (p. 181), make three more identical drafts. Tape all four together to make sure you like the effect. You may find that you want to shift colors and shades.

Finally, make templates for each shape, cut the pieces of fabric for one block, and stitch it together. This serves as a final test of the color combination and also as a check on the accuracy of the templates.

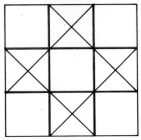

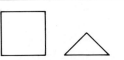

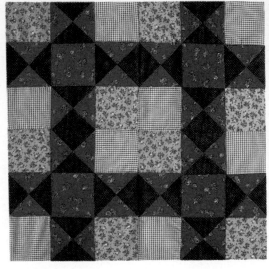

Analyzing a block. Variable Star is called a nine-patch block because its shapes are derived from a grid of nine equal squares. Each block has 21 pieces in two shapes: a triangle and a square (left). Four blocks together (above) reveal the dominant verticals and horizontals in this color scheme.

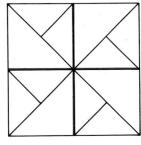

Windmill, a four-patch block, has large pieces that require a minimum of stitching.

Grandmother's Choice fits a grid of 25 squares the size of the center one.

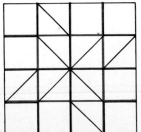

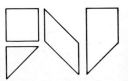

Clay's Choice, a 16-patch block, can be varied by making the rhomboids light.

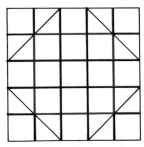

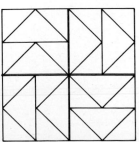

Dutchman's Puzzle is a four-patch block; use a grid of 16 squares to draw triangles.

182

Making patchwork blocks

As many seams as possible in a block should parallel the straight grain of the fabric—either the warp or the weft, which run at right angles to each other. Square or rectangular pieces are easily aligned and cut with the grain of the cloth, but triangles, diamonds, and rhomboids will unavoidably have one or more edges cut on the bias—at an angle to the warp and weft. A bias edge stretches easily, so whenever possible try to join a bias edge to a straight edge. Place a right triangle on the fabric so that the two sides forming the 90° angle are aligned with the warp and weft. However, there is one overriding rule: always make the block's outside edges on the straight grain.

The battle plan. Even though you cut first and join last, in planning a patchwork top you have to start by thinking about the final step—seaming the pieces—in order to cut the pieces correctly. Once you know where you want the straight edges to fall, mark patterns and templates with arrows accordingly. The arrows serve to indicate correct placement of the template on the fabric for cutting. When calculating yardage (p. 181), remember to arrange the pieces on the paper the same way.

Hand or machine stitching. Purists maintain that a patchwork top should be sewn by hand with the running stitch, but most quiltmakers today opt for the faster machine method. However, if a block has many tiny pieces, hand stitching may take no longer than the machine. Whichever way you sew, allow 1/4 inch all around for the seams. Usually quilting is done by hand (p. 187) because quilting stitches show, unlike the stitches that join patchwork pieces.

Pressing seams. As each seam is sewn, iron both seam allowances in the same direction, preferably toward the darker fabric. Iron the completed block before setting it (p. 186).

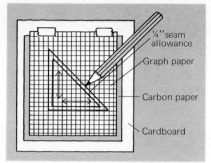

Making templates. With a straightedge draw each shape on graph paper; add lines 1/4 in. outside first lines. Trace second lines onto cardboard as shown. Cut out cardboard template.

¼″ seam allowance
Graph paper
Carbon paper
Cardboard

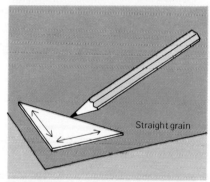

Straight grain

Marking fabric. Outline templates on wrong side of fabric with back side of template facing up. Align pieces with straight grain of fabric (arrows). Cut one thickness of fabric at a time.

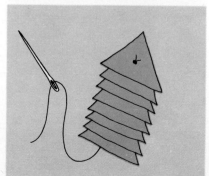

Storing patches. Run thread, knotted at one end, through centers of all patches of the same shape and color. Leave other end of thread unknotted; pull off patches as needed.

Sequence of seams

Follow two rules in deciding order of joining: join smaller units to make progressively larger ones, and always sew seams in a straight line; do not turn corners. Sequence for Variable Star block (p. 182) is shown above. **1.** Stitch together two pairs of triangles. **2.** Sew resulting two triangles together. **3.** Sew resulting squares to square patches. **4.** Sew three strips horizontally.

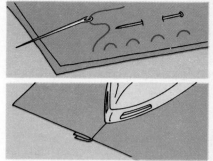

Joining patches. Pin right sides of fabric together with edges aligned; sew 1/4 in. from edges with running stitch. Press seam flat with seam allowances in same direction.

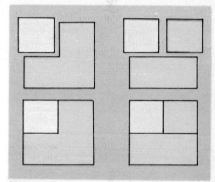

Right-angle corners. Sewing patch into right angle, easily done by hand, is difficult by machine. For machine stitching cut patches so that all stitching is in straight lines.

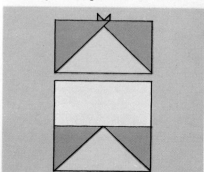

Joining triangles to a right-angle corner. The overlap at the top looks uneven, but the asymmetry disappears when the next piece is joined. Shown is part of Dutchman's Puzzle.

Quiltmaking

Appliqué: quilts with pictures

Whereas patchwork is geometric, appliqué is pictorial. Appliqué quilts, like patchwork, are most easily made in blocks, which are then sewn together and quilted. Appliqué differs from patchwork in that the pieces are sewn onto a background cloth, rather than allowing the patches themselves to form the cloth.

The blocks can be a traditional design such as Oak Leaf; a combination of patchwork and appliqué such as Dresden Plate; or a Hawaiian design in which the pattern is cut from a square of paper folded into eighths, much like a child's snowflake design. For the presentation quilt each block is made by a different person.

Contemporary quiltmakers use appliqué to sew pictures in cloth. The shapes can be abstract, but more often they are inspired by a fondness for certain objects or scenes—birds, animals, flowers, mountains, the sun, faces, or figures.

An appliqué quilt designed as a wall hanging—as many of them are—need not be of washable fabric. Rich textural effects can be obtained with a wide range of fabrics, provided they are not too stretchy or slippery. The quilt can even be given a three-dimensional look by stuffing some of the appliqués.

Making patterns. Follow the directions in *Drawing,* page 212, to enlarge the designs below, or invent your own.

Draw the block to full size on graph paper. Trace each pattern piece separately as it appears in the block pattern (p. 183), using sturdy paper instead of cardboard. Add a 3/16-inch turnunder allowance all around unless you are appliquéing by machine or making a Hawaiian design. Cut out the paper pieces for templates. Generally, threads in the appliqué fabric should run in the same direction as those in the background cloth; mark templates with arrows to so indicate.

Cutting the fabric. Pin the paper template, right side up, to the right side of the fabric. Cut around the template. Next cut out background blocks, allowing 1/4 inch all around for seams.

The block. As you arrange the pieces on the background cloth, allow for the 3/16-inch turnunder. Small or intricate shapes are more manageable if you put a line of machine stitching around the edge close to the turnunder line. Where pieces overlap, leave the edge of the underlying piece flat and unsewn. Common sense usually indicates how pieces should overlap. A flower, for example, must appear to grow from the ground. Sew with thread the same color as the appliqué, unless you want to emphasize the stitching. When all pieces are attached, remove basting threads. Lay the block face down on a bath towel to prevent flattening the appliqué, and press on the wrong side.

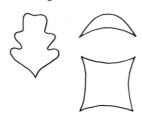

Oak Leaf is a beautiful traditional pattern that appears in many variations. It is usually done in greens and reds placed on a white or off-white background cloth.

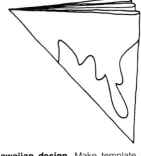

Hawaiian design. Make template by folding a square of paper vertically, horizontally, and diagonally. Draw and cut design; leave folded edges uncut. Herringbone stitch over raw edges.

Bird in a Tree. This one-of-a-kind block would be appropriate for a quilt made of blocks donated by a number of people—a presentation quilt. Quilt with echoing outlines (p. 187).

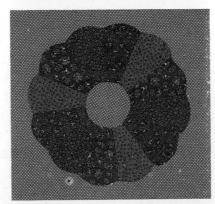

Dresden Plate, an old favorite, combines patchwork and appliqué. Cut and sew the 14 wedges as a patchwork; appliqué to background. Then appliqué the center round over the wedges.

Preparing to sew

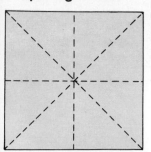

Background cloth. Fold the fabric in quarters lengthwise and across, diagonally, or both. Press lightly; unfold. Use the lines as guides for placing appliqués.

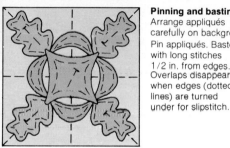

Pinning and basting. Arrange appliqués carefully on background. Pin appliqués. Baste with long stitches 1/2 in. from edges. Overlaps disappear when edges (dotted lines) are turned under for slipstitch.

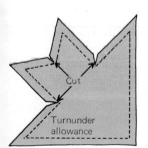

Right angles. For inside corner cut diagonally into the 3/16-in. turnunder allowance.

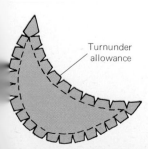

Curves. Clip 1/8 in. into turnunder allowance on inside and outside curves so that fabric does not pull or bunch. Gentle curves and bias edges need no clipping.

Appliqué stitches

Appliqué by hand

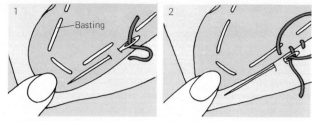

Slipstitch. Fold under appliqué edge 3/16 in. Knot thread. **1.** Bring needle up through background close to folded edge; pull through. From just above take a stitch through appliqué and background. **2.** Insert needle in background just below last stitch, and take one stitch in background only. Repeat first step. Make stitches 1/8 in. long.

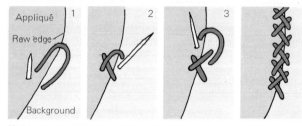

Herringbone stitch. Knot thread. **1.** Pull needle from beneath through background and appliqué 1/8 in. from edge. Insert needle in background only diagonally behind. Bring needle to top 1/8 in. to left. **2.** Make stitch diagonally ahead of first stitch. Return needle to top 1/8 in. behind. **3.** Repeat first step.

Appliqué by machine

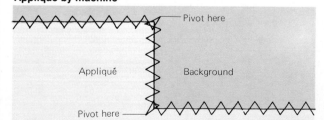

Appliqué is cut without turnunder allowance; stitching, often of contrasting thread, covers raw edges. Pin appliqué, or fuse it to background with iron-on interfacing. Use fairly long and close zigzag stitches. Set machine for 20 stitches per inch. At corners stop with needle in cloth at pivot point; turn fabric and resume stitching.

Points

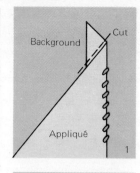

1. Stop sewing 1/4 in. short of point. Remove the raw-edged point that sticks out by making a cut parallel to the next edge to be stitched.

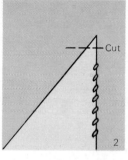

2. Cut off the apex of the remaining point. Leave just enough fabric so that the fold shown in the next step can be made.

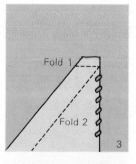

3. Make a fold that is parallel to the cut made in the second step. Fold under the turnunder allowance along the other edge.

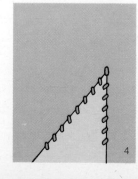

4. Stitch around the point. Be sure to take a stitch at the tip of the point in order to tack it down firmly.

Quiltmaking

Setting the quilt

Quiltmakers call joining the pieced or appliquéd blocks *setting*. The set must be planned in the design stage; for example, if lattice strips are included, they must be added to the dimensions of the quilt. Three ways of setting a quilt are shown below.

Lay out the finished blocks as they will be sewn together. Review the color arrangement and make any changes necessary. If the quilt is to have a pieced or appliquéd border (p. 188), stitch it in pieces to the outside blocks, a block at a time, in the same manner as lattice strips (below).

Next prepare the backing and filling. The backing should be at least 2 inches larger than the top on all sides; trim

excess later according to how the edges will be finished (p. 188). If the backing requires seams, sew with 1/4-inch seam allowance. Press seams open. The filling should be 1 inch larger on all sides than the top. Before finishing edges, trim any excess.

If you want your quilting to be portable, you can sew the blocks in strips the width of the quilt, quilt them off frame, then join the sections as shown below, right. The backing for each strip should be cut 2 inches larger than the top on all sides and trimmed later for the 1/2-inch turnunder. Filling can be cut the same size as the top strip; trim so that fillings abut when strips are sewn together.

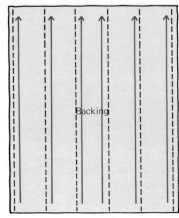
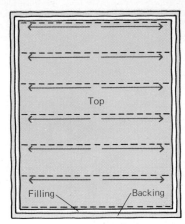

Assembling the layers for quilting off frame

Making the sandwich. Lay filling on table or floor. Place backing on top. Beginning 1 in. from edge, pin and baste rows 9–12 in. apart for length of quilt (left). Keep smoothing backing as you work across. Turn over basted backing and filling so that filling faces up. Lay top over filling; smooth it. Pin and baste all three layers in rows at right angles to first basting (right). Start each row of top basting in center and sew to edges. Basting may be omitted when quilting on frame.

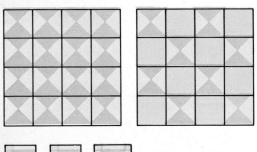

Arranging blocks. Set blocks side by side (far left), or alternate pieced or appliquéd blocks with plain blocks (left). Quilt the plain blocks with a motif such as the star illustrated on page 187.

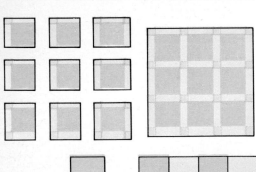

Lattice strips. Attach strips and corner squares to blocks like patchwork pieces in the manner shown at far left. Then stitch the blocks together to form the top as at left.

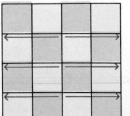

Stitching the blocks together. Hold two blocks with right sides facing. Sew from midpoint to one edge, then from midpoint to other edge. Make strips of blocks. Join strips together by starting at midpoint and sewing to edges.

Quilting in portable sections

Sew with running stitch from midpoint out.

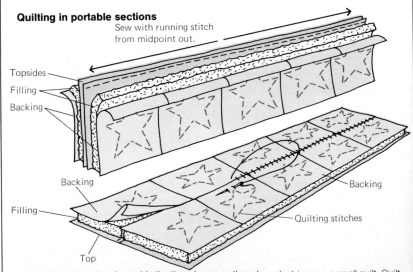

1. Join blocks in strips. Assemble the three layers as though each strip were a small quilt. Quilt strips (p. 187). To join strips, place two with top sides facing. Fold or pin backing out of the way. Join tops with 1/4-in. seam, sewing from midpoint to outside edges. Trim excess backing and filling. **2.** On back of quilt seam backing by folding under one raw edge 1/2 in. and slipstiching it to fabric beneath (p. 185).

Quilting the layers

The quilting stitch that holds the three layers of a quilt together is simple enough—a running stitch, ideally sewn eight stitches to the inch. In days past the expertise of the quilter was measured by the smallness of the stitch and the complexity of the quilting patterns. Often these were intricate designs—feathers, leaves, birds, hearts. Today elaborate, close quilting is unnecessary, in part because polyester fiberfill batting holds its shape through many handwashings with rows of quilting as much as 6 inches apart.

Marking patterns. Allover patterns such as clamshell or diagonals (p. 190) should be marked on the quilt top with pencil or dressmaker's pencil; the marks will disappear with the first washing. For curved lines make a template, or use some household object such as a teacup or saucer to outline the curves. You can buy perforated patterns for fancy designs, or make your own by drawing on tracing paper and making holes through which to mark the quilt. Outline quilting is done freehand with the seams as guides.

Methods. Some quilters prefer to work off frame, either on the whole quilt or on sections (p. 186). Others like the slight puffiness that results from having the work held taut in a hoop or quilting frame. Probably most would opt for a frame if they had space to leave it up for a period of time. The quilt on pages 190–191 was quilted in a hoop. Whichever method you choose, do not quilt into the 1/4-inch seam allowance around the edges, which must be left free for finishing (p. 188).

You may want to try quilting on the machine, but be prepared for disappointment. For one thing, your quilt will not look handcrafted. For another, it is not easy to keep the layers smooth unless they are so thoroughly basted that the time might better have been spent quilting by hand.

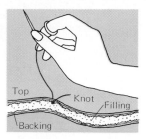

The running stitch. Knot thread at the end cut from the spool; thread needle on other end. Pull knot through backing and filling, or insert needle through a seam between patches. Catch the knot beneath the quilt top.

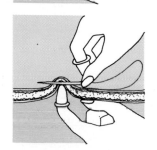

Wear thimble or rubber finger pad on sewing hand. Hold other hand beneath the quilt. With a seesaw motion push needle through layers until you feel point.

Bring needle back to top. Off frame you can do several stitches at once; on a frame or a hoop do only one at a time. Secure end of thread by reversing it through last few stitches.

Quilting on the frame

- Quilted portion wound onto second roller
- Quilting area stretched between tack bars
- Tack bars
- Take-up roller
- Unquilted portion

With rustproof tacks or pushpins, tack backing to one of the tack bars. Lay the backing across the other tack bar. Place the filling and then the quilt top on the backing. Remove tacks and replace them so that they hold all three layers. Make sure layers are correctly aligned by stretching them out to full length. Then tack them tautly to other tack bar. Roll quilt around take-up roller on one side of frame; tack it to roller if necessary. As quilting progresses, remove tacks, advance the quilt, and roll it around other roller. Quilt should be stretched tightly between tack bars; rollers serve to hold quilted and unquilted portions out of the way.

A variety of quilting designs

Allover quilting. Clamshell pattern is made with a semicircular template. The quilt on pages 190–191 is quilted with diagonals, another allover pattern.

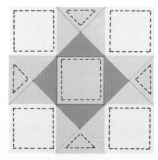

Outline quilting. Choose certain pieces and outline the same ones in all blocks. Sew 1/4 in. from seam line; avoid quilting in seams and seam allowances.

Pattern quilting. The star might fill plain blocks in an alternate-block set (p. 186). To make templates, enlarge pattern by method described in *Drawing,* page 212.

Echoing outline. Used to outline appliqués, this technique is sometimes done with quilting lines close together near appliqué, then widening for a ripple effect.

Quiltmaking

The final touch

A border is optional; use it to set off the quilt or to extend its dimensions. A border can be pieced, appliquéd, or plain fabric. Generally, the design should echo a motif in the quilt. For example, a Variable Star quilt (p. 182) might be rimmed with square patches of the same size and fabrics as in the block or with a row of triangles, as pictured at right. An appliquéd border for Oak Leaf pattern (p. 184) might be strips of the background cloth with a scattering of leaves. Make the border in strips the length of the quilt's block, and sew the strips to individual blocks with 1/4-inch seams before the quilt is set. Extend the filling into the border, and quilt the border with the rest of the quilt (p. 186).

   The edge finish. This final step in quiltmaking can be accomplished in three ways. Easiest is to make a self-edge by simply turning under the two edges and whipstitching them. The quilt on pages 190–191 is finished this way. Making a border of the backing is effective when the backing fabric is decorative and repeats one of the fabrics in the top. Straight-cut binding works well for a straight-edged quilt; use bias binding only if the edge is curved or jagged.

   Trimming the layers. Since the backing and filling are initially cut somewhat larger than finished quilt size, they must be trimmed before the edges are finished. For a self-edge, trim the backing to the same size as the top, the filling to 1/4 inch smaller all around. When using binding, the top, filling, and backing are all the same size. When the backing is turned over as a border, the filling is the size of the top plus the intended width of the border; be sure to plan for the additional width when setting the quilt. Make the backing the size of the top plus twice the border's width each way plus 1/2 inch per side for turning under edges.

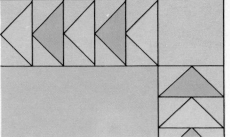
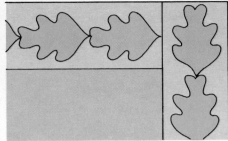

Borders. Piece borders in strips, and sew to blocks before setting. Pattern seldom reaches exactly to corner, so corners can be pieced with a square. Patchwork border (far left) repeats a geometric shape from block. Appliqué border (left) would be appropriate for Oak Leaf block shown on page 184.

Edge finishes

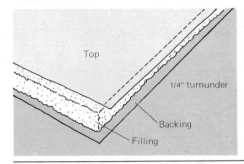
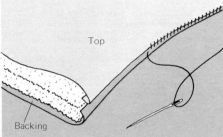

Self-edge. Quilted layers at far left are ready for a self-edge. Backing and top are trimmed so that they are same size. The filling is cut 1/4 in. shorter all around. Bring the backing around the filling (left). Fold under 1/4 in. of the top. Whipstitch along the edge, making the stitches as small and invisible as possible.

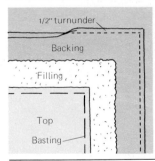
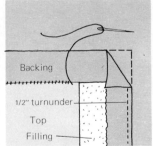
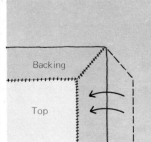

Backing as a border. Far left drawing shows layers ready for finishing. Fold backing over filling, turn under edge of backing 1/2 in., and stitch to edge of top with slipstitch (p. 185). Stop sewing 1/4 in. short of corner of top. Fold the backing corner diagonally (left, center). Then fold the next side's backing over filling. Continue slipstitching backing to top (left).

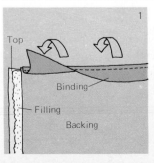
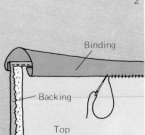
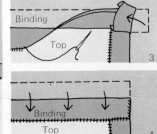

Straight-cut binding. Cut strips 1½ in. wide along straight grain of fabric. Sew together to make four strips slightly longer than quilt's sides. **1.** With backing and right side of binding face-to-face, sew 1/4 in. from edge. **2.** Bring binding over edge to top, press 1/4-in. turnunder allowance with fingers, sew to quilt top with slipstitch. First bind opposite edges. Cut flush with unbound edges. **3.** Extend binding of other edges 1/2 in. beyond corners. **4.** Sew flush with bound edges.

Quiltmaking/project

Patches with papers

Baby Block pillow. One of the more famous persons to have made a quilt of this pattern was President Calvin Coolidge, who pieced a Baby Block quilt in 1882 at the age of 10. In a bed quilt, quilting lines would follow the diamond shape 1/4 in. inside the seam lines.

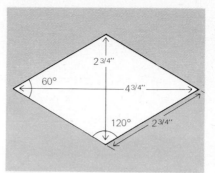

1. Template. On cardboard draw a diamond with dimensions and angles indicated in the diagram. Establish the angles with a protractor. Cut out the diamond for use as a template.

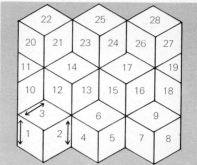

2. Fabric diagram. With template draw pillow to size on heavy tracing paper. Number diamonds as shown on front and on back of paper. Arrows show placement on straight grain of fabric.

A pillow cover is a good way to start quiltmaking. It allows you to practice with small amounts of material and a minimum investment of time. The directions here are for a cover for a 16- by 16-inch pillow, but you can expand the pattern to make an entire quilt. Conversely, any of the blocks on pages 182 and 184 could make a pillow cover.

The patches in the Baby Block pattern are made and sewn together by a method different than the one described on pages 182–183. Each patch is lined with a paper pattern over which the seam allowance is turned and basted. Then the patches are whipstitched edge-to-edge. When all blocks have been joined, the papers and basting are removed.

Materials. Dark, medium, and light fabrics create an illusion of three-dimensional cubes. You will need three of each depth of tone, nine fabrics in all. Buy 1/4 yard of each, and designate each by a letter, as shown in the chart

below, which serves as a cutting guide.

Also buy 1/2 yard of background fabric, thread to match, a 16-inch pillow form, and a 16-inch zipper if you want to be able to remove the pillow cover for washing. Appliqué the finished patchwork to a 16½ inch square of the background fabric, and seam it to another square the same size. Insert zipper in one seam, if used.

COLORS		DIAMONDS
Dark	a	1, 15, 20
	b	4, 18, 23
	c	7, 12, 26
Medium	d	2, 13, 27
	e	5, 10, 24
	f	8, 16, 21
Light	g	3, 14, 19, 28
	h	6, 17, 22
	i	9, 11, 25

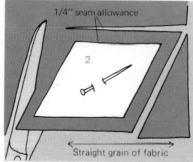

3. Cutting fabric. Cut tracing paper diagram into diamonds. Pin to wrong sides of fabrics indicated by chart. Follow arrows for straight grain. Add 1/4-in. seam allowance as you cut.

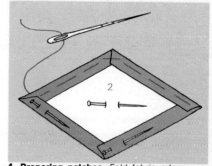

4. Preparing patches. Fold fabric edges over paper diamond. Pin and baste them. Follow directions on page 185 for trimming and folding points. Remove stitches and papers after Step 6.

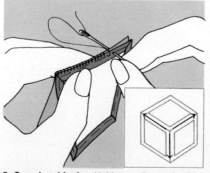

5. Seaming blocks. Hold two diamonds right sides facing and edges parallel. Whipstitch edges, sewing in direction of arrows. Make stitches small, and try not to perforate the papers.

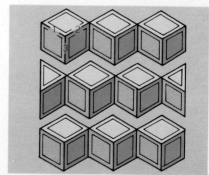

6. Seam sequence. Sew seams of each block in numbered order (upper left). Then join blocks in horizontal rows. Finally, stitch rows together using technique shown in Step 5.

Quiltmaking/project

A traditional way to a modern look

Quilt in Propeller pattern. As the name implies, Propeller is a relatively modern quilt block, but it stems from a popular old block known as Pinwheel. The pattern of quilting lines, shown in red in the cartoon above right, accentuates the strong diagonals of the propeller blades. Patches were stitched on a sewing machine, but the quilting was done by hand.

The patchwork block known as Propeller is full of dynamic movement. One set of triangles whirls around a central square of the block, while another set of whirling triangles is created by the junction of the corners of four blocks. Strong diagonals of color run from upper right to lower left through the block's central squares.

This quilt, 66 by 96 inches, is sized for a twin bed with a dust ruffle. There are 24 blocks in all—4 across and 6 down—each of which is a 15-inch square. A 3-inch-wide border of squares all around echoes the central squares of the blocks.

Twelve of the blocks, "A" above and in the diagram on page 191, are the same throughout the quilt. They run in alternate diagonal rows from upper right to lower left (see cartoon above). The other 12 blocks, referred to as the B block, are nearly the same, but their centers and two blades of the propellers change colors.

Two basic shapes compose the block: a 3-inch square and a right triangle that is 6 inches on two sides and 8½ inches on its hypotenuse. (See page 183 for how to make templates.) Because the patches were pieced by machine, four seams were added to each block to avoid sewing into a corner.

Materials. There are 10 fabrics in the patchwork blocks, identified by lowercase letters in the diagram on page 191. The yardage requirements for 45-inch-wide fabric and the pieces to be cut are listed in the chart below the diagram.

This quilt is backed with the light green fabric designated "a" in the A block. Buy 5½ yards of 45-inch fabric; cut two strips 34 by 99 inches and seam them lengthwise. The filling is 1/4-inch polyester fiberfill batting. Machine piecing was done with light blue thread, of which you need two large spools. For basting you need one large spool of white thread, and for quilting, one large spool of a thread that will show up against most of the fabrics— bright green was used here.

The border is 104 squares of the 10 fabrics in the blocks. Use the same template as for the square block pieces, and sew the squares to the edges of individual outside blocks. The order of the fabrics in the border, starting one square in from the upper left-hand corner and going clockwise, is: e, f, g, a, b, c, d, x, y, z.

Should you wish to substitute an entirely different color scheme, see the suggestions for composing blocks on page 182 and the chapter *Color and design,* pages 220–221. To alter the quilt for another size bed, refer to the ways of modifying quilt sizes on page 181. When making any changes, draw a cartoon to follow as you cut and sew patches. Be sure to continue the diagonal arrangement of the A and B blocks whenever you add rows of blocks lengthwise or crosswise.

Putting the quilt together

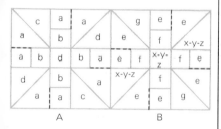

Sequence of seams. Join the patches with machine stitching following the numbered order of seams. In general, small units are sewn together into larger ones.

A					B	
c	a	a		g	e	e
a	b	d	e	f	x-y-z	
a	b	d	b	a	e	f	x-y-z	f	e
d	b		x-y-z	f	
	a	a	c	e	e	g

A   B

FABRIC / PIECES TO CUT

Fabric	Yards needed	For blocks		For borders
a	1 2/3 yd	48 ■	48 ▲	11 ■
b	2/3 yd	48 ■		11 ■
c	2/3 yd		24 ▲	11 ■
d	3/4 yd	12 ■	24 ▲	11 ■
e	1 2/3 yd	48 ■	48 ▲	10 ■
f	2/3 yd	48 ■		10 ■
g	2/3 yd		24 ▲	10 ■
x	1/2 yd	4 ■	8 ▲	10 ■
y	1/2 yd	4 ■	8 ▲	10 ■
z	1/2 yd	4 ■	8 ▲	10 ■

▲ = triangle   ■ = square

The two blocks. A twin-bed quilt requires 12 blocks of each, A and B. Lowercase letters signify various fabrics; see list of materials in chart for how many of each piece to cut. Dashed lines are seams added for machine piecing. Patches marked x, y, and z change with each diagonal row of B block. In upper corner B block (cartoon, opposite), use fabric y for these patches; in second row, fabric x; in third row, z; then start again with y.

1. Making the cartoon. Color the patches on tracing paper laid over a line drawing of the quilt. The cartoon is scaled so that 1/4 in. equals 3 in., or 1 in. equals 1 ft.

2. Making pattern pieces. Draw a right triangle 6 by 6 by 8½ in. and a 3-in. square on graph paper with four squares per inch. Draw lines 1/4 in. outside all edges for seams.

3. Marking cloth. Using templates, mark wrong side of cloth with ballpoint pen. On dark fabrics use dressmaker's pencil. Align pieces with straight grain of fabric (see text, p. 183).

4. Piecing blocks. With all patches laid out in correct order, stitch seams following the sequence in diagram at upper left of page. Here the second seam is in progress.

5. Ironing. Press blocks on back side. Do not try to press seams open. Press toward dark fabric as a rule, but seams tend to fall naturally to one side. Join blocks as shown on page 186.

6. Basting. If quilting off frame or on a hoop, baste layers according to instructions on page 186. Keep smoothing top ahead of needle. No basting is required for quilting on a frame.

7. Marking quilting lines. Use straightedge and dressmaker's pencil to mark quilting lines. Follow diagram on opposite page. When using a frame, mark top before assembling layers on frame.

8. Quilting. Place hoop in center of quilt. Use a needle for each quilting line within hoop. Sew, then park needles at hoop. Move hoop to next section and sew. Quilt the border without hoop.

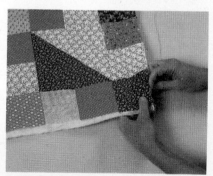

9. Finishing the edge. For a simple self-edge (p. 188) fold under the 1/4-in. seam allowance of the top. Fold backing around filling so that it is even with top. Sew with a whipstitch.

Modeling, moldmaking, and

From clay to bronze

Modeling, moldmaking, and casting are the three steps in one of the most popular methods of creating sculpture. In the first step the form is modeled in a plastic, impermanent medium, such as clay (the clay is impermanent because it is never fired). Then a mold is made of the modeled form by surrounding it with a material (usually plaster) that faithfully reproduces every detail of the model. After the impermanent model is removed from the mold, the mold is filled with a casting material. When that material hardens, the resultant casting is an exact replica of the original model.

Modeling is an easier method of shaping than carving, the other popular sculpture technique (see *Wood sculpture,* pp. 268–275). In carving, the shape is cut from a hard block of stone, wood, or other rigid medium. In modeling, because the medium is plastic, the sculptor has greater freedom in shaping; he can add more of the material if he chooses, or even redo parts of the sculpture as it takes form. Because of the flexibility of the medium and of the techniques, effects are possible in modeling and casting that are impractical or impossible in carving.

Casting traditions. Bronze has been the favorite casting metal of sculptors since ancient times. Small cast-bronze statues have been found in the Middle East dating from about 4000 B.C. Chinese bronze statues dating from about 3000 B.C. have been found in tombs, and fragments of bronze found in India and Afghanistan date from about 2000 B.C.

During the fifth and fourth centuries B.C. the classical Greek ideals of beauty found expression in their superb bronze sculptures. Unfortunately, few authentic Greek bronzes remain, because, unlike stone, bronze can be melted down and used again for new castings or other purposes. The Romans continued in the Greek tradition and brought even greater technical perfection to the art of bronze casting.

Bronze casting lost popularity for about a thousand years, but it flowered again during the Italian Renaissance. Lorenzo Ghiberti, Filippo Brunelleschi, Donatello, and Benvenuto Cellini are only a few of the great bronze sculptors of the era. The rebirth of bronze sculpture that started in the Renaissance has continued through modern times. Edgar Degas, Auguste Rodin, Frederic Remington, Pablo Picasso, Alberto Giacometti, and Henry Moore are among the most popular bronze sculptors of this and the last century. Modern sculptors have introduced new casting materials, such as aluminum and polyester-resin compounds.

About this chapter. The tools used in modeling and moldmaking are shown on page 193. Modeling a head out of clay is illustrated on pages 193–197, and modeling a figure in plaster is demonstrated on page 197. Making a plaster mold is shown on pages 198–201. Casting in wax, clay, polyester-resin compounds, and concrete is illustrated on pages 202–205. Pewter and molds for reproducing small articles in pewter are shown on pages 206–207. A discussion of finishes for castings appears on page 208. Bronze casting is illustrated on page 209.

In the case of bronze, most sculptors send their molds to foundries for casting. Although foundry procedures are described later in this chapter, the beginner should not attempt to cast in bronze. Wax, clay, polyester, plaster, and concrete are suitable mediums for home casting, however, and the procedures for working with these materials are illustrated in detail.

The antiquity of this Greek bronze is evidenced by a rich green patina, which builds up with age. About 2,300 years old, piece is in collection of Boston Museum of Fine Arts.

casting sculpture

Tools

The tools needed for modeling, mold-making, and casting are few and inexpensive. All can be found at a crafts supply store, or perfectly acceptable substitutes can be made at home.

Clay-modeling tools are made of loops of serrated wire attached to wooden handles. It is useful to have both a large and a small modeling tool. A modeling tool can be made at home by attaching a thick wire loop to a wooden handle; simply attach it with a firm wrapping of wire or string.

A special knife called a plaster knife is used in moldmaking. Any stiff kitchen knife will do.

Spatulas are used to apply plaster in moldmaking and for some detail work in modeling. It is best to have one large and one small spatula, but you can make do with only a small one. A butter knife makes a perfectly acceptable substitute for the small spatula.

Flat-bottomed plastic buckets are used for mixing plaster. The cheaper, and thus the more flexible, they are, the better. (It is easiest to remove dried plaster from a flexible bucket.)

A common combination rasp is used in modeling plaster.

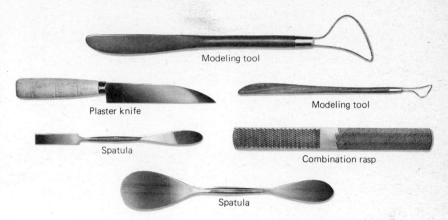

Modeling tool

Plaster knife

Modeling tool

Spatula

Combination rasp

Spatula

Modeling a clay head

Modeling a form in clay is the first step in the process that eventually produces that form in a permanent medium.

Any plastic, water-based clay can be used for modeling. (For information about obtaining, preparing, and storing plastic clays, see *Pottery,* pp. 133–135.) Clays without grog or other nonplastic materials are the most pleasant to work with. Oil-based clay, which never dries out, is also fine for modeling, but it is far more expensive than regular clay.

Because a large clay form will slump under its own weight, some extra support is needed to help the model retain its shape. This is provided by a rough skeleton, called an armature, upon which the clay is packed and modeled. The size, shape, and material of the armature varies with the size, shape, and material of the model to be built upon it. The wooden armature for the clay head shown on the next four pages is illustrated at right.

The modeling process is basically a building up of a succession of clay shapes on top of the armature. Large volumes of clay are attached to the armature to make the rough form of the model. Smaller volumes of clay are added for features and detail. Final details are created by working on this clay with a modeling tool.

It is important to view your model from different perspectives as you work

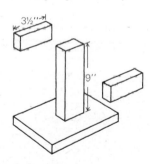

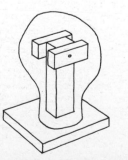

This armature is for a life-size modeled head.

so that you can capture accurately a three-dimensional figure. For a small model the work itself can be rotated (this can be facilitated by using a special modeling stand), whereas it is easier to walk around a very large model.

The clay must be kept moist at all times, or it will lose its plasticity and eventually shrink and crack. When you are not working on your model, wrap it with a moist towel and cover the towel and model with a plastic bag.

Modeling a head. On the following four pages detailed illustrations for modeling a woman's head in clay are given. The basic shape of the head is built up from three major forms (see box, p. 194). The facial features are created by adding and tooling smaller pieces of clay. The basic proportions of the facial features are illustrated in the drawing by Leonardo da Vinci, reproduced at right.

If you are a novice at modeling clay, you may find that by imitating the steps in the illustrations you can gain a familiarity with the medium of clay and with the proportions of a head. Once these methods and proportions become familiar to you, your own departures and variations will be much easier.

Facial features

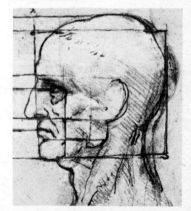

Leonardo da Vinci, the seminal figure of the Italian Renaissance, is famous for his application of mathematics to the study of human anatomy and proportion. His studies led to a new era of realism in representational art. This sketch by Leonardo establishes the proportions of the facial features. Basically, the line of the eyes is halfway between the top and bottom of the face. The nose ends halfway between the eyes and the bottom of the face. The mouth is halfway between the bottom of the nose and the bottom of the face. These proportions are drawn on the model in Step 7, p. 194.

Modeling, moldmaking, and casting sculpture

Modeling a clay head (continued)

Three major shapes of the head

The head is made up of three major shapes. The first, a truncated egg shape, forms the cranium. The second, the neck, is a cylinder that intersects the first shape at a slight angle. The third, a large inverted triangular shape, forms the basic surface of the face.

1. To begin the head, take handfuls of clay and pack them tightly around the top of the armature.

2. Continue adding clay and shape it so that it looks like an egg truncated at both ends.

3. To make the neck, pack clay around the vertical piece of the armature.

4. Thicken the neck, as shown. The neck should intersect the cranium at a slight angle.

5. To make the third shape (see diagram, left), add clay to the front of the head.

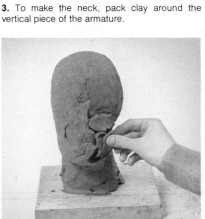

6. Continue attaching pieces of clay to create the general contour of the face and chin.

7. Draw lines for the eyes, nose, and mouth. (For proportions, see drawing, p. 193.)

8. To make ears, take small slabs of clay and attach them to the sides of the head.

9. Trim ears with modeling tool. Top of ears should be about level with line of eyes.

10. For the nose, first make a small triangular slab of clay and attach it as shown above.

11. Trim off the nose at the line drawn in Step 7. Smooth the connection with modeling tool.

12. Roll a small ball of clay almost as wide as the triangle and attach it to the bottom of the nose.

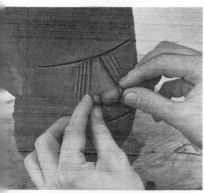

13. Roll two smaller balls of clay and attach them to the sides of the large ball.

14. Smooth the three balls and the triangle of clay with your hand to shape the end of the nose.

15. With the tool, draw a circle around the slit for the mouth, as shown.

16. Add clay to build up a small, flat cone inside the circle drawn in Step 15.

17. Complete building up the cone. Smooth it out with the modeling tool as shown.

18. Draw a flattened "M" in the center of the cone with the modeling tool.

19. Lips are shaped by tooling clay away from the line drawn in Step 18.

20. Continue shaping the lips. The top lip is slightly wider than the bottom lip.

Modeling, moldmaking, and casting sculpture

Modeling a clay head (continued)

21. A small gouge above the center of the upper lip can be cut out with the modeling tool.

22. Cut the line for the bottom of the eye sockets halfway down the length of the nose.

23. Use the tool to cut two fairly deep rectangular gouges for the eye sockets.

24. Roll two balls of clay about the diameter of the sockets and press them into place.

25. Press a small, narrow slab of clay to the bottom of the eye to form the lower eyelid.

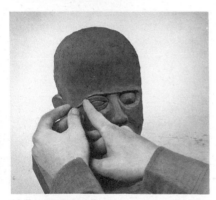

26. Trim the first lid. Then place another small slab on the top of the eye for the upper lid.

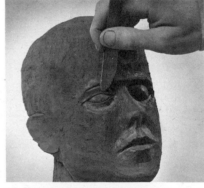

27. Shape the lids with the handle of the tool, as shown. Then make the lids for the other eye.

28. Draw a line that runs parallel to the jaw, then comes up and intersects the socket under the eye.

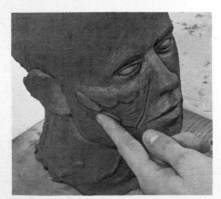

29. Add clay to the model inside the line drawn in Step 28 to make the cheekbones.

30. Add small bits of clay to finish shaping the eyebrows and forehead.

31. The rounded end of a small spatula can be used to finish shaping the eyes and eyelids.

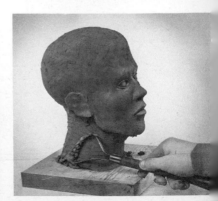

32. Use a large modeling tool to remove excess clay and to shape the neck.

33. Add small bits of clay for the hair. The hair is treated as a volume, not as individual strands.

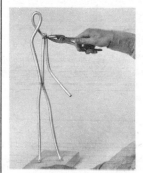

34. This head has been given a ponytail by adding a mass of clay to the back.

35. The mass of hair can be smoothed or given a texture (as shown) with the modeling tool.

36. The hair is given a part by inscribing a line with the wooden end of the tool.

37. Once the hair is finished, final touch-ups of the face can be done with the spatula.

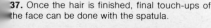

38. Holes can be made in the eyes with a pencil to delineate the irises and to give the eyes focus.

Modeling a plaster figure

Plaster can also be used as a modeling material. A plaster model can be either preserved as a finished work or used as a model for making a mold and, ultimately, a casting.

As with modeling in clay, plaster models are built on armatures. For the figure shown below, the armature is made of thick electrical wire. Arms are made by attaching extra pieces of wire to the main part of the armature.

Strips of burlap are dipped in plaster (see p. 198) and wrapped around the armature, giving the figure its basic shape. As the plaster in the bucket thickens (see Step 10, p. 200) it is applied over the burlap with a spatula. Because plaster only retains this workable, thick consistency for a short while, it is important not to mix too much at a time.

The figure takes form as the plaster is built up over the burlap. Final shaping and texturing are done with the plaster knife, spatula, and rasp.

The basic proportions of the human figure are illustrated in the chapter on *Wood sculpture*, p. 272.

1. Armature for plaster model is made of heavy electrical wire, shaped and nailed to a wooden base. Arms are attached with pieces of wire.

2. Cut strips of burlap about 1 in. thick and dip them in plaster. Wrap the strips around the armature to begin shaping the body of the figure.

3. After the armature is covered with burlap, the shape is built up by the application of thick plaster over the burlap with a spatula, as shown.

4. The rough plaster can be shaped and refined with tools. A combination rasp, with different faces, can create various shapes and textures.

5. The spatula is good for working on such small details as the facial features (as shown) as well as for applying plaster to the whole model.

6. The plaster knife is another tool that can be used on the moist plaster. Here, it is being used to give a smooth, finished texture to the figure.

Modeling, moldmaking, and casting sculpture

Moldmaking

After the model is completed, it is covered by a molding material that faithfully reproduces every detail of the model. The mold is removed from the model and is filled with a casting material to make an exact replica of the model in a permanent medium.

Waste molds. Molds for clay models are usually made of plaster. There are two types of plaster molds, the waste mold and the piece mold. The waste mold is formed on the model and removed in two pieces, usually destroying the clay model, parts of which have to be pulled out of the recesses of the mold. After a casting material has been poured into the waste mold and has set, the mold itself is chipped away in little pieces, hence the name "waste mold."

Because of this chipping away, the waste mold can be used only once and is difficult to remove from castings of delicate materials, such as wax.

Piece molds. The piece mold (which is shown on the following three pages) is the more versatile of the plaster molds. It is designed so that it can be removed from the model, and later from a casting, in pieces, without damage to the mold or casting. Therefore, the piece mold can be used many times, with delicate as well as durable casting materials. Piece molds, unlike waste molds, can be made on rigid objects, such as plaster models or pieces of sculpture that are to be reproduced.

Undercuts. What determines the number and shapes of the pieces of a piece mold is their ability to be removed without either being broken or breaking the model or casting inside. A configuration of the model that prohibits a piece of the mold from being removed without damage is called an *undercut* (see box, below). A piece mold must be designed so that no piece has an undercut.

Learning to discern undercuts takes time, and it is good to practice making piece molds on simple shapes before making one on a complex model. When you are ready to make a mold, look at the model and determine where the divisions in the model must be to prevent undercuts. This determination must be quite precise. For example, in the mold shown on the following pages, the section of the top of the head is necessary because without it the part in the hair would make undercuts for the pieces of the mold on the sides of the head. Also, if the boundary of the front piece of the mold had been moved back a little, the hollows on the sides of the eyes and behind the cheekbones would have created undercuts.

Fences. After you decide on the number and positions of the pieces, you can start making the mold. The first step is to make slabs of clay that will form temporary boundaries for the plaster as it is applied to the model. These clay slabs, called fences, are pressed to the model, smoothed together carefully, and trimmed so that they follow the contours of the mold.

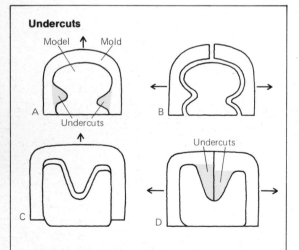

Undercuts

An undercut is a configuration that prevents removal of a mold without damage to the mold or to the model it covers. In Diagram A, a one-piece mold cannot be removed from the form without tearing off the shaded areas—these are the undercuts. This difficulty can be circumvented by making a two-part mold (Diagram B) and removing pieces sideways.

Making more pieces is not always the answer—they must be designed and removed correctly. In Diagram C, for example, a one-piece mold removed vertically will cause no undercuts, but a two-piece mold removed horizontally (Diagram D) will.

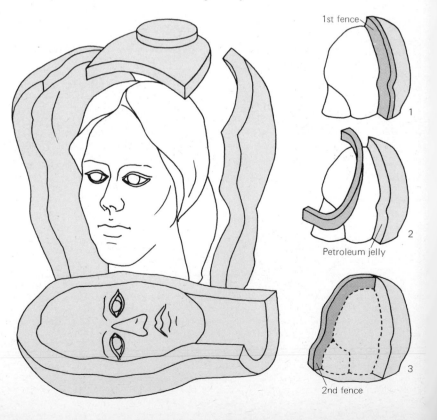

Piece mold. The piece mold, at right, is designed so that no section has an undercut. Sections are made by applying plaster to the model in areas bounded by clay fences attached as seen above, right (Diagram 1). When the plaster hardens, the fence is removed, and the edge of the hardened plaster is coated with petroleum jelly (Diagram 2). When the plaster for the adjacent section of the mold is applied (Diagram 3), no fence between it and the hardened section is necessary because the petroleum jelly prevents the second section from sticking to the first. When the mold is completed, it is pried open along the seams between the sections. The pieces are later reassembled for casting.

The smooth sides of the slabs (the sides that were pressed to a flat surface when the slabs were made) should face the part of the mold that is being filled with plaster. There is always a temptation to smooth the interstices between the fences and the model with a tool—don't; any marks you make will be picked up by the mold and will show up on the surface of the castings.

Applying the plaster. Only molding or pottery plaster, available at crafts supply stores, should be used for moldmaking. The plaster is mixed following the directions given by the manufacturer (usually approximately equal volumes of water and plaster). Plaster is always added to water, not the other way around. While the plas-

ter is still very fluid, a layer is brushed on the model and on the inside of the fence. This layer, called the splash coat, fills the recesses of the model so that the mold will capture small details. The splash coat also allows you to see and break air bubbles in the plaster that otherwise would remain and mar the surface of the mold.

After the plaster in the bucket thickens somewhat, it is applied over the splash coat to build up the mold to a thickness of 1 inch. The mold surface should roughly conform to the shape of the model—the more even the thickness of the mold, the stronger it is.

When the plaster of the first section of the mold sets, the fence around it is removed and the next section of the

fence is attached to the model. Where a section of the mold abuts an already finished section, no fence is necessary, since the thickness of the already hardened plaster will act as the fence. However, the hardened edge should be coated with petroleum jelly so that the adjoining section does not stick to it after hardening.

The third and any additional pieces are made in a similar manner, completing the mold. After the mold sets, it is opened with small wedges of wood. These wedges, about 2 inches long, 2 inches wide, and 1/2 inch thick at the base, can be made from scrap wood. One wedge several inches longer is used to pry the mold sections apart.

After the mold is opened, any clay

that has stuck in it is removed. The thin layer of clay residue is washed off. Air holes in the plaster can be patched, but this should be done in moderation; too much repair work will spoil the details of the surface.

When the mold is not being used, it should be assembled and tied together with rope or elastic cable to prevent the pieces from warping.

In the mold shown on the following three pages a pedestal is shaped on the top of the head so that the mold will balance when it is turned upside down for casting.

Rubber molds. Commercial foundries now make excellent molds of rubber. Rubber molds can be made at home, but to do so is very expensive.

1. To make the fence for the mold, press a mass of clay down on a flat surface until the clay becomes a uniform slab, about 1/2 in. thick.

2. Use a knife to cut the slab into 1-in.-wide strips. It is a good idea to make all of the strips at one time, before starting the mold.

3. After deciding how the mold will be constructed (see text), place the first fence on the model and press it down so that it adheres firmly.

4. Add slabs until the fence is complete, as shown. The smooth sides of the slabs face forward, and the joints between the slabs are smooth.

5. To make the plaster, place about 1 in. of water in a bucket. Slowly sprinkle the plaster into the water as you swirl the bucket.

6. Continue sprinkling in plaster until the plaster ceases to sink into the water and just floats on the surface, as shown.

7. Put your hand into the mixture and mix it thoroughly, breaking up the lumps. The plaster should leave an opaque covering on your skin.

8. Brush the plaster over the part of the model enclosed by the fence. Carefully work the plaster into all of the small recesses. *(Continued)*

Modeling, moldmaking, and casting sculpture

Moldmaking *(continued)*

9. Completely cover the section of the model and the inside of the fence. Look for air bubbles in the plaster and break them with the brush.

10. Let the plaster in the bucket sit until it becomes thick enough to sit on the spatula, as shown. This usually takes about 10 min.

11. Use the spatula to apply the plaster to the model. Build up the plaster until it is 1 in. thick and roughly follows the shape of the model.

12. As the plaster hardens, trim it with the plaster knife so that the surface is fairly smooth. Trim plaster off the outside edge of the fence.

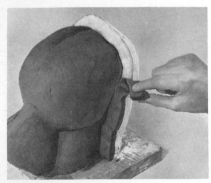

13. Plaster heats up as it sets. When it feels warm, usually in about 20 min, gently pull the pieces of the fence off the model.

14. Apply the next section of fence to the model, just as in Steps 3 and 4. Leave no gap between the fence and the hardened plaster section.

15. Coat the edge of the hardened plaster with petroleum jelly or shortening to prevent it from sticking to the next section of the mold.

16. Mix up more plaster. Apply one coat with a brush, then build up the mold with the spatula, as shown in Steps 8–11.

17. The top of this piece can be fashioned into a pedestal, which will facilitate balancing the mold when it is inverted for casting.

18. Trim plaster off the fence. Wait for the plaster to heat up, then gently remove the fence from the model, as shown.

19. Take the strips of clay for the fence for the third section of the mold and press them firmly into place on the model.

20. For this head it is necessary to place a small slab of clay beneath the back fence so that the mold can be properly formed.

21. Coat the edges of the first two mold sections with a separator such as petroleum jelly or shortening, just as in Step 15.

22. Mix more plaster and brush on a first coat. Apply thickened plaster with spatula. Trim plaster off fence. Remove fence, as shown.

23. Apply a separator to the edges of the hardened plaster as in Step 21, and fill in the last section of the mold with plaster.

24. After the last section heats and cools, open the mold by gradually knocking the six wooden wedges (see text) into the seams.

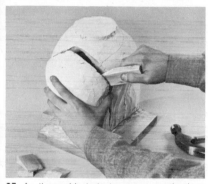

25. As the mold starts to open, use the long wedge to gently pry the first section of the mold from the model.

26. Carefully pull the piece of plaster from the clay and put it safely aside. In this mold the model remained pretty much intact.

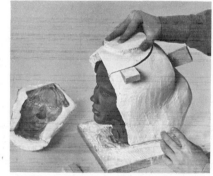

27. After removing the front piece of the mold, knock two wedges into the seam for the top piece and carefully remove it from the model.

28. Drive several wedges into the seam between the last two sections. Then gently pull them apart with your hands.

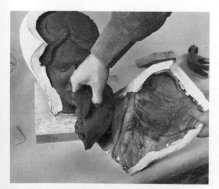

29. If the clay does stick to the mold, gently remove it. Little bits of clay can be removed by blotting them with larger pieces of fresh clay.

30. The thin residue of clay in the mold should be removed by brushing the clay with a paintbrush while the mold is immersed in water.

31. Air pockets on the surface of the mold can be patched with fresh plaster. First apply a small amount of plaster with the spatula.

32. After the plaster sits for a few minutes, smooth it onto the contour of the neighboring area of the mold with a paper towel.

Modeling, moldmaking, and casting sculpture

Casting in wax and clay

Casting is the process by which the mold is filled with a casting material to make a copy of the original model in a permanent medium.

Castings can be either hollow or solid. A hollow casting is usually made by first applying the casting material to the pieces of the mold, then assembling the mold and sealing the seams so that the casting will hold together. Examples of this method of casting are wax casting (this page), clay press molding (facing page), and casting with a polyester-resin compound (pp. 204–205).

Solid castings are made by first assembling the mold, then filling it with a casting material. An example of this is concrete casting (p. 204).

Casting in wax. A wax casting is normally used as an intermediate stage in the course of casting in a metal, such as bronze. A bronze casting is an exact duplicate of the wax casting used to make it (p. 209).

Prepare the mold for a wax casting by soaking it in cold water and wiping any water off the surface before applying the wax.

The wax generally used for casting, called microcrystalline wax (available at crafts supply stores), comes in slabs that must be broken up and melted. (If a wax slab is put in a freezer, it becomes brittle and can easily be broken with a hammer.) The wax is melted in a pot on a hot plate or stove over very low heat. Do not let the wax burn.

The melted wax is carefully brushed into the sections of the mold to capture the fine details, somewhat like the splash coat in moldmaking (p. 199). The wax is built up until it is 1/4 inch thick. The mold is then assembled and tied together. Melted wax is poured in and swirled around, covering the seams between the pieces of the mold. When there is an even coat, about 1/4 inch all around, the excess wax is poured out. The wax coat should not be much more than 1/4 inch thick—the thicker the wax is, the more bronze will be needed to cast it, and bronze foundries charge by the weight of the casting.

When the wax has hardened (you can feel this with your fingers), gently pry the sections of the mold apart, using the plaster knife if necessary.

Clay press molding. In press molding, slabs of clay are pressed into the pieces of the mold, which are subsequently assembled. Clay can also be cast in liquid form (a process called slip casting), but because the castings are very fragile, they are difficult to remove from the mold without damage.

After clay castings are made, they are fired in a kiln to make them hard and inert. Therefore, the clay must be formulated and prepared so that it will fire well (see *Pottery,* pp. 134–135). The clay should contain about 30 percent grog. Before the casting is begun, the clay should be wedged (pp. 140–141). The addition of grog and the wedging process help prevent the casting from distorting or exploding during firing.

The wedged clay is rolled into slabs, which are carefully pressed into the clean, dry pieces of the mold. The clay is trimmed flush with the edges of the pieces; no more clay can be trimmed away, or the casting will not hold together when the mold is assembled. Slip, which is made by repeatedly squeezing a piece of clay submerged in water until it dissolves, is brushed on the edges of the clay to promote adhesion of the sections.

The pieces of the mold are assembled, and the seams are smoothed. In 4 to 8 hours the clay becomes leather hard, a state in which it is stiff but has not yet begun to change color. The mold is then carefully opened, and the fragile casting is put on a board or a plaster bat so that it can be transported without being touched. Several holes should be made in the casting with a pin to help prevent explosions during firing (see *Pottery,* pp. 167–168).

Casting in wax

1. Brush melted wax into the cold, wet pieces of the mold. Build up a wax layer 1/4 in. thick.

2. Using the plaster knife, trim away any wax that has run onto the edges of the mold.

3. Tie the mold together. Pour wax into the mold until it is about one-third full.

4. Swirl wax around to cover seams and to make casting a uniform thickness. Pour out excess.

5. Trim wax off the underside of the mold. After the wax hardens, carefully open the mold.

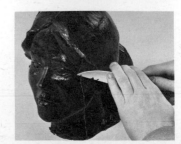

6. Remove the lines caused by the seams (called *flashings*) with the plaster knife.

Casting in clay

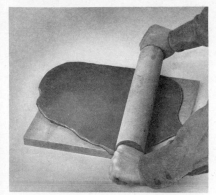

1. Wedge some clay and flatten it out with a rolling pin into a slab 1/2 in. thick.

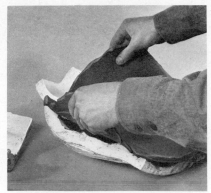

2. Place the slab into a piece of the mold. The mold should be clean and dry.

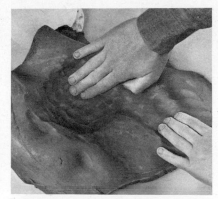

3. Gently push the clay with your fingers so that it fills every recess of the mold.

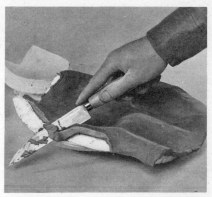

4. Trim the edges of the slab of clay parallel with the edges of the piece of the mold.

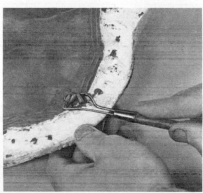

5. Make ridges in the edges of the clay with the serrated edge of the modeling tool.

6. Repeat Steps 1–5 for the other sections. Brush slip on the edges of the first two sections.

7. Assemble these sections. Fuse the clay over the seam with your thumb.

8. Apply slip to edges of third section, and fit it into mold; again fuse edges with your fingers.

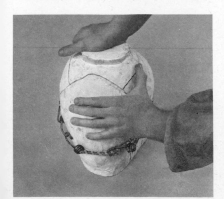

9. Apply slip to the edges of the last section and press it into place. Then let the clay dry.

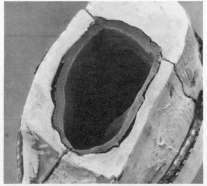

10. When clay shrinks and separates from mold, as shown, casting is ready to be removed.

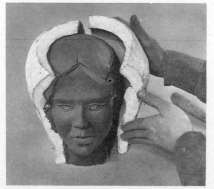

11. Carefully open the mold. You can use the plaster knife to help pry the pieces apart.

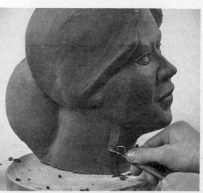

12. Remove flashings on the casting with the modeling tool. Fire finished casting.

Modeling, moldmaking, and casting sculpture

Casting in concrete and polyester-resin

Concrete and polyester-resin compounds are two materials that are easy to cast, and both make very hard, durable castings.

Separators. Unlike wax and clay, polyester-resin compounds and concrete will stick to plaster. Therefore, provision must be made for removing the casting from the mold without breaking or chipping either. This can be done by applying a separator to the plaster before the casting is made, which will seal the pores and make the plaster impervious.

The most effective separator is a combination of materials. First the plaster is given three coats of shellac. (The shellac can be removed with alcohol for casting in clay at a later time.) Then a layer of paste wax (do not use liquid waxes or car waxes that have detergents in them) is applied. The wax should be applied evenly, leaving a shine on the surface; if the wax remains in blobs, it will disfigure the surface of the casting. A coat of silicone spray is applied over the wax.

Casting with polyester-resin. A polyester-resin compound that makes a light and durable casting is the autobody putty used to fill dents and cracks. It is available at any auto supply store. The putty comes in gallon cans along with a small tube of promoter that is mixed into the putty to promote its solidification.

Although auto-body putty makes a nice casting, it is an unpleasant material to work with: wear gloves at all times while using it. Noxious fumes make good ventilation an absolute necessity; if you will be exposed to the compound for a long period of time, wear a chemical mask.

Once the promoter is added to the putty, the putty hardens quickly. Therefore, a lump of putty about the size of a tennis ball is all that should be mixed and applied at one time. Follow the manufacturer's directions for mixing the proper proportion of putty with the promoter.

Once a tool has been used to mix the putty and promoter, do not use that tool in the fresh can of putty, or it will promote hardening of the entire can. Putty can be cleaned off tools with lacquer thinner.

Putty is applied to each section, the sections are assembled, seams are touched up, and the casting hardens in about 1/2 hour. The casting process is much like clay press molding (p. 203).

Fiberglass can be embedded in the polyester-resin compound to give it greater strength, which is needed in the casting of large pieces.

Casting with concrete. Concrete makes a solid casting that is cheap, heavy, and durable. If you mix your own concrete, use one-third Portland cement, one-third sand, and one-third gravel. If you use a commercially prepared mix, choose a sand mixture rather than a gravel mixture. If castings made with the commercial mixture are crumbly, enrich the mixture by adding cement. You can also buy a concrete mixture that contains acrylics, which make the concrete stronger and more resistant to weathering if the casting is to be left outside.

After a separator is applied to the pieces of the mold, they are assembled and tied tightly together and the mold is inverted. If it balances on its top, no further support is needed, but if it does not balance, it must be placed in a bucket or tied to the leg of a table.

Concrete is poured into the inverted mold. The concrete should be agitated by plunging a spoon or stick in and out of the mold for about 5 minutes to break up air pockets.

The concrete should be left to set for several days before the mold is opened. Flashings on the casting can be removed with a chisel, file, or sandpaper.

Solid castings in plaster can be made in much the same way as in concrete.

Casting in concrete

1. To cast in concrete, put water in a bucket and add the dry concrete mix.

2. Before it is poured, the concrete should be thick enough to hold its shape, as shown.

3. Tie the mold together very firmly. Then start to fill the mold with concrete.

4. Periodically stop and agitate the concrete with the spoon to break up air pockets.

5. Fill the mold to the top. Cover it with a damp cloth, and wrap mold and cloth with plastic.

6. Open the mold after several days. Chisel, file, or sand flashings off the casting.

Casting in polyester-resin compound

1. To prepare mold for polyester-resin or concrete casting, first brush on three coats of shellac.

2. Apply a uniform layer of paste wax as shown. Then coat each section with silicone spray.

3. For polyester-resin compound casting, first mix a small amount of putty with promoter.

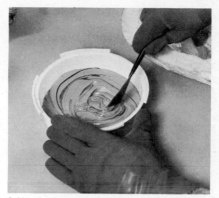

4. Use the spatula to mix the promoter and putty into a completely homogeneous mass.

5. Pour enough of the mixture into the first piece to cover it with a 1/4-in. coat.

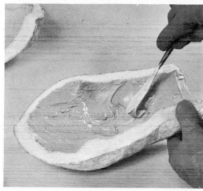

6. Spread polyester-resin over mold so that it fills each recess. Do the same for other mold pieces.

7. Leave a little extra putty on the edges, and put the first two pieces of the mold together.

8. Add the third piece, and tie the three together. Add putty to fuse the seams from the inside.

9. Apply putty to the top section, leaving a little extra around the edges, and press it in place.

10. Use the spatula to add putty, fusing all the seams and leaving an even 1/4-in. layer.

11. After about 1/2 hr, when the putty hardens, gently open the mold.

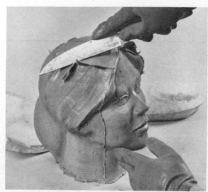

12. Remove any flashings from the casting with the plaster knife.

Modeling, moldmaking, and casting sculpture

Working in pewter

Pewter spoons are thicker than silver or stainless steel because the metal is very malleable.

Pewter is a soft, silver-white alloy of tin and other metals. Because of its silvery sheen, low melting point, and relatively low price (compared to the precious metals) pewter is an excellent metal for casting at home.

Chemical and physical properties of pewter. Until modern times pewter was composed of tin and lead (about 80 percent tin and 20 percent lead). Lead caused the pewter to darken with age.

Because of its toxicity, however, lead is no longer a component of pewter. Most modern pewter is composed of tin (91 to 93 percent), antimony (6 to 7 percent), and copper (1 to 2 percent). Tin is a brittle metal that gives pewter its sheen and resistance to corrosion. Antimony hardens and whitens the alloy and also has the unusual property of expanding as it cools, which preserves the sharpness of the casting. Copper increases ductility and malleability, especially important when hand forming pewter (see *Metalworking*, pp. 276–289); copper also makes the pewter harder. Modern pewter is harder than old pewter, and it does not lose its silver-white color.

The melting points of different pewters vary with their compositions. Most pewter melts between 227°C and 243°C, well within the range attainable on a home kitchen gas or electric stove.

Casting pewter. Historically, most pewter has been cast in permanent brass or bronze molds. These molds can be heated to the melting point of pewter, reducing thermal shock during casting. They can also be reused indefinitely. Unfortunately, they are difficult to obtain. Frequently you will see them at demonstrations at craft fairs or at exhibitions of technology used in colonial times. They sometimes turn up in antique shops or attics.

Brass and bronze molds are not necessary for pewter casting, however. You can make molds using techniques much like those shown on pages 198–201. Plaster molds are quite easy to make, and they will capture fine detail from the model. One disadvantage of a plaster mold, however, is that before it is used for casting pewter, it must be heated in an oven to vaporize the latent water in the plaster. As a result, the mold becomes very brittle, and it is difficult to get more than a few castings from it without breaking it.

Molds can also be made from the polyester auto-body putty that is shown being used to make a casting on page 205. Polyester putty is harder and more durable than plaster but does not capture fine details as well. Unlike plaster, polyester putty cannot be used to make a waste mold (see below) because it is too hard to be chipped into pieces.

Waste-mold method. Pewter can be cast into any shape. A popular use of pewter casting is to reproduce such objects as candlesticks and utensils. You can also fashion a shape in clay, make a mold, and cast the shape in pewter. If you are casting a complicated shape, you can make a two-piece plaster waste mold instead of making a piece mold with many different pieces. A waste mold is made by placing one fence down the middle of the model and making the mold in two pieces (see pp. 198–201). After the mold sets, open it and pull the clay out. Prepare the mold for casting, pour the pewter, let it cool, and carefully chisel away the plaster from the pewter casting.

Piece-mold method. Instructions for casting a spoon, or any utensil, appear on the facing page. Pewter is a soft metal, so if the pewter utensil is intended to have more than a decorative function, it must be quite thick. Choose a utensil with a muted, gentle decoration—pewter will not reproduce extremely fine detail.

The moldmaking process is similar to that shown on pages 198–201. Basically, the same methods are used for making molds out of both plaster and polyester auto-body filler. (Differences are discussed in the captions on the facing page.)

After the mold is made, surface flaws are repaired. A passage is then cut for pouring in the molten pewter. This passage, called a *sprue*, should have a wide mouth on the outside of the mold to permit easy pouring.

The plaster mold is then put in an oven and heated to about 205°C for 20 to 30 hours. This evaporates water from the plaster which, if allowed to remain, would vaporize on contact with the hot pewter and create incomplete castings, bubbles in the pewter, and other flaws. As noted, plaster becomes very brittle when it is heated like this, so you must be careful with your mold. Special plaster that retains considerable strength when heated is available at some crafts stores; however, it is much more expensive than regular plaster.

Polyester compound molds do not have to be heated, but they should sit for a few days before being used for casting. Before casting, the inside of the polyester mold can be coated with carbon by holding each piece over a candle flame. The carbon acts as a separator, easing the removal of the casting, and it helps make the surface of the casting very smooth. If there are areas of design in the mold, clean them of carbon with a toothpick.

Pewter, in ingot form, can be bought at some crafts supply stores and from companies that manufacture the metal. Pewter can be melted over a stove, torch, or bunsen burner in an iron ladle, skillet, or a pot such as the ones plumbers use to melt lead in.

The halves of the mold are clamped together and set on a cookie sheet to collect any pewter that runs off during casting. Pour the molten pewter into the sprue in one continuous flow until the mold and the sprue are completely filled. The pewter cools very quickly—the mold can be opened about 30 seconds after pouring.

If you get incomplete castings in a mold, it may be because the pewter is cooling before it reaches the far recesses of the mold. If this happens, try heating the mold to about 205°C before you pour the pewter.

Finishing. The pewter that hardens in the sprue is removed from the casting with a pair of tin snips, and the edge is filed. Surface flaws and rough edges can be removed with steel wool, followed by a buffing with tripoli. For more information about chasing, see *Metalworking*, pp. 276–289, and for information about finishing and polishing, see *Jewelry*, pp. 324–347.

Care of pewter. Although modern pewter does not darken as older pewter containing lead does, you may wish to clean or polish the surface of your pewterware. Wash pewter with warm water and soap or mild detergent and dry it immediately with a soft cloth. Pewter can be polished with a mild pewter or silver polish.

Do not put pewter into a dishwasher or polish it with steel wool. Never use pewter for cooking.

Casting a pewter utensil

1. Roll a slab of clay 1/2 in. thick. Embed the spoon in the clay. Work the clay so that it comes halfway up the side of the spoon all around. Fill any gaps beneath the spoon in order to prevent undercuts (see p.198) in the mold.

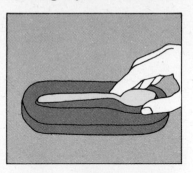

2. Apply a mold separator—oil, shortening, green soap, or petroleum jelly—to the exposed areas of the spoon. Do not apply the separator thickly or let it pool inside the spoon, or it will mar the surface of the mold.

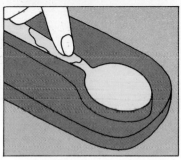

3. Roll a clay slab 1/2 in. thick and 1½ in. wide. Wrap it around clay in which spoon is embedded to make a fence (see p. 198) to hold the mold material. Be sure the fence is attached securely so that no mold material will leak.

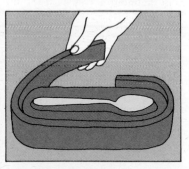

4. Pour the wet mold material, either plaster (see p. 199) or polyester auto-body filler (see p.204) into the area enclosed by the fence, to a depth of 3/4 to 1 in. Jar the table to break air bubbles.

5. After the mold sets, peel off the clay fence. Clay will separate from plaster, but it has to be washed from polyester putty with warm water and detergent.

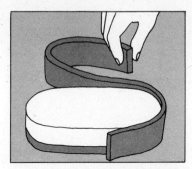

6. Gently pull the spoon out of the mold. If it sticks, scrape away the obstructing plaster or putty. Air holes or other flaws in the mold can be fixed by adding small amounts of the mold material.

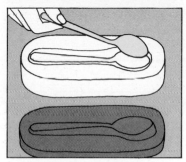

7. To make the second half of the mold, put the spoon back in the first half and coat the spoon and the entire surface of the mold with separator. Build a fence, as in Step 3, and pour the material, as in Step 4.

8. After the mold sets, remove the fence and carefully pry the pieces apart. Remove the spoon. Make any necessary surface repairs on the mold.

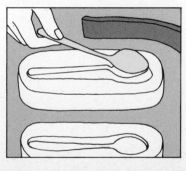

9. Cut a channel (called a sprue) for the molten pewter to enter the mold. A wide sprue opening will facilitate pouring. Use a plaster knife for a plaster mold and a saw or file for a polyester mold.

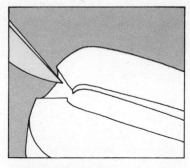

10. Prepare plaster mold for pouring by heating it (see text). After a polyester mold sits for a few days, give it a carbon coating by holding each piece directly over the flame of a candle.

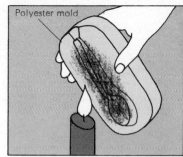

Polyester mold

11. Melt the pewter (see text). Clamp the two pieces of the mold together. Set the mold on a cookie sheet, and pour the pewter quickly and continuously into the mold until it is full.

12. Open the mold and remove the casting. Trim and file the casting, then rub it with steel wool and buff it with tripoli to give it a smooth, lustrous finish.

Modeling, moldmaking, and casting sculpture

Chasing and patining

After a casting is removed from a mold, it generally requires two types of finishing. First, the flashings have to be removed and other surface flaws, such as pits and holes, have to be repaired. This physical finishing is called *chasing*. After chasing, the surface is usually given a color treatment, both to homogenize the surface if it was disrupted during chasing and to generally enhance the appearance of the piece. This color treatment of the surface is called *patining* (or giving it a *patina*).

Patinas can range from very light, simple coloring (as in the plaster model at far right) to dense, opaque, variegated coloring (as in the polyester-resin compound casting at right). In some cases, as in the clay press molding, no patina is necessary.

A patina is intended to enhance, rather than to obscure, the form and medium of the piece. Attempts to make concrete or plaster castings look like bronze usually result in precisely that—plaster or concrete castings intended to look like bronze.

Patinas are generally homogeneous—that is, although they can be variegated, they are not splotchy. Much ancient sculpture was given lifelike coloring (light skin, dark hair, etc.), but this is rarely done today.

Chasing. Flashings are removed from the castings as described on pages 202–205. Air pockets and other surface flaws are then repaired. In a polyester-resin casting, holes can be filled with the polyester putty or with lacquer-spotting putty (if the patina will be opaque). Clay castings should be repaired with bits of the same clay while the casting is still wet. Concrete castings should be repaired with a putty of pure cement; the casting is wetted so that the cement repairs will adhere.

Patining. Patining on polyester-resin compound, plaster, or concrete is done with oil or acrylic paints. Clay castings can be patined with anything that is used to decorate pottery (see *Pottery*, pp. 163–176), as well as with paints. The treatment of metal castings is fundamentally different (see p. 209).

The paints can be applied directly to the casting, or they can be thinned first, depending on the intended density of the patina. After the paint dries, a layer of shellac is applied to seal the surface. A coating of paste wax will give the finish a warm glow.

The complete chasing and patining of the polyester-resin casting is shown at the bottom of the page. Other patinas are shown on the concrete casting and the plaster model at right.

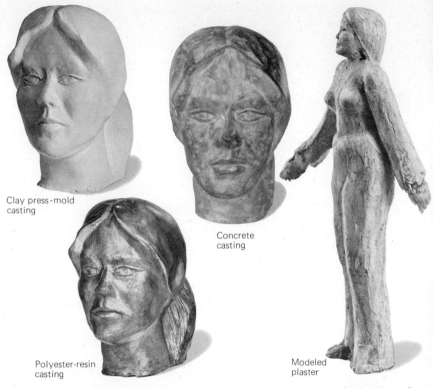

Clay press-mold casting

Concrete casting

Polyester-resin casting

Modeled plaster

Clay press-mold casting was fired to maturity; no patining was done. Any pottery finish—glazes, slips, etc.—can be used on a clay casting. **Modeled plaster figure** was given a light patina in brown acrylic paint thinned with water. A plaster casting can be treated in the same way. **Concrete casting** was given a patina of oil paint thinned with turpentine. It was then given a thick coat of paste wax. **Polyester-resin casting** was patined with spray paint, acrylic paints, lacquer and paste wax (see illustrations below).

Chasing and patining the polyester-resin casting

1. Fill any surface holes with auto-body putty or lacquer-spotting putty.

2. Trim off the flashings, and sand them until the surface is smooth.

3. Spray on a light layer of silver paint to make the surface shine.

4. Squeeze on some brown acrylic paint and spread it around.

5. Use a wet brush to get an even coat of color all over the casting.

6. Dab on green paint and smear it around. Repeat with black paint.

7. Coat the casting with lacquer. Then apply a layer of paste wax.

Lost-wax bronze casting

Bronze head was made by the lost-wax method.

The most popular of the various techniques of bronze casting is the lost-wax method. First a wax casting is surrounded by a shell of refractory material called the *investment*. The invested casting is then heated, and the wax melts out (is "lost"), leaving a cavity. Molten bronze is poured into the cavity, creating a bronze replica of the original wax.

Bronze casting can be done in some homes, but do not attempt it before you thoroughly research the techniques and consult experts and fire officials. The descriptions and illustrations on this page depict one method of lost-wax bronze casting (there are several) done in a professional bronze foundry.

Gate assembly. Rods of wax are attached to the wax casting. After all the wax melts away during burnout (see below), the rods leave cavities through which the molten bronze will flow. These openings, or *runners,* lead from the main opening called the *gate* (the large pyramid of wax at the bottom of the casting in the first illustration at right) to various points in the mold cavity that receive the bronze. The gate and runners must be designed so that the molten bronze reaches all parts of the mold cavity before the bronze cools and hardens.

Other wax rods are attached to the wax casting to make cavities called *risers* through which hot gases from the mold can escape when the bronze is poured. An example of a wax rod that will form a riser is the one attached to the chin in the first illustration at far right. The entire wax assembly—the gate, the runners, and the risers—is called the gate assembly.

Pins. Metal pins are put through the wax to keep the inside and outside investments from shifting after the wax is melted away. The holes in the bronze created by the pins are later hammered closed. The wax model with the pins in place is shown in the first illustration at right on this page.

Investment. The wax is dipped in a ceramic mixture to form a shell that will reproduce accurately the surface of the wax and retain strength when the wax is burned out. This investment material is applied by dipping the wax casting once or twice a day for several weeks into a mixture of water, silica, and other chemicals. Fiberglass is added for strength. The second illustration at right shows the wax casting after the first dipping.

The top of the wax head was cut off when the gate assembly was attached so that the investment would coat both the inside and outside of the wax casting as it was dipped. This process makes possible a thinner investment shell and shorter burnout time (see below) than if the investment were to entirely fill the inside of the wax casting. The top of the head is cast separately and is later welded into place.

Burnout. The invested wax is placed in a kiln and heated to about 870°C. Most of the wax melts and runs out, and the remainder burns out, leaving the cavity in the investment into which the molten bronze is poured.

Pouring the bronze. Bronze, an alloy of copper, tin, zinc, phosphorous, and sometimes other metals, is melted in a graphite crucible. The red-hot mold is placed in sand with the gate facing up. When the bronze reaches about 1205°C, it is poured into the mold in one continuous stream, filling the entire mold and gate assembly (below).

Molten bronze is poured into red-hot investment.

Chasing. After the mold and bronze cool, the investment is hammered away. Then the gate assembly, which has been filled with bronze, is cut from the casting. The rough casting requires a great deal of work with rotary abrasive tools and a hammer and special chisels to repair surface flaws caused during pouring. Separated parts, such as the top of the head in this piece, are also welded together at this point (see third illustration at right). In casting figures, the limbs are frequently removed and cast separately.

Patining. Bronze is usually patined by applying chemicals while the bronze is heated with a torch (see fourth illustration at right). The patina on this head (see above, left) is called French bronze. The bronze is then given a coat of wax for luster and protection.

Four stages of bronze casting. The first head has the gate assembly and pins in place. The second shows the wax casting after the first dipping in the investment material. The third head shows the bronze after the gate assembly is cut from the casting and the top of the head is welded back in place. The fourth head is being given a patina with a torch and brush.

Drawing

Drawing as an art

Pictures scrawled on sandstone, bones, and cave walls indicate that man has been drawing almost since he developed the opposable thumb. For millenia only pointed tools, charcoal from the hearth, and natural chalks were available, and the art was primitive—in ancient Egypt craftsmen sketched on broken pieces of earthenware. Drawing as a fine art, done on silk and paper with ink and brushes, first appeared in China in the fourth century A.D. In the West, however, it was held to have little intrinsic value and was done on wax tablets and other erasable surfaces.

In the 15th century, when paper became commonly available, drawing began to flourish. By then the quill, which was ideal for sketching, was in general use, and the versatility of pen and paper was demonstrated in many drawings of the old masters.

The discovery of graphite in England in the 16th century gave artists a new medium for drawing. Two centuries later this was much improved by the invention of the "lead" pencil (actually graphite mixed with clay encased in a wooden stick).

For a long time serious artists considered drawing preparatory to other forms of art, such as painting and architecture. Renaissance artists used pen or chalk sketches to plan their compositions and to work out the details of major paintings. During that period drawings were also extensively used as adjuncts to scientific treatises. The greatest of these were Leonardo da Vinci's architectural, anatomical, and mechanical studies.

Today drawings are valued in their own right and often form an integral part of the work of 20th-century artists. Notable examples are the simple, evocative drawings of Paul Klee, Henri Matisse, and Pablo Picasso.

Basic techniques. To portray three-dimensional objects in two dimensions, an illusion of contour, distance, and depth must be created. The basic techniques available to the artist to achieve this are outline and proportion, perspective, and light and shade.

The *outline* is a representation of the outer edge of the subject and of the meeting points of adjacent surfaces, color zones, and areas of light and shade. Inherent in the outline is *proportion*, which indicates the relative sizes of the elements in the drawing.

Perspective is the technique used to give flat surfaces the sense of distance and depth naturally perceived by the eye. The use of perspective was formally developed in 15th-century Florence. It was largely absent in the art of non-Western cultures, where elaborate conventions often evolved to resolve the problem. Drawings in ancient Egyptian tombs depict the human figure with the head, legs, and feet in profile; eyes, shoulders, and chest facing front; and lower torso in three-quarter view. In old Persian drawings distance is suggested by objects at different levels, and carpets appear as simple rectangles. Traditional Chinese mist-veiled landscapes have virtually no perspective.

The advent of photography contributed much to the understanding of perspective by its ability to mechanically and objectively render three-dimensional space on a flat plane. Subsequently, cubists and abstract artists abandoned perspective in order to express what has been called a non-visual, inner reality.

Light and shade can be developed in a drawing to suggest contour, color, and mass (solidity), as well as to illustrate actual areas of light and shadow around the objects depicted.

"Ruins of a Courtyard," a pen drawing in brown ink with gray wash over graphite by Venetian painter Canaletto (1697–1768), utilizes linear perspective and strong light and shade.

Tools and materials

Drawing implements

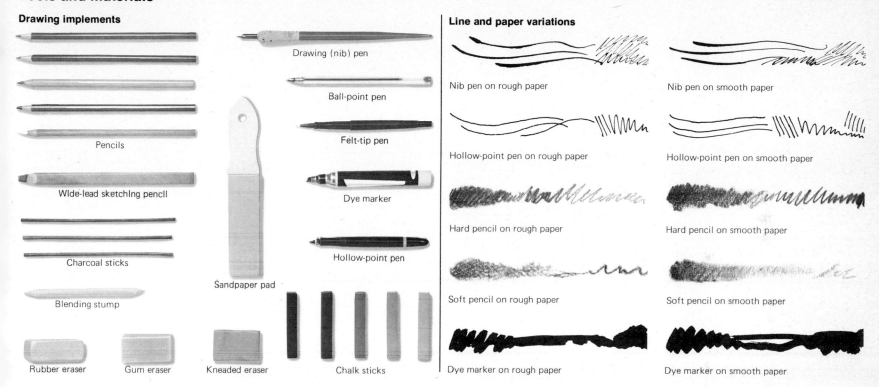

Pencils

Wide-lead sketching pencil

Charcoal sticks

Blending stump

Rubber eraser

Gum eraser

Kneaded eraser

Chalk sticks

Sandpaper pad

Drawing (nib) pen

Ball-point pen

Felt-tip pen

Dye marker

Hollow-point pen

Line and paper variations

Nib pen on rough paper

Nib pen on smooth paper

Hollow-point pen on rough paper

Hollow-point pen on smooth paper

Hard pencil on rough paper

Hard pencil on smooth paper

Soft pencil on rough paper

Soft pencil on smooth paper

Dye marker on rough paper

Dye marker on smooth paper

The most popular and versatile drawing implements are pencils, which come in 17 degrees of softness, from 9H to 6B, with HB and F in the middle. However, these designations are not precise; the exact degree of softness varies with manufacturers. Soft pencils (2B–6B) are best for freehand sketching. For making very broad strokes use wide-lead sketching pencils or carpenter's pencils, both of which have flat leads. Your results will also depend on the type of paper you use.

Graphite. Graphite sticks are essentially naked pencil leads. They come with square, rectangular, and round cross sections fit into graphite holders, and are excellent for covering large areas. Sharpen graphite sticks frequently. Cut them at 90° angles with a

razor blade, or sand them to shape with a fine sandpaper pad.

Charcoal. Charcoal in stick form is crumbly and messy. Charcoal pencils and black chalk give similar effects and are easier to control. Chalk should be snapped into thirds for easier handling.

Pens. Several types of pens are available for ink drawing. The fountain pen has interchangeable nibs, which makes it adaptable to a wide variety of purposes. Ball-point drawing pens are the same as those for writing, except that they contain special drawing inks. The hollow-point pen, used extensively by commercial artists, has a thin tube for a nib, with a very thin wire inside the tube to facilitate the flow of ink. It produces lines of uniform width regardless of the angle at which the pen

is held. Felt-tip pens are refillable and have interchangeable tips.

Drawing papers. A drawing is affected as much by the surface it is drawn on as by what it is drawn with. Besides color, the most important characteristic of paper for drawing is the degree of roughness of its fibers, called tooth; tooth determines "bite" (the amount of graphite, charcoal, or chalk taken up by the paper).

For practice you can use a cheap paper stock, such as newsprint. For finished work, however, use either drawing paper or the more expensive bristol paper. Both come in sheets or pads of several sizes. Bristol paper is available with two surfaces: plate (smooth) and kid, or vellum (matte). Both are good for soft graphite leads.

Erasers. Use ink eraser, art gum eraser, or kneaded eraser to correct errors, depending on your medium. The kneaded eraser, which should be stretched and kneaded often, is good for lightening pencil shades or for emphasizing highlights. To clear away eraser crumbs, use a dust brush.

Art supply stores carry tools for various purposes. A drawing board facilitates moving the paper to different angles for easier sketching. A French curve, a square, and a compass can be useful for precision work. To keep a finished drawing from being smeared or soiled, spray it with a fixative. Pastel and acrylic fixatives are also good for pencil and charcoal drawings. Avoid charcoal fixative, which may eventually turn an amber color.

Drawing

Grid copying

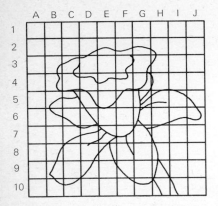

You can easily make a same-size copy of a picture simply by tracing it. But if you need a precise scale copy (larger or smaller) of a picture, the grid method is the easiest way to draw it accurately and in the right proportions.

Begin by lightly penciling a grid on the original, or draw a grid on a piece of tracing paper and superimpose it on the picture. (Examples of designs with such overprinted grids are found as patterns in other chapters of this book.) The copy can be exactly the same size as the original, or enlarged or reduced, depending on the dimensions of the squares in the copy's grid.

Draw the grid for your copy lightly in pencil so that it can be erased later. It is absolutely essential that the grid on the original picture and the grid on the copy be proportional to each other (that both have the same ratio of length to width) and that each grid be formed of the same numbers of vertical and horizontal lines and thus have the same number of squares.

Here the original drawing (above) has been overprinted with a grid, and a larger grid (right) has been constructed, with the same proportions and the same number of lines but with larger squares, to make an enlarged copy of the picture.

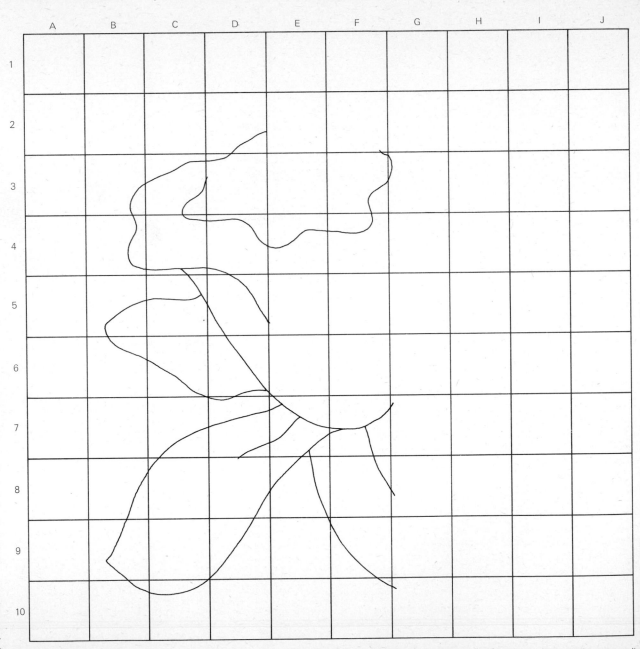

Transfer design one square at a time, starting with any square such as D-2. Mark copying grid wherever a line in original intersects corresponding square. Then, guided by these marks, draw the lines inside each square. You can make an accurate copy of any picture in virtually any size.

Outline and proportion

To draw accurately from life, it is necessary to first construct a freehand outline establishing the general proportions of the object or figures in the scene you are observing.

For a beginner this can be a major stumbling block. Normally, when we look at an object, our eyes take in all its details as part of the whole. In sketching a simple object, such as a pitcher, the beginner would probably draw its outline by tracing from a particular point, continuously and in faithful detail, all around the outer perimeter. But such an outline invariably warps the object's proportions, resulting in an incorrect interpretation of its shape.

To construct an outline properly, you must learn to use your vision analytically. First look at the general shape, ignoring such features as, in the case of the pitcher, the spouts and the handle. Ask yourself: Can the object be enclosed in a square, circle, triangle, or rectangle? What is the rough ratio between its height and width?

To translate your perceptions onto drawing paper, first make light marks at the top and bottom and on both sides to define the boundary of the outline. Then, using many separate, intersecting straight lines, block out the whole shape, keeping all the major proportions in mind. These lines should be drawn lightly and quickly, with the arm sweeping from the shoulder.

If the whole shape fits into, say, a large rectangle, then in your mind's eye divide the rectangle into smaller rectangles. These smaller units will help you establish the proportions of the parts of the object within the outline of its overall shape. Depending on the shapes involved, you can also use squares, circles, or ovals to block out these parts. In this way, working from the largest shape gradually to the smaller details, you can construct a reasonably accurate freehand outline.

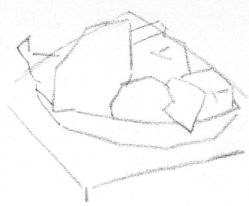

In drawing from life, as in the case of this still life (shown in the photograph at left), begin by marking off the boundaries of the overall shape with four short lines. Employ a series of intersecting straight lines—not one continuous line—to block in proportions of smaller shapes within the outline. Finally, begin to sketch the picture in full detail.

Drawing a human figure is made much easier by first sketching a stick figure. The stick figure determines the right proportions for the torso and limbs and properly places the joints. Note that the walking figure at left has its gravity line (the vertical line through the center of gravity) midway between its two feet.

To draw a face, begin by drawing an oval. Next, determine the proportions of the features. Mark a horizontal line across the middle to indicate position of eyes and tops of ears. Draw a vertical line down the center. Midway between eyes and chin draw a horizontal line for base of nose. One-third to one-half way from nose to chin draw line for mouth.

213

Drawing

Perspective

A drawing is done on a piece of paper, a two-dimensional surface. To suggest three-dimensional reality, the artist employs perspective.

Perspective simulates the way things appear at various distances from and angles to the viewer. For example, buildings at the end of a street look not so tall as those nearby, even when all are of the same height. And when a cylinder is tilted, its circular base appears oval, not circular. A realistic drawing utilizes special techniques to show these effects.

The theory of perspective is based on complex mathematical principles. Only the most basic aspects of the subject are covered here.

One-point perspective. Perspective is most obvious in pictures containing forms with straight lines, such as houses, straight highways, or railroad tracks. When one side of such a form—say, a house—is perpendicular to the line of sight, the other visible sides (those parallel to the line of sight) appear to recede toward a vanishing point on the horizon. At this point, all these lines, or their extensions, meet. This is called one-point perspective.

Two-point perspective. When the vertical planes of an object—say, the walls of a house—are at angles to the line of sight, these lines or their extensions will meet at two different points on the horizon. The drawings on this page illustrate the sketching techniques used in blocking out scenes in one- or two-point perspective.

Three-point perspective. A third vanishing point comes into play when the walls of a house are at angles to the line of sight and the top is tilted toward or away from the viewer. This would occur on the street looking up at a tall building or in a plane looking down, situations more suited to wide-angle photography than to drawing.

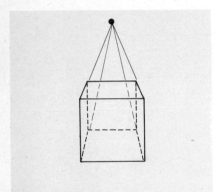

One-point perspective. The sides of a cube (or the walls of a room) are blocked out using one-point perspective. Because the cube is seen head-on, there is only one vanishing point.

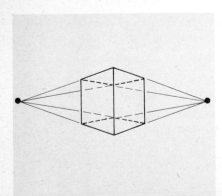

Two-point perspective. Because cube is seen at an angle, lines extending from its walls meet at two vanishing points on the horizon. Tilt cube to see three-point perspective.

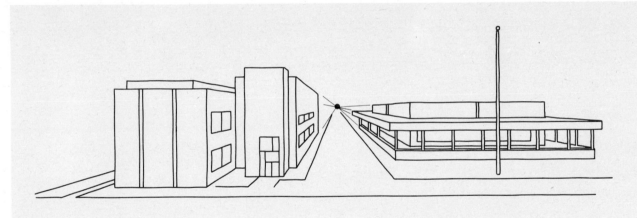

In this drawing using one-point perspective, the line of sight parallels the street; all "parallel" lines would meet at one point on the horizon.

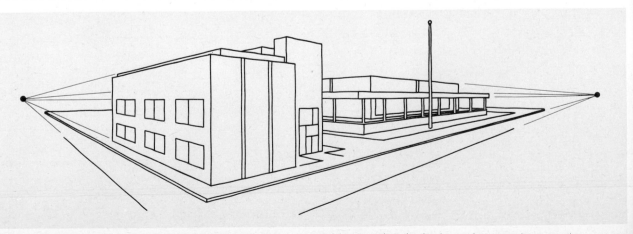

In this view of the same street scene as above, the line of sight does not parallel the street; thus, the drawing employs two-point perspective.

Light and shade

A line drawing, even with proportion and perspective, may not convey a convincing illusion of depth. And perspective is of no use in imparting a three-dimensional effect to rounded or spherical forms rendered in two dimensions. An illusion of depth and of modeling can be created through high-lighting and shading.

Cross-hatching, stippling, and other shading and highlighting techniques are illustrated on the following page.

The illustrations on this page show where the darker and lighter areas will occur on different forms and surfaces with respect to the direction of the light source illuminating them.

The technique of creating dramatic contrasts with light and shade, called *chiaroscuro* (an Italian word meaning, literally, "bright-dark") was highly developed by Renaissance artists in drawings and paintings. Rembrandt was the greatest master of chiaroscuro.

Top-lit vase has mostly quarter tones.

Side lighted, its pattern of darks changes.

Light shines from above on a cube and a sphere, creating highlights and shadows.

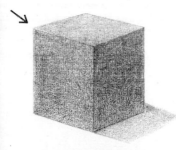

Light shines down at a 45° angle.

Vertical planes of top-lit book show halftones.

Side lighting results in intense darks.

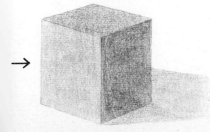

Light shines from the side.

Drawing

Drawing techniques

The vocabulary of drawing consists of a variety of lines, thin or thick, straight or sinuous, bold or delicate. Different kinds of strokes can be used to suggest the solidity of granite slabs, the surface texture of Ming porcelain, or the sun-dappled foliage of a maple tree.

To depict areas of varying brightness resulting from an interplay of colors and lighting, the artist makes use of a technique called *toning*. So-called true tone is attained by a form of shading in which the individual pencil lines are merged. In the case of charcoal, the lines can be smudged. So-called illusory tones are obtained by means of closely spaced lines or dots. The dot method is known as *stippling*.

Tones can be flat, as on a wall receiving and reflecting the same amount of light across its entire area. Graded tones, on the other hand, are used for uneven effects. For example, shading can suggest shadow on a sphere.

A drawing can be elaborately delineated like a painting, with detailed renderings of textures, color tones, and patterns of light and shade. Or a drawing may be just a few well-placed, spontaneous lines that bring out the essence of the objects depicted. A good drawing is an effective orchestration of lines. Even a simple work may combine two or more shading techniques to suggest light, shadow, and form. The apple drawing on this page, for instance, done with graphite pencil on bond paper, contains both simple strokes and crosshatches (patches of fine intersecting lines).

Papers. A variety of drawing papers are available in art and stationery stores. These include bond papers with a high rag content, which, like vellum, offer a smooth, nonporous surface that is ideal for pen-and-ink. Vellum has the additional advantage of being transparent, so that it can be used for tracing. (The finished drawing is then mounted on an opaque white paper or board.) Bond is also ideal for pencil drawings, but interesting effects can be achieved by experimenting with pencil on rougher papers, such as those traditionally employed for charcoal. The apple drawings on this page demonstrate the different effects of using pencil, pen-and-ink, and charcoal on smooth and rough papers.

Pencil drawing. Make your first drawings using just three grades of graphite pencil: HB, 2B, and 3B. Experiment with both round and flat leads. Sharpen leads into conical as well as chisel points.

Charcoal drawing. Charcoal offers a soft texture and a deep black that are not easily achieved with other drawing mediums. Charcoal pencils are used like graphite pencils, but charcoal sticks require a quite different technique. The sticks should be used in 1-inch lengths, broadside, for toning and for merging tones. Do not draw lines between two tones. Use lines only when absolutely necessary. To merge or soften tones, smudge them with your finger. To highlight dark areas, use a piece of kneaded eraser. An easily smudged charcoal drawing can be protected by spraying it with a fixative after its completion.

Pen-and-ink drawing. Ink lines are sharp and precisely defined. The techniques for drawing with a pen are similar to those for pencil, but with ink you cannot differentiate tones by varying the pressure and the grade. You can, however, vary the thickness and spacing of pen strokes. Lightly sketch the outline with an HB pencil beforehand.

Graphite pencil on bond paper

Charcoal on bond paper with smudging

India ink on bond paper with crosshatch

Graphite pencil on rough paper

Charcoal on rough paper with smudging

India ink on bond paper with stippling

Stages in sketching

Shown on this page are two parallel sequences of three stages in the execution of a still life. One is done in charcoal, the other in colored pencil.

The outline in the charcoal sketch is a flat and totally linear portrayal of a bowl with pears, apples, and bananas. The outlines of the bowl and of the fruit are formed by many short, straight lines, revealing the rough shapes and proportions of the objects. Initial toning is done in the second stage—closely spaced strokes are used to fill in all areas except those with highlights. As part of this process, some of the outline is merged with the strokes.

In the final stage the finished toning is achieved by smudging the charcoal with a finger to give uniformity and gradation to the shading. Additional highlights are created with a piece of kneaded eraser. The tones are then graded further by adding charcoal to deepen the darkest areas. These steps result in a suggestion of depth and contour in the still life.

The first sketch in colored pencil is outlined in a similar manner to the charcoal sketch, except, of course, that colors are used. In the initial toning the artist uses "true" tone (see p. 216) for the bananas and the bowl, parallel strokes for the apples, and a mixture of strokes and crosshatches in green and yellow for the pears. In the final stage the bananas are shown to be ripening by the addition of spots of brown toning, and the pears and apples are made to stand out realistically with further toning by means of strokes as well as crosshatches.

In drawing with colored pencils, it is not necessary to use the exact shade of a particular hue, as essence may be more important than photographic accuracy. Because it is difficult to apply colored pencils evenly to large areas, close parallel strokes, repeated without excessive pressure, are generally used.

Charcoal

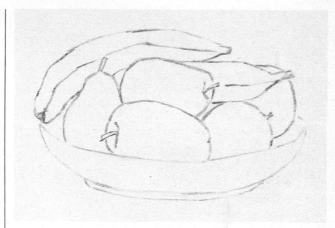

Colored pencil

Drawing

Pastel

In its soft brilliance, pastel differs from colored pencil (see p. 217). Pastel can be classed either as painting, when blending and smudging achieve the effects of paint, or as drawing, when linear features predominate.

Originating in northern Italy in the 16th century, pastel reached an early peak of popularity among portrait painters in 18th-century France. By the late 19th century Degas and other French impressionists had begun to develop a new approach to pastel, which emphasized individual strokes and the juxtaposition of colors with little or no blending.

Pastels are pure pigment powders mixed with a light binder and shaped into soft sticks. They are used on charcoal and pastel papers that have pronounced tooth (see p. 211) or on velour papers with flocked finish.

Minor errors in pastel strokes are not corrected by going back over them, as this would result in a nonuniform tone. Rather, the sticks are held over the area and rubbed on a clean, fine sanding pad to produce loose powder; the powder is then rubbed with the finger to achieve an evenly tinted area. More serious errors can be corrected by blotting them with a piece of kneaded eraser until the loose pastel particles are removed. The area is then rubbed gently with powder as described above.

The disadvantage of pastel is that the dusty powder does not adhere well to paper, and spraying with fixative alters the colors. The best way to preserve a pastel is to frame it tightly under glass.

A sketch is made of a pepper, an artichoke, tomatoes, carrots, and radishes with a sepia conté crayon on steel-gray paper.

The sides of pastel sticks are worked along the edges of the vegetables to fill in the darker parts and some middle tones.

More colors are added to the tomatoes and carrots while middle tones are given to the bodies of green vegetables.

A white pastel stick is used to add highlights to the vegetables where some reflected light rays are observed by the artist.

Most parts of the drawing are smudged gently with a stump (pointed rolled paper) or with the finger for larger areas.

Blue is given to the background and parts of the vegetables. The highlights are put in again and all vegetable edges are refined.

Dye marker

A dye marker is a small cylinder of liquid dye topped with a felt or nylon tip. It is a relatively new drawing implement that is used extensively by poster and commercial artists.

The techniques of using the dye marker are relatively simple. It produces strokes that are dictated by the size and shape of the felt or nylon nib. The color intensity of any one marker cannot be varied, but a large and growing assortment of colors is available. The markers come with water-soluble or oil-based dyes; the two kinds should not be mixed in the same work, as they have very different characteristics and do not blend.

Dyes soak through papers and tend to bleed into one another. A special dye paper, which is relatively nonporous, can be used to limit soaking; however, this paper may cause drawings to appear thin and streaky.

Another problem in using markers is that the dyes are so volatile that they evaporate quickly. It is therefore a good practice to uncap a marker only when it is to be used and to recap it immediately after use. It is possible as an emergency measure to revive briefly a marker showing signs of dryness; simply moisten its tip with a few drops of some solvent such as acetone, lacquer thinner, or pen cleaner.

The intensely colored dyes, once put on paper, are impossible to erase except with a bleach. Such a practice is not advisable, as the bleach must be used with great care and skill to produce acceptable results.

Working in a broad, comic style such as might be employed in a children's book illustration, the artist sketches the dancing bear and stars in soft pencil.

The artist fills in the large areas of color. First, the bear's body is colored in light and dark brown dyes. Its skirt is done in red-violet, snout and eye in black, and stars in yellow.

A border of blue-violet is applied to the skirt. A sharp-tipped black dye marker is used to draw the pleats of the skirt and the paws, as well as to create shaded areas.

219

Color and design

Understanding color

White light is made up of light of different colors. Anyone who has seen a rainbow has seen white light divided into its component colors, the colors of the spectrum. The red petals of a rose look red to us because they absorb all wavelengths of light except those in the red part of the spectrum; only the red wavelengths are reflected to our eyes. The color we call black is theoretically the total absence of light. A pure black ink would be one that absorbed all light, reflecting nothing.

But to appreciate color and to make use of it, it is not necessary to understand the scientific and optical principles of light and color. One need only be aware of why colors relate to one another as they do and of how these relationships can be handled in mixing paints, in dyeing one color over another, or in planning the design, for example, of a woven fabric or a collage.

Hue, brightness, and saturation. When we talk about color, we are really speaking of three different elements that combine to produce the visual effect we perceive as color.

The first of these elements is hue. Red is a hue, green is a hue, violet is a hue—indeed, all of the colors of the spectrum are, strictly speaking, hues, not colors. In the creation of a color, hue is just the starting point.

In addition to hue, there is the element of brightness, or value. Brightness results, for example, in darker or brighter shades of red. In a magazine illustration of an apple, the value or brightness is often controlled by printing gray dots over the red. The more gray dots crowded into the area, the darker the red of the apple will appear. In mixing paints, however, gray would not necessarily be added to the red to darken it; instead, brown or green pigments might be added.

Brightness, or value, scales are based on a progression from black to white.

Black has the lowest value, 0; grays are in the middle; white is usually assigned a value of 10. If the artist is attempting to lower the intensity of a color by adding a neutral gray, he must take care that the gray is of the same brightness as the color or he will find he has also altered the value of the color, producing an effect totally different from that which he intended.

Besides hue and brightness, a color also depends on saturation (intensity) for its visual effect. Saturation, or intensity, refers to how much of the hue is present in the color. When we speak of a pale color or a strong color, we are acknowledging the effect of saturation. For instance, pink is generally a red of low saturation (although it can be of greater or lesser brightness, as previously discussed). Crimson and scarlet are reds of high saturation.

The color wheel and color chart on the facing page should help you understand the effects of hue, brightness, and saturation in the creation of colors.

Color harmony. For most designs you will prefer colors that work well together; in other words, colors that are harmonious in their relationships, like notes in a chord of music.

You need not rely on trial and error in choosing colors for harmony. The color wheel can be used to select harmonious hues; the color value chart will help you select hues that will also be harmonious in terms of their brightness and saturation.

There are 12 hues in the color wheel on the facing page. The three primary hues—red, yellow, and blue—are the basis of the wheel. In addition, the wheel contains the three hues derived from the primary colors: violet (equal parts red and blue), orange (equal parts red and yellow), and green (equal parts blue and yellow). Violet, orange, and green are called secondary hues.

The remaining six hues on this wheel

are called tertiary hues. They are obtained by mixing each primary color with each of the two secondary colors derived from it. A wheel with more than 12 hues can be created, of course, by continuing the recombination of primary, secondary, and tertiary hues.

Complementary hues. Several methods can be employed to identify harmonious hues on the color wheel. The simplest is to choose hues that are immediate neighbors on the wheel, such as violet, red-violet, and blue-violet. Another simple method is the selection of complementary hues or colors. Complementary hues are those that lie directly opposite one another on the color wheel. They can be identified simply by laying a straightedge on the wheel through the center point and rotating the straightedge. Red and green are complementary, as are orange and blue. When mixed together, complementary colors will make a neutral gray. Thus, red and green will produce gray. And since green is created by mixing yellow and blue, red, when mixed with yellow and blue, will also produce gray.

More complicated methods of identifying harmonious hues on the wheel involve the rotation within the wheel of triangles and rectangles. These techniques yield harmonies called triads and tetrads; they are explained in the captions accompanying the illustrations on the facing page. Harmony can also exist among variations of a single hue that differ in value (brightness) or in saturation (intensity).

"Contrast" is a term applied to the way in which colors alter one another when they are viewed at the same time. The strongest contrast exists between primary colors and, in brightness, between black and white. A few of the many additional ways in which colors influence one another are suggested by illustrations on these pages.

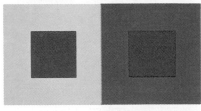
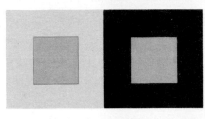

In planning a design, remember that each color is influenced by the colors next to it and by the background against which it is placed. In these examples the inner panels in each pair of rectangles are the same color, although they do not appear so because of the change in background color. You can discover many more effects by experimenting with squares of colored paper.

The color wheel

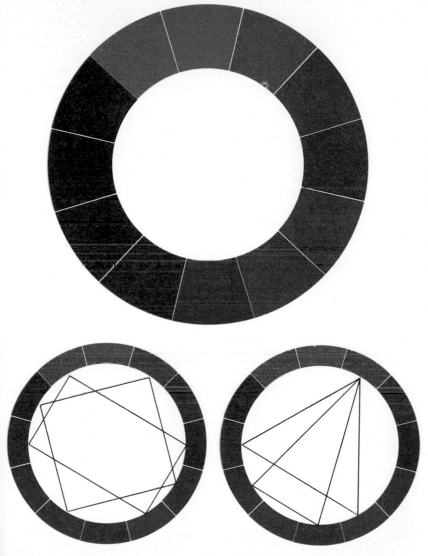

Using the color wheel. The large color wheel at top contains 12 hues obtained from the primaries (red, yellow, and blue) as described in the text on the opposite page. Color wheels with a theoretically limitless number of hues of finer and finer distinction can be created by following the procedures discussed in the text. The two small wheels at bottom illustrate the use of triangles and rectangles to identify hues that are in harmony with one another. Triads are groups of three harmonious hues; they are identified by rotating either an equilateral or an isosceles triangle within the circle. Tetrads are groups of four harmonious hues; they can be picked out of the wheel by placing a square or a rectangle within it, as shown, then rotating the figure.

Color values

Each of the 12 hues of the color wheel appears in the middle row (fourth from the top). In the three rows above the middle one, the pure hues are uniformly tinted with increasing percentages of white to lighten their values. In the rows below the middle, uniform percentages of black (grays) are added to produce shadings darker in value. All colors in the same row have the same value.

Harmony and contrast

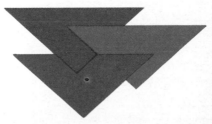

Harmony and contrast can be achieved within the same hue, as seen in the two configurations at left. At top, small variations in the value of a pure blue hue create a sensation of harmony. In the configuration below it, much greater variations in value create a sense of contrast, yet the harmony remains. In the third configuration (above), neighboring hues on the color wheel are employed to produce another type of harmony.

Painting

Changing styles of modern painting

The paintings found in museums around the world range from the rigid, conventionalized tomb paintings of ancient Egypt through the formal but realistic works of the Renaissance masters to the dizzying proliferation of art fashions and fads in our time.

Modern Western painting has its roots in antiquity, but it began to emerge as we know it today in the Middle Ages under the influence and patronage of the Christian Church. Most early Church-inspired works—altar panels, frescoes, and manuscript illuminations—were highly stylized, emphasizing religious symbolism rather than realism. The first attempts at realism are usually associated with Giotto, an Italian master of the early 14th century. While Giotto's works have religious themes, his subjects are rendered with an anatomical accuracy and a personalized sense of emotion. His scenes look real, and his innovations influenced what has come to be called international gothic style, which reached its zenith with the 15th-century Flemish masters. Jan van Eyck, a founder of the Flemish school, pioneered in the then relatively new technique of painting in oil. Florentine masters, meanwhile, were introducing mathematical perspective, even closer anatomical accuracy, and chiaroscuro—the effects of light and shadow.

During the Renaissance (15th and 16th centuries), Western art advanced with unprecedented splendor. Painting reached a new level of authority and grandeur under such towering masters as Leonardo da Vinci, Michelangelo, Raphael, and Titian. The ensuing centuries saw the rise of a number of new painting styles, each a reaction against its immediate predecessor. The lurid colors and anguished forms of post-Renaissance mannerism were replaced by the exuberant richness of the baroque style. When the baroque turned to an overripe and pompous opulence, it gave way to the beguiling sensuousness of rococo. After rococo degenerated into inconsequential frothiness, artists returned to nature and to classical ideals in the style of neoclassicism. Among the great names of these centuries are Peter Paul Rubens, the Flemish genius; Rembrandt van Rijn, the renowned Dutch master; and Francisco de Goya, perhaps the greatest Spanish master.

By the mid-19th century the most innovative movement was impressionism, pioneered by Pierre Auguste Renoir, Claude Monet, and Edouard Manet. Georges Seurat, a neoimpressionist, invented pointillism—using tiny dots of pure pigment that fuse into solid colors when seen from afar.

The pace of change quickened in the 20th century. Two early movements, though short-lived, have had a lasting influence on the modern approach to form and color. Henri Matisse's fauvism arbitrarily distorted natural colors, while cubism, pioneered by Pablo Picasso, Georges Braque, and Marcel Duchamp, fractured solid form, rearranging it in two-dimensional shapes as if it were seen from more than one vantage point. A major art movement native to the United States, abstract expressionism, occurred in the late 1940's.

Given so varied a legacy, the artist today has complete freedom to paint the subject matter of his choice in the style of his choice, naturalistic or primitive, realistic or abstract, representational or nonobjective.

Four painting styles: Thomas Cole's (1801–1848) romantic landscape (upper left) is filled with deep shadows; Pierre Bonnard's (1867–1947) river scene (upper right) emphasizes texture; Claude Monet's (1840–1926) impressionist "Landscape at Giverny" (bottom left) is a dazzle of light; and Vincent Van Gogh's (1853–1890) "Les Chaumes" shows a bold use of brushstrokes.

Painting mediums

A painting's stylistic effects derive not only from the artist's purpose and vision but also from the painting medium. The brushstroke textures of oil paints, the airy moods of watercolor washes, and the blond highlights of tempera are all characteristics of those mediums that would be difficult to reproduce by other means. Paintings using most of the mediums described below are shown later in this chapter.

Oil. This remains the most versatile painting medium and the most highly developed. Oil paint consists of a pigment, a ground, an oil (usually refined linseed oil), and a drying agent. Although it is possible to mix oil paints from scratch, few artists do so. Most buy the paints as tubes of paste. The paste can be applied just as it comes from the tube, or it can be diluted with thinners such as linseed oil, turpentine, and varnish.

Exposure to the air chemically transforms the oil into a solid, transparent, malleable film; the film acts as a protective coat over the bound pigments. The artist may vary his texture from delicate tonal gradations to impasto hillocks (solid piles of oil paints on canvas); he may apply the paints with brushes, palette knives, or wood laths, or he might even pour and drip the paint onto the canvas.

Watercolor. These transparent, water-soluble pigments are used on special watercolor papers. The pigments are bound with gum arabic or other water-soluble agents. Pigments come in both pans and tubes. Watercolors dry rapidly and demand different techniques than oil paints do.

Tempera. A medium for opaque water-soluble colors, temperas, unlike watercolor pigments, cannot be redissolved with water once dry. Originally "tempered" with egg white or yolk (which protects the painting from heat and humidity), tempera paint today often comes in fatty emulsions. The paints are available in trays, jars, or tubes. This quick-drying paint can be applied with any tool. Since it stiffens upon drying, the surface used is usually a stiff board that has been gessoed (coated with a plasterlike substance).

Gouache. Another medium for watercolor pigments, gouaches consist of transparent watercolors mixed with opaque Chinese white. Gouaches have some of the transparency of watercolors and some of the opacity of temperas. These paints dry rapidly to a matte finish and are ideal for commercial illustrations and posters.

Casein. Casein is tempered with a substance derived from cheese or milk curd. It is applied on rigid surfaces in thin washes and dries quickly to a lighter tone. It can be applied with a brush to create an impasto effect. Casein has been used as a substitute for oil, but it is being replaced for this purpose by acrylic paints.

Acrylic. Pigments are mixed into an acrylic polymer resin emulsion to create this new synthetic paint. It has many of the expressive characteristics of oil paint, yet dries more quickly than oil and with less change in color than casein. Acrylics produce a matte finish without brush marks, but the lack of texture can be compensated for by building up impasto or by diluting the paints to obtain transparent color glazes. Acrylics come in a wide range of intense colors, including metallic and fluorescent hues. This paint dries into an elastic, durable, waterproof film that can be cleaned easily.

Aniline dye. Used largely by commercial artists and illustrators, aniline dye offers intensely bright colors but no opacity. It penetrates into paper fibers and can only be removed with bleaches. Colors should not be blended or overpainted, as aniline dyes have a propensity to bleed.

223

Painting

Preparing the canvas

Canvas for oil painting comes in various grades, ranging from bold-textured linen through the less expensive cotton duck to the cheapest, but not too satisfactory, plain cotton canvas.

To assure the proper adhesion of the paint, all grades of canvas should first be sized, then primed. The traditional sizing consists of a diluted solution of rabbit-skin glue. The rabbit-skin glue comes in a concentrated form that must be mixed with water and cooked before it can be applied. The traditional primers for oil painting are gesso or white lead in linseed oil. Ready-mixed primers are available at art supply stores. The new acrylic primer developed for acrylic paints is adequate for oils and is very easy to use.

You can buy ready-to-paint canvas from art supply stores, either oil primed ("single primed" or "double primed") or acrylic primed ("all-purpose canvas"). It comes in rolls or already stretched on a frame.

Many artists prefer to buy untreated canvas at cheaper prices and to stretch, size, and prime it themselves, as illustrated below. It is not necessary to size canvas when using acrylic primer.

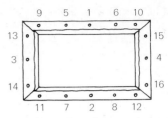

When stretching a piece of canvas, staple opposing sides in an alternating sequence.

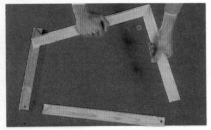

1. Assemble ready-made stretcher bars into a stretcher frame for canvas by fitting the tongue-and-groove ends into each other tightly.

2. To make sure that all corners are square, check the frame with a triangle or a carpenter's square or, as an alternative, against a doorframe.

3. Cut canvas from roll. Put it face down flat, with frame (beveled face down) on top of it. Trim canvas to within 1½ in. of frame edge all around.

4. Fold canvas back against one long side of frame and staple into edge at middle of the side. Instead of staples, carpet tacks may be used.

5. Pulling canvas tightly against the other long side with a pair of canvas webbing pliers, staple into edge at the middle of the other long side.

6. Staple the middles of the short sides. When pulling canvas against the second short side, use the pliers to make sure that canvas is taut.

7. From the middle of each side, staple at 3-in. intervals outward while pulling the canvas tightly. Leave a 3-in. length near the corners unstapled.

8. At one corner, fold canvas and tuck one part under another. Be sure the tucked-in part is folded snugly and neatly against the frame.

9. Staple the folded canvas at the corner. Take care to shoot the staple into the widest portion of the corner wood. Repeat at the other corners.

10. Fold surplus strip of canvas around frame edge and staple it to frame back at 3-in. intervals. Staple all sides in the same manner.

11. At each corner, fold the surplus canvas against the back of the frame, continuing the line of the creases along the sides. Staple all corners.

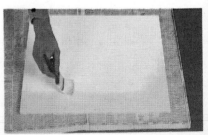

12. Use a flat varnish brush to prime the canvas with one or two coats of ready-made acrylic polymer gesso. Canvas is now ready for painting.

Preparing hardboard

A panel primed with acrylic gesso can be used for any paint. The panel should be made with a piece of untempered hardboard (Masonite or similar brand). If the board is larger than 24 inches on any side, back it with a frame. Lightly sand the smooth side with extrafine sandpaper. Scrub it with denatured alcohol mixed with a little ammonia. Gesso as shown below.

Thin the acrylic gesso slightly with water and brush it on the sanded hardboard, using a wide brush. Remove bubbles with fingers.

Apply one or two additional coats. Brush each in one direction only, at right angle to previous coat. Let each coat dry before applying the next.

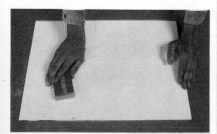

When the final coat is thoroughly dry, remove brush marks and other irregularities by sanding until smooth with fine (4/0) garnet paper.

Equipment and supplies

An oil painter should have a stable and adjustable easel to hold the stretched canvas. A palette is necessary for holding and mixing pigments. Although the traditional oval palette with thumb hole is convenient, many painters prefer a piece of glass, marble, or some other suitable surface placed flat on a table for use in the studio.

Brushes come in flats (flat, square-edged), brights (shorter flats), longs (longer flats), and rounds (rounded, ending in a point). In general, the broader flat brushes are used for working larger areas; the round, pointed brushes are for finer work. Brushes are made of stiff hog's bristles, soft camel or squirrel hair, and springy sable hair. Bristle emphasizes the texture of brushstrokes, while sable allows for very smooth blending.

Painting knives, flexible and trowel-shaped, are ideal for spreading paint thickly on canvas. Palette knives are stiff, blunt instruments for mixing colors on the palette.

Oil paints come in tubes and fall into three price ranges: professional quality for serious artists; intermediate grade; and student's grade.

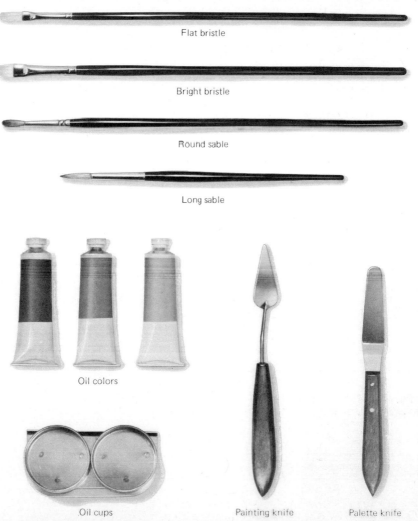

Flat bristle

Bright bristle

Round sable

Long sable

Oil colors

Oil cups

Painting knife

Palette knife

Care and cleaning

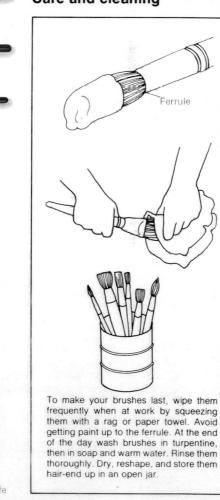

Ferrule

To make your brushes last, wipe them frequently when at work by squeezing them with a rag or paper towel. Avoid getting paint up to the ferrule. At the end of the day wash brushes in turpentine, then in soap and warm water. Rinse them thoroughly. Dry, reshape, and store them hair-end up in an open jar.

Painting

Oil painting techniques

Oils are more durable than paintings done in most other mediums. A finished painting, particularly when protected with a coat of final varnish, will last for a long time without any loss in the vividness or richness of its color. It need not be covered with glass, as is necessary with a watercolor. Any grime, dust, or grit that accumulates on the surface over the years can simply be wiped away with a dampened cloth or a mild solution of soap and water.

No other painting medium is so versatile in its effects or so expressive of nuance. Unlike watercolor and tempera, for instance, the physical properties of oil paints impose almost no restrictions upon the artist. They can be applied to the canvas in many different ways to achieve a wide variety of effects, as suggested by the photographs of masterworks on this page and the illustrations on pages 228–229.

Furthermore, oil is a medium that is kind to beginners yet challenging to seasoned artists. A serious painter, whether a novice or an accomplished artist, can choose from among all the methods and techniques in the rich body of painting knowledge developed by his predecessors over centuries. No single artist could or should use all the techniques known. He needs only those few that best suit his personal style.

Direct painting. An oil painting is usually done by one of two major methods: direct painting (*alla prima*), or indirect painting—underpainting with overpainting. In the first method the artist aims at his final effect by simultaneously dealing with the problems of color, value, modeling, and texture as he progresses with the painting. Depending on his personal preference, he may work from the darks to the lights or vice versa and from less intense colors to brighter ones or from brights to subdued colors.

Indirect painting. Direct painting has been the more popular method in oil for the past century. In earlier times, however, indirect painting was the more widely used technique.

In the indirect method the artist builds his surfaces in a series of layers. After making the sketch, he first executes a monochrome underpainting. The underpainting establishes the basic gradations of light and dark, solving the problems of both composition and value. When the succeeding layer or layers are painted, the artist concentrates on color, modeling, and texture. The painting can be elaborated with such touches as impasto, glazing, and scumbling (see pp. 228–229).

An important consideration in the

A tonal painting is one that employs a limited range of colors to attain its effect. This is a detail from "Self-Portrait," a tonal painting in browns by the greatest of all tonal painters, Rembrandt van Rijn.

Scumbling is the technique of dragging a topcoat of paint over the partially dried canvas to create uneven texture. This famous example is a detail from Claude Monet's "Rouen Cathedral, West Facade, Sunlight."

Impasto—the technique of piling thick paint on the surface of the painting to create coarse textures—is shown off to fine effect in this detail from "Oysters" by pioneer French modernist Édouard Manet.

To achieve the brilliant glazing seen in this detail from his "The Annunciation," Flemish master Jan van Eyck mixed colors with varnishes and special oils, building up several layers of semitransparent paint.

indirect method is that the underpainting must be sufficiently dry before it can be painted over; otherwise, the paint may eventually crack. For this reason many painters like to use fast-drying paints for the underpainting. Such paints include the traditional temperas and the newer acrylics. An oil underpainting may require several weeks of drying before overpainting.

Another traditional method, wiping out, often achieves a unique appearance. The canvas is covered with a flat tone of a neutral color, such as raw umber. The sketch is scratched gently into the paint with the end of a brush handle. Then dark accents are painted in and light areas are wiped out with a rag dampened with turpentine.

Heightening effects. Aside from the major methods of building up an oil painting, many techniques are used to heighten the desired effects. The technique of color mixing is more complicated than it may seem. A particular hue—say, red—has no fewer than 70 different gradations that are recognizable to a trained artist. When these gradations are further differentiated by variations in tone (light and dark values), some 700 color variations of red result. If a red is mixed with a blue (which also has some 700 variations), the number of combinations becomes astronomical. The illustrations at right suggest what you can do to vary one single color of your palette (see also *Color and design,* pp. 220–221).

Other techniques. An intriguing technique of color mixing was devised by the French impressionists (including pointillists), who applied paint to the canvas as dabs or minute flecks of pure, bright color. Like the tiles in a mosaic, the colors are not blended on the canvas but in the viewer's eye—an effect called optical mix.

During the heyday of indirect painting, two major techniques, glazing and scumbling (see p. 229) were favorite devices for achieving varied color effects. Glazing is the use of smooth, transparent layers of paint mixed with a medium such as resin ethereal varnish to produce a glowing, burnished surface, as in the canvases of Rembrandt, Vermeer, and other Dutch masters. Scumbling involves the dragging of a light, opaque paint over darker areas, creating broken patches of color, as in Claude Monet's famous cathedral series. The two techniques yield striking color and light effects.

Interesting textural effects can be achieved by brushwork (see p. 228), and by the use of palette and painting knives, rollers, rags, fingers, dripping paint from cans, and many other unconventional means. One such time-honored effect is impasto (p. 229), the thick piling of paint on the canvas with brush or palette knife. Old masters such as Rembrandt and Rubens made brilliant use of impasto, especially for light areas and highlights.

Tonal techniques are used to create a picture rich in values and restrained in color effects; a painting may be rendered out of a single dominant color tone. Rembrandt is known for his brown tonal paintings dramatized with strong chiaroscuro (see p. 215).

Varnishing. When a painting is finished, certain areas may be absorbed into the canvas more than others, giving them a dull, lifeless look. The problem can be remedied by brushing or spraying these areas with retouch varnish (a very thin solution of nonyellowing resin). To protect a painting as well as to preserve the richness of its color, a final varnish is evenly applied when the painting is reasonably dry—after about six weeks, or better still, several months. If it is varnished too soon, the binding medium will still be contracting and will cause the layers of color to crack.

Color modification

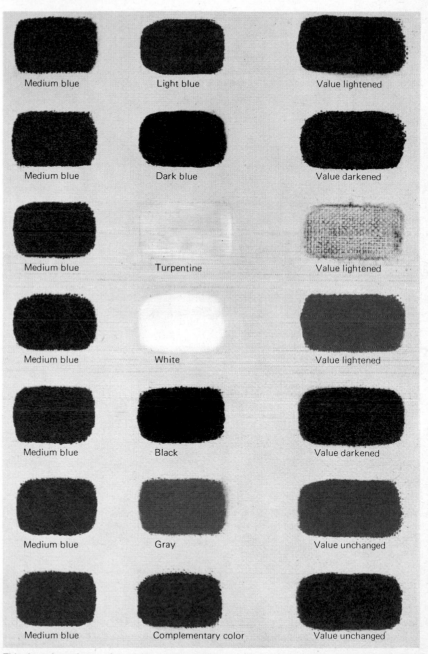

This chart shows how a given color can be modified and still remain basically a color of the same hue.

Painting

Texture and modeling

An oil painting can have a smooth or a textured surface, depending on the way the paint is applied to the canvas. Many sorts of brushwork are possible, including wet and dry brush techniques, cross-hatching, pointillism, glazing, scumbling, and impasto. Examples of such brushwork appear on this and the facing page.

Paint, of course, can be applied to the surface with implements other than a brush. Great bas-relief ridges of im-pasto can be piled up with palette knives, fingers, trowels, spatulas, or by squeezing paint onto the canvas directly from the tubes. When working with the palette knife, large quantities of paint are first squeezed onto the palette; the knife is used to pick up paint from the palette and to press it onto the canvas. Washes of diluted paint can be applied with rags.

Modeling is the process of grading color values in a painting to portray solid form and receding planes with an illusion of three-dimensional depth. The technique involves the blending of adjacent areas of unequal value by creating transitional zones, as seen on this page in the step-by-step illustrations of the modeling of a sphere.

Without modeling, the planes of surfaces of objects would look like cardboard pieces. Faulty modeling, on the other hand, upsets the tonal balance of a painting, resulting in an un-natural look. Modeling is found in what is perhaps its most dramatic use among the works of the Venetian masters who worked under Titian. These paintings are characterized by the contrast of closely modeled shapes in light tones with large, flat, dark areas. However, some painters, including Paul Cézanne and Vincent Van Gogh (see illustration, p. 222), intentionally ignored modeling in developing their own personal styles of painting.

Some types of brushstrokes

Dry-brush strokes

Pointillist strokes

Linear strokes

Undulating strokes

Cross-hatching

Graded wash

Contour-following strokes

Wet-to-dry strokes

Modeling techniques

A sphere is painted with its shadow cast on the table (1). The surface of the sphere is given a band of shadow below and a circle of highlight above (2). Modeling takes the form of blending the color and tone of the shadow (3) and the highlight (4). As a result, the original disklike object appears as a sphere.

Impasto, glazing, and scumbling

Of all the traditional oil painting techniques, impasto, glazing, and scumbling are among the best known. They were extensively used in previous centuries when indirect painting was the dominant method of working (see text, p. 226). Painters still make use of these techniques for special effects.

Impasto. The word "impasto" is used to denote both the technique of impasto painting and the resulting masses of paint on the canvas. Paint is piled and pressed onto the canvas (see opposite text) and is left to dry, preserving a rich texture of palette knife marks or brushwork. Drying may take several weeks or even months.

Glazing. In glazing, a transparent color such as burnt sienna is thinned with a glaze medium, which can either be bought ready-made or mixed in the studio. A popular recipe is 1 ounce stand oil, 1 ounce 5-pound-cut damar varnish, 5 ounces pure gum spirits of turpentine, and 15 drops cobalt drier. The glaze is applied thinly over the selected area of a painting. Light penetrates the transparent coating and is reflected by the underside of the glaze layer. This lends a brilliance and luminosity to the undercoat color. Peter Paul Rubens' favorite technique of laying several glazes on top of one another is still used by many artists.

Scumbling. In this technique a light, opaque color is painted over a dried undercoat of a darker color. The overpainting can be applied irregularly by dragging a heavily loaded flat bristle brush very lightly and quickly over the area. The countless broken patches of pigment combine with the darker undercoat to add a sparkle to an otherwise flat color tone. Scumbling may also be in the form of a coat thin enough to allow light to reach the undercoat. Optical grays, a unique effect of scumbling, are achieved this way.

Impasto

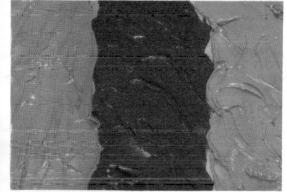

This impasto consists of thick masses of oil paint pressed onto the canvas with a palette knife, forming ridges.

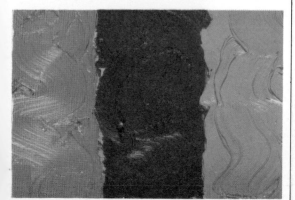

A brush rather than a palette knife is used to create this impasto effect, more supple than that pictured above.

Glazing

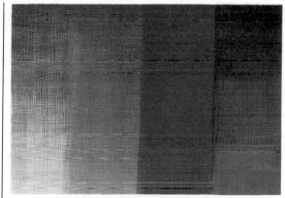

A glaze of transparent burnt sienna is painted over bands of white, yellow, red, and blue underpainting.

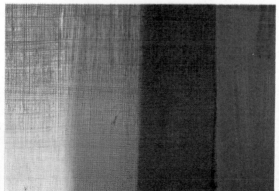

Viridian green, another transparent color, is used to glaze the same bands of color that were overpainted above with burnt sienna.

Scumbling

These scumbling effects result from dragging a brush thickly loaded with brown and then yellow across underpainted color bands.

Five colors are scumbled over burnt sienna. A moist brush is used to work in the pigments, yielding a more refined effect than above.

Painting

Stages in an oil painting

The best way to learn to render portraits in oil is, of course, to study with an experienced portrait painter. But considerable insight can be gained simply by looking over the shoulder of an artist at work. Such an opportunity presents itself on these two pages.

The artist used cotton-duck canvas that was stretched on an 18- by 24-inch frame and double-primed with acrylic. Her equipment and materials included a studio easel, a disposable paper palette, a cup of turpentine mixed with linseed oil for thinning paints, and another cup of turpentine for cleaning brushes. The brushes used were Nos. 1,3,4,5, and 7 filbert-bristle brushes and a large, flat, sable brush. The basic palette consisted of ivory black, titanium white, Naples yellow, yellow ocher, cadmium red (light), Venetian red, alizarin crimson, raw umber, ultramarine blue, viridian green, and cadmium yellow-orange.

She mixed several basic colors on the palette to be used with touches of this or that additional color. Among the basic colors were three different flesh tones for the model's skin: light (Naples yellow and cadmium red light); medium (yellow ocher and cadmium red light); and dark (Venetian red and ultramarine). A mixture of ultramarine, viridian green, alizarin crimson, and white provided the background paint. Raw umber was used for the hair; white with dashes of viridian, Naples yellow, ultramarine, and raw umber were mixed for the blouse.

When any basic mixture was found to be too intense, the artist neutralized it with a little complimentary color (see *Color and design*, pp. 220–221). Throughout the painting the artist worked from the largest to the smallest shapes, from the simple to the complex, and from darks to lights. She built up the image from the background to the foreground, first using only average

colors and average values of light and shadow. She used the largest possible brush for any given area to avoid the creation of distinct lines.

First session. As can be inferred from the first photograph, the artist studied the model after she was seated comfortably in an armchair; she then placed the head slightly off dead center of the canvas and fixed the line of gesture or pose (in this case, the midline from the pit of the neck down the torso to the crotch). Then she sketched rapidly with a brush, relating the largest shapes to each other and to the line of gesture. While at work, the artist frequently stepped back from her canvas to grasp the totality of the picture.

After the initial sketching, the artist painted in the hair mass and laid in the background. Then she began colorkeying (testing her color mixtures) with small patches of paints at strategic spots. During the next stage she used average colors and values, ignoring nuances and details. Starting from the general shadow areas and going to directly lit areas, she massed as many shapes, colors, and values as she could, covering the entire canvas with paints.

After putting in the averages, the artist restated the accents (darkest darks and lightest lights). These acted as constants in the value scale and were used as references for creating gradations. Finally, the artist used a clean brush to soften boundaries so that no distinct edges were left.

Second session. The artist began her second painting session by refining shapes and colors that had been only loosely defined in the first session. She proceeded to define details that had not been painted in previously. During the later stages she used her clean, dry sable brush for fanning (sweeping all edges lightly), blurring and softening them to create the illusion of rounded forms receding into the background.

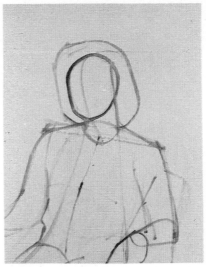

1. With a No. 4 brush dipped in diluted raw umber, the model's head is drawn as a simple oval. The "line of posture" is established by a line down the center of the model's face, another line along the shoulders, and a third down the torso.

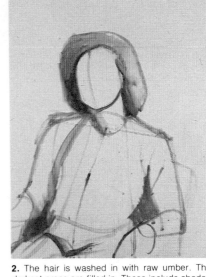

2. The hair is washed in with raw umber. The darkest areas are filled in. These include shaded parts of the hair near the neck; shadows under both arms, on left side of neck, and in the lap; and a large crease in the blouse.

7. The mouth and folds in the blouse are defined as clearer shapes. The whitest white is given to the lightest blouse area (center plane facing the light). Red is put into nose and cheeks. Hair is softened over forehead. Nostrils are softened.

8. After the design on the blouse is roughed in, the mouth, nose tip, and a nostril are further refined. The dark accents in the hair are deepened. Red is added to the forehead, cheeks, nose, and hair. Eyebrows are defined.

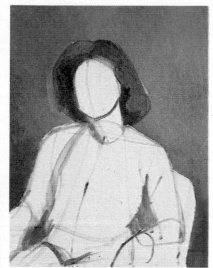

3. The background is washed in thinly with a color slightly darker than what the eye actually perceives, which makes it appear to recede from the viewer. Then the background is blurred into the edges of the hair to avoid a cutout effect.

4. Major darks are filled in—the shadow side of the face and neck, the underarm areas, the chair, the model's slacks, and the shadow above her right shoulder. Color-keying the painting now begins on the light side of the cheek and neck.

5. Directly lit areas on skin and blouse are given average color and value variations. Shadows in light areas, always lighter than those in dark areas, are added to model's left eye socket and left side of forehead and neck.

6. With the whole canvas covered, the process called blending the poster begins—introducing gradations and interchanges between major darks and lights. Darker colors are brought into light areas of lips, nostrils, and blouse shadows.

9. The painting now progresses to smaller forms. The chin and cheek creases are defined. The side of the nose is blended with the rest of the face. More color is put into the mouth. The softening of edges and refining of light and shadow continue.

10. Irises are painted into the eyes in a dark hue, which has the effect of making the whites of the eyes look whiter. The left arm is darkened to conform to the rest of the painting. Highlights are added to the hair and nose.

11. The left wrist is given a center light, suggesting that the hand is advancing toward the viewer. The design on the blouse is more sharply delineated. Highlights are refined, then softened by fanning with a dry sable brush.

12. During the final stage the artist finds it desirable to redefine the outlines of the chin, cheeks, and hair, making the face slimmer and thus heightening the resemblance to the model. Facial features are softened with a sable brush.

Painting

Watercolor

Painting with water-soluble colors has been done in many lands since antiquity: on papyrus in ancient Egypt, on silk and rice paper in China, and on illuminated manuscripts and tempera panels in medieval Europe. Watercolor as we know it today, however, grew out of the work of Rembrandt and other 17th-century Dutch masters who used pen and ink with monochrome washes. Eighteenth-century English artists perfected watercolor as an art in its own right, with unique characteristics.

With its pigment bound by gum arabic and thinned with water, watercolor has a soft luminosity and gentle airiness unequaled by other forms of painting. Its effects result from the near-transparency of the colors, the dazzling white of all-rag paper that sparkles as highlights, and the merging and interflowing of colors from saturated brushes. Once on paper, the effects are almost impossible to alter through overpainting.

Watercolor paints come in cakes, pans, or tubes. Those in tubes are easiest to use and are usually of better quality. They are often sold in metal boxes whose lids have mixing wells or depressions, which serve conveniently as palettes. It is usually sufficient, especially for beginners, to have a dozen or so basic colors. These paints fall into two general grades and price ranges: professional, or artist's, and student's.

Watercolor brushes are mainly the round variety that taper to a point. In addition, an oval-shaped ("sky") brush is used, mainly for washes. Some artists prefer flats to ovals for applying washes. The best brushes are made of soft, resilient red-sable hair. Expensive but long-lasting and versatile, these brushes are used for both fine work and washes. The least expensive brushes are of ox-ear hair; in between are those of mixed ox-ear and red-sable hair.

Tools and equipment

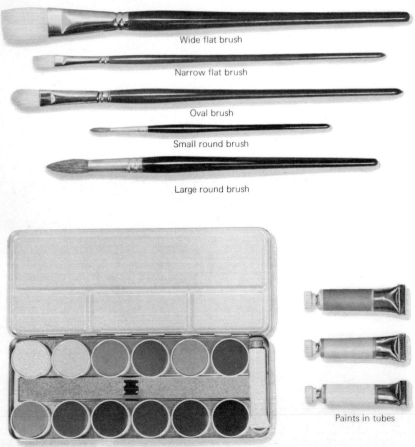

Wide flat brush

Narrow flat brush

Oval brush

Small round brush

Large round brush

Watercolor set

Paints in tubes

Brushstrokes

Flat wash

Graded wash

Wet-on-wet wash

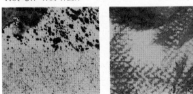

Spatter

Dry-brush effect

Broad linework

Thin linework

Undulating linework

Care and cleaning

An essential item for watercolor painting is a container of clear water. After the application of a color, it is imperative that the brush be rinsed clean before being dipped in a new color. Rinse it frequently even if it is used for the same color for an extended period. Colors are mixed in the mixing wells or on some other surface serving as a palette, not by dipping the brush directly and consecutively into different pigments. After a day's work, brushes and palette (or the box lid with wells) are washed with mild soap and warm water. A hair-shedding brush can be fixed by hammering on the ferrule.

Watercolor paper

Paper for watercolor painting comes in many varieties. All are made of 100 percent rag, as wood-pulp paper will discolor and deteriorate with age. The most expensive papers are handmade by European manufacturers with long traditions as makers of quality papers. Most artists find that better quality machine-made domestic papers are perfectly suitable for their best work.

Papers come in three finishes: *rough* (R) for bold effects and dry-brush techniques; *fine*, or *cold-pressed* (C.P.), for all-around purposes; and *smooth*, or *hot-pressed* (H.P.), for fine brushwork. The smooth finish is more likely than the others to betray signs of an erasure in the pencil sketch or any accidental scuffing. Although watercolor paper is sold in a number of colors, white is the most popular and effective because of the dazzling highlights that result from unpainted areas.

Papers are sold in rolls, pads, and sheets of several sizes. The most common size is imperial (22 by 30 inches), which can be used for a single painting or cut into smaller pieces. Other available sizes are royal (19 by 24 inches), double elephant (27 by 40 inches), and the largest of watercolor papers, antiquarian (31 by 53 inches).

Paper weights. Another feature of watercolor paper is weight, indicated by the number of pounds per ream (500 sheets). This ranges from 72-pound (the flimsiest) through 140-pound (medium) to 300- or even 400-pound (the thickest). The weight is important because most types of paper must be stretched before use. The reason is that wet paint causes the paper to wrinkle and buckle, making colors streak into rivers and lakes. The 300-pound and heavier papers, being as stout as thin cardboard, need no stretching. Some thinner papers also require no stretching because they come in blocks (pads glued on four sides). When a finished painting has dried, the top sheet is easily sliced off from the rest of the block with a knife.

Stretching. Wet paper is stretched on a wooden drawing board or frame by fastening it to the wood with tape, glue, or tacks so that when it dries and shrinks it becomes a drum-taut surface. Painting is done on this paper when it is quite dry but while it is still stretched tightly on the board. When the painting itself has dried, it is cut from its taped edges with a sharp knife or razor blade. For beginners the easiest procedure is to stretch half a piece of imperial-size paper (15 by 22 inches) on a 16- by 23-inch drawing board. A simple method of stretching watercolor paper is illustrated below.

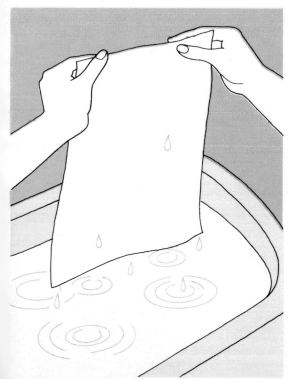

1. Soak the paper in cold water in a clean sink until it is saturated (about 15 min). Grip the paper at its corners; lift it up and allow excess water to run off.

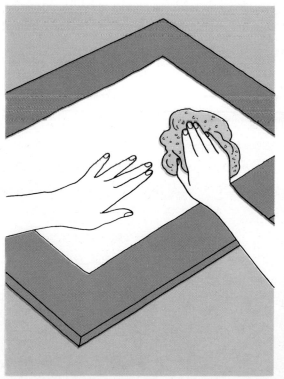

2. Lay wet paper on a drawing board. Sponge off any remaining excess water, smoothing wrinkles from the paper. Dab dry about a 1-in. margin all around the paper.

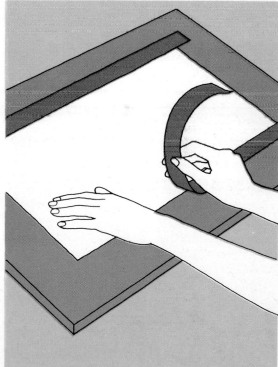

3. Wet a wide strip of gummed paper tape and apply it to the board and the margin of a long side of the paper. Then tape opposite edge and short edges. Press tape firmly outward from the paper.

233

Painting

Stages in a watercolor painting

The photographs on these two pages show typical stages in the development of a watercolor landscape. For the landscape shown here the artist used a 17- by 22-inch sheet of French hand-made, cold-pressed, 300-pound watercolor paper which, because of its thickness, required no stretching. To introduce a variety of brushstrokes, he used several types of brushes, including round red-sable brushes in three sizes—small (No. 3), medium (No. 5), and large (No. 12)—as well as 1-inch, 3/4-inch, and 1/4-inch square, flat, ox-hair brushes.

The artist employed 10 watercolor paints in tubes: Hooker's green (light), Windsor blue, ultramarine blue, Payne's gray, burnt sienna, burnt umber, cadmium yellow, yellow ocher, vermillion, and alizarin crimson. He purchased them in an enameled box whose cover wells served as a palette in which to mix paints and make color washes. A white enamel palette tray was also used for these purposes.

A watercolor can be painted directly from life or copied from a photograph or another painting. For representational subject matter, such as this landscape, the artist first draws a sketch on the paper, either in light pencil or charcoal, then paints over the sketch. In this case a very light pencil sketch was first made on the paper. The paper was then attached to a drawing board with masking tape.

The artist began by filling in the sky and mountains with washes. The top of the dark tree in the foreground was later overpainted on the light sky, but unpainted voids were left in the darker mountain wash for the trunk of the tree and for the house. To prevent unintentional mingling of colors while wet, the paint of one area must be allowed to dry before another color is painted either on top of or adjacent to it. Here the artist accelerated the drying by using a hair dryer.

Dry-brush strokes—achieved with a half-dry brush and painted with ragged, broken strokes—were used to depict the rough texture of the lower trunk of the big tree. The foliage, just beginning to turn color in the fall, was dabbed with paint while varying the pressure on the brush. For the foreground twigs and the house porch, very fine, precise lines were painted with the point of a red-sable brush. To test the color mixtures, the artist dabbed them on the paper's margin (eventually covered by the mat).

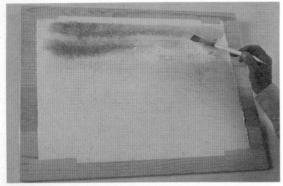

1. First the paper is wetted with water so that the color can flow out freely. Then the sky is painted with an even wash.

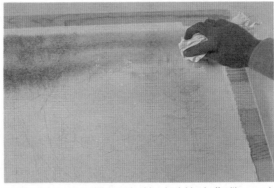

2. While the wash is still wet, the blue is dabbed off with a rag in areas that are to appear as cloud.

3. The hills are first painted with a flat wash on dry paper; darker areas are achieved by overpainting with a wet brush.

4. A wash is used to fill in background meadows, then those in the foreground. Bushes are done with a medium brush.

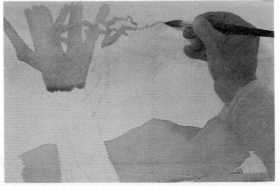

5. The darkest portion of the landscape is the big tree. A wash is used for the upper part, a small brush for the twigs.

6. To emphasize the gnarled bark of the lower trunk, the dry-brush effect is applied, resulting in a very rough texture.

7. Parts of the tree are darkened to complete the bark surface. Slanting brushstrokes suggest a twisted tree trunk.

8. Dabs with a not-too-wet brush suggest foliage. Occasionally the artist places mat frame on painting to study its development.

9. Background trees are painted with a small brush; details are smudged with the finger to create the illusion of distance.

10. House is now meticulously painted in (with pointed brush for porch, windows, and shadows) in area left untouched by hill wash.

11. The road area is wetted, then washed with diluted colors. Ruts and bumps are created with dark lines and dabs of paint.

12. Shadow cast by tree is painted dark gray. Great care is taken to depict distortions caused by uneven road surface.

13. By scraping away paint lightly with a razor blade, highlights on some twigs are created here.

14. Foreground bushes are completed with a small brush over dried painted areas. Finishing details are added here and there.

15. Framed with a mat, the completed landscape is a well-composed pastoral scene, delighting the eye with vibrant fall color.

Painting

Aniline-dye watercolors

The totally transparent liquid watercolors known as aniline dyes have more brilliance and radiance than any other form of water-soluble color. The dyes require a somewhat different painting technique than ordinary watercolors, however. To demonstrate this, the same subject—a pot of Egyptian lilies—was painted twice, once using dyes (below) and again with semiopaque gouache paints (opposite). Six stages are shown for each painting.

The artist used long-haired spotter brushes to work the dyes onto the paper. To avoid blotching, she moved her brush in only one direction within a given area. To avoid bleeding, she worked from the edges of a color area toward the center. To darken a color in a large area, the dye was brushed on diluted, then overpainted repeatedly.

A china (not plastic) watercolor palette is used for the dyes, which stain virtually anything else.

1. Diluted cerulean blue is used for the sky, terra-cotta for the bricks, and light gray for the mortar seams between the bricks.

2. Nile green is blended with yellow ocher for the lawn. This blended color, with an added touch of blue, is used to paint the leaves.

3. Cadmium yellow is used for the flower pistils; then it is blended with cadmium orange for the petals. Bricks are overpainted.

4. After the flowers are painted, additional toning of the leaves and leaf veins is rendered with Nile green blended with sepia.

5. Flower petals are toned with fine strokes of cadmium orange. To make the lines very fine, a small, pointed brush is used.

6. Finally, brown dye is applied with the same small brush to shade the flower pistils, completing this painting in aniline dyes.

236

Gouache

The term "gouache" is applied to the technique of painting with either transparent watercolors mixed with opaque white (see text, p. 223) or with special paints sold in art supply stores as designer's colors or poster paints.

Gouache has varying degrees of opacity, depending on its degree of dilution during application.

Shown on this page are six stages of a gouache painting of Egyptian lilies. The painting was done with an assortment of designer's colors thinned with water. The paints were applied with round red-sable brushes.

Like traditional watercolors and aniline dyes, gouache can be applied in thin washes, as in the sky in this painting. But unlike the other two, it can also be brushed on thickly into a quick-drying matte finish, as in the bricks here. Corrections, alterations, and additions can be done by overpainting, as in the mortar seams in the bricks.

1. Diluted ultramarine blue is used for sky; lemon, ocher, emerald green for lawn; vermillion, burnt sienna for bricks.

2. Leaves are rendered with a blend of green, cobalt blue, and lemon; veins are darkened by adding more green to color mixture.

3. The flower petals are painted with vermillion, then overpainted with the same paint to obtain a deeper color.

4. Pistils are first done with ocher and burnt sienna; each flower is then overpainted with lines of gold, yellow, and vermillion.

5. To darken the bricks and to shade parts of the lily pot, areas are overpainted with burnt sienna and a touch of black.

6. The picture is completed by painting mortar seams with white blended with burnt sienna over the darker brick color.

Painting

Tempera

Tempera painting was popular in Europe until the advent of oil painting during the Renaissance. A 20th-century revival of tempera has restored the medium to popularity.

Traditionally, tempera meant water-soluble paints bound in an oil-and-water emulsion, with the aid of egg yolk as an emulsifier. But the term as used currently covers a variety of paints emulsified with any natural or synthetic substance. Because temperas characteristically dry into a stiff, matte finish, they are usually painted on a rigid panel.

The various stages in two tempera paintings employing entirely different techniques are illustrated on these pages. The first picture (below) was painted with the regular tempera technique on a piece of gessoed Masonite board (see p. 225). The artist made a sketch of her subject—a vase of flowers on a table against a wallpaper background—using a soft pencil to delineate meticulously the entire outline. She then filled in the sketch with all the details of the design. Then she executed the painting in a systematic, deliberate manner, which suits the characteristics of tempera paints. Except for the first diluted coat of the background, the paints applied were completely opaque.

Wet tempera. The second painting, of a tree in a meadow (opposite), was done in a very different manner. The artist first used a large sable brush saturated with water to wet a piece of white paper liberally. Next she diluted her tempera paints and employed the wash technique to lay them on the wet paper quite rapidly. This wet-on-wet technique created a soft, diffused painting suggestive of a landscape done in a watercolor wash. A small brush was used to fill in a few details on the tree trunk.

1. A sketch of a vase of flowers is drawn lightly in soft pencil. Next, background is painted with diluted chrome yellow pale.

2. Vase is painted in light green-blue; tabletop is Bordeaux red, raw umber, and white; leaves and stems are brilliant green.

3. Light blue is used for the flower petals, and the centers of the flowers are painted yellow ocher.

4. After the wallpaper design is completed with yellow ocher, the vase and the table are toned with darker shades of their own hues.

5. A small pointed brush is used to tone the flowers with fine strokes of Cyprus blue and the delicate leaf veins with olive green.

6. Tiny dots of chrome yellow pale, with a touch of cadmium orange on the flower centers, complete this delicate and precise painting.

Wet tempera

. A very thin blue wash is laid on a piece of wet
watercolor paper with a large sable brush. Then a
green wash is used for the foreground.

2. Another green wash is added for the foliage.
The tree trunk is defined in diluted gray with a
small brush and is filled with a gray wash.

. Part of the foliage is painted with a darker wash.
Smaller branches are detailed with a pointed
rush. The texture of the trunk is refined.

4. After further refining, background grass is
painted in dark green. Red apples on the tree and
grass are painted over the green washes.

Acrylics

Acrylics have the expressive characteristics of oils, but they dry very
quickly, usually within half an hour.
They are synthetic paints, manufactured by combining pigments with
acrylic-polymer and vinyl-polymer
resins. The paint dries to form a glossy,
elastic, waterproof film that is highly
durable and easy to clean. Acrylics
come in a wide range of brilliant
colors; they will not fade or yellow with
age. But because acrylics are opaque, it
is not possible to blend colors by overpainting unless the paint is first thinned
to form a wash or a glaze.

Acrylics are sold in tubes, squeeze
bottles, and jars. For the thicker tube
and squeeze-bottle paints a sheet of
glass makes the best palette. Squeeze
colors onto the glass and recap the
tubes immediately. Work from the
glass. Later, the glass can be stripped of
dry paint with a razor blade. A container of water is kept beside the palette to keep the brushes wet: if the
paint hardens on a brush, the brush
may be ruined, although it is possible
to remove dry paint from brushes with
a special solvent sold by art shops. To
use the more fluid acrylics, simply dip
your brushes directly into the jars.

Some precautions. Because of
acrylics' characteristics, certain precautions should be observed when
using the paints. Acrylics are harsh on
natural hair, so many artists use only
nylon brushes. Because of their quick-
drying nature, acrylics are difficult to
keep for long once the tube or jar has
been opened and used. Only the small
amounts needed for each session
should be squeezed onto the palette.

Acrylics can be applied with rags,
sponges, kitchen forks, and even
combs. Paper, canvas, hardboard (Masonite), wood, metal, and burlap are all
suitable painting surfaces. A coat of
acrylic gesso will make the paint adhere to very porous surfaces.

Painting techniques. Acrylics can be
applied in thin, transparent washes like
watercolors (p. 232). Light areas can be
rubbed out with a soft rag or cotton
while the wash is still wet. An acrylic
painting can also be scumbled or
glazed just like an oil painting (see
p. 229). Acrylic glazes are made by
mixing colors with *acrylic medium*.
Acrylic medium comes in matte or
gloss finish. The glaze can be applied
an hour after the underpainting is
done, and several glazes can be laid on
top of one another on the same day.

Unlike oils, acrylics do not retain
brushmarks. Texture can be achieved
by modeling the painted surface before
it dries with such implements as combs,
serrated cardboard edges, or crumpled
paper, or by stippling the surface with
pointed brushes. Impasto can be given
more bulk by adding *inert extenders* to
the paints; these include marble dust,
fine sawdust, kaolin (clay), whiting,
and clean sand. Some artists build up
impasto by first laying a modeling
paste on the canvas, then applying
paints over it. The paste can be bought
ready-made or prepared at home by
mixing an extender with acrylic medium, either matte or gloss. The extenders should never make up more
than 25 percent of either the paint or
the paste.

Acrylics are particularly suitable for
precise shapes and hard edges. An area
can be isolated by brushing around it
with rubber cement before painting.
Later the rubber cement is erased
gently with art gum. Hard edges are
painted using masking tape, as seen in
the illustrations on page 241. Tones can
be blended and hard edges softened by
pressing a piece of cellophane onto the
wet paint, then peeling it away. Corrections are made by scrubbing the
paint lightly with a soft brush dipped in
denatured alcohol and blotting away
the unwanted paint.

Painting

Free-form acrylic painting

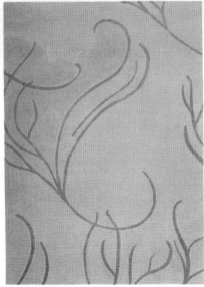

1. For this free-form, highly stylized, Art Nouveau trellis design, a pale green wash is applied to the canvas panel before the vines are sketched.

2. Vines are overpainted with darker green. Stylized morning glories in opaque white and blue are painted within the vines, using a soft brush.

3. Two glaze layers—each made of white, green, and gloss medium—are laid over the entire painting to mute colors and hide small imperfections.

4. Stylized petals are painted in opaque white with a stiff brush, which is twisted and turned to suggest the texture of the petals.

5. More petals are added. Slender stripes in blue, suggesting part of the trellis on which the vines are growing, are painted with a pointed brush.

6. The trellis is completed with blue, then the stamens of the white flowers are painted in dark red with a pointed soft sable brush.

7. Red mixed with orange creates the flower pistils. Graceful tendrils from bases of flowers are rendered in a deep green, using a small brush.

8. A final glaze of gloss medium covers the painting. Each glaze is allowed to dry completely before it is covered with another glaze.

Hard-edge acrylic painting

1. Artist follows a small color sketch in laying out a full-size geometric abstract painting on a panel of gessoed hardboard.

2. The central shape is clearly delineated on all sides with masking tape. It is painted with the brush moving inward from the tape.

3. When shape is painted in, strips of tape are gently peeled away from center outward. Effect of masking is to leave sharp edges on all sides.

4. Each straight-edged shape is similarly taped and painted. Acrylics dry fast; tape can be applied over painted areas in about half an hour.

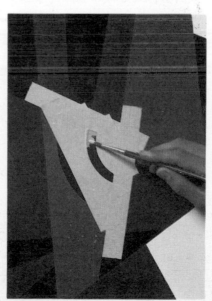

5. A curved area is completely covered with tape. Arcs are drawn on the tape with a compass, then cut out with a sharp knife.

6. The area cut out is overpainted in dark blue. Because of the opaque nature of acrylics, the underlying brown will not show through the blue.

7. Fresh tape is applied, and a second arc is drawn and cut bordering on the first. It is overpainted with the next color, light blue.

8. The hard-edged acrylic is seen completed. Note that the artist has left some of the geometric shapes an unpainted white.

Printmaking

The art of making prints on paper

The printmaking methods described in this chapter are suitable for fine-art prints, not for the mechanical mass production of printed matter. Prints made solely for esthetic purposes are often printed by hand by the artist or on simple presses. Generally produced in signed, limited editions, they are valued by collectors and museums as multiple originals, not as copies. The printing media most commonly employed by artists include wood engraving, woodcut, etching, drypoint, aquatint, linoleum block, lithography, and silk screen. These techniques are described on the following pages. *Printing on fabric* is a separate chapter, beginning on page 254.

The distinction between fine-art prints and commercially reproduced prints has not always been easy to make. Most forms of printmaking were at one time or another used for commercial reproduction. However, after the invention of photo-mechanical reproduction in the late 19th century, most of the traditional processes of printmaking enjoyed revivals as purely creative arts.

Woodcut and silk screen. The earliest known prints were made in China in the second century A.D. Damp paper was placed against stone carvings and seals and rubbed with ink to reproduce relief images. In the sixth century the Chinese began to make woodcuts by pasting illustrations drawn on rice paper onto smooth wood blocks. The rice paper served as a guide for cutting the design into the wood. The blocks were later inked and pressed against paper to make relief prints. The earliest known woodcut print with an authenticated date is in the oldest known printed book, *Diamond Sutra,* a Buddhist scripture printed in China in 868 A.D. Woodcut spread to Korea, then to Japan. Japanese prints from cherry-wood blocks are admired all over the world.

Stenciling (see p. 258), the forerunner of silk screen, originated in China in the eighth century A.D. Some prints of Chinese stencils show no sign of connecting ties or bridges between design elements, suggesting that the stencils were held together with fine strands of hair or silk. Whatever the actual Chinese technique was, it was greatly improved in the year 1907 when an Englishman, Samuel Simon of Manchester, obtained a patent for the modern silk screen. Although initially used for textile printing, silk screen eventually became an artistic medium. As a fine-art form it is called serigraphy.

In Europe the first woodcut prints appeared in the early 15th century as playing cards. There followed pictures of saints and religious scenes. Initially a craft of reproductive printing, woodcut was perfected as an art form in the 16th century by such master painters as Albrecht Dürer and Hans Holbein.

Woodcut declined rapidly during the next two centuries; by the late 18th century wood engraving (end-grain cutting) began to take its place. During the 19th century, especially in the United States, leading publishers used wood engraving extensively to illustrate books and periodicals. Then, when modern photoengraving halftone processes were introduced around the turn of the century, wood engraving was abandoned by commerical printers. However, woodcut has been enjoying a revival ever since such painters as Paul Gauguin and Edvard Munch began working in the medium.

Etching and engraving. Dürer, who earlier popularized woodcut, was also proficient in the then-new art of etching. Making prints from engraved and etched metal plates originated in Europe a few decades after the woodcut. These graphic arts evolved almost accidentally. For centuries goldsmiths had been engraving their wares, but when medieval knights demanded engraved armor designs, armorers found themselves in difficulty. Engraving on iron and steel was not easy, given the crude tools of the time. However, it was found that acid could bite into tough metals. An acid-resistant stencil was placed on the metal (see *Metalworking,* pp. 276–289), and intricate designs could be etched into the armor.

To show up their designs, armorers rubbed black ink into the etched depressions. From that practice it was a small leap to copying and preserving designs by pressing a piece of paper against an inked etching or engraving.

The oldest surviving dated etching was made in Switzerland in 1513. Etching was soon taken up by artists throughout Europe.

Lithography. Lithography, or "stone printing," was invented by a Bavarian, Aloys Senefelder, in 1798. Areas on a flat stone are treated with chemicals to make them more or less absorbent to printer's ink, and paper is pressed to the inked stone. The form spread across Europe in the 19th century, reaching its peak of artistic popularity among printmakers in France.

Lithography and the other printmaking methods fall into one of three categories: relief printing, in which the inked printing area is raised above the background surface; intaglio printing, in which the inked area is depressed; and flat-surface printing, in which the printing surface is isolated either chemically or mechanically.

Relief printing media include woodcut, wood engraving, and linoleum block. Intaglio printing embraces engraving, etching, drypoint (a plate is scratched with a steel needle, resulting in a burr), and aquatint (a plate is grained by applying rosin powder before etching, creating a watercolor effect). Flat-surface printing includes stenciling, silk screen, and lithography.

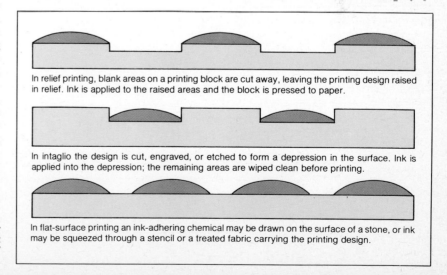

In relief printing, blank areas on a printing block are cut away, leaving the printing design raised in relief. Ink is applied to the raised areas and the block is pressed to paper.

In intaglio the design is cut, engraved, or etched to form a depression in the surface. Ink is applied into the depression; the remaining areas are wiped clean before printing.

In flat-surface printing an ink-adhering chemical may be drawn on the surface of a stone, or ink may be squeezed through a stencil or a treated fabric carrying the printing design.

On the facing page are three prints executed by artists of widely varying periods. They present a variety of styles in printmaking: *"Landscape With Cottage and Large Tree"* (1641), an etching by Rembrandt (upper left); *"Spring Fantasy"* (1978), a serigraph by Kensuke Wakeshima (lower left); and *"Peonies"* (c. 1830), a woodcut by Utagawa Hiroshige.

Printmaking

Silk screen

Silk screen, or serigraphy, can be done on fabric, paper, cardboard, and wood, as well as on nonporous surfaces such as glass and metal. The mechanics of silk screen are quite simple: ink is forced through a porous screen on which the nonprinting areas of the design are blocked with a stencil or a coat of resist medium, such as glue. Multi-color prints are not difficult to make, provided that the print paper is accurately registered (see p. 246). Each color is printed separately.

Beginners may prefer to buy a silk-screen kit from an art supply store. Anyone can easily make a low-cost screen set at home by referring to the illustrations and instructions on the opposite page. A homemade screen frame should be sanded and shellacked before use.

Screen size. The size of the screen governs the size of the prints. For prints up to 6 by 9 inches, a 10- by 17-inch frame (inside measure) is necessary. These dimensions allow for 2-inch margins on both sides along the length of the frame and 4-inch margins along both endpieces. The wider margins act as ink reservoirs where the ink can be piled on the screen between sweepings of the squeegee (see p. 246, Step 6). The squeegee is a thick strip of stiff rubber embedded in a wooden bar. Its length should be slightly shorter than the width of the screen (9½ inches for the above frame), so that it can sweep the length of the screen basin without scraping the sides.

Screen fabric. The standard material for the screen is silk bolting cloth, which comes in widths of 40, 45, 50, and 54 inches. It can be bought in lengths of 1/2 yard and up. For general use, No. 12 mesh, XX grade is best. Organdy and taffeta are cheaper but do not last long. Dacron, nylon, and alloy wire mesh have excellent tensile strength but are more expensive.

Resist methods. A paper stencil can be placed directly under the screen; it will adhere to the inked fabric. Another simple method is to paint the resist area directly onto the screen, using a block-out fluid such as glue, shellac, or lacquer. Ink will pass through only the unpainted areas.

A traditional resist method, good for the detailed designs of fine-art prints, is the tusche-and-glue technique. Tusche (lithographer's ink) is a greasy liquid that is not water-soluble. A brush is used to paint the printing design directly on the silk with tusche; then the entire screen is coated with water-soluble glue. When the design is wiped with kerosene or turpentine, the area covered with tusche becomes open mesh while the rest remains blocked by glue (see p. 247).

Inks. Various water-soluble paints are available, as are special oil paints. The former can be set with heat to make them colorfast if printed on fabric. Water-soluble inks must be used with non-water-soluble block-out fluids (e.g., shellac, lacquer), and oil paints must be used with water-soluble block-out fluids (e.g., glue). Otherwise, the block-out mask will be dissolved by the ink, and the entire screen will become an unworkable mess.

Film stencils. For precise details and sharp lines, the film stencil method is used. The design is cut on film that has a glassine backing sheet. The finished stencil is bonded to the screen with an acetate thinner, and the glassine sheet is peeled off for printing.

Photographic facsimiles. Very refined pen-and-ink drawings or minute lettering can be reproduced in exact facsimile by the photographic method. A transparent positive photograph is made of the design. From it a specially sensitized film is made into a negative that, upon washing with warm water, turns into a stencil for the screen.

Silk-screen printing frame

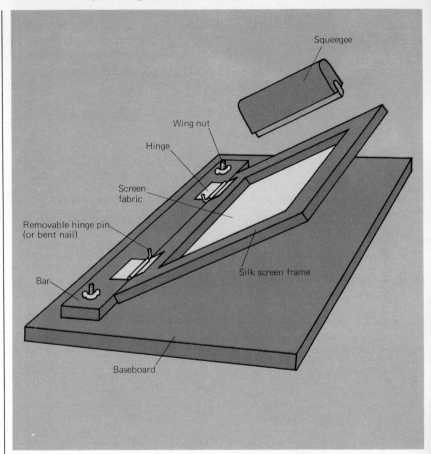

Squeegee

Wing nut

Hinge

Screen fabric

Removable hinge pin (or bent nail)

Silk screen frame

Bar

Baseboard

The basic silk-screen printing equipment is pictured above. Instructions for making it are on the opposite page. The set consists of a rectangular frame on which a fine mesh of silk or some other material is stretched; the frame is hinged to a slightly larger baseboard.

Ink is forced through the screen by the pressure of the squeegee. The ink passes through only those parts of the screen that are not blocked by a stencil or a resist medium (see text, left).

To print, ink is first ladled onto one of the margins (ink reservoirs) at the ends of the screen. The ink is then swept across the length of the screen firmly and evenly with the squeegee. Depending on the amount of ink and the pressure used, each print requires from one to three sweepings of the squeegee. According to the serigrapher's working style, the squeegee may be used without a handle, for two-handed operation, or with a handle, for one-handed operation.

A properly prepared screen may last for hundreds or even thousands of prints. After each print run, the screen is cleaned of ink and resist medium by washing it with water and/or solvents.

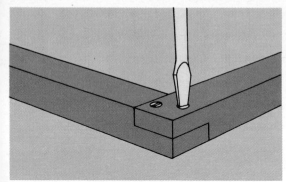

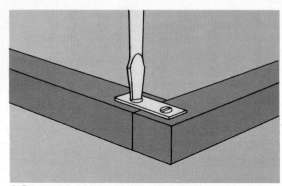

1. Cut white pine 1-by-2 strips to the proper lengths for the size frame you desire for your screen. Here screws are driven into one of the frame's four corner lap joints.

2. Frame can be constructed with simpler joints than the lap joints seen in Step 1. Here a metal fastener is used to reinforce a butt joint. Sand and shellac the frame.

3. Cut silk to allow an extra inch on each side of frame. Fold one edge into double thickness; staple it to one side of frame, working from center toward ends.

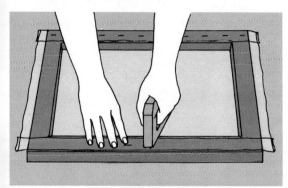

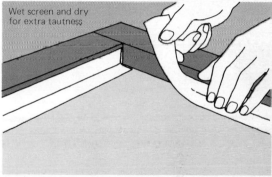

4. Fold the opposite edge of the fabric, pull the silk tight, and staple it to the opposite side of the frame, working from center toward ends. Staple the two remaining edges in the same way.

5. With all four sides of the fabric stapled, the silk screen should be drum-taut on the frame. Reinforce the screen's edges by covering them firmly with masking tape.

Wet screen and dry for extra tautness

6. Turn the screen so that it lies basin up. Apply strips of masking tape inside the frame with half the width of the tape on the frame and the other half on the screen.

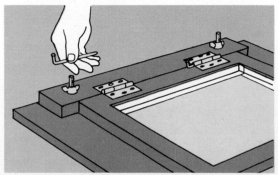

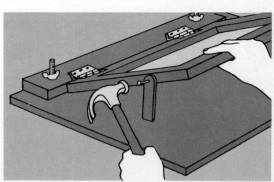

7. Attach a 1-by-2 white pine wood bar of slightly greater length than frame to a drawing board or other wood base with wing nuts. Locate them at extreme ends of bar to provide clearance for screen.

8. With a pair of hinges attach the frame to the bar. Use bent nails or removable hinge pins to join the hinges so that the frame can be removed easily.

9. Nail a drop stick loosely to one side of the frame so that when the frame is raised, the stick will drop down by itself to support the frame in a raised position.

Printmaking

Two-color silk screen

1. Design is drawn on paper. Colored pencil indicates areas to be overprinted in second color.

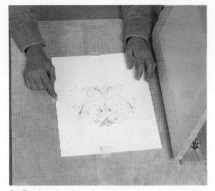

2. Design is placed on board as for printing; position is marked with tape registration tabs.

3. Screen is dropped on top of design. A soft pencil is used to trace outline of design.

4. The background area around the design is painted with brown lacquer block-out fluid.

5. When the block-out fluid is dry, blank printing paper is placed within the tape registers.

6. With the screen in place, water-based red ink is spooned onto an end margin inside the frame.

7. Squeegee is pressed firmly to screen and pulled across it; then it is pushed back again.

8. The print is taken off the board to dry. Other prints are made in the first color.

9. After screen is removed, washed, and dried, second color pattern is traced as in Step 3.

10. The area not to be printed in the second color is blocked out with lacquer.

11. When block-out fluid dries, yellow ink is squeegeed across screen. It prints over the red.

12. Finished print shows two-color design. After use, screen is washed with water, then kerosene.

Tusche-and-glue silk screen

1. With the tusche-and-glue method, oil-based tusche is used to paint the design on the screen.

2. The liquid tusche must be thick and thoroughly stirred. Paint it thickly on the fabric.

3. When the tusche is dry, pour a mixture of 1 part Lepage's glue and 1 part water on screen.

4. Spread glue mixture over entire screen with a piece of cardboard. Let dry. Apply second coat.

5. When glue is dry, pour mixture of half kerosene and half benzine on tusche to dissolve it.

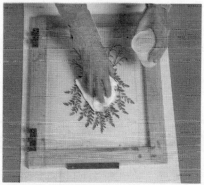

6. Scrub design with paper towel to remove the tusche, creating a stencil on the glued screen.

7. Brush stubborn spots gently with a nailbrush. The glue remains in the area without tusche.

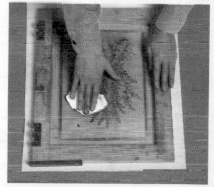

8. Clean screen with turpentine or varnolene. Dab off the solvent; then let dry in the air.

9. Spoon silk-screen ink onto the screen along a short side of the frame. Use only oil-based ink.

10. Squeegee the ink across the screen. Ink will go through area formerly painted with tusche.

11. Push the squeegee back once. If glue coating has pinholes, ink may seep through as tiny dots.

12. Print is finished. Any dots (described in Step 11) should disappear after first few prints.

Printmaking

Woodcut and wood engraving

Woodcut is the classic form of relief printmaking. A design can be traced or pasted on the block as a cutting guide, or the design can be created extemporaneously as the cutting progresses.

Almost any wood is suitable for the block. Hardwoods are better for intricate, delicate designs. Clear, knot-free blocks are usually chosen, but a grainy wood such as Philippine mahogany can give an interesting texture to a print. For very large prints, veneer plywood panels can be used.

Woodcut tools include skew knives (for lines), veiners or V-cutters (for gutters), gouges (for large areas), and square-end chisels (for repairs to the block). A bench hook is useful for stabilizing the block during the cutting (see below and opposite page). A light mallet can be used to strike the gouges and chisels. The block is prepared by sanding with fine sandpaper. A coat of white paint can be applied to dark woods to create a background for tracing the design.

Cutting. In cutting, push the tool away from yourself except when using knives. Your free hand should never be in front of the cutting edge. Shorter tools are held with the palm pushing against the handle. Knives are held like

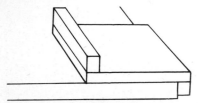

Bench hook rests on table edge.

pencils. Longer-handled gouges and veiners are grasped with the palm and fingers, with the thumb resting on top. Special care is necessary when cutting across the grain: the tool may slip as it cuts through alternate layers of softer and harder fibers.

Correcting errors. Chips can be glued back in place or replaced with plastic wood, which is trimmed flat with a chisel when dry. Mistakes can be cut out of the block. A plug cutter is fitted onto an electric drill, a hole 1/2 inch deep is cut around the mistake, and the part is removed. A replacement plug of the same diameter is then cut from the same type of wood. The plug is glued into the hole (it will be higher than the block's surface). When the glue has dried, the plug is trimmed flush with a chisel and sanded smooth. The plug's grain should run in the same direction as that of the block.

If the block is dented but the wood fiber is not broken, the dent can be raised by covering it with wet cloth and pressing it with a hot iron.

Before printing, rub the block with boiled linseed oil and let it dry overnight to preserve the wood.

Printing materials. Woodcut ink can be purchased in tubes or 1-pound cans. Buy printer's ink, also called job or letterpress ink; do not use offset ink.

Many printmakers prefer soft, fibrous rice paper, which reduces the gloss of the ink. The best papers are imported handmade or all-rag papers. For general use, domestic block-printing paper is adequate.

Prints can be made by rubbing with a wooden spoon, a baren (a padded rubbing disk), or the thumb on a simple homemade press (Steps 13–18, p. 250), or by using the etching press (p. 253). On a platen press, the block must be exactly 0.918 inch thick.

Wood engraving differs from woodcut in that the design is cut into the end grain of the block. The design is carved into the wood rather than raised, and the resulting print is usually a "white line" design as opposed to the woodcut's "black line" design.

Making a two-color woodcut is illustrated on the next two pages.

How to cut correctly

Block is shown in cross section. Undercut edges, seen here, may break after several printings.

If the cuts are vertical, the edges will still be weak and may break off.

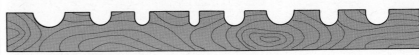

Sloping walls give edges firm bases.

Woodcut tools

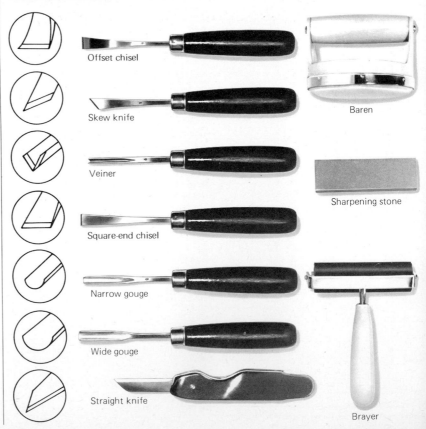

Offset chisel

Skew knife

Veiner

Square-end chisel

Narrow gouge

Wide gouge

Straight knife

Baren

Sharpening stone

Brayer

Two-color woodcut

The step-by-step photographs on this and the following page show the cutting and printing of a two-color woodblock. After the block is cut for the first color, a tracing or a proof is taken from it and used as a guide in cutting the block for the second color. This is done to ensure that the two colors will register precisely when the finished prints are made.

The photographs immediately below show proofs printed with the first block, then the second block, and finally, with both blocks combined for the finished two-color print.

A print of the key block shows the main design.

A print of the color block shows the color areas.

A print of both blocks shows the whole picture.

The key block: 1. A 6- by 9-in. clear ponderosa pine board is sanded silky smooth with 6/0 sandpaper wrapped around a wood block.

2. Carbon paper is laid face down on board, with a pen-and-ink drawing of design over the carbon paper. Trace drawing with a pencil.

3. Here the outline of the drawing has been traced on the wood block. Resulting print will be the exact reverse of this drawing.

4. Ink in tracing with felt-tip pen or india ink. Cover all the printing areas to avoid cutting errors. Blank areas will be carved out.

5. Cut lines in the drawing with a newly sharpened skew knife. A dull knife could chip softwoods such as pine and basswood.

6. Cut broad areas with a gouge. Place the block on a bench hook. One edge hooks onto the table, and the other edge holds the block.

Color block. 7. Place the tracing paper on top of the finished key block. Trace the areas to be printed in the second color.

8. Lay carbon paper on a block identical in size to the key block. Place the design for the color block over carbon paper and trace it onto the block.

9. Ink the areas of the block that will not be carved out (see Step 4), then cut the block with knives and gouges (Steps 5 and 6).

Printmaking

Two-color woodcut (continued)

10. Print the lighter color first. With a rubber brayer roll printer's ink evenly on glass until the ink becomes tacky.

11. Roll the brayer on the color block. All parts in relief are inked in red. Two or three inkings are necessary for the first print.

12. If the brayer inks any gouged areas, then these spots are too high and will smudge the print. Cut them away with the gouge.

13. Lay rice paper on the block, smooth side down, and pin it to the square-edged printing frame. Rub a baren over paper several times.

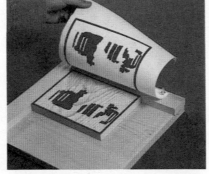

14. After printing the color block, leave the print pinned to the frame but turned face up and held in position with a weight or clip.

15. Cover key block with dark brown ink, using a clean brayer. Key block's darker ink will cover any overlaps with the color block.

16. Put the key block in the frame in the exact position used in printing the color block. Carefully roll the print onto the inked key block.

17. Rub the baren over the print. Since the paper was fixed with pins for the first printing, it is correctly registered for the second.

18. Gently peel print off block; lay it aside to dry. Printer's ink dries in several hours, but it is safer to let prints dry overnight.

Linoleoum block

Linoleum-block printing, or linocut, uses the basic techniques of woodcut (pp. 248–250). Because linoleum is softer than wood and grainless, it is easier to cut; but it does not produce delicate lines or interesting textures.

Linoleum blocks prepared for cutting are available at art supply stores. They come mounted on particle or wood boards in sizes from 3 by 4 inches to 9 by 12 inches.

The design for a linocut is transferred to the block just as in woodcut (p. 249, Steps 2–4). However, the design should not be too intricate, as fine lines cannot be cut into linoleum blocks. Linocut tools, available at art supply stores, are much like woodcut tools except that the latter are stronger and are available in a greater variety of cutting edges and sizes.

Linoleum hardens at low temperatures, which can make cutting difficult. Therefore, in cold weather the block should be placed on a radiator or in a slow oven for a few minutes every half hour to keep it from becoming too brittle. Since most linocut designs are composed of relatively large, simple shapes with few intricate lines, the cutting can often be done with only cutters (veiners) and gouges. Begin by cutting shallow trenches around the areas to be gouged out, then gouge inward from the trenches to the centers of these areas. This technique will minimize accidental cuts into the relief areas of the design. Unlike wood blocks, linoleum blocks cannot be repaired. When the cutting is complete, wash the block with soap and warm water.

Linocuts can be printed with either woodcut ink or water-based block-printing ink. The latter is preferable for children, as it is easier to clean up. All of the woodcut printing techniques can be applied to linocut. A rolling pin can be used to press the paper onto the more resilient linocut block.

Cutting a linoleum block

1. A sketch of the design for the block is made on white drawing or tracing paper.

3. The areas in the design that will be left in relief are painted with india ink.

5. A larger veiner is used to cut along the edges of the entire leaf.

7. The linoleum block is inked with a brayer. Only the raised (relief) areas carry ink.

2. The design made in the first step is transferred to the surface of the linoleum block.

4. The initial carving is done with a veiner along the outlines of the leaf stem and veins.

6. Interior of leaf except for stem and veins is gouged out. Background is crosshatched.

8. The linoleum block is printed as described in the text on the facing page.

251

Printmaking

Etching and engraving

Etching and engraving are two major forms of intaglio printmaking. Both entail cutting a design into a metal plate. The depressed lines of the design are filled with ink, and paper is pressed to the plate to make the print. In etching, the plate is cut with acid; in engraving, with cutting tools.

The illustrations on the facing page show the basic process of etching. This text gives brief descriptions of other intaglio methods. These techniques can be used either alone or in any combination to make a single print.

Etching. In its simplest form, etching can be done by any hobbyist. The basic process consists of coating the printing surface of the plate with a ground—an acid-resistant waxy coating—on which the design is drawn with a steel etching needle. The needle cuts through the ground, exposing the bare metal beneath. The plate is then immersed in a diluted acid bath. The acid bites into the exposed metal, etching the design into the plate. After etching, the ground is removed with turpentine. The plate is then inked and printed.

The apparent simplicity of the etching process belies the subtleties of effect. These depend on the metal, ground, and acid that are employed; on the concentration of the acid; on the length of time the metal is etched by the acid; on the temperature and other atmospheric factors; as well as on the style and experience of the etcher. Minor etching errors can be erased with a scraper, then smoothed with a burnisher (see *Tools,* this page).

Plates. Etching plates are made of copper, brass, zinc, iron, soft steel, aluminum, magnesium, or Plexiglas. The traditional copper plate is excellent for fine lines and delicate texture. Zinc is less expensive than copper, but it tends to give coarse lines. Iron and soft steel yield more prints but are difficult to etch and to correct.

Polished plates can be bought at art supply stores. The most popular etching plate in North America is made of micrometal, an alloy that is often loosely called zinc, although its characteristics are superior to ordinary zinc. Micrometal plates come with the sides and back already protected by a coat of acid-resistant varnish.

Grounds. Hard ground is made of asphaltum, rosin, and beeswax. It comes either as a liquid, which is brushed onto the metal, or as a solid, which is melted onto a heated plate.

A soft ground—one softened with grease, tallow, or petroleum jelly—is preferred by some etchers. A pencil is used to draw on a piece of paper placed on the ground; the ground adheres to the paper wherever there is a pencil impression, exposing the metal when the paper is removed.

Acid baths. The plate is placed face up in an acid bath in a glass, enamel, or plastic tray. Acids are always diluted by adding them to water, never by adding water to the acid (see *Health hazards of crafts materials,* pp. 11–13). A strong solution (1 pint acid to 3–5 pints water) bites quickly and coarsely; a weak solution (1 pint acid to 12 pints water) bites slowly and finely.

Common etching solutions are Dutch mordant (hydrochloric acid, potassium chlorate, and water), diluted nitric acid, and diluted ferric chloride. Although any acid can be used on any metal, ferric chloride is the most easily controlled, and it produces no noxious fumes. However, ferric chloride deposits a sediment of iron oxide on the etched lines, which can slow or stop the biting. This problem can be surmounted by placing the plate face down in the bath and frequently fishing it up and rinsing it with water.

Other grounds, other effects. Sugarlift ground (a mixture of syrup, granulated soap, India ink, and gum arabic) is applied to a naked plate as a painting is done on paper. The entire plate is then covered with hard ground and put in warm water. The water lifts both the sugar and the ground on top of it, leaving the ground where there is no sugar. The resulting etching resembles a brush drawing.

White ground is made of white pigment, soap flakes, and linseed oil. It is first laid thinly and evenly on the whole plate, and the design is then painted with a brush. Areas are then scraped away to make them thinner. As the acid-resistant capacity of white ground is proportionate to its thickness, the finished etching will have variations in tone resembling those of a painting.

Aquatint. Aquatint is used for shading and tones, not for distinctive lines. It is often combined with line etching. Very fine rosin powder is dusted on selected areas of the plate, and the plate is heated, then cooled. When etched by the acid and printed, the areas around the hardened rosin grains yield tones from the lightest gray to the darkest black. Spray paint can be used in place of rosin.

Engraving and drypoint. In line engraving the design is cut into the metal plate with a burin (a cutting tool with a lozenge-shaped cross section). The depth and width of the lines depend on the force applied to the tool. A popular variation is drypoint, in which an abrasive needle is used to scratch the plate, raising a burr along the lines. The burr catches the ink—the lines themselves are too shallow to do so. Drypoint has characteristically delicate, fuzzy lines. Because the burr wears down after a few prints, the method cannot be used for large print runs.

Printing. Most etchers use presses at schools or community workshops or give the plates to commercial printers rather than printing in their studios.

Detail of an etched plate with incised lines.

Detail of plate after inking with dabber.

Detail of the printed etching.

Etching tools

Etching needle

Scraper

Burnisher

Small brush

Flat brush

Flat file

Making an etching

1. Bevel edges of plate with a flat file, then coat the plate with liquid hard ground. Tilt the plate so that the ground will flow easily.

2. Place the sketch over a piece of yellow carbon paper on the dried ground. Trace the design onto the ground with a pencil.

3. Trace the outline of the drawing with a steel etching needle. Be sure that the needle cuts through the ground to expose the metal.

4. Draw fine lines freehand with needle. If you have a simple design with no delicate lines, the entire design can be cut along traced outline.

5. Place plate face up in solution of 12 parts water to 1 part nitric acid (or 3:1 ferric chloride). Brush away bubbles periodically or rinse plate.

6. From time to time paint out delicate lines with ground to prevent further etching. Then return the plate to the acid bath.

7. Rinse the etched plate with water and dab it dry with paper towels. Remove the ground with turpentine-soaked paper towels.

8. Use dabber made of rolled felt to transfer etching ink from a glass palette to the plate. Apply the ink with a circular downward motion.

9. Cover plate evenly with ink, then clean plate with a pad of tarlatan, using a circular sidewise motion. Ink should remain only in etched lines.

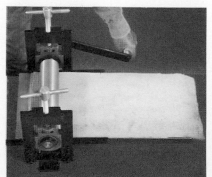

10. Print plate on all-rag paper (soaked for 10 min to remove sizing, then blotted dry). Paper is buffered with felt pads, rolled through press.

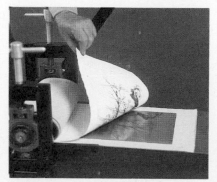

11. Peel the paper gently from the plate. After a trial proof or two, make any necessary corrections by etching parts of the plate again.

12. Apply fresh ink for each print. If dry print buckles, soak it in water and dry it between sheets of blotting paper under a heavy board.

253

Printing on fabric

Stamps, blocks, and stencils

Fabric printing has been practiced since antiquity, notably in India, Egypt, and China. Throughout the centuries it has evolved from a simple process of pressing inked wood blocks on cloth into modern high-speed textile printing by sophisticated photo-mechanical processes, requiring the combined skills of designers, artists, chemists, and machinists. Mass commercial fabric printing may involve the use of engraved printing rollers; mechanized flat or rotary screens; or processes in which designs are first printed on paper, then transferred to polyester and similar synthetic fabrics.

On a much smaller scale, the craftsman employs a variety of printing methods to decorate fabric, clothing, tablecloths, napkins, and draperies. Most of these methods require only minimal equipment and supplies, are accessible to the beginner, yet can yield stunningly beautiful results.

Fabric. Theoretically, any weave of any fabric—cotton, silk, wool, or synthetics—can be printed with a decorative design. In practice the results may vary widely. The colorfastness of pigments and dyes may not be uniform on silk and wool because their natural fibers vary in composition. Some synthetics may not take certain pigments well. Fabrics coated with permanent-press or waterproof finishes repel most pigments and dyes. Coarse weaves do not yield attractive results.

Cotton is the best choice for the beginner. Cotton fabrics include muslin, batiste, denim, and canvas. As you gain experience and self-confidence, you can experiment with different types of fabric and ink combinations.

Before printing, fabric must be washed to remove sizing, then ironed smooth. For a good impression, it should be laid over a soft pad (foam rubber, felt, a blanket, or layers of old newspapers). Pin or tape the fabric in place to keep it from moving.

Inks. Acrylic paints (p. 239) are easy to use, but they dry stiff and may not survive dry cleaning. Oil-based printer's inks and block-printing inks are permanent and easy to apply. Water-based silk-screen inks and textile paints come in brilliant colors and are easy to clean. However, some of these have to be worked onto the printing block carefully because of their squishy, jellylike consistency.

Heat setting. All water-based inks must be heat set 24 hours after printing. For small designs setting can be done with a hot (120°C) iron. Cover the design on both sides with tissue paper. Move the iron back and forth over the work in the conventional way; every area should receive at least 3 minutes of the iron's heat.

For larger designs setting can be done in a home oven. Cover the fabric with tissue paper or cloth and roll it into a loose cylinder. Heat for 10 minutes at 120°C in an electric oven. If you use a gas oven, preheat the oven to 150°C, then turn off the gas and put in the roll of fabric and paper.

Printing methods. Fabric can be printed using stamps, linoleum or wood blocks, stencils, or silk screens (see *Printmaking,* pp. 242–253 and *Stenciling,* pp. 258–263).

A stamp or block is inked either by pressing it on an inking pad or by rolling ink onto it with a brayer. The stamp is then pressed against the fabric. Larger stamps may be struck with a mallet, or the printer can stand shoeless on top of the block (called treading). Stenciling is done with a brayer or a stippling brush, and silk screen is printed with a squeegee, as described in the aforementioned chapters.

The following pages illustrate simple methods of printing on fabric.

Late 18th-century French printed cotton fabric has overlapping floral motifs.

Printing with found objects

Original and interesting designs can be printed on fabric with found objects—objects picked up in the home or purchased from the hardware store.

Anything that has a shape and a surface for printing can be used to print and decorate your fabric: doilies, muffin tins, wrenches, sewing machine treadles, storm-drain grates, gear wheels, bottle caps, or tree leaves. Intricate patterns can be created, and the same object in the hands of different people can yield unique results in composition and coloring.

Any found object should be carefully assessed to evaluate its printing potential. An object may have more than one surface good for printing. The object should be washed or cleaned before use. In most cases the simplest way to ink a stamp is with a brayer, as shown at right. The illustrations below show different methods of printing with found objects.

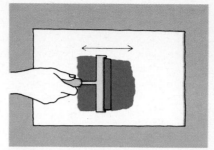

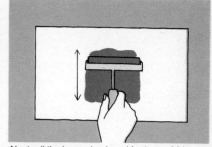

Inking the brayer. First spread ink on a glass palette, then roll the brayer over the ink.

Next roll the brayer back and forth at a 90° angle to its previous line of motion.

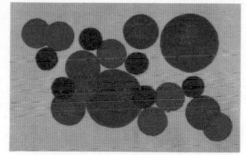

Simple impressions. The mouth of a drinking glass is pressed on an ink-saturated pad of felt or foam rubber. Glass is used to print fabric with a design of circles. Jar and bottle tops print colored disks.

Masking tape. Tape is used to make a pattern on the fabric. The brayer is inked and rolled firmly over the fabric. The tape is then peeled away. The areas underneath are shielded from the brayer's ink. Grid pattern and squares were made this way.

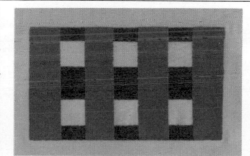

Found objects. A plastic doily is inked with the brayer; the doily is placed on a flat surface, inked side up. Fabric is laid over it and rolled with a rolling pin to create the print. Second pattern employs artist's French curves.

Printing on fabric

Stamping

Aside from the use of found objects (see p. 255), carving stamps is the simplest method of printing on fabric. The printing block is merely inked and pressed to the fabric. Elaborate patterns can be built up by repeated printings with a single stamp. The stamps can be made from many materials, including rubber, styrofoam, wood, linoleum, and plaster of Paris. Two basic stamps, a potato and an art-gum eraser, were used here.

To make a potato stamp, slice a large potato in half. Carve a simple relief design into one of the raw faces. Dry the face with a paper towel, and ink it with water-based ink (do not use oil-based ink). A potato stamp can be kept for several days by wrapping it in plastic and refrigerating it. A stamp cut from art-gum eraser will last much longer and is compatible with both water- and oil-based inks. Carve either with a razor blade or utility knife.

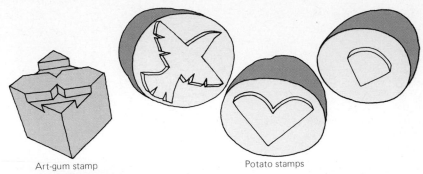

Art-gum stamp

Potato stamps

Art gum. These stamps are suited to neat, geometric patterns. Here, a basic design of three parallel diagonals is cut into one stamp. The same stamp is rotated four times to create each print at left; it is printed in different combinations below.

Potato. These stamps are ideal for quaint designs for everything from children's clothes to kitchen curtains. As suggested by the pictures below, just one or two stamps can be used to create a variety of whimsical patterns.

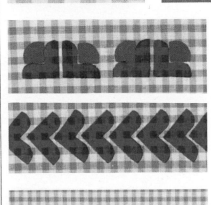

Linoleum-block printing

A linoleum block can be used for larger and more elaborate designs than a potato or an art-gum stamp. The drawing at right shows the linoleum block that was used to print the fabric samples depicted below.

To prepare and print the block, follow the instructions given in *Printmaking*, pp. 250–251. Keep in mind that fabric does not present as smooth a printing surface as paper; therefore, the block should be carved deeper.

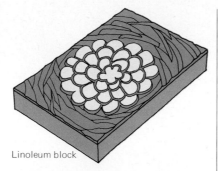
Linoleum block

The floral design linoleum block is printed on fabric in a straight line.

The same flowers are arranged here in an uneven pattern.

Leaves, printed with an art-gum stamp, are added to the flowers on checkered cloth.

Stenciling

A design can be printed on fabric by using a stencil in combination with a silk screen, as discussed in the text in *Printmaking*, p. 244. Or the stencil can be employed alone with ink and a brush or a brayer to stencil the design directly onto the fabric.

Choose a stencil material such as acetate, cardboard, or stencil paper. Cut the stencil as described in *Stenciling*, pp. 258–263. In using the brayer to print the design, be sure that the roller is heavily and uniformly inked. Roll the brayer across the full length of the stencil and then back again before lifting it. The brayer is ideal for creating interesting color effects, as in the striped pattern pictured below.

The elephant design was printed by repeating a single stencil across the fabric. The printing was done by dabbing the design with a large, round stippling brush saturated with ink, using an up-and-down motion.

Stripes. To print striped design shown below, squeeze inks of three different colors side by side on a glass palette. Then roll the brayer over the palette, forming three color bands on the brayer. Roll these across the stencil.

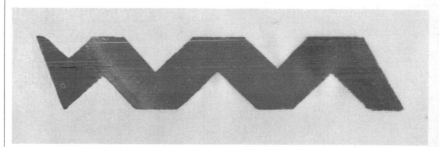
A rainbow of colorful inks is printed with a brayer over a stencil.

A parade of pachyderms is created by repeating a single stencil.

Detail from 18th-century Japanese stenciled costume design; gold leaf painted on silk.

Stencils around the world

Stenciling, the craft of applying color through a precisely cut design onto almost any surface—cloth, paper, walls, furniture—has been practiced since ancient times.

In China stencils were used by monks to produce some of the many images of the Buddha in the Caves of the Thousand Buddhas. From early in their history the Japanese decorated their clothing by means of stencils. Both the Chinese and Japanese devoted attention to creating elaborate and subtle designs. The most delicate of all stencils, these early Oriental examples of the craft were cut from finely pressed mulberry fiber, which was waterproofed with persimmon juice and held together by threads of silk or hair.

Stencils were used in Europe during the Middle Ages to decorate church walls and wooden screens and to color inexpensive, popular prints of the Virgin Mary and the saints. At the end of the 17th century the French developed stencils for coloring the first wallpaper, which imitated luxurious contemporary fabric wall hangings.

Few of the early settlers in North America were able to afford costly imported wallpaper and furniture; thus, wall and furniture stenciling flourished. Artisans traveled extensively, carrying their designs and the dry pigments to make up paint. In return for decorating the rooms of the house, the stenciler was given room and board and a small wage. When wallpaper was manufactured locally and became inexpensive, these designs were often covered over.

At the end of the 19th century, architects revived the use of stencils for the decoration of public buildings in Europe and North America. Today stenciling is undergoing another revival as part of the present widespread interest in folk crafts.

Tools and materials

To create decorations with stencils, all you really need is stiff paper, plastic, or cardboard from which to cut the stencil; a sharp knife; and some form of colorant. Stencils can be made from materials as commonplace as grocery bags, and the color can be applied with felt-tipped marking pens or crayons. Such materials are most useful in experimenting with designs. For more elegant finished results choose the appropriate tools and materials for your project from the following list.

Stencil paper. This semitransparent waxed paper permits a stencil to be cut directly from a design placed under it. It is good for stenciling furniture and for other projects that do not require much repetition, but it deteriorates rapidly with repeated use.

Stencil board. A flexible, oiled board more durable than stencil paper, stencil board is recommended for projects on walls and floors. As it is not transparent, the design must be transferred onto the board before cutting.

Acetate. A transparent, stiff plastic, acetate is long-lasting and suitable for any frequently repeated design. When starting to cut in acetate, it is advisable to use simple, straight-sided designs. Buy .005-gauge sheets.

Frisket paper. This is a pressure-sensitive acetate film that adheres to the object being stenciled. It is especially useful for airbrush work.

Architects' linen. This cloth can be cut into elaborate designs with manicure scissors; it lasts well.

Craft knife. This knife with replaceable blade is recommended for all stencil cutting. The blade must be kept very sharp; either replace it often or sharpen it frequently on a whetstone or knife sharpener.

Single-edged razor blade and utility knife. These can be used to cut large, simple designs.

Stenciling

Tools and materials (*continued*)

Tracing paper and carbon paper. These papers are used to transfer designs onto stencil board.

Masking tape. This is the best tape available to hold stencils in place.

Nonpermanent spray adhesive. This prevents seepage of spray paints.

Metal-edged ruler. When cutting straight lines, use a metal-edged ruler as a guide.

Paper punches. They are useful for making small round dots.

Acrylic paints. Good multipurpose paints for stenciling, acrylics dry quickly and can be used directly from the tube for a sharp design or can be mixed with water and other colors for more subtle effects. Acrylics will adhere to any nonslick surface and can be used on washable fabrics. However, they deteriorate when dry-cleaned.

Latex paints. These can be used as widely as acrylics. They dry quickly, but as they have a runny consistency, care should be taken to apply them with an almost dry brush, as described on page 263. In floor and wall stenciling latex paints will blend well with background paint.

Japan colors. These paints dry very quickly and will adhere to slick surfaces such as glass, polished metal, enamel, varnished furniture, and glazed ceramics. As the consistency is very thin, two or three coats should be applied with an almost dry brush.

Oil paints. Oils are slow-drying, but they can be used on both slick and nonslick surfaces.

Patio and deck paints. Often used for floor stenciling, they dry very slowly, so care must be taken in planning and applying the design. They have a thin consistency.

Spray paints. These require wide margins on the stencil. If the stencil material is lightweight, it should be stuck down with masking tape or nonpermanent spray adhesive.

Watercolors, colored inks, marking pens, and crayons. All can be used for stenciling on paper or for testing a design. Apply watercolors and colored inks with sponges or fine brushes.

Poster paints. These are effective for use on paper or cardboard.

Stencil brushes. Their bristles have blunt ends. Select brushes with soft bristles, which preserve the stencil better. Use a separate brush for each color.

Sponges. These can be used with watercolors and thinned acrylics to create soft, mottled effects. Cut a flat sponge into strips about 1 inch wide and dip one end into the color.

Fine brushes. They are useful for details and retouching.

Paint rollers and glue brushes. Use these on large stencils. It is important to remove excess paint from the saturated roller before using it. To do this, roll it on newspaper.

Airbrushes. These special-purpose tools are used for misted effects.

Fine brushes

Utility knife

Craft knife

Stencil brush

Cutting stencil paper, acetate, and stencil board

It is very important to use a sharp knife for stencil cutting. A new or freshly sharpened blade should be used for each cutting session, and it should be replaced or resharpened during a long work session.

Begin by cutting a piece of stencil material larger than the design by at least an inch all around. Then, with a craft knife, cut cleanly through the material, pressing down firmly on the stencil with the other hand. Always cut toward your right elbow (if right-handed), moving the stencil around to maintain this cutting direction. Go over any ragged edges or untidy corners and make them neat.

As cutout areas weaken a stencil, start by cutting out the smaller shapes and do the large shapes last.

Transparent materials, including stencil paper, can be cut over a design. Tape stencil material to design and use a piece of firm board as a base. Hold knife perpendicular to stencil. Press firmly to make a clean cut, following outline beneath.

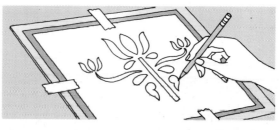

When cutting stencil board, it is necessary to transfer the design onto the board before cutting. Trace the outline of the design on tracing paper, then place the tracing over carbon paper on the board and retrace the design.

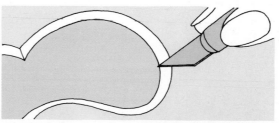

With stencil board, the edges of the design should be beveled to make a neat outline when it is painted. Cut with the knife almost perpendicular but leaning slightly away from the design.

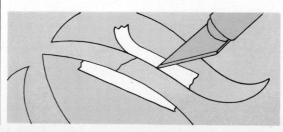

If part of the outline is broken or cut through, it can be repaired with masking tape. Do not fold the extra tape over; turn the stencil over and trim off the tape neatly in line with the design.

Stenciling

Designing and cutting a simple symmetrical stencil

Cutting a symmetrical shape from folded paper is a simple, effective method for designing a stencil. Choose an interesting but uncomplicated silhouette with matching sides. Cut half of the outline from the folded edge of a piece of paper. When opened, the paper will have the form of a stencil; however, the design should be transferred to flat, waterproof stencil material, as illustrated at right.

Suitable outlines can be derived from flowers, trees, or the human figure. To make borders on walls or a floor, cut designs on one large stencil.

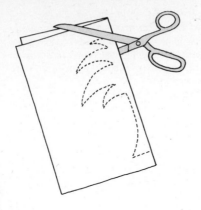

To make a simple symmetrical stencil, draw half the design along the fold of a piece of paper. Cut the outline with scissors or a craft knife. Open the design and place it over a contrasting piece of colored paper and under a piece of stencil or tracing paper. Using a craft knife, cut out the design, or trace the outline onto stencil material before cutting, as shown here.

More complex symmetrical stencils

By folding a square piece of paper three times, it is possible to produce complicated and delicate stencils that are symmetrical on all four sides. After the designs have been cut in the folded paper, it is important to transfer them to flat, waterproof stencil material for the final stencils.

Designs can range from a simple four-petal shape—made by cutting a single shape along the long folded edge, being sure not to cut across either corner—to subtle designs made from shapes cut into both folded edges.

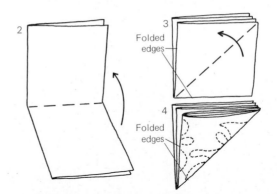

For a complex stencil that is symmetrical on all four sides, take a large, square piece of paper and make clean folds—first in half (1), then into quarters (2). Make one more fold (3), joining the folded sides of the square to form a triangle (4). Cuts are made along the folded edges only, as indicated by the dotted lines. Instructions for creating the stencil are illustrated below.

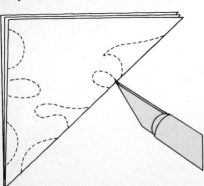

To create a stencil with a radial pattern, cut undulating serrations along both folded edges. Do not cut the unfolded edges.

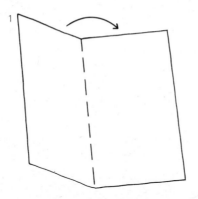

Open the design and lay it flat on a contrasting piece of colored paper. Tape a piece of stencil paper over it, then trace the design underneath.

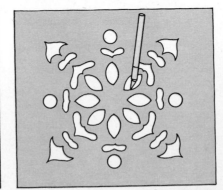

Remove the stencil paper and cut along the traced lines with a craft knife. Rotate the stencil paper as you work.

The finished image of the painted stencil can be approximated by laying the stencil over colored papers. Paint can be protected with shellac.

Designing and cutting a stencil with ties

When designing an asymmetrical stencil, it is important to find a strong, interesting outline. If it represents an object, the outline should be easy to recognize. Sources for designs include old stenciling, prints, magazine illustrations, and your own drawings.

To show details inside the outline, it is necessary to use ties—thin strips of material that bridge cutout areas of the design and connect to the edges of the stencil. With a line drawing, follow the contours or natural shading of the object and expand these lines to strips about 1/8 inch wide. Many intersecting lines are difficult to render.

Ties are also useful for strengthening a stencil. Long, wavy outlines or intricate designs are liable to warp when painted unless ties are used.

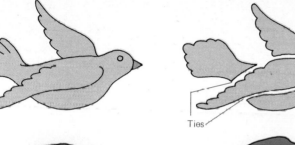

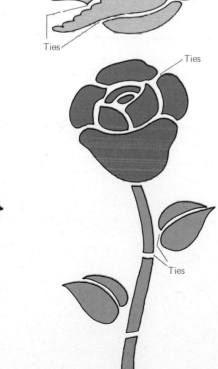

Ties

Painting

Before starting to paint a stencil, test your paints on the intended background material. (If you are stenciling furniture, for example, test a piece of wood with the same finish; if you are stenciling a wall, test a hidden area, such as the back of a closet.)

Mix the paints to a creamy consistency. Thin paints should be applied in several light coats with an almost dry brush to prevent seepage under the cut edges of the outline. The chapters in this book entitled *Color and design* (pp. 220–221) and *Painting* (pp. 222–241) contain information on the selection, mixing, and application of paints.

After each stenciling, wipe off any wet paint on the stencil and check to be sure the back side is clean before applying it to another surface.

Paint should be applied with an almost dry brush. The brush can be dried by dabbing it on newspaper before painting with it.

With your free hand, press the stencil firmly against the surface underneath. Apply the brush to the center of a painting area first to remove any excess paint.

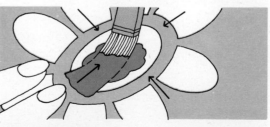

When painting a stencil, always brush from the outside into the middle of each area. Avoid bumping against the edges. If the area is very small, brush across it gently.

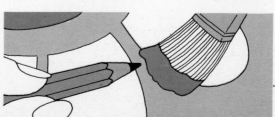

When painting near a tie, the tie can be pressed down with a small, sharp object, such as a pencil.

Stenciling

Using two or more stencils

More than one stencil is necessary for designs that have several colors or that have so many small details that the large number of ties would break up the design on a single stencil. The outline of the first stencil is traced in position on all secondary stencils. Four or five small triangular *registration marks* are then cut along this outline, pointing inward. After the first stencil has been painted, the others can be accurately positioned by checking for the color of the previous stencil through the registration marks.

Where two colors meet, provide for an overlap of about 1/8 inch so that they will join neatly. Pale colors do not cover darker ones well unless several coats of paint are used, so it is better to paint dark colors over light ones.

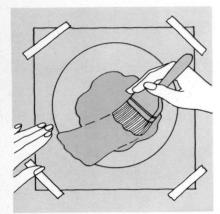

1. When using a series of superimposed stencils, design the first stencil to apply the basic outline and the main background color.

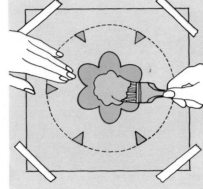

2. The second stencil is in the correct place when all the registration marks show only the color of the first stencil.

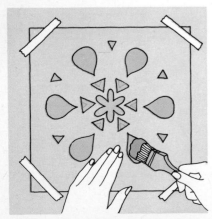

3. A third and any additional stencils are also positioned with the registration marks. First allow preceding paint to dry completely.

4. By using several stencils, a complicated, multi-colored design can be built up without the interruption of too many stencil ties.

Stenciling/project

Stenciling painted furniture

Painted wooden furniture provides a good surface for stenciling, lending itself to bright, multicolored designs. This project makes use of a small, unfinished bench, which is first sanded and given two background coats of latex paint. The stencil is cut from heavy stencil paper, and acrylic paints are used to apply the design.

Before stenciling any such surface, make a full- or reduced-scale plan to help determine the position and sizes of the patterns. For a large surface, such as a door, several separate bordered panels can be designed. For a very large surface, such as a wall, the main design can be adapted to serve as a border stencil.

Drawing the stencil. The design in the grid on the facing page can be drawn to any size (see *Drawing*, p. 212). For the top of this bench, which measures about 1 by 2½ feet, the design is enlarged to twice its size on the right-hand half of a piece of tracing paper. The other half of the design is drawn by folding back the paper exactly along the left edge of the design and tracing through the doubled paper. The design is then unfolded and laid out flat under a sheet of transparent stencil paper, which is cut following the outline of the design beneath.

Border corners. To make neat corners on a border, measure the edges exactly before stenciling so that the designs will be spaced evenly. Use either a complete design or a special motif in each corner. Here the border leaf motif was repeated in the corners, but the leaves in the corners were positioned at 45° angles.

Applying paint. Work with one color at a time, using as little paint as possible on the brush. The dry-brush technique will give a smoother surface as well as neater outlines.

The border stencil should be applied to the short sides first, then extended along the long sides from each corner.

Uneven edges can be touched up with a fine brush, using either the acrylic or the background latex paint. A knife or razor blade can be used to remove a ragged acrylic edge.

To protect the stenciled surface, apply a coat of clear shellac when the paint is completely dry. For the sake of a uniform appearance, you may want to shellac the entire bench.

Alternate to design on p. 262

1. Tape both design and stencil paper (stencil paper on top) to piece of cardboard so that stencil can be turned as it is cut.

2. For this border with leaf motif draw one leaf in each corner. Then space the others evenly along edges with a ruler.

3. Check that the painted surface of the furniture is clean and dry, then tape the main stencil in position on the wood.

4. Acrylics can be used from the tube or mixed to a creamy consistency. When painting each area, brush from outside inward.

5. Stencil should always be pressed down to give a crisp edge. Here the end of a second brush is used to apply pressure in small areas.

6. Paint in blue areas of main stencil after red dries. When blue dries, remove main stencil. Paint border corners, then short sides.

7. On long sides, first paint border inward from each corner; then place stencil across remaining gap, adjusting for even spacing.

8. When border is dry, a second stencil of smaller leaves can be applied over first in a different color to give border added interest.

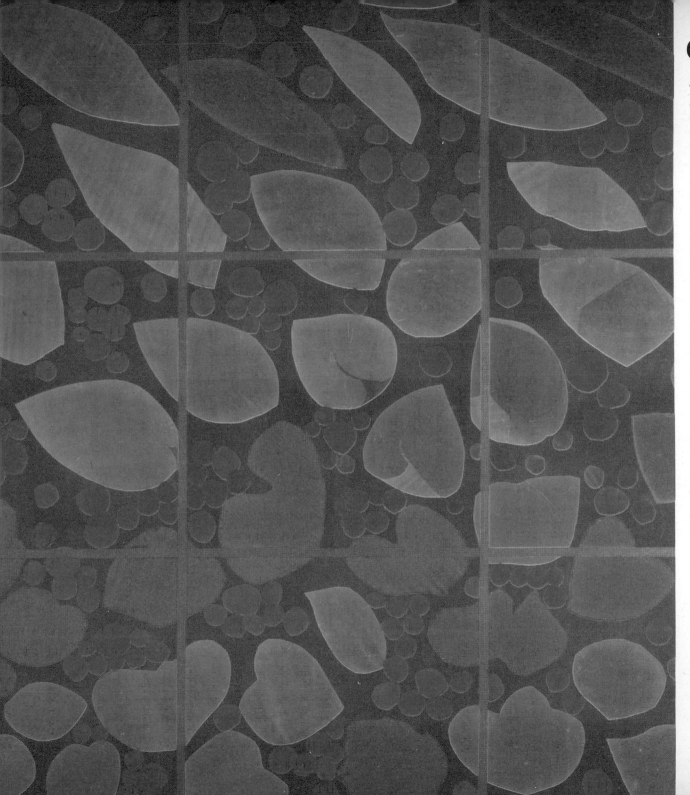

Collage
A contemporary art form

Collage, from the French verb *coller* ("to glue") is the general term for an artistic arrangement of various materials glued to a surface. Just about any material—fabric, wood, metal—can be used in making collages. When more than one type of material is employed in the same work, the product is called an assemblage. An assemblage may incorporate such found objects as nuts and bolts, doorknobs, rag dolls—whatever the artist finds pleasing.

Collage has long been a popular hobby because no special training as an artist is required to practice the craft. When early in the 20th century Georges Braque and Pablo Picasso began to incorporate collage into their paintings, this former folk art quickly attained the level of a serious art form. Other artists soon turned to collage, and it has exerted an important influence on 20th-century art.

Apart from the materials of the collage itself (discussed on the following pages), you will need glue, brushes, and a mounting support. Supports are normally made either from Masonite, particle board, or plywood. A support 1/8 to 1/4 inch thick will suffice for most work. A large assemblage incorporating many heavy materials may require a thicker support and special fastening techniques, as discussed on page 267. Though more expensive than the above materials, canvas can also be used as a support—either mounted on a stretcher or glued to a board. It is the obvious surface to use when combining collage and painting.

The adhesives most commonly used in collage are polyvinyl acetate (PVA), or white glue, and acrylic polymer. Both are normally thinned with water in a ratio of 1 part glue to 1 part water. Acrylic polymer also acts as a varnish, giving the surface a polished look.

The detail of the Henri Matisse "Lierre en Fleur" (1953) is an arrangement of bright paper cutouts.

Working with paper

Any kind of paper can be used in collage. Popular choices include newspaper, magazine illustrations, postcards, photographs, greeting cards, posters, billboard signs, gift paper, old letters, and wallpaper. Wrappers from candy bars have been used, as well as labels from bottles and soup cans. Finely textured tissue papers are available in a range of colors from art stores. For paper with body and texture you can use paper napkins and paper towels. Japanese rice papers also have interesting textures and possess their own intrinsic beauty. Rice papers, available in most art stores, come in different weights, colors, and textures.

Experimentation. Tissue papers change color to lighter shades when they are glued. Two pieces of the same color glued together will produce an interesting mottled pattern. Gluing tissue papers of different colors on top of one another yields a variety of interesting effects, owing to the translucency of the paper.

The key to collage is experimentation. Begin by selecting papers with colors and textures that interest you. Cut out illustrations you like, or cut silhouettes from different kinds of papers. Lay them on your support and experiment with different arrangements. A design may grow as you shift and rearrange the cutouts.

When you have arrived at a pleasing arrangement, glue it down, but don't feel bound by the finished result. If after several days you are dissatisfied, add other shapes and papers.

Sizing and priming. PVA and acrylic polymer adhesives will cause the thinnest (1/8 inch) Masonite to warp as it dries. To prevent this, size the board before applying the collage. Sizing consists of coating both sides of the Masonite with a diluted solution of the same adhesive you plan to use in the collage, then letting the board dry before you proceed. Dilute the adhesive with water until it has the consistency of light cream. Adhesive sizing dries clear, leaving the background the brown color of the Masonite underneath the sizing.

As an alternative to sizing with adhesive, the surface can be primed with gesso. Gesso is a white primer painters use to seal canvases; it gives the support a white background.

1. Using a wide brush, apply primer to the smooth side of the support. Here gesso is applied to Masonite. PVA and acrylic polymer will dry in about 30 min, gesso in about 2 hr.

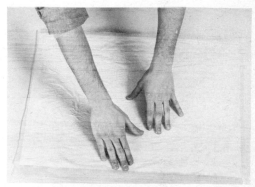

2. Brush adhesive onto the support. Then lay down a background paper, such as this lightly shaded tissue paper. Wrinkles contribute a sense of texture.

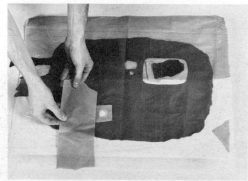

3. Allow the background paper to dry, then cut out the elements of your design. Place them on the background. Experiment with arrangement until design satisfies you.

4. Since this tissue paper is so light that the adhesive permeates it, brush it on top of the paper rather than underneath. Coat the finished surface with adhesive.

Collage

Working with fabrics

Fabrics—textiles—are often used to great effect in collage work. They contribute organic textures and a weighty appearance that are totally different in effect from anything that can be achieved by using paper.

The fabrics appropriate for collage are varied and numerous. Burlap and canvas are excellent for their obvious, rough-hewn textures; both also make good background materials. When applied on top of these heavier fabrics,

lighter, more colorful materials such as silk, cotton, and nylon provide interesting contrasts. Other fabrics suitable for collage include brocade and upholstery material, chair caning, gauze and netting of various kinds, string and rope, lace, ribbons, velvet, old flannel shirts, denim, old towels, and quilts.

As with paper, fabrics need not be new or in perfect condition to be usable. In fact, old ripped, faded, and damaged fabrics often possess an in-

trinsic symbolic and textural value lacking in new fabrics. You may want to buy new material to obtain certain textures or to realize a particular idea. But frequently the fabrics you need will be no farther away than your closets, drawers, basement, or attic.

Fabric tends to lend itself to larger work than paper used alone. In general, therefore, you should use at least a 1/4-inch-thick sheet of plywood, Masonite, or particle board as a support.

Prime or size the board as for paper (see p. 265), then apply any background material you like. You can use the same adhesives as those used for paper. PVA is better than acrylic when gluing larger, heavier pieces, though acrylic is acceptable for smaller pieces. When gluing fabrics, do not dilute the adhesive. Apply it liberally. As with paper, a final coat or two of acrylic will produce a glazed finish that accentuates the textures.

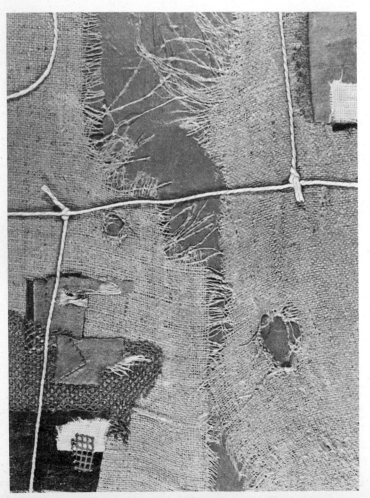

1. Arrange the various pieces of fabric you have selected for the design on the support. The board used for this support is 1/2-in. plywood.

2. The larger background pieces, such as the burlap and canvas used here, are laid down first. Smaller fabrics are glued on top of these.

3. Since PVA is stronger than acrylic, it is used for the heavier pieces. For lighter pieces, such as string, you can use acrylic adhesive.

4. After front is complete, turn board over. Trim most excess fabric. Fold remainder over. Paste it to back of board, then tack fabric down.

Assemblage

An assemblage is a collage incorporating materials or objects other than paper and fabric. Although an assemblage often makes use of paper and fabrics, objects predominate, since the purpose is to create an architectonic effect of three-dimensional space.

These objects are customarily called "found objects," from the French *objets trouvés*. As with collage, the origins of assemblage are associated with Picasso and Braque. "Found object" is usually interpreted to mean any utilitarian object that has outlived its purpose. As an expression of our technological age, manufactured mechanical objects have been used with telling effect: watch mechanisms, clock and watch faces, gears, springs, washers, sheet metal, hubcaps, eyeglasses, jewelry. But the objects need not be strictly utilitarian. You could use eggshells and seashells, pinecones, dried leaves, pebbles, fishbones. Wooden spools can be most effective, as in the assemblage pictured below. The true grist of assemblage is junk—junk put to a new, creative use.

As with paper and fabrics, you should experiment with an assortment of objects to determine design possibilities. The construction of an assemblage differs from other collage work primarily in that adhesives are not always the best means for attaching objects to the support. Although undiluted white glue will bind many lightweight metal pieces to wood or fabric, there may be times when you will want to nail, tack, or screw things into place, depending on their weight and texture. Objects can also be embedded in a thick coat of modeling paste (see below), an adhesive used for heavier metal articles.

The weight of the objects and the screws or nails used to hold them determine the thickness of the support.

1. In this assemblage, PVA adhesive is used to glue the various small outer wooden pieces to the support, which is a piece of 1/2-in. plywood.

2. The outer wooden pieces and the support background are sprayed with white spray paint. Use spray paint carefully, as it is flammable.

3. The larger frame is nailed down with small brads (as the propeller will be). The other metal objects are embedded in modeling paste.

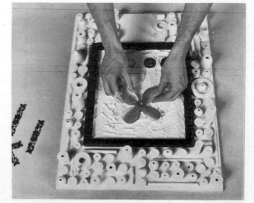

4. The smaller frame (see large photo, left) is glued to the support with PVA. The finished work can be coated with acrylic polymer adhesive.

Wood sculpture

Before the dawn of history

The oldest known stone carvings date back more than 25,000 years. Although no examples of prehistoric wood sculpture remain (wood decomposes much faster than stone, usually in a few generations), it is reasonable to suppose that early man began to carve wood at least as early as he began to carve stone, considering the relative hardness of the two materials.

The oldest extant wood sculpture comes from Egypt, where the hot, arid climate has helped to preserve it. A small statue discovered in 1860 in Karnak, on the Nile River, is at least 4,500 years old. Wood sculpture is thought to have been produced in many of the great ancient civilizations. For example, great classical Greek statues were carved of wood, painted, and overlaid with ivory and gold.

As with many art forms, wood sculpture went into a decline in the Middle Ages but then arose in splendor during the Renaissance, especially in Spain and Italy. Such sculptors as Michelangelo and Donatello, known primarily for their work in other mediums, also sculpted wood. Sculptors in Europe as well as in North Africa and the Far East frequently worked in close conjunction with architects for secular and religious purposes.

Wood sculpture became part of the popular North American culture in the 19th century. Examples of fine wood sculpture (which are frequently overlooked as fine art) are figureheads from sailing ships and cigar store Indians.

Although the use of new mediums has contributed to the decline of wood sculpture in modern times, it remains a vital art form. The tools and techniques have changed little since its beginning, so the art of wood sculpture gives the sculptor an artistic link with his prehistoric ancestors.

Fifteenth-century Chinese wood carving is in collection of London's Victoria and Albert Museum.

Tools

Most wood carving is accomplished with tools called gouges, which are chisels with curved cutting edges. Gouges come in scores of shapes: there is variation in the size of the cutting edge (from about 1/8 inch to 3½ inches); the arc of the cutting edge (shallow, medium, or deep); the shape of the shank (straight, long bent, or short bent); and the shape of the cutting edge (there are special shapes, such as the spoon gouge, the V-gouge, and the fishtail gouge).

It is best to start with a few basic gouges, for example a wide, flat gouge, a medium gouge (about 3/4 inch), a spoon gouge, a V-gouge, and a flat chisel. As you gain experience, your work will dictate which of the more exotic gouges you will need. Also buy a round wooden mallet for striking the handles of the gouges.

Buy high-quality tools, as they will save you the trouble of having to sharpen the cutting edges every few min-utes, as happens with cheaper tools.

Abraders are used to finish the surface of the sculpture. They include wood files and rasps (buy them separately or in the form of a combination rasp, which has several different faces) and rifflers—smaller finishing tools with finer teeth than rasps. Gouges, chisels, mallets, and rifflers are available at crafts supply stores.

Buy a sharpening stone (oilstone) with both a coarse and a fine face.

A wire brush or file card is used to clean the wood from the teeth of files, rasps, and rifflers.

Clamps are needed for laminating wood blocks (see p. 270) and for holding the sculpture stationary during carving (a woodworking vise is good for this, but not necessary). The size and shape of your work will determine the size and shape of the clamps.

A crosscut saw is used to make the first cuts into a block of wood, and sandpaper is used during finishing.

Sharpening tools

The cutting edges of gouges and chisels must be kept very sharp while you are carving. Dull blades will tear the wood, which will cause damage to the wood, inaccurate cuts, and surface mars.

To sharpen your tools, put some light machine oil on the sharpening stone. If the tool is quite dull, start with the coarse face of the stone; if not, you can use just the fine side.

All cutting edges should be sharpened to 25° angles. Hold the tool on the stone so that when you push the tool across the stone it will form a 25° angle. The sharpening motion is circular—the tool is pressed forward across the stone, then pressure is eased as the tool is dragged back (Steps 1 and 2, below). Gouges must be rotated as they are pushed across the stone to make the curved edges sharp and even (Step 3).

If the tool has to be razor sharp, as for final surface finishing, the edge can be stropped on a piece of leather.

Wide gouge

Medium gouge

Flat chisel

Spoon gouge

V-gouge

Combination rasp

Wood file

Mallet

Rifflers

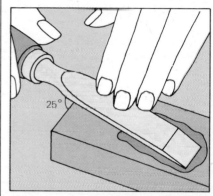

1. Place oil on the sharpening stone. Hold the tool so that the stone will sharpen a 25° angle on the tool. Push the tool forward across the stone, applying pressure with your fingers.

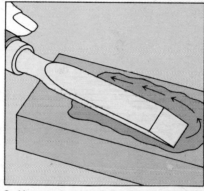

2. After you have pushed the tool all the way forward, ease up slightly on the pressure and pull the tool back across the stone. The motion of the sharpening process should be circular.

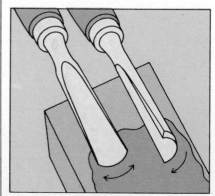

3. When you are sharpening a gouge, you must rotate the tool from side to side as you push and pull it across the stone. Try to keep the edge as sharp and even as possible.

4. In order to get a 25° edge, different tools must be held at different angles. For example, this spoon gouge must be held at a greater angle to stone than the chisel in Steps 1 and 2.

Wood sculpture

Reinforcing handles of tools

The handles of gouges and chisels wear down under continual pounding with a mallet. You can prolong the lives of your tool handles by reinforcing them with wire.

A groove is cut into the handle with a saw so that when the wire is laid in, it will be flush with the rest of the handle. The wire (preferably brass) is laid in, twisted together at the ends, and the twist is pushed down into the groove. The twist is then soldered.

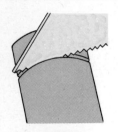

1. Cut a groove in the handle with a saw.

2. Lay in the brass wire.

3. Twist the ends and tuck them into the groove.

4. Solder the ends of the wire.

Choosing a wood to carve

Any wood can be carved. However, woods vary radically in their constitution, cell structure, and grain pattern, all of which affect the wood's appearance and carvability. For example, woods with uneven, coarse grain will be more difficult to carve than woods with close, even grain. For general information on woods and woodworking, see *Woodworking*, pp. 360–403.

When you are choosing a wood to sculpt, the carvability is an extremely important consideration. The finished appearance of the wood—color, grain, and texture—is also an important criterion. Unfortunately, probably the most crucial considerations in choosing a wood for carving are availability and cost. If you are unfamiliar with a certain type of wood, find out about it before investing your time and money. Among the most popular choices for carving are mahogany, walnut, cherry, oak, and white pine.

Seasoning wood

Before any piece of wood is carved, it must be carefully dried, or seasoned, to help prevent it from cracking and splitting. Splits and cracks can result from uneven evaporation of water from the various levels of the wood as it dries. Commercially seasoned logs are dried in a kiln, but such logs are expensive and difficult to obtain.

Unless you have access to a wood-drying kiln, the only way for you to season a log you cut down or find is by

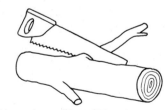

Cut log and saw off branches.

Coat ends and cuts with shellac or end-sealer.

air drying. There is no sure way to air dry without causing cracks, but there are ways you can improve your chances of ending up with a carvable log.

The heartwood, the very center of the log, is always the last part to dry. The chances of seasoning logs without cracks are greatly improved if you drill

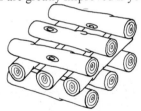

Stack wood so that air can circulate freely.

out the entire heartwood before you seal the ends. Coat the ends of the logs and any points where branches have been cut off with shellac or commercial lumber end-sealer (see diagram, below left). This prevents the ends from drying faster than the centers, which would cause splitting in the ends. Then stack the logs in a manner that permits free circulation of air (see diagram above). The best spot for seasoning is a dry area free from extreme temperature changes, such as a basement, attic, or shed. Seasoning can be done outdoors if the logs are kept covered. The wood should not be exposed to sunlight, rain, or direct heat, such as radiators. It takes at least several years to season a log.

Laminating a block of wood

Even if you season a log correctly, after it is carved it will almost invariably develop splits and cracks as the temperature and humidity change. Logs, especially of carvable hardwoods, are expensive and difficult to obtain, and the failure rate involved in seasoning logs that you prepare yourself can be very discouraging.

These difficulties can be circumvented by creating wood blocks by laminating boards. Boards are far easier to obtain and far cheaper than logs of the same volume. Hardwoods must be bought at a special hardwood dealer, but clean white pine can be bought at any lumberyard. Boards season in a small fraction of the time it takes for logs to season. A well-laminated block of wood will withstand the ravages of time—warping, splitting, cracking—far better than a log. And the

Making a laminated block

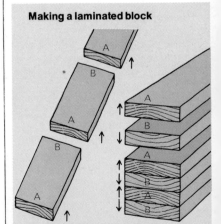

Each piece of cut board has an A end and a B end; stack the pieces as shown, alternating the direction of the grain. Boards frequently have a concave and convex side. The arrows indicate the side facing up in the original board. When the pieces are stacked, every other piece is rotated, as indicated by the arrows in the picture above.

lamination lines in a well-laminated block are practically invisible.

Boards that are to be laminated must be planed flat so that the surfaces will adhere to one another. It is easiest to buy wood that is already planed. If you buy rough wood, the lumberyard may have a power planer you can use. Planing by hand is extremely difficult.

The boards are cut to size and stacked up so that the grain runs in opposite directions in alternate pieces. This prevents the expansion and contraction that occur in wood during changes of temperature and humidity from tearing the block apart. Directions for cutting and alternating wood for a laminated block are given at left.

The boards are arranged in the block roughly in the shape of the sculpture's final form. For the torso on pages 271–275 the block is rectangular because the

basic shape of the torso is rectangular. If the figure had an extended limb, an additional piece of wood would be laminated onto the block, and the limb would be carved from it. This kind of planned lamination saves a lot of wood, time, and effort.

The boards are covered with white wood glue (PVA) and are stacked up. The stack is compressed with as many clamps as possible, because the greater and more even the pressure is, the more sound and secure the lamination will be. If you don't have any large clamps, such as the bar clamps shown in Step 4, p. 273, you can make a perfectly acceptable substitute out of pieces of wood and threaded steel bars (see illustration below).

After the laminated block sits for a day, the clamps are removed and the wood is ready to be carved.

Clamps for laminating blocks

Nut

Fender washer

Threaded steel rod

Clamps for laminating blocks of wood can be made at home. Drill holes in 2 by 4's cut to needed length. Place 1/2-in. threaded steel rods (available at hardware stores, usually in 36-in. lengths) or threaded pipe through the holes. Attach fender washers and nuts. Tighten the clamp by turning the nuts with a wrench. Use several of these clamps to laminate a block, as shown above.

Carving a torso

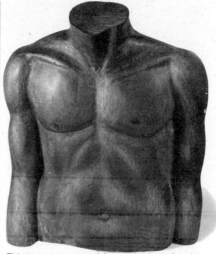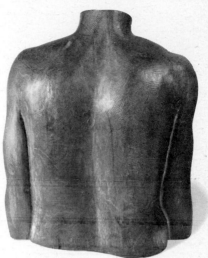

This torso was carved from a laminated mahogany block, then stained and waxed.

On this and the following four pages instructions and illustrations for carving a wood sculpture of a male torso are given. There is no one "right" way to carve a sculpture; the illustrations on pages 273–275 are intended to depict the general techniques and procedures of wood sculpture. Almost any form can be carved in wood: the torso is a popular choice, as is the human head. (For a description of the forms and proportions of the human head, see *Modeling, moldmaking, and casting sculpture,* p. 193.)

Wood. The torso shown on the next four pages is carved from a laminated block (see opposite page ; Steps 1–4, p. 273) of 1- by 6-inch mahogany boards. If you are carving from a log, be sure that it is properly seasoned before you begin (see p. 270).

The torso. The illustration on page 272 shows the torso in proportion to the entire male figure. The figure's sense of motion is a result of its weight being on its front foot. This causes an asymmetry in the position of the head, shoulders, and hips, resulting in a gentle S-curve down the center of the

body. This posture is referred to as *contraposto* ("counterpoise"). This illustration is a sketch taken from the statue that is considered the canon of classical beauty, "Doryphorus" ("spear bearer"), carved by the Greek sculptor Polyclitus in 450–440 B.C.

After the wood block is laminated, a sketch is chalked onto the front, sides, top, and back of the wood. You can use "Doryphorus" or some variation of it as your model.

The carving of the block is guided by the sketch. Despite this guide, however, novices tend to be reluctant to carve away enough wood, which results in their figures retaining a blocklike feeling. One way to avoid this is to think of the torso in terms of its basic volumes (see small illustration, p. 272) as the sculpture takes shape.

Sawing the wood block. When you have drawn the sketch onto the wood block, you will see that there are large volumes of wood that must be removed before you reach what will become the surface of the torso. Saw off as much of this excess wood as you can—it is much

(continued on next page)

271

Wood sculpture

Carving a torso *(continued)*

easier to remove wood by sawing than by carving with gouges.

Carving the torso with gouges. If you picture a three-dimensional torso, you will realize that the interior lines in the sketch on the block of wood represent the intersections of convex surfaces of the torso. The first step in carving is to begin to form the convex surfaces by cutting in on these lines. The interior lines are carved with a medium gouge (Steps 11–18). Large volumes on the outside of the piece can be removed with a wider, shallower gouge (Step 19). Because shallow gouges make less pronounced ridges in the wood than deep gouges, shallow gouges are also used to begin to refine the forms that are roughly defined by the first cuts (Steps 20, 23, and 24).

The V-gouge is used when you want to cut sharply into the wood in order to make very concisely defined lines (Steps 21 and 22).

The spoon gouge is used to remove wood from enclosed hollows where other gouges cannot cut (Step 25). It is also good for general hollowing, because it does not leave ridges as the other gouges do (Step 26). The spoon gouge cuts more gently than the other gouges and should be used if there is any danger at all of splitting or cracking the wood.

The technique used for cutting with a gouge is to hold the gouge in one hand and to hit it with short, crisp strokes of the mallet. As you carve, your work will dictate whether you will need more exotic tools for special purposes (see *Tools*, p. 269).

In general, then, a combination of gouges is used first to cut basic shapes, then to round the forms delineated by the first cuts, and finally to give proportion and detail to each shape.

Immobilizing the work. The sculpture must be held steady at all times. This can usually be done with clamps until the last flat plane on the top of the sculpture is removed. When the torso is lying flat, it can be propped against a piece of wood that is held steady by a clamp. When the piece can no longer be held by a clamp, it can be screwed onto a board of wood, then the board can be clamped to the table or bench (Steps 31–32). A woodworking vise is quite expensive but is probably the best tool for holding the wood.

Opposing cuts. Wood cuts best across the grain. When you are cutting with the grain, you must be careful that you cut the wood rather than cracking or splintering it off. To prevent the wood from cracking along the grain, first make cuts across the grain at right angles to the cut, along the entire length of the cut. These are opposing cuts (see below and Step 27, p. 275).

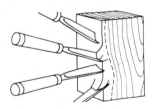

Opposing cuts, across grain, prevent splitting.

Finishing. The surface of a wood sculpture can be left in almost any state of finish, from one that shows every gouge mark, to a satiny smooth surface. Wood is made progressively smoother by the use of shallow gouges, spoon gouges, and flat chisels, which remove the ridges left by the deeper gouges (Step 29). The abraders—rasps, files, and rifflers—followed by sandpaper, can be used to make the surface even smoother (Steps 33–35).

The torso shown on page 271 was given an oil stain, then coated with a thick layer of paste wax. Any finish used in woodworking can be used with a piece of wood sculpture (see *Woodworking*, pp. 390–391).

The sketch at right, adapted from the sculpture "Doryphorus" ("spear bearer") by Polyclitus, shows the principal features of the male torso (the part of the body enclosed by the block).

The gentle mid-line S-curve (1) corresponds with the backbone. The pubic arch (2) is also the base of the pelvic bone. The waist (3) coincides with the top of the pelvic bone. The navel (4) is at the intersection of the waist and the mid-line S-curve. The base of the rib cage (5), the base of the pectoral muscles (6), the collarbones (7), the outline of the upper abdominal area (8), the outline of the lower abdominal area (9), the neck (10), the neck and shoulder muscles (11), and the arms (12) complete the definition of the basic shapes of the torso.

The principle volumes of the torso (shown above) are the pelvic area (A), the connecting form between pelvis and rib cage (B), the rib cage (C), the neck (D), the neck muscles (E), and the arms (F).

1. To laminate a wood block, cut and stack the pieces as discussed on page 270. Pour PVA glue on the first two boards, and spread the glue.

2. Press the glued faces together. Rub them together to break up air pockets and to ensure that the surfaces make complete contact.

3. Pour glue on top of the second board, and spread it around. Pour glue on the third board, spread the glue, and stack the wood as in Step 2.

4. Continue to build up the boards to finish the block. Line up the pieces; attach as many clamps as possible to make the lamination secure.

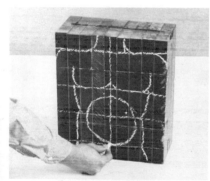

5. Let the laminated block sit for a day, then remove the clamps. Using a grid as a guide, draw the front sketch on the block (see p. 272).

6. Sketch the torso from the sides and back, as shown. The circle on top of the block is the top view of the neck.

7. Saw excess volumes of wood off the block wherever possible to save yourself from having to carve them off with gouges.

8. This illustration shows block with wood already removed from top of shoulders and sides of neck. Excess from arm is being sawed off.

9. Angled cuts can be used to remove excess wood from hollows. Here the hollow between the shoulder blades is cut away with the saw.

10. This illustration shows the block after sawing is completed. Notice how great a volume of wood can be removed with different cuts.

11. Use a medium gouge for the initial carving. Hold it in one hand and give it short, crisp strokes with the mallet.

12. Initially, use the gouge to cut into the lines drawn on the block. The interior lines are the intersections between surfaces. *(Continued)*

Wood sculpture

Carving a torso *(continued)*

13. Make cuts between the arm and side and around the pectoral muscle. Then make cuts into the perimeter of the stomach muscles.

14. Carve a layer of wood off the entire stomach area, as the stomach projects less than the rib cage or chest.

15. Make cuts on the other side of the torso, forming the collarbone and outlining the other pectoral muscle.

16. Define the bottom of the rib cage by carving as shown. This cutting also begins to give shape to the stomach muscles.

17. After the outlining is finished, lay the piece flat so that the contours of the parts can be created. Here work is done on the rib cage.

18. Incise a line to define the parts of the stomach muscle, as shown. While the piece is reclining, add detail to the collarbone.

19. Stand the piece up again. Use a wide, shallow gouge to remove volumes of wood from the sides of the arms, as shown here.

20. Also use the wide, flat gouge to carve and refine areas in which the deeper gouge leaves pronounced lines and grooves.

21. The V-gouge cuts sharp lines into the wood. Use it to more sharply define the boundaries of the different forms of the torso.

22. The V-gouge is also used to make incisions where other tools cannot reach. For example, cut line between arm and body with V-gouge.

23. Create more refined contours by carving with the flat gouge toward the lines cut with the V-gouge in Steps 21 and 22.

24. Use the flat gouge to make small cuts that give shape to the top of the shoulders, the collarbones, and the sides of the neck.

25. The spoon gouge can carve inside hollows where other tools cannot reach. Use it for hollows between the neck and collarbones.

26. The spoon gouge removes wood without leaving lines that the other gouges leave. Use it to begin detail on the stomach muscles.

27. Use opposing cuts (p. 272) whenever it is necessary to cut parallel with the grain; otherwise there is danger of splitting the wood.

28. Use the spoon gouge and the V-gouge to create detail in the various features. Here the spoon gouge cuts lines that delineate the ribs.

29. Use the flat chisel for surface finishing. Take very small bites with the flat chisel, or you will tear, not cut, the wood.

30. Use the saw to cut off the top part of the neck. The part of the neck you leave should incline toward the front of the torso.

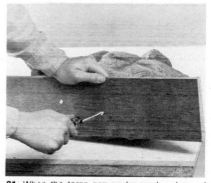

31. When the torso can no longer be clamped directly to the table, you can secure it by first screwing it to a wood board.

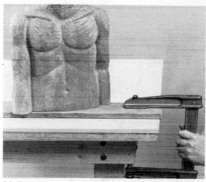

32. Then clamp the board to the workbench. This makes the piece almost as secure as if it were clamped directly to the table itself.

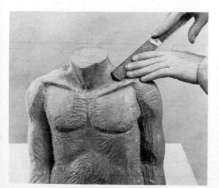

33. If you wish to refine the finish of the wood, first go over the surface with a rough abrader—a wood rasp or a wood file.

34. Rifflers in various shapes are used to refine the finishing started with the rasp and file and to reach places not accessible with those tools.

35. If you want the finish to be even smoother, go over the surface of the sculpture with sandpaper of varying grades.

36. The wood can be given a stain, as shown. It can then be given a layer of paste wax for luster and protection.

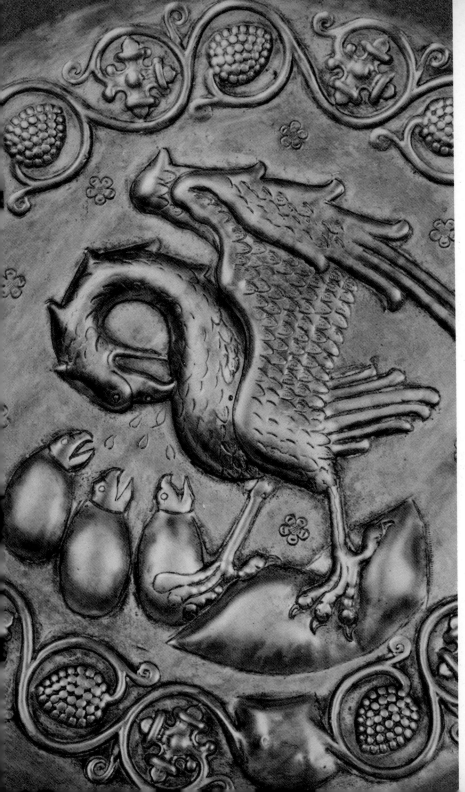

Metalworking

The art of metalcraft

The rise of human culture and civilization is closely related to the development of man's ability to work with metals. Indeed, some of the very stages by which scholars mark the evolution of civilization are named according to the prevalent metal in use at the time: Copper Age, Bronze Age, Iron Age.

Metal, then, has been in use since prehistoric times. Gold and copper were probably the first metals to be discovered, and man could have begun to use them ornamentally at least 12,000 years ago, during the Old Stone Age. Both are found in their pure metallic form, and both are soft enough to be worked with the crudest tools. A gold nugget lying in a streambed could very well have attracted the eye of an early caveman, who might have kept it as a jewel or charm, or even hammered it with a piece of stone, bone, or wood to form a shape. Archeological sites of prehistoric origin have yielded many small copper artifacts, such as pins and fishhooks, that had been twisted to shape, probably from strands of native copper gouged out of exposed cliffside veins. An inch-long copper pendant, hammered into an oval, found in what is now Iraq, is the oldest known manmade metal object. Archeologists have established that it was made about 11,500 years ago.

The first age of metal—the Copper Age—had its beginnings some 8,000 years ago. Around that time man learned to extract metal from ore and to fashion metal implements that made more effective tools than their stone counterparts. By the fourth millenium B.C., or 6,000 years ago, the technique of smelting copper from ore to obtain the pure metal was being practiced throughout the Middle East. Many of the basic processes of working with metal were developed and refined dur-ing this time as well. In fact, most current metalworking techniques are quite old. Methods of beating copper into hollow vessels and of raising copper into the elaborate relief patterns that today are called by the French term *repoussé* were practiced by the artisans of Sumeria nearly 5,000 years ago. The ancient Egyptians, who were inheritors of Sumerian technology, brought the craft of hammering metal to perfection only a short time after the decline of Sumerian civilization. The quality of Egyptian gold and copper fashioned before 1000 B.C. remains in many respects unsurpassed even today.

By the 15th century A.D. artistic hand metalworking had attained a high degree of refinement in Europe. Much of it, of course, reflected methods that had been in use since the classical periods of Greece and Rome, and even earlier. Almost all common modern craft metals were in use, with the notable exception of aluminum. Bronze-workers had more than 4,000 years of experience behind them. Brass had been introduced at least by the time of the Greeks; pewter had appeared during the Middle Ages. Iron, traditionally used only for heavy tools and weapons, was by the 15th century widely used in decorative work, often replacing bronze in large-scale pieces. Most of the metalworking techniques that we know today were then in use, as were methods of enameling, inlaying, chasing, embossing, engraving, and etching.

With the advent of the Industrial Revolution, metalworking became increasingly the province of specialized machines. Today, however, metalcraft is witnessing a revival, combining the sophisticated processes that have come with our advanced technology with many of the time-honored skills that are as old as civilization.

A classic example of the metalworking technique known as *repoussé* is seen in this detail from a 15th-century bronze plate, a product of the Dinant area of Belgium.

Tools and materials

The projects in this chapter all make use of sheet metals, especially copper and brass. Two projects are made of tin-can metal, which is actually thin sheet steel coated with tin. Copper and brass are readily available from crafts stores and are sold according to Brown and Sharp gauge numbers. Higher gauge numbers designate thinner metals. Most craftwork requires metal between 18 and 26 gauge. Thicker metal is difficult to cut with hand shears, while thinner sheets are suitable for decorative work but lack the rigidity needed for most pieces.

Copper. An excellent craft metal, copper is very similar in its properties to silver but much less expensive. It is easily worked into shapes, annealed (softened by heating), planished (hardened by hammering), and joined by soldering. Copper will not rust. Although it will darken, polishing easily restores its warm reddish-gold luster. Copper can be purchased soft, half-hard, or hard. For crafts purposes always specify soft copper.

An important hazard to keep in mind is that a poisonous green oxide—verdigris—forms on copper exposed to acids in the air. Any cooking and eating utensils made of copper must be coated on the inside with a thin layer of pure tin (by a process called tinning) to prevent this oxide from forming.

Brass. Brass is a man-made metal, an alloy of copper and zinc. Brass is harder than copper, and thus more difficult to work, but it is treated in the same way as copper. Like copper, it can be heated to make it softer and hammered to make it harder and more brittle. Soldering brass requires about the same heat as soldering copper, which makes possible attractive projects combining both metals. Brass withstands dampness somewhat better than copper and takes a brighter polish. Like copper, it is sold by gauge

number. The same caution concerning verdigris applies to brass.

Tin. Tin-plated metal, as explained earlier, is difficult to obtain in small quantities suitable for the home craftsman. In fact, empty tin cans may prove to be your best source of this metal. Round cans are usually ribbed for strength, but the square 5-gallon cans available from restaurants and other institutions are not ribbed, and these are easily cut and opened out into smooth, flat sheets.

Old-fashioned tinplate, the kind used by tinsmiths until the early 20th century, was made by dipping sheets of thin wrought iron into a vat of molten tin. The resulting metal was softer than the product made today by electroplating sheet steel. Modern tinplate is easily punched, pierced, and soldered; however, it is not so easily chased (inscribed) or formed into shapes as the old variety. On the other hand, tin-can metal takes and retains a high polish. Its extreme hardness allows sharply defined bends and impressions, which show off such features as crimping (see p. 279) more effectively than old-fashioned tinplate.

Aluminum and pewter. These are also popular craft metals. Both are soft and easy to form, although aluminum is not easily soldered or kept bright.

Pewter is a silver-white alloy containing tin, antimony, and copper. The lead formerly used in pewter is now excluded from the compound, making it safe for tableware. Pewter generally remains soft when hammered. Its melting point is low; soldering is easy, but it must be done with care, using only a small flame.

Special fiber mallets are used to form both aluminum and pewter. Special files made for soft metals are employed for trimming. Both metals are sold at crafts stores by gauge number. Most projects require 14 to 20 gauge.

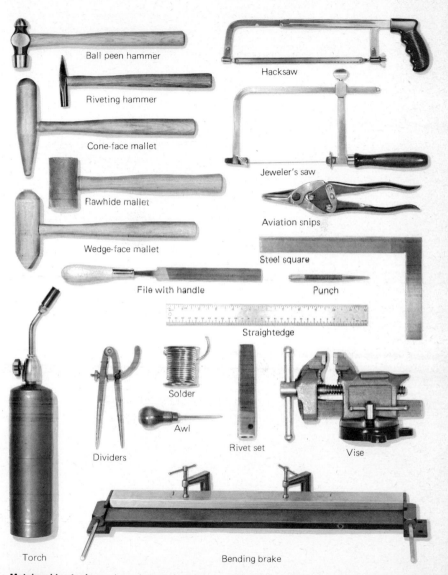

Ball peen hammer

Hacksaw

Riveting hammer

Cone-face mallet

Jeweler's saw

Rawhide mallet

Aviation snips

Wedge-face mallet

Steel square

File with handle

Punch

Straightedge

Solder

Dividers

Awl

Rivet set

Vise

Torch

Bending brake

Metalworking tools are shown here and on page 282. The most specialized, which may not be in hardware stores, can be obtained from crafts and industrial suppliers. The techniques for using tools are illustrated throughout this chapter.

Layout tools include an awl for scribing lines and a punch for centering drill holes. Cutting tools include aviation snips (see p. 278), saws, and files. A jeweler's saw is employed for piercing work and for complicated patterns. Files remove small amounts of metal. Forms, forming stakes, and a bending brake are used together with mallets and hammers for shaping. Wood blocks held with clamps offer an alternative to the brake. Riveting and soldering tools are essential.

Your workshop should have a sturdy workbench and vise. Lighting should be subdued so that glare will not obscure scribe lines.

Metalworking

Basic techniques

Two important rules to remember in metalworking are: go slowly and use the right tool for the job. Always be sure that measurements are correct and clearly scribed before cutting. Snip away excess metal first, then gradually cut closer to the cut line in several passes, removing the last bits of metal with a file if necessary. Bend metal slowly and in stages, using light hammers and light, careful blows.

Using snips. Use snips only for cutting sheet metal; never for wire or tubing. For accuracy align the *tips* of the blades along the direction of the cut and focus your eyes on this point, not farther back where the jaws contact the metal. Avoid cutting all the way to tips of the blades on long cuts, as to do so causes splinters and tiny bends that spoil the smoothness of the edge. When notching corners, keep the tips of the blades just short of the point where the cut will end in order to avoid cutting beyond the line.

The difficulty in cutting metal with snips comes in making long cuts: the metal must make way for the shears as they move through. Position the snips with the narrower side of the cut resting on the bottom blade so that it will curl out of the way as the cut is made. Right-handed and left-handed aviation snips are specially designed to facilitate this action. If the top blade is on your right, the snips are right-handed; if on the left, left-handed. With right-handed snips, the blade position causes the waste metal to curl away to the left; with left-handed snips, the waste metal curls off to the right.

Bending. The line along which metal is bent must be held firmly in place at all times. Clamp the sheet metal between two carefully aligned blocks of wood, or use a bending brake. The brake simultaneously clamps the metal and folds it evenly along the desired line. Blocks, however, permit folding angles impossible on most brakes.

Clamp the entire block assembly—with the scribed lines visible on the metal—to the top of your workbench or between the jaws of a vise. Hammer along the line with a mallet to gradually turn the metal and form the angle.

Hemming. Edges of sheet metal are usually hemmed to strengthen them, to make them smooth, and to provide rigidity to the piece of metal as a whole. A hem is made by folding the edge over

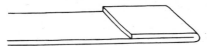

Hem strengthens edge, giving rigidity to metal.

on itself and hammering it flat. After bending the edge to form an angle of 90 degrees or more, disassemble the blocks and clamp a thin strip of metal or an old straightedge along the fold in place of the top bending block. Hammer the edge gradually down to it, then

remove the strip and hammer the folded metal down completely. For additional strength leave the actual edge of the hem unhammered to form a *beaded edge*.

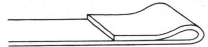

Edge of beaded hem is not hammered.

Wiring an edge. Extra strength can be obtained in hems by curling edges around a piece of wire. After an angle bend is formed in the edge, a length of smooth wire is held against the inside of the fold by clamping a strip of metal or an old metal ruler or straightedge against it. The edge of the metal is beaten down over the wire, then the metal ruler is removed; finally, the hem is curled tightly around the wire with the flat end of a riveter's hammer, as seen in the last illustration on this page (at bottom right).

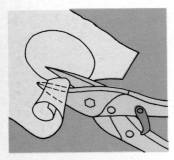

When cutting be sure blades are on waste side of pattern. Never cross scribed lines. Narrow waste piece should rest on bottom blade. Sight along blade tips for accuracy. Wear gloves when cutting difficult patterns. Rest if you become tired.

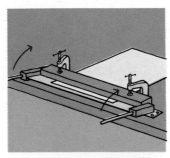

Bending brake will simplify folding. Hinged-angle iron draws metal upward at crease line, folding it along edge of top block. Unlike wood block method, no hammering is required. Beveled top blocks allow reverse angles, some complex folds.

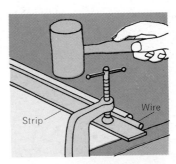

Wire edges for maximum rigidity. **1.** Determine amount of overlap for the curl by testing with scrap, or simply allow slightly less than four times the diameter of the wire. Fold edge, press wire into crease, and clamp strip as in hemming. Make curl as shown below.

Strip

Wire

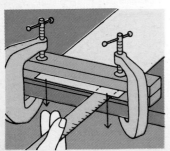

Place metal between blocks for bending. Clamp to bench or between vise jaws. Check bottom block for squareness with rule held beneath metal against block at both ends. Hammer downward with mallet along line to fold metal.

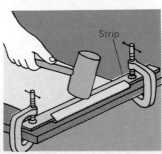

Strip

Make hems 1/4–3/8 in. wide. After forming angle in brake or with blocks, clamp a thin metal strip inside fold; hammer edge down gradually, pulling mallet away from edge on each stroke. Remove strip, hammer hem flat, but leave edge of crease unhammered.

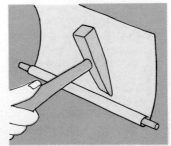

2. Hammer edge down, then remove backing strip from fold. Use riveter's hammer to gently turn edge around wire, curling it underneath. Mask surface with tape to avoid marking it. Cylinders should be wired while metal is flat; allow extra wire for bending.

Shaping with forms

A unique property of metal is that for all its apparent rigidity, it is really a flowing material. It can be spread, stretched, compressed, shrunk, bent, beaten, and twisted into a multitude of shapes without cutting or joining separate pieces. Shaping metal requires knowledge of the metal itself—how much it will stretch, how long it can be hammered before becoming work-hardened, and how it can be resoftened so that the work can continue. The techniques involved can be perfected only with practice; basic procedures are shown below, however, and in the instructions accompanying the projects that come later in the chapter.

Annealing copper and brass. Repeated hammering hardens most metals. When metals harden, stretching stops; cracks may develop in the metal if the hammering is continued. When copper and brass become work-hardened in this way, they must be *annealed*. Place the metal in an anneal-ing tray (see *Jewelry,* p. 331) or on an asbestos pad and heat the metal with a propane torch until the metal glows dull red. Remove the flame and let the metal cool. The fire scale that forms on the piece can be dissolved by immersing the metal in pickling solution (pp. 330–331). The annealed metal is now soft and clean and hammering can be resumed. Repeat the process whenever work-hardening occurs.

Molds. These are hollow forms into which metal is beaten. Two easily constructed molds for making shallow bowls are shown in use below. The first can be turned on a lathe, or it can be made by cutting a circular hole with a keyhole saw in one piece of wood and gluing it down on a second, solid piece. The second mold is a block of wood cut away on one side to the depth of the bowl; a pair of nails or screws are located in from the edge a distance equal to the width of the lip of the bowl, as shown below.

Stakes. Metal forms for shaping are called stakes. They can be purchased at crafts stores specializing in supplies for

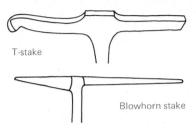

T-stake

Blowhorn stake

T-stake and blowhorn stake are used in shaping.

silversmiths. Most beginning craftsmen start their collections by accumulating a variety of common wooden and metal forms—angle iron, an old rolling pin, hollowed or fluted wood blocks—and a number of mallets and hammers with which to shape metal over the forms. Cylinders and scrolls are made by curling metal around a length of pipe held in a vise. Flat pieces can be crimped with long-nose pliers.

Filing

Files are used to remove burrs, to smooth edges, and to remove small amounts of metal. *Single-cut* files have a single set of teeth cut at an angle across the blade. *Double-cut* files have two sets of crisscrossing teeth.

Double-cut files remove metal quickly; they are used for rough cutting. Special files—sometimes called dreadnoughts—with a single set of teeth arranged in semicircular rows across the blade are used for filing very soft metals such as pewter. Copper and brass are best filed with coarse-grade new tools that have not been used on steel. Prevent them from clogging by cleaning them with a file card. Chalk applied to the file helps keep metal bits from sticking.

Clamp the piece to be filed flat on the

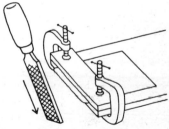

Clamp metal for filing; file cuts downward.

bench top, with the edge of the metal protruding beyond the bench's edge. Hold the file with one or both hands and push it downward and along the metal at a steep angle. Remember that files cut only on the downstroke.

Draw filing. To finish an edge, sometimes metal is held vertically and draw-filed. Here the file is held flat across the edge, parallel to the floor, with both hands. With the front end of the file tipped slightly down toward the floor, push the file down along the length of the edge with no side-to-side filing motion. Draw filing yields a neat edge, though smoothing with steel wool or emery paper is recommended.

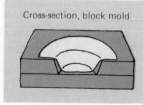

Cross-section, block mold

To form shallow bowl in block mold, position metal disk over cutout. Define perimeter of bowl with mallet blows widely spaced along rim. Stretch metal down and into sides of mold. Deepen bowl by hammering in spiral pattern outward from center.

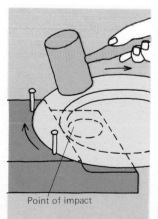

Point of impact

Sinking method calls for steady hammering only at the single point of impact, as shown above. Position metal disk against nails or screws located in cutaway block at distance equal to width of bowl lip. Rotate disk as hollow forms inside lip. Flatten lip if folding occurs.

Scrollwork

Length of pipe secured in vise jaws is handy stake for shaping scrolls and cylinders. Metal is held flat across pipe. Let hammer blows fall vertically, just to one side of center line. Twist thin metal by hand around stake. Work gradually to avoid wrinkles.

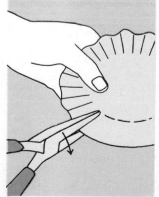

Crimping raises rim of disk into the shape of a bowl. Slide edge of metal between jaws of long-nose pliers, inserting to same depth each time. Point jaws toward center; keep ridges nearly parallel. Squeeze jaws and twist pliers a quarter turn. Rotate the disk and repeat.

Metalworking

Joining metal

Seams can be used to join metal, either by themselves or in combination with solder. Seams that are secure by themselves are called mechanical seams.

Lock seam. The simplest mechanical seam is the lock seam, shown at right. Two pieces of metal are hemmed (see p. 278); the edge of one piece is folded upward, and the other piece is folded down. These "hooks" are overlapped and hammered flat with a mallet. The seam can be made flush by hammering on a block of wood as illustrated at right. Use the lock seam to joint metal edge-to-edge or to form the corners of rectangular boxes and containers.

Soldering. A joining process by itself, soldering can also be used to strengthen and waterproof mechanical seams. Sheet metal is usually soft soldered with low heat, using solder with a low melting point made of tin and lead. Very heavy work is brazed, using much higher heat and molten brass. Only soldering is used in this book's projects.

Either a soldering iron or a propane torch can be used as a heat source. The torch is recommended, as it is difficult to keep the metal at a high temperature with an iron. In either case the metal in the areas to be joined is first thoroughly cleaned, then coated with flux (see illustrations below and *Jewelry*, pp. 330–331). After this the metal is heated and the solder is applied.

Rivets. Rivets provide maximum strength for joints. Their use is generally reserved for heavier work or for decorative effects. A rivet set is used to draw the metal tightly around the rivet and to form the finished head, as illustrated below. Where the head will not show, the flat end of the riveter's hammer is used simply to spread the rivet end over the surface of the metal.

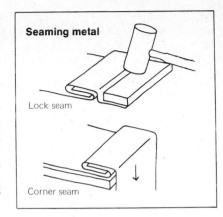

Seaming metal

Lock seam

Corner seam

Soldering metal

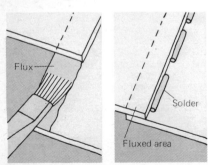

Flux

Solder

Fluxed area

To soft solder, clean metal and apply flux to areas to be joined. Use acid flux for sheet metal. Clamp pieces in soldering position. Lay pieces of solder along fluxed joint.

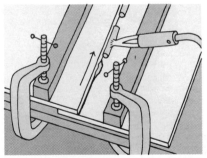

Heat entire area with torch until flux bubbles. Then focus flame on solder, drawing torch along seam as solder melts and flows into joint. Wash excess flux off joint with detergent.

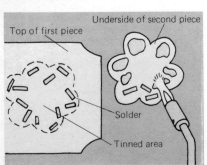

Top of first piece

Underside of second piece

Solder

Tinned area

To sweat-solder, first "tin" areas to be joined: clean and flux metal; heat each piece over torch flame; apply solder and spread evenly over surface. Clean again and reflux.

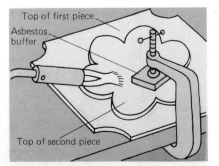

Top of first piece

Asbestos buffer

Top of second piece

Clamp tinned pieces together. Reheat joint area until thin line of shiny solder is visible along seam. Allow to cool. Wash finished joint thoroughly with detergent to prevent corrosion.

Riveting metal

Rivets come in several shapes: flathead, countersunk, and roundhead. All must rest on sturdy metal surface plates when being hammered. To make surface plate for roundhead rivets, drill a small depression to fit the head of the rivet in a piece of steel or an angle iron; this will hold head while other end of rivet is being shaped. You will also need a rivet set and a riveter's or ball peen hammer.

The length of the rivet is important. Its shank should protrude through the metal being joined by a length 1 to 1½ times the diameter of the shank; this will provide enough material for shaping the end.

Insert the rivet through holes drilled in the pieces to be joined. These holes should be just large enough to allow a snug fit. Place the long shaft of the rivet set over the shank (A) and hammer it once or twice firmly to draw the pieces tightly together.

Remove the rivet set. With round face of hammer carefully mushroom the end of the rivet by tapping in a circle (B) around top edges of shank. Hammer only enough to form a full head, slightly higher than the hollow of the rivet set.

Place hollow depression of the rivet set over newly formed head and strike set with one or two sharp blows (C). Too much hammering crushes the metal between the rivet heads, weakening the riveted joint.

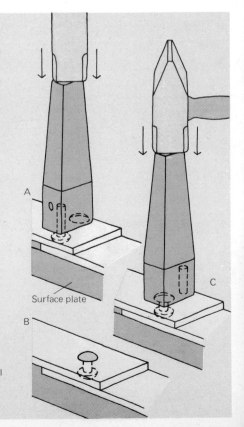

A

Surface plate

B

C

Laying out the design

"Measure twice, cut once" is a craftsman's motto that is especially germane to metalworking. Mistakes in cutting are difficult to hide; carelessly scribed lines cannot be erased. Always plan your projects thoroughly, and scribe measurements accurately onto the metal before any shaping is begun. Test your designs by making paper models of them before creating them in metal. In cases where pieces must be cut and fitted together, templates made of heavy paper—the pieces of your preliminary model—are invaluable as patterns, contributing to a smooth, craftsmanlike job.

Layout techniques. Start your layout in the lower left corner of the metal. Use a steel square to check edges for squareness before you begin. If the sheet is not square, scribe your own base and side lines with an awl, scribing along the inside edges of the square to form a large right angle. Make all subsequent measurements from these lines, not from the edges of the metal.

When laying out lines, measure and mark both end points, then connect them. Distinguish lines for bending as opposed to cutting by pricking bending lines with the point of the awl along their length and scribing cutting lines with an unbroken line.

Using a rule. Always use a quality metal rule for layout work; never use a wooden ruler. Accurate measurements are made by holding the rule on its edge, with the markings facing you and

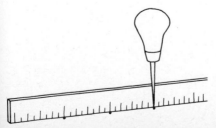

Hold rule on edge for accurate markings.

the lines of measurement actually touching the metal.

Scribing. Mark the beginning and end points of the line with the awl while holding the rule on edge. Then lay the rule flat as close to the marked points as possible without obscuring them. Press the rule down firmly to prevent shifting. Scribe a line between the two points with the awl, drawing it along the bottom edge of the rule. Be careful not to let the awl wander. Do not scribe beyond the marked points.

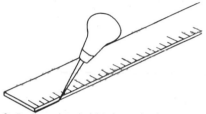

Scribe line using straightedge and awl.

Wing dividers. These are used to scribe circles. Use a sharp pair, with legs that can be tightened in position. Mark the center of the circle first with the awl, then dimple the spot with a center punch lightly struck with a hammer. This depression will keep the dividers from slipping. On plates, bowls, etc., make this mark on the outside surface, on what will be the underside of the object. It is traditional among silversmiths that the center

Dimple center point when scribing with dividers.

point be left visible on a finished piece of handcrafted hollowware.

Carbon paper. Many designs do not

lend themselves to layout with a rule or dividers. Carbon paper is often used to transfer designs directly onto the metal. With fine emery paper or steel wool, thoroughly scrub the metal, then wash it clean with soap or cleanser. Water should not bead on the clean surface. Paint the metal with opaque white watercolor (poster paint). When the paint is dry, place the carbon paper, carbon side down, on the white surface. Place the design to be transferred on top. Secure both sheets to the metal with tape. Trace the design with a hard pencil or pen. Remove the carbon paper and the design sheet. With an awl, trace the pattern left by the carbon paper, scribing the design through the paint into the metal. Wash the paint off the scribed metal.

Templates. Designs can also be drawn on templates made of heavy paper such as oaktag. A design found in a magazine, for instance, can be traced from the page and transferred to the template paper using carbon paper. Trace over the carbon lines with a pencil or pen to make sure they are sharply delineated.

Another way to transfer the traced design to the template paper is to rub the back of the tracing paper with soft pencil lead, then place the design face up on the template paper and trace over the design. The soft lead leaves a carbonlike impression of the design on the template paper.

Traced designs can be enlarged or reduced by redrawing them on graph paper before transferring them to the template paper (see *Drawing*, p. 212).

The finished template is then cut out. It can be pressed against the metal and its outline scribed with an awl, or, after cleaning the metal, it can be glued directly to the surface with rubber cement. The metal is then cut using only the template as a guide. Templates that are not glued can be reused.

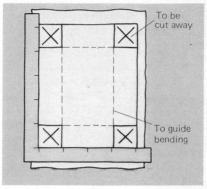

Square lower left corner to begin layout. Scribe lines for cutting; prick those for bending.

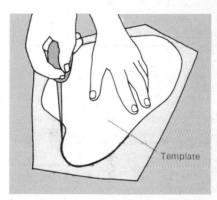

Scribe outline of template with awl, or glue template to metal with rubber cement, then cut.

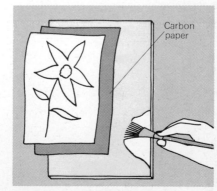

To transfer a design using carbon paper, first paint metal with white poster paint.

Metalworking

Decorating metal

Designs and textures can be added to metals in a variety of ways.

Planishing. Often, smooth pieces of metal are decorated simply by hammering. This process, called planishing, ripples the surface with overlapping rows of hammer spots, hardening the piece as well as producing an evenly faceted texture. A *planishing hammer* (pictured below) is used. It has slightly curved faces of very hard steel, polished smooth to prevent marring the metal as it strikes.

With the metal resting on a steel surface plate, light blows produce small planish marks. Stronger blows and softer plates of lead, hardwood, or leather result in greater stretching of the metal and produce larger spots. Beginners should planish with the round end of a ball peen hammer because with this tool there is less chance of accidentally scarring the work with a glancing blow. Polish the hammer face with fine emery paper, and use it only for planishing, not striking tools.

Crafts stores carry both types of hammers. They can also be found in hardware stores. Choose a 6-ounce size of either type for general work.

Chasing and embossing. Chasing is the technique used to indent a design into the top surface of the metal. The design is worked into the metal by tracing the outline with chisellike

Chasing tool indents design in top surface.

chasing tools struck lightly with a chasing hammer. Tools and hammer are shown below. Chasing tools have dulled edges to avoid actually piercing the metal. They are ground to a variety of shapes and patterns, which can be used to highlight a basic design or to stamp texture into the background.

Embossing is similar to chasing, except that the design is worked into the metal from the back; features are

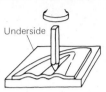

Embossing raises relief on top surface.

raised in relief on the front. Embossing tools are much the same as chasing tools—many are interchangeable—but are even more blunt and rounded.

When chasing and embossing are combined, the effect is called *repoussé.* By repeatedly embossing the design in relief from the back and by further defining it with chasing tools on the front, extremely intricate and beautiful work can be created. Expert repoussé done in high relief resembles sculpture.

Technique. Hold chasing and embossing tools almost vertically, as shown below. Hold the hammer with the end of the handle fitted into the palm of your hand. Extend your index finger along the top of the hammer shaft. Tap lightly with regular blows delivered from the wrist. Fix your attention on the cutting edge of the tool, not on the point of hammer contact.

Chase the outline first, anneal the work if necessary, then place the work face down for embossing. You should repeat these procedures until the design is well defined and raised in sharp relief. Flat pieces can be worked on wood, leather, or lead surface plates. Drive nails around the edges of the piece to hold it firmly. A *pitch bowl* (pictured below) holds hollowware. The pitch is softened by heat, then the work is pressed into it. As the pitch cools, it supports the work firmly. The circular base of the bowl permits it and the work to be tilted in any direction.

Chasing hammer

Planishing hammer

Chasing and embossing tools

Cold chisel

Surface plate (steel)

Pitch bowl

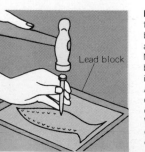

Planishing hardens metal, giving it a faceted texture. Hold hammer as shown. Deliver blows from elbow, not wrist. Strike metal squarely with uniform pressure, overlapping the areas of impact.

Lead block

Improvised tools like this blunted nail can be used for chasing and embossing. Notched screwdriver blades also create interesting patterns. A ball peen hammer can substitute for a chasing hammer. Wood, leather, or lead can be used in place of pitch bowl.

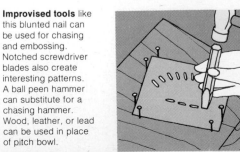

Pitch bowl

Embossing and chasing are done on pitch bowl. Hold tool between thumb, and index and middle fingers. Rest bottom finger on work. Guide tool toward you with steady blows of hammer. Shift position of work when necessary.

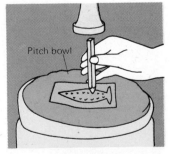

Piercing. Thin metal is often pierced to create distinctive designs through which light can pass, as in a metal lampshade. Place work on wood surface. Use sharp nails or cold chisels as piercing tools; strike tool with the flat end of ball peen hammer.

Etching

Etching is a way of creating designs on metal by using acid to eat away unprotected portions of the surface. If the protected portion of the metal forms the design, the process is called *relief etching*. If the design itself is etched into the metal, the work is termed *intaglio etching*.

Materials. Etching supplies, including acids, are available from crafts stores. A safe acid to use on copper and brass, the most commonly etched craft metals, is ferric chloride. It can be purchased in lump form to be dissolved in water or as liquid ready to use. It is often called *copper etching mordant*. Ferric chloride is slow acting, often requiring 8 hours for a deep etch. It is not dangerous to use if the precautions listed on the package are followed.

Asphaltum varnish is used as a *resist* to the acid. It is a tarlike substance thinned with turpentine. Apply it thickly with a brush to metal that has been cleaned with detergent. Be sure that all parts of the metal to be protected with asphaltum are thoroughly coated, including the back and the edges of the piece. Reddish areas of metal showing through the asphaltum indicate that the coat is too thin. Asphaltum requires 6 to 10 hours to dry.

A Pyrex glass container serves as an etching bin to hold the acid. Use a loose net of ordinary string to immerse the object and to raise it for inspection. A feather or a cloth-wrapped stick is used to brush away bubbles and sediment from the design as it etches.

Preparation. To prepare for simple intaglio etching, cover the metal completely with resist, then scribe the design into it with any sharp tool, such as an awl. For complex work cut a stiff paper template of the design and glue it to the bare metal with rubber cement. Apply asphaltum to the remaining areas. Remove the template by slicing around the edge with a crafts knife or razor blade after the asphaltum is dry.

Peel the template off, then remove the rubber cement by rubbing it away with a soft cloth.

Prepare for relief etching by first painting the entire back of the piece with asphaltum. When it is nearly dry, lay the piece face up on a sheet of blank newsprint. Paint the parts of the design to be protected from the etching acid with asphaltum. Remember that if you paint around a template to create the design, it is the metal underneath the template that will be etched by the acid. Finally, paint a border of asphaltum around the piece, overlapping the brush onto the newsprint to seal the edges of the metal completely. When dry, trim the newsprint to within 1/2 inch of the metal's edge.

Etching. Fill the tray with enough water to cover the design plus 1/2 inch. Add acid to the water in a 1:3 proportion. Stir the solution gently to dislodge bubbles. As the piece etches, brush it frequently with the feather or stick to remove sediment. Objects may be etched upside down to allow sediment to fall away naturally. Rest a resist-covered portion of the metal on a small

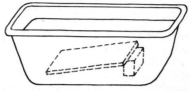

Metal etched upside down rests on support.

support block to raise it off the bottom of the etching tray.

Inspect after an hour, then every half hour, by rinsing the piece in running water. Retouch the asphaltum if necessary. Etching is finished when one-third of the thickness of the metal has been removed. Multilevel etching is done by interrupting the process of the work, adding asphaltum to partially etched areas, then replacing the piece in the acid.

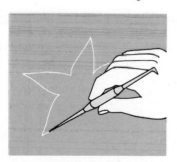

Intaglio etching is scribed in asphaltum covering the metal. Use any sharp tool. Before etching, inspect metal for accidental scratches. Retouch surface with asphaltum if necessary.

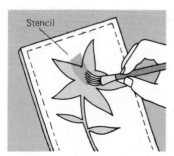

Stencil

Relief-etched design will stand out above level of etched background. Paint the raised areas of the design with asphaltum, as shown. Borders are also painted to prevent pitting of edges.

Bowls serve as their own etching containers. Paint design inside and fill with acid. Clean away sediment from design every half hour with a feather. If bowl is very shallow, build up its walls with modeling clay or paraffin wax.

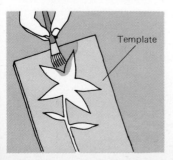

Template

Template can be used to mask large areas when applying the asphaltum. Stencils offer accuracy in painting difficult patterns. Cut template to design shape for intaglio etching and to background shape for relief etching (see text); cement to metal.

Lower work into acid bath using a homemade string net. Here piece rests at one end on a support of wax or clay (see text). After an hour remove piece, rinse, and check. Replace with opposite end on support to ensure even etching.

Remove asphaltum with turpentine and steel wool. Acid can be reused. Add fresh acid to strengthen an old solution. To dispose of acid, neutralize with baking soda in wide-mouthed jar. When bubbling stops, discard.

Metalworking/project

Copper tea tray

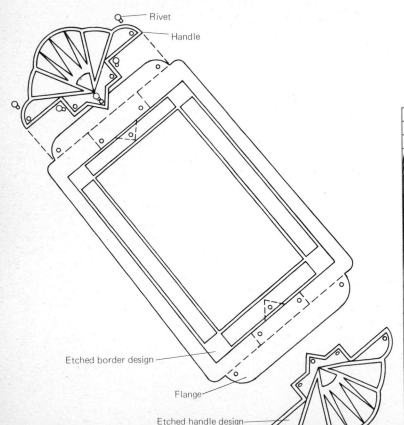

Rivet

Handle

Etched border design

Flange

Etched handle design

All of the pieces for this large tea tray can be cut from a single square sheet of heavy, soft copper. The handles are etched and decorated with chasing tools as described on page 282. Rivets (p. 280) anchor the handles securely and decoratively to the raised sides, as shown in the exploded view at left. Read page 283 to learn more about etching, then study the etching sequence on page 289 before beginning the project.

This particular tray has a simple design etched into the bottom where the sides are raised from the base. You can alter the design in any way you choose—for example, by adding a central monogram or a more elaborate border. Stippling the background areas of the handles after they are etched enhances their appearance. Stippling also covers minor surface irregularities left by the etching process. The ham-mered handles require annealing (p. 279) before they can be formed to fit the tray's inside dimensions.

The tray is folded on bending blocks cut to the dimensions given in the list of materials below. The blocks are cut 2 inches shorter than the distance between the outside etching lines, which mark where the sides of the tray are folded up. Support the tray on wide blocks, raising it high enough off the work surface to allow the sides to bend all the way down as they are hammered. Bend the metal in gradual stages, using overlapping mallet strokes. Do not hammer beyond the ends of the bending blocks. The corners will form automatically as you fold first the sides and then the ends.

Do not try to raise the corners to the same height as the sides. This would require shrinking the metal by working it into the adjacent sides and ends.

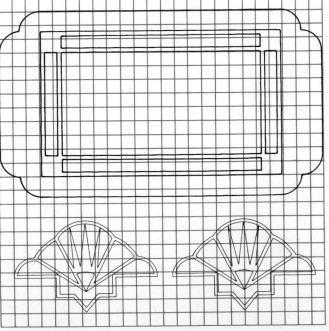

A tea tray measuring about 29 in. handle to handle and 13 in. in width can be made from a single 24- by 24-in. sheet of soft, 18-gauge copper. Bending and hammering may result in slight variations in dimensions of the finished tray. Cardboard templates are made by enlarging patterns (left) within a grid of 1-in. squares as described in *Drawing*, p. 212. These templates are used to scribe outlines onto the metal. A second set of templates, used to facilitate the etching process, is cut from stiff paper; these templates are rubber cemented to the metal, as shown in Steps 4 and 8 on the opposite page. They are then trimmed with razor blade to serve as stencils for application of asphaltum, which resists etching fluid, creating the relief.

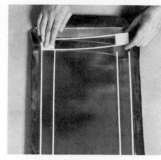

1. Using cardboard templates made by enlarging patterns in grid (opposite), scribe outline of tray and then of etching design onto metal. Cut out tray with snips; file edges.

2. To form sides, clamp metal between blocks (p. 278). Center blocks so that they fall 1 in. short of corner lines at each end. Support tray and hammer sides to 50° angles.

3. Hammer ends of tray to 50° angles, as in Step 2. Corners form automatically. Brace ends against wood block or table and fold flanges to 90° angles as shown at right.

4. Glue paper templates to scribed areas inside tray with rubber cement. Inspect to make certain bond is tight. Remove any excess rubber cement by rubbing area with fingertips.

5. Paint entire tray with asphaltum. When dry, lift template edges with a razor blade and peel off (right). Rub off cement to expose metal. Clean up asphaltum edges with turpentine.

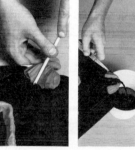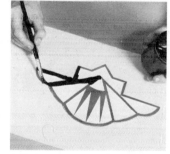

6. Build up corners with plasticine. Mold inner plasticine fence to form channel for etching fluid. Pour fluid to depth of 1/2 in. Stir often with feather to clear design of sediment.

7. When etching is complete, form corner spout in plasticine and pour off fluid. Then remove plasticine. Clean off asphaltum with turpentine. Wash tray; polish with steel wool.

8. Cut out both handles. Paint their backs with asphaltum. Glue templates to faces. With razor, cut along all lines; remove strips, leaving sections in place. Rub off extra glue.

9. Paint all exposed strips and triangles with asphaltum. Seal edges with asphaltum, as described on page 289, to prevent pitting. Inspect work; retouch if necessary.

10. When asphaltum is completely dry, remove remaining template sections as explained in Step 5. Clean ragged edges by scraping or by using fine brush dipped in turpentine.

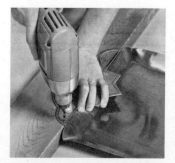

11. Etch handles in glass tray filled with fluid to depth of at least 1/2 in. Inspect often; wipe away sediment. Remove handles when one-third of their thickness is etched away.

12. Clean metal with turpentine; polish with steel wool. Stipple background using chasing tool (see p. 282). When finished, anneal and pickle (p. 279). Repolish handles.

13. Mark rivet locations in handle corners with center punch. Drill holes. Using handle as template, mark and drill rivet holes through flanges on ends of tray, as shown.

14. Rivet handles to flanges using method described on page 280. Use roundheaded rivets if possible. Rivet set shown here is not necessary if you prefer a hand-formed effect.

15. Brace handle against block or table end. Use rawhide mallet to shape inner section to tray contour. When fit is flush, rivet remaining corners. Repeat for other handle.

Metalworking/project

Hanging ivy planter

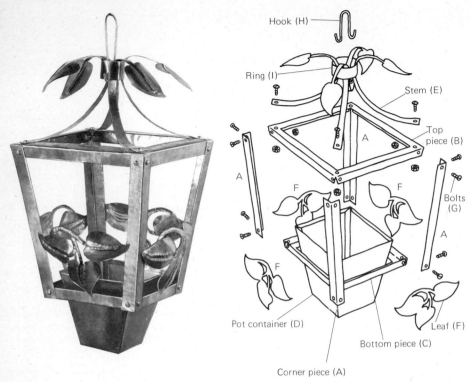

Hook (H)

Ring (I)

Stem (E)

Top piece (B)

A

A

F

F

Bolts (G)

A

F

Pot container (D)

Bottom piece (C)

Leaf (F)

Corner piece (A)

This planter is made of copper and brass, metals that complement each other nicely. Accurate cutting and folding are the keys to success here. Begin by making full-size templates by enlarging the patterns below within a grid of 1-inch squares (see *Drawing,* p. 212). Use a protractor to obtain correct angles. Cut the pieces out of sheet metal, flatten them with a mallet, and planish them lightly (p. 282) before drilling or bending. This minimizes distortion, preventing misalignment of holes. Solder the retaining ring from leftover 20-gauge brass. Bend the hook in a vise. This design can be adapted to a lantern simply by adding glass panels to the sides and using a flat base with a candleholder soldered to its center.

Four corner pieces (A) are cut from single 12- by 12-in. sheet of 24-gauge copper. Top piece (B) and bottom piece (C) are also 24-gauge copper. Pot container (D) and leaves (F) are 24-gauge brass. Stems (E) are 20-gauge brass. You will need 20 brass machine screws to use as bolts (G) and about 10 in. of 1/8-in.-diameter brass rod for the hook (H). Ring (I) is made from leftover 20-gauge brass.

1. Scribe corner pieces on 24-gauge copper using template made by enlarging pattern on this page (see text). Cut piece, flatten with mallet.

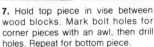

7. Hold top piece in vise between wood blocks. Mark bolt holes for corner pieces with an awl, then drill holes. Repeat for bottom piece.

13. Solder (p. 280) leaves to corner pieces of planter. Take special care with torch to avoid unsoldering leaves that have already been attached.

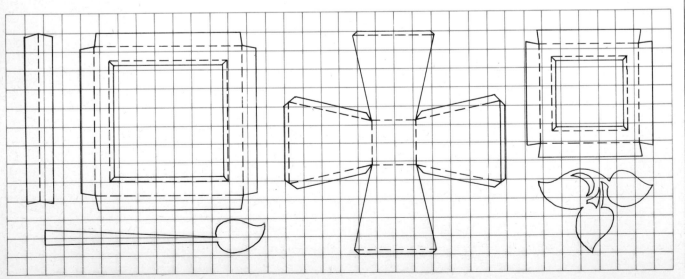

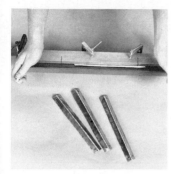

2. Drill bolt holes at ends, each 3/8-in. from corner edges. Then bend each piece along center line at right angle, as shown here.

3. Use template to scribe bottom piece on 24-gauge copper, then lay corner template flush on scribed line to lay out miters. Scribe top piece.

4. Cut top and bottom pieces with shears. Remove inner sections by saw piercing with a jeweler's saw as described in *Jewelry*, p. 329.

5. Smooth inside edges with file. Hem or bead each edge by hammering metal with mallet over bending blocks and straightedge (p. 278).

6. Fold sides of top *down*, sides of bottom *up*, until corner notches close. Metal is clamped between two wood blocks; top block is visible here.

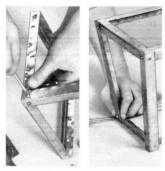

8. Assemble top, bottom, and corners with brass screws. File ends of corner pieces flush with top and bottom, taking care not to mar metal.

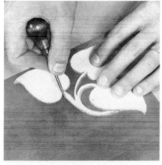

9. Scribe leaf patterns on 24-gauge brass, using template. Cut metal with shears; pierce inner sections with jeweler's saw. File edges smooth.

10. Chase vein pattern on leaves (p. 282). Use sharp tool to outline, blunt tool to depress metal. Work on block of lead or softwood.

11. Turn leaves over and emboss additional contours from beneath. Allow metal to curl. Light planishing (p. 282) gives leaves final texture.

12. Scribe stems on 20-gauge brass. Repoussé (p. 282), then drill bolt holes (see exploded view, opposite). Planish underside to curl metal.

14. Scribe pot container pattern on 24-gauge brass; cut. Hem edges; fold appropriate corner flaps (see exploded view) to right angles.

15. Flux and tin unfolded edges of container piece; hold fluxed edge over flame of torch as shown and draw solder along it. Polish; reflux.

16. Fold sides of pot container into position over wooden stake held in vise: stake width must equal the width of the container bottom.

17. Clamp tinned corners of pot container (see Step 15) against scrap iron as shown. Sweat-solder, adding additional solder to fill seam.

18. Assemble planter: insert container; thread stems through brass ring, then bolt to top as shown; pass hook through ring from below.

Metalworking/project

Candle sconce

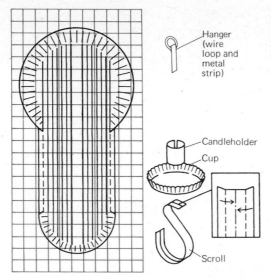

Hanger (wire loop and metal strip)

Candleholder

Cup

Scroll

This candle sconce, made entirely of tin-can metal, is a traditional piece styled after the designs of early American tinware. The reflector back protects the wall from the candle flame as well as increasing the available light.

The template pattern in the grid at left can be enlarged to any size by following the directions in *Drawing*, p. 212. The sconce can be made about four times the size of the pattern at left, using the metal from a 48-ounce juice can. Most cans of this size have ribbing worked into them by the manufacturer for strength. This ribbing becomes part of the finished design; it also serves as an easy guide for making layout measurements directly on the metal.

One end of the can is used to make the candle cup, and a piece of metal left over after cutting the pattern can be used to make the candleholder. An extra strip of tin, 8 by 1¾ inches, is required for the S-shaped scroll, and a 1-inch length of thin wire is needed for the small loop that is soldered to the back of the sconce for hanging. Tools needed are snips, a rawhide or wooden mallet, long-nose pliers, soldering torch, solder, and acid flux. You will also need an awl for scribing the pattern on the metal and a small ball peen or riveter's hammer for hemming and folding seams on several pieces.

To make the bright tin less shiny, oxidize the metal by heating it with the torch before any soldering is done. Final burnishing with steel wool then produces a metal with a warm gray luster resembling antique pewter.

1. After removing ends with can opener, use snips to open can and remove seam. Also remove rims. Handle carefully to avoid cuts.

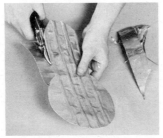

2. Gently flatten metal with rawhide mallet, then scribe template of sconce on the metal with an awl. Cut metal with snips. File edges smooth.

3. Hem each side by turning edge to right angle with bending blocks, then hammering it over straightedge (see p. 278). Finally, hammer hem flat.

4. Crimp evenly with long-nose pliers all around rim of reflector and base. Aim pliers toward center and twist each crimp one-quarter turn.

5. Hem edges of strips (p. 278) for scroll and candleholder. Scroll is so narrow that hems meet to form strip of double thickness.

6. Use can end for candle cup that contains candleholder (see Step 8). Trim it neatly all around with shears, then crimp as in Step 4.

7. Form scroll and candleholder by bending metal around tool handle. Press metal tightly against wood, working carefully to avoid wrinkling.

8. Solder candleholder to cup. Be sure metal is clean and fluxed. Lay solder around joint. Apply heat gradually to avoid discoloring metal.

9. Turn candle cup over. Solder scroll to underside. Take care to avoid unsoldering candleholder on other side. Wash all joints free of flux.

10. Solder scroll to sconce. Solder cup edge to reflector for added strength. Solder hanger to back of sconce. Wash joints; polish.

Metalworking/project

Copper bowl

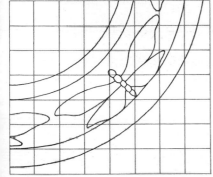

Rim design

This shallow copper bowl is an excellent beginner's project. Any design can be etched around the rim; a name or a personalized inscription would make it a special and thoughtful gift. Only two tools are needed to form the bowl itself: a block mold (see p. 279) and a rawhide mallet. Copper disks of various sizes and gauges (20–24 gauge is best) can be purchased at crafts stores. To decorate the rim, you will need basic layout tools (p. 281) and etching materials (p. 283). Enlarge the design above to the size of your disk as explained in *Drawing*, p. 212, and transfer the pattern onto the disk as shown in the step-by-step illustrations.

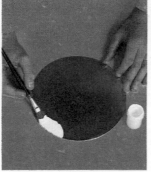

1. Clean disk with detergent; cover one face with white poster paint as a tracing background.

2. Place pattern over carbon paper on painted surface. Trace design firmly to obtain clear impression.

3. Remove carbon paper and pattern. Carefully scribe transferred design into metal with sharp awl.

4. Wash metal free of paint. Place disk facedown on blank newsprint; cover entire back with asphaltum.

5. Before drying is complete, place metal faceup on fresh newsprint. Paint relief design with asphaltum.

6. Seal edge by overlapping brush onto paper while painting rim. Dry overnight. Trim excess paper.

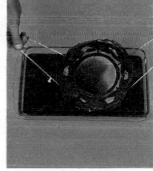

7. Suspend disk in looped string to immerse it in etching bath. Inspect often, wiping away sediment.

8. When one-third of metal is etched away, remove disk. Rinse. Scrub with turpentine.

9. Give etched background a stippled texture. Use matting tool or homemade punch on a hard plate.

10. Align disk on mold. Mold is made of two laminated wood blocks as described on page 279.

11. Seat bowl with firm blows around perimeter. Then hammer in spiral from center outward.

12. Turn bowl over to flatten rim. Before hammering deeper, anneal metal (p. 331) to avoid cracking.

Peperomia, jade, spider, and ivy are all part of this windowsill community, viewed here from above.

Living with houseplants

Living with plants can be an enriching experience even for the novice gardener. A gloriously red amaryllis set against drifting snowflakes outside the window, the sensuous fragrance of jasmine blossoms in a spring evening, or the feel of the gnarled trunk of a bonsai juniper 10 inches tall and 90 years old offer elusive but endless pleasures in our increasingly technological mode of modern living.

Although gardens and potted plants have been kept for millenia, the practice of growing plants inside the house during all seasons has its origins in relatively recent history. European interest in indoor gardening arose about the time of Columbus, when explorers and ship captains brought home plants from far-flung quarters of the globe. By the 17th century many tropical and subtropical plants were being imported into Europe, where greenhouses and conservatories were built to provide artificial environments for the growth of these plants.

In Victorian England the use of sheet glass in conservatories, improved heating, and the Wardian case (the forerunner of today's terrarium, devised by London surgeon Nathaniel B. Ward) all contributed to the success of contemporary indoor gardens.

Many of today's houseplants were developed from specimens brought back from other lands in the 19th century: bougainvilleas, fuchsias, and philodendrons from tropical America; spider plants, African violets, black-eyed Susans, and gladioluses from Africa; hydrangeas, chrysanthemums, and (rather belatedly) the art of bonsai from Japan; gardenias, lilies, azaleas, and bamboos from China.

The great plant hunt in the 19th century was part scientific pursuit, part big business. The horticultural scouts were mainly English and French. They included botanists, gardeners, missionaries, traders, diplomats, and sea captains. In spite of pirates, shipwrecks, and other assorted perils, the expeditions were almost always productive and at times were very colorful. A Scottish gardener, sometimes in Chinese clothes and pigtail, spent 19 years searching for tea plants, blue peonies, and yellow camellias in China and for chrysanthemums in Japan. An English collector roamed the Far East early in the 20th century, traveling in sedan chairs and houseboats, always accompanied by his dog, his bed, and an enormous box camera.

One of the greatest horticultural coups is credited to a 17th-century French Jesuit missionary. He presented two mimosa plants, native to the West Indies, to the emperor of China. The emperor was so intrigued by the bashful mimosas, whose leaves shrink when touched, that he threw open the gates of the imperial gardens to the plant-collecting priest.

European botanists and nurserymen improved many of these exotic species through selection and crossbreeding, creating new hybrid specimens. As a result, today's houseplants need much less pampering than their ancestors did a century or so ago.

The artificial environment. As the house is not a natural habitat for vegetation, any plant you bring home must adapt to a man-made environment. This is where you, the indoor gardener, can help your plants in their adjustments. Besides soil, or potting mix, water, and nutrients (see pp. 292–293), houseplants need warmth, moisture, and, above all, light. Requirements for these essentials may vary (see pp. 304–

Indoor gardening

307), but basically they are similar for most houseplants and are almost identical for species within the same genus.

Plants need light to produce their own food by the process of photosynthesis, to grow, and to bloom. But a house—even a greenhouse—never has as much light as the outdoors. In addition, the intensity of light varies within a house. Window exposure also decisively affects light conditions: a south window has greatly varying light, usually bright and at times hot; an east window gives strong morning sun but no scorching rays; a west window means warmer, brighter evenings, thus prolonging the day for plants; a north window yields a steady, gentle light.

Some plants are tolerant of shade and cannot withstand direct light. Others thrive in strong light. The listing on pages 304–307 details the lighting conditions required by a variety of common and exotic houseplants.

The duration of daylight signals the blooming time for many plants. Thus we have "long-day" plants such as fuchsias, and "short-day" plants such as chrysanthemums. Most plants are "day neutral," showing no definite response to the length of day. It is possible to control the growth and flowering

cycle of some plants by altering the length of the "day" through the use of window drapes and/or artificial light.

In indoor gardening artificial light can substitute for sunlight. Plants need the blue rays in sunlight for foliage growth and the red rays for flowering. Incandescent light has little blue, so it should be used only as a supplementary light source. Fluorescent light, however, can be used as the only "sun" for most plants. You can combine *daylight*-type tubes (more blue rays) with *warm white* tubes (more red rays) or simply use *cool white* tubes (balanced rays) or special plant-growth lamps.

Temperature varies within a house or an apartment from room to room and within a room according to the proximity to windows, heating registers, or radiators. Placing a plant in its preferred "climatic zone" will help ensure that it thrives.

With winter heating, our dwellings are too dry for most plants except cacti and other succulents. This condition can be improved by frequent misting of plant foliage, by humidifying a room, or by standing a potted plant on a tray of pebbles partially covered with water or inside a bigger pot lined with slightly moistened peatmoss.

Natural light

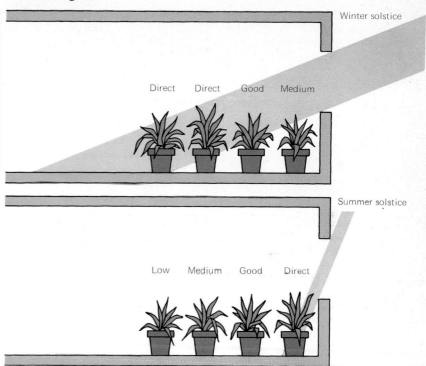

The angle of the sun's rays varies according to latitude and season. Sunlight penetrates deepest into a south-facing window at winter solstice in the northern hemisphere (top). At summer solstice it enters the same window only slightly (bottom). Such wide fluctuations in the sun's position require a seasonal movement of houseplants to maintain their preferred lighting conditions. The time of day and the exact direction of any obstruction to the window further affect lighting. The drawings above show the approximate angle of sunlight at latitude 40° N.

Artificial light

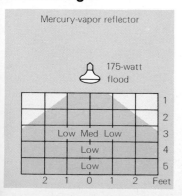

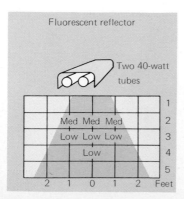

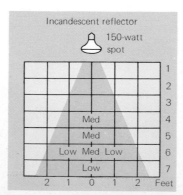

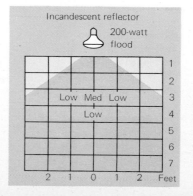

The four charts at left are a guide to placing plants under various types of artificial light. The rating depends on the distance from the lamp, both below and sideways. A mercury-vapor bulb, like a fluorescent tube, can be the sole light source for most plants. Like an incandescent bulb, it creates a decorative accent. It is more expensive but has a longer life than a fluorescent tube, and it consumes little electricity.

Indoor gardening

Plant containers and watering

Plant containers come in many varieties. Wooden boxes and straw baskets make attractive containers for indoor shrubs. But to prevent any water damage to the container or the floor, you should also use inner pots or plastic liners. For trailing and cascading plants you may prefer hanging containers. These range from wire baskets lined with peatmoss and plastic to pots held by macramé plant hangers (see *Macramé,* p. 34) and fitted with drip trays to catch any water overflow.

The most commonly used containers are, of course, fired clay pots. Unglazed clay pots are good for indoor gardeners who tend to overwater their plants, as the water evaporates easily through the porous pottery. Modern plastic pots are lighter, easier to clean, and more durable than clay pots; since plastic is non-porous, plants in these pots require less frequent watering. Plants kept in glazed ceramic pots, which usually have no drain holes, need even less watering than those in plastic pots.

Hanging plants are usually located high up in a warmer zone of the room, where evaporation is rapid; thus, they should be watered more frequently than plants at lower levels.

Generally, all houseplants should be watered thoroughly and infrequently, rather than being given small amounts of water often. No rigid schedule is possible, as the need differs according to the plant, the container, the potting mix, the location, and the air in the room. Where convenient it is better to water plentifully: stand the plant in a sink to drain away any overflow. Water again when the soil *surface* is dry. A rule of thumb, except for cacti and other succulents, is that the soil should stay nicely moist but not wet. Water all plants more frequently during the growing season, but do not water often if the plant is sick. Use water at room temperature to avoid shocking plants.

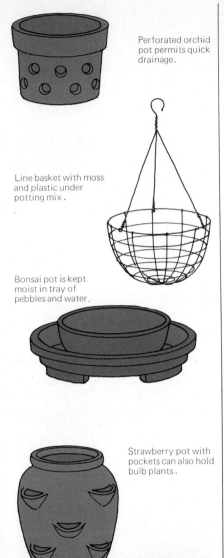

Perforated orchid pot permits quick drainage.

Line basket with moss and plastic under potting mix.

Bonsai pot is kept moist in tray of pebbles and water.

Strawberry pot with pockets can also hold bulb plants.

Nursery plants often come in plastic pots with drain holes

Vacation care

A winter vacation a week or two in duration poses no problem to the indoor gardener, as most plants are dormant in winter and need little watering. When going off on a summer vacation, you can seal plants in clear plastic bags, as illustrated below, to create self-contained tropical environments.

Wicks can be used to provide a continuous supply of water to the soil from a reservoir, as seen below, or the pots can be placed on an absorbent capillary mat moistened by a dripping faucet. Several pots can be put in a bathtub on a blanket supported by bricks, with water just below the blanket line.

Blanket and bricks

Capillary mat

Plastic bag for large plant

Plant wicks

Plastic bag for small plant

Plastic reservoir

Potting and repotting

A potted houseplant, unlike a plant in nature, cannot send out its roots in search of food and water. What is available to it depends on you.

The soil in the pot—the potting mix—should be absorbent enough to store nutrients and water, yet loose and fluffy enough for adequate drainage and to allow the roots to breathe. An all-purpose mix can be made by combining equal parts of sterilized soil, peatmoss, and washed sharp sand or perlite. You can sterilize soil yourself by baking moistened garden soil in a covered, but not sealed, oven utensil. Bake it at 70°C–82°C for 25 minutes. Let the soil cool overnight before mixing it with other ingredients.

Ready-made potting mixes are generally available in four types: all-purpose mix, a balanced soil for most foliage plants; African violet mix, for all flowering plants; cactus mix, a quick-draining soil; and terrarium mix, with absorbent characteristics suitable for a self-contained environment.

When transplanting and repotting, employ a mix similar to the one the plant is accustomed to. Check your plants annually, in the spring, to determine whether the roots are pot-bound (see drawings at right). If you want to repot a pot-bound plant in the same pot, adding nutritious fresh soil, first trim back the root ball as illustrated below. If you want to give more root space to a growing plant, repot it with more soil in a slightly larger container.

Nutrients in the potting mix are normally used up by the plants in six months or less. Thus, adding plant food during the growing season may be necessary to keep your plants healthy. Plants need three essential chemicals: nitrogen for foliage growth, phosphorus for root growth, and potassium for flowering and fruiting. Commercial plant foods contain these elements in varying proportions. They come in tablet, powder, and liquid forms. Liquid acts fastest and, if used while watering, according to instructions on the bottle, is the most convenient and safest for amateur gardeners. For most foliage plants use an all-purpose plant food. For flowering and fruiting plants use African violet food. Do not feed plants when the soil is dry or if they are sick or dormant. For luxuriant growth, spray foliage plant food on leaves.

Needs no repotting

In early spring take the root ball of a plant out of its pot. If only a few roots are exposed on the root ball, the plant needs no repotting. If tangled growth covers the ball, the plant is pot-bound and should be repotted.

Repotting required

To repot, first cover drain hole with shards or pebbles. Then put in a layer of fresh potting mix so that the top of the root ball is about an inch below the pot rim. Fill the sides with more fresh potting mix and water the plant.

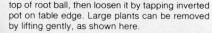

To remove a plant from its pot, put a hand on top of root ball, then loosen it by tapping inverted pot on table edge. Large plants can be removed by lifting gently, as shown here.

When adding fresh potting mix and repotting a plant in its original container, the root ball should be reduced in size. Remove part of the old mix and trim off some of the roots.

Place the root ball on a layer of fresh potting mix similar to the old mix. Then fill the gap on the sides with more fresh mix. Press down the fresh mix firmly but not too forcefully.

After repotting, immerse small pot in water to soak soil. When bubbles stop coming out, set it aside to drain for an hour. Leave in shady spot. Water large pots with vessel, as shown here.

Indoor gardening

Plant propagation

Like animals, plants reproduce themselves sexually—that is, through seed. Many plants can also propagate through a variety of forms of vegetative reproduction. It is far easier to multiply houseplants by vegetative propagation than by attempting to raise them from seeds. Seedlings demand very tender treatment; moreover, they tend to lose special characteristics that were originally created through hybridization—crossbreeding with other strains and species—at a professional seed house.

Reduced to basics, vegetative propagation involves cutting off a part of a plant and planting the cutting. The cutting is planted in a moist rooting mix (equal parts of peatmoss and washed sand, no fertilizer) and is kept in a warm, humid, and bright (but not sunny) place until roots form.

Various methods of propagation are used, depending on the type of plant. Plants that form tufts or clumps of shoots, such as African violets, can be multiplied by cutting through the top growth all the way down through the roots with a sharp knife to produce two plants, then planting each clump in an individual pot as described above.

Plants that form tubers and corms can be divided easily by plucking off baby corms and bulbs and planting them separately. These plants include tuberous begonias and some ferns.

Spider plants, other plants that send out plantlets or runners, and plants with aerial roots can be propagated by soil layering. Simply pin a plantlet onto the top of moist rooting mix with a wire loop. When new roots form on the plantlet, cut it off the parent plant.

If you have a plant that has grown too large and ungainly, or if you simply want to multiply some plants you like, vegetative propagation is the answer. On this and the opposite page, three popular methods of such propagation are illustrated in detail.

Stem cuttings

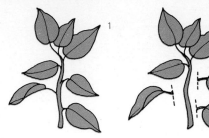

Take hardwood cuttings in spring or summer. Cut off young shoot several inches long (1). Strip lower leaves (2). Dip cut end in rooting hormone powder and insert in moist rooting mix (3). Cover with plastic (4). Soft stems will root in water any time of year. They can be planted in two to three weeks. Keep all cuttings out of direct sunlight.

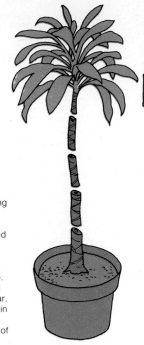

A plant that has grown leggy and lost its lower leaves (left) can be multiplied into smaller plants through stem cuttings. Cut long stem into 4-in. segments. Partially embed them in rooting mix (above). When new sprouts grow to 2 in., replant them separately. Root top as hardwood cutting. Bottom segment may send up a new sprout, but whether it is worth keeping or not depends on its growth.

Leaf cuttings

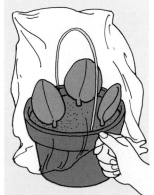

New plants can be grown from the leaves of such plants as the African violet and begonia rex. Pluck leaves, including their stems.

Make holes in a moist rooting mix with a stick or pencil. Insert the stems into the holes. Press mix gently around leaves.

Erect a small wire frame over the leaves. After watering the mix, cover the pot with a clear plastic bag to create a humid atmosphere.

Baby plants will sprout up in two to three weeks. When plantlets grow bigger and stronger, transplant them into individual pots.

Air layering

1. Woody plants that have grown too tall can be rejuvenated by air layering. Slice upward halfway into stem below top leaves, or peel off some bark partway around stem.

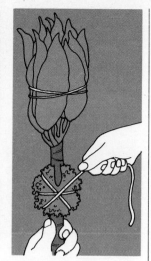

2. After dusting the cut with hormone rooting powder, gently insert some damp sphagnum moss into the cut, or wrap it around the peeled strip. New roots will grow from cut.

3. Wrap more damp moss around the cut, forming a ball the size of a small grapefruit. Tie the ball of moss in place with a string. Ball should be tight and compact to hold moisture.

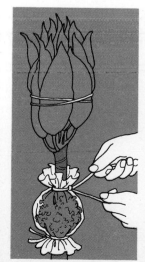

4. Wrap plastic around the moss ball. Tape shut the seam of the plastic and secure it tightly to the stem with adhesive tape or string. This is done to seal in moisture.

5. In about six to eight weeks new roots will grow into moss ball and will be visible through plastic. Cut stem below new roots. Unwrap plastic and string holding moss ball.

6. Plant the newly rooted specimen in a pot that is slightly larger than its root ball. Use a loose, fluffy potting mix. Water. Repot plant in larger pot the following spring.

Plant pests

Aphids are the most likely insect pest to be found on houseplants. Usually green, but sometimes gray, brown, or black, they suck the sap of the plants, causing yellowing leaves and warped growth. They secrete a sticky substance called honeydew, which is often covered with a black mold. Wash the plant and spray with malathion.

Spider mites have white or red oval bodies and are so small that they are virtually invisible except in groups. They spin webs on the undersides of leaves, which become mottled with yellow or brown spots. As the mites thrive in dry, hot air, misting discourages them. Liquid rotenone and malathion are effective sprays against this pest.

Mealybugs are insects with white, wooly hair covering their bodies as well as their eggs. Although they are not small, they are often hard to spot because they hide in stem crotches and on the undersides of leaves. These bugs suck the sap and secrete a honeydew. They can be washed off with a hose or a cotton swab dipped in denatured alcohol.

Scale insects have hard, shiny, brownish-green shells in adult form. They usually congregate on plant stems and the undersides of leaves. They suck plant juice and also produce a honeydew. When infestation is severe, the leaves are encrusted with scales, resembling fern spores. Spray with malathion or scratch off with a fingernail.

White flies are tiny insects with white bodies and wings. They fly off in a white spray when the plant they rest on is disturbed. Most damage is done by the green, nearly transparent larvae, which attach themselves to the undersides of leaves to suck the sap. Leaves yellow and drop off. Wash off larvae. Spray with malathion or rotenone.

Thrips are small, black-winged, fast-moving insects. Although not usually found on houseplants, they can migrate into the house on a new plant. They feed on foliage and flowers. Infested leaves show a white mottling. Wash the thrips off with a hose or sprayer, then spray the plant with rotenone, malathion, or pyrethrins.

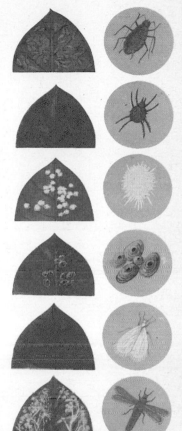

Plant diseases

Botrytis, or gray mold, is a brownish-gray furry fungus that affects leaves, stems, flowers, and fruits with patches of grayish mold. It is found in cool, moist rooms with still air. Remedy by lowering humidity and ventilating room.

Virus diseases deform both leaves and flowers. Healthy plants can easily catch the viruses if you handle infected plants. There is no cure for these diseases. Once a sick plant is diagnosed, it should be burned immediately.

Mildew comes in many varieties. It covers stems, leaves, and buds with patches of gray, powdery mold. Among the possible causes are overcrowding and overwatering of plants. Prevent this with better ventilation.

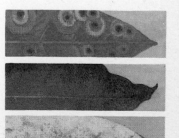

Indoor gardening

Greenhouses and conservatories

For those who go into indoor gardening in a big way, greenhouses and conservatories are the answer. Strictly speaking, a greenhouse is where plants are propagated and raised, and a conservatory is where they are displayed. In modern homes the trend is to combine them with a living area and call it a garden room.

Home greenhouses range from fully equipped professional structures of glass with wood or metal frames to humble pole supports draped with plastic sheets. Both types consume much energy for heating. In between are the modern, versatile prefabricated greenhouses. These come in kits and can be built as lean-tos against walls or freestanding on rooftop terraces. One company makes a heat-retaining greenhouse with panels of double-pane rigid acrylic in aluminum frames.

A greenhouse should be equipped with sturdy potting benches and an array of seed flats. It should have a gravel or sand floor to maintain humidity and a concrete or brick walk that can be hosed off. In cool and temperate regions a greenhouse requires a heating system during the colder months. Sunshades and ventilators are necessary in summer. Better-equipped greenhouses have fluorescent lighting and perforated watering pipes that drip water on all plants.

You can connect a lean-to greenhouse with your house, separating it from the house with sliding glass doors. Equip it as a conservatory but furnish it with garden furniture. Pave the floor with tiles or bricks over sand. In cooler seasons this expanded living area can be used as a sunroom where you will be surrounded by lush foliage and fragrant flowers. A more elaborately equipped modern conservatory or garden room might have a fountain or an in-floor pool with water lilies.

Indoor gardening tools

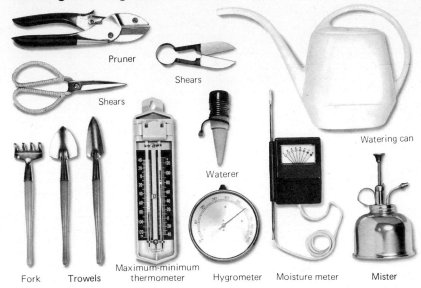

Pruner

Shears

Shears

Watering can

Fork   Trowels   Maximum-minimum thermometer   Waterer   Hygrometer   Moisture meter   Mister

Besides basic tools shown, an indoor gardener with many plants to care for may want the specialized tools shown: maximum-minimum thermometer, plastic reservoir for self-watering, hygrometer to check humidity, moisture meter to probe soil, and misting gun.

Louvered sunshades are adjustable to control amount of entering sunlight.

Sliding ceiling and roof panels admit sunlight into this modern garden room.

Terrariums

All terrariums have in common an enclosed area that light can enter but from which warmth and moisture cannot easily escape. Moisture rises from the soil and from the leaves of the plants, condenses on the terrarium ceiling, and trickles down the sides as a constant "rain." Plants breathe in carbon dioxide and breathe out oxygen during the day, then reverse this process at night. Thus, a sealed terrarium is a self-contained microworld in which the atmosphere is recycled by the plants. After the initial moistening of the soil, it needs almost no watering.

A terrarium should be of untinted glass or plastic. It should not leak. It should never be placed in direct sunlight. At normal room temperature the humid atmosphere inside resembles that of a tropical rain forest. Tender houseplants originally from the steamy jungle and ferns, lichens, and mosses make ideal members of the terrarium community. To plant a terrarium, first put down a 1-inch layer of gravel and an equal layer of charcoal chips. Top this with an inch or so of potting mix low in fertilizer, and decorate it with small rocks. In a tank terrarium make the soil surface slope upward toward the back, where taller plants are placed. In a round terrarium locate smaller plants around the edge.

To create a bottle garden, the soil and plants must be inserted through the narrow neck. You can easily fash-

Homemade tongs use wood strips.

ion homemade tongs for this purpose, using two long, narrow, flexible strips of wood; bolt them together and insert a small wooden wedge, as seen in the illustration.

A spherical terrarium can be fashioned from a goldfish bowl, a brandy snifter, or some other round glass container. The bowl at left does not have a lid and therefore, strictly speaking, is not a terrarium. (Being lidless, it does not have a closed environment and so requires frequent watering or misting.) Terrariums and bottle gardens should be located in a bright place that is not in direct sunlight, such as a north window.

A tank-type terrarium (right) can easily be created using a fish tank and a glass or acrylic lid. Plant as described in text at left.

Planting a bottle terrarium

Bottle gardens require special techniques. Use funnel and paper tube to pour in charcoal layer, then mix of peat moss and sharp sand.

Most of the soil should be shaken from plant's roots. Use tongs to insert plant into the bottle and to put it in position.

With a long stick, such as a yardstick, gently press roots into soil, straightening plant. Allow a few inches between plants.

Water with sprinkler or mister. Do not overwater. Moderate condensation on glass indicates enough moisture. Water again if necessary.

Indoor gardening

The art of bonsai

Bonsai ("tray planting" in Japanese) is the Oriental art of cultivating dwarfed trees in shallow pots. Although to the Oriental bonsai embodies a whole complex of esthetic and philosophical concepts, for the Western hobbyist it can provide unique decorative plants rather than objects of meditation. Bonsai originated in China well over 1,000 years ago and was perfected subsequently in Japan. Today it is increasingly popular in the West. Bonsai clubs and publications cater to both connoisseurs and beginners. Bonsai plants are available at many nurseries, garden centers, and even department stores.

The art of bonsai evokes the spirit of dwarfed and deformed trees and shrubs growing on craggy peaks and windswept cliffs in China and Japan. Eking out a precarious living in marginal soils and surviving severe weathering, these plants, with exposed roots and gnarled, twisted trunks, cling to life tenaciously. Some centuries-old trees never grow more than 2 feet high. Others slant so much that they grow almost horizontally or cascade down overhanging precipices.

Originally these naturally dwarfed trees were dug out and transplanted into pots. Through the centuries this practice evolved into an elaborate set of techniques for artificially dwarfing trees, simulating age, and creating illusory perspectives.

The intrinsic idea of bonsai is not an imitation but an evocation of nature. A few diminutive Japanese maples in a single bonsai pot can transform the several square inches of moss-covered soil into a realistic landscape of trees with budding leaves in spring, brilliantly colored foliage in the fall, and gray, leafless, stark forms in winter.

Bonsai plants can be conifers or deciduous. Traditionally they are hardy trees and shrubs, normally kept outdoors and only brought inside for brief periods. There is a developing trend in North America toward cultivating tropical plants as bonsai. These can be kept indoors the year round just like other houseplants (p. 303).

Importance of proportion. Traditional bonsai emphasizes proportion. The height of the tree should be about six times the diameter of the rooted trunk base. The diameter of the trunk base should equal the depth of the pot. The length of a rectangular pot should be about two-thirds the height of the tree. Trees with small leaves, flowers, or fruits are preferred.

Balance is as important as proportion. A large branch on the left should be balanced by a similar one on the right. But balance does not mean symmetry, which is avoided in bonsai. Thus a tree with a perfectly cylindrical trunk is considered undesirable.

The shape of the branches and of the foliage of a bonsai tree (except for cascading types) should resemble a triangle with unequal sides. In a multiple planting the number of trees is always odd. Trees are never equal in size; each pot has a dominant individual.

Traditional bonsai has five basic styles: formal upright (straight up), informal upright (trunk slightly curved), slanting (treetop leaning outside tree base), semicascade (tree curves downward, but not lower than the pot), and cascade (tree cascades way below the pot). These basic styles are depicted on the opposite page, together with five additional styles: windswept (trunk almost horizontal), raft (multiple "trunks," really branches of a horizontally placed trunk), grove (a group of individual trees), and on-the-rock (roots in rock crevice or hugging a rock and reaching into the soil).

The Sargent juniper bonsai (top) is more than 250 years old. Japanese maple (bottom) is some 30 years old. The methods by which such specimens are created are described in these pages.

Ten styles of bonsai

Formal upright

Informal upright

Cascade

Semicascade

Slanting

On-the-rock

Grove

Raft

Double trunk

Windswept

Indoor gardening

Bonsai potting

The trees cultivated as bonsai would, in their natural state, have deep roots. Cutting the roots to plant the tree in a shallow bonsai pot is traumatic for it, so you must be very careful when transplanting. The greatest challenge in bonsai is to keep the plant alive and thriving in its artificial environment.

A bonsai connoisseur sifts his mix and separates it into several sizes, putting the coarser grains at the bottom of the pot and finer ones progressively toward the top. It is not necessary for the beginner to do so. You can make potting mix for bonsai from equal parts of clay, peat moss, leaf mold, and washed coarse sand. Pot the mix dry in the normal way for better filling and packing. Use distilled water, unpolluted rainwater, or dechlorinated faucet water (tap water left exposed to the air for a few days).

The planting position of a bonsai is intimately related to the shape of the pot and the planting style. For esthetic reasons a tree should be planted about one-third of the way along the length of a rectangular or oval pot. This rule also applies to the biggest tree in a grove planting. In a round, square, or hexagonal pot, plant the tree in the center, or slightly off center for the windswept, semicascade, and cascade types. Shallow pots are used for the grove, landscape, and other traditional styles. Cascading bonsai require deeper pots to show off the cascades.

After potting or repotting you may want to plant a fine layer of moss on the soil surface. You can peel fresh moss off rocks in shaded woods or buy powdered dry moss and plant it, watering with frequent mistings. A favorite practice in bonsai is to place small rocks beside a tree, creating the sense of a life-size landscape. If several rocks are used, place them so that the grain goes in the same direction.

Pruning the root ball

To move a plant from a nursery pot to a shallow bonsai pot, take the root ball out of the old pot (p. 293). Soak it in a bucket of water and spray some water on its branches and foliage. Slosh the root ball around to loosen the soil among the roots. Wash off as much soil as possible, using a stick to remove any hard lumps without damaging the minute root hairs.

Lift plant from bucket. Untangle, tease, and comb the roots with a stick, a pair of chopsticks, or your fingers. Remove most of the leftover soil while combing the roots. Immerse the roots in water and slosh them around at intervals. After spreading out the roots you will have a clear idea of the root system.

Prune all large roots with sharp shears. (If taproot is heavy, cut it back only slightly and plant the tree in a deep pot; a year later prune it further, then still further in future years, before finally potting it in a shallow pot.) Pruning larger roots stimulates the growth of fine root hairs, which are efficient in absorbing water. Trim off a third of root mass along sides and half on bottom. Plant is now ready for bonsai pot.

Anchoring bonsai

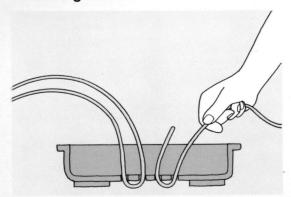

A plant with pruned roots is anchored in its tray to prevent its toppling over. Slip lengths of wire through the drain holes. Spread a layer of gravel, then one of potting mix, on the bottom of the tray.

Place the root ball in position in the tray. Fill in potting mix between the roots, then wrap the wires around the root ball and tie wires together. Fill in more mix, packing root spaces with stick.

Fill pot with mix, covering wires on top of roots. Soak pot in a sink up to the level of the surface of the soil for 15 min. Spray foliage and soil several times daily for next 10 days.

Bonsai training

The ultimate appearance of a bonsai is a product both of the plant's natural characteristics and of training it to attain a desired style. Some techniques, such as pruning, are common. Others, such as wiring, are more sophisticated. But a beginner, with care and practice, can train a bonsai to achieve the shape he wants. Avoid excessively bizarre shapes for your trees. No really beautiful bonsai drastically violates the traditional esthetic rules—which are, after all, elegant simulations of extremes occurring in nature.

Bonsai pruning is normally a one-time basic procedure. It is a drastic step, so prune only if the plant is in good health. After pruning, further shaping is done mainly by pinching back—that is, by nipping off growth buds. Nipping off new buds on one branch stimulates growth on neighboring branches. If all the plant's stem-tip growth buds are pinched off, the whole plant will become bushier. Pinching buds controls the shape of the plant without scarring it.

Wiring a bonsai controls the direction it will grow. Wire a deciduous bonsai when its leaves are fully grown and an evergreen in fall or winter. Use paper-wrapped wire on tender-barked maples and beeches. Remove the wire when the new growing season begins to avoid harming the bark and buds. Some plants need annual rewiring for several years. Bigger branches and even the trunk can be bent with weights or with tension devices, but use only slight tension.

Leaf cutting reduces the size of leaves so that they are more proportionate to the dwarfed tree. However, this should not be attempted on a young plant. Age can be simulated by creating a portion of dead wood on a branch or by wiring tightly to create a gnarled appearance. The latter device is risky and not for beginners.

Initial pruning of bonsai plant shapes it roughly to the style you want to create. Prune in spring or summer with a sharp knife, leaving concave cuts for better healing. Do not keep more than one branch at any given level of the trunk. Remove large branches on side from which tree will be viewed. Balance branches left and right. Trim all superfluous branches.

A wired trunk or branch can be gently bent to the desired shape. To do so, anchor aluminum or annealed copper wire in drain hole or root ball. Wind it evenly upward at a 45° angle around the trunk and the branches to be reshaped. Choose wire size so that wire tension is only slightly greater than branch tension. Never crisscross the wire.

Leaf size of a deciduous or broadleaf evergreen bonsai can usually be significantly reduced by leaf cutting. In early or mid-summer (but not earlier or later), snip off all the leaves, but not the leaf stems. A month later smaller leaves will appear from the dormant leaf buds. This can be repeated each year. Do not cut flowering and fruiting trees.

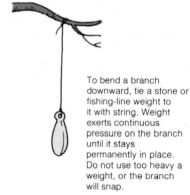

To bend a branch downward, tie a stone or fishing-line weight to it with string. Weight exerts continuous pressure on the branch until it stays permanently in place. Do not use too heavy a weight, or the branch will snap.

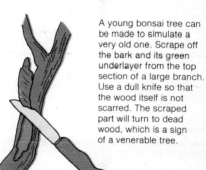

A young bonsai tree can be made to simulate a very old one. Scrape off the bark and its green underlayer from the top section of a large branch. Use a dull knife so that the wood itself is not scarred. The scraped part will turn to dead wood, which is a sign of a venerable tree.

If a pair of trunks or large branches are too close together, you can wedge them apart permanently simply by inserting a piece of notched wood or plastic between them. Remove the wedge after a few months. Reinsert it if the trunks spring back toward each other.

If trunks or branches are too far apart and you want them to be closer to each other, tie a piece of string or padded wire around them tightly. Untie them after a few months. If they do not remain in position, tie them together again.

Indoor gardening

Advanced bonsai planting styles

With the knowledge of how to plant and train individual bonsai trees (pp. 300–301), an ambitious gardener may want to attempt a more sophisticated and dramatic project. Three advanced planting styles are briefly described here: raft planting, grove planting, and what may be called bonsai on-the-rocks (see pp. 298–299). Beginners are advised to master simpler planting styles before attempting these, especially the on-the-rock types.

Raft planting is the easiest among the three. It creates a "grove of trees" from a single trunk. A tree with a mature trunk from which several large branches point in one direction is used. All branches except these main ones are cut off, leaving small stumps. After the roots have been thinned, the trunk is planted horizontally in a shallow pot with the stumps buried and the roots flattened and covered with soil. The top surface of the trunk is usually exposed. The large branches now stand up as

individual "trees." Japanese maples and Japanese white pines are good candidates for this style. Raft planting, however, is not so esthetically pleasing as the genuine grove style because its "trees" all have to be in a straight line.

A grove planting actually uses a number of individual trees in a shallow rectangular or oval pot. It suggests a small forest viewed from some distance. For this style the trees chosen, always an odd number, are upright and slender. No tree with unusual or outstanding characteristics is used, since a group effect is desired.

Before planting, the exact positions of all trees are carefully plotted. The biggest tree is planted first, either slightly off center or about one-third of the way along the length of the tray. The remaining trees are placed in an uneven, nongeometric pattern. Put bigger trees in front and smaller ones at the back. This creates a sense of natural perspective, since in a real landscape

the trees nearest the viewer always look biggest. A cover of moss and a rock or two are often added to suggest a woodsy terrain.

The most difficult of the three styles is on-the-rock. The tree requires up to 10 years of training. It is done in one of three ways. The simplest is to start with a concave rock that has a sizable crevice. The crevice is filled with soil, and a small tree is planted in it. This method, in effect, uses the crevice as a pot.

A second method involves training the roots to cling to the rock. Wires are first anchored to the rock surface with metal pins or epoxy glue. A wet pasty mix of half clay and half peat is smeared over the rock, then the roots are carefully draped all over its sides. More mix is smeared over and among the roots, which are then firmly fastened onto the rock with the wires. The wires can be removed only when the roots are well established. A carpet of fine moss is usually pressed over the

roots and temporarily anchored with U-shaped copper wires to prevent its erosion as a consequence of watering. These two types of rock plantings can be placed in a tray of damp sand or on a marble slab, as the roots do not go beyond the rock.

For the third type of rock planting the roots are similarly trained to drape over the rock, but they extend beyond it to penetrate into the soil in the bonsai pot. No moss should cover the exposed roots. The rock is embedded in the soil to a depth of about one-third or one-fourth of its height.

To give a realistic touch, trees for rock plantings must be types naturally found on rocky sites. The rocks should be craggy and pitted but not too soft, as they would deteriorate with age. When the roots have taken hold, wires can be removed. All on-the-rock bonsai plants should be sheltered from the weather for about a month and sprayed with water daily.

This five-needle pine is 25 in. tall. It is an excellent representative of the bonsai rock-planting style.

In this bonsai grove-style planting there are two types of trees: Japanese white pine (center) and beech.

This 23-in.-tall raft-style bonsai planting consists of branches from the single trunk of a holly tree.

Suggested bonsai plants

Adventurous bonsai lovers often find satisfaction in taking a young tree or shrub from a nursery or the wild—or raising one from a seed or a cutting—and training it as a bonsai, even though no one may have trained this particular species as bonsai before. Most trees and shrubs can be adapted for bonsai, except for a few species that grow too vigorously, have long leaves, or have large fruits or flowers that cannot be miniaturized. However, not all plants are equally adaptable to life in a bonsai tray or to a particular style of bonsai.

Two favored plants for classic bonsai are the Sargent juniper and the Japanese white pine, both needle-leaf evergreens. Among traditional flowering bonsai, Japanese flowering cherries are difficult to train, but Japanese flowering apricots adapt more easily and have smaller blossoms. North Americans have successfully trained many native species, including bald cypresses, Canadian hemlocks, and red maples.

Beginners have better chances if they start with plants that can be more easily turned to bonsai, such as fire thorns, dwarf hemlocks, and some varieties of cotoneasters and junipers.

This page contains several lists of plants recommended for bonsai. They are by no means rigid, as much depends on the plant and the gardener. The main list includes traditional and popular plants and those generally available in North America. Some plants are especially good for certain styles. They appear in the three shorter lists. A few plants are versatile enough to appear in more than one list.

The final list contains plants suitable for indoor bonsai. Like other houseplants, they can be left indoors most of the time. The price one pays for indoor cultivation is that the trees often lack the venerable gnarled look, and many do not live for centuries as do hardy traditional bonsai trees.

Traditional and popular bonsai plants

Azalea (Rhododendron genus)
Bunchleaf English ivy (Hedera helix conglomerata)
California scrub oak (Quercus dumosa)
Chinese elm (Ulmus parvifolia)
Chinese hackberry (Celtis sinensis)
Chinese wisteria (Wisteria sinensis)
Cotoneasters: Cranberry contoneaster (Cotoneaster apiculata), Rock cotoneaster (C. horizontalis), Rock spray cotoneaster (C. microphylla)
Cypresses: American cypress (Chamaecyparis thyoides), Bald cypress (Taxodium distichum), Montezuma cypress (T. mucronatum)
Dawn redwood (Metasequoia glyptostroboides)
English hawthorn (Crataegus oxyacantha)
Flowering quince (Chaenomeles lagenaria)
Gray-bark elm (Zelkova serrata)
Heavenly bamboo (Nandina domestica)
Japanese cedar (Cryptomeria japonica)
Japanese flowering apricot (Prunus mume)
Japanese larch (Larix leptolepis)
Japanese weeping cherry (Prunus subhirtella pendula)
Junipers: Blaauw's juniper (Juniperus chinensis blaaui), California juniper (J. californica carriere), Chinese juniper (J. chinensis), Prostrate juniper (J. squamata prostrata), Sargent juniper (J. chinensis sargentii)
Maidenhair tree (Ginkgo biloba)
Maples: Japanese maple (Acer palmatum), Red maple (A. rubrum), Trident maple (A. buergerianum)
Mayflower rhododendron (Rhododendron racemosum)
Midget crab apple (Malus micromalus)
Pines: Japanese black pine (Pinus thunbergii), Japanese white pine (P. parviflora), Mugho pine (P. mugo mughus)
Sargent crab apple (Malus sargentii)
Scarlet fire thorn (Pyracantha coccinea)
Spruces: Dwarf Norway spruce (Picea abies maxwellii), Dwarf white spruce (P. glauca conica), Ezo spruce (P. jezoensis)
Star jasmine (Trachelospermum jasminoides)

For grove style

Chinese elm (Ulmus parvifolia)
Deodar cedar (Cedrus deodara)
Ezo spruce (Picea jezoensis)
Fir (Abies genus)
Hemlock (Tsuga genus)
Japanese cedar (Cryptomeria japonica)
Japanese hornbeam (Carpinus japonica)
Maidenhair tree (Ginkgo biloba)
Maples: Japanese maple (Acer palmatum), Trident maple (A. buergerianum)
Oaks (Quercus dentata, Q. serrata)
Sweet gum (Liquidambar genus)

For cascade style

Atlas cedar (Cedrus atlantica)
Azalea (Rhododendron genus)
Cascade chrysanthemum (Chrysanthemum morifolium)
Coast live oak (Quercus agrifolia)
Dwarf Japanese yew (Taxus cuspidata nana)
English hawthorn (Crataegus oxyacantha)
Fig (Ficus carica)
Honeysuckle (Lonicera japonica)
Japanese white pine (Pinus parviflora)
Japanese wisteria (Wisteria floribunda)
Junipers: Creeping juniper (Juniperus horizontalis), Prostrate juniper (J. squamata prostrata), Sargent juniper (J. chinensis sargentii)
Rock cotoneaster (Cotoneaster horizontalis)

For on-the-rock style

Bald cypress (Taxodium distichum)
Chinese elm (Ulmus parvifolia)
Chrysanthemum (all woody varieties with small blossoms)
Ezo spruce (Picea jezoensis)
Pines: Dwarf stone pine (Pinus pumila), Japanese red pine (P. densiflora), Japanese white pine (P. parviflora), Mugho pine (P. mugo mughus)
Rock cotoneaster (Cotoneaster horizontalis)
Sargent juniper (Juniperus chinensis sargentii)
Trident maple (Acer buergerianum)

Plants for indoor bonsai

Arizona cypress (Cupressus arizonica)
Camphor tree (Cinnamomum camphora)
Chinese date (Zizyphus jujuba)
Crape myrtle (Lagerstroemia indica)
Dwarf pomegranate (Punica granatum nana)
English ivy (Hedera helix)
Figs: Mistletoe fig (Ficus diversifolia), Strangler fig (F. aurea), Weeping fig (F. benjamina)
Geometry tree, or black olive (Bucida buceras)
Grape ivy (Cissus rhombifolia)
Hong Kong wild kumquat (Fortunella hindsii)
Japanese flowering quince (Chaenomeles japonica)
Japanese privet (Ligustrum japonicum)
Norfolk Island pine (Araucaria heterophylla)
Olive (Olea europaea)
Pinwheel jasmine (Jasminum dichotomum)
Sea grape (Coccolobis uvifera)
Singapore holly (Malpighia coccigera)
Southern yew (Podocarpus macrophylla maki)
Tourist tree (Bursera simaruba)

Indoor gardening

Concise guide to houseplants

This and the following three pages contain an indoor gardener's guide to houseplants commonly available from florists and commercial greenhouses. The plants are divided into seven categories: foliage plants, flowering plants, cacti and other succulents, ferns, climbers and trailers, food plants, and novelty plants—those with odd and intriguing characteristics.

Each plant is introduced with both its common and its botanical name.

The botanical name is necessary because common names often vary widely from one region of the country to another. Where space permits, the brief descriptions of the plants include information on watering and on light and temperature requirements. When this does not appear, follow the instructions on the general care of plants in previous pages, including those on potting (p. 293), propagation (p. 294), and plant health (p. 295).

Foliage plants

Aluminum plant (*Pilea cadierei*). Green quilted leaves marked with patches of silvery sheen. Does well in bright north window, in filtered sunlight, or in fluorescent light. Keep soil evenly moist at all times. Mist often. Temperature: 18°C–30°C.

Begonia rex (*Begonia rex*). Comes in many hybrids; leaves have pink, red, lavender, silver, or gray markings. Bright north window or winter sun. Let soil dry out moderately between thorough waterings. Prefers temperature of 13°C–18°C, tolerates 4°C–32°C. Likes humid air.

Chinese evergreen (*Aglaonema sinensis*). Popular, large-leafed plant, related to the jack-in-the-pulpit. The genus has many other species in shades of green and white with cream or silvery markings. Thrives 20 ft from a bright window or in a dark corner. Keep out of direct sun. Place pot on wet pebbles or in moist peatmoss, or grow in water. Suffers below 13°C.

Copperleaf (*Acalypha wilkesiana macafeana*). Gets its name from the red, pink, and metallic copper mottling of its leaves. Prefers sunny window in winter, bright indirect light in summer. Keep soil evenly moist. Mist often. Temperature: 13°C–24°C.

Elephant-foot tree (*Beaucarnea recurvata*). Brownish-gray trunk swells at the base, hence the common name. Topped with a rosette of long, slender leaves; reaches 7 ft. Likes full sun; tolerates north window. A mature plant can go months without watering, as it stores water in its bulbous base. Temperature: 13°C–24°C.

False aralia (*Dizygotheca elegantissima*). An elegant, delicate-looking plant from the New Hebrides. Has feathery, tooth-edged leaves; turns coarse as it grows older. To check height, nip new tips. Cut a leggy plant in early spring to induce young shoots. Bright north window or filtered sunlight. Keep soil evenly moist. Mist often. Temperature: 18°C–30°C.

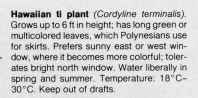

Hawaiian ti plant (*Cordyline terminalis*). Grows up to 6 ft in height; has long green or multicolored leaves, which Polynesians use for skirts. Prefers sunny east or west window, where it becomes more colorful; tolerates bright north window. Water liberally in spring and summer. Temperature: 18°C–30°C. Keep out of drafts.

Heavenly bamboo, or Chinese sacred bamboo (*Nandina domestica*). Slow-growing evergreen whose leaves turn red in fall. Propagate by stem cuttings in summer. Prefers partial shade. Water liberally in summer but little in winter. Although a hardy plant, young shoots are best nurtured in a cool room (7°C–13°C).

India rubber plant (*Ficus elastica decora*). Tree with glossy, dark-green leaves. Prefers sunny east or west window; tolerates bright north window. In spring and summer water liberally; feed every 2 weeks. Mist often. Keep above 16°C.

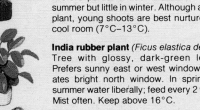

Kashmir cypress (*Cupressus cashmeriana*). A graceful Tibetan plant with delicate, blue-green leaves hanging down like fronds. Grows to 6 ft and is good for a picture window. Bright indirect light or partial sun. Water liberally in spring and summer; feed monthly. Keep soil moist in winter. Likes cool room at 7°C–13°C.

Norfolk Island pine (*Araucaria heterophylla* or *A. excelsa*). Tiered branches and evergreen needle leaves. Indoors the young plant looks best when 4–6 ft tall. Tolerates north window the year round, but prefers winter sun. Keep soil moist in summer. Temperature: 4°C–21°C.

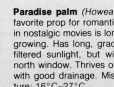

Paradise palm (*Howea forsteriana*). This favorite prop for romantic hotel orchestras in nostalgic movies is long-living and slow-growing. Has long, graceful leaves. Likes filtered sunlight, but will adapt to bright north window. Thrives on liberal waterings with good drainage. Mist often. Temperature: 16°C–27°C.

Parlor palm (*Chamaedorea elegans*). A dwarf mountain palm from Mexico; grows no higher than 4 ft. Slender leaves hang gracefully from arching stalks. Does best in bright north window or partial shade. Keep soil moist but not wet. Mist often in summer. Temperature: 13°C–27°C.

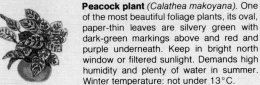

Peacock plant (*Calathea makoyana*). One of the most beautiful foliage plants, its oval, paper-thin leaves are silvery green with dark-green markings above and red and purple underneath. Keep in bright north window or filtered sunlight. Demands high humidity and plenty of water in summer. Winter temperature: not under 13°C.

Piggyback plant (*Tolmiea menziesii*). Sprouts baby leaves at the base of mature leaves, which are downy and long-stemmed. This luxuriant but short-lived plant prefers bright north window but tolerates shady spots. Needs moist soil. Likes temperature 10°C–21°C.

Snake plant, or mother-in-law's tongue (*Sansevieria trifasciata laurentii*). An extremely tough houseplant that can survive dry air and low light. Has thick, sword-shaped leaves bordered with yellow and striped with snakelike markings. Thrives on full sun or partial shade. Tolerates a wide range of temperatures above 10°C.

Split-leafed philodendron (*Monstera deliciosa,* or *Philodendron pertusum*). This Mexican evergreen can support itself on a slab of bark wood with its aerial roots. Bright north window, filtered sunlight. Water liberally spring, summer. Temperature: 18°C–30°C.

Umbrella plant (*Cyperus alternifolius*). Has long, thin stalks from whose tops arching green bracts radiate in all directions like umbrella spokes. Propagate by root division. Prefers bright north window or filtered sunlight. Keep soil wet for this water-loving plant by placing the pot in a dish filled with water. Temperature: 10°C–21°C.

Flowering plants

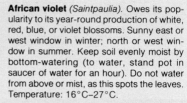

African violet (*Saintpaulia*). Owes its popularity to its year-round production of white, red, blue, or violet blossoms. Sunny east or west window in winter; north or west window in summer. Keep soil evenly moist by bottom-watering (to water, stand pot in saucer of water for an hour). Do not water from above or mist, as this spots the leaves. Temperature: 16°C–27°C.

Amaryllis (*Hippeastrum*). Has large trumpet-shaped flowers of white, pink, or deep red. Beginning in November put potted bulb in warm place (16°C–24°C) and keep it evenly moist. When leaves appear, water more and move to a sunny window. While in bloom, keep plant in bright light but not direct sun. After flowering, continue watering; feed monthly until end of August. Then leave in dark, cool closet for 8-week rest.

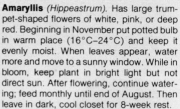

Angel's tears (*Billbergia nutans*). Among the easiest bromeliads to grow. Has narrow gray-green leaves, rosy bracts, and blue-green flowers. Prefers sunny window and filtered sun in midsummer. Keep soil moist and the leaf cup filled with water. Prefers temperature of 16°C–21°C. Tolerates wide ranges of temperature and light.

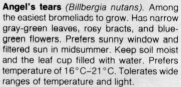

Camellia (*Camellia japonica*). Has glossy, dark, evergreen leaves and large white, pink, red, or variegated flowers. Bright north window or filtered sunlight. Keep soil evenly moist. Mist often and feed acid food. Prefers temperature of 4°C–16°C in winter and fresh air.

Chenille plant (*Acalypha hispida*). Draping, fuzzy, red flower spikes in fall and winter. Prune top shoots and repot in February. Prefers filtered sunlight or bright north window. Keep soil moist. Likes 16°C–24°C and high humidity.

Chinese hibiscus, or rose of China (*Hibiscus rosa-sinensis*). Blooms year-round with large, lovely, fragile-looking, white, yellow, pink, or scarlet flowers. This long-living bush must be pruned to keep it small. Sunny east or west window. Water well spring and summer. Likes temperature 16°C–21°C and fresh, humid air.

Flamingo flower (*Anthurium scherzerianum*). Has bright-red heart-shaped bracts and yellow tassels. Sunny window in winter; bright indirect light in summer. Keep soil moist by putting pot on saucer of wet pebbles or in damp sphagnum moss. Temperature: not below 16°C.

Gardenia (*Gardenia jasminoides*). This fussy plant rewards careful indoor gardeners with large, white, waxy flowers with sweet fragrance in winter and spring. Sunny south window. Keep soil moist but well drained, or buds will drop off. Demands temperature around 21°C by day and 16°C–18°C by night. Dislikes dry, stale air.

Geranium (*Pelargonium hortorum*). This is one of the most popular houseplants in the world. Ranges from 3 in. to 3 ft in height with pink, red, white, or lavender flowers. Sunny window except in summer. Water well, but let soil dry out moderately between waterings. Temperature: 18°C–24°C.

Guzmania (*Guzmania monostachya*). This popular bromeliad has bayonet-shaped yellow-green leaves and a stem with red bracts and white flowers. Prefers a very light potting mix. Filtered sun or bright light. Keep leaf rosette filled with water. Night temperature not lower than 16°C, daytime temperature over 21°C.

Jasmine (*Jasminum polyanthum*). Like the gardenia, indigenous to China. Small, pinkish-white blossoms with a sensuous fragrance come out in spring. May be trained upright or on a wire loop inserted in the pot. Care and conditions are the same as for the gardenia, which flowers in winter.

Lady's slipper orchid (*Paphiopedilum*). Named for its shape; comes in many species and hybrids. The best orchid to grow as a houseplant because it tolerates a heated house in winter. Keep in sunny east or west window (not south window) or in fluorescent light. Prefers moist but not wet soil and humid, fresh air.

Laelia pumila (*Laelia pumila*). This South American orchid is good for beginners. Has 4-in. flowers of rose-violet color with deep crimson lips and yellow ridges. Use a potting mix of 2 parts osmunda fiber to 1 part sphagnum moss. Sunny window except in midsummer. Water liberally in spring and summer. Temperature: not below 13°C in winter. Needs warm, humid, fresh air.

Mum (*Chrysanthemum*). Comes in some 200 species, but the commonest indoor variety is the short-day treated type (given artificial short days by florists to promote flowering). Discard these after blooming. (Other varieties may be propagated by cuttings.) Sunny east or west window. Water well. Temperature: 7°C–18°C.

Narcissus (*Narcissus*). Bulbs are planted in early fall in a bowl of sand or pebbles covered with water and are kept in a cool dark place (10°C). When growth is 4 in., move to a cool but light place. After budding, move to a warmer room (up to 18°C) with filtered sunlight or bright indirect light.

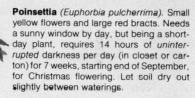

Ornamental pepper (*Capsicum annuum conoides*). A perennial grown as an annual for its colorful fruits in summer and fall. The peppers are white, yellow, green, red, or purple. Sunny south window except in summer. Keep soil evenly moist. Do not fertilize. Temperature: 16°C–24°C.

Poinsettia (*Euphorbia pulcherrima*). Small yellow flowers and large red bracts. Needs a sunny window by day, but being a short-day plant, requires 14 hours of *uninterrupted* darkness per day (in closet or carton) for 7 weeks, starting end of September, for Christmas flowering. Let soil dry out slightly between waterings.

Shrimp plant (*Beloperone guttata*). Has drooping spikes of brown-red bracts and small white flowers. Sunny window; less direct sun in summer. Keep soil evenly moist April to December. Water less the rest of year. Winter temperature: 13°C–21°C.

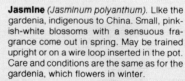

Temple bells (*Smithiantha zebrina*). Mexican plant with heart-shaped leaves and pink, yellow, orange, or scarlet bell-shaped blossoms. Blooms from summer to fall. Filtered sunlight. Keep soil moist and feed in the growing season. A month after flowering has stopped, keep barely moist. Likes temperature of 18°C–27°C, but when dormant keep at 10°C–13°C.

Wax begonia (*Begonia semperflorens*). This and its hybrids are the most popular group of indoor begonias. Have small pink, red, or white flowers and waxy green or bronze leaves. Propagate by stem cuttings. Sunny east or west window in winter. Keep soil moist between thorough waterings. Likes cool room (16°C–21°C).

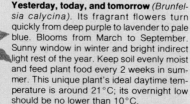

Yesterday, today, and tomorrow (*Brunfelsia calycina*). Its fragrant flowers turn quickly from deep purple to lavender to pale blue. Blooms from March to September. Sunny window in winter and bright indirect light rest of the year. Keep soil evenly moist and feed plant food every 2 weeks in summer. This unique plant's ideal daytime temperature is around 21°C; its overnight low should be no lower than 10°C.

Indoor gardening

Cacti and other succulents

Basketball plant, or Turkish temple (*Euphorbia obesa*). Ball-shaped succulent with small, sweet-smelling flowers in summer. Sunny south window. Keep soil moist in spring and summer; from late fall through winter keep in dryish soil at 7°C.

Bunny ears (*Opuntia microdasys*). A dwarf variety of prickly pear cactus with jointed, pad-shaped stems. Its hooked bristles are difficult to get out of the skin, so handle with thick gloves. Best avoided in households with small children. Sunny south window. Drench; water again only after soil is dry. Temperature: above 4°C.

Christmas cactus (*Schlumbergera bridgesii*). Has flat, segmented, spineless stems tipped with dark-red flowers around Christmas. In spring keep soil moist and put plant in bright indirect light. Let soil dry during July and August; thereafter, water sparingly and keep in a cool but sunny place. Flowering requires 40 days of cool, 12-hour nights.

Devil's backbone, or redbird cactus (*Pedilanthus tithymaloides variegatus*). Not a true cactus. A succulent with distinctive zigzag stems, leaves with white and rosy markings, and scarlet flowers. Sunny window. Temperature: 10°C–30°C.

Donkey tail (*Sedum morganianum*). Tear-shaped succulent leaves on pendulous stems growing as long as 6 ft make it a favorite in Mexican gardens. Sunny window; tolerates bright indirect light. Let soil dry moderately between thorough waterings. Temperature: 13°C–24°C.

Golden barrel, or mother-in-law's chair (*Echinocactus grusonii*). A very popular globular cactus with golden spines and edible flesh. Grows up to 3 ft in diameter; used as a water reservoir in the desert. Must be repotted every 2 or 3 years, but be careful of its brittle roots. Likes sunny window, but introduce it to the full sun gradually. Keep soil moist in summer and dry in winter. Prefers cool night temperatures, but not below 4°C.

Hearts entangled, or rosary vine (*Ceropegia woodii*). Has long wiry stems strung with heart-shaped succulent leaves and tiny beadlike bulblets. Flowers resemble purple lanterns. Plant in sandy soil in a hanging basket or place the pot on a shelf. Prefers sunny window, but tolerates bright north window. Temperature: 13°C–24°C.

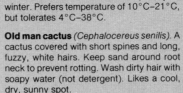
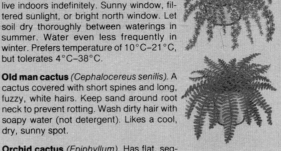

Jade plant (*Crassula argentea*). A small treelike plant with succulent leaves. Can live indoors indefinitely. Sunny window, filtered sunlight, or bright north window. Let soil dry thoroughly between waterings in summer. Water even less frequently in winter. Prefers temperature of 10°C–21°C, but tolerates 4°C–38°C.

Old man cactus (*Cephalocereus senilis*). A cactus covered with short spines and long, fuzzy, white hairs. Keep sand around root neck to prevent rotting. Wash dirty hair with soapy water (not detergent). Likes a cool, dry, sunny spot.

Orchid cactus (*Epiphyllum*). Has flat, segmented, scalloped stems and gorgeous, brilliant flowers. Sunny east or west window or filtered sunlight. In summer let dry between liberal waterings and keep in a sheltered outdoor spot. In winter keep cool and dry, but mist occasionally. Needs winter temperature of 10°C (night) and 21°C (day) for spring blooms.

Panda plant (*Kalanchoe tomentosa*). Fleshy, pale-green leaves covered with a silvery-gray felt. Young plants good for dish gardens or windowsills. Older ones dramatic when lighted. Sunny south window. Water well; let dry between waterings. Temperature: 13°C–21°C.

Powder puff cactus (*Mammilaria bocasana*). Resembles a pile of powder puffs with its globular bodies and white, silky hair. May produce small yellow flowers and purple berries if kept in full sun. Water well and feed monthly in summer. Keep dry and above 4°C in winter. Occasionally turn pot in the sun to avoid uneven growth.

Rattail cactus (*Aporocactus flagelliformis*). Has cascading stems 1/2 in. thick and up to 4 ft long, short thorns or spines, and pink flowers in spring. Best shown in a hanging container or grafted on top of a tall, straight cactus. Requires coarse, heavy potting mix with good drainage. In winter keep above 4°C in a dry, bright place.

Tiger's jaws (*Faucaria tigrina*). Has gray-green leaves dotted with white and edged with sharp "teeth." Although only a couple of inches tall, this South African succulent has large yellow flowers in the fall. Propagate by cuttings in summer. Sunny south window. Keep soil moist in late summer and fall. In winter let soil dry and keep temperature 4°C–7°C.

Ferns

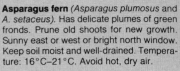
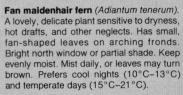
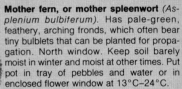
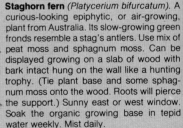
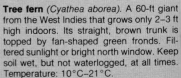

Asparagus fern (*Asparagus plumosus* and *A. setaceus*). Has delicate plumes of green fronds. Prune old shoots for new growth. Sunny east or west or bright north window. Keep soil moist and well-drained. Temperature: 16°C–21°C. Avoid hot, dry air.

Boston fern (*Nephrolepis exalta bostoniensis*). Was fashionable around the turn of the century and is now popular again. Has sword-shaped fronds a couple of feet long with stiff, closely spaced leaves. Filtered sunlight or bright north window. Keep soil evenly moist at all times. Mist often. Temperature: 13°C–24°C.

Fan maidenhair fern (*Adiantum tenerum*). A lovely, delicate plant sensitive to dryness, hot drafts, and other neglects. Has small, fan-shaped leaves on arching fronds. Bright north window or partial shade. Keep evenly moist. Mist daily, or leaves may turn brown. Prefers cool nights (10°C–13°C) and temperate days (15°C–21°C).

Mother fern, or mother spleenwort (*Asplenium bulbiferum*). Has pale-green, feathery, arching fronds, which often bear tiny bulblets that can be planted for propagation. North window. Keep soil barely moist in winter and moist at other times. Put pot in tray of pebbles and water or in enclosed flower window at 13°C–24°C.

Staghorn fern (*Platycerium bifurcatum*). A curious-looking epiphytic, or air-growing, plant from Australia. Its slow-growing green fronds resemble a stag's antlers. Use mix of peat moss and sphagnum moss. Can be displayed growing on a slab of wood with bark intact hung on the wall like a hunting trophy. (Tie plant base and some sphagnum moss onto the wood. Roots will pierce the support.) Sunny east or west window. Soak the organic growing base in tepid water weekly. Mist daily.

Tree fern (*Cyathea aborea*). A 60-ft giant from the West Indies that grows only 2–3 ft high indoors. Its straight, brown trunk is topped by fan-shaped green fronds. Filtered sunlight or bright north window. Keep soil wet, but not waterlogged, at all times. Temperature: 10°C–21°C.

Tsussima holly fern (*Polystichum tsussimense*). A miniature fern good for terrariums and fluorescent gardens, as it usually grows only 5 in. high. Shadowless north window. Temperature: 13°C–21°C. Prefers humid air; tolerates cold drafts.

Climbers and trailers

Firecracker vine *(Manettia inflata).* Can be trained on a small trellis in the pot. Has fleshy leaves, and from spring through fall blooms with tubular red flowers tipped with yellow. Shadowless north window or light shade. Water well. Feed biweekly, except in winter. Temperature: 13°C–21°C. After it flowers, keep it at 10°C.

Heart-leaf philodendron *(Philodendron oxycardium* and *P. cordatum).* One of the most popular indoor plants, it tolerates dim light, heat, and neglect. Thin stems can climb up to 6 ft on stakes or barked slabs, or can cascade from a hanging basket. Bright north or sunny east window. Mature plant can live in dim light but needs bright periods to recuperate. Keep evenly moist. Mist often. Temperature: 18°C–30°C.

Lipstick vine *(Aeschynanthus lobbianus* and *A. parvifolius).* So named because in late spring its trailing stems are tipped with glistening red flowers amid dark green leaves. Propagate by stem cuttings in spring or summer. Sunny east or west window; filtered sunlight in summer. Keep soil evenly moist, but keep dry in May for budding. Temperature: 18°C–24°C.

Purple passion vine *(Gynura sarmentosa).* A fast-growing, easy-to-care-for plant whose wine-red leaves look iridescent with purple, velvety hair. Tends to entwine. Sunny window for brilliant color but tolerates bright north window. Keep soil evenly moist at all times. Feed every month. Temperature: 18°C–30°C.

Spider plant *(Chlorophytum vittatum).* Long arching stems, with slender green-and-white striped leaves, sprout plantlets in midair. North window or winter sun. Keep evenly moist and avoid acid soil. Temperature: 10°C–24°C.

Tahitian bridal veil *(Gibasis geniculata).* Has thin, trailing stems with small green leaves brushed purple on their undersides. Blooms with clouds of tiny, delicate, white flowers. Filtered sunlight or bright north window. Keep soil evenly moist at all times. Mist in winter. Suffers below 13°C.

Wandering Jew *(Tradescantia fluminensis* and *Zebrina pendula).* A name given to many similar trailers with variegated leaves. Prefers filtered sunlight. Avoid strong sun. Tolerates bright north window. Keep soil evenly moist. Mist often. Temperature: 18°C–30°C. Likes humid air.

Food plants

Bean sprouts, or mung beans *(Phaseolus aureus).* Easily grown in the basement or a closet, for the cooking pot or the salad bowl. Get dried mung beans from a garden shop or a Chinese grocery. Soak them in cold water overnight, then spread them out on cheesecloth in a shallow pan. Keep in total darkness at 21°C and sprinkle with tepid water several times daily. In about a week the sprouts are ready to eat.

Eggplant *(Solanum melongena ovigerum).* Can be grown indoors either from young plants or from seeds. For fruit, pollinate blossoms with fine brush. Needs at least 6 hours per day of direct sunlight. Water liberally. Temperature: above 16°C.

Onion *(Allium cepa).* Grows in a pot on a sunny windowsill like any other bulb. Its mauve flower is showy, but odor may be a problem. One solution is to grow it in the kitchen where its scent will blend with cooking aromas.

Parsley *(Petroselinum crispum).* A popular flowering kitchen-window plant that garnishes many dishes. Its curled leaves on ribbed stems should be picked regularly when mature to promote new growth. Sow seeds in seed mix from mid to late spring. Transplant seedlings into small pots. Partially shaded windowsill. Keep evenly moist.

Pepper *(Capsicum annuum acuminatum).* Has colorful green, red, or yellow fruits and is grown mainly for culinary purposes. Pollinate blossoms with brush. Sunny south window; filtered sunlight on very hot days. Feed weekly when flowers appear. Keep temperature around 21°C.

Sweet basil *(Ocimum basilicum).* A spice herb with a faint peppery flavor. Has light-green leaves and tiny lavender-tinged white flowers. Sow seeds in seed mix at 13°C in spring. Transplant seedlings into small individual pots and keep evenly moist. Leaves are available in summer and early fall as spice. Sunny south window. Do not overfeed, or flavor may be reduced.

Tomato *(Lycopersicon esculentum).* Often grown in a pot indoors either from seed or from young plant. Stake the plant. Water daily in hot weather. Prune side shoots and yellowing leaves. Sunny south window; needs at least 6 hours of direct sun per day to blossom. Pollinate flowers with fine brush. When fruits appear, feed liquid tomato food weekly. Keep above 16°C.

Novelty plants

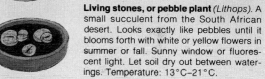

Artillery plant *(Pilea microphylla,* or *P. muscosa).* Has fleshy stems, fernlike leaves, and small, insignificant-looking flowers. From late spring through summer the flowers, when touched, puff out ripened pollen like exploding gunpowder. Sunny east or west window. Keep soil evenly moist. Mist often. Suffers below 16°C.

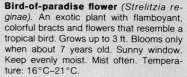

Bird-of-paradise flower *(Strelitzia reginae).* An exotic plant with flamboyant, colorful bracts and flowers that resemble a tropical bird. Grows up to 3 ft. Blooms only when about 7 years old. Sunny window. Keep evenly moist. Mist often. Temperature: 16°C–21°C.

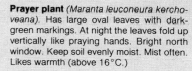

Living stones, or pebble plant *(Lithops).* A small succulent from the South African desert. Looks exactly like pebbles until it blooms forth with white or yellow flowers in summer or fall. Sunny window or fluorescent light. Let soil dry out between waterings. Temperature: 13°C–21°C.

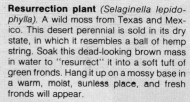

Prayer plant *(Maranta leuconeura kerchoveana).* Has large oval leaves with dark-green markings. At night the leaves fold up vertically like praying hands. Bright north window. Keep soil evenly moist. Mist often. Likes warmth (above 16°C.)

Resurrection plant *(Selaginella lepidophylla).* A wild moss from Texas and Mexico. This desert perennial is sold in its dry state, in which it resembles a ball of hemp string. Soak this dead-looking brown mass in water to "resurrect" it into a soft tuft of green fronds. Hang it up on a mossy base in a warm, moist, sunless place, and fresh fronds will appear.

Sensitive plant *(Mimosa pudica).* Folds its small, feathery leaves when touched or blown on. A tender perennial grown as an annual. Sunny east or west window or bright north window. Keep soil evenly moist. Likes warmth and humidity.

Venus's-flytrap *(Dionaea muscipula)* Called "the most wonderful plant in the world" by Charles Darwin. Grows wild in the swamps of the Carolinas. Its leaves are shaped like jaws with long, sharp teeth. When an insect touches a sensitive hair, the jaws spring shut and a juice is secreted to digest the prey. Plant in a mix of peat moss, sphagnum moss, and vermiculite. Sunny window. Keep moist all the time. Feed with insects, ground meat, cheese, or egg white—not plant food. Keep above 10°C.

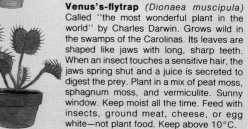

Drying and preserving flowers

Gathering and drying methods

Marigolds and delphiniums; wheat, oat, and barley grasses; larkspurs and buttercups—all can be enjoyed in or out of season. Practically every kind of plant material can be preserved so that it retains its natural color and form.

There are three basic ways to dry and preserve flowers: by hanging and air-drying them, by pressing them, or by treating them with a variety of chemical compounds.

When to gather. Some plants, such as ball thistle, honesty, and yucca (which turns naturally from green to gray), can simply be left in the garden to dry out. Collect seedpods and grasses in midsummer—while the plant is still absorbing moisture and before its color begins to fade. Leaves should be gathered in autumn if you want to press them. Pick green leaves in spring when they are young if you plan to treat them with glycerin.

Snip roses, daffodils, daisies, and other single blooms just as they are about to open, at their very freshest. Cut long spikes of flowers such as delphiniums before the top buds open. Thistles, bulrushes, and pampas grass should also be collected when they are only half developed because the mature pods fall apart easily.

Choosing the appropriate drying method. Hang-drying is the most convenient method to preserve such seed heads as teasels, foxgloves, poppy heads, iris pods, barley, oats, majoram, and wild oregano. Drying goldenrod, lavender, garlic, pinks, and sweet William upright preserves their colors best.

Delphiniums, larkspurs, bells of Ireland, and hydrangeas dry well when left standing in 1/2 inch of water in a dark corner until the water evaporates.

Small, delicate wild flowers and grasses can be dried flat on trays and box lids, in shallow boxes, or on thick sheets of brown paper. Use this method if you find that the stems are too weak to support the weight of the flower heads when hung upside down.

Flowers suitable for pressing include buttercups, wild thyme, clover, barberries, dogwood, roses (press each petal separately), grasses, and honeysuckle. Do not attempt to press wet blooms (gathered after a rain), as the moisture will produce mold.

A simple solution of glycerin (available in drugstores) and water or antifreeze and water will give leaves and berries a permanent glow. Use this method for young beech, maple, and oak leaves; for ivy; and for seed heads such as old-man's beard and sorrel. Prepare the leaves by cutting off damaged parts. Scrape the bark and split the ends of the woody stems about 2 inches up. Put them in a well-mixed solution of 1 part glycerin to 2 parts hot water or of equal parts antifreeze and hot water. Let plants soak until leaves are pliable. Except for ivy, which keeps its natural color, plant colors will deepen to russet, black, dark blue, reddish-brown, and orange.

Household borax, silica-gel crystals (available in hobby shops and florist shops), and treated sand are especially good for preserving flower heads of roses, daisies, daffodils, marigolds, and carnations. These materials will absorb the moisture while leaving the flower's form intact and deepening the color.

Constructing flowers. After drying flowers you may want to combine different parts of them with other plant materials, such as cones, small pods, nuts, and berries, to "construct" your own flowers. For example, cones and honesty petals were used to construct the flower shown on page 311, with only such simple materials as adhesive, floral tape, and wire.

Exquisite floral display is detail from *Still Life: Flowers*, by 19th-century American painter Severin Roesen. Work is in collection of Metropolitan Museum of Art.

Hanging and air-drying

Drying shrinks plants; hang more than you need.

To hang-dry flowers, strip the leaves from the lower part of the stems. (These can be pressed and restored later with floral tape.) Tie the flowers in small bunches with gardener's tape or string. Use a slip knot—the stems will shrink and you will need to tighten the string. Hang the bunches in a dark, warm, dry place where the air circulates freely. Leave them until they rustle when touched.

To air-dry flowers, place the sprays in an open jam jar, pail, or basket and put the container for two or three weeks in an open cupboard or on a shelf where the air can circulate.

As each batch dries, gently cut the tape or string and separate the stems carefully. If you want to store the flowers for a time before making an arrangement, keep them upright if possible. If not, pack them in crumpled tissue paper in boxes or leave them on open shelves. Keep the flowers in a dry place away from direct sunlight.

Pressing flowers

Successful pressing depends on collecting fresh materials. Place them carefully between two sheets of blotting paper or waxed paper (newspapers shed ink); then weight them down with bricks or heavy books and leave them in a warm, dry place for at least four to six weeks. Use blotting paper for very fleshy flowers, such as daisies; use waxed paper for delicate petals, such as baby's breath. The longer the pressing time, the stronger and more resistant to fading the colors will be when the pressed flowers are once again exposed to the light of day.

Hardy ferns and heavy green leaves can be pressed by placing them between sheets of writing paper or paper towels and putting these on the floor under a heavily trafficked area of rug for an entire summer.

Delicate flowers can be pressed between the pages of a heavy book, such as a dictionary. Line the pages with wax paper or blotting paper. Press only a small amount of material on each page, arranging the plants so that no single petal or leaf touches another.

Tease stalks of wild flowers, clover, and buttercups into soft curls to avoid harsh angles in pressed-flower compositions.

Inspect fleshy flowers once or twice during the pressing period and change the blotting paper if it is saturated. Put each flower or leaf in a separate transparent envelope, available in photography shops; store all pressed material in a dry place to avoid mildew formation. You can create an infinite variety of delicate pressed-flower compositions by following the illustrated instructions below.

Fold waxed paper (or blotting paper) so that crease falls in center of book. Put similar plant material—delicate or fleshy—together on same page.

Remove pressed flowers with tweezers. Arrange them on heavy paper. Dab a bit of latex adhesive behind flower centers and backs of stems.

Gently press flowers into position with fingers. When completely dry, place composition on a stiff backing. Lower glass over the arrangement.

Tape the glass, the composition, and the backing together. Use plastic electrician's tape or a brighter colored tape of similar strength.

Drying and preserving flowers

Drying with desiccants

1. Cut off stem 1/2 in. below bud. Make a hook in the end of a 10-in. piece of wire. Put the straight end of the wire into the center of the bud. Pull through until the hook rests in the bud.

2. Coil the wire under the bud. Pour a 1-in. layer of silica gel into an airtight container, such as a polyethylene bread box or a cake tin. Insert the flower, coil first.

4. When all the flowers are in the container, make sure no two flowers are touching. Using a small paper cup or coffee measuring spoon, trickle the gel onto the petals.

5. Continue to build up the layer of silica-gel crystals. Make sure all plant surfaces are covered. If you wish, add leaves cut from their stems and cover them with crystals.

7. Hold each flower by its base and straighten the coiled wire. Blow away gel. Prepare leaves by gluing piece of wire to back center veins, leaving 1/2 in. of wire extending from each base.

8. Wrap floral tape around the base of the flower. Continue wrapping tape all along the wire stem in a downward spiral, pulling the tape snug with your fingers as you twist it.

A desiccant is a drying agent used to gradually draw out moisture. Flowers are buried in granular desiccants for a period of up to four days to preserve them in such a way that they will still look natural and fresh. Desiccating causes reds, blues, and yellows to deepen in tone, while other colors will fade slightly.

There are several types of commonly available desiccants; the method illustrated at right is appropriate for all.

Household borax, available in drugstores and hardware stores, has the lightest granular formation and is best suited to fragile wild flowers. Because borax is so light, it may be difficult to work into the smallest crevices. Use a small paintbrush to sweep the borax into the centers and folds of flowers, or mix in a little cornmeal to add weight.

Sand is a readily available desiccant, but it has one major drawback: it has to be thoroughly washed before it can be used. Washing and drying may take half a day. To begin, put the sand into a bucket, fill it with water, and stir well. Pour off excess water, refill the bucket with water, and add several handfuls of household detergent. Stir again and pour out the excess water. Rinse the sand in fresh water over and over until the water poured away is clear. Spread the sand in a shallow container, and dry it in the sun or in a 120°C oven. Since sand is heavier than borax, take care to pour it slowly and to support the flowers with your hands as you pour.

Ground silica-gel crystals are an effective and popular desiccant because they are easy to use and can be reused indefinitely. The blue crystals turn pink when they have absorbed as much water as they can. To reactivate the crystals, spread them out in a shallow pan and put the pan in a 120°C oven until the crystals turn blue again (about 30 minutes).

Constructed flowers

3. With your fingers, gently push the silica gel up under the flower until it is well supported. Prop up each petal in exactly the position you want it to be in when thoroughly dried.

6. Cover container and put a band of tape around the lid. Place container in a dry room. Remove flowers carefully after two days or when they are crisp and papery to the touch.

9. To attach leaves, wrap floral tape around wires extending from them, then wind tape around flower stem until leaves are securely affixed. Bend leaves to desired angles.

Flowers constructed from natural materials, ordinary household supplies, and items available at your local florist can be made more durable than flowers that are simply dried. These sturdy constructions are suitable for everything from decorative wall hangings to boutonnieres.

Honesty, Chinese lantern, iris, yucca, lily, poppy, mallow, and wild cucumber seedpods are particularly adaptable to constructed flowers. Tulip, magnolia, larch, mahogany, coconut, and sandalwood tree pods are also durable and decorative. Save cones and berries found on field hikes to make flower centers.

Besides the natural materials you gather, you will need scissors, a sharp knife, wire, wire clippers, brown floral tape, PVA glue, and masking tape.

When constructing flowers, always try to build them up the way the petals being used would actually grow. For example, honesty petals naturally grow opposite one another.

Opposing petals may best simulate nature.

In order to give a constructed flower a natural appearance, you may need to add paper appendages to the plant material. You can make a conelike

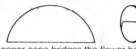

A paper cone bridges the flower head and stem.

calyx, for example, from a piece of construction paper cut in a semicircle. Step-by-step instructions for making a constructed flower appear below.

1. Anchor a 12-in. wire at base of small pinecone. Wrap wire around cone several times to be certain it is secure. (The smaller, more rounded the cone, the easier it is to use.)

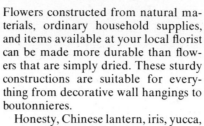

2. Make a paper cone as illustrated in the drawings that appear with the text. Glue end of a long strip of brown floral tape to the cone and begin wrapping cone as shown here.

3. Slide the paper cone up the wire stem so that the wider end of the paper cone meets the pinecone. Wrap tape tightly, on the bias, until the stem is completely covered.

4. Separate honesty petals carefully from stems. Petals will be brittle; any wrong pull will cause a rip. Dab glue on small end of a petal and on pinecone where you plan to place a petal. Begin gluing petals at base of cone, placing one opposite another.

5. Continue working around the base of the pinecone. Once the base petals are in place, add petals above the base in same way as shown in the last step.

6. Continue working around flower, placing final petals nearest the center of flower. About 10 petals will make a full flower. Overlap petals on both edges to avoid a propeller-like appearance.

Mosaics

Pictures from fragments

Mosaics are made up of bits and fragments of colored stone, glass, ceramic tile, and other materials. From close up these fragments may make no visual sense. Viewed from a distance, however, they arrange themselves into colorful pictures or designs. In this, mosaic technique is similar to pointillism, the 19th-century school of art in which whole scenes were painted with clusters of dots, or points, which resolve themselves into a picture only when seen from afar. Television pictures operate on the same principle: the screen actually shows only a mass of tiny dots of colored light, which appear to the eye as a coherent moving picture.

Origins. Mosaics seem to have originated in the Near East. Some 5,000 years ago in Erech, Sumeria, long terra-cotta cones with colored heads were driven into walls and columns in decorative patterns. But mosaics did not become popular until the eighth century B.C., when a good number of nonfigural mosaic floors were laid in Crete and Asia Minor.

Among the earliest known figural works are 18 pebble mosaics at Olynthus, Greece, dating back to the fourth century B.C. These mosaics, which decorated the floors of private homes, depict scenes from Greek myths. One shows the hero Bellerophon astride Pegasus, the winged horse, fighting the monster Chimera.

In classical times new materials were introduced, including glass, colored marble, and limestone. Uniform rectangular pieces of material, called tesserae, were also introduced. Their regular shapes made it easier to fit pieces close together.

Wall mosaics became common in the Roman Era. The mosaics discovered in the ruins of Pompeii—one of the cities destroyed by the eruption of

Birds are seen boarding Noah's ark in 13th-century mosaic in St. Mark's Basilica.

Tools and materials

Mount Vesuvius in A.D. 79—incorporate great color and detail in their scenes from myth, history, and everyday life. As the Romans went about conquering the world, they brought the art of mosaics with them everywhere, from Africa to Britain.

Byzantine mosaics. The early Christians began using mosaics in churches as early as the 4th century, and the art of mosaics reached its peak during the time of the Byzantine Empire—the 4th through the 15th centuries. The walls and ceilings of Byzantine churches were covered with great mosaics depicting scenes from the Bible and from the lives of the saints. These mosaics were important not only for their great beauty, but also for their instructional value in a largely illiterate society.

Some of the greatest examples of early Byzantine mosaics can be seen in Ravenna, Italy. The magnificent mosaics in the Hagia Sophia in Constantinople (now Istanbul) date from the 6th century to the 12th. St. Mark's Basilica in Venice has fine examples of late Byzantine art.

Decline and revival. By the end of the 12th century Gothic architecture was taking over, and stained glass windows replaced mosaics in the churches. Thereafter, mosaics remained largely unpopular until our own time, except for a brief revival in the 19th century. Now once again they are being created with style and imagination.

The New World. The mosaic technique was developed independently in pre-Columbian Mesoamerica by the sixth century. The Mayas and Aztecs decorated masks, shields, and helmets with mosaics of turquoise and other materials. Latin America is also a center of the current revival. The exteriors of the buildings at the University of Mexico are covered with mosaics of great beauty and diversity, designed by Diego Rivera and other leading artists.

Many of the tools and materials used for mosaics are items you probably have already, such as a hammer, nails, and bits of wood. All specialty items required are described below.

Tesserae and cutters. Mosaics are made up of small, varicolored units called tesserae—from the Latin word *tessera* ("four sided"). An uncut tessera is generally square or rectangular. Ceramic tiles and glass tiles are the most common tesserae, but almost any material can be used, including shells, wood, and plastic.

Glazed ceramic tiles about 3/8 inch square are available in crafts and hobby shops and in art supply stores. You can also make your own (see p. 317). Commercial tesserae that may be

harder to find include opaque glass tiles, porcelain tiles, and smalti (glass tiles with irregular surfaces that increase the reflective properties of the piece). Smalti resemble the tesserae used in the great Byzantine mosaics, but they are expensive. Stained glass cut to various shapes and sizes can also be used as tesserae. When handling small tesserae, use tweezers.

For cutting the tesserae you will need a good pair of tile nippers (a tool resembling pliers), which have sharp jaws for cutting ceramic or glass tiles. (For directions on their use, see the illustrations below.) If you use glass in your mosaic, you will need a glass cutter. (For directions on cutting glass, see *Stained glass,* p. 106.)

Adhesives and grout. You can use any adhesive that will bind the materials involved. Cement is the traditional adhesive, but it makes the mosaic extremely heavy. Polyvinyl acetate (PVA), or white glue, is best for small mosaics, and it is easy to use.

After the mosaic has been put together and glued or cemented to its backing, the spaces between the tesserae should be filled with grout—a creamy cement mixture. Buy a commercial mosaic grout or make your own by mixing 1 part lime to 5 parts Portland cement, then stirring in water slowly until the mixture attains the consistency of sour cream. Cement dyes are also available. To color the grout, add dye to the dry ingredients.

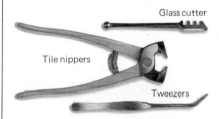

Glass cutter

Tile nippers

Tweezers

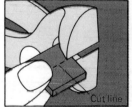

Cut line   Cut line

Cut tiles at any angle with a pair of nippers. Hold tile at one end of proposed line of cut between thumb and forefinger. Place nippers with jaws along cut line, but cover only part of it. Squeeze nipper handles firmly together until tile snaps in two. **Caution: Wear protective glasses, as pieces may fly into your eyes.**

Direct and indirect methods

Two basic methods are used today for creating mosaics: the direct and the indirect. The methods vary only in the manner in which the tesserae are assembled and laid in the adhesive.

In the direct method the tesserae are placed down one by one. In the indirect method they are first arranged loose on another surface exactly as they will be in the finished mosaic. A frame of lathing strips is nailed around the arrangement to keep the pieces from shifting. Then a piece of tracing paper is pasted to the tops of the tesserae with water soluble paste. When the paste has dried, the entire mosaic—or a section of it if it is a large work—is lifted up and placed into position on the per-

manent adhesive. When this adhesive has dried, the paper is moistened and carefully removed.

General procedures. To make a mosaic by either technique, first complete your design and draw its outline full size on a piece of paper. This is called the cartoon. Cut the tiles you will be using and fit them into place on the cartoon to help you judge the spacing and overall effect. The small tesserae and the spaces between them must be manipulated to give the most pleasing appearance. Generally, if you want a lot of detail in the mosaic, you should use smaller tesserae of various shapes so that you can more easily fit them close together.

If you are using the direct method, copy the cartoon onto the surface that will be used as backing for the mosaic. Apply the adhesive to the surface, and set the tiles into place one by one. Do large mosaics one section at a time.

Let the adhesive dry overnight. Then rub grout into the spaces between the tesserae, scrape off the excess, and clean the surface with a damp sponge. Let the grout dry for at least 4 hours, preferably overnight. Grout and clean the mosaic again. When the second coat of grout is dry, smooth it down with a stiff-bristled brush. Sponge the surface clean and apply liquid floor wax to the finished mosaic. These final steps are the same for both methods.

Mosaics/project

Making a table by the direct method

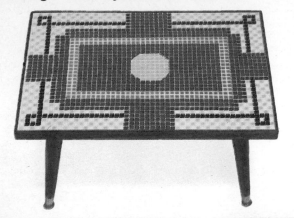

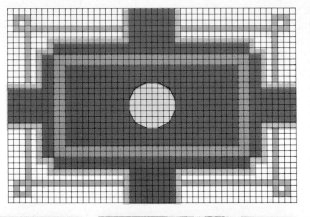

Cover an old tabletop with a ceramic tile mosaic or make your own table. The geometric pattern at left is a good design for a beginner.

To make your own table, get a piece of 3/4-inch plywood, enough 1-inch-wide decorated wood stripping or molding to go all around the edges of the plywood, and four ready-made table legs with connecting brackets. Measure and cut the edging to fit around the plywood as an apron. Sand the edging and legs, stain and varnish them, and set them aside. Then follow the illustrated directions below.

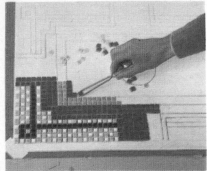

1. Draw cartoon, testing measurements by placing tiles down on it from time to time. Tape completed cartoon to a board and position all tiles on it, using either tweezers or your fingers.

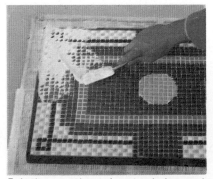

2. Draw a copy of cartoon on base you will use for tabletop. Use a ruler and compass to get design straight. Inaccurate measuring could ruin a geometric design such as this.

3. Place board with tiles over one end of base or right beside it so that you will not have to carry tiles too far. With a brush, spread white glue evenly over one corner of base.

4. Transfer tiles from board to prepared section of base one at a time. Apply glue to a second section and transfer tiles to it. Proceed in this same manner until all tiles have been glued down.

5. Let glue dry overnight. The next day mix grout in a bowl until it has consistency of sour cream. Spread it generously over entire surface of mosaic with a rubber scraper.

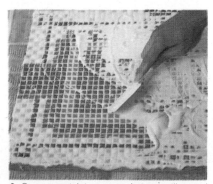

6. Force grout into spaces between tiles and scrape off excess. Wipe surface clean with a damp sponge. Let grout dry overnight, then nail on wood siding strips prepared earlier.

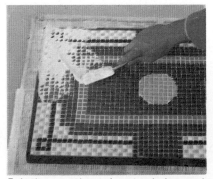

7. Apply a second coat of grout and rub as much of it as you can down between the tiles. Scrape off any excess grout and sponge the surface clean. Let the grout dry overnight.

8. Vigorously brush mosaic with stiff-bristled scrub brush to smooth out grout. Sponge clean. Apply coat of liquid floor wax to mosaic and wood. Attach leg brackets and screw in legs.

Making a trivet by the indirect method

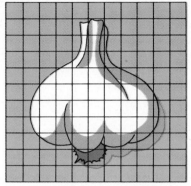

Each square in grid equals a ½-in. square.

The indirect method is best for mosaics that require a large number of tesserae. The trivet shown at left is made up of many tiny pieces of glazed ceramic tile. The small, close-set tesserae make the head of garlic appear realistic, even at relatively close range. This project should give you a good idea of how to design representational mosaics—how to make a fairly realistic picture with tiny colored fragments. Use a small piece of 3/4-inch plywood for the base of the trivet and 1-inch-wide decorated wood strips or molding for the edging.

This can be a project for the entire family. Begin by enlarging the design at left. (see *Drawing*, pp. 210–219). Then let one member of the family cut the tiles while another places them on the cartoon. When the workers get tired, let someone else relieve them.

Note that although there are curved lines in the design, you cannot cut curves into the tiles. Instead, you must arrange a number of tiny squares, triangles, and other shapes made up of straight lines in such a way as to approximate a curve. When the mosaic is grouted, the lines will appear curved from a distance.

1. Draw cartoon and tape down wood slats around outside border to keep tiles from slipping. Place cut fragments of tile onto cartoon, positioning them to fit together.

2. When all tiles have been positioned, check carefully for gaps. If design is alright, cut tracing paper to size of mosaic and liberally brush it on one side with library paste.

3. Place paper, paste side down, onto tiles. Being careful not to disturb any tiny tile fragments, smooth paper down over entire mosaic with your hands. Let paste dry thoroughly.

4. Loosen taped slats from working surface and turn mosaic over. Apply white glue to plywood base, and place plywood, glue side down, squarely over backs of tiles.

5. Press plywood base into tiles and weight it down with books or something else of substantial weight. Leave it for 24 hr or more, to be sure glue cures properly.

6. Turn mosaic right-side up again and pull wood slats away from its sides. Gently peel off tracing paper. If it is stubborn, wet surface. Sponge off any paste residue.

7. Using piece of heavy cardboard or rubber scraper, apply grout generously to surface, forcing it down into spaces between tiles. Scrape off excess; sponge mosaic clean.

8. Let grout dry overnight. Meanwhile, measure sides of mosaic and cut, sand, stain, and varnish edging. When grout and varnish are dry, nail edging onto sides of base.

9. Apply second coat of grout. Once again force as much grout as you can into spaces between tiles. Scrape off all excess grout and sponge surface of mosaic clean.

10. Vigorously brush surface with stiff-bristled scrub brush to wear down any unevenness in grout. Sponge mosaic clean. Give mosaic and wood a coat of liquid floor wax.

Mosaics/project

Mixing glass and tile tesserae

Each square in grid over this pattern equals 1 sq in. on panel.

Glazed ceramic tiles are the most commonly used tesserae, and pieces of stained glass are the second most commonly used. The floral mosaic panel shown at far left incorporates both. The flowers themselves are made up of brightly colored pieces of glass, and the background is filled in with a variety of tile chips of neutral colors.

To make the panel, enlarge the cartoon at left (see *Drawing*, pp. 210–219) and copy it onto a piece of plywood 9 by 13 inches. Cut the paper cartoon of the flowers into individual patterns for each piece of glass in the design. Following these patterns, cut the glass carefully. (For a full discussion on types of glass and on how to cut glass, see *Stained glass*, pp. 105–106.) Apply adhesive to the floral part of the panel and position the glass. Apply the rest of the adhesive and fill in the panel with tile chips. When the panel is fully covered, grout and clean the mosaic.

As in the preceding projects, add decorated wood strips to the edges of the panel or, if you prefer, put the mosaic into a more elaborate frame (see *Picture framing*, pp. 404–408) and hang it on a wall. It can also serve as a bright and decorative trivet.

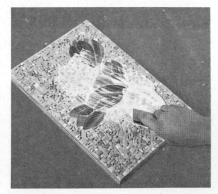

1. Copy cartoon onto plywood base and cut glass to exact sizes and shapes needed. Using direct method, begin mosaic. Apply white glue to floral section and position all the glass first.

2. Cut tiles into chips of various sizes and shapes. A section at a time, add white glue to base and fill in with tile chips. Fill in around flowers first, then edges, then center.

3. Let glue dry overnight, then apply grout to entire mosaic, forcing it down between pieces of glass and tile. Scrape off excess grout, sponge mosaic clean, and let dry overnight.

4. Nail on edging if you plan to use it, then apply second coat of grout. Clean as before and let grout dry thoroughly. Brush dry surface vigorously, sponge clean, and apply liquid wax.

Mosaics/project

Making your own ceramic tiles

If you have access to a kiln, you can make your own ceramic tiles for use in mosaics. By etching or sculpting the tiles, you can create your own original designs. The table shown at left was inlaid with homemade tiles.

Begin by removing the air bubbles from the clay and making it pliable by kneading it—a process called wedging. (For a discussion of wedging, see *Pottery*, pp. 140–141.)

Press mold. Any number of tiles can be manufactured with a plaster press mold. The mold is easy to make and inexpensive. Begin by positioning two wood slats parallel to each other over a piece of burlap. The length of the slats and the distance between them depend on the size and number of tiles you want to make. The burlap will prevent sticking. Fill the space between the slats with clay and smooth it with a rolling pin until it is even with the tops of the slats over its entire surface.

Cut out tiles with a knife or a cookie cutter. You can make them all alike or cut them to different sizes and shapes. If you want them to be perfectly symmetrical, carefully measure them with a ruler and square and etch the cutting lines into the clay with the point of a nail. For more decorative tiles, sculpt a design on top of each with more clay.

Place the cut tiles in a box and cover them with plaster of Paris. When the clay is leather hard and begins to pull away from the plaster mold, the mold is dry; remove the tiles. The plaster mold can be used over and over. Each batch of tiles made will be exactly the same. The tiles must then be fired and glazed (see *Pottery*, pp. 167–176).

1. Position two parallel wood slats over piece of burlap. Slats must be of same thickness as tiles will be. Press wedged clay between slats and roll it out flush with tops of slats. Remove slats.

2. Mark off edges of clay with point of nail at uniform distances. (Distance should equal width of tile you are making.) Cut out tiles with knife, using long stick across marks as guide.

3. Remove tiles you have cut out of block of clay and place them inside a shallow box with at least 1/2 in. of space around each. Put in as many as you can, but do not crowd them together.

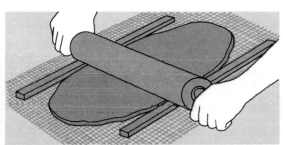

4. Mix a batch of plaster of Paris to consistency of thick soup and pour it over clay tiles in box. Smooth plaster out with a spatula or putty knife. Let dry until clay is leather hard (about 2 or 3 hr).

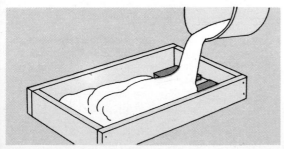

5. When clay is thoroughly dry, it will shrink away from sides of mold slightly and be easy to remove. Remove mold from box and tap it lightly on bottom; tiles will fall out.

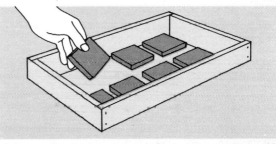

6. Press more clay into mold with fingers and smooth off top with a stick. Let clay dry overnight; remove tiles. Make as many batches as needed, then fire and glaze tiles (see *Pottery*, pp. 167–176).

Nature, the first lapidary, fashioned these minerals. These museum specimens would not be cut and polished, but the earth contains myriad specimens of suitable gemstone materials.

Working with gemstones

Lapidary is the art of cutting, shaping, and polishing gemstones. The word "lapidary" comes from the Latin *lapidarius* ("of stone"); it is used for the artist-craftsman who does the work, for the work itself, and for the place in which the work is done.

The development of lapidary. Nature herself was the first lapidary. Since the world was formed, raging rivers have been cutting deep canyons into rock and shaping and polishing stones into works of great beauty, and the grinding action of the surf and sand on seashores has been transforming pebbles into forms that would grace any piece of man-made jewelry. Far back in prehistoric times man took the hint from nature and used beautiful stones, pebbles, and shells to adorn himself. First he probably took those he found in nature, but soon he learned to bring out the beauty of the gemstones himself.

In Mesopotamia, as long ago as 4000 B.C., stones were being shaped by hand. By 3000 B.C. lapidaries were using wheels to shape gemstones into flat and rounded forms.

Lapidary work was widespread throughout the ancient world from Egypt to China. The Greeks and Romans were adept at engraving gems for use in rings and other jewelry. The Bible (Exodus 28:9-20) gives a detailed description of how the vestments of the priests should be decorated with gems engraved with the names of the 12 sons of Israel and set in gold filigree. The stones, which are all named, included lapis lazuli and amethyst.

Gemstones continued to be shaped during the Middle Ages. Not only was lapidary work done throughout the known world, it was also done in many parts of the unknown world. The Maoris of New Zealand and the Incas

and Aztecs of South America and Mesoamerica were carving jade long before the arrival of the Europeans.

In the 15th century it was discovered that diamond powder fixed to the rim of a rotating metal wheel could be used to cut and shape diamonds. Soon after, the technique of faceting was developed, which shows off to full advantage the brillance of diamonds and other transparent stones.

In the late 19th or early 20th century electric motors began to be used to drive lapidary wheels. In the second half of the 20th century lapidary became popular with hobbyists, and lapidary clubs were formed in many parts of the world.

Classes of gem cuts. The most common classes of gem cuts are lapped, faceted, cabochon, and tumbled. Lapped stones are perfectly flat. Faceted stones have a network of flat

surfaces arranged around the surface of the stone in such a way that light will be reflected and refracted in the stone to bring out the full beauty of the gem. Cabochon stones have smooth, rounded surfaces. Tumbled stones are smooth but irregular in shape. Gemstones can also be engraved or carved.

Faceting stones is an advanced technique. Although cutting a single facet is easy enough, cutting a large number of perfectly matched facets at the required angles takes a great deal of experience and is generally done only by professionals. Lapped stones are used mainly for special purposes, such as inlay. Engraving and carving are also special techniques. Consequently, faceting, lapping, carving, and engraving are not dealt with in this book; but full directions for tumbling stones and for cutting and polishing cabochons are given in the following pages.

Lapidary

Tools and materials

The simplest of all lapidary techniques is tumbling. It also requires the least amount of equipment: a tumbling machine, a collection of small gemstones in the rough, some abrasive grits, and a polishing agent. Cutting a cabochon requires a saw; machinery for grinding, sanding, and polishing; a few hand tools and materials; and gem materials.

If you wish to try cutting a cabochon before investing in lapidary machinery, take a course in lapidary at a crafts school or join a lapidary club. Many lapidary clubs have workshops and charge members a small fee for the use of their equipment. Some supply free instruction. If not, there is often a member who will be glad to show you his equipment, to advise you what to buy to suit your needs, and to give you hints on using the equipment.

Gem materials. The lapidary's basic materials are gems, which should not be confused with rocks. Gems are stones that are exceptionally beautiful, relatively rare, and comparatively hard and durable. A few stones that are not very hard or rare but that are of great beauty, such as malachite, are also considered gems. Gems are generally made up of single minerals. Rocks are aggregates of minerals and are usually too soft to be polished. However, single-mineral gems are sometimes found embedded in rocks, and a few rocks of particular beauty and durability, such as lapis lazuli (a mixture of lazurite, iron pyrites, and limestone), are treated as gems. In addition, a few organic materials, such as amber, coral, and pearl, are considered gems.

The hardness of gems is measured on the Mohs' scale, which was devised by the German mineralogist Friedrich Mohs in 1822. The scale (at right) consists of 10 carefully selected minerals arranged in decreasing order of hardness. It measures the ability of one mineral to scratch the next softest. The

scale is not calibrated. The difference between the hardness of 10 (diamond) and that of 9 (corundum) is greater than that between 9 and 1 (talc).

Stones with a hardness of 7 or more are best for lapidary work, but a few softer stones—including opal and turquoise –are also used. Ruby and sapphire (both of hardness 9) should be worked only by experienced lapidaries, and diamond, because of its extraordinary hardness, is cut only by specialists.

You can buy gem materials at lapidary supply houses or rock shops. They are sold in chunks and slabs and in pebbles for tumbling or in small, rough chunks not deemed suitable for slabbing but still good for tumbling into free-form gemstones.

You can also collect your own stones, but it is difficult to know which ones will polish well. Whenever possible consult an experienced lapidary.

Mohs' scale of hardness

10	Diamond	5	Apatite
9	Corundum	4	Fluorite
8	Topaz	3	Calcite
7	Quartz	2	Gypsum
6	Feldspar	1	Talc

Hardnesses of some popular gemstones

Agate	7	Moonstone	6
Amber	2-2.5	Nephrite jade	6-6.5
Amethyst	7	Opal	5-6.5
Carnelian	7	Ruby	9
Coral	3.5-4	Sapphire	9
Diamond	10	Serpentine	2-4
Emerald	7.5-8	Tiger's-eye	7
Garnet	7-7.5	Topaz	8
Lapis lazuli	5-6	Tourmaline	7-7.5
Malachite	3.5-4	Turquoise	5-6

Otherwise, use the hit or miss method, following these hints: Using a penknife, scrape off any surface accumulations from the stone you are considering and examine the stone carefully. If it is porous, granular, or flaky, or if it has raised veins on its surface, reject it. If it has none of these defects, try to scratch it with the steel blade of the penknife. If you cannot scratch it, the stone is probably hard enough to use.

Tumbling equipment. A typical tumbling machine consists of an electric motor, a barrel, and a frame with rollers. One of the rollers is connected to the motor by a belt and pulley. During operation, the stones are placed inside the barrel with an abrasive grit and water, the barrel is placed on the rollers, the motor turns the roller it is attached to, and the roller turns the barrel. The movement of the barrel causes the stones and grit to knock against each other, and the resulting abrasion wears the stones smooth.

Many models of tumbling machines are available. Since tumblers must operate continuously for weeks at a time, be sure to get one with a good motor, sturdy parts and bearings, and a strong, leakproof barrel lining.

Choose the size tumbler you will need based on the amount of tumbling you expect to do. Sizes are measured by the capacity of the barrel, ranging from 1½ to 12 pounds. But bear in mind that only a full load can be tumbled—never a partial load. (A full load consists of enough stones to take up a little less than three-quarters of the barrel. The weight specified in the barrel capacity is the weight of the stones, grit, and water together.) Only small stones can be tumbled in small tumblers.

Tumbling machines are also available with two barrels. Since stones must be tumbled in two separate groups (moderately hard and very hard), a double-barrel machine is

Tumbler with two 2½-lb barrels

Tumbler with single 2⅛-lb barrel

handy, as it allows you to tumble both groups at the same time or to reserve one barrel for polishing only.

In addition to a tumbler you will need various silicon-carbide grits for grinding down the stones. For rough grinding use a grit of 80 or 100 mesh; for fine grinding use a grit of 400, 500, or 600 mesh. (Experience will teach you which grit is best for which stones.) An 80-mesh grit is one that has been passed through a screen with 80 holes per square inch. The higher the mesh, the finer the grit. You will also need cerium oxide for polishing.

Lapidary saws. Gems are generally found in large chunks that must be cut down to a workable size. First the chunk must be cut into slabs, then the slabs must be cut close to the size the finished stone will be. The first of these cuts is made with a slabbing saw; the second, with a trim saw.

Slabbing saws are very expensive and are rarely found in home workshops. You can buy gem materials in *(continued on next page)*

Lapidary

Tools and materials (continued)

precut slabs or have them slabbed for a nominal charge at a lapidary club, school, or dealer.

A trim saw is a small power saw with a circular blade that is charged with diamond dust. The blade of the saw is set into a metal table. The blade cuts the stone on the surface of the table, then passes through a tank of water below the table. The water acts as a coolant to keep the blade from overheating due to friction. You will need a trim saw and a blade to fit it.

Grinding and polishing machines. The ideal lapidary shop has separate machines for grinding, sanding, and polishing cabochons, but a beginner can make do with a single lapidary arbor, a motor with a double shaft, and the necessary wheels (wheels 6 inches in diameter are ideal for home shops).

A lapidary arbor consists mainly of a hood, a spindle with a pulley, tubes with spigots to let water flow over the wheels when they are in place, and a basin to catch the water.

Some models come equipped with motors, but most come without them. You will need an electric motor that runs at 1,725 revolutions per minute, a double spindle for the motor, and a belt. The motor and pulleys should be such that the surface speed of the wheels, when attached and running, is

2,250 feet per minute for grinding and between 1,000 and 2,000 feet per minute for polishing. Revolutions per minute are not the same as surface speed. The surface speed varies with the diameter of the wheel being used.

To operate the machine with a 6-inch wheel at the proper grinding and sanding speed, use a motor pulley 1/4 inch smaller in diameter than the pulley on the arbor. To operate the machine at the proper polishing speed, use a motor pulley that is 1¼ to 2 inches smaller than the arbor pulley. The smaller the motor pulley in relation to the arbor pulley, the higher the surface speed of the wheel will be. Use a 5/8-inch-thick belt; the top of the belt should be flush with the tops of the two pulleys. Once the machine is set up, you can change speeds easily by switching the belt from one motor pulley to the other.

Water can be fed into the arbor with a recirculating pump or with plastic tubing connected to a faucet. Or you can position a container with a spigot at the bottom above the arbor.

To complete the machine, you will need the various wheels. Get a 100-grit silicon-carbide lapidary wheel for rough grinding and a 220-grit wheel for fine grinding. Silicon carbide is a man-made abrasive with a hardness of 9¼ on the Mohs' scale. The higher the grit number, the finer the grit.

After grinding, a stone must be sanded and polished. You can get a 6-inch flexible rubber drum that can be mounted on the arbor and fitted with sanding belts of various grits. You will need a 320-grit belt and a 500- or 600-grit belt. For polishing get an end plate that can be screwed onto the arbor and two leather polishing disks that can be glued onto the spongy face of the end plate. If you prefer not to invest in a rubber sanding drum, use sanding disks on the same end plate.

Trim saw

Lapidary arbor with grinding wheel and sanding drum

Grinding wheel   Rubber sanding drum   Sanding belt   End plate   Leather polishing disk

Combination machines are available that have a trim saw and grinding, sanding, and polishing wheels all on one axle, but these can present problems. The entire machine must be disassembled to change an inside wheel.

Other tools and materials. In addition to the gem materials and machinery, you will need a few miscellaneous tools and materials to fashion a cabochon. Get a template for tracing the shape of the stone you wish to cut onto the rough slab of stone. The template is merely a piece of plastic or metal with various shapes and sizes of cabochon stones cut out of it. Each is labeled with the size of the stone. (Stones are always measured in millimeters with the larger dimension written first.) To scribe the shape onto the stone, you will need an aluminum pencil 1/8 inch in diameter. The pencil can be sharpened to a fine point on a 100-grit grinding wheel. If the scribe

mark is too faint, use a fine-pointed felt marking pen with water-resistant ink. A bit of acrylic spray fixative will keep the mark clear.

Tripoli (a fine-grained silicon powder) and cerium oxide are used for polishing stones. Get separate small brushes for applying each one.

A dop stick is used to hold the stone after the rough grinding. It is simply a short length of wooden dowel 1/8 or 1/4 inch in diameter, depending on the size of the stone. Dopping wax—a combination of wax and shellac—is used to hold the stone to the dopping stick. The wax is melted over an alcohol lamp. Tweezers are needed to hold the stone while dopping it.

Finally, get a 2½- to 4-power jeweler's loupe for examining the stone while you are grinding, sanding, and polishing it. A loupe is a magnifying glass in a plastic case that is held in the eye like a monocle.

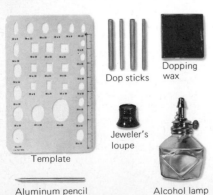

Template

Dop sticks

Dopping wax

Jeweler's loupe

Aluminum pencil

Alcohol lamp

Tumbling gemstones

In tumbling, rough stones are placed in a rotating barrel with water and an abrasive grit and are left there until the stones become smooth and polished. Tumbling is done in several stages. The stones are tumbled first with a rough grit of silicon carbide, then with a fine grit. They are then tumbled with a polishing agent and, finally, with clean water and a bit of detergent. Some lapidaries add a tumbling with a medium grit between the first two steps, but this is not necessary. The entire process takes several weeks.

The finished stones will be irregular in shape. If you want to control the shapes of the stones to a certain extent, grind them to a rough shape (pp. 322–323) before tumbling them.

Although tumbling is basically simple, care must be taken to use only hard stones, to load the barrel correctly, to cull out pitted or deeply scratched stones, and to thoroughly clean both the stones and the barrel after each stage of tumbling.

Use only stones of a hardness of 6 or more, and tumble stones of the same hardness together. If you have collected your own stones, use only the ones you cannot scratch with a penknife, then separate these into groups of moderately hard and very hard. If you can scratch the stone with a hard steel file, put it into the moderately hard group; if you cannot, put it into the very hard group. Examine all the stones carefully, and discard any that have deep pits or scratches.

Mix stones of different shapes and sizes for the best results, but do not use too many large stones. If your tumbler has a capacity of 3 pounds or less, use stones 1/4 to 1 inch in diameter; if it has a larger capacity, you may include larger stones.

For your first tumbling you should have enough stones in each group for two batches. After the first stage of tumbling you will have to cull out stones that have developed deep pits and scratches, and even the good stones will be smaller. Consequently, you will not have enough stones left for a full load for your second stage of grinding. You must therefore rough-grind a second batch of the same group in order to have a full load. Without a full load, the stones will not tumble correctly. Once you have a supply of tumbled stones, you can add finished stones to the barrel to complete the load for the second stage. If you do not have enough stones for two batches of each group for your first tumbling, you can leave the bad stones in after the first stage, but the results of this first tumbling will not be as good.

Moderately hard and very hard stones are both tumbled in the same way, in the following four stages.

Rough grinding. Wash the barrel of the tumbler and put enough stones into it so that it is a little less than three-quarters full. Do not handle the stones roughly or throw them into the barrel, or you may damage them.

Add the proper amount of rough silicon-carbide grit and enough water to barely cover the stones. If your tumbler barrel has a 2½-pound capacity, use about 1/2 pound of grit. If it has a different capacity, use the amount recommended by the manufacturer. Close the lid of the tumbler tightly (to keep it from leaking), place the barrel on the rollers, and start the motor.

There is no set amount of time for tumbling gemstones. Different stones take different lengths of time. Fairly smooth quartz pebbles may take only three to six days, while harder, rougher stones may take weeks. Check the progress of the stones every 24 hours.

To check the stones, remove the barrel from the rollers, open it, and take out about half a dozen stones. Rinse these stones under running water, dry them, and examine them under a good light. If they are ready for the second grinding, they will have no pits, cracks, or blemishes. If they have, return them to the barrel and tumble them another 24 hours, then check again.

When at least four of the six stones examined are ready, remove all the stones from the sludge in the barrel, pour the sludge into a plastic bag, and dispose of it with the garbage. Never pour the sludge down a sink, as it will stop up the plumbing.

Carefully wash the stones and the barrel. Even a trace of grit can damage your stones during the second grinding. Dry the stones and carefully examine each one. Remove any that contain pits, deep cracks, or blemishes. These can be rough-tumbled again with your next batch. If left in for fine grinding, they may ruin the good stones.

Fine grinding. Put the good stones back into the barrel and add enough other rough-ground or polished stones to make the barrel nearly three-quarters full again. Add the correct amount of fine grit (about 1/2 pound for a 2½-pound load) and enough water to barely cover the stones.

Cover the barrel and tumble the stones, checking them every 24 hours. Again, there is no set amount of time for tumbling. The time required will depend upon the stones being tumbled, but it will probably take at least a week. The fine grinding is finished when the stones are perfectly smooth and without the slightest blemish. The stones should look as they will when polished, except that they will have a matte finish instead of a shiny one.

When the stones are ready, carefully remove them and wash and dry them. Dispose of the sludge as before and wash the barrel thoroughly.

Polishing. Return the stones to the barrel. Add the proper amount of cerium oxide (1 heaping tablespoon for

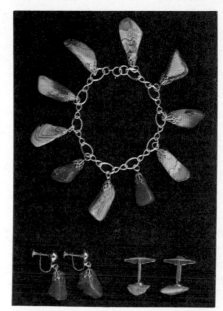

Tumbled stones can be made into beautiful jewelry like the pieces shown here by simply attaching them to findings (see *Jewelry*, p. 337).

a 2½-pound load) and enough water to barely cover the stones. Tumble the mixture until the stones attain a uniform high polish (from three or four days to a week or more). If, during the polishing, the stones make harsh or unrhythmical sounds as they tumble, add a little wallpaper paste to the mixture to bring the consistency of the liquid to that of thin cream. This will cushion the stones and protect them from damage.

Final washing. Wash the polished stones and the barrel. Return the stones to the barrel and add 1/2 teaspoon of detergent and enough water to barely cover the stones. Tumble this mixture from 4 to 8 hours to remove the film left on the stones by the polish.

Remove the washed stones from the barrel and rinse them under running water. Wrap them in a soft cloth and allow them to dry.

Lapidary

Cutting and polishing a cabochon

Cutting a cabochon requires a steady hand and an artist's eye. Basically, you need only grind out the shape, then polish the shaped stone, using a variety of surfaces; but you must be able to visualize the final shape of the gem in the rough stone, and you need a hand steady enough to bring out that shape.

The word "cabochon" comes from the French *caboche* (a slightly derogative term for "head"). It was probably named for the round cabochon, which resembles a bald pate, but cabochons can be cut into a variety of shapes, including ovals, squares, rectangles, teardrops, hearts, and crosses.

Using silicon-carbide grinding wheels, you can cut a cabochon of any shape from any gemstone material except ruby, sapphire, and diamond. A good stone for a beginner is an agate, and the easiest shape to cut is oval.

Begin with a slab of agate a little more than 1/4 inch thick and small enough to fit comfortably on the table of your trim saw. Select the size and shape stone you wish to cut. An 18- by

13-millimeter stone is a popular size for rings; good sizes for pendants are 25 by 18 millimeters, 30 by 22 millimeters, and 40 by 30 millimeters. Locate the size you want on the template and place that opening over the least attractive side of the agate, as the side with the marking will be the base of the finished stone. Position the opening in the template so that the design on the other side of the agate is centered in the most attractive way; if possible, position heavy markings at the center of the opening. Holding the template firmly in place, scribe the outline of the opening onto the stone, then lightly coat the scribe mark with acrylic spray.

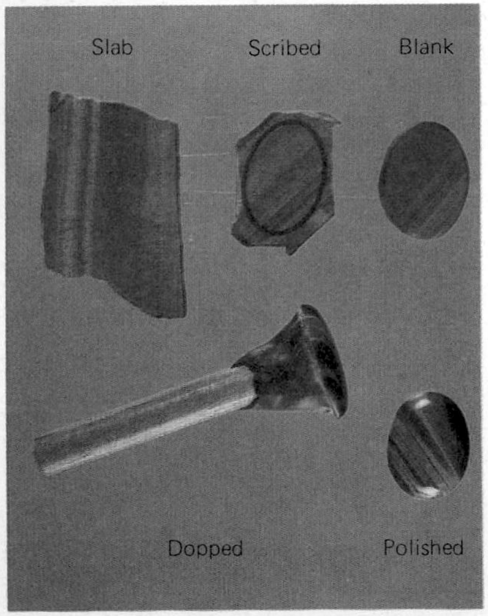

Place the stone slab on the trim saw and saw out a rectangle around the scribe mark. Leave the least possible amount of material outside the scribe mark, as this material will have to be ground away on the wheel.

When working with lapidary machines, remove all jewelry from your hands and wrists and anything else that may get caught in the wheels. If you have long hair, tie it back. By taking these precautions, you will avoid accidents. It is also a good idea to wear washable clothes and a rubber apron, as cutting a cabochon is messy work.

Begin the rough grinding on a 100-grit wheel. Turn on the motor of the grinding machine and the water supply. Do not forget the water—all grinding must be done wet. Although you can see your progress better if the work is dry, the resulting dust may get into your lungs and cause silicosis. Holding the cabochon blank (the cutout stone) in both hands, carefully grind it down to the scribe line.

When grinding, apply moderate pressure. Do not press hard. The wheel must do the work. Excessive pressure may overload the motor. Keep the stone moving at all times, twisting and turning it and moving it across the

entire width of the wheel. If you keep the stone in one place on the wheel, you will wear a gutter in the wheel, which will make it useless for later work. If you hold one part of the stone to the wheel for too long, you may create unwanted flat areas.

Change to the 220-grit wheel, turn the water on over it, and cut out a 45° bevel around the base of the stone. Wash the stone and attach a dop stick to its base (see Steps 6 and 7 on the facing page). Wash the stone again.

Grind the stone to shape on the 100-grit wheel, working from the top of the stone to the bottom (see sketches at right). Hold the stone by its dop stick so that you can see the edge of the base of the stone. Be very careful not to cut through the edge or you will ruin the shape of the stone.

When the stone is within 1/16 inch of completion, wash it thoroughly and switch to the 220-grit wheel. Bring the stone to its most symmetrical shape, carefully grinding down any high parts.

Remove all scratches from the stone on the sanding machine—first with a 320-grit sanding belt, then with a 500- or 600-grit belt (Step 10). Scrub the stone with soap, water, and a brush.

Mix up a slurry of a heaping teaspoon of tripoli and a half cup of water. Apply the slurry to the polishing wheel with a small brush. Prepolish the stone on the wheel with firm pressure and a circular motion. When the stone begins to take on a gloss, wash it again.

Mix another slurry of a heaping teaspoon of cerium oxide and a half cup of water. With a clean brush, apply the slurry to a clean buffing wheel and polish the stone to a high sheen.

Remove the dop stick by heating the wax and lightly prying the stone off with a knife blade. Remove any remnants of wax with alcohol. For ideas on how to set the stone, see *Jewelry*, pp. 324–347.

Cut blank into cylinder and bevel bottom.

Remove top corners, rounding off edges.

Gradually round off stone from the top down.

Round off top completely, then grind bottom.

Grind bottom to 15° slope all around stone.

Finished bottom should resemble this detail.

A cabochon is ground down from a blank from the top down, following the sequence shown.

Caution: Always turn off the water before leaving the grinding wheel. Water seeping down on an unused wheel will settle in the bottom of the wheel and make it lopsided. If enough water collects, centrifugal force will burst the wheel when you start it again. If you accidentally leave the water running, stand to the side of the wheel when you turn it on again.

Slab   Scribed   Blank

Dopped   Polished

Steps in cutting a cabochon tiger's-eye are shown here, from slab to polished stone.

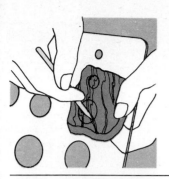

1. Place template over less attractive side of stone and trace outline with aluminum scribe. Hold scribe so that point is directed away from center, against edges of hole in template. Apply acrylic spray to scribe mark to keep it from wearing away later.

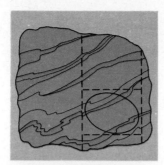

2. Excess material must be cut away. Most of it can be cut off with trim saw. But trim saw can cut only straight lines, so material must be cut away so as to leave oval marked by scribe line in smallest rectangle that will contain it, as shown. Rest of excess is ground away later.

3. Fill tank of saw with water to act as coolant. Turn saw on and let it run until water drips from spash shield above blade. Place stone flat on bed of saw, hold stone down with one hand on each side. Make notch in edge of stone, then feed it gently into blade to cut lines around oval.

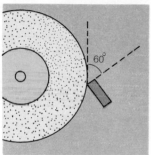

4. Turn on grinding machine and adjust water to trickle over entire edge of 100-grit wheel. Hold stone to wheel at 60° angle and keep turning stone and moving it across entire width of wheel rim until stone is ground down to within a hair of scribe mark.

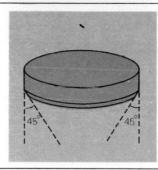

5. Move to 220-grit wheel and adjust water to flow over its edge. Grind a 45° bevel around base of stone. When completed, stone should be in the shape shown here. Wash it thoroughly with soap and water.

6. Light an alcohol lamp and heat some dopping wax over the flame. (Do not hold wax in flame, or wax will become brittle.) When wax softens, pick up some of it on end of dop stick. Put just enough wax on stick to cover three-quarters of base of stone.

7. With tweezers, pick up stone and heat it top and bottom. Press hot wax onto base of stone, and mold wax around stick and stone with butt of tweezers. Base of stone must be at right angle to stick. When wax is cool enough, finish shaping it with fingers. When fingernail cannot penetrate wax, set stone aside to cool to room temperature.

8. Wash stone and return to 100-grit wheel. Hold stone by dop stick so that you can see base of stone. Move stone in rotating pattern over entire width of wheel, shaping stone from top to bottom as shown on facing page. Stop when within 1/16 in. of completion.

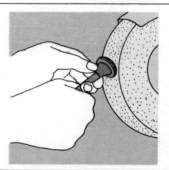

9. Wash stone. Complete shaping on 220-grit wheel. Do not press hard or stay in one place too long, or flat areas will result. Dry stone off occasionally and examine with loupe. Stop grinding when stone is perfectly symmetrical and without flat areas or deep scratches. Wash stone thoroughly.

10. Sand stone on 320-grit belt. Keep sander wet with trickling water or moist sponge. Applying firm pressure, move stone in a rotating pattern. Do not hold it too long in one place or it might develop flat areas. When stone has no visible scratches, wash and then sand it on a 500- or 600-grit belt until it takes on a gloss.

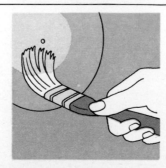

11. Prepolish the stone on polishing wheel with a slurry of tripoli and water. With clean brush, paint slurry over wheel, then turn wheel on. Apply stone to wheel with firm pressure, rotating stone against wheel. Continue until stone is glossy and almost perfectly polished. If scratches show up, return to sander.

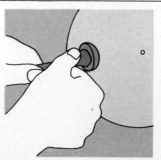

12. Scrub stone and go to a clean polishing wheel. Using a clean brush, paint wheel with slurry of cerium oxide and water, then polish stone. Again use firm pressure and circular motion. Stone should get hot, but not hot enough to melt wax. When stone is perfectly polished, wash it and remove dop stick.

Jewelry

The ancient art of self-adornment

Jewelrymaking is among the most ancient of crafts. Man has been adorning himself with some type of jewelry since far back into prehistoric times. More than 10,000 years ago the cave-dwelling hunters of the Old Stone Age were wearing necklaces of shells or ivory. Since it is unlikely that there were professional jewelers in such primitive societies, we can safely assume that these cavemen were the first do-it-yourself jewelrymakers.

Jewelry in antiquity. The oldest jewelry surviving intact, dating back to about 2500 B.C., was found in the tomb of Queen Paubi of Ur, Sumeria. In the tomb were earrings, bracelets, rings, an elaborate necklace, and other jewelry made with the same techniques that have been used throughout history, including soldering, the cutting and setting of stones, and filigree.

The rulers of Babylonia and Egypt wore elaborate jewelry of gold, copper, coral, turquoise, lapis lazuli, quartz, pottery, and glass. Jewelry found in the tomb of Tutankhamen, the young pharaoh who died in the 14th century B.C., is of unexcelled beauty.

Ancient Greek jewelry was frequently made of stamped gold. Hunting and battle scenes were often depicted in high relief on ring bezels. In the fifth century B.C. Greek jewelry took on the character of sculpture, with designs derived mainly from the human form and mythological figures.

The Romans used more jewelry than any civilization before them. Engraved gems and the coiled serpent armband were especially popular.

European modes. The use of jewelry declined in the fourth century of the Christian Era, when it was worn mainly by the very wealthy. Bishops wore rings that symbolically wedded them to the Church. Kings and nobles wore jeweled armor into battle.

During the Renaissance jewelry again became popular. The rich weighted themselves down with jewelry. The elaborately ornamented baroque style was popular in the 17th century, and there was a return to the classical style in the late 18th century.

During the Industrial Revolution in the 19th century, jewelry began to be mass produced. As a result, all but the very poor could afford to wear it.

Eastern and African jewelry. Ancient Chinese jewelry utilized metal inlay and filigree. The Japanese wore elaborate headdresses. In India gold and silver jewelry carried designs of flowers or animals—especially dragons.

The tribal jewelry of Africa included large ear and nose rings and tightly woven necklaces. Silver and/or gold were used, depending upon the resources of the area.

American jewelry. The Indians of South America and Mexico produced magnificent gold jewelry before the arrival of Columbus, but almost all of it was destroyed by the Spanish. North American Indians worked in copper. Fish-shaped copper necklace beads have been found that date back to the fifth millenium B.C. Later, Indians made necklaces and pendants of turquoise and coral. Wampum—small beads made from shells—were worn in necklaces and belts or used as money.

European settlers brought jewelry with them from the Old World and through the years continued to copy European styles. Recently, however, a new awareness of non-European heritages has resulted in the use of African, Oriental, and other styles, and new forms have been derived from modern art and space-age materials.

Necklace, earrings, and button (above) were created by Thracian goldsmiths of fifth century B.C. Ancient pectoral (below) is Scythian in design but Greek in workmanship.

Tools and materials

Although you would need a fairly large store of tools and materials to work in all of the techniques described in the following pages, you can make a great deal of jewelry with only a few simple tools. To make the no-solder bracelets on page 342, for example, you need only two pairs of needle-nose pliers and some ready-made jump rings. If you prefer to make your own jump rings, you also need a jeweler's saw, a hand drill, a metal rod, and a vise. But even the full set of tools listed here is not as formidable as it might seem at first glance, as most of the tools are inexpensive and easily stored.

Before beginning a project, read the instructions carefully to see what tools and materials you will need to complete it. Then buy only those tools you will need. Before you know it, you will have a well-stocked jewelry workshop.

Most of the tools and materials you will need are available at jewelry supply houses. Some items can be found in hobby shops or hardware stores.

Basic materials. Metal, polished stones, and ready-made findings (see below) are the most widely used materials in making jewelry. The most common metals are silver and gold.

Silver is a soft material that is generally mixed with small amounts of other metals to form alloys. Silver alloys are measured in terms of fineness, or parts

of silver per 1,000 parts of total metal. Fine silver is pure, 100 percent silver. Sterling silver is 925 fine—it contains 925 parts silver and 75 parts copper. The copper increases the metal's mechanical strength and lowers its melting point.

Sheets of silver are available in 10-inch-wide rolls of various gauges; the higher the gauge, the thinner the silver. Silver wire is either spring hard or spring soft. Spring hard is used for pieces that should be less malleable, such as jump rings. Spring soft is used for pieces that must be shaped. Both are available in various gauges and shapes—round, square, and so on.

Pure gold is even softer than silver and is rarely used in jewelry. Its alloys are measured in karats: 24 karat is pure gold, 18 karat is 18 parts gold and 6 parts other metals. The most commonly used alloys are 14 and 18 karats. The alloys are available in sheets or wire. Gold is almost twice as heavy as silver. Even though pure gold is very soft and malleable, the alloys are more difficult to shape than silver alloys, and gold is far more expensive than silver, so it is seldom used by novices. Gold-filled (heavily plated) wire and findings are also available.

Findings are any small accessories used in jewelrymaking, such as jump rings, clasps, pins, earring posts, cuff link bars, teardrop cups, spring rings, and chains, all of which can be bought ready-made. If you prefer, you can make your own jump rings, chains, and teardrop findings (see p. 337).

Buy stones ready for mounting, or shape and polish your own (see *Lapidary,* pp. 318–323). Use enamelwork in your jewelry if you have a kiln (see *Enameling,* pp. 348–359).

Beads of all types are sold ready for stringing. Beading cord is available in a variety of types and thicknesses. Beading needles are sold in packets.

If you plan to make models for casting, you will need wax. Wax comes in a large variety of shapes and densities. Buy the wax that will be easiest to carve into the shape you need.

Holding tools. While working on a piece of jewelry, you will need a number of holding tools. Equip your workshop with a good vise with a jaw opening of about 2½ inches. It will prove invaluable. A ring clamp will make holding rings and other objects much easier. A wedge inserted at one end of the clamp forces the jaws on the other end down onto an object and holds it firm.

Jeweler's pliers come with jaws in any of several different shapes. You will need several types of smooth-jawed, 4½-inch pliers: two pairs of needle-nose, or chain-nose, pliers for closing jump rings and for other jobs; round-nose pliers for working with round wire; flat-nose pliers for working with flat surfaces; and half-round pliers for working with curved surfaces. Do not use ordinary household pliers—they have ribbed jaws that will scratch jewelry. You may also need a pair Bernard pliers, which have slits in their jaws for holding wire.

Three types of tweezers are needed. Jeweler's precision tweezers can be used to hold any small object, but they cannot be used in soldering work, as they are not fireproof. Cross-lock tweezers are fireproof and will lock onto the object being held. Fine-point tweezers, also fireproof, are used on objects being soldered.

You will also need copper tongs for use in pickling soldered metals. Iron tongs cannot be used, as they would contaminate the pickling solution. If you are setting stones in pieces that are hard to hold on to, you will need a pitch bowl—a metal bowl filled with tar—in which to anchor the piece.

(continued on next page)

B & S GAUGES

Round wire		Sheet metal
14	●	▬▬▬▬▬▬
18	●	▬▬▬▬▬
20	·	▬▬▬
26	·	—

The thickness of metal is generally measured by the Brown and Sharpe gauge system. A few of the gauges in wire and sheet metal are shown above (actual size).

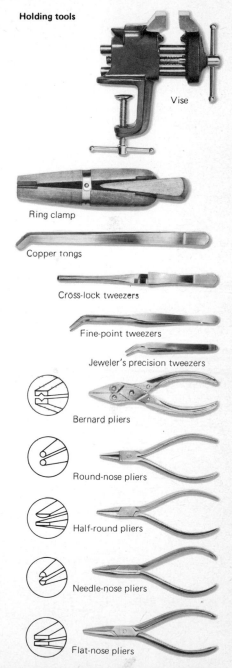

Holding tools

Vise

Ring clamp

Copper tongs

Cross-lock tweezers

Fine-point tweezers

Jeweler's precision tweezers

Bernard pliers

Round-nose pliers

Half-round pliers

Needle-nose pliers

Flat-nose pliers

Jewelry

Tools and materials *(continued)*

Cutting tools. A jeweler's saw is indispensable for cutting sheet metal. Get a 5-inch-deep saw frame with an adjustable length. The adjustable length will allow you to use part of a broken blade. Blades are graded according to fineness. The finest of all is No. 8/0 (shorthand for eight zeros); the larger the number of zeros in a grade, the finer the teeth in the blade will be. The next coarsest blade after No. 0 is No. 1. The grades then proceed numerically to No. 14, the coarsest of all. Use No. 0 or No. 1 blades for general silverwork, No. 2 for coarser work, and No. 2/0 or No. 3/0 for general goldwork.

A slotted bench pin is used as a cutting surface. The metal is sawed vertically on top of the bench pin. The slot allows the saw to cut the metal without cutting the work surface. Buy a bench pin or make one (see below).

A divider is useful in making parallel lines on metal as a guide to cutting. To transfer designs onto metal, you will need a scribe—a kind of metal pencil. Buy one or use the pointed end of a compass or some other sharp-pointed metal object. Metal snips, or shears, are necessary for cutting wire and thin sheets of metal. A craft knife is useful for cutting paper patterns.

Get a punch for making dents in areas to be drilled and a hand drill and drill bits for drilling the holes. The larger drill bits are measured according to their diameters. The very fine bits are measured by a system of numbers ranging from 1 to 80. No. 80 is the thinnest; it is less than half the thickness of a straight pin.

Shaping tools. Metal is shaped with a rawhide mallet on a flat metal surface or on a mandrel. The rawhide mallet is a hammer with a head made of tightly rolled leather. The ideal flat surface is a bench anvil, which is really just a thick square of heavy metal, but any smooth, sturdy metal surface will do. Mandrels are steel rods used for shaping metal jewelry. You will need an oval bracelet mandrel for shaping bracelets and a ring bezel with graduated ring sizes. You may also want to use a bezel mandrel for working with bezels (the rims that hold stones in settings).

For setting stones you will need a burnisher, a setting nail, and a ball peen hammer. The burnisher is a tool of hard polished steel with a handle, resembling a short blunt knife with a curved-up tip. It is used to press the bezel down against the stone. The setting nail is a concrete nail that has been worked on a grinding wheel to give it a smooth, polished tip. It is used for the same purpose as a burnisher on harder bezels or to finish settings begun with a burnisher. The ball peen hammer, which has a head with one flat end and one round end, is used to drive the setting nail and to shape metal.

If you want to draw your own wire— to make it thinner and stiffer—you will

The bench pin

Make bench pin from piece of hardwood about 8 in. long, 3 in. wide, and 1 in. thick. Drill 5/8-in. holes 3 in. from each end of wood. On one end cut out V-shaped section between hole and end. Pass C-clamp through other hole and clamp bench pin to table.

C-clamp

Cutting tools

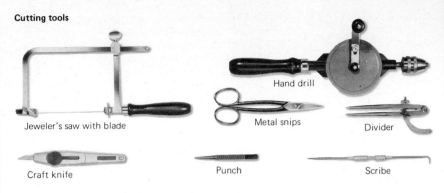

Jeweler's saw with blade

Hand drill

Metal snips

Divider

Craft knife

Punch

Scribe

Soldering equipment

Shaping tools

Wire screen

Annealing dish

Bracelet mandrel

Graduated ring mandrel

Burnisher

Bench anvil

Drawplate

Silver solder

Poker

Alcohol lamp

Mapp gas canister torch

Propane canister torch

Charcoal block

Waxworking tools

Ball peen hammer

Rawhide mallet

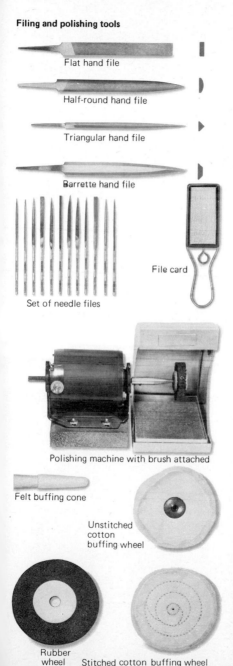

Filing and polishing tools

Flat hand file

Half-round hand file

Triangular hand file

Barrette hand file

File card

Set of needle files

Polishing machine with brush attached

Felt buffing cone

Unstitched cotton buffing wheel

Rubber wheel

Stitched cotton buffing wheel

need a drawplate—a flat piece of metal with a series of holes graduated in size. Wire is pulled through a succession of increasingly smaller holes until it reaches the gauge needed.

To make wax models for casting, you will need a wax carver (a knifelike tool) and a small assortment of waxworking tools that resemble dentist's probes. You will also need an alcohol lamp for heating the wax.

Soldering equipment. All but the simplest metal jewelry requires soldering. The most important soldering tool is the torch used to heat the solder and make it flow. A gas-air torch is ideal, but a propane canister torch will do for most jobs, and a mapp gas canister torch will suffice for soldering jobs requiring more heat. When a canister torch is empty, the top can be detached and screwed onto a full canister.

Silver solder is used to bind silver, copper, and brass. It comes in four grades, easy, medium, hard, and IT, determined by their melting points. The type of gold solder to be used depends upon the karat of gold being soldered (see *Soldering*, pp. 330–331). All solder is sold in sheet or wire form, which must be cut, or in chips.

Before metal can be soldered, it must be covered with flux, which prevents oxidation and helps the solder flow. Yellow-gold flux is the easiest to work with, but any type can be used. The flux is applied with a small brush. You will also need a small piece of hard asbestos and a piece of soft asbestos to protect your work surface while soldering. If you need a great deal of heat to solder a piece and the asbestos seems to be drawing some heat away, substitute a charcoal block, or work on a small wire screen that rests slightly above the asbestos. Another handy tool is an annealing dish. A metal bowl on a swivel that is filled with charcoal chips or a similar substance, an annealing

dish is an ideal and convenient surface for annealing and soldering.

You will need a nickel-chrome wire poker for handling molten solder. You can make one by sharpening a piece of wire coat hanger. Get some iron binding wire to hold together pieces that are being soldered. Pieces that have been soldered with easy solder can be insulated with yellow ocher to prevent the solder from remelting when heat is applied nearby.

Finally, soldered pieces must be pickled to remove the flux and fire scale. Commercial pickling powders are available. The pickling must be done in a glass pot that can be placed on an open flame.

Filing and polishing tools. A variety of different files are needed for shaping and smoothing metal. Files vary in shape and roughness. The roughness is generally graded by cut numbers. Cuts 1 and 2 are best for jewelry. A number of different shapes are used. You should have at least four 6-inch hand files: a flat file; a triangular, or three-square, file; a barrette file; and a half-round file. You will also need an assortment of small needle files, including round, half-round, square, barrette, flat, knife, and triangular (three-square) files. If you work with wax, get a second set of needle files.

It is a good idea to get a file card for cleaning metal particles out of the files. A file card is a brushlike tool with a fine abrasive material in place of bristles. You will also need emery paper of various grades.

One of the most important tools is the polishing machine. It consists of a motor that turns at about 3,450 revolutions per minute (rpm), a spindle, and a number of polishing wheels, including a brush with two or three rows of bristles, a felt cone, a stitched wool or cotton buffing wheel, and an unstitched cotton buffing wheel. If you want to

inlay onyx into metal (see *Inlaying*, p. 338), you will also need a ½-inch-wide rubber wheel that is made for a maximum speed of 3,800 rpm. To complete the machine, get a metal shield to catch flying dust particles. The shield should have a light in it. A vacuum attachment to suck up the dust is recommended. The abrasive compounds used with the polishing machine include tripoli (a powder or silicone mixed with tallow or wax) and red jeweler's rouge.

Care of tools. If you care for your tools properly, they will last indefinitely. Regularly lubricate any moving parts. When you are not using your tools, always pack them away in a toolbox that has been lined with felt and sprayed with gun oil. If they are not to be used for a while, keep a block of camphor in the tool box to absorb moisture and to prevent the tools from rusting. Never store files one on top of the other, or you will dull them.

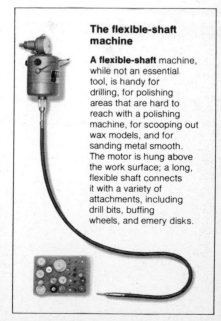

The flexible-shaft machine

A flexible-shaft machine, while not an essential tool, is handy for drilling, for polishing areas that are hard to reach with a polishing machine, for scooping out wax models, and for sanding metal smooth. The motor is hung above the work surface; a long, flexible shaft connects it with a variety of attachments, including drill bits, buffing wheels, and emery disks.

327

Jewelry

Designing metal jewelry

Jewelry can be made of almost any material, but most good jewelry utilizes silver or gold. A few basic techniques are used in fashioning metal jewelry. By combining these techniques in different ways, you can make an unlimited variety of beautiful pieces.

The basic techniques are: (1) sawing; (2) saw piercing—a method of cutting a design out of the center of a piece of metal; (3) shaping metal with a mallet; (4) simple soldering and sweat-soldering—combining two pieces of metal to give them the appearance of one solid piece; (5) setting stones; (6) inlaying stone into metal; and (7) filing, sanding, and polishing. All of these techniques and others are demonstrated on the following pages. Although silver is used in the illustrations (silver is the metal most used by hobbyists), the same techniques can be used for gold or other metals.

With these techniques you can create all the basic forms you will need, including bracelet bands, ring shanks, bezels for holding stones, and findings and decorations, including filigree. A few of the many possibilities for combining the basic cuff bracelet form with the various techniques are shown below. The same principles can be applied to pendants, rings, earrings, cuff links, and belt buckles.

Basic bracelet form is made by sawing out a rectangle of silver, shaping the silver on a mandrel, filing and sanding it smooth, and polishing it to a high gloss.

Saw curves along sides of basic bracelet form to alter shape. Circles or complex patterns can be cut out of center of bracelet by saw piercing. Innumerable designs can be created in this way.

Give the bracelet a slightly raised design by adding a second piece of metal to its surface. Saw a design out of gold, copper, brass, or another piece of silver and sweat-solder it to the basic bracelet form.

Make a bezel (p. 332), solder it to the basic form, and set a stone in it. You can then decorate bracelet with silver balls (p. 333), sweat-soldered forms, or saw-pierced patterns on each side of stone.

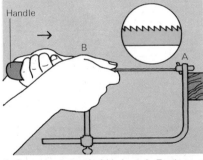
Solder a frame of square wire around edges of basic form, inlay the frame with chips of onyx (p. 338), and bring the entire piece to a high polish.

Add enameled plaque to bracelet. Bend piece of sheet metal to fit on bracelet. Enamel bent metal (see *Enameling*, pp. 348–359). Make bezel to fit around enameled piece, solder bezel to bracelet, and set piece in it.

Sawing

Metals that are too heavy to be cut with metal snips or shears must be sawed to the size and shape needed. You can saw metal into almost any shape, from a simple rectangle for a ring shank to an intricate animal form for sweat-soldering onto another piece.

Blades used in jeweler's saws are very thin and break easily. You will probably break a lot of blades, especially at the beginning, so buy a large supply of them. They are usually sold by the dozen, as even the most experienced jewelers break blades often. The sizes most commonly used in jewelry-making are No. 0 through No. 3. The higher the number, the heavier the blade. Use a No. 2 for general work.

Use a saw frame with an adjustable length, and adjust it so that when one end of the blade is in place, the other end does not quite reach the other side of the frame. Press the frame against the edge of a table to bend it slightly, then screw the other end of the blade into place. When plucked, the blade should make a light pinging sound.

Make a paper pattern of the shape you want and transfer the design to the metal. Place the work on a bench pin. Hold the saw vertically and begin sawing with one sharp upward stroke. Move the metal into the saw as you proceed, not the saw into the metal.

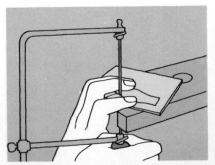
1. Screw in one end of blade at A. Teeth must point toward handle. Brace frame against table and push in on handle until the blade bows slightly. Screw in blade at B.

2. Attach pattern to metal with transparent tape, trace pattern onto metal with scribe. Or cover metal with water-soluble white paint and trace pattern onto dry paint with carbon paper.

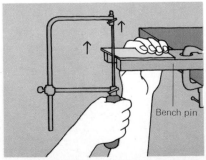
3. Hold metal in place over slot in bench pin with one hand. With other hand hold saw vertically and make one sharp upward stroke to cut a small channel in which to begin sawing.

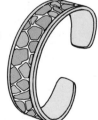
4. Saw along scribe or carbon marks, keeping saw vertical. Move saw up and down with slight forward pressure and move metal into saw. When finished, wash off paint, if used.

Saw piercing

Jewelry can be made by cutting a design out of the center of a piece of metal in a process called saw piercing. A piece of metal is saw pierced by drilling a hole in it, inserting the blade of the saw through the hole, then fastening the blade into the saw frame and sawing out the design.

Saw-pierced bands can be bent into bracelets or rings. Pendants, earrings, and cuff links can be made by saw piercing a shape and soldering on the appropriate findings. A saw-pierced piece can also be sweat-soldered onto another piece as a decoration.

All of the techniques used in regular sawing are used in saw piercing. The only additional steps are those required to insert the saw in the metal without cutting through the edges. After you have transferred the design to the metal, drill the hole at the point where you will begin cutting, and thread the saw blade through the hole. The hole should be just large enough to accept the blade. Make a slight indentation in the metal before drilling to keep the bit from slipping.

When saw piercing very lightweight metal, you can make the hole with a punch and hammer. However, the punch will cause the metal to pucker a little in the back, and the pucker will have to be filed smooth.

Shaping metal

The next basic technique in fashioning metal jewelry is shaping the metal. Shapes that cannot be formed with pliers must be beaten into the metal with a rawhide mallet on a metal surface. Rings and cuff bracelets are shaped on mandrels. Bent metal can be restraightened by hammering it with a mallet on a bench anvil. Metals that are to be sweat-soldered must fit together snugly, without gaps, or the solder will not hold or will result in an irregular surface. Always hammer the pieces flat before sweat-soldering them.

To make a cuff bracelet, first measure the wrist it is being made for with a tape measure and subtract the amount of space needed for the opening used to slip the bracelet on and off. If you are making the bracelet for someone whose wrist measurement you do not know, make it 5½ inches long, which is a good average size for a lady's bracelet. Draw the design to size and cut out a pattern. Transfer the pattern to the metal and cut it out. Bend the metal around a bracelet mandrel and hammer it snugly around the mandrel with a rawhide mallet. Take it off the mandrel, put it back on upside down, and hammer it again to counteract the tapering caused by the tapered mandrel. Ring shanks are formed in almost the same way (see *Ring shanks*, p.333).

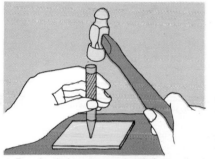

1. Transfer design onto metal and place point of punch where you want to begin cutting. Tap head of punch with ball peen hammer to make a slight indentation in metal to guide drill bit.

2. Hold metal firmly in place by pounding nails partway in around it. Place drill with bit in indentation made in Step 1 and drill hole through metal. Back out drill bit and remove nails.

1. To flatten out a piece of metal, place it on a bench anvil and hammer it flat with a rawhide mallet. Treat all metals to be sweat-soldered in this way to be sure that they are perfectly flat.

2. To shape a bracelet, cut out the shape from flat sheet metal and hold the cut metal against a bracelet mandrel. With your thumbs, push the ends of the metal around the mandrel.

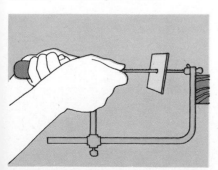

3. Screw one end of blade into saw frame. Slip other end through hole in metal and fasten blade into frame in usual way. Pick up saw and metal and position metal over bench pin.

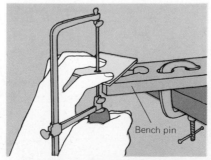

Bench pin

4. While sawing, hold metal with two fingers, one on each side of blade. Move the metal into the blade. When done, remove the metal from saw. **Caution: Keep fingers out of path of blade.**

3. Continue to push metal around mandrel. About halfway around, reverse positions of your thumbs and fingers to give you more leverage, and push metal around to make it hug mandrel.

4. When you have pushed metal as snugly around mandrel as you can with your hands, hammer it closer with a rawhide mallet. Turn bracelet upside down on mandrel and pound it again.

Jewelry

Soldering

Soldering is the most important technique in making jewelry. Joints in rings and bezels must be sealed with solder, bezels and findings must be soldered into place, and flat pieces of metal must be joined by sweat-soldering. A soldered joint should be smooth and even so that it will be invisible after filing and polishing. Practice soldering scrap metal until you get the feel of the process. Knowing how much solder to use, where to place the solder (see below), and how much heat to apply comes only with experience.

The process. Always work on a fireproof surface. For most work use a piece of soft asbestos placed on top of a piece of hard asbestos that is propped up on wood or bricks.

Be sure that the pieces of metal being soldered are clean and that they fit together snugly. Brush them with flux and dry the flux with the torch.

Place the solder on the fluxed metal and apply heat to it until it flows (becomes fluid enough to spread along a seam). Keep the torch moving in a figure-8 pattern to distribute the heat evenly. If you want to draw the molten solder in a certain direction, move the heat in that direction and the solder will follow. Watch the metal being soldered. If it begins to glow red, it is in danger of "burning up" (melting). Move the heat away instantly and let the piece cool before resuming work.

After you have soldered a piece, pickle it to clean off the flux and some of the fire scale created by the torch. Mix a commercial pickling powder with water as directed on the package, bring the solution to a slow boil in a flameproof glass container, and put the soldered piece into the boiling solution, using copper tongs. Do not use a metal container or iron tongs, as they will contaminate the pickling solution and discolor the piece being pickled.

Preparing solder. You can buy solder in ready-to-use chips or in wire or sheets that must be cut. To cut a sheet of solder, make partial cuts every 1/32 inch along its width with wire snips. Then cut across these cuts, bracing the

Cut sheet solder into squares of about 1/32 in.

Placing solder

Bezels: Place chips of solder around inside perimeter of bezel, leaving about 3/8-in. space between chips.

Ring shanks: Place one chip of solder over top of seam in shank.

Sweat-soldering: Scatter chips of solder 3/8 in. apart over area to be covered by second piece of metal.

Adjusting gas-air torch

Too much gas

Too much air

Correct

Gas-air torch must be adjusted to get proper flame. Top flame at left is burning too much gas; middle flame has too much air; bottom flame has correct mixture of gas and air. Canister torches need no gas-air adjustment.

1. With a small brush generously apply flux to the surface of the metal being soldered. Without flux the metal will oxidize and the solder will not flow properly.

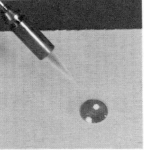

2. Light torch. To light propane canister torch (shown), turn on gas and slowly bring lighted match into gas stream from below. Regulate length of flame to about 3 in.

3. Direct flame of torch over entire surface that has been fluxed until flux is thoroughly dry. Flux is dry when it becomes crystalline and turns white.

4. For sweat-soldering, position top piece on bottom one before drying flux. Mark position with scribe, remove top piece, dry flux, and position hard or medium solder.

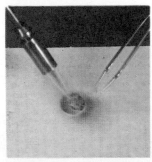

5. Heat solder until it begins to glisten and melt. Move torch away occasionally to keep metal from "burning up." Turn piece, if necessary, with fine-point tweezers.

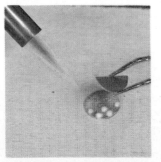

6. Position fluxed and dried top piece of metal over molten solder, using scribe mark as guide. Both pieces of metal must be perfectly flat, or they will not adhere.

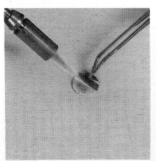

7. Hold top piece in place. Keep moving flame around bottom piece until solder flows to edges and joins the two pieces so that they look like a single piece of metal.

8. Bring pickling solution to a slow boil and place soldered piece into it with copper tongs. Remove piece when it turns cloudy white; rinse it under running water.

cut edge with your finger to keep the chips from flying in all directions.

Types of solder. Solder is an alloy of the metal being bound. Silver solder is an alloy of silver, copper, and zinc. Gold solder is an alloy of gold and whatever metals will make it match the color of the metal being soldered.

Solder must melt at a lower temperature than the metal being soldered; otherwise the entire piece would melt when the solder was heated.

Gold solder must be matched to the karat and color of the gold being soldered. Both gold and silver solder come in four forms: easy, medium, hard, and IT. Each has a successively higher flowing point. When you are working on a piece that requires two or three different solderings, use hard solder first, then medium, then easy. The higher flowing points of the earlier joints will allow you to make the later ones without melting the earlier solder. IT solder is used for enamelwork and other special applications.

In general, use hard solder for joints that will be banged on a mandrel or that will be under stress, or in moving parts, such as hinges. Use hard or medium solder for sweat-soldering, as easy solder flows too fast.

MELTING POINTS OF METALS	
Fine silver	961°C
Sterling silver	893°C
Pure gold	1063°C
18-k white gold	943°C
18-k yellow gold	927°C
14-k white gold	996°C
14-k yellow gold	879°C

FLOWING POINTS OF SOLDERS	
Easy silver solder	718°C
Medium silver solder	754°C
Hard silver solder	774°C
18-k white-gold solder	680°C-730°C
18-k yellow-gold solder	730°C-780°C
14-k white-gold solder	655°C-740°C
14-k yellow-gold solder	690°C-770°C

Annealing

When metal is worked, it becomes hard and brittle. If it is to be worked further, it must be annealed to make it malleable again. Metal can also be annealed before it is worked if greater malleability is desired.

Flux the metal and place it in an annealing dish (or on asbestos). Heat the metal with a torch, turning the annealing dish as you do to reach all sides, and bring the metal to a dull-red glow. Do not let it turn bright red, or it may "burn up" (melt). Work in dim light so that you can see the glow. Let the annealed metal cool completely before working with it.

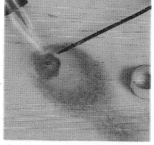
9. A bezel or ring shank may be too narrow to hold solder chip. Place chip on asbestos and apply heat until it forms a ball. Hold a poker close to solder while working.

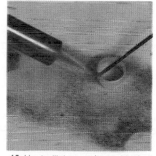
10. Heat will draw molten solder ball onto end of poker. Transfer solder from poker to top of bezel and move flame down line to be soldered. Solder will follow heat.

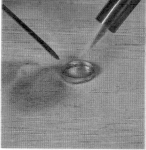
11. To solder bezel to plate, position solder chips around inside perimeter. Move torch inside and outside of bezel until solder flows. Use poker to turn piece while working.

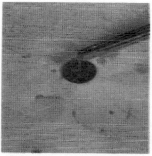
12. To solder on an earring post, place one solder chip in center of baseplate. Heat solder until it flows, then quickly place post in position before solder hardens.

To anneal flat silver, flux the metal and place it in annealing dish. Keep moving flame back and forth along entire length of piece until it glows dull red. Let it cool.

13. More heat is required to solder heavy metal. Asbestos drains away some heat. Work on charcoal block. Wrap sides of block with iron binding wire to keep it intact.

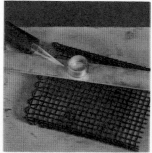
14. If even more heat is required, place work on a raised wire screen and heat it from underneath by passing the torch under the screen as well as over the top of the work.

15. If you cannot hold pieces together with cross-lock tweezers, tie them with iron binding wire. Hold top-heavy pieces upright by wedging them into annealing dish.

16. If easy solder has been used on a piece and you want to solder on another part, insulate area already soldered with yellow ocher and proceed with new soldering.

To anneal silver wire, coil it and wrap coil with iron binding wire. Heat coil evenly to dull-red glow and let it cool. Remove binding wire, and pickle annealed wire to help remove fire scale.

Jewelry

Bezels

The most common setting for unfaceted stones is the bezel setting. A bezel is a metal band that fits snugly around the stone. The bezel is soldered to the piece of jewelry, the stone is placed inside the bezel, and the top edge of the bezel is crimped down over the stone.

The bezel is often soldered directly onto the jewelry, but sometimes it is first wrapped around a baseplate of the same circumference as the stone. This type of bezel is used for rings in which the shank (band) is narrower than the stone and for earrings, cuff links, or pins with nothing surrounding the bottom of the bezel. The appropriate finding is soldered to the back of the baseplate, and only the stone and bezel show when the piece is worn.

Silver bezels are made of fine (pure) silver. The height of the bezel depends upon the height of the stone being set. Commercial bezel wire is available in widths of 1/8, 3/16, and 1/4 inch. You can make your own bezel wire by cutting it out of 28-gauge fine sheet silver. Use 26-gauge silver for heavy bezels.

Ascertain the length of the bezel wire needed by wrapping the wire around the stone and marking off the proper length with a metal scribe. Cut the wire and fit the ends snugly together. Place one jaw of a pair of flat-nose pliers above the joint and one below it, then squeeze to be sure the ends are perfectly flush. If they are not, the solder will not hold. Solder the seam between the abutted ends with hard solder. Keep the stone away from the soldering area or the heat may crack it.

Let the solder cool, then push the stone through the bezel, first in one direction and then in the other to be sure it fits and to reshape the bezel. The stone should fit snugly, but if there is a tiny bit of play between it and the bezel, it is alright. If the bezel is a little too small, put it on a bezel mandrel and hammer it with a rawhide mallet in the direction of the thick part of the mandrel. Keep turning the mandrel and pounding the bezel until it stretches to the right size. (If you do not have a bezel mandrel, you can use a ring mandrel if the bezel is large enough.)

With the stone removed, solder the bezel to the piece of jewelry the stone is being set in or to the baseplate. Use medium solder. Then solder on any findings needed with easy solder. Remember always to use flux and to pickle the piece after each soldering. Set the stone only when all the soldering has been completed.

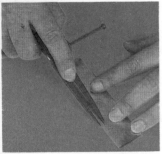

1. To make your own bezel wire, set divider to desired width and move it along one edge of the metal, one pointer riding against the edge and the other marking a straight line.

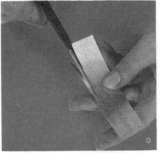

2. Using metal snips, cut along the line as closely as possible. Move along the entire line and beyond it without completely closing the snips, or you will create little nicks.

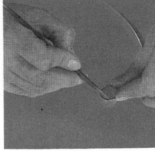

3. Wrap the bezel wire completely around the stone. Using a scribe, punch, or other sharp metal object, carefully mark the place where the wire overlaps. Remove the stone.

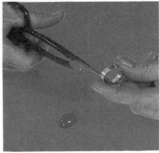

4. Snip off the bezel wire at the mark, then wrap the cut piece of wire around the stone again to check its size. If it is too long, trim it as needed. If it is too short, cut a new piece.

5. Manipulate ends of bezel wire until they are perfectly flush and tighten joint with flat-nose pliers. Otherwise solder will not hold, and you may wear a hole in bezel when polishing it.

6. With stone away from heat, solder ends of bezel together with hard solder (pp. 330–331). Watch metal. If it turns a light red, remove heat immediately or bezel may "burn up."

7. To make a bezel with a baseplate, place the stone on sheet metal and scribe its shape onto the metal, or use a template the size of the stone and scribe along the template.

8. Position scribed metal on a steady bench pin and carefully saw out the baseplate, using the scribe mark as a guide. File the plate smooth with a 6-in. hand file, cut No. 2.

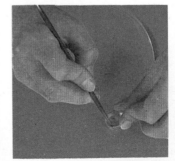

9. Wrap bezel wire around baseplate and mark place where wire overlaps. Remove baseplate and cut wire at mark. Test the fit of the wire and adjust it if necessary.

10. Solder ends of bezel with hard solder. Place bezel over baseplate and put several chips of medium solder around its inside perimeter. Apply torch until solder flows.

Ring shanks

Ring shanks, or bands, are made basically in the same way as bezels, but they are shaped on a mandrel. For most, 18- or 16-gauge metal is used.

To make a standard closed band, measure and cut the metal and shape it on a ring mandrel. Then manipulate the shank with your fingers, bringing one end above the other and then below it until they fit together snugly. If the metal is too stiff, anneal it (p. 331).

If a bezel with a baseplate or some other piece with a flat metal bottom is to be soldered onto the shank, a slightly open shank is generally used. The open shank is shaped in the same way as the cuff bracelet (p. 329), and its ends are filed down to fit snugly against the flat top of the ring.

To ascertain the length of a closed shank, multiply the ring size by 1/8 inch and add 1½ inches to the product. Cut the shank a bit longer to leave room for filing the ends. Cut an open shank about 1/2 inch shorter and trim as needed after the shank is shaped.

Manipulate ends of shank until they are aligned.

Silver ball ring

This attractive ring is made by soldering together a group of silver balls and attaching them to a shank. Form the balls by holding the flame of a torch on bits of silver until they melt and curl up into balls. Use silver bits of the same size if you want balls of uniform size. Use hard solder to connect the balls to each other. Make a closed shank and flatten it slightly on top with a file, then attach the balls to the flattened spot with medium solder. File the ring smooth and polish it (pp. 334–335).

Silver balls can be used to decorate any jewelry. For example, you can surround a bezel with them. The grouping used on this ring could also be attached to a baseplate with medium solder and made into earrings, cuff links, a pendant, or a pin by attaching the appropriate finding to the baseplate with easy solder.

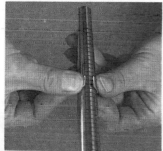

1. Measure and cut metal for ring shank, and press metal into shape on ring mandrel. If mandrel is graduated, middle of shank should end at mark for size you want.

2. Complete shaping with rawhide mallet. When shank fits snugly around mandrel, take it off, put it back on upside down, and pound it again to correct taper from mandrel.

3. If you are fashioning a closed shank and the ends do not meet exactly, take shank off mandrel and pound it with mallet until ends fit smoothly and snugly together.

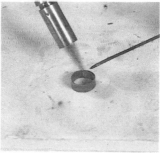

4. Put shank on asbestos, apply flux, dry flux with torch, solder ends together, and pickle shank (pp. 330–331). File soldered seam smooth with 6-in. hand file, cut No. 2.

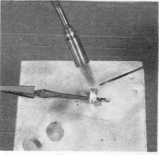

5. To add top to closed shank, place shank on asbestos, soldered seam up, and anchor it with cross-lock tweezers. Position medium solder chips over seam and heat them.

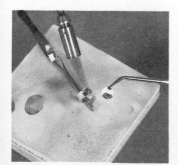

6. When solder begins to melt, pick up top with fine-point tweezers and place it over solder. Press top down with tweezers and heat with torch until solder flows completely.

7. To fashion an open shank, cut the metal a little shorter than finger size to allow for gap on top. Shape it on ring mandrel, as above, first with your hands, then with mallet.

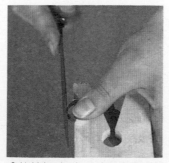

8. Hold the shank on a bench pin with one hand. With the other hand file the open ends flat with a 6-in. hand file, cut No. 2. Ends must be flat to accept baseplate or other top.

9. Make baseplate with bezel or other top for ring and place it face down on asbestos. Flux top and shank; dry flux. Position shank and place a medium solder chip at each corner.

10. Heat solder with torch, moving flame from solder chips along lines to be sealed. Solder will flow in direction of heat. Use poker to turn ring as needed. Pickle ring.

Jewelry

Setting stones

Before setting a cabochon stone, place it into its bezel and check its height. The top of the bezel should be a hair above the place where the stone begins to curve. If necessary, raise the stone by soldering bits of silver inside the bezel or by packing the bezel with sawdust. The latter method is unconventional but easy and effective.

Hold the piece, with the stone in place, in one hand and hold the burnisher in the other. Applying firm, even pressure with the flat side of the burnisher, work your way around the stone, pressing the edge of the bezel down onto it. Do not work too fast or press too hard, or the metal may pucker. To complete the setting, put the piece into a vise or wedge it into a pitch bowl and finish it with a hammer and setting nail.

Faceted stones are generally put into prong settings, but making a prong setting requires great skill and is usually done only by professionals. However, you can buy a ready-made prong setting. Simply solder it to your jewelry, position the stone in it, and press the prongs down over the stone with a burnisher.

1. Push top edge of bezel down over stone with flat side of burnisher. Use firm, even pressure and work slowly. Turn piece over and press bezel from opposite direction.

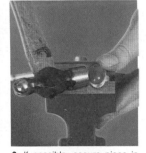

2. If possible, secure piece in vise with bezel completely exposed and gently tap all around top of bezel with flat end of a ball peen hammer to help close bezel tighter over stone.

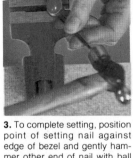

3. To complete setting, position point of setting nail against edge of bezel and gently hammer other end of nail with ball peen hammer until no gaps remain between stone and bezel.

4. Some pieces, such as bezel settings with no trim or border, cannot be positioned in vise without damaging piece. With a torch, heat tar in a pitch bowl to soften it, and wedge piece in.

5. When tar is cool, complete setting of stone as described in Steps 2 and 3. Be careful when using setting nail not to gouge silver or stone. Hold nail steady and tap gently.

6. Heat tar with torch, being careful not to let flame hit bezel or stone, or heat may crack stone. Gently pry piece out of tar. File, sand, and polish it as shown at right.

Filing, sanding, and polishing

After a piece of jewelry is completely put together, the metal must be filed, sanded, and polished. It can also be oxidized to emphasize certain areas by darkening them.

Filing and sanding. File down the finished piece of jewelry to make it as smooth as possible. Use a 6-inch hand file for large areas and needle files for delicate and hard-to-reach areas. Choose whatever shape file works best in a given area. For general work, use cut No. 1 or No. 2.

When filing, brace the piece of jewelry on a steady bench pin and apply light pressure to the file. If it does not cut sufficiently, increase the pressure little by little until you ascertain the ideal pressure to use. If you begin by using too much pressure, you may create unsightly grooves in the piece. If your files become clogged with filings, clean them with a file card.

When you have smoothed out the piece as much as you can by filing, go over it with fine emery paper or sandpaper. For some pieces you may have to use a medium paper first.

Polishing. Most polishing is done on a polishing machine, but if you have a flexible-shaft machine, you can use it to polish hard-to-reach areas, such as the openings in saw-pierced pieces, tight corners, and deep grooves.

The fine metal dust that is raised in polishing can be unhealthy if breathed in, so wear a surgical mask while polishing. Also wear rubber tips on the fingers you use to hold the jewelry to the wheel, as the friction from the wheel can be unkind to bare fingers. If you have long hair, tie it back so that it cannot get caught in the machinery. Finally, wear washable clothes and an apron—polishing can be messy.

Place the motor of the polishing machine so that the wheel attached to it fits under the dust shield. If the shield has a pan underneath, fill it with water to help minimize flying dust. When operating, the polishing wheel should turn toward you in a downward motion. Always hold the piece you are polishing about three-quarters of the way down between the highest and lowest points on the wheel. While polishing, keep the piece moving continuously. If you hold it too long in one place, you may create a depression in the metal. Always grip the piece firmly, or it may be pulled out of your hands by the moving wheel. Wrap chains around a piece of wood to keep them from becoming entangled in the machinery. If a piece does get caught, let it go at once and quickly turn off the motor. If you continue to hold onto it, your hand may be pulled in with it.

The steps to be followed in polishing are shown at right. If your buffs get too clogged with tripoli, clean them with a comb made of a board with nails pounded through one end.

Oxidizing and cleaning. If you want to create dark areas on your silver jewelry, heat the silver slightly with a torch and paint the areas to be darkened with liver of sulfur (potassium sulfide) before buffing the piece with rouge. This process is called oxidizing, although, in fact, no oxidation takes place. Commercial oxidizing solutions are available for silver and other metals. Oxidation is used primarily for grooves in metal, for bottom layers of multi-layered surfaces, and for twisted wire.

After a piece of jewelry is completely polished, it should be soaked in ammonia for a few minutes, scrubbed with an artist's brush or toothbrush, rinsed in clear water, and patted dry with a lint-free cloth. However, if a piece contains soft stones, such as malachite or turquoise, do not soak it in ammonia, which could penetrate the stones and damage them. Merely scrub the piece with ammonia, and rinse and dry it immediately.

1. Cover soft stones, such as malachite or turquoise, with several layers of cellophane tape. Trim tape away from metal before filing, sanding, or polishing piece. Remove tape after polishing.

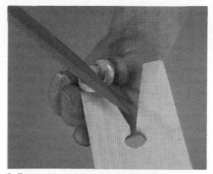

2. Taper sides of ring shank with a file to make it narrower at bottom. This facilitates finger movement when worn. Move file from front to back but apply pressure only to back.

3. File smooth all soldered seams and any other rough areas. Use a needle file for delicate and hard-to-reach places. Choose whatever shape of file best fits into the area being smoothed.

4. When you have smoothed out piece as much as you can with files, finish job with fine-grit emery paper. Some pieces of jewelry may need preliminary sanding with medium-grit paper.

5. Attach brush to spindle of polishing machine and turn machine on. Brush should spin in direction of arrow. Hold block of tripoli against brush until bristles are lightly coated with it.

6. Hold piece being polished firmly against brush and keep moving it around. Polish back, then crevices and other areas buff cannot reach. Add more tripoli if brush does not cut properly.

7. Put stitched wool or cotton buff on machine and coat buff with tripoli. Keep moving piece against buff until all sharp edges are rounded off. Apply more pressure to remove fire scale.

8. To polish inside of ring shank or bracelet, use felt cone with tripoli. Hold piece on moving cone. If you prefer a highly polished inside, sand it first with cone wrapped in emery paper.

9. When you have polished entire piece with tripoli, attach unstitched cotton buff to machine, and coat with red rouge by holding rouge against moving wheel. Polish entire piece with rouge.

10. Wrap chain around piece of wood to keep it from getting tangled in machinery. Polish as usual with tripoli and rouge, but keep changing position of chain on wood to reach all parts.

11. To create darkened areas on silver, heat metal slightly and brush with liver of sulfur before polishing piece with rouge. Darkening low areas will give piece an antiqued look.

12. Soak polished jewelry in ammonia for a few minutes, then rinse and pat dry with lint-free cloth. If piece contains soft stones, do not soak. Scrub with ammonia and rinse immediately.

Jewelry

Twisting, drawing, and flattening wire

It is sometimes necessary or desirable to change the shape or gauge of wire to make it fit a project. Wire can be twisted for decorative use, it can be drawn to make it thinner and stiffer, and it can be flattened.

A single length of wire can be doubled and twisted, or several lengths of similar or dissimilar wire can be twisted together, as shown below. By using different types of wire, a large variety of twists can be made.

Wire is drawn by passing it through successively smaller holes in a drawplate. The drawplate has several series of graduated holes numbered on the face of the plate. The numbers correspond to the gauge the wire will be when pulled through the holes. Each series of holes has a different shape (square, round, or half-round), corresponding to the shape of the wire.

Before drawing a length of wire, rub it with beeswax to reduce friction. File

one end of the wire to a tapered point about an inch long and insert it into the smallest hole the wire will not fit into easily. Screw the drawplate securely into a vise horizontally. If you position it vertically, the pressure of drawing may snap it in two. With wire-holding pliers, pull the wire through the hole. Use a good deal of pressure and pull in one continuous motion to avoid making ridges in the drawn wire. Then pull the wire through the next smaller hole and then the next until the wire reaches the desired gauge. Do not skip holes, or you may break the wire.

In the process of drawing, wire becomes stiff. If it becomes too stiff to handle, anneal it before continuing (see p. 331). You can repeat the annealing as often as necessary.

Flatten regular or twisted wire by pounding it on a metal surface with a ball peen hammer. Flattened wire is used in filigree work (see pp. 340–341).

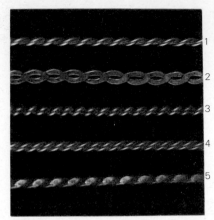

Both like and dissimilar wires can be twisted together and can even be reshaped after twisting. A few possibilities are shown here: single length of brass wire can be doubled and twisted (1); same wire can be flattened after twisting (2); length of brass wire can be twisted with length of copper wire (3); three lengths of brass wire can be twisted together (4); round copper wire can be doubled and twisted, then passed through square holes in a drawplates (5).

Hinges

Hinges are made of metal tubing and wire that fits snugly into the tubing but is a fraction of an inch longer. The tubing serves as the body of the hinge; the wire acts as the hinge pin.

Trim the tubing to size and cut it into three equal sections. Solder two of them with hard solder to one side of the piece being hinged, flush with the edges of the piece. Position the center section of tubing on the other side of the piece and test its fit between the other two sections. Mark its exact position with a scribe and solder the final section into place. Fit the sections together, push the wire through the tubing, and flatten the ends of the wire with a ball peen hammer. When making a hinge, be careful to solder the tubing in the right positions, or the hinge may not work.

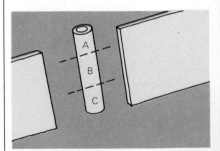

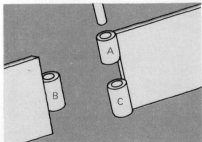

To make hinge, saw off length of tubing equal to length of piece being hinged. Saw tubing into three equal sections (top). File down rough edges. Solder two outside sections of tubing to one side of piece; solder middle section to other side (bottom). Fit pieces together, slip wire into tubing, and flatten ends of wire with hammer.

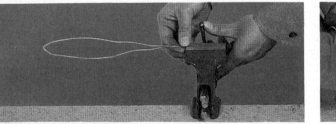

To twist single piece of wire, fold it in half and insert loose ends in vise. Tighten vise to hold wire firmly. Secure a hook in chuck of a hand drill and slip doubled end of wire over hook.

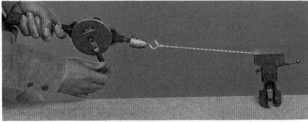

Pull drill away from vise until wire is taut, then turn handle of drill until wire is fully twisted. To twist separate pieces of wire, place them side by side, insert ends in vise, and use drill without hook.

To draw wire, rub with beeswax and file one end to a point. Secure drawplate in vise and push pointed end of wire into smallest hole you can. Pull through with pliers. Repeat through successively smaller holes.

To flatten wire of any shape, simply place it on a bench anvil or some other flat, smooth metal surface and pound it all along its length with a ball peen hammer. Be sure to hammer it evenly.

Findings

Except for rings and cuff bracelets, most jewelry utilizes some kind of findings to keep it together or to hold it on the wearer. You can buy findings ready to use, or, if you prefer, you can make some types yourself.

The jump ring is the most important of all findings. It is used alone or in combination with other findings to hold pendants to chains; to make chains, bracelets, or necklaces; and to hold parts of a piece of jewelry together. If you make your own jump rings, use spring-hard silver wire and anneal it, then follow the instructions below. Annealing makes the silver more pliable, but not as pliable as spring-soft silver, which is too soft for use in jump rings. To open a jump ring, hold it with two pairs of flat-nose pliers and twist it open at a slight angle; move the ends of the ring in opposite directions (forward and backward) and slightly outward at the same time. Reverse this motion to close a jump ring.

You can attach a pendant to a chain with jump rings only, but a more attractive connector is the teardrop. Make your own as shown below.

The uses of a few other findings are also shown below. A number of findings need only be positioned and soldered into place with easy solder.

 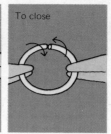

Open and close jump rings at a slight angle.

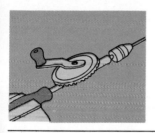

To make jump rings, insert metal rod of same diameter you wish rings to be into chuck of hand drill. Tighten chuck over rod and secure drill in a vise.

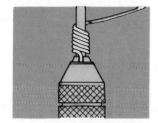

Anneal the wire, straighten it, and insert one end into chuck of drill next to rod. Turn handle of drill to tightly coil entire length of wire around rod.

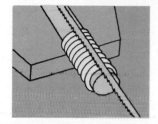

Brace rod with wire coil on bench pin and saw through one side of each ring. Be sure to cut all the way through wire, or you will create burrs on ends that will keep you from closing rings properly. Place a container under bench pin to catch falling rings.

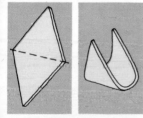

To make a teardrop, use metal snips and neatly cut a diamond shape out of thin (about 25-gauge) metal. Fold metal in half with round-nose pliers. Try to bend piece exactly in half to avoid having to file it down later.

Wedge wide part of teardrop into pitch bowl and solder a closed jump ring to the top with seam of jump ring close to top of teardrop. Remove soldered teardrop from pitch bowl, and pickle, polish, and clean it.

If opening in jump ring has been soldered shut, cut it open again at a slight angle. Solder another jump ring to top of pendant and connect the two jump rings. Thread chain through teardrop.

Make your own chain by connecting large number of jump rings. Simply open a jump ring, slip a second ring onto it, and close both. Then open a third jump ring and connect it to second. Proceed until chain is of desired length, then add a spring ring in same way.

Spring ring

Half jump ring can also be used as pendant finding. Cut jump ring in half with snips, and solder one half to pendant. Attach whole jump ring to soldered-on half jump ring, and thread chain through whole ring.

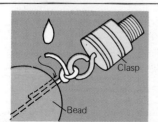

Clasp

Bead

To attach screw-type clasp to bead string, pass end of cord holding beads through link on clasp and knot clasp against last bead. Clip off most of excess cord. Stiffen rest by applying glue and letting it dry. Slip stiff cord into last bead. Repeat with other half of clasp.

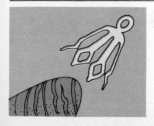

Tumbled stones are usually odd shapes that cannot be set in a bezel. Attach a bell cap to any tumbled stone by spreading arms of cap to fit snugly against stone and securing cap to stone with a drop of instant glue. Add a jump ring and use stone as pendant or drop.

Wire setting can be made for tumbled stone to be used as a pendant. Bend length of spring-hard wire into shape shown, then place stone on top of it and bend four points over stone to hold it. The size of the setting will depend upon the size of the stone.

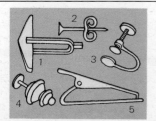

Many findings need only be soldered into place on piece of jewelry. These include cuff-link finding (1), earring post (2), screw-type earring back (3), tie tack (4), and tie-clip back (5).

Jewelry

Inlaying

Beautiful jewelry can be made by inlaying chips of stone into a bezel or a metal frame. The technique of inlaying resembles that of mosaic, except that no particular pattern or picture is formed by the stone.

The best stone to use for inlaying is onyx, which can be polished with tripoli and rouge. If you substitute another stone, you must polish it with lapidary equipment (see *Lapidary*, pp. 318–323).

Begin with a pair of earrings or cuff links. Make a bezel with a baseplate soldered to it and solder on the appropriate posts before you begin the inlay work. Otherwise the heat from the soldering could harm the stone. While inlaying, hold the piece steady by fastening cross-lock tweezers onto the post. Instead of using a bezel, you can make a frame by soldering wire to a baseplate; then fill the frame with stone chips, as was done for the belt buckle on pages 346–347. You can make inlaid bracelets or pendants utilizing the same principles.

The inlaid stone is held in place with instant glue. Read the directions on the glue container carefully, as instant glue dries quickly. If used carelessly, it could glue your fingers together. If this should happen, soak your fingers in acetone (nail-polish remover) to dissolve the glue.

1. With hammer, break onyx into rough chips. Place several chips into bezel, using tweezers. Hold bezel steady with cross-lock tweezers.

2. Add a few drops of instant glue to top of onyx chips. Glue will seep down between chips and cement stone to bezel. Let glue dry.

3. Add more onyx, fitting chips together as closely as possible. Add more glue and let it dry. Repeat until bezel is full of onyx chips.

4. When glue is thoroughly dry, attach a rubber wheel to polishing machine and grind down tops of stone, applying firm pressure until smooth.

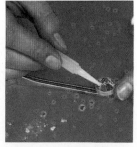

5. When grinding is finished, small gaps will be left on surface. Completely fill in these gaps with tiny chips of onyx and add more glue.

6. When glue is thoroughly dry, grind stone smooth on rubber wheel again. File and sand metal, and polish entire piece with tripoli and rouge.

Beads of all kinds

Beads can be made of any material, including glass, ceramics, shells, plastic, wood, paper, coral, amber, pearls, gemstones, and silver, gold, and other metals. They can also be of any shape—round, oval, cylindrical, square, triangular, tapered, free form, or in the shapes of animals, flowers, or anything else. All types of beads, including pearls, are available ready for stringing, with the bores (holes) already drilled through them.

Beads can be strung on almost any kind of filament. They can also be made into chains with interlocking wire eyes, as in rosaries, or prayer beads. In fact, the modern English word "bead" comes from the Middle English *bede* ("prayer"), which came to mean "prayer beads." Only later was the word used for jewelry beads.

When stringing or wiring beads, it is a good idea to work on an inverted, velvet-lined box lid. The velvet keeps the beads from rolling around and makes them easier to pick up.

Stringing beads. The type of filament, or cord, used to string beads depends on the design of the jewelry and the size of the bores in the beads being used. The cord should be thick enough to hold the beads fairly snugly, but narrow enough to pass through the bore at least twice in order to accommodate interconnecting rows of beads and to accept the cut-off ends of the cord, which are tucked in to keep them out of sight in the finished jewelry. Commercial nylon beading cord is available, but any sturdy thread, cord, string, wire, or chain can be used. Waxed dental floss works well. It is sturdy, and the wax further strengthens and helps preserve the cord.

Use any kind of needle that will fit through the bores of the beads you are stringing. Use an ordinary sewing needle for small beads, a darning needle for beads with large bores, or a commercial beading needle. You can make your own beading needle by bending a length of wire in half and twisting it together, leaving an eye at the place where the wire is bent. To string beads, thread the needle and slip the beads over the point of the needle onto the cord. If you are stringing pearls or expensive beads, knot the cord between each bead. Then, should the string break, the beads will not spill all over the floor and get lost. If you are making a necklace consisting of a string of beads that can be slipped over the head, no clasp is necessary—you need only tie the ends of the string together. If you are making a short necklace or a bracelet, add a screw-type clasp or a box clasp. (For directions on attaching screw-type clasps, see *Findings*, p. 337.)

Wiring beads. For wiring beads you will need various wire connectors, including jump rings, spring clasps, head pins, and eye pins. All of these are available commercially in any type of metal you wish to use.

An eye pin is a short piece of wire with a loop on one end. A bead is slipped onto the eye pin, the straight end is cut off a little above the top of the bead, and the cut end is twisted into a second loop with round-nose pliers. The loops hold the bead in place and connect to other eye pins, which hold other beads. You can make your own eye pins with any flexible wire and a pair of round-nose pliers.

The head pin is a short piece of wire with one end flattened like the head of a straight pin. Head pins are used to form dangles. One or more beads are slipped onto the head pin and are held there by the flattened end. The other end is bent over to form a loop, which connects the pin to the piece of jewelry. Drops are used as pendants, attached to necklaces and bracelets, or are connected to earring findings to make drop or chandelier earrings.

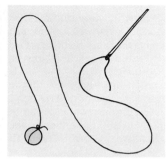

Stringing beads. 1. Pull cord through eye of needle, letting 2–3 in. hang down free. Tie a bead to other end of cord to keep strung beads from falling off while you are working.

2. Push one or more beads over point of needle and let them slide down to end of cord. Keep adding beads until piece is finished. Remove bead that was tied on in Step 1.

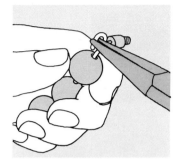

3. Add screw-type clasp (p. 337) or tie remaining string ends to pull beads tightly together. Snip ends of string off short and push into bores of end beads. Secure knot with glue.

4. To add a second row of beads to bottom of first row, thread needle and pass cord through bores of beads on bottom of first row, then string second row as you did first.

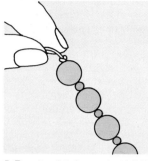

5. To get variety in your beaded jewelry, use beads of different shapes or colors on the same string. If the main beads are large, string small seed beads between the large beads.

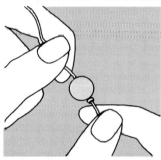

Pearls and costly beads. 1. Thread needle with cord that fits fairly snugly into bore of beads. Make a knot in cord at least 1½ in. from its end, then slide on first bead.

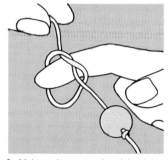

2. Make a loose overhand knot in cord. Insert index finger through knot and slide knot carefully down cord until it rests against bead. Do not let knot tighten before reaching bead.

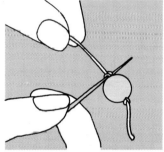

3. When knot is near bead, slip your finger out and insert point of a darning needle. Push knot firmly against bead with needle and pull knot tight at same time. Remove needle.

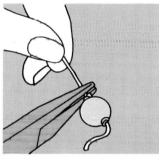

4. Hold cord in your fingers a few inches from bead. With needle-nose pliers grasp cord near knot and push knot gently but firmly against bead to tighten it securely.

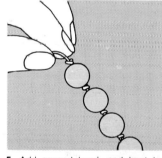

5. Add second bead, and knot in same way. Continue stringing one bead at a time, knotting each one into place until all beads are strung. Then add screw-type clasp (p. 337).

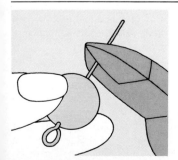

Wiring beads. 1. Slip first bead onto an eye pin and snip off all but short piece of protruding straight end. Leave enough to form a hook eye of same size as the one on eye pin.

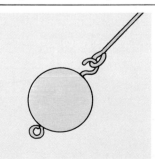

2. Bend cut end of eye pin with round-nose pliers to form second hook eye. Before eye is completely closed, add second eye pin and then tighten hook eye to hold eye pin.

3. Slip second bead onto second eye pin. Repeat Step 2. Add other beads in same way, then add jump ring to one end of piece and spring ring to other (see *Findings*, p. 337).

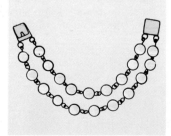

4. If you want to make a piece with several rows, make each row as described at left and attach rows to jump rings on a box clamp instead of attaching jump ring and spring clasp.

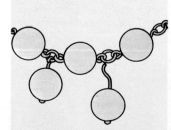

5. To make a drop, slip one or more beads onto a head pin, then cut off all but a bit of protruding straight end of head pin. Bend cut end with round-nose pliers to form hook eye.

339

Jewelry

Casting

Jewelry can be sculpted from wax and cast in metal. Rings and bracelets can be made in this manner, ornaments can be cast and soldered onto other pieces of jewelry, or jump rings or pin backs can be soldered onto cast pieces to create pendants, charms, or pins.

Casting is an advanced technique that requires special tools, but you can make your own wax models and send them to a professional caster—many professional jewelers send their work to casters. The caster will use the lost-wax technique—one of the processes used in sculpture (see *Modeling, mold-making, and casting sculpture,* pp. 192–209). When you get the piece back from the caster, merely file, sand, and polish it. If you want to make more than one copy, send the polished metal piece back to the caster and have him make a rubber mold from it. The mold can be used to make an indefinite number of pieces, all exactly alike. The copies made in the mold will be slightly smaller than the original casting, due to shrinkage, but all pieces made in the mold will be of uniform size.

Making a wax model. There are no set rules for sculpting wax models. Choose the type of wax that is easiest to work into your design. Scribe the design onto the wax, then use various waxworking tools to carve, scrape, and cut the wax into shape. If you want to build up more wax on the surface of the model, heat the tool you are using in the flame of an alcohol lamp, scoop some wax onto it, and press the wax into place on the model. Use files to add detail. If you are putting in a lot of detail, paint the wax white to make the lines easier to see.

Smooth the finished model with emery paper. If it is still not smooth enough, pass it lightly over the flame of an alcohol lamp or rub it with a cloth soaked in lighter fluid.

Unless you want a heavy, solid piece, turn the finished model over and carefully hollow it out, using a flexible-shaft machine with a burr attachment. Hold the model to the light as you work to help you see when it is uniformly thin. The finished model should be 1 to 1½ millimeters thick. Work carefully, as the wax is fragile at this stage. If too much pressure is exerted, the model may crumble.

Cast rings. To make a wax model for a ring, begin with a piece of ring tubing (wax with a small finger hole cut into it) or take a block of wax and cut a hole through it a little smaller than the finger the ring is being made for. Heat a ring mandrel in the flame of a torch and force the cut-out hole in the wax over the mandrel, first in one direction and then in the other (to make up for the taper in the mandrel). Twist the wax down to the marking for the correct ring size. Remove the model from the mandrel and carve the outside of the ring in the usual way.

Filigree

Filigree pendant was made from heart-shaped forms filled with coils and soldered together.

Filigree is a fine, intricately wrought network of coiled silver or gold wire that is contained within forms, or frames. These individual forms are soldered together to create a pattern. A number of filigree units can be connected to make bracelets or necklaces, or single units can be used as charms, earrings, or pendants.

The forms are made of flattened round wire and can be of any shape you choose. (A few of the many possible forms are shown below.) A piece of sheet metal is cut out to the shape of the desired form, and the round wire is flattened and then pulled around the sheet-metal template to give the wire the proper shape. The wire is then slipped off of the sheet metal, and its ends are soldered together. Each form is then filled with coils of flattened twisted wire. If you wish, fill in the areas between the coils with flattened twisted wire in the shape of scrolls or other curved figures.

The first step in putting together a filigree piece is to design it. You must decide what shapes you want the forms to be and how to fit the forms together into an attractive pattern. Draw the design larger than the finished piece will be to make it easier to work with. Once you have drawn the overall pattern, draw the coils that will fill in the forms. Draw lightly in pencil so that you can erase and redraw the coils if you need to change their arrangement to get a better pattern. When you are satisfied with the pattern, draw it to size, then make the piece by following the steps illustrated at right.

If you find it difficult to solder this fine wire without "burning it up," paint the surrounding areas with yellow ocher before soldering.

When the piece is completely soldered together, file and sand down any rough areas and polish it. Be careful when polishing not to apply too much pressure to the piece, or it may break. Attach a jump ring to the wire in one corner of the piece and connect it to a chain, earring, or other piece of jewelry, or connect several filigree pieces together with jump rings to make a bracelet or necklace.

Step-by-step process of carving wax shell is shown here, with cast piece.

Filigree forms can be made in innumerable shapes, which can be arranged into virtually any pattern.

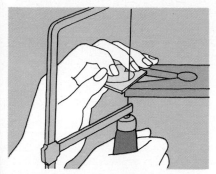

1. Cut the pattern of the entire design into patterns for the individual forms. Glue the form patterns to 16-gauge sheet metal and saw out the different templates from the metal.

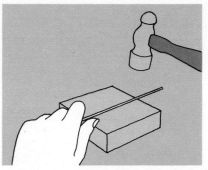

2. Flatten a length of 22-gauge round wire by placing the wire on a bench anvil or some other flat, smooth metal surface and hammering it evenly all along its length.

3. Press the flattened wire snugly around sheet-metal templates with fingers or pliers. Bring ends together flush on a straight part of the form, not at a corner or a sharply curved section.

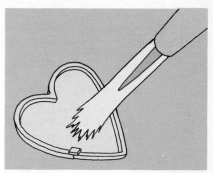

4. When wire fits snugly against all parts of template, carefully slip wire off sheet metal, place it on asbestos, and solder its ends together with a tiny chip of hard solder.

5. Loosely coil a length of 27-gauge round, spring-hard silver wire and place it on an annealing dish. Anneal it by passing flame of torch back and forth over it until it glows a dull red.

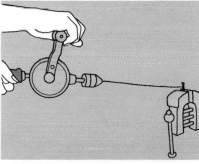

6. Uncoil annealed wire when cool, then double it and twist it (p. 336). Loosely coil twisted wire and anneal it (carefully, or it may "burn up"). Uncoil and flatten it with a hammer on an anvil.

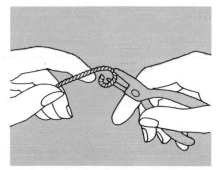

7. Grasp one end of flattened twisted wire with round-nose pliers and wind wire into coils of desired sizes to fit designs for interiors of forms. Snip off excess wire.

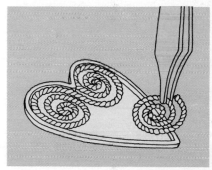

8. As you complete each coil, position it in form according to your design. Use tweezers to move the coils into the correct positons inside the form. When finished, coils should fit snugly together.

9. When all coils are in position, brush entire surface of piece with flux to get it perfectly clean. The least bit of dirt or corrosion can keep solder from binding these delicate joints.

10. Place tiny chip of medium solder over each point where two or more coils touch and where coils and frame touch. Heat carefully in flame of torch until flux dries and solder flows.

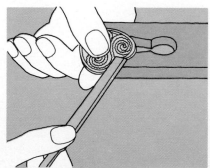

11. Assemble all the soldered frames, following your design. File and sand off any excess solder, rough edges, and irregularities. Place the entire assembly on asbestos for soldering.

12. Place tiny chips of easy solder over points where frames meet. Paint piece with flux and heat with torch until all solder flows. File, sand, and polish the finished piece.

Jewelry/projects

No-solder jump-ring bracelets

Jump rings are woven together in a regular pattern to make the bracelet shown at near right. Make the jump rings from 20-gauge spring-hard silver wire twisted around a rod 5/32 inch in diameter (see *Findings*, p. 337). Directions for weaving are given below. The bracelet shown at far right is a variation. It is made by weaving 20-gauge jump rings made on a rod 1/8 inch in diameter in a slightly different pattern.

The bracelets can be made of jump rings of other sizes, but the gauge of the wire must be in the same proportion to the diameter of the rings to give the bracelet flexibility. Copper, brass, gold, or gold-filled wire can be used to make the bracelets instead of silver wire.

Basic bracelet is shown here with magnified detail. Weaving pattern, explained below, is to add two pairs of jump rings, drop two, peel two, pull up two. You will need about 12 ft of wire to make this bracelet.

Variation of basic bracelet is made by using smaller jump rings and changing pattern to add three pairs of jump rings, drop two, peel two, pull up two. You will need about 9 ft of wire to make this bracelet.

Weaving the basic bracelet

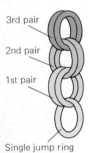

1. Make jump rings. Connect three pairs of them and add a single jump ring to first pair to mark beginning of chain. Thereafter, always work away from single ring to keep the weaving pattern intact.

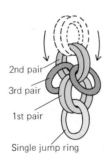

2. Hold connected jump rings vertically to form chain with single jump ring on bottom. *Drop* two top jump rings (third pair)—that is, push one of them to one side and other to opposite side.

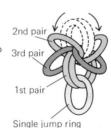

3. Still holding chain vertically, *peel* the pair then on top (second pair)—that is, grasp chain just below top pair and force one ring of the top pair to one side and the other to the opposite side.

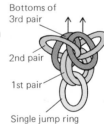

4. Reach down between peeled pair of jump rings with needle-nose pliers and grasp the two rings nearest the top. Carefully pull up these rings and hold them with the pliers. (You will be pulling up bottoms of third pair—pair that was dropped in Step 2.)

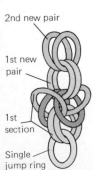

5. Begin regular weaving. While still holding pulled-up jump rings with pliers, attach to them another pair of jump rings (first new pair). Then add yet another pair of rings (second new pair) to the first new pair.

6. Still holding the chain in a vertical position with the single jump ring (beginning of chain) at bottom, drop the two top jump rings (the second new pair), one in each direction.

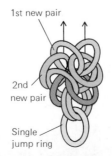

7. Peel the two rings that then appear on top (first new pair), then reach between them and pull up the next pair (the upside-down second new pair, which were dropped in Step 6.) Add two more pairs of jump rings to these. Keep repeating this pattern until the bracelet is of the desired length.

8. Add spring ring to end of bracelet. Single ring at beginning serves as other half of clasp. Wrap bracelet around piece of wood and polish it, using brush and buffs (pp. 334–335).

Jewelry/projects

Jewelry from beads

A large variety of jewelry can be made by stringing or wiring beads, using the techniques described on pages 338–339. The pearl bracelet shown below can be made of imitation, cultured, or real pearls, or of beads of any other kind. The earrings here are made of store-bought cloisonné beads, but any other type of bead can be substituted. Beads of different sizes can also be used, and the number of beads on each earring can be varied. The three necklaces shown at right are all slight variations of one design made with different types of beads. Any other beads can be used, the number of jump rings between the beads can be varied, or the necklace can be shortened and a spring clasp added. The type of metal used for the findings can also be varied.

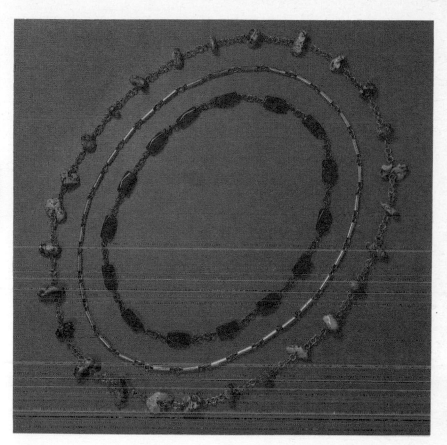

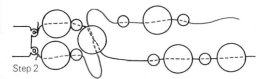

Step 1

Step 2

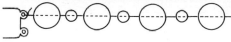

Step 3

This bracelet is made from 29 pearls of medium size, 36 seed pearls, and a sterling-silver box clasp with two hook eyes on each side. Tie a length of nylon beading cord to one loop in clasp. String 19 medium pearls on it, with a seed pearl separating each pair. Tie second length of cord to other eye of same half of clasp and string one medium pearl and one seed pearl onto it. Bring second cord (red in sketches) up through bottom of second medium pearl on first cord, then begin regular weaving pattern. String a seed pearl, a medium pearl, and another seed pearl onto second cord, pull up next three pearls on first cord, then pass second cord up through bottom of next pearl on first cord. Repeat until all pearls are strung. Pull cords to tighten weave and tie off loose ends to other half of clasp.

The drop earrings at left consist of four ready-made cloisonné beads, a pair of gold-filled screwback findings with loops for attaching dangles, two head pins, and two eye pins. To make each earring, slip one bead onto a head pin and cut pin off 1/4 in. or so above bead. With round-nose pliers bend cut end into a loop, inserting loop of an eye pin before closing it. Slip second bead onto attached eye pin, trim straight end of eye pin, and bend it into loop over loop in finding.

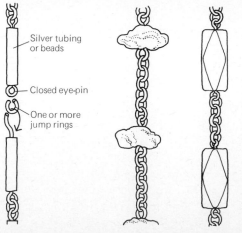

— Silver tubing or beads

— Closed eye-pin

— One or more jump rings

Three contrasting necklaces are made by slightly varying single design and changing types of beads. Innermost necklace shown above is of carnelian, center one is of silver tubing, and outermost one is of turquoise nuggets. All three necklaces are made by slipping beads onto eye pins, closing the eye pins, and connecting them with one or more jump rings. To make silver necklace, cut 16 in. of silver tubing into 1/2-in. lengths and connect them with silver eye pins and single jump rings. To make turquoise necklace, use chain of six jump rings between nuggets. On carnelian necklace, use gold-filled eye pins and chains of five gold-filled jump rings. Number of beads depends on their size and on desired length of necklace.

Jewelry/project

Ring with cabochon stone

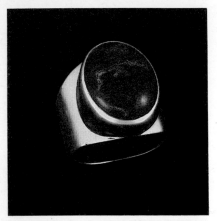

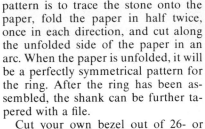

Stone

Bezel

Shank

Ring utilizes large cabochon stone and tapered shank. Sketch at right shows construction.

The variety of possible ring styles is almost infinite. The one shown at left is a variation of the simple ring with a cabochon stone. This ring, however, is larger and heavier than usual, with a higher bezel. Because of the width of the stone and bezel, the shank must be tapered so that it is much narrower at the bottom to allow the wearer freedom of finger movement.

It is almost impossible to make a perfectly symmetrical tapered shank if you draw and cut it freehand. Therefore, you must make a paper pattern first, tape the pattern to the silver, and saw out the shank using the pattern as a guide. The easiest way to draw the

pattern is to trace the stone onto the paper, fold the paper in half twice, once in each direction, and cut along the unfolded side of the paper in an arc. When the paper is unfolded, it will be a perfectly symmetrical pattern for the ring. After the ring has been assembled, the shank can be further tapered with a file.

Cut your own bezel out of 26- or 28-gauge fine silver 5/16 inch wide and about 2 inches long. Make the shank from a piece of 18-gauge sterling silver about 3/4 inch wide and 2½ inches long. Use any 18- by 13-millimeter cabochon stone. The stone used here is a brecciated jasper.

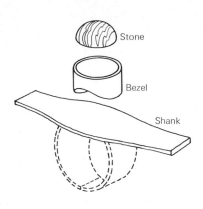

1. Place the stone you have chosen on the center of a small piece of thin white paper. With a pencil, trace a heavy line around the stone, then remove the stone from the paper.

2. Carefully fold the paper in half, with the drawn oval inside. Watch the oval as you fold, making sure that its two halves come together exactly and are perfectly congruent.

3. Fold the paper in half lengthwise, being sure that all edges are aligned. With scissors, cut the unfolded edges of the paper in a slight arc, beginning at the edge of the drawn circle.

4. Unfold paper and fasten it with transparent tape to a piece of silver a little larger than pattern. Put silver on a bench pin and saw out shank, using pattern as guide.

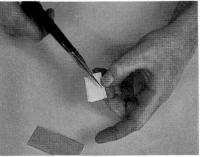

5. Remove paper pattern from silver and trim ends of silver to length needed for the size ring you are making (see p. 333). Shape the shank on a mandrel and solder its ends together.

6. Cut 5/16-in.-wide bezel wire and make bezel, using stone as guide to size. Brace half-round file flat side down on bench pin and file arc in bottom of bezel to make it fit contour of shank.

7. Tie bezel in place on top of shank with iron binding wire and wedge bottom of shank into annealing dish. Place several chips of solder around inside of bezel and heat until solder flows.

8. File edges of shank to smooth soldered connection and to emphasize taper near the bottom. Put ring into vise and set stone (p. 334), file and sand ring, then polish and clean it.

344

Jewelry/project

Watchband-style bracelet

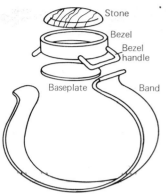

Stone
Bezel
Bezel
handle
Baseplate
Band

Bracelet hooks closed on top at side of stone. Sketch at right shows how bracelet is put together.

The watchband-style bracelet consists of a silver band that goes all around the wrist and hooks into two small handles on the sides of the bezel. One end of the band is permanently linked to one of the bezel handles, while the other end can be unhooked from the other bezel handle for putting the bracelet on or taking it off. When the bracelet is closed, the spring tension of the band holds the removable hook in place in the bezel handle.

To make the bracelet, you will need a stone, some sheet silver, and a bit of silver wire. The stone used here is a 25- by 18-millimeter cabochon chryso- colla, but any cabochon stone of that size can be substituted. The band is made of 16-gauge sterling silver 6½ inches long and 1/2 inch wide. The bezel is made from about 3¼ inches of 3/16-inch-wide bezel wire, and its baseplate is made from a piece of 22- gauge silver about 1 by 1½ inches. The handles are made from about 1½ inches of 14-gauge round wire.

The inside of this bracelet is difficult to polish, so polish the back of the band with tripoli before shaping it. To pro- tect the polished surface while shaping the bracelet, wrap the mandrel with a soft cloth. When you polish the com- pleted bracelet, polish the back with rouge on a felt cone.

1. Scribe shape of stone onto 22-gauge sheet silver and cut out baseplate for bezel. Make bezel to fit around baseplate, using 3/16-in.-wide bezel wire. Solder bezel to baseplate.

2. Make two bezel handles. Scribe marks 1/8 in. from one end of 14-gauge round wire and 1/2 in. from first mark. Place jaws of round-nose pliers just inside each mark, and bend to right angles.

3. Check size of short end of each handle and cut other end to same size. File ends at angle to fit onto bezel. Position handles along bottom of long sides of bezel and solder them into place.

4. Put bezel into vise with handles touching jaws of vise. Tighten vise enough to hold bezel se- curely, but do not overtighten, or handles may bend out of shape. Set stone (p. 334).

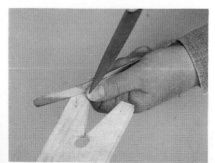

5. On 16-gauge silver, measure and scribe a 6½- by 1/2-in. rectangle. Saw out rectangle and file its corners round to form bracelet band. Polish back of band with tripoli (pp. 334–335).

6. Hold bracelet band with polished side down. With round-nose pliers curl one end of band nearly into a circle, leaving gap for bezel handle to pass through. Curl other end into U-shape.

7. Wrap soft cloth around a bracelet mandrel and bend bracelet band into shape as much as you can with your hands. Use rawhide mallet to force band into shape, leaving ends a bit too far open.

8. Hook one handle of bezel into one hook of band and hammer end of band completely closed. Remove bracelet from mandrel and test- fit other end of band. Adjust if necessary.

Jewelry/projects

Inlaid belt buckle

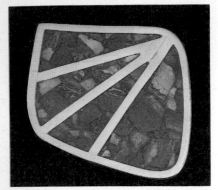

Belt buckle is made by soldering wire frame to baseplate and inlaying frame with onyx.

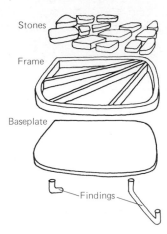

Stones

Frame

Baseplate

Findings

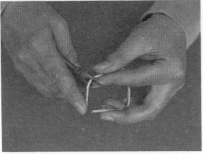

1. With round-nose pliers, bend 6-in. length of 10-gauge square wire into four-sided frame with rounded corners, making one side wider than others. Frame determines size and shape of buckle; you may redesign it to suit your taste.

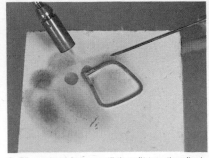

2. File ends of frame until they fit together flush. Apply flux to joined ends and dry flux with torch. Place chip of hard solder over joint and heat with torch until solder flows, turning frame with poker if necessary. Pickle frame.

Belt buckles are generally made entirely of metal—usually brass or some other relatively inexpensive metal. An outstanding buckle can be made of silver inlaid with onyx. The buckle shown above left is made by sweat-soldering a frame of square silver wire onto a baseplate of sheet silver, inlaying the interior cavities of the frame with chips of onyx, and bringing the entire piece to a high polish. The sketch above shows the different parts and how they fit together. The finished buckle looks deceptively like a solid piece of silver that has been carved out and inlaid with stone.

To make the buckle as shown, you will need about 14 inches of 10-gauge square silver wire for the frame, 2 square inches of 18-gauge sheet silver for the baseplate, about 4 inches of 10-gauge round wire for the findings, and about 4 square inches of onyx. This will make a buckle about 1½ inches long and 1¼ inches wide at its broadest part. This size is ideal for a narrow belt. If you prefer to make a larger buckle, merely increase all the measurements given in the instructions proportionately. If you are making the buckle for a fairly thick belt, increase the height of the findings by using slightly longer

pieces of round wire in Step 9 and bending their ends a little more than 1/2 inch from the ends. You can also alter the general shape of the buckle or change the number or design of the interior wires of the frame to suit your taste. The buckle can be made round or oval, or the inside wires of the frame can be curved. The techniques used for making these variations are the same as those described at right.

Although it is possible to cut the baseplate for the buckle first and then shape the wire frame to fit it, you will probably find it easier to shape the outside of the wire frame first and then use the frame as a pattern for cutting out the silver for the baseplate. The wire must be bent freehand with pliers, and it may be difficult to twist it to the exact contours of a baseplate. It is much easier to saw the shape of the frame out of sheet metal.

When sweat-soldering the wire frame to the baseplate, be sure to draw the solder out to the edges of the buckle. The outside edges of the buckle should have no holes or gaps. If you find gaps in the silver after your first attempt, apply more heat to the piece. If there are still gaps, fill them in with tiny chips of solder and heat again.

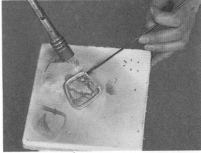

5. Using medium solder and mapp gas canister torch or gas-air torch, solder wire frame to baseplate as you would a bezel. Draw solder out to edges with flame of torch to make piece look solid. Pickle soldered buckle.

6. Check soldered seam. If it is not solid all the way around, add more solder and pickle again. Then grind edges of buckle smooth on rubber wheel, dipping buckle into water occasionally to keep it from getting too hot from friction.

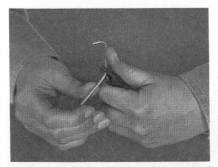

9. To make findings, cut 2½ in. of 10-gauge round wire and scribe marks 1/2 in. from each end. Place round-nose pliers 1/8 in. in from marks and bend ends to right angles. Cut 1 in. of wire and bend at center to right angle. File all ends smooth.

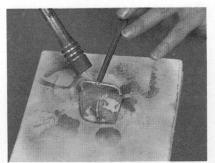

10. Scribe locations of findings on buckle. Solder on findings one at a time with chip of easy solder at each joint. When soldering second and third joints, keep flame away from joints already soldered or they may come loose.

3. Place frame on sheet of 18-gauge silver and scribe line on sheet silver around outside of frame. Brace sheet silver on bench pin. Using scribe mark as guide, cut out baseplate about 1/16 in. larger than wire frame all around.

Cuff links

Beautiful cuff links can be made with only a minimum of silver and a pair of matching stones. Black onyx buff-top (flat) stones 14 millimeters in diameter were used here, but any 14-millimeter buff-top stones can be substituted.

To make the cuff links, you will need about 1¾ inches of 1/8-inch-wide bezel wire (buy it or cut your own from 28-gauge silver), about 1/2 square inch of 22-gauge sheet silver to form baseplates for the bezels, the two stones, and a pair of cuff-link findings. Make two bezels with baseplates, solder on the findings, set the stones, and polish the finished cuff links.

4. Place wire frame on a bench anvil and hammer it with a rawhide mallet until it is perfectly flat. Then place frame on a sheet of emery paper and rub it back and forth to make the bottom of the frame perfectly smooth.

Cuff links are made from small amount of sheet silver and bezel wire, two stones, and findings.

7. Measure inside of buckle to determine sizes of inside diagonal wires. Cut wires a bit longer than needed and place them inside buckle. With a scribe, mark where wires meet inside edges of buckle. Remove wires and file them to fit.

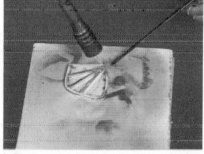

8. Flux baseplate and wire, dry flux, and solder wires into place with medium solder. Fill in any gaps with solder, and pickle buckle. Grind down any rough edges and fill in any gaps with more solder. Pickle the buckle again.

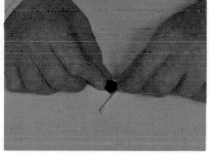

1. Wrap a length of bezel wire around each stone and mark with a scribe where wire begins to overlap. Remove stones and snip off wire at marks. Shape bezels and solder their ends together with hard solder.

2. Measure and cut two squares of 22-gauge sheet silver a little larger than bezels to form baseplates. Pickle bezels and file joints and bottoms smooth, then solder bezels to center of baseplates with medium solder. Pickle cuff links.

11. Pickle buckle, and inlay top with onyx (p. 338). Put in several chips of onyx and add few drops of instant glue. Keep adding onyx and glue until all frames are filled. Grind down stone on rubber wheel, fill gaps, and grind again.

12. Polish inlaid buckle. Use brush and tripoli to polish around findings, then buff entire piece, first with tripoli, then with red rouge. Soak buckle in ammonia for a few minutes, then scrub with small brush, rinse, and pat dry.

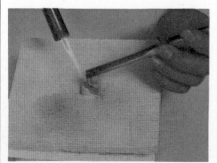

3. Check cuff links to be sure solder has flowed evenly. If there are gaps, apply more heat to draw solder out. Add more solder if necessary. Turn cuff links over and solder findings to centers of baseplates with easy solder.

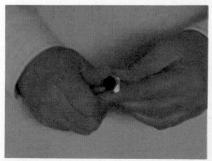

4. Pickle cuff links, then set stones (p. 334). Polish both cuff links: use brush and tripoli around findings and buff all parts with tripoli, then red rouge. Soak cuff links in ammonia and scrub them with a small brush. Rinse them and pat dry.

Enameling

The marriage of glass and metal

Enameling is a form of decoration or painting produced by the fusion of glass and metal. Gold, silver, and copper have been the metals most widely used in enameling, but others have been used as well. The glass used is a special vitreous enamel. Vitreous enamel should not be confused with the glossy paint called enamel. This paint, as well as the smooth substance that covers our teeth, was named "enamel" because of its smooth, glassy, enamel-like surface. (The word "vitreous" is from the Latin *vitrius,* meaning "glass.")

The enamelist applies the ground glass, or enamel, to metal and "fires" the metal and enamel in a kiln until the two materials fuse together. Other layers of enamel are added to the first layer, and the resulting work is a marriage of metal and glass that produces pictures or patterns of great beauty, vivid color, and enormous durability.

Only a special type of glass can be used in enameling. Glass and metal expand and contract at different rates when heated and cooled. When glass and metal are fired together, the different rates of expansion and contraction create pressure between the two materials. To prevent the glass from cracking under that pressure, enamels must be made following a special formula to produce a glass that melts and fuses with metal at a lower temperature than most glass would.

Clear, colorless vitreous enamel (flux) is made by mixing the proper proportions of flint, sand or silica, borax, and lead, soda, or potash; bringing the mixture to a molten state; then cooling it. Colored enamels are made by adding different metallic oxides to the clear enamel while it is in its molten state. The color produced depends upon which metallic oxide is added. The glass is subsequently ground into crystals or a powder.

Enameling in the ancient world. The oldest type of enameling is cloisonné, in which fine wires are twisted into patterned webs of small cells that are filled with enamel. The oldest extant pieces were made in Greece, Crete, and Cyprus from the 13th to the 11th centuries B.C. Enameling then fell into disuse until the sixth century B.C., when cloisonné work was used in Greek jewelry. A few centuries later, enameling spread to the rest of Europe.

In about the third century B.C. Celtic craftsmen of the British Isles developed a new enameling technique. As a substitute for coral inlay, they fired enamels in bronze molds—a technique now known as champlevé.

Later developments. Enameling became very popular in the Middle Ages and spread throughout the world, including the Byzantine Empire, China, and Japan. Although enamel had no intrinsic value, it was greatly admired for its extensive range of long-lasting, brilliant colors. Unlike those of paintings, the colors of enamels remain unfaded for centuries.

Four new techniques were developed in Europe in the 14th to the 16th centuries. These were basse-taille, plique-à-jour, and the painting techniques—limoges and grisailles (see opposite). The excellence of the painted enamels done at Limoges, France, in the 16th century made the town famous throughout the world. Superb enameled vases were produced in China during the Ming and Ch'ing Dynasties (1368–1911).

Enameling has continued to be widely popular through the present time. New enameling techniques and improvements in the six classic techniques are still being developed today.

This 18th-century, 27-in.-high cloisonné vase with its strong dragon motif is an exquisite example of the magnificent enameling work that was done in China during the Ch'ing Dynasty (1644–1911).

Enameling techniques

There are six classic enameling techniques; they are determined by the way the metal is treated before it is enameled and by the method in which the enamel is applied to the treated metal. Because of the outstanding reputation earned by the enamelists of Limoges and other cities of France during the Middle Ages, the six techniques are still known by their French names. A single enameled work may employ one or more of these techniques.

Cloisonné ("partitioned"). Fine wire is twisted into a patterned web of *cloisons* ("cells") and is attached to the metal. The cloisons are filled with layers of enamel until the enamel is flush with the tops of the wires.

Champlevé ("raised field"). Areas of the metal are etched out to form a design. These areas are filled with enamel until the surface of the enamel is flush with the unetched (raised) parts of the metal.

Basse-taille ("low cut"). The metal is etched, engraved, carved, hammered, punched, or stamped to establish a design, then the metal is covered with several layers of transparent enamel. The varying depths of the enamel that result from the uneven metal surface produce variations in the shades of color in the enamel and bring out the underlying design.

Plique-à-jour ("braid-filtered daylight"). A design is cut completely through the metal, and the openings are filled with transparent enamel. The light can shine through the unbacked enamel, producing an effect similar to that of a stained glass window.

Limoges. Many layers of enamels are applied to the metal in a painterly fashion to establish the design.

Grisaille ("gray"). Black enamel is applied to the metal, then layers of white enamel are added over the black, producing subtle shades of gray.

The enameled pieces shown here illustrate the six classic techniques. They are, from left to right, plique-à-jour, limoges, basse-taille, grisaille, champlevé, and cloisonné.

Tools and materials

To do enameling work, you will need metal, various enamels, a kiln, and a number of special materials and hand tools. All these supplies (discussed below) are available at enameling or jewelry supply houses. You will also need a few household supplies.

Enamels. Enamels are sold in powdered form or in lumps that can be ground down with a mortar and pestle. Flux is a clear, colorless enamel. Colored enamels are of three basic types: opaques (solid enamels that cannot be seen through); transparents; and opals, or opalescents (iridescent enamels).

Flux and black and white enamels are available in soft-fusing, medium-fusing, and hard-fusing powders, indicating the relative amount of heat needed to fire them. A special hard-fusing white enamel is available for use as an undercoat with transparent enamels or for backgrounds. A special flux used as an undercoat with silver is also available. Small plastic pill bottles with tight-fitting covers can be used for storing the enamels.

Metals. Copper and fine (pure) silver are the metals most commonly enameled. The ideal thickness for enameling is 18 gauge. It is best to use only electrolytic copper, which is 90 percent pure; roofing and etching coppers contain alloys that may cause the enamels to pit or crack. Preformed copper bowls and jewelry blanks are available. When firing copper, all exposed areas of the metal can be painted with scalex, a liquid insulator, to prevent fire scale, a discoloration due to oxidation, from building up.

Gold is an ideal base for transparent enamels, but only 24-karat (pure) gold or a special 18-karat nontarnishing gold can be used. Sterling silver (92.5 percent silver and 7.5 percent copper) can be used when extra strength is desired, but it is difficult to fuse red and yellow enamels onto it. Steel, aluminum, and iron can also be enameled. Gold and silver foil (paper-thin sheets of metal) can be applied to an enameled metal surface and covered with transparent enamels.

The kiln and its accessories. Although it is possible to fire some enamels with a propane soldering torch and a tripod, you will need a kiln for most enameling work. Get one with a pyrometer—an instrument for measuring the interior temperature of the kiln. The kiln should have a door that opens toward you, not one that opens from the top. Before using a kiln for the first time, paint its interior with a creamy mixture of kiln-wash powder and water to keep enameled pieces from sticking if they should fall.

(continued on next page)

Kiln with pyrometer; door opens out.

Enameling

Tools and materials (continued)

Enameled pieces must be placed on some type of support for firing. The most widely used supports are a stainless-steel screen firing rack, an iron planche, and a metal stilt with adjustable wings (the wings adjust to accommodate smaller or larger pieces). Use the support that holds each piece best. You will also need a spatula of the appropriate size for transferring pieces to and from the support and a firing fork (a large two-pronged fork) for moving the pieces and the support into and out of the kiln. Wear an asbestos glove when firing to protect your hand. When the hot work is removed from the kiln, it must be placed on a sheet of hard asbestos to cool.

Tools for applying enamels. You will need sifters of various meshes for separating and applying enamels. Sifters are plastic cylinders with screen bottoms. They are graded by mesh numbers, which correspond to the number of holes per square inch in the screen. The higher the mesh, the finer the enamel must be to pass through the sifter. If you cannot find sifters of the mesh you need, make your own. With a jeweler's saw, cut the top off of a large plastic spray-can cap. Cut a piece of screen of the right mesh a little larger than the cap, then heat the wire and press the cap firmly down onto it. The heat will partially melt the plastic cap and seal it to the wire. Trim away the excess wire.

A liquid binder is needed to make the enamel adhere to the metal until it is fired. Klyrfyre is the most widely used binder today, but gum tragacanth can be used instead. You will also need an assortment of paintbrushes, ranging from very small to 2 or 3 inches in width. You may also want to get an enameling spoon—a long, thin spoon with a tiny bowl—for picking up enamels. If you apply the enamels wet, you will need a palette of some sort on which to mix them.

Get or make a bridge to support your hand while scribing designs into the metal or enamel. A bridge is a piece of metal with its ends bent down.

Other tools and materials. Metal must be cleaned thoroughly before it can be enameled. To clean it, you will need a supply of fine pumice (an abrasive powder) and a nylon abrasive pad. The metal is sometimes further brightened by rubbing it with a glass brush—a sheaf of glass bristles bound into a cylinder. Finished enameled pieces are generally "stoned" smooth with carborundum stones—blocks composed of an abrasive grit. You will need three grades of stone: coarse, medium, and fine (scotch stone).

If you work in champlevé or basse-taille, you will have to etch the metal. To do the etching, you will need asphaltum varnish (a black, tarlike, acid-resistant substance) and ferric chloride (for flat copper) or nitric acid (for copper bowls and silver). If you work in cloisonné, you will need copper, silver, or gold cloisonné wire—a special thin wire used to build the cloisons. For working in plique-à-jour, you will need a piece of maranite (a fibrous, non-combustible material) or kiln brick and a piece of clear mica. The maranite is used to support the enamel during firing, and the mica is used to keep the enamel from sticking to the maranite. You will also need T-pins to secure the work to the maranite.

For special effects you can draw designs on the enamel with ceramic pencils, which come in various colors, or use ceramic decals as collage materials. Both are available at ceramics supply houses. Glass threads—thin strands of glass—and low-firing glass beads can also be fired onto a piece.

Finally, you will need an assortment of jewelry tools and materials, including a jeweler's saw, a bench pin, a hand drill with bits, a flat hand file, a set of needle files, a burnisher, smooth-jawed pliers, jeweler's precision tweezers, a small bench vise, pickling powder, copper tongs, iron binding wire, a metal scribe, and soldering equipment. For a full discussion of these supplies, see *Jewelry*, pp. 325–327. When soldering metal that will be enameled, always use IT solder. Its high flowing point (793°C) makes it safe for use in a kiln. The hard, medium, and easy solders commonly used for jewelry might melt in the heat of the kiln.

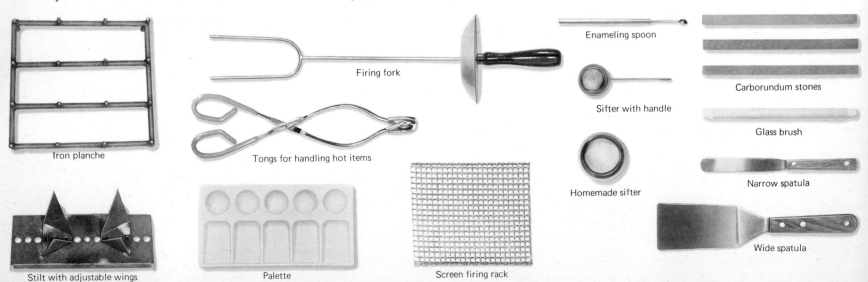

Iron planche

Firing fork

Enameling spoon

Sifter with handle

Carborundum stones

Glass brush

Tongs for handling hot items

Narrow spatula

Homemade sifter

Stilt with adjustable wings

Palette

Screen firing rack

Wide spatula

Working with the metal

The first step in enameling is preparing the metal. Select the metal you will use and saw it down to the size and shape you want the enameled piece to be. If your design calls for any cutout areas, saw pierce them by drilling holes in the metal, inserting the saw blade, and sawing (see *Jewelry*, pp. 328–329).

The metal must then be annealed—heated to a red glow to soften it. Remove the fire scale that builds up during the annealing by soaking the metal in a hot pickling solution. (Some pickling solutions need not be heated. Always follow the directions on the package.) If you are fashioning a piece of jewelry that requires soldered-on findings or a plaque that needs a picture hanger on the back, solder on these pieces before proceeding further (see *Jewelry*, pp. 330–331 and 337).

Before adding any enamels, thoroughly clean the metal. If you are working on a basse-taille piece, engrave, carve, hammer, punch, stamp, or etch the metal as needed at this point (see *Metalworking*, pp. 276–289).

When heated, enamel and metal expand at different rates, and the resulting pressure may cause the metal to warp. To equalize this pressure and to reduce the warping, the metal should be counterenameled—that is, a coat of enamel should be fired onto the back of it. Clean the counterenameled metal when it has cooled, then etch it if etching is called for (see *Metalworking*, p. 283). Finally, enamel the front of the metal as described on pages 353–355.

If any unenameled metal shows in a finished piece, you may want to polish it as described in *Jewelry*, pp. 334–335. If you do not have a polishing machine, wrap a stick with felt, apply tripoli to the felt, and vigorously rub it over the metal. Clean the metal with warm, soapy water, then repeat the polishing with a clean piece of felt and red jeweler's rouge.

1. Place metal on support. Wearing asbestos glove, pick up support with firing fork and put it into 815°C kiln. When metal glows red, transfer support to asbestos sheet. Pick up annealed metal with tongs and plunge it into cold water.

2. In flameproof glass saucepan mix pickling powder and water as directed on package and heat solution. Using copper tongs, place metal in hot solution and leave there until metal turns pink. Remove piece with copper tongs.

3. Submerge metal in water or hold it under running water and scrub it briskly with fine pumice and a nylon abrasive pad (if you use steel wool, be careful not to use it near the enamels). When metal is perfectly clean, rinse it in clean water.

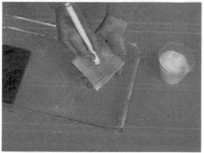
4. If transparent enamels are to be used, allowing metal to show through, bring out shine in metal by rubbing it with a glass brush. Douse metal in ammonia to alkalize it, and rinse it until water runs smoothly over its surface.

5. With a clean brush, give the top of the metal a heavy coat of scalex to protect the surface from building up excessive fire scale while metal is being fired with counterenamel. Place the metal on top of the hot kiln and let it dry.

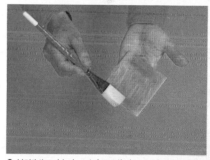
6. Hold the dried metal gently in one hand. Using clean brush, paint a coat of binder over the entire back of the metal. Cover the edges first. Binder is used to hold the powdered enamel to the surface of the metal until it is fired.

7. Hold 60-mesh screen over paper and put hard-fusing black or other enamel into it. Shake sifter over metal to cover it with heavy coat of enamel. Cover edges first. Gently blow off excess enamel. Return enamel that spilled to container.

8. Dry metal on top of kiln. With spatula, transfer metal to support. Wearing asbestos glove, pick up support with firing fork and put it into kiln. Fire metal until enamel is glossy (see p. 353). Remove support and metal to asbestos.

9. When the piece is cool, file its edges to get rid of all traces of fire scale. Remove scalex from front (it will lift off in a thin sheet like onion skin). Clean the metal with fine pumice and water, alkalize it with ammonia, and rinse it.

Enameling

Preparing the enamels

Enamels range in grade from crystals to fine powders, and the different grades result in different effects when fired, offering the enamelist a wide choice of possibilities. Generally, 60-mesh enamels are used as counter-enamels and for ground coats—the first coat of enamel applied to the front of the metal. A variety of grades can be used over the ground coat. The coarser the enamel, the clearer it will fire. Very fine enamels are ideal for establishing detail. Enamel grades range from 60 mesh, the coarsest, to 600 mesh. The 600-mesh enamels can be applied in much the same way as tempera paints, or they can be applied by airbrushing.

Enamels are generally sold in 60-mesh powders. Finer enamels are also available, but the 60-mesh enamels contain these finer mesh enamels as well as the coarser ones. By sifting the 60-mesh enamels through screens of various finer meshes, you can separate the different grades of enamel into coarse grains for use in jewelry and fine powders for painting with enamels.

If you do a lot of sifting at one time, wear a mask to avoid breathing in the fine dust. To clean a sifter after using it, tap it against the edge of the worktable to dislodge any grains of enamel that are caught in it.

Manufacturers grind down their enamels in a ball mill that leaves a certain amount of residue in the powdered enamels. Wash any transparent enamels you are preparing for jewelry application to get rid of this residue. Otherwise, the clarity of the fired enamels will be lost.

Always keep your enamels in clean, covered bottles that are carefully labeled. Colored enamels are given numbers by their manufacturers. Include this number on the label together with the grade number. A typical label might read "60-mesh transparent imperial blue (No. 122)."

1. Place a 200-mesh sifter in the center of a clean piece of paper. Open a bottle or package of 60-mesh enamel and pour it into the sifter. Keep a few clean bottles nearby.

2. Shake the filled sifter from side to side over the paper. The fine grains of enamel will sift through onto the paper and the enamel that is coarser than 200 mesh will remain in the sifter.

3. Open a clean bottle. Pick up paper with sifted enamel, fold it in half, and pour enamel into open bottle. Cap bottle and label it, listing color, color number, and mesh number of the enamel.

4. Pour the enamel remaining in sifter into a second clean bottle. Holding something under the empty sifter to catch remainders of enamel, tap the sifter against edge of table to clean it.

5. Pour enough distilled water into the bottle containing the 60-mesh enamel to almost fill it. Do not use tap water; it may contain minerals that will contaminate the enamel.

6. Cover bottle and shake it vigorously for a few seconds. Powdered residue from manufacturer's ball mill will become suspended in water. Clean enamel will sink to bottom of bottle.

7. Pour off dirty water before residue has time to settle back into enamel. Repeat washing with clean distilled water until water stays clean when shaken with enamel—about three times.

8. With an enameling spoon, scoop wet enamel out of bottle into a clean, ovenproof glass dish. Cover the dish, put it into an oven at low heat, and leave it there until enamel is completely dry.

9. Pour dried enamel onto clean sheet of paper. Pick up paper and pour enamel into a clean bottle. Label bottle. Note: the 60-mesh enamel is darker in color than the sifted 200-mesh enamel.

Applying enamels

In enameling, a design is built up by layering the enamels over the metal base. The first layer, or ground coat, is applied to all parts of the metal that are to be enameled. Generally, 60-mesh enamel is used for the ground coat. If you want part or all of the underlying metal to show through, use flux; otherwise, use black, white, or colored transparent or opaque enamels. You can either use a single color for the ground coat or apply different colors to different areas.

Subsequent layers of enamels can be added to parts of the ground coat or over its entire surface. Several thin layers should be built up. The thinner the layer and the coarser the enamel, the clearer the fired enamel will be.

The techniques for applying enamels are outlined below. More specific directions, with illustrations, are given on the following two pages. Some related techniques are also described on the following two pages.

Sifting and wet inlay. Powdered enamel can be sifted onto metal that has been painted with binder, or it can be mixed with binder and water and applied by wet inlay. Either method can be used exclusively or both methods can be used together.

Sifting is commonly used to establish a design with the use of stencils or by sgrafitto—cutting into unfired sifted enamel with a scribe. Sifting allows for enormous versatility, as it can be used to cover large areas or can be applied with a very fine sifter to establish intricate designs.

In *wet inlay* the moistened enamel is applied with a paintbrush. Detail can be added by painting with finely ground enamels and by mixing enamels or, when clarity is desired, by building up layers of glass.

Firing. After each layer of enamel has been applied, it is left to dry before it is fired. Enamels all fire at different temperatures, depending upon the color and thickness of the coat of enamel and the weight of the metal. Begin with a 815°C kiln and adjust the temperature as needed.

Fire each layer of enamel separately. Place the piece on a support and put the support and the piece into the kiln with a firing fork. Close the kiln door. Check the progress of the firing after about 90 seconds by opening the door a crack and looking in. Keep checking every 30 seconds or so.

During firing the enamel will go through three stages. First it will look grainy, then it will develop an uneven orange-peel texture, and finally it will glow slightly and become smooth and shiny. When it reaches the third stage, it is fired to maturity. Remove the piece and its support and put it on a sheet of asbestos to cool. The colors will be off at first, but the true colors will emerge as the piece cools. If a slightly uneven texture is desired, the piece can be taken out of the kiln when the enamel is still underfired–between the orange-peel stage and maturity.

If you do not have a kiln, you can fire a piece by placing it on a wire screen, putting the screen on a tripod, and passing the flame of a soldering torch back and forth under the piece. However, torch firing does not offer the control possible in a kiln.

Cleaning. After each firing, the edges of the metal must be filed to get rid of fire scale. This step can be eliminated if the metal is fine silver or gold, as these metals do not acquire fire scale.

All pieces must be washed thoroughly after each firing. Use soap and water, then rinse the piece and douse it in ammonia to alkalize it. Otherwise, grease collecting on the surface may react with the enamels and create problems. Rinse the alkalized piece and dry it. Touch the clean piece as little as possible, as oil from your fingers can contaminate it.

Finishing. After the last firing, the enameled surface will be a little uneven. Unless you prefer to retain this uneven surface, you can smooth it by stoning—filing it down with carborundum stones. Stoning dulls the glossy finish of the enamels. To restore the gloss, you can polish the piece with a jewelry polishing machine, using a felt buffing wheel and cerium oxide (see *Jewelry,* pp. 334–335), or you can rub it by hand with a moist felt buff and cerium oxide. Alternatively, you can flash fire the piece, which is done simply by putting it into a very hot kiln until its gloss returns.

Test tiles. It is impossible to judge the exact color an enamel will be after firing. The colors of powdered enamels and color charts are inadequate indicators. Consequently, it is helpful to make test tiles to be certain of how the enamels will look after firing.

If you want to make a test tile, cut out a 2-inch-long rectangle of copper. Drill a hole in one end of the rectangle for attaching the tile to a ring or hook, then counterenamel the metal. To make a test tile for a transparent enamel, first wet inlay white enamel to the top 1/4 inch of the tile, flux to the next 1½ inches, and the enamel being tested to the bottom 1/4 inch. Fire, cool, and clean the tile, then fire 1/4-inch strips of silver and gold foil to the top of the fluxed area (see p. 354). Finally, sift a coat of the enamel being tested over the entire tile and paint the color number onto the bottom of the tile with fine black enamel. Fire, cool, and clean the tile. The finished tile will show how the transparent enamel looks over the various surfaces.

To make a test tile for an opaque enamel, sift the enamel over the entire surface of the counterenameled tile and fire it; then paint on the color number with fine black enamel, and fire, cool, and clean the tile.

Enamels change color and texture during firing. These copper circles with flux demonstrate three stages of firing: orange-peel stage (left), underfiring (center), and firing to maturity (right).

Three test tiles at left are of opaque enamels. Three at right are of transparent enamels fired over white enamel, silver and gold foil, flux, and bare copper. Color numbers are painted on at bottom.

Enameling

Applying enamels (*continued*)

Sifting. Before beginning to apply enamels to a piece, thoroughly clean and counterenamel the metal, as described on page 351. Then wet a paintbrush with binder and spread a thick coat of binder over the surface of the metal with the brush. Be sure that all areas to be covered with enamel are generously coated with binder.

Put enamel for ground coat into 60-mesh sifter and gently sift it over edges, then rest of piece, until all parts are covered with thick coat of enamel. Binder will hold most of the enamel to metal. Pick up piece with spatula and put it on top of hot kiln to dry. With spatula, transfer dried piece to suitable support.

Wearing asbestos glove, pick up support and piece with firing fork and put them into kiln. Fire until glossy (see p. 353). With firing fork, remove piece and support from kiln and place them on asbestos to cool. File edges of cooled piece to get rid of fire scale. Wash piece, alkalize it with ammonia, and rinse it in water. Add further coats in same way.

Stencils. You can sift any type of pattern onto a ground coat. One way to control design is to use a stencil. Cut out cardboard pattern of areas not to be covered by the next color enamel and place this stencil on metal. Or make stencil by covering metal with masking tape and cutting out areas to be enameled with a utility knife, as shown here.

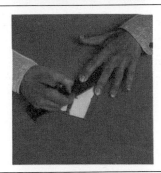

Brush binder onto areas not covered by stencil and sift enamel over entire piece. Blow away excess enamel. (You may also wet inlay enamels around a stencil.) Let piece dry. Do not put a piece with tape on top of hot kiln, or heat may soften tape's adhesive and leave a residue on the enamel.

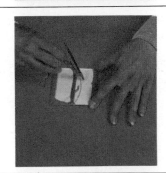

When dry, carefully remove stencil. If you have used tape, grasp one corner of tape with tweezers and slowly peel off stencil. Fire piece. When it is cool, file its edges (unless you are working with fine silver), clean it, and alkalize it with ammonia. Add next layer of enamel.

Sgrafitto. A common way of establishing a design with sifted enamels is sgrafitto—a method of scribing designs directly into sifted enamels before they are fired. Begin with piece that has at least a ground coat fired onto it. Brush binder over piece and sift on enamel. (Use a 100-mesh screen to get a thinner enamel grain that is easier to handle.)

Blow off excess enamel and let piece dry. Draw design by scraping away portions of enamel with a scribe or other clean instrument that will give the desired effect. When working on center of piece, rest your hand on a metal bridge placed over the work to keep hand from touching the surface and smudging it.

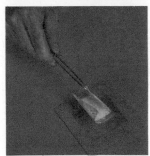

Use a compass with a metal scribe inserted into it to draw curves into pattern. Finish establishing design with more scribing, if desired. Blow off excess enamel and put piece on top of kiln to dry (providing there is no tape on it). When dry, fire and clean it in usual way.

Foil. Silver or gold foil fired under one or more coats of transparent enamel adds brilliance to an enameled surface. Place foil between two pieces of paper, as it is too delicate to handle alone. Cut foil with scissors or hole punch and slide it out from between pieces of paper.

Brush binder onto area to be covered with foil. (Metal must have at least one coat of enamel fired onto it before adding foil.) Dip brush into binder. With wet brush, pick up cut-out foil and position it on piece. Smooth foil down with brush and put piece on top of hot kiln to dry.

With a needle, prick holes in large pieces of foil to keep air bubbles from forming during firing. Fire piece until foil adheres to enamel but is not sunk in. Let piece cool and file its edges. Using moderate pressure, massage foil with burnisher to bring up its luster. Clean piece and add a thin coat of coarse transparent enamel over the burnished foil.

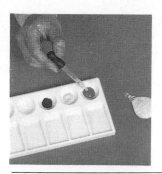

Wet inlay. Enamels used for wet inlay must be mixed with binder and a little water. Place small amounts of enamels on a palette. With an eyedropper, add a few drops of binder and enough water to make each enamel a bit thinner than sour cream.

Pick up small amount of enamel with enameling spoon or brush and transfer it to prepared metal. Smooth out enamel with brush. On cloisonné or champlevé (shown), try not to get enamel on wires or raised parts of metal. When all colors have been added, pick up piece with spatula and put it on top of hot kiln to dry.

Transfer dried piece to support (adjustable stilt is used here) and fire it as you would a sifted piece. Cool on sheet of asbestos, then clean in usual way. (If metal used is fine silver, you need not file edges.) Add further layers of enamel as desired, firing and cleaning each layer in same way.

Stoning. Finished pieces are usually stoned. Cushion piece on leather or balsa wood. Submerge in water or hold under running water to wash away filings while working. Rub briskly with rough then smooth carborundum stone until piece is smooth and even. Polish piece (see *Jewelry*, pp. 334–335) or flash fire it (fire it briefly in a hot kiln).

Copper bas relief. You can make a bas relief piece by cushioning thin (36-gauge) copper on a wad of paper towels or cloth and molding metal to shape with your fingers and a burnisher. Paint back of copper with scalex and let it dry, or, if you plan to fuse copper piece onto another enameled surface, counterenamel the copper.

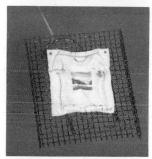

Brush binder over front of molded copper piece and sift on a coat of 100-mesh enamel. Fire, cool, and clean piece. Then paint it with enamels or add decals, as shown below, and fire, cool, and clean it. To fuse enameled copper piece to another enameled surface, place it on that surface and fire the pieces until they adhere to each other.

Transferring a design. To transfer design directly onto piece with ground coat, place carbon paper or white transfer paper over piece and put pattern over copy paper. Trace design onto ground coat, remove pattern and copy paper, and go over traced lines with scribe. Wash piece thoroughly to get rid of all traces of carbon or copy paper marks.

Ceramic pencils. You can also draw a design onto a piece with colored ceramic pencils. Stone an enameled piece to give it a matte surface and draw the design directly onto the enamel with ceramic pencils. Fire piece until pencil marks are glossy, then add enamels over the pencil marks, if you wish.

Painting. Enamels can also be painted onto an enameled ground coat. Simply mix finely ground enamels (200–600 mesh) with a few drops of binder and a little water to make them a bit thinner than for wet inlay, and paint them onto surface with brush. Paint freehand or fill in design drawn with ceramic pencils or scribe.

Decals. Ceramic decals with printed designs can be fused onto an enameled surface as a collage material. Cover metal with ground coat. Cut decals to desired shapes and sizes with a pair of scissors.

Soak cut-out decals in water until paper backing peels away. Pick up decals with tweezers and position them on enameled surface. Carefully correct position of decals by moving them with the tweezers.

With a paper towel, pat the decals to remove all water and air bubbles. Let piece dry 24 hr, then fire, cool, and clean it. Leave piece as is or fire transparent enamels over the decals. Glass threads and low-firing glass beads can also be fired onto enamels. Experiment with different glass beads to find out which can be used for enameling.

Enameling/projects

Cloisonné pendant

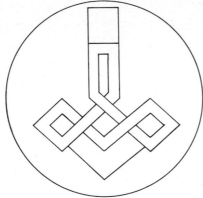

Cloisonné pendant at left can be made by following pattern at right. Pattern is full size.

Cloisonné is the oldest and best known of the enameling techniques. To make the cloisonné pendant shown at left, you need only a circle of 18-gauge copper, about 2 feet of fine silver cloisonné wire, and the enamels. You can buy the copper circle already cut or saw out your own from a sheet of copper. The enamels you will need are hard-fusing black for the counterenamel; hard-fusing flux for the ground coat; and medium-fusing black, transparent garnet, and opaque cream.

Before beginning the enameling, saw pierce a square hole near the edge of the circle. When the pendant is finished, you can loop a satin ribbon through the hole for hanging the pendant around your neck.

The wire is cut into sections and shaped, then it is put in place over the ground coat on the pendant. Since the pendant is flat, the wires can be held in place for firing with a little binder. (For curved cloisonné pieces the wires are sometimes soldered down.)

If, after firing two or more layers onto the pendant, the garnet enamel is becoming too dark, substitute flux for the garnet in subsequent firings. This will give more depth and retain the red where you want it.

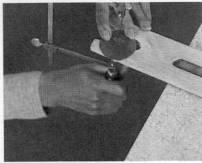

1. Saw pierce a small square hole near edge of copper circle. Counterenamel circle, then sift on and fire ground coat of hard-fusing flux. Cool piece and file its edges, including hole.

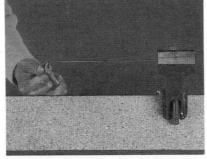

2. Fasten one end of the cloisonné wire in a vise and grasp the other end with pliers. Pull the wire tautly until it stretches slightly. This straightens the wire and makes it longer and thinner.

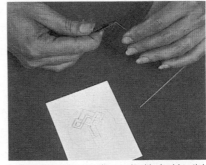

3. Copy the pattern and cover it with double-stick transparent tape. Using pliers, bend stretched wire one piece at a time to match lines of pattern. Put bent wires into place on the pattern.

4. When all wires have been shaped and placed on pattern, remove wires one at a time, dip each into liquid binder, and position them correctly on pendant. Place pendant on top of kiln to dry.

5. Fire the pendant until the wires sink into the ground coat, then remove it from the kiln and place it on a sheet of asbestos to cool. When cool, file the edges and clean the pendant.

6. Wet inlay large border areas of pendant with black enamel. With a 000 artist's brush, fill cloisons with cream and garnet enamels. Try to keep enamel from getting on tops of wires.

7. Allow piece to dry, then fire it. When cool, file its edges and clean and alkalize it, then add more enamels and fire them. Repeat process until enamel is flush with tops of wires.

8. Stone the finished pendant to make it smooth and to slightly flatten the wires. Polish wires with a scotch stone. Flash fire pendant to restore its gloss. Loop satin ribbon through hole.

Plique-à-jour earrings

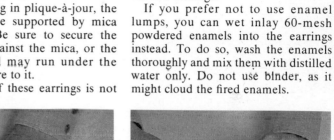

Plique-à-jour earrings at left can be made from pattern shown at right. Pattern is full size.

The stained glass effect of plique-à-jour is well suited to earrings. To make the earrings shown at left, you will need two 1½-inch squares of 18-gauge fine silver and some enamel lumps. Attach the earrings to ready-made findings or make the loops for pierced ears with about 4 inches of 20-gauge silver wire, as shown.

When working in plique-à-jour, the enamel must be supported by mica during firing. Be sure to secure the silver tightly against the mica, or the molten enamel may run under the metal and adhere to it.

The design of these earrings is not symmetrical. Therefore, it is important to make one the reverse of the other so that the same parts of the design will mirror each other when the earrings are worn. When you file down the openings at a slant, as described in Step 2 below, do it so that the wider side of the openings are on opposite sides of the two earrings.

If you prefer not to use enamel lumps, you can wet inlay 60-mesh powdered enamels into the earrings instead. To do so, wash the enamels thoroughly and mix them with distilled water only. Do not use binder, as it might cloud the fired enamels.

1. Make and cut out two tracings of pattern. Attach them to silver with water-soluble white glue. Saw design out of metal (see *Jewelry*, pp. 328–329). Pull off patterns and clean metal.

2. Brace each earring blank on bench pin and file edges smooth. With needle files, file interior openings at slight angle to give enamel chips some support when added. Anneal the silver.

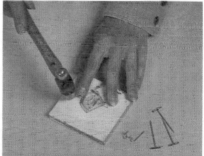

3. Place mica on maranite and earring blanks over mica. Wide sides of interior openings in blanks should face up. Bend T-pins and drive them into maranite around blanks to hold metal.

4. When blanks are held firmly against mica with T-pins, wrap iron binding wire around maranite and over pins to keep pins from moving. Twist ends of wire tightly together with pliers.

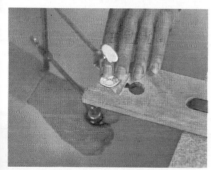

5. Put enamel lumps into a mortar one color at a time and grind the lumps down into small chips with a pestle. **Caution: Wear goggles or protective glasses, or chips may fly into your eyes.**

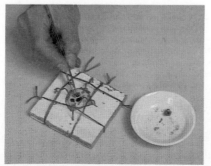

6. Using tweezers, fill openings in silver to heaping with enamel chips, then fire in a hot kiln. When cool, add more chips (shown) and fire again. Repeat until openings are filled with enamel.

7. Stone enamel down even with silver. Sand with No. 500 then No. 600 emery paper. Polish both glass and metal on earrings with a felt buff and moistened cerium oxide.

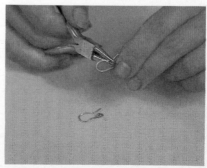

8. Make each ear loop by holding soldering torch to end of 2-in. lengths of 20-gauge silver wire until metal melts into ball at end. Bend rest of wire into shape (see pattern) and attach to earrings.

Enameling/projects

Champlevé bowl

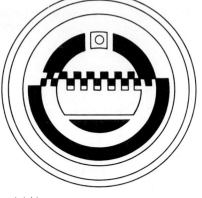

Champlevé bowl at left can be made following pattern at right.

A simple copper bowl can be made exquisite by etching out sections of the copper and filling the recesses with enamels. To make a bowl similar to the one shown at left, you can use a round bowl of any size. You will also need opaque evergreen enamel for the outside of the bowl and various opaque enamels for the inside. In addition, you will need asphaltum varnish, beeswax, and nitric acid for etching the metal. (Although ferric chloride is normally used to etch copper, it does not etch evenly on a curved surface.)

To etch the bowl, cover the areas that will not be etched with asphaltum and protect the rim of the bowl with a covering of beeswax. Measure the holding capacity of the bowl, then pour three-quarters of that amount of water into a large glass container. Carefully add the equivalent of one-quarter of a bowlful of nitric acid to the water. Stir the solution gently with copper tongs, then carefully pour it into the bowl until it reaches the wax on the rim. Allow the solution to stand in the bowl until it is etched. Occasionally use a feather to brush away any bubbles that rise to the surface, as the bubbles will impede the bite of the acid. Use the handle of a disposable artist's brush to

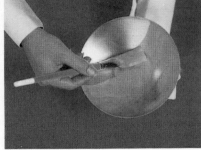

1. Anneal the copper bowl and let it cool. Clean the bowl thoroughly, using fine pumice and glass brush, as described on page 351. Alkalize the cleaned bowl with ammonia and rinse it. Brush a thick coat of scalex over inside of bowl.

2. Turn the bowl over, being careful not to get finger smudges on it, and brush the entire exterior with binder. Using a 60-mesh screen, sift on a heavy coat of opaque evergreen enamel. Transfer the bowl to the top of the kiln to dry.

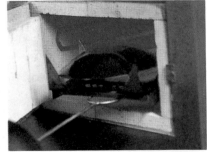

3. Fire the bowl when it is dry, then transfer it to asbestos to cool. Clean the cooled bowl inside and out, being sure to remove all the scalex and fire scale from the inside. Alkalize the bowl with ammonia again and rinse it.

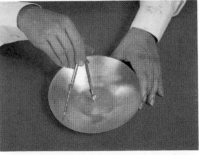

4. Using above pattern as guide, scribe design onto inside of bowl. Use a compass fitted with a metal scribe to draw circles; fill in rest of design with scribe alone. (Use a flexible straightedge as guide when drawing straight lines.)

6. Melt wax over alcohol lamp, scoop it up with waxworking tool or narrow spatula, and apply it to entire rim of bowl. Prepare acid solution in a glass container, then carefully pour it into bowl until it reaches wax on rim. Stir gently.

7. Check progress of the etching every 15 min. Use feather to break bubbles that rise to top. If some parts etch faster than others, remove solution, cover those parts with asphaltum, and return solution to bowl until all parts are etched equally.

8. Empty acid solution into glass container, add baking soda and water to neutralize it, then dispose of it. Clean asphaltum from bowl with paint thinner and steel wool. Clean bowl thoroughly and wet inlay first layer of enamels.

9. Paint exposed metal with scalex to keep fire scale from building up on it during firing. Be careful not to get scalex on the enamel. Let bowl dry, then place it upside down on a support and fire it. When it is cool, clean it thoroughly again.

check the depth of the etch every 15 minutes or so. For more complete directions on etching, see *Metalworking,* pp. 276–289.

Caution: Always add the nitric acid to the water; never add the water to the acid. Adding water to acid may cause the acid to sputter, which could burn you. When etching, place the bowl in a glass baking pan or other glass receptacle to catch any acid that spills over the sides of the bowl. Always wear rubber gloves when handling acid and when cleaning the etched-out metal. Neutralize the acid by adding baking soda and water before disposing of it.

5. Clean bowl again until it is immaculate. Paint asphaltum over entire outside of bowl and over parts of inside that are not to be etched. It is better to paint on several thin coats of asphaltum rather than one thick one. Let asphaltum dry overnight.

10. Apply additional layers of enamel until enamel is flush with level of exposed metal. Remember to paint exposed metal with scalex before each firing. Stone enamel to make it smooth and even, then flash fire bowl. Polish exposed metal.

Grisaille plaque

Grisaille is a painting technique, and painting is a highly individualistic art. If you work in grisaille, you should create your own designs. However, if you prefer to begin with a given design for your first grisaille project, copy the pattern shown at right to establish your design as described in Step 2 below. Add your own details and shadings as you proceed. The pattern is half size. To copy it exactly, double all the measurements. To make the plaque, you will need a 4-in. square of 18-gauge copper, 60-mesh hard-fusing black enamel, and 100-mesh and 300- or 400-mesh grisaille white enamel. A finished plaque made from this pattern is shown at right.

1. Clean the copper and counterenamel it with 60-mesh hard-fusing black enamel. Add a ground coat of the same enamel, then sift on a light coat of grisaille white enamel. Use a 100-mesh screen and hold it high above the piece when sifting to ensure a thin coat. Let the enamel dry.

3. Mix some 300-mesh or 400-mesh grisaille white enamel for wet inlay and use it to build up white areas by painting it on plaque. Fire plaque and add four or five more applications of white enamel to produce desired shadings. As you work, wet enamel will look as it does after firing, but unfired dried enamel on plaque will not.

2. Establish the design by cutting lines into the white enamel with a scribe. Do not add details at this point; they will be added later. Blow off excess enamel, fire plaque, and let it cool.

4. Clean plaque and add highlights with the white enamel. Fire plaque, let it cool, and clean edges.

Grisaille is an excellent medium for painting portraits and realistic still lifes. The blending of black, white, and shades of gray inherent in this medium produces the effect of a black and white photograph. The classic grisaille technique can be modified, if desired, by dusting light touches of color onto the finished piece and firing it.

Instructions for making the plaque shown at left are given below. Follow the pattern given here to establish the overall picture. Fill in the details yourself. If you plan to hang the finished plaque, bend a short piece of heavy copper wire into a loop and solder it to the back of the cut-out copper plaque with IT solder before adding any enamels (see *Jewelry,* pp. 330–331). Or you can mount the finished plaque on a sheet of Plexiglas and frame it.

Woodworking

Making fine furniture

Woodworking has different meanings to different people. To some it is building kitchen cabinets; to others it is turning a bowl of rare wood; to still others it is carving sculpture, a subject treated elsewhere (see *Wood sculpture*, pp. 268–275). The subject of this section is the making of fine furniture and furnishings, a challenging and totally absorbing craft. Much of today's commercial furniture is flimsy; by making your own you get lasting quality and superior materials.

Carpentry and cabinetry. The tools and many of the techniques of carpentry and cabinetry are similar; the two differ in the degree of accuracy required in measuring, marking, and cutting. The tolerances for deviation in carpentry may be 1/16 inch; in cabinetry the tolerances are 1/32 inch and, in very fine work, 1/64 inch. (Building a harpsichord requires tolerances of 1/128 inch.)

Woodworking began in prehistory when man fashioned adzes, chisels, gouges, and awls of stone and used them for cutting and shaping wood. Bronze Age man invented the saw, metal chisels, and files. The ancient Egyptians used the same joints we know today: butt, miter, rabbet, dovetail, and mortise. By the time of the Roman Empire most hand tools had been invented. The plane, lost during the Dark Ages, was rediscovered in the 12th or 13th century. Medieval carpenters added a crank to the drill bit, thus inventing the brace.

Today's woodworker has available not only hand tools but an array of machines, ranging from light and portable to large, stationary floor models. For all their precision and speed, these machines perform the same age-old techniques as hand tools: sawing, planing, drilling, and sanding.

Detail is of drawers, shelves, and pigeonholes inside New England secretary, c.1745.

Tools

Hand tools (see opposite and p. 362) are the safest, the least expensive, the slowest to work with, and their accuracy depends on the sureness of the hand guiding them. Portable power tools (pp. 364–365) are faster, more hazardous, and require careful setting of guides to achieve sufficient accuracy. Stationary power tools involve a considerable investment—worthwhile only if you are certain you will make enough use of them. When efficiency in making a number of identical, perfectly matched cuts dictates their use, try to locate a workshop where you can rent bench time—adult education centers often offer such facilities.

Workbench. The most basic tool, the workbench, should be of hardwood and should have at least one vise and holes for bench dogs (rectangular metal pegs that act as stops to hold the work in position). A ready-made bench is expensive; you can save money by buying metal legs and constructing the wood surface. Or make your own bench referring to the drawing on p.9.

Storing tools. You can lose much time looking for a misplaced tool or sharpening a blade that has been dulled through improper storage. A pegboard rack with hooks and attachments for holding screwdrivers and chisels is quick and easy to use. Replace each tool as you finish with it. Clamps can be suspended from horizontal strips of wood nailed to verticals to hold them away from the wall surface; use thin strips for small clamps, thicker strips for heavy bar clamps.

Caring for tools. Dirt and rust are the enemies of smoothly operating tools. Clean tools after use. In a damp climate a thin coat of light oil prevents rust on saw blades, chisels, and planes. Remove rust by rubbing surfaces with kerosene and fine steel wool; a heavy coat of rust may require a commercial rust dissolver.

Hand tools

Top-quality tools are expensive; so beyond the necessary saws, hammers, drills, screwdrivers, and measuring and marking devices, acquire tools as the need arises. Look for well-known brands and buy the best you can afford—quality tools will give better results and enhance your enjoyment of the craft. Do not be lured by bargains in a bin; they will not perform well or stand up to hard use.

Pick up a tool the way you will use it to test it for good balance and for comfortable fit in the hand. Hammerheads should be drop-forged steel; saw blades should be tempered steel; screwdriver blades should be crossground. Handles must be securely fastened. Page numbers in a caption indicate where tools are shown in use.

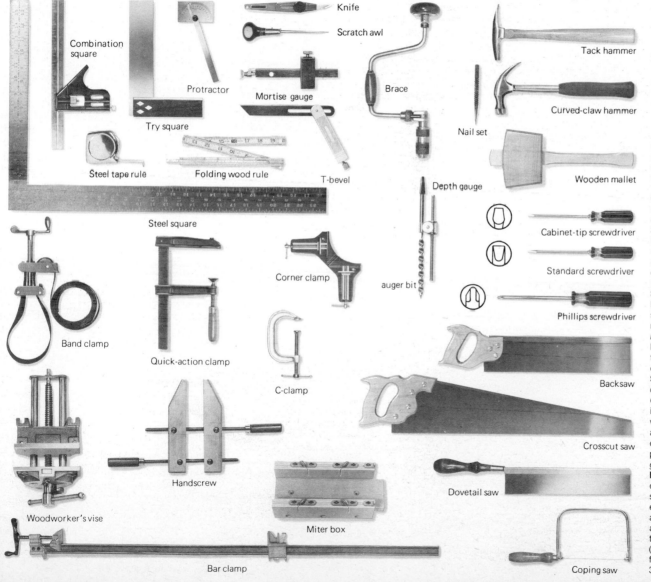

Knife

Scratch awl

Combination square

Protractor

Mortise gauge

Brace

Tack hammer

Try square

Nail set

Curved-claw hammer

Steel tape rule

Folding wood rule

T-bevel

Steel square

Depth gauge

Wooden mallet

Cabinet-tip screwdriver

Corner clamp

auger bit

Standard screwdriver

Band clamp

Quick-action clamp

Phillips screwdriver

C-clamp

Backsaw

Woodworker's vise

Handscrew

Crosscut saw

Miter box

Dovetail saw

Bar clamp

Coping saw

Measuring and marking tools. Squares are for checking squareness and flatness and for marking lines: *try square* (p. 372); *steel square* for large pieces; *combination square* (p. 370) also measures depth of hole and 45° angle; *engineer's square* for checking blade and fence settings on large power tools (not shown). Rules: *steel rule* in various lengths (not shown); *folding wood rule* with sliding extension for measuring inside cabinet or drawer; *steel tape rule* for long spans; *6-in. rule* with 32nds of inch on one side, 64ths on other (not shown). *T-bevel and protractor* are for drawing angles other than right angles. *Knife* (p. 370) is for marking lines. Single pin of *mortise gauge* (p. 370) marks line for cut; double pins mark for a mortise (p. 380) *Scratch awl* makes starter hole for drill bit.

Clamping devices. A range of jaw openings is available in *bar clamps* (p. 374) *C-clamps, quick-action clamps* (a short bar clamp) (p. 375), and *handscrews* (p. 381). Buy sizes, at least two of a size, as needed for your work. *Corner clamp* holds miter joint for gluing. *Band clamp* encircles and holds large or irregular objects. Mount *woodworker's vise* on edge of bench with jaw tops flush with bench top.

Striking tools. *Curved-claw hammer* should have beveled and slightly rounded striking surface. Striking end of *tack hammer* is a magnet to hold tack while starting it. *Wooden mallet* (p. 375) is for striking chisels and for knocking joints together. *Nail set* (p. 368), with tip diameters ranging from 1/32 to 5/32 in., drives finishing nails below wood's surface.

Screwdrivers and drill. Standard *screwdriver* comes in range of blade widths and lengths. *Cabinet-tip screwdriver* has straight-sided tip for inserting a recessed screw without damaging wood and a flat shaft to which wrench can be applied for turning. *Phillips screwdriver* fits cross-slotted screws. *Brace and auger bit* provide control for centering holes. *Depth gauge* (p. 373) attaches to bit, controls depth.

Handsaws. *Crosscut saw* (p. 370) makes crossgrain cuts and cuts lengthwise if no rip saw is available. Most useful size is 26 in. with eight teeth per inch. *Backsaw* has rigid spine for accurate cutting of thick stock, deep tenons, and other joints on large pieces. Small version is tenon saw (not shown). Still smaller *dovetail saw* (p. 375) has narrow kerf, makes smooth cuts for joints. *Coping saw* cuts curves. *Miter box* (p. 379) angles backsaw at 45° angle.

Woodworking

Chisels, planes, and shaping tools

Mastery of the tools on this page is essential to making fine furniture. Planes smooth and level wood; chisels cut and trim for joints; scrapers and rasps shape and smooth.

Chisels. These tools are classified according to blade thickness and how they are used—paring cuts with hands only or chopping cuts by striking with a mallet. A paring chisel is thinnest, beveled on sides and end, and is for paring only. A firmer chisel, of medium thickness, may come with or without a side bevel and is for paring or chopping. Heavy-duty and mortise chisels, thick and extra-thick respectively, have no side bevel and are for chopping. Other chisel terms refer to the length of the blade: butt is 2½ to 3 inches, cabinet is 4½ to 5 inches, and long is 6 to 7 inches. Tang and socket describe the method of handle attachment. Often sold in sets, chisels are better bought individually as needed.

Keep chisels razor sharp (p. 363). Lay them on the bench bevel side down to protect the cutting edge. When removing waste, place the chisel perpendicular to the wood on the waste side of the marked line with bevel edge facing the waste. For a paring cut to remove thin shavings, lay the chisel almost parallel to the wood with bevel side up, unless you are working in a confined area or on a curved cut. Drive the chisel with hands only.

Planes. The cutting blade of a plane is simply a chisel held stationary in a rigid body. The bottom of the plane should be perfectly flat and square with its sides; sometimes old metal planes bought at tag sales or flea markets are more accurate in this respect than new ones. Some woodworkers find that a corrugated bottom makes for easier planing than a smooth bottom. Either kind can be lubricated with a coat of wax or paraffin.

Wood vs. steel bodies. Even though they are more expensive, wood planes are preferred by some woodworkers because they are lighter and less tiring. Others prefer the heft and long-lasting quality of a steel body.

Plane blades are sharpened like chisels (p. 363). Adjustments to a bench plane are explained on page 371. Generally, move a bench plane in the same direction as the wood's grain (pp. 366–367). Level the plane's bottom on the wood surface by rocking it slightly before starting a pass until you feel its entire width is in contact with the wood's surface.

Two special planes for cutting or trimming joints are shown in use on pages 375 and 376. Tools for turning on a lathe are shown on page 388.

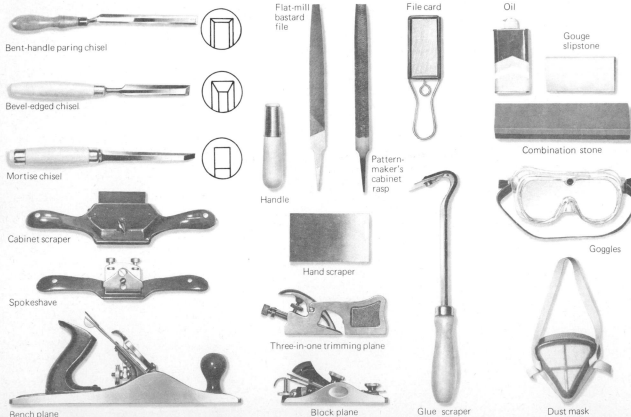

Bent-handle paring chisel

Bevel-edged chisel

Mortise chisel

Cabinet scraper

Spokeshave

Bench plane

Flat-mill bastard file

Handle

Pattern-maker's cabinet rasp

Hand scraper

Three-in-one trimming plane

Block plane

File card

Hand scraper

Glue scraper

Oil

Gouge slipstone

Combination stone

Goggles

Dust mask

Chisels. Most useful widths of *bevel-edged chisel* (p. 375) are 1/8, 3/8, 3/4, 1¼, and 2 in. Best size of *mortise chisel* (p. 380) is 5/16 or 3/8 in. *Bent-handle paring chisel*, 1/4 or 1/2 in. wide, permits working in tight situations.

File and rasp. For sharpening cabinet scraper, circular saw blade, and drill bits, use *flat-mill bastard file*. For shaping and smoothing curved surfaces, *patternmaker's cabinet rasp* No. 50 has finest teeth. Wire teeth of *file card* clean files and rasps. *Handle* fits files and rasps.

Planes and scrapers. *Bench plane* (pp. 371–372) comes in four types by length: smooth, 9 or 9¾ in.; jack, 14 or 14¾ in.; fore, 18 in.; jointer 22 or 24 in. Except for length they are similar in appearance; thus only one is shown here. Block plane has blade at low angle for planing end grain. *Three-in-one trimming plane* trims side of a rabbet or tenon; with small nosepiece (not shown) replacing large one, it planes close to obstruction; without nosepiece it planes into corner. *Hand cabinet scraper* smooths and shapes curves. *Cabinet scraper* mounted in metal body smooths level surfaces. *Glue scraper* removes glue that has inadvertently dried on wood's surface. *Spokeshave* is for smoothing and shaping curves; blades come in various shapes for concave and convex curves, but most common is flat-bottomed blade for convex surfaces. Look for one with blade-adjustment nuts.

Sharpening equipment (p. 363). *Oilstone* hones chisels and plane blades. Lubricate stone with *oil*. Finish honing on *leather strop* (not shown). *Gouge slipstone* sharpens both sides of gouge.

Safety equipment. Wear *goggles* when using power tools. *Dust mask* filters out sawdust.

Honing chisels, plane blades, and lathe tools

Cutting tools frequently need the keenness of their edges renewed while you are working with them. This is best done on an aluminum oxide combination oilstone for preliminary honing and a soft Arkansas stone for refining the edge. The procedure is the same for chisels and plane blades. Gouges and skew chisels (p. 388) are sharpened on a slipstone.

The bevel on a newly purchased tool is generally machine-ground to a 25° angle. You must bring the tool to cutting sharpness by honing the edge at the same angle. Then, to give the tool a finer edge that lasts longer, a microbevel of 5 degrees, just a hairsbreadth in width, can be added. This is visible only as a glint on the tool's edge.

Grinding need be done only if a new chisel has not been ground to the correct angle or if the edge has been nicked or honed to a rounded cross section. Unless you have a grinding wheel, have this done professionally.

Before you start honing, put a few drops of light mineral oil on the stone and spread it with your fingers. After each use clean the stone by patting it with a rag until the dirty oil is blotted from the stone. Leave a coat of clean oil on the stone.

Sharpening a chisel or a plane blade

1. Honing. Hold blade lightly. With index finger press bevel flat on oilstone and rub until burr—a wirelike residue—appears; repeat on Arkansas stone for 20–30 strokes.

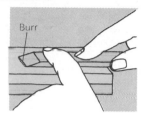

2. Removing burr. Rub flat side on Arkansas stone; press down firmly. Burr will shift to bevel side. Reverse tool; rub bevel. Repeat until you no longer feel burr with fingers.

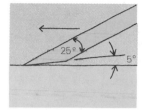

3. Microbevel. With bevel down raise chisel handle 5 degrees. Rub on Arkansas stone five strokes with forward motion. Rub flat side of chisel as in Step 2 to remove burr.

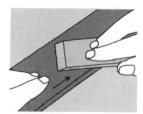

4. Stropping. On a smooth, hard piece of leather, strop the bevel and the flat side, moving tool in one direction only with its edge trailing. Do not dress leather with oil.

Sharpening a gouge or a skew chisel

1. Honing. Hold gouge or skew in one hand; rub bevel with flat part of slipstone. Move slipstone around to whet all of bevel, taking care to keep slipstone at same angle as bevel.

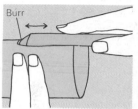

2. Removing burr. Rub slipstone back and forth on other side of tool. Alternate sides until burr is gone. Strop on leather, folding it for inside edge of gouge.

Running a safe woodworking shop

Careless operation of power tools is the most frequent cause of woodworking accidents, but even hand tools, when improperly used or left in the wrong place, can cause injury. For safety's sake, observe these precautions: Never work in the shop when tired. Concentrate on your work. Do not smoke in the shop. Keep the floor and bench top swept clean and tidy. Do not wear loose clothing or jewelry—roll up sleeves or button them snugly around the wrists. Long hair should be tied back. Whenever there is danger of flying chips or particles, use safety goggles; eyeglasses are not a substitute. And always have a first-aid kit handy.

Power-tool safety. In addition to the usual precautions, when using power tools, keep them clean and properly maintained. Ground all power tools; if you have no outlet for a three-prong plug, use an adapter and connect the ground wire to the screw in the receptacle faceplate. Alternatively, buy double-insulated tools. Never use power tools while standing on a wet surface. Always disconnect the cord before changing a blade or making adjustments. Make sure that the chuck or blade-lock bolt is firmly tightened. Stand to one side of a cutting blade. Use a push stick to push wood past a blade when a hand would come dangerously close to the blade.

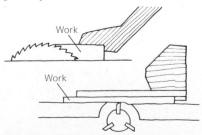

Push sticks: table saw (top); jointer (below)

Guards and shields should be left in place unless the operation cannot be performed without their removal. When using a table saw, wear a full face shield that wraps around the face—it gives better protection than eye goggles(p. 362).

Solvents. Other hazards result from working with solvents and thinners for finishing and for stripping old finishes. Their vapors are highly flammable and are toxic in varying degrees. Adequate active ventilation prevents problems—this means an exhaust fan placed close to the work area so that it pulls vapors away from the worker's face, or a fan that blows air past the worker, taking the vapors with it. Just opening a window is not enough. A fire extinguisher is another good precaution.

Solvents can also cause drying and cracking of skin; wear rubber gloves if your hands will be in contact with a solvent for more than a few minutes.

Noise. Extensive work with power tools can cause hearing damage. Keeping machines well oiled and in good repair helps somewhat, but the best protection is a pair of earplugs or, even better, ear protectors that muffle noise but allow you to hear voices.

Sawdust. The dust from power planing, sawing, or sanding is a nasal irritant that can be alleviated by wearing a dust mask (p. 362).

Woods. Some woods or the chemicals or molds in them can cause skin or respiratory allergies in sensitive people. Following is a partial list of woods—mostly exotic or tropical varieties—that may cause allergic reactions: boxwood, western red cedar, ebony, mahogany, rosewoods, satinwoods, and teak. Some of these woods are toxic on first contact, others only after repeated exposure.

Woodworking

Power tools

Power tools fall into two broad categories: portable ones (opposite page, left column) guided by hand and large, stationary floor machines. Before you spend several hundred dollars for one of the latter, learn what these machines can do and how to operate them safely. A good way to do this is to take a woodworking course at a crafts or adult education center.

Drills. A drill press bores a hole perpendicular to the wood and adjusts to three or four speeds. A portable drill can be carried to the job and accepts attachments for such chores as sanding, buffing, and paint mixing. With the addition of a drill stand, available for some models, a portable drill performs as accurately as a drill press.

Portable drills are available with 1/4-inch, 3/8-inch, and 1/2-inch chucks. The smaller the chuck, the higher the speed of the drill, but a larger chuck provides more torque for drilling large holes. Slow speed is better for inserting screws, and reversibility allows removing screws. Variable-speed models permit adjusting speed.

Orbital sander. A model that can be switched from a circular motion for sanding joints to straight-line sanding parallel to the grain is preferable. The motor should drive the pad directly. The pad should make 4,000 to 12,000 orbits per minute and have an orbit of approximately 1/8 inch.

Router. A wide variety of bits allows this tool to cut rabbets, dadoes, grooves, bevels, shaped edges, moldings, and dovetails. A router with high horsepower works better.

Hand-held saws. A circular saw should be capable of cutting a 2 by 4 at a 45° angle and should have a blade diameter of 7 inches or more. The saber saw is slower but cuts curves too. A variable-speed motor of 1/3 horsepower or more performs well. The saw should be able to cut nominal 2-inch stock and make bevel cuts.

Stationary saws. The table saw is very accurate and versatile. It should have at least 1/3 horsepower for an 8-inch blade; blades range from 7½ to 10 inches. A band saw, the only stationary saw capable of cutting curves, should have at least 1/3 horsepower; the table's size and the distance between blade and post control the size of the work it will take. A radial-arm saw, most expensive of the three, usually has a 10-inch or 12-inch blade and a motor of 1½ horsepower or more.

Jointer. This planing machine levels and squares one face and the edges of a board by means of revolving blades set between the infeed and outfeed tables. It can plane the second face, but it cannot mill an irregular board to uniform thickness. The blade width is the width of the board it can level.

Lathe. A lathe appears on page 387.

Operating the tools

Power tools come with directions that differ from model to model. Because certain tools are less familiar than others or because they call for special safety measures, procedures for operating the circular saw, router, jointer, and table saw are given here. The chart shows adjustments for various saw cuts.

Circular saw. Operate this tool with extreme care. Support and clamp work firmly so that it will not shift. Have a helper support waste from a long cut. Grip saw handle firmly and keep other hand well away from blade. Start saw before blade enters work and do not allow it to veer. Do not let the saw drop at end of cut.

Router. Insert appropriate bit in collet and tighten two nuts with wrenches supplied with tool. Adjust depth of cut by turning the adjusting collar. Use router guide (purchased), or clamp straightedge to wood. Distance from edge of cut to straightedge should be same as from edge of bit to outside edge of base. Make test cut and check depth with a rule marked each 1/64 in. Set up work so that router moves away from you from left to right in a straight-line cut. If cutting an arc or a rectangle on an outside edge, move router counterclockwise; on an inside edge, move it clockwise. Turn the router on before touching the bit to wood. Too rapid movement may burn the motor; too slow, the wood. Practice on scrap wood until you get the feel of the tool.

Jointer. Outfeed table must be at same level as the three-bladed cutter edge; raise or lower infeed table according to how much wood you wish to remove—generally no more than 1/16 in. at a pass. Press wood against fence with both hands as it feeds across blades from infeed to outfeed table. As work moves onto outfeed table, keep pressing it to fence, one hand behind the blade and one ahead of it. Use push stick to push board across table when you are planing its face. Plane concave face of board first; then press that face against fence to plane edge. (See text, p. 372, for how to square wood.) The guard swings aside just enough for passage of the wood and closes behind the wood.

Table saw. Use guard and slitter, a device that holds stock open after it is cut. Stand to one side of blade, never directly behind it, in case of kickback. Do not reach hand over blade. Set blade so that it protrudes 1/8 in. above work as it cuts. When ripping narrow work, use a push stick like the one shown on page 363. Let saw reach full speed before moving work into blade. Wait until blade has halted before removing work. A deep cut is better done in more than one pass; raise the blade slightly for each pass. Many woodworkers attach an auxiliary wood fence to the miter gauge to hold long pieces of wood square to blade.

How to make cuts with power saws

SAW	CROSSCUT	RIPCUT	BEVEL CUT	DADO OR GROOVE	CURVE
Circular	Clamp straightedge to wood as guide	Use rip fence or straightedge for guide; rip or combination blade	Loosen blade-tilt lock, tilt blade, tighten lock; make test cut	Use guide; adjust baseplate. Saw on lines; remove waste with parallel cuts	Cannot be done readily with this saw
Saber	Clamp straightedge to wood as guide	Use accessory rip fence, or clamp straightedge to work as guide	Loosen bevel-cut adjustment, tilt base, tighten; make test cut	Cannot be done with this saw	Use narrow blade for small radius; clamp wood to work surface
Table	Hold board against miter gauge at 90° angle; move across blade	Use combination or rip blade and rip fence	Adjust blade tilt; make test cut	Use dado head; adjust blade height; test cut	Limited to mild curves; check with the maker's instructions
Radial arm	Hold work against fence; move blade across work	Turn blade parallel to fence; hold work against fence; push work through	Tilt blade to angle indicated on bevel gauge; make test cut	Use dado head or saw on lines; remove waste with parallel cuts	Mild curves possible with some saws; check maker's instructions
Band	Do freehand or use miter gauge; upper blade guide ¼"-½" above work	Do freehand or use fence; wide blade preferable	Tilt table; set angle by tilt gauge; test cut	Cannot be done with this saw	Use narrow blade; be sure work fits between blade and post

Hand-held power tools

Circular saw

Saber saw

Drill

Router

Orbital sander

Stationary power tools

Jointer

Table saw

Radial-arm saw

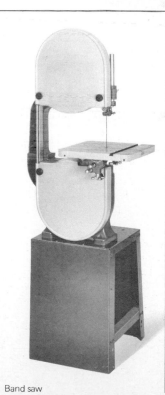

Band saw

Drill press

Woodworking

Materials: wood

For woodworking projects you will be dealing with three kinds of wood: hardwood from broad-leaved, deciduous trees; softwood from conifers, or cone-bearing trees; and plywood, which is made of thin sheets of wood, called veneers, glued together. Hardwoods—e.g., mahogany, oak, cherry—are the usual choices for fine furniture, but auxiliary parts, such as cabinet backs, drawer bottoms, and bracing, can be made of less expensive softwoods or plywood. Some softwoods —e.g., redwood—are harder than some hardwoods, such as basswood.

Wood characteristics. Color is a matter of personal choice. Grain, texture, and figure affect how you work with wood. Look at the edge of a board to determine the direction the grain runs. If it runs at a slight angle to the surface, plane it in the direction of the rising lines of grain; otherwise, you may roughen the surface. If grain changes direction in a board, change the direction of planing.

The closeness or openness of the cells, or pores, in the wood affects the way you finish the wood. Figure results from circumstances of the tree's growth: placement of the annual rings, knots, and deviations from normal growth. Figure should be considered when choosing and arranging boards.

The chart on this page lists some commonly used hardwoods and one softwood—pine. Do not be put off from using a wood termed difficult to work. Its relative hardness means that cutting tools must be sharp, but it will finish well and make a fine, durable piece. Other hardwoods to consider are those known as exotics. Rare and expensive, they are available in stores that specialize in supplying woodworkers. They include teak, satinwood, rosewood, zebrawood, padauk, purpleheart, and bubinga.

Drying. Make sure the wood you buy is dried to reduce its moisture content. Kiln drying, done under controlled conditions, is preferable to air drying for wood to be used immediately. All lumber, even after drying, is subject to distortions—shrinkage, swelling, warping, cupping, and bowing (see drawings, opposite)—caused by moisture changes in the air in which it is stored.

Buying hardwood. Hardwood is sold three ways: rough, dressed to specified thickness and width, or cut to exact dimensions—length as well as thickness and width. Unless you have access to a jointer and a thickness planer (a ma-

Common woods for furniture

WOOD	CHARACTERISTICS	FINISH
Ash, white	Off-white to dark brown; open grain; hard and tough; difficult to work; holds shape well after forming; often used for sports equipment	Paste filler; fairly difficult to stain; penetrating or surface finish (pp. 390-391)
Cherry, black	Light to dark reddish-brown, darkens with age; close grain; medium hard; moderately difficult to work; resists warping and shrinkage	Filler unnecessary; stains well but not often done; penetrating or surface finish
Mahogany, African, Honduran, Philippine	Pink to dark reddish-brown; open grain; medium density; tough and strong; easy to work; resists warping; Philippine not true mahogany, known as lauan, coarser in texture, less stable	Filler optional—paste if used; stained only to deepen natural color; penetrating or surface finish
Maple, hard and sugar	Light tan; close grain; hard and strong; dulls tools fast; excellent for turning; needs generous amounts of glue; interesting figures available	Filler unnecessary; does not stain well; penetrating or surface finish
Oak, red and white	Light tan (white oak) to light reddish-brown (red oak); open grain; hard and very tough; somewhat difficult to work; tends to warp; white oak has finer texture	Paste filler; stains well; sometimes fumed with ammonia to darken; penetrating or surface finish
Pine	Cream to light reddish-brown; close grain; soft; easy to work; often knotty; very little figure; sugar pine or yellow pine best	Filler unnecessary; stains surface finish; takes paint well
Poplar	Light yellow-brown, sometimes tinged with green or purple; close grain; soft; easy to work; excellent for turning; many prefer it to pine for inexpensive work	Filler optional; stains well; surface finish; takes paint well
Walnut, black	Gray-brown to dark brown; open grain; hard; easy to work; saws and planes well; little shrinkage and expansion	Filler optional—paste if used; stains well; penetrating or surface finish

Logs into boards

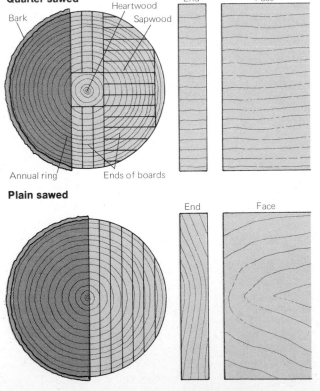

Quarter sawed

Bark · Heartwood · Sapwood · Annual ring · Ends of boards · End · Face

Plain sawed

End · Face

The method of sawing affects a board's resistance to distortion and its appearance. Most shrinkage occurs in the circumference of annual growth rings. A plain-sawed board is likely to bend or warp away from tree's center and shrink in width; a quarter-sawed board will shrink most in thickness. On a quarter-sawed board annual rings appear as nearly parallel lines the length of surface and across end. Lighter sapwood surrounds darker heartwood. On plain-sawed board annual rings appear as V-shaped figure. Quarter-sawed wood is rare and costly.

chine that mills boards to required thickness), the extra cost of dressed or cut-to-size lumber is worthwhile.

Specify "dressed two sides" for lumber surfaced on two faces or "dressed four sides" for lumber dressed on faces and edges. The edges are merely rip cut on a saw and may require planing. Dressed lumber may have some unusable portions, so order about 10 to 20 percent more length than you need. Lumber cut to exact size is the most expensive and requires only smooth planing.

Lumber dimensions are always expressed in this order: thickness by width by length. The cost of hardwood is calculated by board feet (see drawing) or by lineal, or running, feet.

Hardwood grading is as follows: FAS, which stands for firsts and seconds, is the top grade, about 90 percent usable. No. 1 Common and Select contains some knots and defects. No. 2 Common has many defects and is suitable only for cutting into small pieces.

Softwood. Softwood is sold in boards by board feet and lineal feet and, in addition, in standard widths and thicknesses, called dimension lumber. The nominal sizes of dimension lumber are just that—sizes in name only; in reality the lumber is smaller. For example, a 2 by 4 is actually 1½ by 3½. There are several categories of grades of softwood; the only one suitable for fine work is Select. Within the Select category the grades are A, B, C, and D; grades A and B, sometimes called 1 and 2 Clear, are suitable for natural finishes, C and D for painting.

Plywood. Plywood is usually sold in 4- by 8-foot sheets ranging in thickness from 1/8 to 1⅛ inches. It is composed of an odd number of layers of veneer. Lumber-core plywood, with its solid-wood center, holds nails and screws better than veneer-core but is more expensive. The outside faces of either kind may be softwood or hardwood, each of which has its own grading system. For hardwood plywood the grades are, from best to worst, Premium, Good, Sound, Utility, and Reject. Specify the grade you want for both faces, e.g., G1S (one Good side) or G2S (two Good sides) and whether the plywood is for interior or exterior use.

Fir plywood for cabinet backs and bottoms is labeled A through D in descending order of quality. Specify the grade for both faces, e.g., A–C for a piece of top quality on one side and lower quality on the reverse.

Anatomy of a board

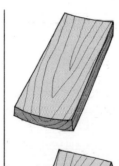

A board's parts—faces, edges, and ends—are referred to in this section as labeled above. Always plane or sand in same direction as grain, as seen on board's edge. Annual rings show on plain-sawed board's surface as figure.

A board foot

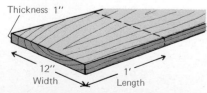

A piece of lumber 1 ft long, 12 in. wide, and 1 in. thick equals 1 board foot. To calculate board feet, multiply length *in feet* by nominal thickness *in inches* (the board may actually be thinner) by width *in inches* and divide by 12.

Lumber distortions and defects

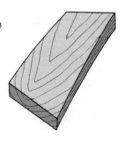

Cupping. This form of warping produces rounded edges. Slight cupping can be corrected by planing (pp. 372–373) or by sawing board lengthwise and reversing every other piece as in edge joint (p. 374).

Bowing. Ends of board curve up and board is bowed through its length. May also occur as a series of small bows. Use in short lengths; plane level. A thin board can be straightened by attaching it to a framework.

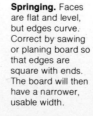

Springing. Faces are flat and level, but edges curve. Correct by sawing or planing board so that edges are square with ends. The board will then have a narrower, usable width.

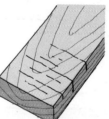

In wind. When a board is twisted diagonally from corner to corner lengthwise, it is said to be in wind (rhymes with dined). Correct by planing diagonally from one high corner to the other.

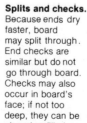

Splits and checks. Because ends dry faster, board may split through. End checks are similar but do not go through board. Checks may also occur in board's face; if not too deep, they can be planed or filled.

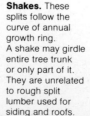

Shakes. These splits follow the curve of annual growth ring. A shake may girdle entire tree trunk or only part of it. They are unrelated to rough split lumber used for siding and roofs.

Cross shakes. Splits across the grain or width of board are caused by compression from strain in the living tree or from the impact as felled tree hit the ground. Wood with cross shakes is usable for hidden parts.

Wane edge. Where board's edge was cut too close to tree's outer circumference, sometimes bark and paler sapwood remain on edges. Board is usable if resawn to a narrower width.

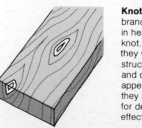

Knots. The base of branch embedded in heartwood forms knot. In hardwood, they weaken the structure of wood and detract from appearance. Often they are desired for decorative effect in pine.

Woodworking

Materials: glues, fasteners, and abrasive papers

Choose a glue according to the properties listed in the chart at right. If you have a complicated clamping arrangement, you may do a better job with a glue that has a long assembly time. Allow more clamping time than the glue manufacturer states and more for pieces under stress. Do not work on a piece until the curing time is over. High humidity will lengthen curing time; a warm temperature will shorten it.

Fasteners. Nails are sized by the penny system, abbreviated *d* after a number, the smallest generally being 2d (1 inch) and the largest 60d (6 inches). Finishing nails go to 20d (4 inches), and box nails—similar to common nails but better for hardwoods because their shanks are thinner—run to 40d (5 inches). Wood screws have greater holding power than nails. Bolts are used where the fastener can pierce the work, where extra strength is required, and when the parts will be disassembled frequently.

Abrasive papers. Flint paper is the cheapest but wears out soonest. For cabinetwork, garnet paper is a better choice. If tool marks are visible, start with 50- or 60-grit paper; otherwise, use 80, then 120 for initial sanding. Finish with 220 for softwoods and 280 for hardwoods. (In an older grading system for abrasive papers, the equivalents are 1, 1/2, 0, 3/0, 6/0, and 8/0.) A sanding block is essential if the resulting surface is to be perfectly smooth and even. Make one of wood or cork, with the sanding face 3 by 5 inches, 1½ inches thick, and rounded on the top edges for a handhold. Glue felt to the face of a wooden block.

Wet/dry sandpaper. For sanding between coats of finish (pp. 390–391), use silicon-carbide paper in very fine grits—400, 500, or 600. Use it dry, or soak it in water, which makes it cut faster. Steel wool in No. 3/0 or 4/0 completes the kit of abrasives.

GLUE TYPE	SAMPLE BRANDS	ASSEMBLY TIME (min)*	CLAMPING TIME (hr)*	CURING TIME (hr)*	FILLING ABILITY	WATER RESISTANCE	SOLVENT	REMARKS
Polyvinyl resin emulsion (PVA, or white glue)	Elmer's Glue-All; DuPont or Sears White Glue; Franklin Evertite	25-30	4	24	Fair	Low; do not use where exposed to water	Soap and warm water before hardening	Ready to use; clogs sandpaper; stress causes creeping over time
Aliphatic resin	Franklin Titebond; Elmer's Professional Carpenter's Glue; Wilhold Glu-Saver	15	2-4	Overnight	Poor	Medium; do not use on outdoor furniture	Warm water before hardening	Ready to use; fast set; sands easily; less creep than white glue
Resorcinol formaldehyde	Elmer's Waterproof Glue; Sears, Franklin, Wilhold, or U.S. Plywood Waterproof Resorcinol Glue	45-50	8-12 (must be at 21°C)	Same as clamping	Good	Waterproof; also resists high temperature	Cool water before hardening	Two parts; mix amount needed; bonds other materials to wood
Liquid hide	Franklin Liquid Hide Glue	45	Overnight (must be at 21°C)	Same as clamping	Poor	None	Warm water before hardening	Ready to use; leisurely assembly time
Urea formaldehyde	Weldwood, Elmer's, or Craftsman Plastic Resin Glue; Wilhold Marine Grade	15	12 (must be at 21°C)	12	Good if sawdust added	Good when cured	Soap and warm water before hardening	Comes in powder; mix with water before use

* at 21°C

Nails

Common nail

Box nail

Finishing nail

Brad

Setting a nail

Use common and box nails where heads will not show. Stop striking finishing nails and brads before hammer mars wood. Drive the nail below wood's surface with nail set (p. 361). Fill hole with wood putty; smooth with putty knife.

Screws and braces

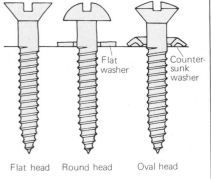

Flat head   Round head   Oval head

Flat washer

Counter-sunk washer

Corner iron   T-brace

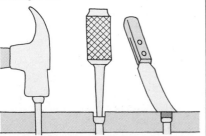

Flat-head wood screw is countersunk (p. 381). Use round-head screw with flat washer if wood is soft or thin. Oval-head screw can be countersunk in wood or in special washer. Braces substitute for joints; other types are available.

Bolts and nuts

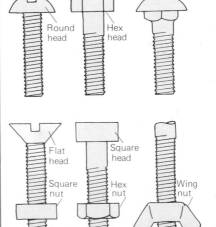

Round head   Hex head

Flat head   Square head

Square nut   Hex nut   Wing nut

Stove bolts   Machine bolts   Carriage bolt

Bolt heads vary; those most often used in wood are shown with three nuts. Length should be thickness of wood pieces plus 1/2 in. Drill hole slightly larger than shank. Use washer between wood and metal unless head is countersunk.

Planning your own project

Time and care spent in planning pay off later in smooth step-by-step operations and in avoiding running short of wood. Deciding what to make may be easy, but do not be overambitious if this is your first project. To ensure success and enjoyment, it is better to make a small and fairly simple project—for example, the box on page 392 or the wall-hung rack below. Even after some practice, do not attempt a large piece that requires hours of laborious hand planing unless you have access to power tools.

Once you have decided what to build, look for design ideas in books, magazines, stores, and furniture catalogs. Consider what kind of wood you want to work with; style and material should be consistent with the surroundings in which the piece will be displayed. Make rough sketches to determine basic proportions, then translate the rough sketches to scale drawings (see below).

At this point some woodworkers make a full-scale drawing of the project, perhaps front and side views, on large paper to determine whether the scale and proportions are pleasing.

Next, determine the thickness, width, and length of each piece of wood; be sure to include the parts that extend into joints. Label each part in the drawing with a letter or its name, such as "top shelf" or "left side"; later, write these designations on the wood.

Work out a shopping list of wood by thickness, width, and length in that order. Unless you are ordering all pieces cut to exact size—possible but expensive—allow extra for planing and for saw kerfs (1/16 inch in thickness, 1/4 inch in width, and 1/2 inch in length for each board). If you are using plywood, make a cutting diagram of the 4- by 8-foot plywood sheet (see p. 386); allow at least 1/8 inch for the saw kerfs between pieces. List other materials, such as glue and hardware, and make sure you have all tools.

Plan and list procedures step by step. Generally, you will perform operations in the following order: measuring and marking; cutting boards to size (p. 370); squaring boards (pp. 372–373); cutting and fitting joints (pp. 374–380); gluing joints (p. 381); sanding; and finishing (pp. 390–391). Before gluing joints, sand inner surfaces, shelves, panels, and surfaces that will be intersected by other members. After the glue has dried, plane to smooth joints and corners, then sand outer surfaces, cleaning off any dirt and glue before you begin to apply the finish.

Typical dimensions

Item	Height	Depth	Length
Bedside table	23″-25″	18″-23″	optional
Book	32″-84″	8″-18″	optional
Chest of drav	32″-54″	18″-24″	optional
Coffee table	14″-18″	18″-24″	36″-60″
Desk	30″	24″-30″	40″-60″
Dining table	29″	30″ or more	allow 23″ elbow room per person
End table	27″	15″-24″	24″-26″
Kitchen cabinet	36″	12″-24″	optional
Straight chair	16″-18″ seat	14″-18″	12″-16″
Workbench	32″-34″	24″	optional

Making scale drawings

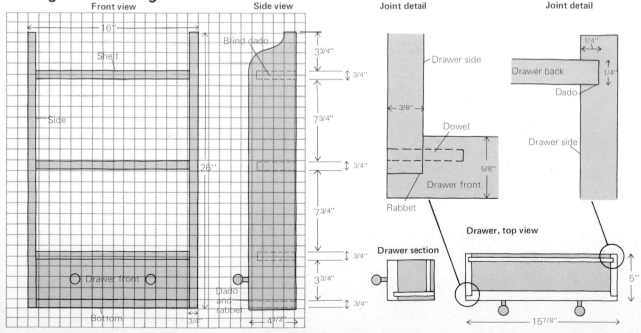

After you have made rough sketches, draw the project on graph paper—eight squares to the inch is a good size. Let each square represent 1 square inch. Start by drawing the front and side views, then, if necessary, draw top, bottom, and back views by extending lines from all the corners and other features on the front view. Features that are hidden can be represented by dashed lines. This is called an orthographic projection. For a piece that has interior framing or drawers, draw a line through one or more views and extend from that line a so-called *section* showing the various members in relationship to each other. Take into consideration appropriate joints (pp. 374–380) and their application in various furniture parts (pp. 382–385). Make larger scale drawings of joints. Write all dimensions beside the parts, using small arrows and extended lines to indicate the area encompassed by that measurement. Mark drawings of joint details in the same way. Recheck all measurements carefully; it is important to be accurate at this stage so that you can use the drawings to calculate your lumber order. As you work on your project, you will constantly refer to the drawings and will possibly revise them. Shown are plans for a wall-hung cabinet with three open-back shelves and a single drawer.

Woodworking

Measuring, marking, and sawing

Measure boards for cutting to size with a rule, square, and pencil. When marking a dressed board for cutting into pieces for a project, allow 1/32 to 1/8 inch—depending on the saw—for the saw cut, called the *kerf,* plus a scant 1/16 inch on each side of the kerf for planing off the saw marks. Rough lumber, to be dressed with power tools (p. 364) or by hand, should be cut an extra 1/2 inch long and 1/4 inch wide.

Sawing. A crosscut is sawed across the grain; a rip cut is along the grain. Recheck measurements before sawing. Mark waste material with X's. Place the good side up when using a handsaw or table saw; place the good side down for a radial arm, circular, or saber saw. Saw on the waste side of the line.

Marking and cutting joints. More precision is required for joints. Use a knife blade instead of a pencil to mark lines. Use a squared piece of wood (pp. 372–373) as a saw guide.

Squaring a line. Joint cuts often must be marked on three or four surfaces with a continuous line. Called squaring a line, this is done with a square and knife. The lines should meet at the fourth corner; if they do not, check the board for squareness (pp. 372–373).

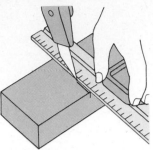
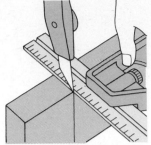

Marking lines for a joint. In marking for a saw or chisel cut, hold the handle of a combination or try square flat against the board. Mark with knife blade flat against square (left). At corners of board press knife in to deepen the line. To square the line across board's edge (right), place knife blade in deepened line, butt square up against knife, and continue line.

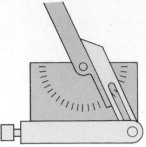

Marking an angle other than a right angle. Set protractor to desired angle. Loosen thumbscrew at base of T-bevel, butt the handle against bottom of protractor, and match T-bevel blade to protractor blade (left). Tighten the thumbscrew. Hold the T-bevel handle squarely against the wood (right), and mark the angle on the wood with a knife.

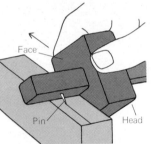

Marking gauge. Use only on squared wood (pp. 372–373). Set pin correct distance from face. Hold gauge by head and press it flush to wood. Move gauge away from you.

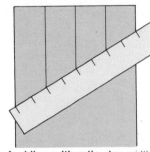

Avoiding arithmetic. Any width can be divided equally by tipping rule till it gives equal increments between edges. Mark points, draw lines with square.

Marking identical pieces. For uniform saw cuts or joints, clamp pieces (e.g., shelves or legs) with edges and ends aligned. Mark across all simultaneously.

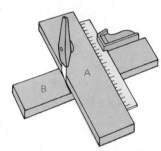

Using a board as a measure. Mark desired position of A on B. Use A instead of a rule to mark its own width. Square holds A perpendicular to B in correct position.

Sawing techniques

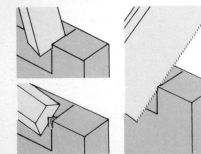
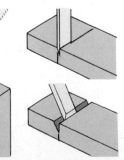
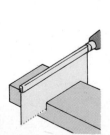

Notching for saw cuts for joints. To hold saw on marked line, make a notch by pressing a chisel, bevel side toward waste, into line made with knife; then chisel out a small wedge as shown (left). For a cut made across grain with a backsaw or dovetail saw, chisel vertically into knife-marked line across board, then lift out a thin sliver of wood (right).

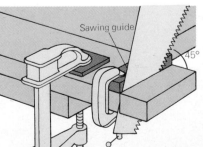
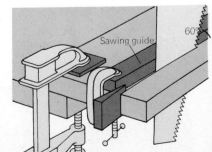

Cutting boards to size. Clamp board in vise or to bench. To start crosscut (left), pull saw toward you in short strokes until kerf is established. Gradually lengthen strokes until saw is cutting more on push than pull. Saw at 45° angle. Toward end of cut take shorter strokes, saw vertically, and support waste with hand. Rip cut (right) is made at a 60° angle. If saw binds, wedge open kerf.

Essentials of the bench plane

To plane with ease, keep the blade sharp (p. 365), and have the plane's blade and blade cap properly adjusted for the kind of wood you are planing. The harder the wood, the less blade should protrude beyond the cap and the shallower the cut should be. A coating of wax or paraffin on the plane's sole helps reduce friction.

Even when all adjustments have been made and the blade is sharp, the plane may be difficult to push if you try to take too thick a shaving. To decrease the cut, raise the blade higher than necessary, then lower it, so that the last adjustment of the blade is always downward. In practice, start planing with the blade raised so that it does not cut at all, then gradually lower it by turning the adjustment wheel the equivalent of one hour on a clock.

Because adjusting the width of the throat is difficult, move the frog only as a last resort. If the throat chronically becomes clogged with shavings, widen the opening. But to switch from coarse softwood cuts to hardwood and vice versa, it is better to have two planes.

When not in use, the plane should be laid on its side to avoid damage to the blade or to the surface on which it rests.

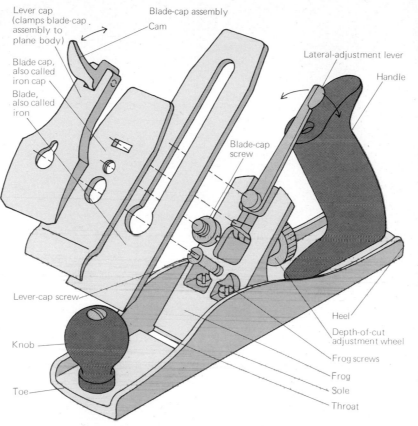

Lever cap (clamps blade-cap assembly to plane body)

Cam

Blade-cap assembly

Lateral-adjustment lever

Handle

Blade cap, also called iron cap

Blade, also called iron

Blade-cap screw

Lever-cap screw

Knob

Toe

Heel

Depth-of-cut adjustment wheel

Frog screws

Frog

Sole

Throat

Removing and setting the blade

To remove a blade, lay plane on side. Raise the cam on lever cap, lift off cap (foreground), and remove blade assembly as shown.

Turn blade assembly over so that blade is on top. Loosen blade-cap screw; move blade forward, away from end of blade cap.

Swivel blade to a right angle to blade cap, slide blade back to enlarged end of slot, and lift blade free of blade cap. Reverse procedure to remount blade.

Position blade cap 1/32 in. from edge of blade for softwood, 1/64 in. for hardwood. Edge of blade cap must be flush against blade and exactly parallel to it.

Making adjustments to the plane

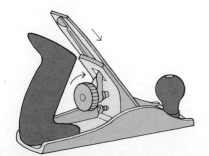

Depth of cut. Turn the depth-of-cut adjustment wheel clockwise to lower the blade, counterclockwise to retract it. The final adjustment should always be to lower the blade (see text).

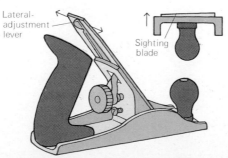

Lateral-adjustment lever

Sighting blade

Aligning the blade. If one corner of blade is lower, move lateral adjustment lever toward lower corner; this action raises corner. Test by sighting along bottom of plane and by planing a piece of scrap wood.

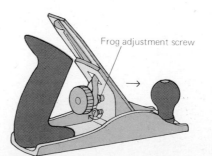

Frog adjustment screw

Width of throat. Loosen frog screws. Turn frog adjustment screw clockwise to move frog forward for a narrower throat (for hardwoods or smoothing cuts); turn counterclockwise to move it backward for a wider throat (for softwoods or coarse cuts). The relationship of blade setting and width of throat to a coarse cut and a fine cut is shown at right.

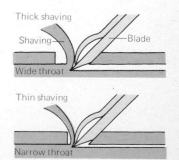

Thick shaving

Shaving

Blade

Wide throat

Thin shaving

Narrow throat

371

Woodworking

Squaring wood with hand planes

Dressed lumber is seldom square. After sawing boards to size and before cutting joints, check all six surfaces for squareness and plane them as shown below. Allowances left when you cut the wood to size are then removed.

The work of trueing a surface is best done with a long plane, which levels the high spots and does not follow the dips in the wood's surface. However, the longest plane, the jointer, is heavy and tiring to use for long. Save this plane for the final trimming, with blade set for a fine shaving. Do most leveling on small work with a jack plane and on longer lengths with a fore plane.

After all surfaces are square, you can use a smooth plane, the smallest of the bench planes, to remove plane marks and minor blemishes. The blade should be set for a fine cut (p. 373).

If you own or have access to stationary power tools (p. 364), you can buy rough lumber and square it in the following sequence: square the first face and one edge on the jointer; square the second edge by a rip cut on the table saw, and plane the edge with a pass through the jointer; then square the second face on the thickness planer; square the ends by crosscuts with a table saw or radial-arm saw.

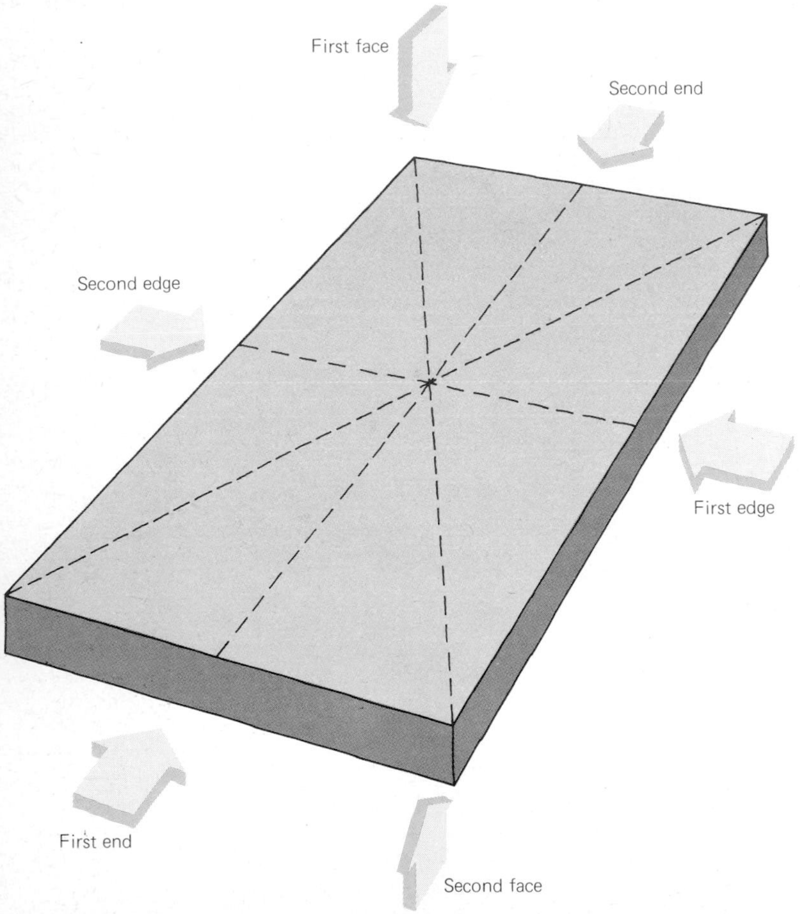

First face
Second end
Second edge
First edge
First end
Second face

Squaring sequence. Each surface as it is squared becomes reference for squaring next surface. Follow order in columns at right. Always butt try or combination square against previously squared surface. Dashed lines (above) indicate directions in which to check two faces. On edges and ends plane a few passes, check with square, mark high spots with X's, then plane level. Pencil an identifying mark on each surface after it is squared.

First face

With strong light and a straightedge, look for low spots where light shows through; mark high spots with X's, then plane. Board is level when no light shows at all.

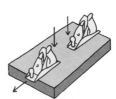

Start pass with slight pressure on toe. Equalize pressure in middle; end with pressure on heel. Keep sole flat on wood; angle plane slightly to its own path.

First edge

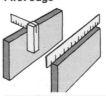

Move square along length of board, checking for high spots (mark with X's) and for squareness of corner. Check lengthwise with straightedge.

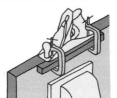

Use a shooting board (p. 373) or clamp a squared piece of wood to the bottom of the plane as a guide to keep the plane level and square to board's edge.

First and second ends

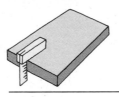

Check ends for squareness. Move square along end. Use first face as reference. Check also from first squared edge. Mark high spots with X's.

Scrap wood

Plane edges with block or smooth plane. Beveled scrap wood is clamped to edge to prevent tearing end grain at corner.

Second edge

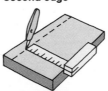

If board is to be rip cut to width, mark line. Saw, leaving 1/8 in. extra to be planed. Check edge for squareness same way as first edge.

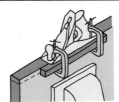

Plane with jack or fore plane to line marked. Use guide or shooting board, as for first edge. Last stroke should split the line.

Second face

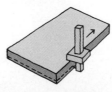

If board is correct thickness, check as for first face. If board is too thick, mark correct thickness, using first face as reference.

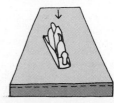

Plane as for first face. If planing to thickness, take off high spots and plane to line. Square face with edges and ends. Recheck flatness with straightedge.

Planing aids

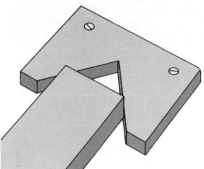

A stop for planing. If your bench lacks dogs to hold board for face planing, nail or screw a V-shaped board to flat surface. Jam board's end into V; clamp scrap wood to hold other end.

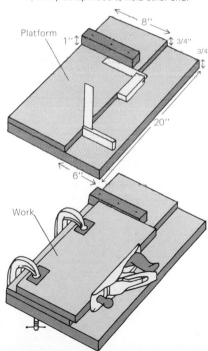

Shooting board. To square a board's edge, make a shooting board of scrap wood (top). Square all parts and make sure they are square to each other as shown by the try squares. Drill holes, and screw parts together. Dimensions shown are for small work; for larger work increase size. Clamp work to platform (below); plane with plane's side flat on base.

Cutting joints

Whether you choose to cut joints with hand or power tools depends on how you prefer to work and what tools you own. A table saw is expensive but unexcelled for cutting dadoes, grooves, rabbets, and miters with accuracy. However, it takes time to set guides for each cut and to test the cuts on scrap wood. The power router, not as accurate, also requires careful setting and testing.

All joints can be made with hand tools, provided you measure, mark, and cut carefully. Traditional dovetail and mortise-and-tenon joints are best made with handsaw and chisels. Spe-cial planes, such as the hand router (p. 375) and rabbet planes (p. 377), make fast work of cutting certain joints.

Saw cuts for joints are best made with the dovetail or tenon saw. Chiseling may involve two kinds of cuts: paring cuts to remove thin slices of wood, usually done with the hands alone; and chopping cuts, in which the chisel is pounded with a mallet. Both kinds of cuts are demonstrated in making the various joints (pp. 374–380).

If a joint's fit is extremely tight, a coat of glue may be enough to ruin its fit. To avoid this dilemma, plane or sand the entering piece very lightly.

Selecting joints. The joints in a project should be the simplest that will provide the necessary holding strength and the most appropriate to the project. A birdhouse, for example, does not require a dovetail joint; for that you can use the simplest joint of all, the butt joint—two flat surfaces butted against each other and glued.

The butt joint is inherently weak: it has the least glue surface and no interlocking parts. Seldom used in fine cabinetry, it is nevertheless useful for knocking rough work together quickly. It must be reinforced with screws, nails, glue blocks, or dowels (see below).

A doweled butt joint

The trick in installing hidden dowels is to align dowel holes perfectly. Boring holes from outside and inserting dowels after glue in joint has dried is easier, and visible dowel ends can be decorative. Purchase birch or maple dowel rods and cut them to length, or buy ready-made dowel pegs with a spiral groove that allows glue and air to escape. Dowels range from 1/8 to 1 in. in diameter; use a size that is one-third to one-half the thickness of the pieces being joined. Dowels make a fast but relatively weak substitute for a mortise and tenon (p. 380).

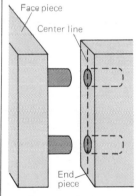

1. Marking. Set marking gauge to half thickness of end piece; mark center line on end piece. With same setting mark face piece. With square, mark lines for dowels' positions (shown). Where lines cross, punch shallow starting hole for drill bit with awl.

2. Boring holes. Use brace and auger bit with bit depth gauge. For face piece set depth gauge so that point of bit will not bore through board. Center the bit. Stop every few turns and sight from front and side to make sure bit is perpendicular. Dowel can penetrate end piece an inch or more.

3. Dowels. Cut dowels 1/8 in. shorter than combined depth of opposing holes. Sand ends round. Cut a lengthwise groove in each dowel by running it along saw blade. Test fit; if a hole is misaligned, plug it with a dowel and bore hole again.

4. Gluing. With a small brush or bottle's applicator, put glue in holes of end piece. Dip dowels in glue, insert in holes, and pound with mallet. Put glue in holes of face piece and on protruding dowels. Join pieces, and clamp until glue is dry.

Woodworking

Edge joining

For a cabinet top or sides or a table-top—wherever a wood surface is wider than 9 to 12 inches—you will have to join boards side by side in edge joints. Hardwood boards are not generally available wider than 12 inches, and beyond 9 inches they are likely to be badly cupped and expensive.

The wider a wood surface, the more it tends to warp. By ripping a board lengthwise and rejoining the pieces with the annual rings alternating in opposite directions (see drawing below), a surface that might warp can be made more stable. Butcher-block tops are one common example of edge joining many strips of wood.

In deciding how to join two or more boards, you will want to consider the grain and the figure of the boards (p. 366). Planing is easier if the grains run in the same direction. However, if you match or contrast the figures for appearance and as a result the grains run opposite ways, you can reverse the direction of planing for each board.

Cut the boards 1/2 inch longer than the finished piece to allow for slippage caused by wet glue and clamping. Square all boards (pp. 372–373) and decide on their order (see below). Mark the boards across the joints with pencil slash marks—one mark across the first joint, two across the second, and so on—to identify the order. Check all edge joints (see below) and plane the edges square if necessary.

C-clamps and bar clamps. Do a dry run of the gluing procedure with all the necessary clamps, using scraps of wood to protect the surfaces from the clamps. To hold the joints with even pressure, you need bar clamps spaced no more than 12 inches apart, alternating one on top and one beneath the piece. Tape wood scraps to the jaws of the bar clamps. Put waxed paper between bar clamps and wood to avoid stains.

At each end of each joint use a C-clamp to pull the faces into alignment. For each C-clamp prepare two wood scraps by rubbing them on both sides with paraffin so that they will not stick to the dried glue.

Because some glues dry in as little as 15 minutes, you must work with speed and accuracy. If the boards are large and require more than three bar clamps, it is a good idea to have a helper. Depending on glue type (p. 368), air temperature, and the warp of the boards, clamping time is 2–8 hours. Saw to final length and wait 24 hours before planing (Step 6).

Arranging boards

Boards warp in the direction opposite the curve of the annual rings. If boards are joined with annual rings in same direction, the natural trend of the warp is amplified (top). To counter this warping, arrange boards with annual rings alternating (bottom).

Checking edges

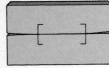

If boards placed edge to edge swivel freely (top), there is a hump in center of one or both. Remove hump with jointer plane. Inspect joint with bright light behind it (below). Bracket points of contact and plane them. Finally, take a long, continuous cut with a jointer or fore plane along full length of the edge.

1. Applying glue. Squeeze glue onto two joint edges. Spread in an even film with fingers or brush. Boards rest on bar clamps ready to be tightened. Marks indicate pairing of boards.

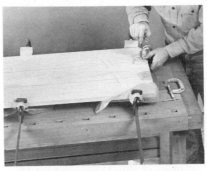

2. C-clamps. Push glued edges together by hand. Tighten C-clamps directly on the joints at both ends to align faces of boards. Paraffin-coated scraps of wood protect surfaces.

3. Bar clamps. With hand, check to make sure that surfaces are flush. To align them, push them with hand or pound with wooden mallet. Tighten center bar clamp first.

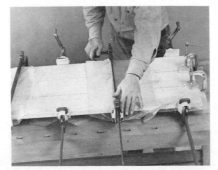

4. Top bar clamps. Add bar clamps halfway between bottom clamps. Press or pound boards into alignment. Tighten clamps from center to ends. Wipe off glue or scrape with glue scraper.

5. Checking surface. After 24 hours scrape glue from both sides. With strong light behind a straightedge, make pencil marks on high points—where no light shows—to be planed flat.

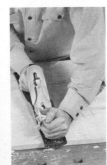

6. Planing. With a long plane, such as a fore or jointer, level surface by planing straight across grain (left). Plane boards lengthwise (right) to remove marks of first planing.

Lap joints

In a lap joint half the thickness is cut from each board to form a cross-, T-, or L-shaped joint in which the upper and lower surfaces are flush. The two boards are of equal thickness. Cut a lap joint with a saw, and remove waste with chisels or a router plane. If you use a power router, be sure to set guides and depth-of-cut adjustment with care.

The edge of the joint is called the shoulder line, and its depth is called the depth of cut. As with any joint, the wood surfaces should be planed smooth and squared (p. 372). Mark all lines with a square or a marking gauge; recheck measurements before cutting.

End lap joint

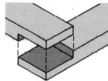

End lap joint is used in chair seats or other places where two boards meet at right angles and must be flush with each other.

Mid lap joint

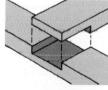

In framework for a cabinet the mid lap joint allows end of one board to be joined into the length of another board. Similar joint below is stronger.

Dovetailed lap joint

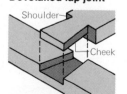

Shoulder

Cheek

Lay out entering piece with T-bevel; saw shoulders, cheek, and angle in that order. Transfer shape to receiving piece; saw and chisel as for cross lap joint.

Cross lap joint

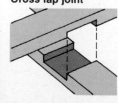

Shown here on faces of boards, joint can also be made on edges of boards. Procedure for making cross lap joint on faces is shown at right.

1. Measure from end of board and mark one shoulder with square and knife. Leave square in place, lay second piece of wood across first against square, and mark other shoulder.

2. If boards are same width, lay side by side, clamp, and continue shoulder lines across second board. If widths differ, transfer width to second piece from first as in Step 1.

3. Set marking gauge to half thickness of boards. Mark for depth of cut on edges of both boards below shoulder lines. With square, join shoulder line to depth-of-cut line. X indicates waste.

4. Score the shoulder lines with wide chisel held vertically (left). Then, with chisel at angle (right), remove a sliver on waste side of line to create a groove for starting saw cut.

5. For a guide, cut a block of wood just thick enough so that rib on top of saw hits the guide when cut is required depth. Clamp guide to board; press saw against it while cutting.

6. Make relief saw cuts at 1-in. intervals to ease waste removal. Use chisel and mallet to remove waste; work from both sides toward center. Chisel is held horizontally, bevel side up.

7. Remove high point that is left in center of joint by paring with a wide chisel. Work from both edges of board toward center. Deepen the shoulder cut with saw if necessary.

8. Router plane gives a smooth finish to cut. Set blade to remove center high point. Lower blade one-quarter turn of adjustment wheel at a time until it reaches depth-of-cut line.

9. Clean out corners of joint with wide chisel held vertically, then lift out waste, holding chisel nearly horizontal, bevel side up. Test-fit joint with light blow of mallet or fist.

Woodworking

Dadoes, grooves, and rabbets

A dado is a three-sided channel cut across the grain on the face of a board. A groove is such a channel cut with the grain. A rabbet is an L-shaped ledge that can be cut either across or with the grain. All are extensively used in cabinets, boxes, drawers, shelves, and frame-and-panel construction (p. 382). They can be cut with hand or power saws, routers, chisels, special planes, or with a combination of tools.

Waste is more easily removed across the grain, as in a dado, which can be hand chiseled. For a long dado you may need a bent-handled paring chisel that will reach into the cut without the handle's bumping the board's edge. A groove is better cut with a plough plane or multiplane, a power router, or a table saw. Chiseling is awkward, especially on a long groove.

When the joined boards must bear considerable weight or stress, all of these joints—especially the rabbet—may require reinforcement with screws or dowels. Drill holes for them with the clamps in place during the dry run.

Although screws and dowels are often interchangeable, dowels grip better in a board's end. And since end grain usually enters into a dado or a rabbet cut across the grain, dowels—not screws—are used for reinforcement.

In a long rabbet cut with the grain, the reinforcing screws can serve as clamps to hold the boards while the glue dries. This reduces the need for clamps to just the two or three necessary to juxtapose the boards. Drill holes and drive the screws during the dry run. Then remove and discard that set of screws. Rub paraffin on a second set to be permanently installed. Glue the joint, then insert the screws at both ends and the center of the joint, followed by the remaining screws.

The visible end of a dado or groove can be masked with veneer tape (p. 386), molding, or wood strips.

Through dado

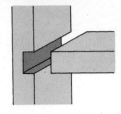

Cut a dado no deeper than half receiving board's thickness. Use dovetail saw and chisel, router plane, combination plane, dado blade of table saw, or power router.

Stopped dado

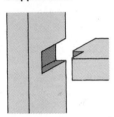

Also known as a blind dado, this dado stops short of board's edge. When glued, notched entering piece appears butted against board.

Rabbet

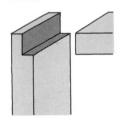

A rabbet is a two-sided cut made on end or edge of a board. It can be cut across or with grain. Cut with dovetail saw, rabbet plane, power router, or table saw.

Dado and rabbet

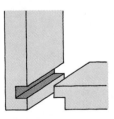

Dado receives half thickness of entering board. Rabbet is same depth as dado. Cut with power router; with dovetail saw, hand router, and rabbet plane; or with table saw.

Dovetail dado

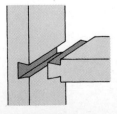

A very strong joint, this is used to hold shelves or to attach legs to a central pedestal. If cut by hand (p.377), make entering part first. If cut with dovetail bit on power router, cut dado first.

Cutting a dado

1. Marking. Measure from end of board to shoulder line; mark. Hold entering board at line and mark second shoulder line (left). Extend lines across edge; mark depth of dado (right).

2. Sawing. Clamp guide at shoulder line; guide can be of such a height that rib on back of saw hits guide when cut is correct depth. Saw both shoulder lines, using guide.

3. Chiseling end of cut. If using a router plane to remove waste, chisel one end of dado to depth of cut to prevent splintering, or plane inward from both edges toward the center.

4. Removing waste with router plane. Set blade just below surface and make cut. Lower blade by quarter turns of depth-of-cut adjustment screw. To hand chisel, proceed as with lap joint (p. 375).

5. Trimming. If fit is tight, plane or sandpaper entering piece. If prior finishing or veneering on entering piece precludes this, trim dado with side rabbet plane (shown).

6. Checking depth. Lower blade of combination square into dado; set at lowest point. Run it length of dado and mark any area of resistance. Hand rout or chisel to uniform depth.

Cutting a stopped dado

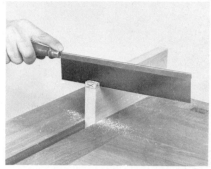

1. Lay out lines as for dado (p. 376), but mark a line for stop 1/4–1/2 in. from edge. Next step shows chiseling out enough wood behind stop so that saw can cut shoulder lines.

2. Chisel held vertically is pounded in just inside lines (left). Masking tape indicates depth of cut; do not try to drive chisel full depth at once. Remove waste with paring cuts (right).

3. Remove rest of waste as for dado. Mark entering piece for notch. Visible line was taken by combination square from depth of dado (p. 376, Step 6). Line being marked is stop's width.

4. Saw notch with dovetail saw or backsaw; clean corner with chisel. If fit is too tight, follow instructions for thinning entering piece or widening dado on page 376, Step 5.

Cutting a rabbet by hand

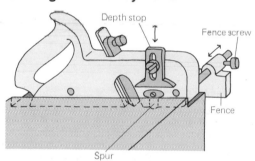

Rabbet width is thickness of entering portion, and its depth is one-half its own thickness. Set width of cut by loosening fence screws and moving fence. Adjust rabbet plane's blade so that it cuts easily; then set depth of cut by adjusting distance from blade tip to bottom of depth stop. Lower the spur only for planing across grain. Start first cut 2 in. from far end; back up a few inches for each subsequent bite until you can make one pass full length of board. Press fence flush against board.

Combined dado and rabbet

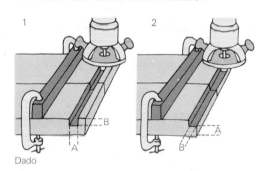

Determine but do not mark rabbet's depth and width—both usually half the thickness of board. Dado will also be that distance from end of board. **1.** Lay out and cut dado. When cutting two receiving boards with power router (p. 363), clamp them front edge to front edge and make both dadoes with one cut. With 6-in. rule marked each 1/32 in., measure A; this becomes A on rabbet. Dado's depth, B, becomes width of rabbet. **2.** Reset the router bit if necessary. Lay out and cut the rabbet. Test fit it; if it is too tight, trim the rabbet with shoulder plane or chisel.

Cutting a dovetail dado

1. Marking. On board's edge mark dovetail with T-bevel at 80 degrees. Continue lines across board's end. Use gauge to mark shoulder line on face.

2. Saw cuts. Hold saw at dovetail angle. Watch edges of board so that saw does not cut beyond shoulder. Lay board on face; saw shoulder.

3. Cleaning cuts. Guide for sawing shoulder line is left in place while corner is cleaned with paring chisel. Trim angled cut as needed.

4. Marking dado. Mark position of entering board. Transfer angle with T-bevel. Mark depth of cut with gauge as set for shoulder line on entering board.

5. Sawing dado. Make a saw guide, using T-bevel to copy the angle marked in Step 4. After sawing shoulders, make two parallel relief cuts in waste.

6. Cleaning dado. Remove waste with router plane or chisel. Clean corners with long paring chisel. If fit is tight, chisel or sand dado's shoulders.

Woodworking

Dovetail joints

The dovetail is the strongest joint for joining two ends at right angles. Practice on scrap wood, as considerable accuracy is required, especially in sawing the pins and tails. Shown at right are the through dovetail, with pins and tails showing, and the lapped, or half-blind, dovetail, usually used for drawer fronts. There are many variants.

Planning a through dovetail. The pieces to be joined must be square and of uniform thickness and width. Identify and mark the inside and outside faces of both boards. In laying out the joint, mark the inside faces first.

Usually the tails will be cut from the board spanning the furniture's front. The more nearly equal the pins and tails, the stronger the joint, but since a dovetail joint is intrinsically very strong, it is customary to use narrower pins so that the amount of end grain showing on the front is reduced. However, make the pins no narrower than 1/8 inch, the width of the smallest chisel available. You will need chisels of several sizes to cut the sockets.

Spacing. Allow one pin per inch on small work; on large work, pins can be further apart. If the board is a fraction less or more than a round number of inches, divide it into equal parts as shown on page 370. The long lines drawn to the board's ends, seen in the step-by-step photographs below, become the centers of the pins. Each edge of the board represents a center, so there will be a half pin at each edge. As you lay out the joint, be sure to mark the waste with X's so that you will not chisel out the wrong portions of wood. Saw and chisel on the waste side of the line, the chisel just touching the line.

Cutting. Two techniques for cutting dovetails make fitting them easier. Cut the shoulder 1/32 inch too deep; this allows you to plane or chisel the protruding pins or tails instead of having to plane an entire board to level the joint. Hollow the joint by pounding the chisel in with a mallet at a slight angle from the vertical to prevent splintered grain from spoiling the fit.

The fit of a well-cut dovetail should be tight. If in test-fitting it gets stuck, clamp the tailpiece in a vise and pull and wiggle the pin piece free.

You can buy a jig for cutting dovetails on a power router. The resulting pins and tails will be identical.

Through dovetail

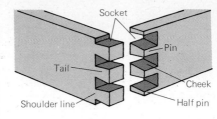
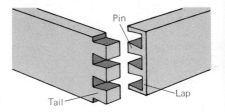

Lapped dovetail

1. Marking. Set gauge to wood's thickness plus 1/32 in. Mark shoulder lines on all four faces (left). Square lines across edges. Mark width of pins both sides of center lines (right).

2. Pins. Set T-bevel on protractor at 75–80 degrees; mark angled line of pins across board's end (left). Extend these lines straight down outside face to shoulder line (right).

3. Sawing pins. Start saw at 45° angle; gradually bring it to right angle and cut straight across as shown. Make sure saw follows cheek line and does not cut below shoulder line.

4. Removing waste. Alternate vertical chopping at shoulder with horizontal cuts. After first cut, angle chisel slightly from vertical to hollow joint. Reverse board halfway through.

5. Cleaning out sockets. With paring cuts, make sure corners are clean and square, and remove any splinters of wood from bottoms of sockets. Trim pin cheeks straight.

6. Marking tails. Clamp boards in handscrew. Hold knife blade flat against pin's cheek and incise outline of pins on tailpiece. With square continue lines across tail board's end.

7. Marking second face. Set T-bevel to angle of tail on first face, then transfer angle to second face. Check the angle of each line and reset the T-bevel if necessary.

8. Sawing tails. Clamp board in vise at angle so that cuts can be made with saw vertical. Tilt other way for other cheek line. Saw out the half sockets at edges of board.

9. Chiseling tails. Clamp board flat; chisel out waste between tails as in pin piece (Step 4). With board vertical, clean out corners with thin paring chisel as shown.

10. Fitting joint. Pound joint together with mallet. If fit is tight, make a jig of scrap wood with cutouts to press pins into socket with aid of a clamp. Use later when gluing joint.

Lapped dovetail

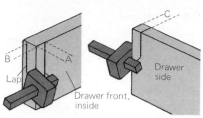

Marking a drawer joint. Front is thicker than side. A equals thickness of drawer side. B is two-thirds thickness of drawer front. C is same as B; mark on faces and edges of side.

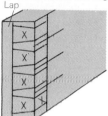

Marking pins. Lay out pins as in Step 2, p. 378. The sockets stop at the line that indicates two-thirds of drawer front's thickness (see above, B).

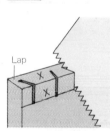

Sawing waste. Saw can cut only part of the waste because of the lap. Watch both ends of the saw carefully. Make additional saw cuts in waste to aid in chiseling it out.

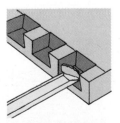

Chiseling waste. Chop out waste with bevel-edge paring chisel. An old chisel ground askew at a 45° angle helps to get into corners.

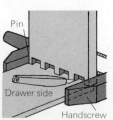

Tails. Clamp pin and tailpieces with bottom of socket at the edge of tailpiece. Mark outline of pins. Saw and chisel waste as in Steps 8 and 9, p. 378.

Miter joint

Two pieces set end-to-end at a right angle with the joining ends cut at 45° angles form an end miter, which is usually flat, as in a picture frame or molding. Two pieces joined edge-to-edge at the same angle form an edge miter, useful in case construction. If pieces are joined in other than a right angle, the miter always divides the angle in half.

The miter joint looks simple, but accurate cuttings of the angle and the length of the joining members is essential. Even with great care, you will probably have to trim with a plane.

Not a strong joint, the miter is almost always reinforced by one of the methods shown at the bottom of the page. It can be glued in corner clamps (p. 361), but they are expensive and do not pull the joints together as well as the device pictured below.

End miter

Edge miter

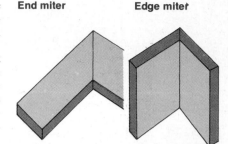

1. Marking. Place pairs of equal-length boards side by side and mark both with 45° angles. This ensures that angled edges and boards' lengths will be identical.

2. Sawing. Clamp board in miter box to steady it. If you have no miter box, use a saw guide of scrap wood. Trim to fit with a shoulder or a smooth plane if necessary.

3. Gluing. Coat surfaces with glue; let dry. Have ready square-cornered scraps of wood with grooves in their outer surfaces to use in clamping. Glue and assemble joints.

4. Clamping. Place scraps at corners. Encircle with strong twine, pull it tight, and twist it with wood tourniquet. Lay tourniquet against a corner to maintain tension.

Reinforcing the miter joint

Veneer feather

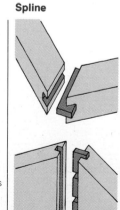

After glue in joint has dried, saw into corner. Cut piece or two of veneer or a thin piece of wood larger than needed. Sand to thickness of saw cut. Coat feather and the saw cut with glue, and slip the feather into place. Trim with chisel when glue is dry. In an edge miter install feathers every few inches.

Spline

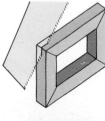

Before gluing joint, cut grooves in the adjoining surfaces with power router or power saw. Measure grooves. Cut spline of similar wood; be sure to cut it across grain. Glue spline in place when gluing joint. In an edge miter, spline can be several pieces; place closer to inside corner.

Dowels

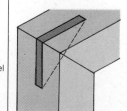

Mark dowel position in Step 1, above; drill at right angle to angled surface. Sand dowel corners. Glue with joint. Dowels that show, inserted after gluing, are easier.

Glue blocks

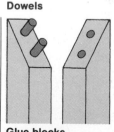

Drill screw holes alternately left and right in block of same wood. Mark through holes for pilot holes in joined pieces. Glue joint; glue and screw block.

379

Woodworking

Mortise-and-tenon joints

One of the oldest joints, mortise and tenon is often used to join narrow pieces in furniture frames—for example, the supports for a tabletop, the legs to the rails of a chair seat, or the frames in panel-and-frame construction (p. 382). Tenons may have three shoulders, as those illustrated below, or two, four, or no shoulders.

To make a through tenon tight, especially when considerable downward pressure will be exerted on it, wedges of the same or a harder wood are sometimes inserted into saw cuts three-quarters the depth of the tenon. The wedges spread the tenon, and a taper is chiseled into the mortise to accommodate the spread. An attractive effect results, particularly if the wedges are darker than the tenon.

Stub (blind) tenon

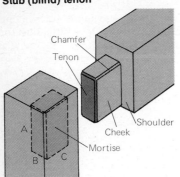

Letters indicate dimensions of mortise and tenon. A is three-quarters width of tenon board; B is one-third thickness of tenon board. C is two to three times B. Marking stub tenon is shown at right. To prevent splitting, mortised wood can be cut to final length after joint is made.

Through tenon

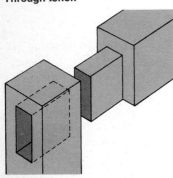

Mark lines as for stub tenon, but carry lines around to second face of mortise piece with square. Bore mortise with auger bit until point appears on second face; reverse wood and bore from other side. Make tenon 1/16 in. too long and plane flush. This is stronger than a stub tenon.

Wedging a through tenon

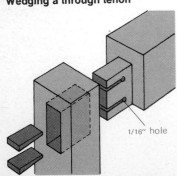

1/16" hole

Saw wedges with grain. Make 4 in. too long. Tape sandpaper to bench; rub wedge to final thickness; cut to 1/4 in. longer than saw cut. Drill holes and make saw cuts in tenon. Taper mortise. Glue joint; glue wedges and saw cuts. Mallet wedges into place simultaneously. Saw off excess and plane flush.

1. Marking. Divide tenon face into four equal parts. Hold against mortise piece at finished-cut line. Mark at bottom of tenon and at three-quarter mark (dimension A).

2. Choosing a chisel. Divide tenon piece into thirds (dimension B). Find a chisel 1/16 in. narrower than middle third, or adjust width for available chisel.

3. Mortise width. Set points of mortise gauge to chisel's width plus 1/16 in. Mark down center of mortise piece from finished-cut line to bottom of mortise.

4. Boring waste. Set depth gauge on auger bit so that mortise depth will be two to three times its width. Draw center line on which to start bit. Make several holes.

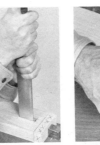

5. Chiseling waste. Mark mortise depth on chisel with tape. Use mallet and mortise chisel to chop out ends and bottom (left), wide chisel without mallet for sides (right).

6. Marking tenon. With tenon piece held against mortise, transfer length to tenon. Measure mortise depth (C) with combination square, and transfer it to tenon piece.

7. Sawing tenon. Cut to shoulder line facing you, with saw at angle as shown; reverse in vise and finish cut with saw horizontal. Make other cuts with saw horizontal.

8. Chamfer. Clamp tenon piece in vise. With paring chisel make a small chamfer around edges of tenon. This helps to make seating it in mortise easier.

9. Test-fit. If tight, trim tenon with chisel; if loose, glue veneer strips to tenon. Pull apart by clamping in vise and rocking tenon piece. Saw off waste on mortise piece.

Gluing and clamping

For permanence most joints must be glued, since no matter how tight the fit, in time the wood will dry and shrink, and the joint will loosen. Clamping the pieces together while the glue sets maintains even and constant contact between the parts. Excess pressure, however, squeezes too much glue from the joint and causes a starved joint, so tighten clamps with your hands only. Refer to the glue chart (p. 368) for the appropriate glue and clamping time.

Surfaces of joints to be glued must be kept clean and free of grease. Before you apply the glue, do a dry run to test the fit and to determine the clamping procedure. Prepare scraps of wood to protect the wood surfaces from the jaws of metal clamps. If the scraps will touch the glue, rub them with paraffin on both sides so that the glue will not bond them to the wood. If metal clamps will touch glue and wood, wrap them with waxed paper to prevent stains.

Some glues dry in 15 minutes, so you must work quickly. If the piece is large, it is a good idea to have a helper. With a brush or fingers spread liberal amounts of glue on all surfaces to be joined. Have a bucket of water handy for washing hands and for wiping off excess glue. Tighten the clamps. A thin line of glue should be squeezed from the joint; if none appears, take the joint apart and add more.

If wood surfaces are ready to be finished, wipe off excess glue with a wet cloth, then wipe dry. If the piece requires further planing and sanding, you can allow the glue to dry and scrape it off with a glue scraper. Then plane off marks of the scraper.

Most clamps have one stationary jaw and another that adjusts. Some C-clamps have a swivel head on the stationary jaw that allows clamping on an angled or irregular surface. The jaws on handscrews are both adjustable. They can be offset and will still remain parallel, or they can be set at an angle to each other. Handscrews are used to hold pieces of wood while you perform other operations (see below); they do not exert enough pressure for gluing large pieces. Some clamping situations are shown elsewhere (pp. 374, 379), and a way to use screws in place of clamps is described on page 376. But there will be times when not enough of the right clamps are available, and you will have to improvise—one possibility is illustrated below.

Installing screws and nails

While major structural parts rely on good joints augmented by glue, subsidiary parts—such as drawer guides, cleats, and small moldings—are affixed with screws or nails, and some joints may require reinforcement with screws or dowels. One-half to two-thirds of a screw's or nail's length should penetrate the second piece of wood unless such length would cause it to protrude.

Predrill a shank hole the diameter and length of the unthreaded portion of the screw and a pilot hole the length of the screw and the diameter of its threaded portion minus the threads.

So that you know when to stop drilling, mark the bit with masking tape at the depth of the hole, or use a commercial depth gauge (p. 361). To ensure that the hole is vertical, use a guide, purchased or made as shown below. Or buy a vertical drill stand for mounting a power drill. Make starter holes with an awl so that the bit will not jump out of position. Start the drill before touching wood.

Flat-headed wood screws can be countersunk flush with the wood's surface. If you do not want them to show, they can be counterbored—the screw head sunk 1/8 inch or more below the wood's surface—and the hole filled with plastic wood or a plug made with a drill attachment called a plug cutter.

To countersink (see below), use two bits plus a countersink bit. To counterbore, use three successively larger bits. You can buy special bits that countersink or counterbore all the holes in one operation. Some of these bits adjust for more than one size screw.

When screwing a wide plank, such as a tabletop, to a frame, make allowance for the wood's shrinking and expansion by drilling an oval shank hole that permits the screw to move. The oval's length runs cross-grain of the plank.

Driving a nail can end in disaster unless a few rules are observed. Blunt the nail's tip with a hammer to avoid splitting the wood. In hardwood, drill a pilot hole slightly smaller in diameter than the nail. Hold the nail beneath the head while starting it. If the nail bends, pull it out and start a new one. Use a nail set (p. 361) to drive finishing nails slightly below the surface. Fill the hole with wood putty, and sand it smooth when dry. Stagger a row of nails; if they are lined up, they are likely to split the wood. Avoid using nails or screws in end grain because they pull out easily.

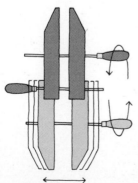
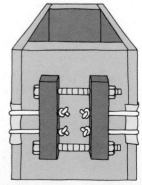
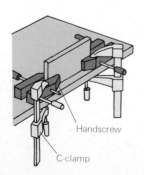
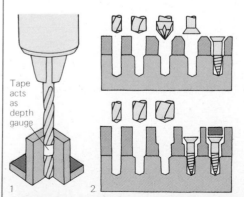

Handscrews. To open and shut jaws, hold one handle stationary and rotate jaws around it with other handle.

Cord clamp. A substitute for bar clamps is made of strong cord, wood blocks, and bolts to tighten it.

Handscrews as hold-downs. Clamp handscrews to bench with C-clamps. Jaws hold board for sawing or chiseling.

Tape acts as depth gauge

Handscrew

C-clamp

1. Drill guide is made of four pieces of wood squared and glued. **2. Countersinking** (top) is done with three bits (see text); screwhead is used to check diameter of countersink; screw is inserted. **Counterboring** (bottom) requires three bits; screw is inserted; wood plug fills hole. **3. Slot-screwing:** Drill holes at both ends of oval; remove wood in between with chisel.

Woodworking

A vocabulary of forms

A case is a boxlike structure that may vary in size from a jewelry box to a ceiling-high wardrobe. A case can be constructed in several ways. In one method the slabs of the top, bottom, sides, and back form the box (generally this works best with small pieces). In another method, known as frame-and-panel construction, a thin sheet is fitted into grooves in heavy surrounding members, which form the frame. The resulting panel is used in place of a solid board. The advantages of frame-and-panel construction are that a large piece can be lighter in weight than one made of solid slabs and that the panels, which are not glued, can move in their frames in response to changing humidity without warping or twisting the whole structure. Slab or frame-and-panel construction can be assembled as four unbraced walls, or they may surround a rigid, strengthening framework of narrow strips called rails. In large pieces, such as chests or desks, the rails support drawers and doors (pp. 384–385). Rails also form the frameworks for tables and chairs, as shown in the illustrations on these pages.

Legs. Legs in a variety of shapes—round or square, straight, tapered, or turned—are joined to table and chair

Solid slabs

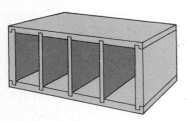

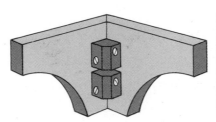

Record cabinet. Corner joints are dado and rabbet. Grain runs in same direction all the way around. Back (not visible) is rabbeted into sides, top, and bottom. Dividers fit into dadoes.

Bracket foot. Detail of leg for chest below shows miter joint and reinforcing glue blocks. Chest could equally well rest on one of the plinths shown on the next page.

Frame-and-panel construction

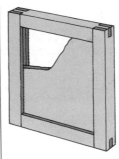

Frame for panel is joined with mortise and tenon. Finish panel before gluing. Avoid letting glue ooze out of joint and into panel groove. Panel should remain loose. Plywood panel can be glued.

Two forms of mortise-and-tenon joint for frame are shown in detail: stub (top) gives effect of a butt joint; open (below) is used in windows, doors, and screens. Make mortise same width as groove that holds panel.

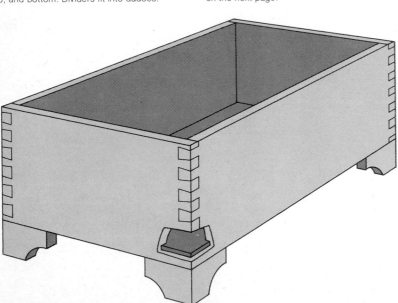

Chest of slabs. Here the box form of the record cabinet is reoriented so that the back becomes the bottom. To support the weight of the contents, the bottom is grooved into the front, back, and sides and may be reinforced with glue blocks if necessary. Note that grain runs in long direction of wood all around so that shrinkage and expansion, usually across grain, occur in same dimension.

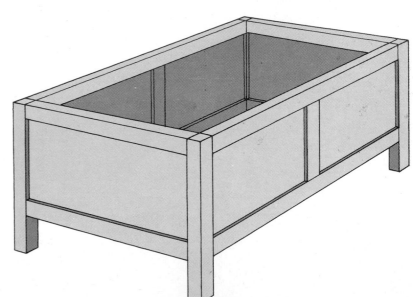

Frame-and-panel chest. A number of panels joined together form a chest; this method of construction is used in the chest on pages 396–397. At the corners the frame is lengthened to form the legs. A chest of drawers or a desk can be constructed by the same principle; doors are often made this way. Lids for both chests would be hinged at the back (see p. 385 for hardware).

rails with mortise-and-tenon joints, dowels, or a combination of the two. Legs can be an extension of the frames in a frame-and-panel piece. You can buy readymade legs in many styles.

Plinths. A large piece, such as a chest, may need firmer support than legs. Such support is provided by a base called a plinth. In traditional styles the plinth is slightly larger than the case, and the two are joined by a molding. In contemporary furniture the plinth is often recessed. The plinth is constructed separately, reinforced with glue blocks, and screwed to a solid wood case; along the side rails, slots should be made for the screws (p. 381) so that the wood can shift.

Cabinet backs. When a piece will stand against a wall, the back is often of plywood or masonite. The back supplies rigidity to the case; its thickness varies with the size of the piece. Sometimes backs are reinforced with *muntins,* grooved vertical strips into which panels of plywood are set.

Tabletops. As the top contracts and expands, it may crack when shrinking or become deformed when expanding if fastened tightly to the rails. Two methods of fastening tabletops are shown on this page.

Rails as reinforcement

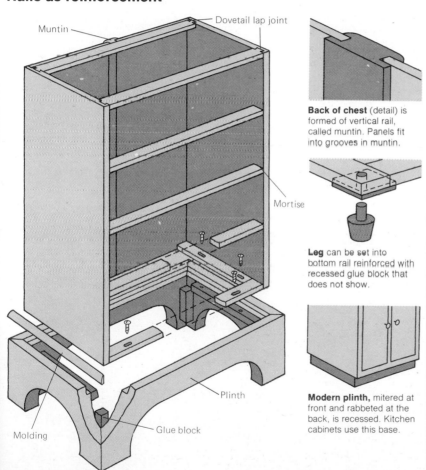

Chest of drawers with solid slab sides has reinforcing rails dovetailed at top and mortised into sides below. A base called a plinth, here in traditional style, supports chest. Plinth is constructed separately and screwed to case; molding covers the joint. Glue blocks reinforce miter joints at plinth's front and back corners. Drawer rails, omitted here, are shown on page 384.

Back of chest (detail) is formed of vertical rail, called muntin. Panels fit into grooves in muntin.

Leg can be set into bottom rail reinforced with recessed glue block that does not show.

Modern plinth, mitered at front and rabbeted at the back, is recessed. Kitchen cabinets use this base.

Tables and chairs

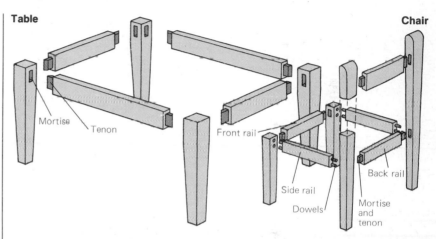

Rails and legs of tables and chairs can be mortised or doweled (see details below). Rails can be the same thickness as legs or thinner. When side rails of chair slant toward back, it is best to mortise front and back rails to legs and to use two dowels to join side rails to legs as shown. Glue blocks (not shown), recessed below rail tops of chair, support the seat and reinforce corners.

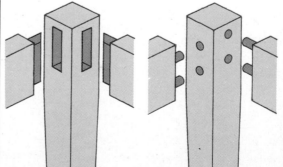

Mortises in legs meet and form L-shape (left). Ends of rail tenons are mitered but need not fit perfectly. Dowels (right) should be staggered so that they will not meet. A third possibility is to mortise one rail and join the other with dowels, as in chair above.

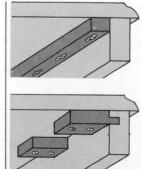

Tabletops are slot-screwed (p. 381) to continuous glue block (top) or are screwed to series of blocks rabbeted to rail (below).

Woodworking

Drawers, doors, and lids

Drawer construction involves making some choices. First, decide on the front: if it is to be flush with the case, it must fit perfectly, with no gaps between the drawer sides and the case; if the front is to overlap the case, fit is somewhat less critical.

There are several possibilities for the drawer joints (see drawings below). Thicknesses of the drawer parts should be within the following ranges: the front at least 3/4 inch to allow for cutting dovetails; the sides and back 5/16 to 1/2 inch; the bottom 1/8 to 1/4 inch, preferably of plywood, since it does not shrink and expand as does solid wood. In a solid wood bottom, the grain should run side to side.

The drawer back often rests on the drawer bottom and is therefore cut narrower than the sides and front. The bottom should measure slightly less from front to back than the drawer. It is almost always grooved into the front and sides. However, the bottom of a small, shallow drawer can be rabbeted to the front and sides. A solid wood bottom that is grooved into place should be glued only to the drawer front, never the sides; a plywood bottom can be glued all around. If a drawer bottom is rabbeted into the sides and front, the joint should be reinforced with screws.

Care must be taken in locating the groove for the bottom in a dovetailed drawer so that the groove does not split the lowest pins in the front but instead passes through the socket above it and the tails in the drawer sides.

Reinforcement. If a drawer is long or its contents heavy, reinforce it across the bottom with a strip of wood dovetailed into the drawer front and rabbeted to receive the drawer back; grooves in the strip's edges hold the drawer bottom's two panels. A solid wood bottom can be reinforced every 6

Drawer construction

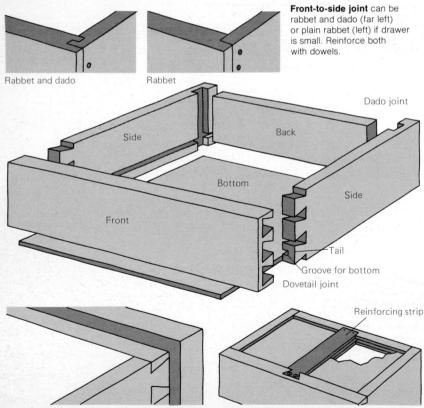

Front-to-side joint can be rabbet and dado (far left) or plain rabbet (left) if drawer is small. Reinforce both with dowels.

Rabbet and dado

Rabbet

Dado joint

Side

Back

Bottom

Front

Side

Tail

Groove for bottom

Dovetail joint

Reinforcing strip

Cut drawer joints in following order: front to sides, bottom into front and sides, and back into sides. Test-fit after each joint. Check fit in opening before gluing; clearance should be a scant 1/16 in. all around. Front-to-side joints in drawer with overlapping front (bottom, left) can also be rabbeted as at top. Back can be joined to sides with dovetail or dado—dovetail is stronger. Wide drawer (bottom, right) should be reinforced across bottom with strip.

Drawer runners and guides

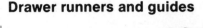
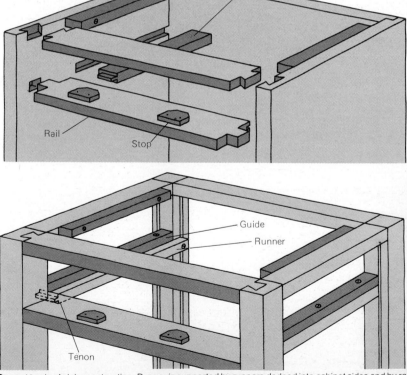

Kicker

Runner

Rail

Stop

Guide

Runner

Tenon

Case at top is of slab construction. Drawer is supported by runners dadoed into cabinet sides and by rail across front mortised into sides. Kicker prevents drawer from tilting as it is pulled out; the stop catches bottom of drawer front to prevent its hitting cabinet back. Frame-and-panel construction (below) requires guides screwed to runners to prevent sideways movement of drawer; runners are rabbeted and screwed to back corner rail and tenoned into front rail.

inches with small, rectangular blocks of wood called cleats. These should be glued and screwed to the drawer sides and slot-screwed (p. 381)—but not glued—to the drawer bottom.

Mounting the drawer. A small drawer set on a solid shelf can simply ride in and out on the shelf. Otherwise, a drawer rides on runners. Unless the case sides are flush with the drawer sides, guides must be mounted on the runners or on the drawer to restrict side-to-side motion. A strip of wood called a kicker is mounted above each drawer side to prevent the drawer from tipping as it is pulled out. A stop, mounted on the front rail, prevents the drawer from hitting the back of the chest when it is pushed in.

Metal drawer slides can be purchased for drawer mounting. They require clearance between drawer and cabinet sides and should be purchased before the cabinet is built so that the drawers can be sized and fitted according to the maker's instructions.

When the drawer is assembled, test its fit. If it is tight, determine where the wood is rubbing; it may be the back, side, or front. Sand or trim with a plane to remove the high spots.

Hinges. Doors, lids, fall flaps (the drop front of a desk, for example), and drop leaves of tables are all mounted on hinges. There are many varieties of decorative, semiconcealed, and concealed hinges, but for most furniture one form or another of the butt hinge will do. A butt hinge has two rectangular leaves that swing on a pin; the pin may be removable—called a loose-pin—or it may be riveted in place. The portion of the leaves surrounding the pin is called the knuckle. Hinges are measured across the width of the two leaves spread open. A variety of hinges and some of the ways they are mounted are shown below.

Alternate runners and guides

Conventional drawer

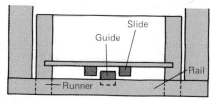

Side-hung drawer

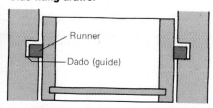

Drawer hung from tabletop

Drawer guide, rabbeted to front and rear rails of case, is centered beneath drawer. Strips of wood for slides are screwed to drawer bottom; slot-screw them if drawer bottom is solid wood (p. 381). The drawer sides—not the bottom—rest on runners like those on opposite page; guide simply restricts side-to-side motion. Side-hung drawer (center) requires very thick and heavy sides. Sides of single drawer beneath tabletop (below) are screwed and glued to runners; drawer is hung from rabbeted guides that are glued and screwed to tabletop.

Hardware for doors, lids, and fall flaps

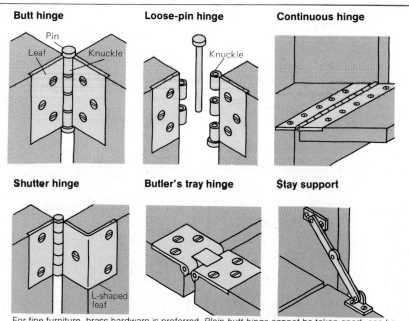

For fine furniture, brass hardware is preferred. *Plain butt hinge* cannot be taken apart, can be mounted on either side of door or lid. Chisel a mortise the exact size of the leaves into door and frame. *Loose-pin hinge* has removable pin, comes apart, and is easier to mount. Make sure pin drops into knuckle from top. *Continuous hinge,* also called piano hinge because it is used on piano keyboard lid, can be used for fall flaps, chest lids, or doors. For lid or doors (not shown) mount as you would a butt hinge, with the knuckle protruding. For fall flap, bevel corners of both edges with plane so that knuckle is sunk below surface and hinge leaves are flush with surface. *Shutter hinge,* so named for its use in mounting window shutters, makes stronger fastening for chest lid than butt hinge because L-shaped leaf is screwed to inside of case as well as to edge. *Butler's tray hinge* holds a fall flap level when open; chisel mortises for the leaves and the knuckle into both surfaces. One arm of *fall-flap stay support* is mounted inside case, other on flap. Position it after flap has been hinged; check position with flap open and closed.

Mounting doors

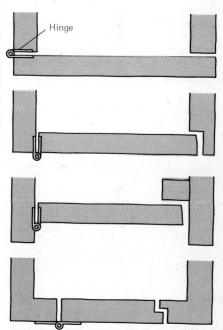

Four ways of mounting butt-hinged doors and four ways of stopping doors are shown. Inset doors (all except top) are angled to prevent binding. Unless hinge is surface mounted (bottom), mortise leaves into both door and case. Place tapered shims—thin pieces of wood—beneath door to position it. Mark hinge locations—two for a door less than 24 in., three for larger door—then remove door. Using hinge as template, draw shape on both surfaces. With chisel, pare out mortises. Screw hinges to case, check alignment, and screw to door.

Woodworking

Working with plywood

Plywood has several advantages over solid wood. Because the grain of its layers runs alternately at right angles, it does not shrink and expand with humidity changes. Plywood can span a wide area and is stronger across the grain than solid wood. In frame-and-panel construction (see chest, pp. 396–397), plywood panels can be glued whereas hardwood ones cannot.

Top-quality panels of plywood with faces of hardwood, such as mahogany or birch, can form a case with rails of solid wood. Often fir plywood is the best choice for the back of a case or the bottom of a drawer. But as a rule do not mix plywood and solid wood in a case, as, for example, by putting a hardwood top on plywood sides.

Before ordering plywood, make a cutting diagram on graph paper (right). Lay out pieces on the sheet so that the grain will run the same way all around the piece of furniture—usually with the longest dimension.

Marking and cutting. Mark the good face of the plywood, and saw with that face up to avoid splintering it, but when cutting with a radial arm, circular, or saber saw, mark the back, and cut with that side up. Placing scrap lumber beneath the plywood and cutting through it prevents splintering. Use saw with fine teeth—10 to 15 per inch—or a special plywood blade; set the saw so that it penetrates to one tooth's depth. With a hand saw, cut at a very shallow angle. Support the sheet of plywood so that it does not flex or jiggle as you saw.

Sanding and planing. If your saw blade is sharp, the edges should require only light sanding. Do not sand the surface; you may wear through the thin face veneer. If planing the edge is necessary, take a light cut with a very sharp plane; better yet, level it by sanding.

Gluing. Plywood edges absorb a lot of glue, so apply a thin coat, let it sink in, then apply a second coat. Joints need reinforcement with cleats and glue blocks; nails and screws do not hold well in veneer-core plywood. Because of its solid center, lumber core holds screws and nails better and is thus preferable for mounting hinges. Veneer core, however, is stronger, less expensive, and preferable to other plywoods for most purposes.

Plywood edges are unattractive; therefore, joints should minimize their exposure. A miter joint (p. 380) hides both edges but is weak unless reinforced. When edges will unavoidably show, cover them with molding or veneer tape.

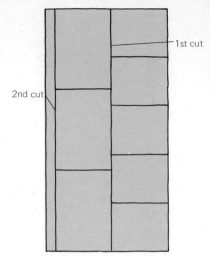

A cutting diagram. Arrange pieces and order cuts so that initial cuts run across length or width of sheet. Allow at least 1/8 in. for saw kerf. Remeasure after each cut.

Plywood joints

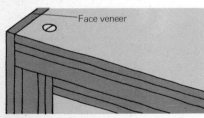

Rabbeting a corner. A regular rabbet joint leaves plywood edge exposed. By leaving face veneer uncut, a minimum of edge is left showing. Reinforce joint with screws or glue blocks.

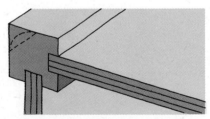

Dado. Entire width of plywood is dadoed into a solid wood rail. If this were a corner post—a leg, for example—outside corner could be rounded or cut at an angle (dashed lines).

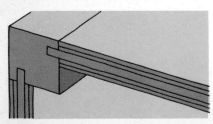

Tongue and groove. A groove the width of center core of plywood is cut into solid wood rail with saw or router. Outer layers of veneer are sawed or routed to leave core as tongue.

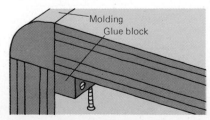

Molding and glue block. Plywood is butt jointed to quarter-round molding of solid wood, which covers end grain of plywood. Glue block is screwed and glued inside for reinforcement.

Edge treatments

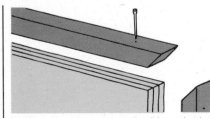

Molding. Cut plain or shaped solid wood strips 3/8 to 1/2 in. thick and slightly longer than edge to be trimmed. Miter corners of molding. Glue; drive finishing nails in predrilled holes.

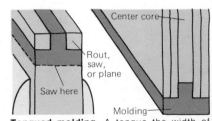

Tongued molding. A tongue the width of plywood's center core holds molding more firmly. In making molding (left), cut tongue, then saw strip. Remove center core with saw or router.

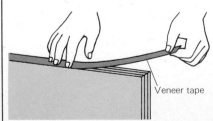

Veneer tape. Purchase in rolls. Iron on tape with glue on back. For tape without glue, cover both surfaces with contact glue, allow it to soak in, apply a second coat, and press tape into place.

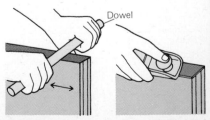

Removing excess. Roll glued tape flat with dowel several times; roll over edges to crease any overhang. Cut away excess with block plane. Sand lightly to blend tape into wood face.

Woodworking

Spindle turning on the lathe

Turning wood on a lathe is perhaps the most satisfying part of woodworking. Causing symmetrical shapes to emerge from a block of wood is somewhat akin to making a beautiful vessel emerge from a blob of wet clay.

Two kinds of turning are possible on lathes. In spindle turning between centers, a square of wood is held between headstock and tailstock; this method is used for making chair and table legs, lamp bases, and bedposts. In faceplate turning (not the subject of this book), a large block of wood is held to the headstock by an attachment called a faceplate; bowls, goblets, and trays are turned by this method.

Lathe speed. On a lathe equipped with four-step motor pulleys, you adjust the lathe speed by moving the belt from one pulley to another. On a variable-speed lathe, you dial the desired speed. Slower speed (900 rpm) is best for rough removal of waste and for large pieces of stock. Speed may be increased to the next step, around 1400 rpm, for shaping and smoothing cuts; higher speeds are usually unnecessary.

Safety. As with all power tools, you must observe certain precautions. Sleeves should be tight or rolled up, collars buttoned. Wear goggles or a face protector. Do not talk—concentrate on the work. Tools must always be sharp (p. 363); keep a whetstone and slipstone handy, and use them often. Adjust the tool rest with the motor off; move it closer as the work gets smaller in diameter. Spin the work by hand before starting the motor to make sure that it clears the tool rest. Stand aside when turning on the motor. Touch the tool to the rest before touching the wood. Hold tools firmly, but do not dig into the wood, as this could cause the tool to be deflected abruptly. Move the tool from a larger to a smaller diameter so that it is always cutting downhill, never uphill.

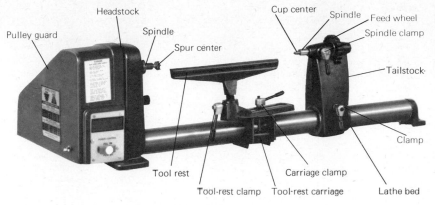

Pulley guard — Headstock — Spindle — Spur center — Cup center — Spindle — Feed wheel — Spindle clamp — Tailstock — Clamp — Tool rest — Tool-rest clamp — Tool-rest carriage — Carriage clamp — Lathe bed

Wood-turning lathe. Headstock contains motor-driven live, or spur, center that turns the work. Tailstock adjusts on bed according to work's length and is locked by tailstock clamp. Dead, or cup, center is tightened into stock by turning spindle-feed wheel; spindle clamp locks spindle into position. Tool-rest carriage adjusts two ways: in position along the bed and in distance from work. The carriage clamp locks it. Tool rest adjusts up or down and is locked by turning tool-rest clamp. Lathe size is indicated by its "swing" over bed, that is, the largest diameter that can be turned, which is twice distance between spur center and bed. Some lathes have bed gap that allows for turning large-diameter pieces by faceplate method. A 24-in. tool rest can be purchased for turning long pieces; it requires two carriages.

Centering and mounting the stock

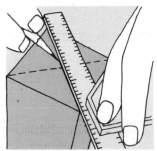

1. On both ends of squared stock, mark the center points by holding a combination square against edge of block with rule running diagonally from corner to corner.

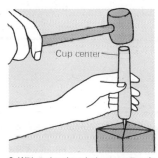

Cup center

2. With awl make a hole at center of cup end. With mallet drive cup center into wood to indent circle in end of stock. Place cup center in tailstock spindle.

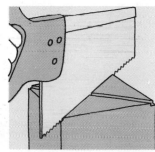

3. On opposite end of stock make saw kerfs with backsaw following diagonal lines drawn in Step 1. Cuts should be 1/16 in. deep. They position spurs of spur center.

Spur center

4. Place spur center in center of end in which saw kerfs were cut. Make sure that spurs will enter saw kerfs. With wooden mallet pound spur center into wood.

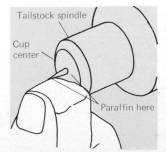

Tailstock spindle — Cup center — Paraffin here

5. Remove tool rest from lathe. Lubricate the cup center with paraffin or a candle. Place spur center in headstock spindle; hold block in position over lathe bed.

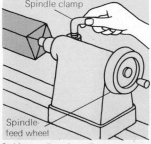

Spindle clamp — Spindle-feed wheel

6. Move tailstock until cup enters indentation made in Step 2; lock tailstock clamp. Tighten cup center against wood with spindle-feed wheel; lock with spindle clamp.

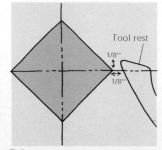

Tool rest — 1/8" — 1/8"

7. Replace tool rest, and adjust it so that its top is 1/8 in. above center of turning block and so that corner of block clears tool rest by 1/8 in. Rotate by hand to check.

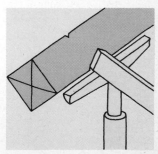

8. Turn lathe on. With skew chisel knick corners. Turn lathe off; if all knicks are same depth, block is centered. If not, lay scrap wood on block and tap with mallet to center.

Woodworking

Making a spindle turning

The secret of cutting—as opposed to scraping—is to lean the bevel of the tool on the revolving wood so that the tool's edge cuts like a plane, creating a thin shaving. Hold the tool's handle in the right hand and the blade in the left. The left hand's index finger rides the curve of the tool rest. Lean the blade on the tool rest, and lay the back of the blade, held at a slight angle, on the turning wood fairly high up. Draw the blade back until its bevel is flat on the wood and its edge engaged. Only a small portion of the edge cuts wood—in the case of the skew chisel, the portion from midpoint to heel. Turning tools must be honed often (p. 363); the edges should not have a microbevel nor be ground hollow.

Cutting vs. scraping. Cutting is the classic woodturner's method; it requires much practice but yields a smooth surface that needs little or no sanding. Scraping is slower; it is easy to learn but dulls tools rapidly, requires a wider range of tools, and leaves a rough surface that needs considerable sanding. Except for parting-tool cuts, techniques on these two pages demonstrate the cutting method.

Tools. Turning by the cutting method calls for five basic tools: a 3/4-inch square-end gouge for roughing out; a 1/2-inch long-nosed gouge for shaping concave curves; skew chisels in two sizes, 1¼ inch and 1/2 inch, for smoothing and for cutting other shapes; and a parting tool for coarse sizing cuts.

Materials. Turning squares—blanks of wood of various widths and lengths—can be bought from stores that supply cabinetmaking woods. They should be fractionally larger than the planned diameter of the turning, free of knots, and square (p. 372). Practice on softwood before trying a hardwood turning. You can also turn a laminated wood block (pp. 270–271).

Turning

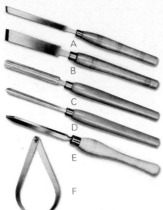

Shapes in turning are traditional and are cut in certain ways. Method for each cut is shown on opposite page.

- Square shoulder
- V-cut
- Bead
- Half-bead
- Cove
- Half-bead
- Urn shape
- Round shoulder

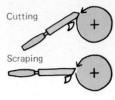

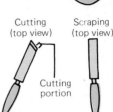

Tools. *Skew chisels* (A and B) have bevels on both faces and angled edges. Cutting is done between midpoint and heel. *Square-end gouge* (C) is for roughing out; *long-nosed gouge* (D) is for coves; both have beveled backs. *Parting tool* (E) makes square cut straight into wood. *Calipers* (F) measure diameters.

Cutting vs. scraping. In cutting (top) blade is held at slightly less than 90° angle to wood. Place it high on cylinder and draw back until bevel rests on turning. Arrow shows direction wood turns. Only small part of blade does cutting. In scraping (below) chisel addresses wood straight on or slightly downward; entire edge touches wood.

Cutting

Scraping

Cutting (top view)

Scraping (top view)

Cutting portion

Turning operations. Turn on lathe at low speed and address blank with large gouge as described in text. **1.** Start at left end, move gouge to right, then reverse. Gouge is held at 90° angle to blank, with cutting edge raised and rolled slightly in direction of travel. Gouge's edge from midpoint to right corner does cutting. **2.** To cut toward spur end, roll gouge slightly other way. Gouge's edge from midpoint to left corner now does cutting. **3.** When blank is rounded but still rough, smooth it with large skew chisel. Lean bevel on wood, angle skew slightly, and start at end. Take one long bite, length of cylinder; reverse, changing angle of skew. Turn off motor. Check cylinder for straightness by holding leg of try square along cylinder's length while revolving it by hand. **4.** Make full-size drawing of planned turning; mark critical diameters and fold pattern in half lengthwise. Hold it above cylinder, turn on lathe, and mark details on cylinder with pencil. **5.** Rough out sizing cuts to within 1/16 in. of final size with skew or parting tool. **6.** Cuts with parting tool are made with blade at 90° angle to work; cut well on waste side of line, as parting tool leaves much roughness to be smoothed. **7.** Measure cuts by holding calipers across critical diameters, then laying them on a rule. Cut final shapes as shown opposite. **8.** Cut out pattern and check final shapes.

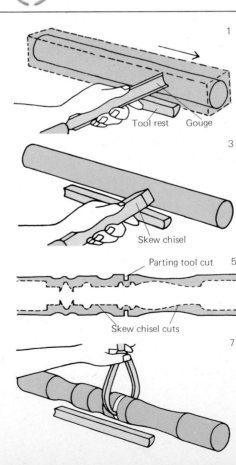

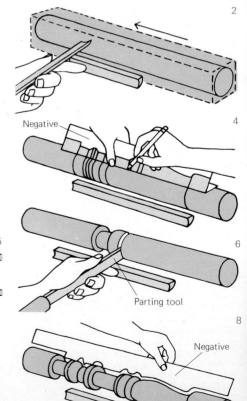

Tool rest   Gouge

Skew chisel

Parting tool cut

Skew chisel cuts

Negative

Parting tool

Negative

Shoulders, beads, V-cuts, coves, curves, and tapers

Square shoulder. Viewpoint is that of worker looking down at lathe. Dashed lines represent shape being cut. **1.** Indent line for cut with toe of skew; do not force it so far that metal burns. **2.** With skew's edge between midpoint and heel, cut away wood leading to shoulder. **3.** With bevel leaning on wood and heel cutting, smooth vertical surface of shoulder. Repeat procedure until shoulder is required depth.

Round shoulder. 1. Indent a line with toe of skew where smallest diameter of the shoulder will be. **2.** At highest point of shoulder lay bevel flat on wood; draw back handle until the skew's edge is engaged near heel. Begin to roll skew in direction of low point. **3.** With continuous arm motion roll skew over so that heel drops downhill into valley at base of round shoulder. Finish with blade's edge vertical.

Bead. Each side of a bead is formed with a quick twist of the wrist that differs from the full arm motion used for round shoulder. **1.** With toe of skew indent lines that mark outside of bead. **2.** Engage skew's heel at high point of bead. **3.** Roll skew over into the valley, ending with edge vertical. This is called a half bead. To complete the bead, lay skew on other bevel and repeat motion in opposite direction.

V-cut. Two V-cuts form a feature similar to a bead. Mark center portion and narrowest diameter of V-cuts. **1.** Indent with toe of skew where narrowest diameters will be. **2.** Lay bevel on wood, and engage heel at line marking start of V-cut. Roll chisel so that edge is at desired angle for V-cut, and cut downward with heel. A shallow V-cut can be cut in one bite; a deep one may take several bites. **3.** Reverse skew and cut other half.

Cove. 1. Lay long-nosed gouge almost flat high up on cylinder; engage edge and make a shallow cut to serve as a flat on which bevel can rest. This flat prevents gouge from jumping sideways. **2.** Roll gouge in scooping motion, making sure that bevel leans on wood. Cut with small portion of edge just below the midpoint. **3.** At bottom of cove gouge has been rolled so that it lies on its back. Cut other side in reverse.

Urn shape and tapers. Make sizing cuts (p. 388) at significant diameters. For curves use skew. **1.** Cut from high to low part, rolling skew in direction of travel. **2.** In a concavity that is too small for skew to maneuver, use long-nosed gouge in motion similar to making a cove but with wider diameter. **3.** For a taper make sizing cuts at each end and at midpoint. Remove waste between with skew, taking progressive bites downhill.

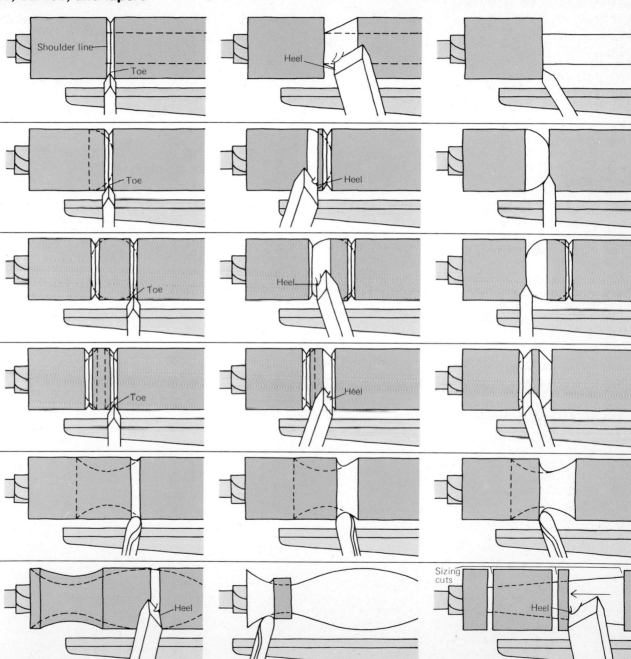

Woodworking

Finishing to enhance and protect wood

Wood finishes fall into two basic categories. One type remains on the surface, sealing the wood and protecting it. Surface finishes are the first three listed in the chart below: varnish, shellac, and lacquer.

The other category can broadly be called penetrating finishes. These sink into the wood, in some instances actually changing the chemical structure of the wood. Among these are boiled linseed oil, tung oil, and the penetrating resins. All of these are described in more detail below, and the chart summarizes their characteristics.

Some general procedures apply to all finishing operations. The room temperature should be at least 18°C. The work area should be clean and dust-free. This is especially important with varnish, which takes longer to dry. Allow more drying time in damp weather. Work in the same direction as the grain when sanding or when applying stain and finish with these exceptions: fillers and the first coat of varnish are applied across as well as with the grain. If possible, the surface to which stain or finish is being applied should be held horizontal.

The steps in finishing are: sanding, staining (optional), applying a filler (done only on open-grain woods; see p. 366), sealing (for surface finish), applying the finish, and rubbing.

Sanding. Actually, the best surface preparation is planing with a smooth plane followed by a minimum of sanding. On a well-planed surface start with 120-grit paper; follow with 220 for softwoods and 280 for hardwoods. When the surface feels satin smooth, wet it to raise the grain, allow it to dry, then sand it again with the final-grit paper. Vacuum the surface with a vacuum-cleaner extension tool to remove dust; wipe with a tack rag, bought in a paint store—it has a "tacky" feeling, and dust particles adhere to it.

Stains. Used basically in two instances, stains can color bland woods, such as pine and poplar, or enhance the figure and deepen the color of most woods. If you decide to stain, test the color first on a piece of scrap wood of the same kind as the project; apply a coat of the final finish over the stain to see the end result. Characteristics of different kinds of stains used on furniture are described below.

When applying the stain, work on an area no larger than can be stained and wiped (if it is a wiping stain) in 15 minutes. First stain the back, then do the sides, the front, and drawer fronts, leaving the top until last. Coat end grain with thinned shellac before staining it; otherwise it will absorb more stain and will appear darker than the rest of the wood. Work with the grain. Start the brush an inch from the edge, and brush in both directions to avoid buildup on the edges.

Penetrating oil stain. Purchased ready to use, this stain is easy to apply and, as its name implies, penetrates deeply into the grain of the wood—more so in open-grain than close-grain woods. Use the stain on the kind of wood indicated by the color—e.g., walnut on walnut—as it will not give the same color on a different wood. Apply it with a wide, flat brush. After allowing the same amount of time for the stain to penetrate all parts of the surface, wipe off the excess with a cloth. One penetrating oil stain, marketed by Minwax, serves as the final finish too, followed by buffing or a coat of paste wax or oil; it can also be covered with other finishes. Penetrating oil stain bleeds through varnish, lacquer, or filler; to avoid this, apply a sealing coat of thin shellac after the stain has dried for 24 hours.

Pigment oil stain. Also applied with a brush and wiped off, this differs from penetrating oil stain in that the pigment remains on the wood's surface rather than penetrating it. Over a long period of time the color may fade. It is easy to apply. Pour a little more than 1 pint of turpentine into a metal container and add 1/2 pound of color, 6 ounces of boiled linseed oil, and 1/2 ounce of drier. Add the ingredients one at a time in that order, stirring after each addition. Stir the mixture frequently while applying it. Be sure to sand evenly, as any area that is not smooth will show up later. Drying time is 24 hours. Cover with a coat of shellac before applying filler. This stain works best on softwoods.

Water stain. This is made by mixing aniline dye with water that has boiled and dropped to just below the boiling point. Because it raises the grain, the wood must first be wetted, allowed to dry, then sanded with the same grit paper as the final sanding. Although not as easy to apply as oil stain, water stain gives a clear, permanent, and deeply penetrating stain. It works best on close-grain hardwoods. Apply it with a stiff brush, and allow 4 hours drying time. Apply two or more successive coats; each will darken the wood a little more. Do not use water stain on previously finished wood.

Alcohol stain. Also known as non-grain-raising stain, alcohol stain is extremely fast drying—nearly instant to 3 hours, depending on the brand—and is therefore difficult to use on a large area without leaving overlap marks. You mix it by dissolving alcohol-soluble dye powder in denatured alcohol—about 1/2 ounce of dye to 1 quart of alcohol. The stain works best on close-grain hardwood. It can penetrate a previous finish and is often used for

Wood finishes

FINISH	SURFACE EFFECT	COLOR EFFECT	SOLVENT/ THINNER	NO. OF COATS	BETWEEN COATS (hr)	APPLY WITH	RESISTS WATER
Varnish	Glossy, semiglossy, or satin	Clear to dark brown	Turpentine	2-3	24 (oil base) 12 (polyurethane)	Brush or spray	Fairly well
Shellac	Semiglossy	Clear; darkens wood slightly	Denatured alcohol	3-4	3 after first coat; 1 hr longer each subsequent coat	Natural-bristle brush	Poorly
Lacquer	Matte to high gloss	Clear; darkens wood least	Lacquer thinner	2-3	5; 24 before last coat	Natural-bristle brush or spray	Very well
Penetrating resin	Wood appears uncoated	Darkens wood most	Turpentine; ready to use—do not thin	1-2	12	Pour on; spread with rag or brush	Fairly well
Tung oil	Flat to semiglossy	Darkens wood slightly	Turpentine	1-2	24 or more	Rub in with rag, hand, or hard felt	Well

touching up damaged spots. Its disadvantage is that it fades in time.

Filler. Usually used to fill the pores on open-grain woods (p. 366), filler is unnecessary on close-grain woods. Although it comes in paste and liquid form, paste is generally recommended. Thin it with turpentine to the consistency of thick wall paint, then apply with a brush, first across the grain, then with the grain. In 10 to 15 minutes, when the filler looks gray or dull, wipe it off with a rough cloth such as burlap, first across the grain, then with the grain. Allow the piece to dry overnight before proceeding with the next step.

Sealer. Applied over stain and filler to prevent bleeding into the final finish, the usual sealer is shellac thinned 2 parts of 5-pound cut shellac (see below) to 1 part denatured alcohol. Lacquer and varnish thinned with equal parts of thinner may also be used, but never over an oil stain.

Final finish. Choose a finish appropriate to the wood and the use to which the piece will be put. A penetrating finish gives a natural wood look; a surface finish, a more traditional look.

Varnish. Many substances are sold under the name "varnish." Polyurethane, a synthetic varnish, is a good choice for tabletops because it gives superior protection against liquids and alcohol. Except when using varnish as a sealer (see above), apply it full strength. Apply the first coat across the grain with a full brush so that it flows on. Then, with an empty brush, rebrush with the grain from edge to edge in a continuous stroke, removing any air bubbles. Between coats rub with steel wool, using number 4/0 for a gloss finish, 3/0 for a satin or flat finish.

Shellac. This is the easiest surface finish to use. Because it dries faster than varnish, dust is not a problem in building a smooth finish. Shellac deteriorates after four to six months, so try to buy it labeled with an expiration date. Shellac is sold by the "cut"—e.g., 5-pound, 3-pound—meaning the number of pounds of shellac resin dissolved in 1 gallon of denatured alcohol. Three to four coats of 3-pound cut shellac, sanded between coats with very fine paper or steel wool, is appropriate; a thinner cut and more coats gives a silkier finish. To 5-pound cut shellac add 1 pint of denatured alcohol to make 3-pound cut; to 4-pound cut add 1/2 pint of alcohol. Do not apply shellac under damp conditions. Between coats wash the brush in warm, soapy water and rinse it. Do not use a nylon brush, as alcohol (as well as lacquer thinner) dissolves the bristles.

Lacquer. Unless you need to remove dust or high spots, lacquer requires no sanding between coats. Glossy lacquer gives a shiny, glasslike finish, while flat lacquer gives a matte finish. Both dry very quickly. Lacquer comes in two forms: for brushing or for spraying. Spraying lacquer dries faster and should not be used with a brush, but brushing lacquer can be sprayed. Stains and fillers tend to bleed through lacquer, as do rosewood and mahogany, so seal these with thinned shellac (see above) and do not sand the sealer.

Penetrating resin. Often labeled "Danish" or "natural" finish, this is the easiest of all finishes to apply. It soaks into the wood and solidifies the fibers, leaving the wood with a mellow patina that resists damage. Saturate the wood with the resin and allow it to penetrate for the time prescribed by the manufacturer; if dull spots appear during this time, apply more finish. At the end of the penetrating time—about 45 minutes—wipe off all excess. Let the finish dry overnight, wipe with a tack rag, apply a second coat, and wipe it after 30 minutes. Scratches can be repaired by rubbing them with steel wool and applying more finish.

Tung oil comes in two forms: pure or combined with varnish and other substances. Pure tung oil is a penetrating finish; tung oil varnish penetrates the wood and coats the surface. Use the pure form for a satin finish; for a semigloss finish use tung oil varnish. Like traditional linseed oil, tung oil must be rubbed hard to generate the heat that helps it penetrate.

Rubbing. The final step for a surface finish, rubbing is unnecessary with a tung oil or penetrating resin finish. Rubbing may involve simply removing the surface imperfections and cutting the high gloss with 4/0 steel wool. Or it can be done with wet/dry sandpaper (p. 368) followed by polishing with a paste wax. Finishes that are to be rubbed should be applied in at least three coats, and the last coat should be allowed to dry for 48 hours.

Make a pad of the steel wool. Rub with the grain, turning the pad as it wears. Rubber gloves will prevent steel slivers from injuring your hand. Do not rub any longer than necessary to reach the desired look. On open-grain woods rubbing should be done with fine-grit wet/dry sandpaper.

Wet/dry sandpaper gives a satin finish. Lubricate the paper with water unless the finish is shellac, for which use oil. Soak fine-grit (No. 500 or 600) paper in the lubricant, then rub the surface with moderate pressure, with the grain, and one section at a time. Keep the paper wet. Wipe off the surface with a clean cloth dampened with water or, if oil was used, benzine. Wet/dry sandpaper can also be used between coats of finish.

For the final coat most professional finishers choose a paste wax or, in the case of a lacquer finish, a rubbing compound similar to automobile wax. Apply the wax or compound with a dampened cloth, rub vigorously, and remove excess with a clean cloth.

Stripping an old finish

To refinish an old piece of furniture, you follow the same procedure as for finishing new wood, except that you must first strip the old finish and make any needed repairs. Paint and varnish remover is the usual method of getting rid of the old finish. Sanding has its role in the cleanup, but if used to remove the finish, it is likely also to remove the patina that has built up over time on the wood's surface.

Paint remover is highly flammable; therefore, work in a well-ventilated room or outdoors, provided you are in the shade. Wear rubber gloves and old clothes. Protect the floor or ground with newspaper. Dispose of all used rags, brushes, and newspaper immediately.

Paint remover comes in liquid or paste form. The liquid is more efficient, but the paste is handy for vertical surfaces if you cannot turn the piece to work on each surface horizontally. Some liquids are scraped off with a putty knife or refinishing scraper; others are washed off with water—you can use a garden hose if you are outdoors. You will need about 1 quart of remover for each 100 square feet of surface. Apply remover generously with an old natural-bristle brush. Follow the maker's directions as to how long to let it soften the old finish. If using a knife or scraper, take care not to damage the wood. Use burlap or coarse steel wool on curves. Clean out crevices in turned parts with coarse string or a piece of twisted burlap. For a thick, stubborn finish, you may have to repeat the application.

When all of the old finish is gone, rub the surface clean with rags and turpentine, lacquer thinner, or a wood cleaner made especially for this purpose. This dissolves any remaining remover, which, if left on, would inhibit the wood from taking a new finish evenly.

Dry the piece overnight, then sand. You can use cheap flint paper, but it will clog quickly and will have to be discarded. Make repairs, such as gluing loose parts. Raise dents in the wood's surface by pressing them with a steam iron set at high temperature and applied over a wet cloth folded double. Fill cracks and holes with wood putty or shellac stick, or make your own filler by mixing sawdust and glue. Sand the repairs smooth and, if necessary, stain them to match the old wood. Then proceed to apply the new finish to the wood.

Woodworking/projects

A knuckle-jointed jewelry box

The joinery of this 9- by 18- by 4⅜-inch box is dramatized by the knuckle joints that hinge the dual lid. The box is ideal for practicing woodworking techniques. Use it for jewelry—the tray with round compartments holds small items—or make a notched crosspiece and line the box with tarnish-resistant cloth to hold silver.

Materials and tools. The wood is dark, oiled walnut. The bottom is plywood. You need 3/16-inch dowel rod for the rabbet joints, screws to attach the knobs, 1/2-inch wire brads for the bottom, 1/16-inch steel rod for the knuckle joint, and velvet to line the bottom of the box and the compartments in the tray. In addition to the tools mentioned, you need four bar clamps with 2-foot openings.

Dual lid opens to reveal a lift-out tray resting on thin ledges (right) that are glued into grooves in ends. Sides are rabbeted into ends; joints are reinforced with dowels. Bottom is rabbeted into sides and ends. When shut, lid rests on 3/4- by 3/16-in. rabbet cut across upper edge of ends.

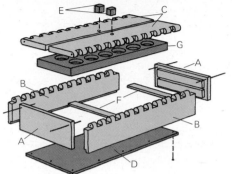

Part	Finished size (in.)	Number
A End	5/8 x 4 3/8 x 9	2
B Side	5/8 x 4 3/8 x 17 1/4	2
C Lid	3/4 x 4 1/2 x 17 1/8	2
D Bottom (plywood)	1/8 x 8 1/8 x 17 1/4	1
E Knob	3/8 x 5/8 x 5/8	2
F Ledge	1/8 x 3/4 x 7 5/8	2
G Tray	1 5/16 x 5 3/16 x 16 1/2	1

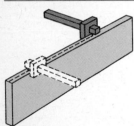

Knuckle joint. 1. On edges of sides and lids to be hinged, mark the center line by holding the marking gauge against one face, then the other, until point marks the same line.

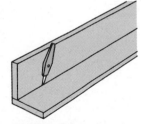

2. Mark the shoulder lines of the joint by transferring the thickness of the lid to side piece and the thickness of side piece to lid. Note that the lid is 1/8 in. thicker than side.

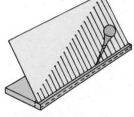

3. Divide lid edges into 23 equal spaces by method shown on page 370. Clamp paired side and lid face to face; transfer lines just drawn. Extend lines to the shoulder lines.

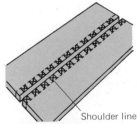

Shoulder line

4. Mark alternate spaces on each edge with X's to indicate waste. Make saw cuts to the shoulder line, cutting on the waste side of the line. Do this on all four pieces.

5. Round corners of knuckle joints with rasp and/or plane. Move rasp back and forth at 45° angle, simultaneously traveling length of edge. See next picture for angle of cuts.

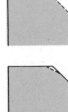

Remove corner with plane or rasp

Remove corners made by first pass

6. First pass removes corner; second pass removes corners created by first pass. Continue making flat areas until surface appears rounded. Use plane in similar way.

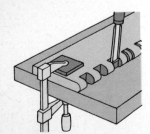

7. Saw relief cuts in waste; remove waste with chisel as for dovetail joint (p. 378). Sand chiseled surfaces with abrasive paper wrapped around square scrap that fits opening.

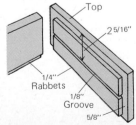

Top

2 5/16"

1/4" Rabbets

1/8" Groove

5/8"

Joints. 8. In ends cut rabbets (pp. 376–377) and grooves 1/4 in. deep and widths shown. Grooves hold ledge. Cut 1/4- by 1/4-in. rabbets in bottom edges of sides.

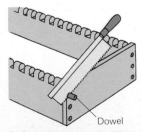

Dowel

9. Glue sides and ends. When glue has dried, drill holes for 3/16-in. dowel. Glue dowels; when dry, trim dowels and sand flush. Glue ledges into grooves in ends.

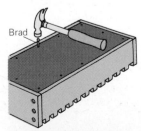

Brad

10. Glue plywood bottom into place in rabbeted sides and ends. After the glue has dried, reinforce joint with 1/2-in. wire brads spaced at intervals of about 4 in.

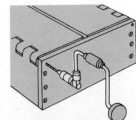

11. Drill 1/16-in. holes in ends. Tap brads into first two knuckles and test lid's action. Remove brads. Drill into knuckles, insert steel rod; cut off. Fill hole with plastic wood.

12. With brace and expansive bit or drill press and multispur bit, cut 12 holes 2 in. in diameter and 3/4 in. deep in tray. Finish box and tray. Line both with velvet. Screw on knobs.

A box of miniature perfection

A single piece of wood 5/4 (1¼ in.) by 6 by 27 in. yields all four parts (right). Plane wood to 1 in. thick before laying out cuts (far right, center). Router jigs (far right, bottom) are of 3/4-in. plywood screwed to 1-in.-thick squared wood. Distance from edge of router base to edge of bit, different for each router, determines inner dimensions of jigs.

A beautiful object to hold and behold, this 5¼- by 5½- by 1½-inch box with leather-lined drawer is made from one piece of purpleheart. Another hardwood, such as mahogany (which is easier to work than purpleheart), could be used. The grain of the wood must be straight and regular.

The box was designed around the power router (p. 364). A router is as precise as the jig guiding it. Be sure that the parts of the jigs are squared (p. 372); test their accuracy on scrap wood. Line each jig with a thin shim of tin or cardboard. Rout the waste with a 1-inch straight bit in several passes, each a little deeper. Remove the shim; make one pass to smooth the wood.

Finish. Apply two coats of penetrating resin (pp. 370–371); after 24 hours apply a third coat with No. 400 wet/dry sandpaper. Apply finish inside box with rags on dowels; wipe dry. The kid-leather drawer-bottom lining is tooled (see *Leatherworking*, p. 20). Stain it and the narrow strip for the drawer sides to match the wood before gluing them with contact cement.

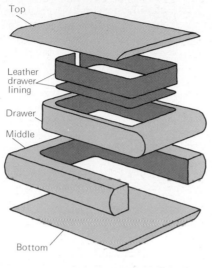

Top
Leather drawer lining
Drawer
Middle
Bottom

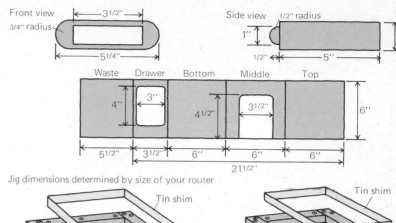

Front view — 3½"
3/4" radius
5¼"
Side view — ½" radius
1"
½"— 5"
1½"

Waste | Drawer | Bottom | Middle | Top
4" | 3" | 4½" | 3½" | 6"
5½" | 3½" | 6" | 6" | 6"
21½"

Jig dimensions determined by size of your router

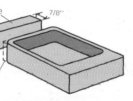
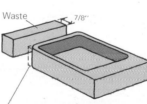

Jig for middle
Tin shim
1" wood
3/4" plywood

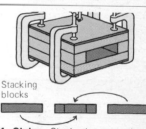

Jig for drawer
Tin shim

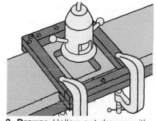

Work
Scrap wood

1. Routing middle. Screw work to like-size scrap wood through portion to be routed. Clamp jig to work and table. Rout waste; remove shim and make final (smoothing) cut.

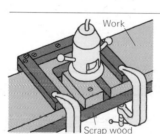

2. Drawer. Hollow out drawer with router. Last pass should be to 11/16 in. Remove shim; make final pass at same depth to smooth wood. Saw pieces apart.

Waste
7/8"
Remove corner with rasp

3. Shaping drawer. Saw off waste. Transfer arc of middle piece to back corners of drawer. Shape with rasp. Test-fit drawer in box (see next step) before gluing box.

Stacking blocks

4. Gluing. Stack pieces so that grain looks continuous at joints. Sand inside lightly. Glue sparingly to avoid drips inside. Clamp with wood scraps to even pressure.

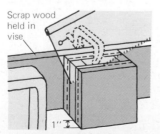

Scrap wood held in vise
1"

5. Cutting to size. Lay out lines for final thickness (see side view above). With backsaw or table saw, cut near lines, leaving 1/32 in. for planing. Plane to lines.

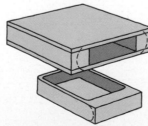

6. Shaping curves. From views at top of page make templates for sides and drawer front. Mark curves on wood. With very sharp plane shape as in Step 6, p. 392.

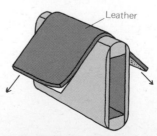

Leather

7. Smoothing curves. Remove plane marks with cabinet scraper. Sand sides and drawer front with abrasive paper backed with leather. Sand drawer to fit opening.

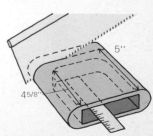

5"
4 5/8"

8. Trimming box to size. Measure depth of drawer opening; mark on box's top. Saw waste, leaving 3/8 in. wood at back and total depth of 5 in. front to back.

Woodworking/project

A Shaker sewing stand

This functional table typifies Shaker design at its best: its lines are simple, its proportions harmonious, and its joinery classic.

Materials. The table is cherry throughout, including the drawer bottoms. The top is three boards edge joined (p. 374). The parts list at the end of this text gives the finished size of each piece of wood. For a discussion of how to buy hardwood, see pages 366–367. For the spindle base buy wood dressed to 2¾ inches square and 22 inches long; for the knobs buy a 1-inch square 6 inches long. If you order wood cut to exact dimensions, request the pieces for the top and drawer fronts 1/32 inch thicker than the finished sizes to allow for planing. Buy ten 1⅛-inch wood screws to attach the runners and four 3/4-inch screws to attach stops.

Procedure. Cut all pieces close to size if they are not so cut. Check for squareness (p. 372) and plane as necessary. Saw the legs with a bandsaw, saber saw, or coping saw; shape them with a rasp, spokeshave, and cabinet scraper. Edge join the top. Plane and sand all parts. Turn the spindle base and the drawer knobs. Then cut the dovetailed grooves that join the legs and spindle base. (A similar joint is shown on page 377.) Here, because the groove is difficult to control on a round surface, cut the groove first and the entering part second. Apply finish to the spindle and legs. Next make the drawers (see opposite); then assemble all parts as shown opposite.

Finish. Sand with 280-grit paper; then wet the wood to raise the grain. When dry, sand lightly with the used paper. Finish the table with any finish.

Part	Finished size (in.)	No.
A Top	9/16 x 6 1/8 x 20	3
B Spindle base	2 5/8 diam x 19 3/8	1
C Legs	11/16 x 12 x 12*	3
D Center guide	7/8 x 3 x 15	1
E Side guides	7/8 x 1 1/2 x 15	2
F Stops	3/8 x 3/8 x 2 3/4	2
Drawers		
G Front	3/4 x 3 1/2 x 5	2
H Sides	1/4 x 3 1/2 x 16 1/4	4
I Back	5/16 x 3 1/2 x 5	2
J Bottom	1/4 x 4 3/4 x 15 3/4	2
K Runners	3/8 x 3/8 x 15	4
L Knobs	7/8 diam x 1 3/8	2

*Board for one leg; see template for shape

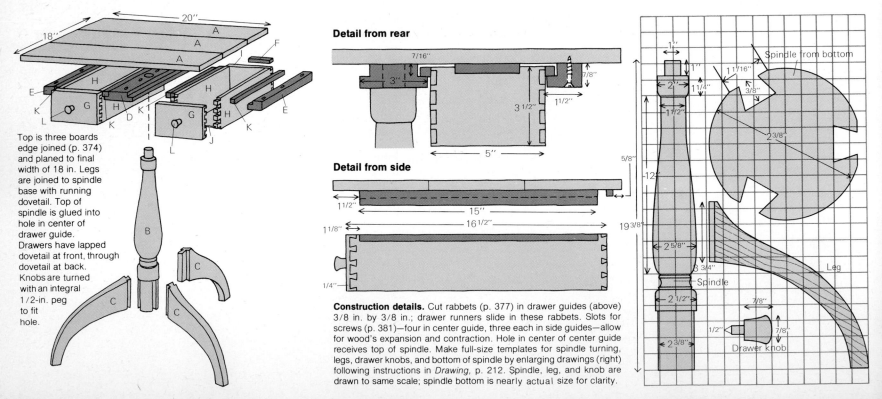

Top is three boards edge joined (p. 374) and planed to final width of 18 in. Legs are joined to spindle base with running dovetail. Top of spindle is glued into hole in center of drawer guide. Drawers have lapped dovetail at front, through dovetail at back. Knobs are turned with an integral 1/2-in. peg to fit hole.

Detail from rear

Detail from side

Construction details. Cut rabbets (p. 377) in drawer guides (above) 3/8 in. by 3/8 in.; drawer runners slide in these rabbets. Slots for screws (p. 381)—four in center guide, three each in side guides—allow for wood's expansion and contraction. Hole in center of center guide receives top of spindle. Make full-size templates for spindle turning, legs, drawer knobs, and bottom of spindle by enlarging drawings (right) following instructions in *Drawing*, p. 212. Spindle, leg, and knob are drawn to same scale; spindle bottom is nearly actual size for clarity.

Spindle from bottom

Leg

Spindle

Drawer knob

Constructing the drawers

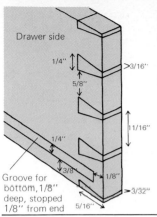

Dovetails. See pp. 378-379 for making dovetail joints. Half pins at top and bottom edges are slim; take extra care not to split wood. Drawing shows dovetail for drawer back; measurements for lapped dovetail at front are same, except pins are 1/2 in. long. Drill holes in drawer fronts for turned knobs before assembling drawers.

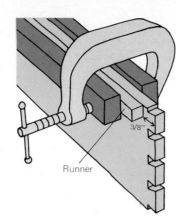

Runners. Prepare runners and drawer sides as for an edge joint (p. 374). Place runners 3/8 inch from back end of drawer sides. Glue runners to drawer sides. Clamp with thicker strips of wood on both sides to spread the pressure from the clamps. Use three C-clamps on each drawer side. No nails or screws are necessary.

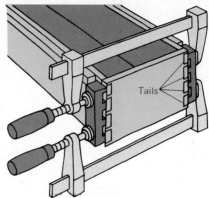

Assembly. Make four jigs of scrap wood cut so that when clamped, pressure bears on the tails only. Glue front and back corners on one side of drawer at a time with other drawer side and bottom in place to hold drawer's shape. Front-to-back clamps may be necessary if fit is loose. Fit the turned knobs into the drawer fronts after assembly.

Cutting the dovetailed groove

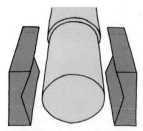 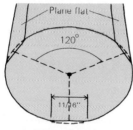 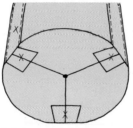 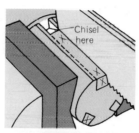 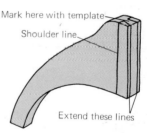 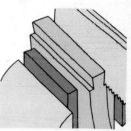

1. From two pieces of softwood cut jigs to hold spindle in vise. Leave one face of each jig flat, and cut other face V-shaped on a power saw.

2. With T-bevel mark three 120° angles at center of spindle bottom. Plane three flat areas 11/16 in. wide up spindle 3¾ in. with a three-in-one plane.

3. From pattern opposite make template for grooves. Center template on each line; mark. With small try square, extend lines 3¾ in.

4. Chisel 3/4-in. mortise at groove's end so that saw can move. Cut sides of groove with dovetail saw; rout or chisel out waste between cuts (p. 377).

5. Check entering ends of legs for squareness. Center template on edges, and mark. Extend lines across ends. Mark shoulder lines on leg faces.

6. With dovetail saw cut away waste. Dovetail should slide into groove with gentle tapping. Clamp spindle in jig made in Step 1; glue legs one at a time.

Assembling the parts

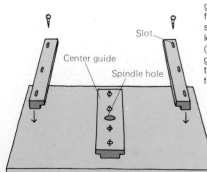

Drill hole in center guide for spindle top; fit must be snug. Drill slots for screws lengthwise in guides (p. 381). Screw center guide to underside of tabletop 1½ in. from front and back edges.

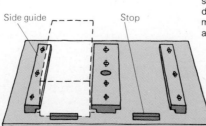

Set drawers in place in center guide; measure and mark for placement of side guides. Attach with screws. Again set drawers in place and mark position of stops; attach with screws.

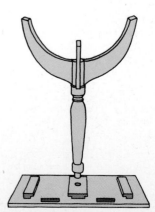

Sand spindle top if too tight in hole. Place level across legs to check that they are level. Glue spindle with one leg parallel to center guide and pointing to rear. Sand and finish the table.

Woodworking/project

A blanket chest

Pale birch plywood panels contrast with deeper brown of the mahogany framework.

Mahogany rails frame birch plywood panels in this chest that exemplifies frame-and-panel construction (p. 382). Its plywood lid, strong enough to sit upon, is edged with solid birch strips that hide the plywood layers. Its dimensions are 44¾ inches long, 18¾ inches wide, and 19⅝ inches high.

Materials. Legs, rails, and muntins (see chart) are solid mahogany; the panels and bottom are from a 4- by 8-foot sheet of 1/2-inch birch plywood, good one face; and the lid is 1⅛-inch birch plywood, good two faces, which may have to be specially ordered. You need solid birch strips for edging the front, sides, and back of the lid. Two brass hinges and two fall-flap stays (p. 385) secure the lid.

Tools. In addition to the usual tools for marking and cutting joints, you will need a minimum of three bar clamps (p. 361) with 4-foot openings, six C-clamps, a smooth plane, a fore plane, and a three-in-one plane (p. 362). Cutting the grooves for the panels and the bottom by hand is time-consuming, so try to obtain the use of a power router or a table saw with dado blades. If the latter is available, by all means use it to cut the tenons for the joints with a tenoning jig to hold the work (see picture, opposite).

Procedure. First mark and cut all mortise-and-tenon joints. If working by hand, follow the procedure on page 379. If using a table saw, cut the tenons first; you will still have to cut the mortises by hand. Dry fit the skeleton frame; check measurements to make sure they are as planned and to ascertain the size to cut the plywood panels. Plane smooth the rails' inner surfaces that will have grooves in them.

Next, cut the grooves for the panels (opposite); make test grooves in scrap wood until you find a router bit or a setting on the table saw that cuts a groove the correct width for the plywood. Round edges of frames with a rasp and scraper (p. 362). Saw the plywood panels and bottom, making sure that the grain will run the length of each panel. Sand the edges and surfaces, and finish the panels with a penetrating resin finish.

Follow the directions opposite for gluing and clamping. Then attach and shape the lid's edging as shown. Install hinges and fall-flap stays. Slightly round the outer corners of the mahogany rails with a rasp. Sand the outer mahogany surfaces and the lid, and apply penetrating resin finish (pp. 390–391). Do not get any finish on the already finished panels.

Part		Finished size (in.)	No.
Mahogany			
A	Leg	1 3/4 x 1 3/4 x 18 1/2	4
B	Rail	1 3/4 x 1 3/4 x 38 3/4	4
C	Rail	1 3/4 x 1 3/4 x 16 3/4	4
D	Muntin	1 3/4 x 1 3/4 x 14 3/4	2
Birch plywood			
E	Lid	1 1/8* x 18 3/8 x 42 1/4	1
F	Panel	1/2* x 13 x 18	4
G	Panel	1/2* x 13 x 15	2
H	Bottom	1/2* x 36 13/16 x 14 13/16	1
Solid birch			
I	Edging	3/16 x 1 1/8 x 42 1/4	2
J	Edging	1 3/4 x 1 1/8 x 18 3/4	2

* Nominal thickness of plywood

Mortise-and-tenon joints

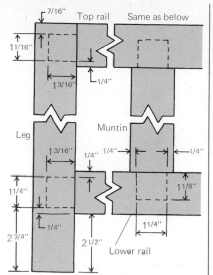

Tenons are 9/16 in. thick and centered on width of work; other dimensions are shown above. Where tenons meet inside mortises at corners, their ends should be mitered (p. 383).

Jig for table saw

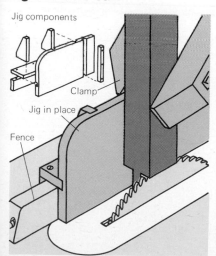

Jig components

Clamp

Jig in place

Fence

Tenoning jig of 3/4-in. plywood (top) fits rip fence, allows safe, rapid cutting of tenons. Each tenon requires eight cuts. Make like cuts on all rails before changing saw's setting.

Cutting grooves for panels and bottom

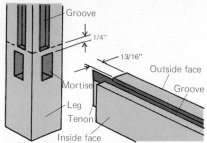

Groove

Mortise

Leg

Tenon

Outside face

Groove

Inside face

Cut the stopped grooves (pp. 376–377) in rails and legs and through grooves in muntins with router or table saw. Grooves are width of plywood, 1/4 in. deep, 13/16 in. from rail's outer surface, and stopped 1/4 in. from mortise. Chisel ends of stopped grooves square.

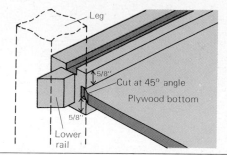

Leg

Cut at 45° angle

Plywood bottom

Lower rail

Cut the grooves in lower rails width of plywood bottom, 1/4 in. deep, and length of rails. Do not cut into legs; saw off corner of bottom at 45° angle, measured 1/2 in. each way. Cut will not show. Round corners of rails and muntins with rasp (p. 392 and next photo).

Assembling the chest

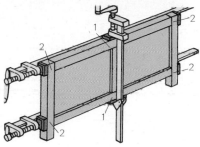

Glue front and back in two stages. 1. Glue muntins into rails with legs and panels in place; clamp horizontally and across joints. 2. Glue rails into legs; clamp across joints. Add bead of glue to panel grooves for rigidity. Scrap wood protects wood from clamps.

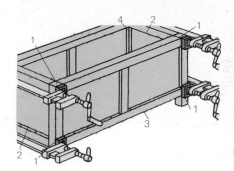

Glue front to back in four stages. 1. Glue side rails into front legs. 2. Remove unglued parts, add bead of glue to side panel grooves, glue all panels except bottom. 3. Glue bottom into front and side rails with back in place. 4. Glue side rails, bottom into back.

Edging and hinges on lid

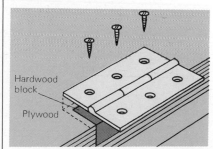

Hardwood block

Plywood

1. To hold hinges securely, sink block of solid wood into back edge of lid inside of where edging will be and 7 in. from side edge of lid. Block should be 1/16 in. smaller than hinge and 3/4 in. deep into plywood. Remove waste with chisel or router.

Bar clamp

Edging

Scrap wood buffer

3. Glue side edging (pieces J) to sides of lid. When glue has dried, plane upper and lower corners of edging to curves as shown in next step. Use rasp if you encounter stubborn grain. Finish with hand scraper and abrasive paper.

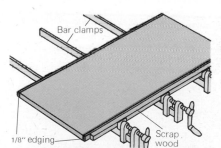

Bar clamps

1/8" edging

Scrap wood

2. Glue solid birch edging (pieces I) to front and back edges of lid. Clamp with continuous pieces of scrap wood as shown. When glue has dried, plane or sand edging flush with lid. Lightly sand corners of edging.

4. Round edging by planing a series of small flats with a plane in the same way a rasp makes a curve (p. 392, Step 6). Refine curve with hand scraper and/or No. 80 garnet paper. Attach hinges and fall-flap stays (p. 385).

Woodworking/project

Slat-backed chair

Here is a chair of unique design and comfort. Made to fit the curve of the human spine, it has a back of slats that ride freely in grooves, allowing for the natural expansion and contraction of wood. All joints are mortise and tenon.

Materials. The framework is cherry and the slats are walnut. The plywood seat platform is covered with leather that matches the walnut. Choose a light cherry to contrast with the dark walnut of the slats. For the seat buy 1-inch-thick foam rubber, a piece of leather 20 by 21 inches, eight No. 10 1½-inch round-head screws, and four No. 8 1¾-inch flat-head screws.

Tools. This chair must be made largely with hand tools—dovetail saw, chisels for mortising, planes, rasp, cab-inet scraper, and the usual measuring and marking tools. To shape the chair parts, a band saw or saber saw is almost a necessity. Use a router to cut grooves for the slats in the back legs and to shape the slats. Cutting the many tenons will go faster if you can use a table saw with tenoning jig (p. 397).

Procedure. Mark and cut all joints before the members are shaped, with one exception: shape the back leg post first. The order of operations is detailed opposite and on page 400.

Finish. Do the initial sanding of all parts before gluing them. The slats should be final sanded and the finish applied before the chair is assembled. Finish the chair with a penetrating resin or tung oil (pp. 390–391).

Part		Finished size (in.)	Number
A	Front leg	1 1/4 x 2 1/8 x 17 1/8	2
B	Back leg post	1 1/4 x 5 3/16 x 45*	2
C	Side seat rail	7/8 x 3 5/8 x 12 5/8*	2
D	Front seat rail	7/8 x 2 1/2 x 14 1/4*	1
E	Back seat rail	7/8 x 3 5/8 x 14 1/4*	1
F	Top back rail	1 1/4 x 4 x 14 1/4	1
G	Cross rail	7/8 x 2 7/8 x 14 1/4*	1
H	Stretcher	7/8 x 3 1/8 x 14 3/8*	2
I	Crosspiece	7/8 x 2 1/4 x 14 1/8*	1
J	Slat	13/16 x 1 1/16 x 13 1/4	14
K	Plywood seat	1/2 x 13 1/2 x 14 5/8	1
L	Corner blocks	1 1/8 x 1 1/2 x 4 1/2	4

* Size of cut lumber; piece is shaped as in drawings within grid (below)

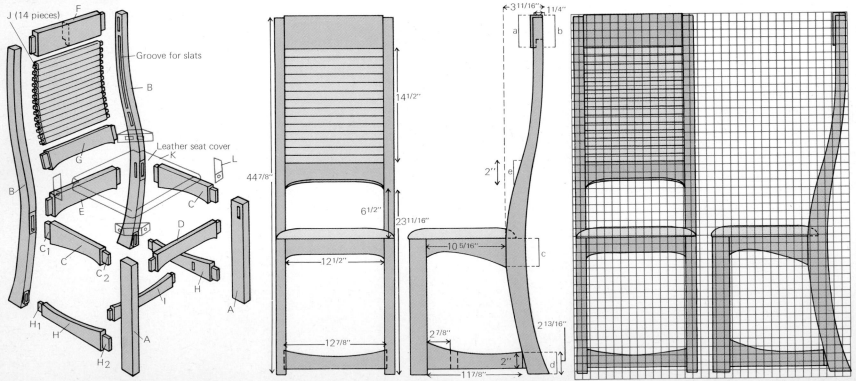

Each square represents 1 sq in.; to enlarge to full size, see *Drawing*, p. 212. Trace templates members before laying out joints.

Marking and cutting mortise-and-tenon joints

Joints. Dimensions of mortise-and-tenon joints are given in chart at right. Rough shaping cuts shown below in two members (C and H) aid in cutting tenons. If making joints by hand, cut mortises first and tenons second. If working with a table saw, cut tenons first and mortises second. Mark and cut joints before shaping pieces (Step 10) except for back leg post, which is shaped first (Steps 5 and 6).

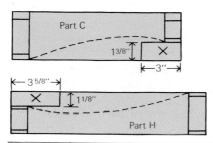

Part C

$1 3/8''$

$3''$

$3 5/8''$

$1 1/8''$

Part H

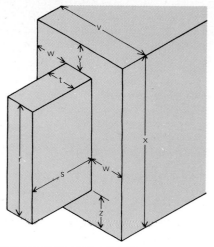

PART (in inches)	r	s	t	v	w	x	y	z
C_1	2 3/4	1 1/4	5/16	7/8	9/32	3 5/8	1/2	3/8
C_2	1 3/8	1 1/4	5/16	7/8	9/32	3 5/8	5/8	1/4*
D	1 3/4	7/8	5/16	7/8	9/32	2 1/2	3/8	3/8
E	2 7/8	7/8	5/16	7/8	9/32	3 5/8	3/8	3/8
F	2 5/8	7/8	7/16	1 1/4	13/32	4	1	3/8
G	2	7/8	5/16	7/8	9/32	2 7/8	7/16	7/16
H_1	1 1/2	1 1/4	5/16	7/8	9/32	3 1/8	1/4*	1/4
H_2	2 1/2	1 1/4	5/16	7/8	9/32	3 1/8	3/8	1/4
I	1 1/2	9/16	5/16	7/8	9/32	2 1/4	3/8	3/8

Chart keyed to exploded view on facing page
1 Tenon into back leg
2 Tenon into front leg
* Size of shoulder after preliminary waste is cut away (see diagrams, left)

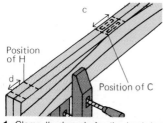

1. Clamp the boards for the back leg posts (B) inner face to inner face. Mark their inner edges for the position of the stretchers (H) and the side seat rails (C). Lay out but do not cut the mortises for the tenons of C.

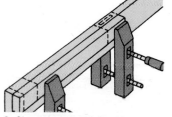

2. Clamp each B with its front leg (A) inner face to inner face, with inner edges aligned; transfer the lines for H and C from B to A. Square these lines (p. 370) and those drawn in Step 1 around all sides of A and B.

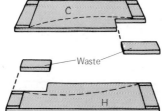

3. Mark and cut mortises for C and H on the front legs; also cut the mortises laid out in Step 1. Lay out the corresponding tenons on C and H. For ease in cutting tenons, saw out a piece of waste as shown; cut the tenons.

4. Clamp two B pieces together. Mark 4 in. from top of B for lower edge of F; mark 23⅝ in. and 26½ in. from bottom of B for G. E intersects B at same level as C. Square all lines just drawn onto both faces of B pieces.

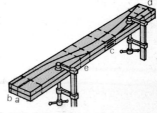

5. With table saw or handsaw make three straight saw cuts in B: one at a, another at b, and a third at d. The edge at c is already straight. If necessary, redraw the pattern of the curve to conform to the saw cuts.

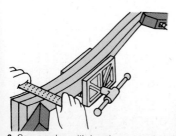

6. Saw one leg with band saw or saber saw. Lay it on other leg; correct lines to match if necessary. Saw other leg. Clamp legs together and shape identically with rasp (p. 392) and scraper except d. Edges at e must be straight.

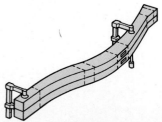

7. Lay each side's parts on full-scale drawing to check joint alignment. Clamp back legs with inner faces together; extend lines for positions of F, G, and H across the sawn and rasped edges. Unclamp the legs.

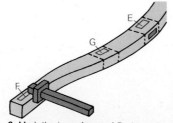

8. Mark the inner faces of B pieces for mortises with the marking gauge set as follows: for G, 1/2 in. and 13/16 in.; for F, 1/2 in. and 15/16 in.; for E, 17/32 in. and 27/32 in. Cut the mortises and tenons (see above).

9. Mortise back legs for stretchers (H); cut tenons in H. Saw off piece in front of back leg, and chisel-trim back leg to meet outside edges of H. Make mortises in H for crosspiece (I) and cut corresponding tenons in I.

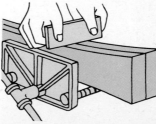

10. One at a time saw shapes of seat rails, stretchers, cross rail, and crosspiece with band saw or saber saw. With like pieces clamped together, finish shaping with rasp and cabinet scraper. Round edges of top back rail (F).

399

Woodworking/projects

Slat-backed chair *(continued)*

1. Cut a rabbet in lower back edge of top back rail 7/8 in. deep and 3/8 in. wide. The rabbet allows space for the slats to expand when the weather is humid.

2. Cut grooves 7/16 in. deep and 1/4 in. wide in inner faces of back leg posts. Groove is 15/32 in. from front edge and extends from cross rail to top back rail. Use router fence designed to follow a curve; bear against front edge of work. Use a 1/4-in. straight bit.

3. Lay out the tenons on each end of the walnut slats. They should be 1/4 in. thick, 1/4 in. deep, and 3/8 in. long. Cut the tenons with dovetail saw if working by hand; if table saw is available, make identical cuts on both ends of slats all at the same time. Number slats on ends in order of fit.

4. Mount router in shaper table (homemade, such as one shown, or purchased), and use a corner round bit with 3/8-in. radius to shape the edges of slats. Sand slats with No. 80 garnet paper to smooth transition between routed surfaces and front and back of slats.

Assembly

1. Do a dry run of the clamping arrangement (left). For the actual gluing, have someone help you. Use a slow-drying glue (p. 368). With the piece sawn out of leg post board as scrap, glue all members of one side into place at one time. Repeat for other side.

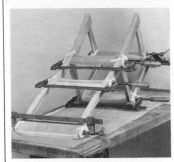

2. Glue lateral pieces —D, E, F, G, and I— into one side only, but with other side in place to maintain squareness of joints. When glue is dry, unclamp and remove the unglued side.

3. Place slats in groove of glued side in numbered order. If fit is tight, trim top slat to narrower width, leaving 1/4 in. space to allow for expansion of slats upward into rabbet in top back rail.

4. Place second side atop lateral members, and barely insert tenons of lateral members into mortises. Spread glue on the tenons—but do not allow any glue to dribble onto slats. Tighten clamps.

The seat

1. Miter corner blocks for seat supports so that they fit as shown. Chisel flats to seat two No. 10 1½-in. round-head screws. In center of blocks drill holes for No. 8 screws 1¾ in. long that will enter bottom of plywood seat. Insert blocks 1/4 in. below chair seat rail. Mark position of screw holes on seat bottom.

2. Cut the 1-in. foam for seat 1/2 in. larger on front and sides than seat platform, flush at back and at L-shaped cutouts. Cover with muslin, pulled tight to round edges of foam. Staple muslin to bottom of seat platform.

3. Cut leather for seat cover 3 in. larger all around to allow for tacking on bottom of plywood. Pull leather smooth. Tack with 3/8-in. upholstery tacks. Work from center of each side toward corners; leave corners untacked for next step.

4. Cut two triangles from leather, one each side of each corner. At L-shaped corners make a slit from corner of leather to edge of seat. Fold corners as though wrapping a package. Tack down; do not tack over marks made in Step 1, above. Screw platform to blocks from underside of chair.

Woodworking/project

A jewelry chest

This jewellike miniature chest, 10 inches across, 7 inches deep, and 7 inches high, is fitted with three drawers. Corners are miter jointed (p.379).

Materials and tools. The chest is cherry; the drawers are of padouk, an exotic wood. Drawer bottoms are of 1/8-inch tempered Masonite. Velvet lines the drawers. The necessary tools are mentioned in the instructions. If a table saw is available, cut the miters on it (and the grooves). If the blade angle is accurately set, you may not have to plane the sawn surfaces. Make a test box of scrap wood to ensure that the saw and plane jigs (Steps 2 and 3) or the saw setting is accurate.

Procedure. Check that all edges, ends, and faces are absolutely square (p. 372)—if they are not, the miters will not match. For the case, follow the steps below. Before making the drawers, measure the width of drawer housings and adjust 9¼-inch dimension of drawers if necessary. Cut drawer miters (p. 379). Drawer bottoms are housed in grooves 1/8 inch from bottom of all parts, 1/8 inch deep, and 9/64 inch wide. Cut these and glue in bottoms.

Sand all parts before assembly except the gluing surfaces, and finish the top with penetrating resin (pp. 390–391). Apply a thin coat of glue to all miter-joint surfaces, let it sink in, and reapply glue before clamping. Finish other parts when glue has dried.

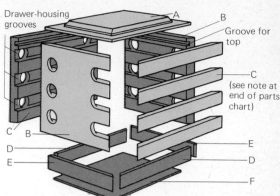

Four strips across front are cut from front board (C) after miter joints have been cut. Drawers fit into grooves on inside of back and sides. Add an extra inch to the lengths (last dimension in chart) of B, C, D, and E to allow for waste from miter-joint cuts.

Drawer-housing grooves

A
B
Groove for top
C
(see note at end of parts chart)
E
D
F

Part		Finished size (in.)	Number
Case:			
A	Top	5/8 x 6 1/4 x 9 1/4	1
B	Side	5/8 x 7 x 7	2
C	Front* & back	5/8 x 7 x 10	2
Drawers:			
D	Front & back	1/4 x 31/32 x 9 1/4	6
E	Side	1/4 x 31/32 x 6 1/4	6
F	Drawer bottom	1/8 x 6 x 9	3

* Later cut into four separate strips

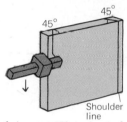

1. Lay out 45° angles on edges of sides, front, and back with T-bevel or combination square; orient boards so that grain runs same way all around. Draw shoulder lines with marking gauge across both faces of each board.

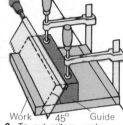

2. To cut miters, make a saw guide of 1- by 3- by 7-in. wood beveled at 45° angle. Clamp it and work to table; cut joint with dovetail saw, leaving 1/32 in. to be planed in next step. If using a table saw, cut on line, allowing for kerf.

3. Make a guide of 2- by 3¼- by 6-in. wood beveled at 45° angle. Clamp to bottom of plane. Test accuracy by planing for duplicate B's and C's and clamping to test fit of miters. Clamp work in vise, and plane down to shoulder line.

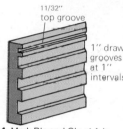

4. Mark B's and C's at 1-in. intervals for drawer housings; mark 5/16 in. from tops for grooves to hold A. Cut drawer grooves in sides and back and groove for A in all pieces by hand (p. 376), router, or table saw. Grooves are 1/4 in. deep.

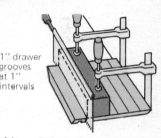

5. On front piece only mark 1-in. interval lines drawn in previous step on outside face. Saw piece into seven strips (three are waste), cutting on waste side of lines to leave enough wood for planing smooth. Plane down to lines.

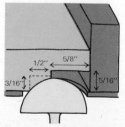

6. On edges of A cut rabbets 5/8 in. wide and 5/16 in. deep. Then mount the router in shaper table (p. 400); use 1¼ -in.-diameter core box bit. Adjust depth of cut and router fence so that bit cuts 3/16 in. deep and 1/2 in. wide.

7. With brace and 1-in. bit or drill press and multispur bit, drill six holes in each side and in back. Drill from each face of 1-in. grooves for drawer housings. In all cases centers of holes should be 1¼ in. from outside corner of piece.

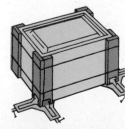

8. At front edge of each side piece (B) draw tangential lines from top and bottom of each hole to edge. Saw on waste side of these lines with dovetail saw to remove section of wood. Use bevel-edge chisel to smooth cuts to lines.

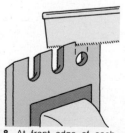

9. Make four corner jigs like those on page 379, but 7 in. high with several grooves to hold twine. Wax jigs' inner surfaces. Place bottom edges of case's back corners in corner clamps. Apply glue (see text); tighten twine around jigs.

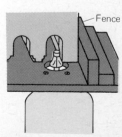

10. Clean surfaces of dried glue by sanding. Using shaper table, rout edges of four front strips, top, and holes with a two-fluted beading bit with 1/16-in. radius. Cut and assemble drawers (see text); line their bottoms with velvet.

Woodworking/project

Zebrawood coffee table

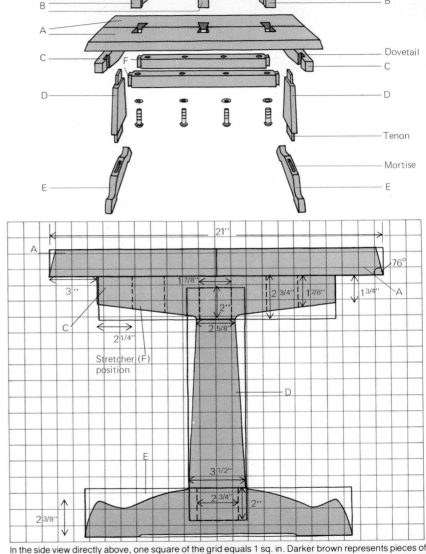

Butterfly joints and strikingly grained zebrawood set this coffee table above the humdrum. The butterflies join the two planks of the top as in an edge joint (p. 374). If a less prominently grained hardwood were used, the butterflies might be of contrasting wood. The tabletop is 21 by 48 inches, and the table's height is 18 inches.

Materials. The two wide planks for the top (see chart, below) may have to be specially ordered; buy at least 6 inches extra length for each so that you have some latitude in aligning color and figure. In addition to the wood parts, eight No. 14 round-head wood screws (p. 368), 3 inches long, and eight 3/4-inch washers are needed.

Tools. A band saw or saber saw is needed to cut curves in the base; a table saw or circular saw is helpful for cutting the beveled tabletop edge. Prepare the planks for the top as if for an edge joint with various lengths of hand planes (p. 372). You need three bar clamps with 3-foot openings, and two quick-action clamps. For cutting the butterfly sockets, you need 3/4-inch and 1-inch chisels. For shaping the curves and rounding edges, a rasp and cabinet scrapers are necessary.

Procedure. Assemble the base first:

cut the joints in the legs, brackets, and feet; shape these parts and shape the stretchers lengthwise to conform to the profile of the brackets; then glue the parts (opposite page, top).

Next, assemble the tabletop. Square the planks (p. 372); then cut and fit the butterflies (opposite). Glue butterflies into sockets, and glue edge joint simultaneously as shown on page 374. Because the planks are likely to expand and contract with changes in humidity, the stretchers must be slot screwed to the top (p. 381). Make the slots in the stretchers; drill corresponding pilot holes in the tabletop bottom at 8½-inch intervals. Sand the table (if it has been well planed, little sanding should be necessary) and finish it with a water-resistant finish, such as tung oil or polyurethane varnish (pp. 390–391).

Part		Finished size (in.)	No.
A	Top	1 3/4 x 10 1/2 x 48	2
B	Butterfly	1 3/4 x 1 3/4 x 2 3/4	3*
C	Bracket	1 9/16 x 2 3/4 x 15	2
D	Leg	1 9/16 x 3 5/8 x 14 1/2	2
E	Foot	1 9/16 x 3 x 16 7/8	2
F	Stretcher	2 x 2 5/16 x 30 1/2	2

* Cut from one piece 1 3/4 x 1 3/4 x 18

In the side view directly above, one square of the grid equals 1 sq. in. Darker brown represents pieces of wood in the sizes given in the parts chart (left) before the wood is shaped. Final shapes are represented in lighter brown. Use these outlines to make full-size templates (see *Drawing*, p. 212) for transferring shapes to wood. Shapes are roughly cut out with band saw or saber saw, then refined with rasp and cabinet scraper. Dashed lines show junction of stretchers and bracket, and position of tenons on legs as they fit into bracket and foot. Bevel on outer edges of top planks is cut at a 76° angle; it continues across ends of planks too. After making and fitting the butterflies (opposite), cut the bevel with a table saw or circular saw, plane off the saw marks with jack and smooth planes, and gently round the edges with a smooth plane.

The base: joints, shaping, and assembly

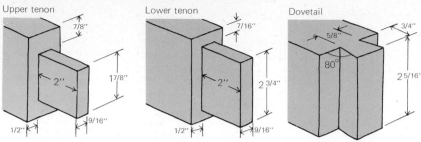

Upper tenon   Lower tenon   Dovetail

Joints. Legs are tenoned into brackets and feet (left and center). Clamp legs face to face and mark tenon shoulders together. By hand, cut mortises first and tenons second (p. 379). On table saw cut tenons first, using tenoning jig (p. 397). Dovetail (p. 378) joins stretchers to brackets (right). Clamp brackets together and transfer socket markings from one to the other so that they are identical.

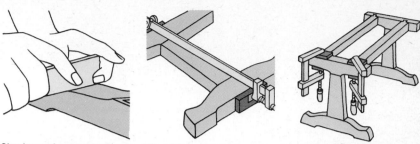

Shaping and assembly. Saw to within 1/16 in. of lines drawn from templates (opposite) on brackets, legs, and feet; shape with rasp and cabinet scraper (left). Shape undersides of stretchers to conform with bracket profile. Glue foot joint with bracket in place; then glue bracket joint (center). Correct shaping. Glue other leg. Glue stretchers into brackets, one end at a time (right).

The top: cutting butterfly joints

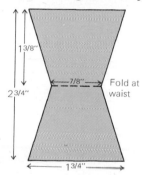

Butterflies. Fold stiff paper in half; draw half the butterfly with the dimensions shown above. Cut template from folded paper. Unfold; trace three times on squared wood 1¾ by 1¾ by 18 in. (left). Square end and waist lines across wood's edges (p. 370); repeat butterflies on other face. Number them—they are not interchangeable.

1. For angled cuts (diagram, left) saw to waist with saw angled (above left) so that it cuts only one face. Reverse wood; saw to waist with saw straight (right). Smooth cut with chisel; trim at waist so that angle is sharp.

2. Align tabletop pieces and saw to length. Clamp face to face and plane to identical length if necessary. Unclamp; plane top faces smooth. Clamp edge to edge and trace butterflies. Number to correlate with butterflies.

3. Square butterfly's waist across edge. With T-bevel transfer angles from top face as in a dovetail (p. 378). With combination square, measure socket's depth on top face; mark on lower face (shown), but draw line with marking gauge.

4. With top face toward you, saw angled lines with dovetail or tenon saw, watching line carefully. If saw penetrates waste on lower face, correct cut from that side. Board is being held in clamping arrangement shown on page 381.

5. Chisel out waste as for dovetail socket, alternating vertical and horizontal cuts. Two chisels are required: one that fits back of socket, one for front. Hollow joint so that it is slightly concave; clean sides with chisel.

6. Tap butterfly gently into corresponding socket (left); trim socket if necessary for fit. Clamp boards edge to edge and fit again (right); use same technique when gluing. Knock out butterflies by tapping on reverse face.

Picture framing

An art that enhances art

Artists have nearly always put borders around pictures to enhance them and to separate them from their surroundings. Geometric borders of contrasting colors often surrounded ancient mosaics; gilded borders set off the pictures in medieval manuscripts; altarpieces were surrounded by frames of supporting architecture. Later, when paintings on canvas or wood became readily portable, the frame not only enhanced the picture but was a deterrent to thievery. By the 17th century, framemaking was a recognized craft guild, an offshoot of cabinetmaking. Carved and gilded wooden frames were later replaced by molded plaster of Paris. Frames became so elaborate that they sometimes subordinated the art. Today's taste is for more simplicity.

Framing works done on paper serves an additional purpose—protecting the art from the ravages of dirt and mold. The mat sets off the picture and keeps the glass from coming in contact with the picture's surface.

As anyone who has had framing done professionally knows, it is expensive. A recent development is the frame-it-yourself shop, where everything is cut to size and you do the gluing and fitting at about one-third less cost than custom framing. Or you can do the whole job yourself, the subject of this chapter.

No hard and fast rules govern the choice of molding. Obviously, it must suit the style of the artwork and the decor of the room. Frame and mat may echo or slightly contrast colors and textures in the picture. Generally, a molding that slopes inward, holding the work at the back of the frame, is best with a perspective picture, one that seems to retreat toward a horizon. A molding that thrusts the work forward suits a picture that appears to lie on one plane, as do many modern works.

Tools and materials

Framemaking is partly woodworking (pp. 360–403) and uses tools shown on page 361: backsaw, miter box, corner clamps, combination square (for checking miter cuts), drill, hammer, and nail set. A table saw cuts accurate miters, but do not use a hand-held power saw—you can do a better job with a backsaw and miter box. A metal miter box with guides to hold the saw steady is preferable. There are special clamps for gluing frames, but the arrangement shown on pages 380 and 406 does just as well.

For cutting glass you need a glass cutter (see *Stained glass*, p. 105), which is used as shown on page 106. For marking mats and as a guide for cutting you need a steel straightedge; this can be a T-square, a framing square (p. 361), or a rule. Although you can cut mats with a utility knife, to cut a perfect bevel on the inside edge of the mat, you will need a mat cutter (p. 405).

Finishing frames (p. 408) requires brushes, abrasive papers, and steel wool. Metal leafing calls for special tools: a gilder's knife, a gilder's cushion—of leather stapled rough side up to a board—and a gilder's tip (a 4-inch-wide camel's hair brush).

Materials. A framing shop or a well-stocked art supply store can provide moldings, mat board, mounting board, and glass or acrylic. Buy 16-ounce picture glass, not window glass, which is thicker. Some people prefer nonglare glass, but it dulls colors.

Ordinary paper, cardboard, and mat board contain acids that over time may adversely affect the paper on which an artwork is painted or printed. However, 100 percent rag materials are acid free and quite safe for mounting and framing purposes. Valuable works should never be glued down, as this reduces their value and may eventually cause deterioration.

Carved and gilded frames such as these are designed for old masterworks.

Matting and mounting

Before putting a tool to mat or molding, you must do some figuring. With a picture that is to be matted, the starting point is what will show through the window of the mat; this is called the *sight size*. Working from the sight size, you compute the mat size (see below).

After you have made these calculations, determine the size of the frame and build it (p. 406). Then measure the inside dimension of the frame's rabbet to ensure that it matches your initial calculations. It is far easier to modify the size of the mat, mounting board, and glass than to adjust the frame once it has been cut and assembled.

Materials. Mat board comes in an array of colors and textures—some 80-odd colors are available in paper mats. Fabric mats are available in a variety of colors and materials, including silk, linen, grasscloth, and burlap. You can even buy suede and cork-textured mats. For matting fine art, all-rag (acid-free) matting is available only in white and off-white. If you want to use a colored or fabric mat, use acid-free barrier paper between the mat and the work. The opening in a mat is usually cut with a bevel sloping inward so that the mat's thickness is visible.

Sometimes an extra mat, called a filet (not shown), sets off the picture from the main mat. Usually 1/8 to 1/4 inch of filet shows. It can be made by cutting a contrasting mat, or use special filet mats, thinner and available in metallic colors, white, and off-white. Its outside dimensions need not be the size of the main mat.

Mounting. Several methods are used to attach the work to the backing. Dry mounting, used for photographs, posters, and art reproductions, permanently bonds the work to the mounting. A plastic-coated paper is placed between the work and mounting board, and the assemblage is heated and pressed in a dry-mount press, an expensive machine that may be available in a do-it-yourself frame shop or in a photo laboratory. An alternative is adhesive-film paper, sticky on both sides, protected by wax paper that is peeled off when you use the paper.

Acid-free mounting. Pictures can be glued to the backing with an acid-free vegetable paste, such as wheat or rice starch. Methyl cellulose paste, a synthetic, is also acid free and is reversible—with enough water to dissolve the paste, the picture can be unglued. However, none of these methods are recommended for original drawings, prints, or watercolors, or even for photographs that are not easily replaceable. Works of value should instead be mounted with gummed Holland tape, sometimes called linen tape, in the manner shown below.

Backing. Mounting, or backing, board, white on one or both sides, comes in several thicknesses and sizes. Acid-free board, called museum board, should be used for works of value. Foam-core board (a sandwich of polystyrene foam between sheets of white paper) is a lightweight backing often used for dry mounting and for passe-partout framing (p. 407).

A frame's parts

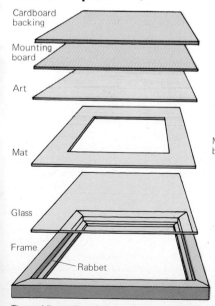

Cardboard backing

Mounting board

Art

Mat

Glass

Frame

Rabbet

The molding, mitered at corners, supports glass, mat, art, mounting board, and—if the frame is deep—cardboard. Gummed tape keeps out dust (p. 406). Push points or brads hold sandwich against rabbet.

Sizing a mat

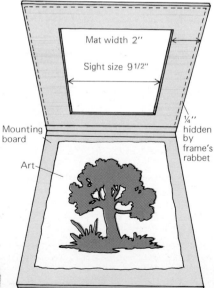

Mat width 2"

Sight size 9 1/2"

1/4" hidden by frame's rabbet

Mounting board

Art

To determine outside edge of mat, add sight size and twice width of mat that will show plus twice rabbet's width. (In this example, formula is 9½ + 4 + 1/2 = 14.) Repeat for length. Mounting board and glass are same size as mat.

Cutting a mat

1. Outside edge. Mark on back of mat. Holding knife on waste side, guide it along straightedge toward you. Two or more passes may be needed.

2. Opening. Mark sight size on back. Adjust mat cutter for bevel. Align on cut. Clamp rule at cutter edge. Start 1/16 in. outside corner; push cutter.

3. Corners. Slit with single-edge razor blade if corners are not cut. Smooth any roughness from bevel with emery board. Remove dirt with gum eraser.

Mounting with gummed Holland tape

1. Top edges. Lay mounting board and mat end to end. Moisten tape; lay over edges and press hard. Fold mat down over mounting board.

2. Taping. Position art in mat. Lift mat and slide clean paper over art, weighting it. Attach moistened gummed tape to back of art along top edge.

3. Fastening tape. Glue strip of tape, adhesive side down, across each strip laid down in previous step. Press firmly with clean paper on top.

Picture framing

Constructing frames

Moldings come in so many shapes and finishes that the best course is to take the picture to the framing supplier to find the molding that most enhances the picture. Until you have gained experience, work with moldings that have right angles between the base and outside leg—they are easier to cut and join.

Molding sources. Consult your telephone directory's yellow pages for picture framing shops and molding suppliers (where moldings are sold by the running foot). You can buy unfinished builder's molding from a lumberyard; as a rule, you will have to make the rabbet by gluing a strip of wood to the base of the molding. You can then apply a wood finish (pp. 390–391) or use one of the techniques shown on page 408. You can make moldings from strips of wood, using various router bits to shape the face of the molding and to cut the rabbet.

Sizing the frame. The frame's inner dimensions are determined by the *rabbet size* (see diagram, below left), which equals the size of the mat (p. 405) plus an extra 1/16 inch of length and width. This allows 1/32 inch of play on all sides of the mat. However, to mark the frame on a visible edge for cutting the miter, you must make still another calculation (below, left).

How much molding to buy. Add together the planned length and width of the mat (p. 405) and multiply by two. To the resulting figure add eight times the width of the molding. This accounts for the four miter joints. As a safety margin, add a few extra inches—more if the molding is carved.

Shadow box. This kind of frame is for three-dimensional objects—shells, bas-relief sculpture, a collage of raised objects, and so on. The glass is placed well forward of the mounting board. Moldings with two rabbets are available in a limited number of designs, so more often than not your choice will be to make a shadow box. The backing must be extra stiff—it can even be wood. Often it is covered with cloth, painted, or stained. The inside surface of the molding should be finished.

Framing an oil painting. The canvas of an oil painting is tacked to wooden stretchers that are roughly 3/4 inch thick. Choose a molding with a rabbet deep enough to accommodate this thickness. Often an oil painting is set

Frame moldings

Marking molding for miter cuts. Mark on inside edge of the molding so that mark is visible when sawing. To calculate length on inside edge, subtract twice rabbet's width from mat's width and add 1/16 in. to ease fit. Below are some typical frame moldings.

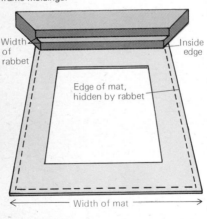

Width of rabbet — Inside edge

Edge of mat, hidden by rabbet

Width of mat

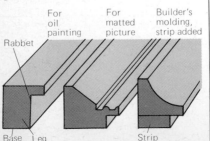

For oil painting | For matted picture | Builder's molding, strip added

Rabbet

Base Leg Strip

Framing a matted work

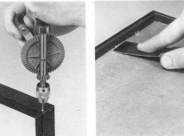

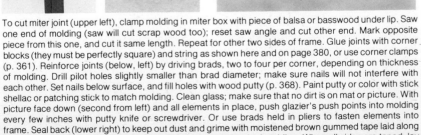

To cut miter joint (upper left), clamp molding in miter box with piece of balsa or basswood under lip. Saw one end of molding (saw will cut scrap wood too); reset saw angle and cut other end. Mark opposite piece from this one, and cut it same length. Repeat for other two sides of frame. Glue joints with corner blocks (they must be perfectly square) and string as shown here and on page 380, or use corner clamps (p. 361). Reinforce joints (below, left) by driving brads, two to four per corner, depending on thickness of molding. Drill pilot holes slightly smaller than brad diameter; make sure nails will not interfere with each other. Set nails below surface, and fill holes with wood putty (p. 368). Paint putty or color with stick shellac or patching stick to match molding. Clean glass; make sure that no dirt is on mat or picture. With picture face down (second from left) and all elements in place, push glazier's push points into molding every few inches with putty knife or screwdriver. Or use brads held in pliers to fasten elements into frame. Seal back (lower right) to keep out dust and grime with moistened brown gummed tape laid along back of mounting board and pressed against inside and back of molding. When all sides are taped, lay straightedge on tape and slit tape with single-edge razor blade to remove excess.

Shadow-box frame

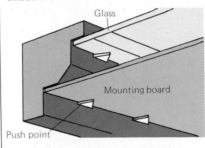

Glass

Mounting board

Push point

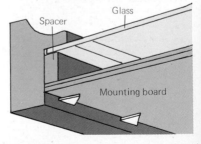

Glass

Spacer

Mounting board

Molding at top has one rabbet at back to hold mounting board and one near front for glass. Paint or stain mounting board and inside surface of molding, or cover mounting board with fabric. Use back rabbet as reference point for cutting miters. Assemble frame; measure front rabbet for glass, which is held in place with glazier's push points. Molding with deep rabbet (below) has spacers of wood or thick mat, which are painted, stained, or covered with fabric. Cut glass and mounting board to same size. With glass in rabbet, glue spacers to molding. Place mounted art on spacers; fasten with push points.

off from its frame by an extra frame called a liner. The liner might be gilded or covered with linen. When using a liner, you must build two frames, making separate calculations for the size of each. The liner's rabbet size (or the frame's if no liner is used) is the outer dimensions of the stretcher plus 1/8 inch. For the outer frame the rabbet size is the outer dimensions of the liner plus 1/8 inch. If the fit is too loose, use shims of wood or cardboard between the stretcher and the frame.

Passe-partout. Simple and inexpensive, passe-partout (literally, "pass everywhere") is a framing method that uses colored cloth or plastic tape to surround and hold together the backing, art, mat, and glass. Because the tape carries the weight of these elements, it must be strong and not stretchy. Eventually it will deteriorate, so this method is used mostly for temporary framing or for small objects.

Passe-partout backing must be stiff and light; foam-core board is an excellent choice. Acrylic may be used in place of glass, as it is lighter in weight. So that the rings from which the work is hung do not touch the work, a protec-

tive layer should be placed between the work and the backing. Use barrier paper or museum mounting board (p. 405) if the work is valuable.

Old frames. You may want to use an old frame found in a secondhand store or a flea market. You will probably have to adjust the mat size to fit the frame by making it wider in one dimension than the other. Antique gold-leaf frames that appear to be carved wood are often molded plaster of Paris. Clean gold leaf with mild soap and water. Minor scratches can be filled with thin plaster of Paris and a brush,

but if a section of carving has been knocked off, repair it as shown below.

Hanging pictures. For the best viewing, hang pictures at eye level. Make groupings of small pictures. Lighting should be adequate, but do not place pictures in direct sunlight, which will cause rapid deterioration. If you use your fireplace frequently, do not hang a valuable artwork over it. Put a small cross of masking tape on the wall before driving a nail into plaster. For a heavy picture on a hollow plaster wall, use a screw and anchor, a molly bolt, or a toggle bolt.

Framing an oil painting

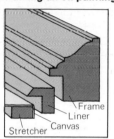

A framed canvas. Outer frame surrounds liner, which fits around canvas stretchers. Make liner first, then make frame to fit liner (see text). If fit is loose, place shims of mat or cardboard between elements.

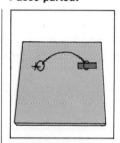

Cutting linen liner. Place liner in miter box. Lower saw until it touches fabric; mark along saw blade with sharp pencil. Raise blade, slit linen with knife, then make saw cut.

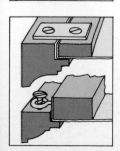

Fastening frame. If back of frame and stretcher are flush, screw flat metal plates across them. If they are uneven, fit screw eyes into projecting part; run screws through eyes into other part.

Passe-partout

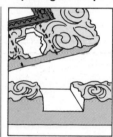

Attaching hangers. Make cross-shaped slits in backing one-third down from top. Insert prongs of passe-partout rings; spread them open. Pass tape through each ring; press down firmly.

Taping. Tape three sides with masking tape. Extend untaped side over table's edge. Cut plastic tape 1 in. longer than side, and with straightedge as a guide, lay it on glass. Smooth over edge and back.

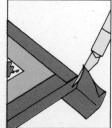

Corners. Remove masking tape from opposite edge and repeat previous step. Trim tape at corners. Tape other two edges; overlap tape at corners and trim even with edges.

Repairing an old plaster frame

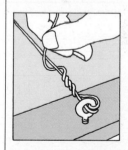

Cutting out damage. With a hacksaw make vertical cut on each side of damaged portion. Remove this portion with putty knife; scrape off plaster that sticks to wooden base.

New piece. Press modeling clay onto identical section of molding. Make impression slightly deeper than removed section. Fill with plaster of Paris to depth of damaged section. Let dry. Peel clay away.

Fitting section. File edges and, if necessary, bottom to fit opening. Glue with white glue. Fill cracks with plaster of Paris. Seal new section with thin shellac. Apply gold-leaf paste; antique if desired (p. 408).

Hanging pictures

Screw eyes. Use short-shanked screw eyes in largest size that will not split wood. Drill pilot holes on inside surface or back of molding one-third of way down from top. For heavy frame, use four screws.

Picture wire. Cut braided wire 8 in. longer than width of frame. Pass it twice through each screw eye, pull 4 in. beyond eye, and twist end around itself.

Other hangers. Sawtooth hanger (top) for light frame is nailed to back of molding at top center and is suspended from nail in wall. Strap or mirror hangers (below) are for heavy pictures.

Picture framing

Finishing frames

Finishes for picture frames can be as simple as any of the wood finishes described on pages 390–391 or as imaginative as your fancy dictates—just don't let the frame overpower the art. As you become familiar with the basic techniques on this page, experiment with your own variations. When shopping for materials, look for products, new and old, that can be adapted to frame finishing.

An old frame will probably require cleaning. Use paint and varnish remover (p. 391) only if you want to strip the frame to bare wood. As with any cleaning or stripping agent, work in a well-ventilated area. Let the frame dry. A gilded frame should be washed with mild soap and water. Dull a shiny painted surface with fine abrasive paper or steel wool before applying new paint or enamel.

Antiquing. To give a frame the mellowness of age, use the process called antiquing, which is nothing more than applying a coat of glaze of a contrasting color over paint or enamel, then wiping some of it off. A raw-wood frame should be sealed with a coat of shellac before you apply the base coat of antiquing paint, which is an extra-thick latex. Two coats may be necessary for good coverage. Let the final coat dry for 24 hours before applying the glaze.

Buy the glaze ready to use, or mix your own by combining oil color, linseed oil, turpentine, and drier. Whites, pale colors, and golds are usually antiqued with brown tones, such as raw umber or raw Sienna; vivid colors and silver or aluminum are usually glazed with lampblack oil color. The antiquing glaze itself may be a color. When the glaze has dried, coat it with varnish unless the glaze contains varnish.

Metallic finishes. You can buy metallic paints in liquid or paste form. Although these are fine for repairs, they do not achieve the luster of a surface covered with metal leaf.

Metal leafing requires a number of preparatory steps. First, apply three coats of gesso (a mixture of powdered whiting and glue). Sand the frame with No. 220 garnet paper until it is perfectly smooth. Finish rubbing with a wet felt pad. If color is to show through the leaf, apply a coat of dark brownish-red paint. Seal the gesso and paint with two coats of thin shellac; sand lightly after each coat. Apply gilder's size, a yellow adhesive for the leaf that dries slowly. Or use quick-drying Japan size, which is clear. Then proceed as shown in the pictures below. Afterward, if red paint is to show through, rub the metal leaf lightly with fine steel wool. Seal with a coat of thin shellac. You can then antique the metal finish or rub it with rottenstone, a decomposed limestone.

An inexpensive, easy alternative to classic metal leafing uses gold or silver foil wrapping paper—easiest to find in the holiday season—or a combination of the two. This technique covers many flaws, and there is no need to strip the old finish. The only materials needed are a toothbrush and white glue diluted with an equal amount of water.

Antiquing a frame

1. After preparing the frame's surface (see text), apply a coat of semigloss enamel or antiquing base paint. Brush on evenly with grain of wood. Use spray can of paint for an elaborately carved frame. Apply a second coat if necessary. Allow to dry 24 hr.

2. Brush antiquing glaze onto one section of the frame at a time. Make sure that all of the surface is thoroughly covered. Before glazing the other sections, proceed with the next step.

3. Wipe off glaze with soft, lint-free cloth a little at a time until you get the desired effect. Remove excess from crevices with a clean, dry brush. As you work, wipe brush on clean cloth. Rub most of glaze from high spots to give look of wear. See text for how to seal the finish.

Metal leafing

1. When gilder's size (see text) is tacky to touch, open book to a leaf. Place suede-covered board on top of leaf. Turn everything over and place board on table. Peel book away carefully; leaf will adhere to suede. If necessary, cut leaf to size on board.

2. Spread a thin layer of petroleum jelly on forearm; rub edge of gilder's tip in jelly. Pick up leaf at edge as shown, and guide it to frame; lay it carefully in place. Once down, leaf cannot be moved. For best results, overlap by half width of leaf.

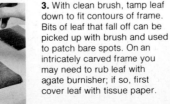

3. With clean brush, tamp leaf down to fit contours of frame. Bits of leaf that fall off can be picked up with brush and used to patch bare spots. On an intricately carved frame you may need to rub leaf with agate burnisher; if so, first cover leaf with tissue paper.

Leafing with foil paper

1. Cut metallic foil wrapping paper into approximately 1½-in. squares. Roll each square into a small ball; this crinkles it and gives it texture. Open the ball of paper flat, but do not smooth out the creases.

2. Dip toothbrush into glue and water mixture (see text). Coat surface of frame and back of paper. Lay paper on frame; edges can overlap. Push paper into contours of frame with brush dipped into glue solution, covering front of paper with glue. If paper tears, put another piece over it.

3. When glue has thoroughly dried, it will be transparent. You can then antique it with antiquing glaze or with artist's oil paints. Finally, cover the frame with two to four coats of high luster or satin varnish.

Preserving fruit

Bottling the freshness of summer

Our rural forebears preserved fruit out of necessity. Fruits that might have withered on the branch in autumn were spread as jam in January. The pure delectability of homemade jams, jellies, and preserves—in contrast to the bland preparations that appear on supermarket shelves—is reason enough to try this once traditional craft of the country kitchen. If you grow your own fruit, you will have even more reason to make your own fruit spreads—to bottle the freshness of summer for use in the barren winter months.

Types of preserved fruit. Fruits can simply be canned (bottled) in syrup, or they can be made into a number of different kinds of spreads or relishes, which are the subject of this chapter. There are eight major types of spreads and relishes. *Jellies* are clear, firm spreads made from strained fruit juice—they contain no actual fruit. *Marmalades* are jellies containing small pieces of fruit and sometimes rind. *Jams* are spreads made from cooked-down fruit; they are softer than jellies. *Conserves* are jams made from mixtures of fruits with nuts and raisins added. *Fruit butters* (such as apple butter) are jams that are cooked down even further to make a denser, richer spread. *Preserves* are thick syrups with large pieces of fruit or whole fruits. *Chutneys* are spiced sweet-and-sour relishes. *Pickles* are whole fruits preserved in sweetened, spiced vinegar.

History of preserving fruit. The problem of keeping fruit unspoiled for consumption during the winter, when fresh food is scarce, is as old as civilization. In ancient times fruit was dried, pickled, fermented (especially for use in wines), or preserved in syrups of fruit juice and honey. About 1,000 years ago the Arabs began to refine sugar and to use it to preserve fruits.

The crusaders probably learned the craft from their enemy and took it back to western Europe, where it became widespread and flourished in the late Middle Ages and after.

The early settlers of North America became especially adept at preserving fruits, which were found in great abundance in the New World. They used honey, molasses, and maple sugar in their spreads and extracted pectin from apple parings to jelly fruits that were low in natural pectin.

In 1810 Nicolas Appert, a French confectioner, published a book on a method he had developed for preserving foods by sterilizing them, then sealing them in bottles. This method made it possible to make jams and jellies that would keep for much longer periods of time than had been possible previously. No one knew why Appert's canning process worked until 1857, when Louis Pasteur discovered that microorganisms cause spoilage in food. Cooking the food killed the microorganisms, and sealing the container kept others from entering.

The last major development in the history of preserving fruit was the invention in 1858 of a new type of glass canning jar by John Landis Mason, an American tinsmith. Mason's jar had a threaded opening that could be sealed with a rubber gasket and a metal screw-on lid. Up until that time, fruits were canned in glass bottles or earthenware jugs that were sealed with cork stoppers and wax; or the fruit was covered with oiled paper, and the containers were sealed by stretching tissue paper that had been dipped in egg white over their tops. Mason's invention greatly simplified home canning. The jars used by home canners today are variations of it, and all of them are generally referred to as mason jars.

Putting up jams, jellies, and other foods has been a part of North American life since the Pilgrims landed at Plymouth Rock. It is one way of storing the riches of the harvest for the winter months.

Preserving fruit

Equipment and supplies

Any reasonably well equipped kitchen will have most of the utensils needed for preserving fruits. The only essential equipment that may be missing is a supply of mason jars for storing the preserves. A few special utensils are recommended, but you can substitute common household items for these.

Equipment. The most important piece of equipment is a large cooking pot. It should be made of heavy aluminum, stainless steel, or unchipped enamel. The pot must be large enough to hold three times the amount of fruit you are putting into it. Otherwise, the food might boil over. You will also need another large pot for sterilizing the mason jars and a small saucepan for sterilizing the jar caps.

The jars for most preserved fruit must be processed in boiling water to keep the fruit from spoiling during storage. Special boiling-water-bath canners are available. These are large pots with tight covers and baskets that separate the jars and hold them off the bottom of the pot (see facing page). You can, however, use any large covered pot with a rack on the bottom; just use some kind of utensil to separate the jars and to keep them from falling over or bumping into each other. The pot should be deep enough to allow at least 3 inches of headspace above the jars. Special jar lifters are available for handling the hot jars.

For making jelly, you will need jelly bags and a stand for the bags. A jelly bag is simply a bag of thin cloth used to juice the fruit. The stand is a wire frame that holds the bag open above a bowl. You can substitute a piece of muslin or finely woven cheesecloth laid in a colander. A jelly, candy, or deep-fat thermometer is ideal for ascertaining the jelling point of fruit juice, but it is not essential. For making jams and fruit butters you will need a food mill to reduce the fruit to a pulp. A food mill is a colander through which food is pressed by means of a plate attached to a rotating handle. If you do not have a food mill, you can press the food through a sieve or strainer with a pestle or wooden spoon. You will also need an assortment of small utensils, including a wooden spoon for stirring, a paring knife, measuring cups and spoons, a slotted spoon, a ladle, and tongs for handling hot lids. You may also need a kitchen scale.

Mason jars can be used for all preserved fruits. The most common type of mason jar has a two-piece vacuum cap. The cap consists of a flat metal lid with a flanged edge, the underside of which has a rubberlike sealing compound, and a threaded metal screw band, which fits over the lid and holds it in place. The screw bands and jars are reusable, but the lids are not. The other type of mason jar has a glass top that is held down by wire bails. Jelly can be stored in jelly glasses and sealed with a thin layer of paraffin.

Supplies. For all preserved fruits you will need sugar and the fruit or fruits being processed. Use firm, unbruised fruit. For the best results, about one-quarter of the fruit should be slightly underripe. Some recipes also call for spices, nuts, or vinegar.

Pectin is a substance found in most fruits that makes the fruit jell. If you are making jelly with a fruit that is low in natural pectin, you will have to mix it with a fruit that is high in pectin (such as apples) or add commercial pectin. Pectin comes in two forms: powdered and liquid. Both are available at well-stocked supermarkets.

Cooking the fruit

Fruit is preserved by cooking it with sugar or sweetened vinegar and sealing it in airtight sterilized jars. Most fruit spreads are jelled to some extent. The jelling is brought about by the interaction of the sugar with the natural pectin and acid of the fruit. Fruits that are low in acid must have a little lemon juice added to them. Fruits that are low in pectin—including blueberries, strawberries, peaches, apricots, and cherries—must have commercial pectin added to them if they are to be used for jellies or other firm spreads.

Prepare the preserved fruits following the recipes on pages 412–413, then seal the preserve in hot containers (see facing page). Be sure to follow the recipe closely if you are using commercial pectin. Powdered pectin must be added and cooked before the sugar is added, but liquid pectin must be added after the sugar has been added and the juice brought to a boil.

To make jelly without adding pectin, boil the sugared fruit juice rapidly until it reaches the setting point—4°C above the boiling point of water. Although the standard boiling point of water is 100°C, it varies with different altitudes and atmospheric conditions, so check it before making the jelly. When using a thermometer, make sure its bulb is completely submerged but not touching the pan. Always read the thermometer at eye level. If you have no thermometer, test the setting point by picking up some juice in a spoon, cooling it slightly, and letting it fall back into the pan. If the juice forms two drops that run together and fall off the spoon in a sheet, the jelly is ready.

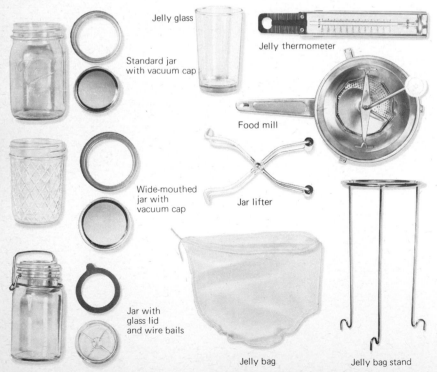

Jelly glass

Standard jar with vacuum cap

Jelly thermometer

Food mill

Wide-mouthed jar with vacuum cap

Jar lifter

Jar with glass lid and wire bails

Jelly bag

Jelly bag stand

Jelly is ready when it sheets from the spoon.

Filling and processing mason jars

As soon as the fruit has finished cooking, it must be put into containers at once and sealed quickly. Otherwise, bacteria may enter the preserve and cause it to spoil.

The containers must also be free of bacteria when you put the preserve into them. Sterilize the jars ahead of time and have them ready for filling by the time the preserve is finished cooking. Just before you begin the final cooking of the preserve, examine the jars you will be using and discard any that have cracks or nicks. Put the good jars into a large pot and boil them for 10 minutes, then let them sit in the hot water. Just before the preserve is ready, remove them from the water with a jar lifter, shake out the excess water, and stand them on a towel to drain.

Similarly, you must sterilize the jar caps. Put the caps in a saucepan with water and bring the water almost to the boiling point, then turn off the heat and let the caps sit in the hot water until they are needed.

The most common type of container and the easiest to use is the jar with the two-piece vacuum cap. Another popular jar has a glass top that is held down by wire bails. Directions for filling and sealing both these types of jar are given at right. Jelly can be put into jelly glasses and sealed with a thin layer of paraffin. For directions on how to use jelly glasses, see p. 412, Steps 8 and 9. If you use any other type of container, follow the manufacturer's directions.

After the containers have been sealed, they must be processed in a boiling-water bath, as described at right, unless they contain jelly. Jelly is the only type of preserve that is not processed. If you live at a high altitude, add 1 minute to the processing time called for in the recipes for every 1,000 feet above sea level. This will compensate for the fact that water boils at a lower temperature at high altitudes.

Jars with vacuum caps. 1. Ladle hot preserved fruit into sterilized jars. For jellies and pickles, leave 1/8 in. headspace (space between preserve and top of jar). For other types of preserve, leave 1/4 in. headspace.

2. Wipe the tops of the jars with a clean, damp cloth or sponge, being sure to get any spilled preserves out of the threads of the jar tops. Use a pot holder to hold the jars as you clean them, or you may burn your hand on the hot jars.

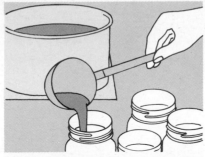

3. Place flat metal lids on top of jars so that sealing compound on underside of lids rests on top edges of jars. Screw threaded bands down tightly over flat lids. Tighten firmly with hand only; do not use jar wrench or other device.

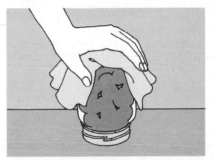

4. Turn the jars upside down and hold them in that position for a few seconds so that the hot preserve can contact the insides of the lids and help destroy any mold or yeast that may have settled on the lids. Then stand the jars upright.

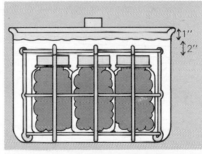

5. Place jars in boiling-water-bath canner or substitute pot (see p. 410). Add water to 2 in. above jar tops, leaving 1 in. or more space between water and top of canner. Cover canner and boil water for time indicated in recipe.

6. Remove jars from bath and let them cool. Vacuum will pull centers of lids down. Check seal by pressing down on lid. If it sinks down and pops up again, seal is faulty—reprocess fruit. Store sealed jars in cool, dark, dry place.

Jars with glass lids and wire bails. 1. Fill the sterilized jars and wipe them clean as you would with vacuum lids. Fit wet rubber rings on mouths of jars, stretching rings only enough to make them fit over the mouths of the jars.

2. Place glass lids on jars so that they rest on rubber rings, then adjust long wire bails so that they fit into center of grooves on top of glass lids. Leave short wire bails up, then process jars in boiling-water bath as you would other jars.

3. Remove jars from boiling-water bath and push short wire bails down to complete seal. When jars are cool, turn them upside down to check for leaks. Repack and reprocess any leaking jars. Store sealed jars in a dark, dry, cool place.

Preserving fruit

Apple jelly and other recipes

The first step in preserving fruit is sorting out the raw fruit. Discard any bruised or overripe fruit, remove the stems and caps, and wash the fruit. Generally, you should not pare or pit fruit that will later be strained or put through a food mill. The skin of the fruit is high in pectin and the pits of many fruits add a nutty flavor to the finished preserve.

For the best results, warm the sugar in the oven before using it and cook only small amounts of fruit at a time. The recipes given here should produce 2 to 4 pints of preserve, depending on the climate, altitude, and the firmness and juiciness of the batch of fruit. The same variables dictate the length of cooking time. Except for jellies with added pectin, the cooking time may range from 10 minutes to an hour.

Always stir the sugar into the fruit or juice over low heat until the sugar dissolves, then boil the mixture rapidly until it is thick or reaches the setting point. Stir the mixture frequently while cooking it, or it may stick to the pan or scorch. Fruit spreads thicken as they cool, so they should be cooked to less than the desired consistency.

What can go wrong. Jellies and marmalades may become tough if too much pectin is added or if they are cooked too long; they may become cloudy if they are not poured quickly or soon enough. Crystals may form in them if they are cooked too little, too slowly, or too long. Mold may form in stored preserved fruits if they are improperly sealed. A preserve may darken at the top of the jar if it is stored in too warm a place or is improperly sealed. Fruit may float in jam if it was underripe or not cooked long enough.

Apple jelly. An illustrated recipe for apple jelly is given at right. The ingredients needed are 6 pounds of apples, 6 cloves, and 6 cups of sugar. Other recipes follow.

1. Wash 6 lb of tart apples (about one-quarter of them should be underripe). Remove the stems and blossom ends from the apples, but do not core or pare the fruit. Cut the apples into small pieces and put the pieces into a large pot.

2. Add 6 whole cloves and 6 cups of water to the apples, and cover the pot. Place the pot over high heat and bring the water to a boil, then reduce the heat and simmer the apples until they are tender. This should take about 20–25 min.

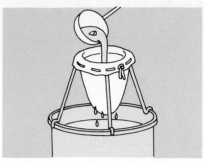

3. Using a ladle or cup, transfer the apples and juice to a damp jelly bag set over a large bowl or pot. Let the juice drip through the bag into the container untouched. Do not press or squeeze the fruit, or you may cloud the juice.

4. Measure 8 cups of the juice into a clean cooking pot. Add 6 cups of sugar, and stir the mixture until the sugar has completely dissolved. Place the cooking pot over high heat, and bring the sweetened juice to a rolling boil.

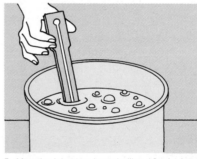

5. After the juice has been boiling 10 min, begin checking it for setting (see p. 410). When the temperature reaches 4°C above the boiling point of water or when the jelly sheets from a spoon, remove the pot from the heat.

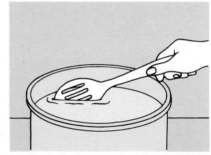

6. Quickly skim away any scum from the top of the jelly. This is best done by passing a slotted spoon across the entire surface of the liquid. Work quickly, or the jelly may set before you can get it into the jars or jelly glasses.

7. Pour or ladle the jelly into hot mason jars or jelly glasses, holding the pot or ladle close to the mouths of the jars or glasses to keep air bubbles from forming. If you are using mason jars, fill them and seal them as shown on page 411.

8. If you are using jelly glasses, fill them to within 1/2 in. of top. Carefully cover the top of the jelly with a single 1/8-in. layer of paraffin. The paraffin should be melted in a double boiler—it should be hot but not smoking.

9. Make sure that the paraffin touches the glass all around, or the seal will leak. With a pin, prick any air bubbles that appear in the paraffin. Cover the glasses with lids or waxed paper held in place with rubber bands. Label the glasses.

Grape jelly with liquid pectin

4 lb Concord grapes
7 cups sugar
3 oz liquid pectin

Crush the grapes and strain them through a jelly bag. To remove the tartaric acid crystals that form in grape juice, let the juice stand overnight—the crystals will settle to the bottom. The next day strain the juice through a clean, damp jelly bag or a double thickness of cloth. Measure out 4 cups of the strained juice and stir the sugar into it. Bring the sweetened juice quickly to a rolling boil. Add the pectin and boil the mixture rapidly for 1 min. Remove the jelly from the heat, skim it quickly, and seal it immediately in hot mason jars or jelly glasses.

Cherry jelly with powdered pectin

3 lb cherries
1¾ oz powdered pectin
4½ cups sugar

Remove the stems, but not the pits, from the cherries. Crush the fruit and put it into the cooking pot with 1/2 cup of water. Cover the pot and bring the cherries to a boil. Reduce the heat and simmer the fruit for 10 min, then pour it into a jelly bag and extract the juice. Measure 3½ cups of the strained juice into the cooking pot and stir in the pectin. Stirring constantly, bring the juice to a rolling boil. Remove the pot from the heat and stir in the sugar, then boil the mixture hard for 1 min. Remove the pot from the heat, quickly skim off the foam, and seal the jelly in hot mason jars or jelly glasses.

Peach jam

2 doz firm, ripe peaches
Sugar as needed

Slice the peaches and discard the pits. Simmer the sliced fruit in a covered pot until it is tender, then put it through a food mill. Measure the pulp and stir in an equal amount of sugar. Cook the mixture, stirring frequently, until it is thick. Seal the jam in hot mason jars and process the jars in a boiling-water bath for 15 min.

Strawberry-rhubarb conserve

1 large orange
3 cups crushed strawberries
3 cups rhubarb cut into 1/4-in. slices
5 cups sugar
1 cup raisins
1/2 tsp salt
1/2 cup chopped pecans or walnuts

Peel the orange and remove the seeds and white membrane. Chop the peel and pulp finely, put it into the cooking pan with 1 cup of water, and cook it until the peel is tender. Stir in the strawberries, rhubarb, sugar, raisins, and salt. Boil the mixture, stirring frequently, until it begins to thicken, then add the nuts and cook for about 5 min more. Skim the conserve, seal it in hot mason jars, and process the jars in a boiling-water bath for 15 min.

Spicy pear butter

2 doz medium-sized ripe pears
Sugar as needed
Juice and grated rind of 1 lemon
1 tbsp cinnamon
2 tsp ground cloves
1 tsp allspice
1 tsp nutmeg

Quarter the pears, core them, and cook them in 1/4 cup of water until they are soft. Put fruit through a food mill and measure the pulp. Stir in 1/2 cup of sugar for every cup of pulp. Add the other ingredients. Cook the mixture rapidly, stirring frequently, until it is a little thicker than applesauce. Seal the pear butter in hot mason jars and process the jars in a boiling-water bath for 10 min.

Pickled apricots

4 cups white wine vinegar
1½ cups light brown sugar
1/2 tsp allspice
1/2 tsp white peppercorns
4 whole cloves
4 lb apricots
6 cups granulated white sugar

Put the vinegar, brown sugar, allspice, peppercorns, and cloves into a bowl and stir the mixture to dissolve the sugar. Cover the bowl and place it in a pan of cold water. Bring the water in the pan to a boil, then remove the pan from the heat. Let the bowl of vinegar stand in the hot water for 2 hr, then strain it.

    Preheat the oven to 175°C. Halve the apricots, remove the pits, and bake the pitted fruit in a covered dish until the skins begin peeling off (about 15 or 20 min). Remove the skins and pack the peeled apricots into hot mason jars. Reheat the spiced vinegar, dissolve the granulated sugar in it, and pour it over the apricots. Seal the jars at once and process them in a boiling-water bath for 20 min. Store the pickles in a dark, cool, dry place for at least a month before eating them.

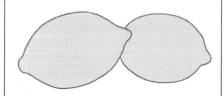

Lemon-lime marmalade

5 large limes
5 lemons of same size
Sugar as needed

Slice the fruit thinly and remove the seeds. Put the sliced fruit into a large cooking pot and add enough water to barely cover the fruit. Cover the pot and cook the fruit until the rinds are tender. Measure the fruit and liquid and stir in an equal amount of sugar. Boil the mixture rapidly until the liquid reaches the setting point of jelly. Skim the marmalade and seal it in hot mason jars. Process the jars in a boiling-water bath for 10 min.

Apple and tomato chutney

2 lb tart apples
2 lb red tomatoes
1 lb onions
1 clove garlic
1/2 lb white seedless grapes
1 tbsp mustard seeds
1 tbsp curry powder
Salt to taste
Pinch cayenne pepper
5 cups white cider vinegar
3 cups light brown sugar

Peel and core apples, cut them into thin slices, and cook them in a small amount of water until tender. Put tomatoes into almost boiling water for 1 min, then peel and halve them, squeeze out the seeds, and chop the pulp coarsely. Peel onions and chop them finely. Mince the garlic, and crush the grapes. Add all these ingredients to the apples, together with the mustard seeds tied in a piece of muslin. Stir in the curry powder, salt, cayenne pepper, and half the vinegar. Bring the mixture to a boil and simmer it until soft, then add the sugar and the rest of the vinegar. Cook the mixture until it is thick and smooth (about an hour). Remove the muslin with the mustard seeds, bottle the chutney, and process the jars in a boiling-water bath for 5 min.

Strawberry preserves

12 cups strawberries
9 cups sugar

Wash and drain the berries and remove the stems. Toss the berries with the sugar and refrigerate them overnight. Bring the sugared fruit to a boil, stirring gently, and cook it rapidly until the syrup is thick and 4°C above the boiling point of water. Skim the preserves and seal them in hot mason jars. Process the jars in a boiling-water bath for 5 min.

In different parts of the world and at different periods of history, bread has been made in an almost limitless number of sizes, shapes, colors, and flavors.

Our daily bread

Man has been making bread of some sort since the end of the last ice age. The earliest breads were undoubtedly crude, unleavened loaves baked on hot stones or in beds of live coals. It is believed that the first raised breads were made in the Near East, where grains containing enough gluten to raise dough were plentiful. The first raised bread probably came into existence by accident. A baker may have used leftover dough that had begun to ferment, and the fermentation caused the bread to rise.

Bread first became prevalent in ancient Egypt. A surviving papyrus describes no less than 30 different kinds of bread baked by the Egyptians, who used bread instead of money to pay their workers and offered bread as a sacrifice to the gods. Other civilizations also used bread in religious ceremonies. Major religious cults developed around Demeter and Ceres, the Greek and Roman goddesses of grain. The Jews used matzo, or unleavened bread (the most ancient bread of the Hebrews), as "the bread of affliction" in celebrating the feast of Passover, and Christians brought new significance to the Passover bread in the Sacrament of the Eucharist.

By the beginning of the Christian Era breadmaking had spread to all parts of the known world, including China. Generally, the nobles ate breads of finely milled wheat, while the poor ate coarse breads. In the New World the Indians ate unleavened corn bread, such as the Mexican tortilla, because they had no grains suitable for raised breads. But Columbus brought wheat to the New World in 1493, and wheat bread became widespread.

Today, bread is important in most of the world's cultures. In the West it is considered not only a type of food but a symbol for food itself.

The basics of baking bread

Bread is made of moistened flour, salt, and yeast. Yeast is a living organism that rapidly ferments the sugar it derives from the starch in the flour, releasing carbon dioxide gas, which permeates the moistened flour. Flour contains a protein substance called gluten. The gluten forms an elastic network in the dough that holds in the carbon dioxide and makes the dough rise. The salt strengthens the gluten and inhibits the action of the yeast, preventing the dough from rising too fast.

Making the dough. To make bread, dissolve the yeast in warm water, mix it thoroughly with the other ingredients, and knead the mixture into a somewhat elastic dough. Put the dough into a bowl, cover it, and leave it in a warm, draft-free place until it rises to double (or in some cases more than double) its bulk. This may take several hours. Deflate the risen dough and form it into loaves, let the dough rise again, then bake the risen loaves. Some doughs must be left to rise a second time before they are shaped into loaves, then left to rise a third time, and baked. Allow the baked bread to cool thoroughly, then wrap it in airtight plastic for storing. If you wish, you can freeze it for later use.

Most breads are left to rise at a temperature of about 27°C, but some breads should rise at about 21°C. Although this cooler temperature slows the rising, it allows the bread to fully develop its texture without souring. You can delay the rising of any bread by placing it in a cooler place—even the refrigerator. You can also freeze the dough before any of its risings for up to 10 days and continue preparing it after it is thawed.

Although the entire process of making bread takes hours, you are busy with the bread for less than half an hour. During the long rising periods you can attend to other tasks or relax.

Breads from around the world

Equipment and supplies

Very little equipment is required to make bread. Aside from a thermostatically controlled oven, all you need are a few utensils, a bowl, baking pans, and the ingredients called for in the recipe.

Equipment. The most important piece of equipment, besides the oven, is a bowl to hold the dough while it is rising. The bowl should have a capacity equal to at least three times the amount of flour called for in the recipe you are using. The sides of the bowl should be fairly straight—not too sloping—to help push the rising dough upward instead of letting it spread outward.

You may also need a pastry scraper—a rectangular piece of stainless steel with a handle running along one of its long sides. The pastry scraper is used to lift doughs that are especially sticky in the early stages of kneading. A wide spatula can be used in its place.

Depending upon the type of bread you are making, you will need either a large cookie sheet or bread pans. You can get special bread pans or use metal, glass, or foil meatloaf pans. The dough should fill the pan two-thirds full. If the pan is too large, the loaf will be a little flat; if it is too small, the dough may spill out over the sides. Breads in unusual shapes may call for special pans.

For most breads you will need only a few further miscellaneous items. These include a pastry board or large chopping board to use as a kneading surface, a rubber scraper or a mixing spoon, and measuring cups and spoons.

For French bread you will also need a spray bottle or atomizer filled with water, a baking pan, and a lame—a metal tool with a razor-sharp point—or a single-edged razor blade for cutting slashes into the loaves before baking them. Special French bread pans are available for holding the shaped loaves during the third rising and the baking. These pans consist of two or more half cylinders that form troughs for holding

the loaves. If you have no special pans, you can place the loaves on a floured canvas pastry cloth for rising and bake them on a large cookie sheet.

If you plan to do a lot of bread baking, you may want to get a heavy-duty table-model electric mixer with a dough hook attachment. The dough can be kneaded by placing it in the mixing bowl and letting the dough hook do all the work. Special bread pails with detachable dough hooks are also available, but these must be cranked by hand.

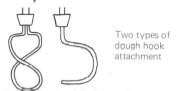

Two types of dough hook attachment

Ingredients. The basic ingredients in bread are flour, water or milk, yeast, salt, and sometimes sugar. Other ingredients that may be used include eggs, seeds, fruits, and nuts.

White wheat flour is the flour most widely used in breads. It is made from the starchy core of the wheat kernel. The bran (the coarse outer layer of the kernel) and the oily germ of the kernel (which spoils rapidly) produce coarser doughs and so are discarded.

There are three basic types of white flour: bread flour, soft white flour, and all-purpose flour. Bread flour is high in gluten, the part of the flour that creates an elastic network in the dough and holds in the carbon dioxide formed by the yeast to make the bread rise. Soft wheat flour is low in gluten and is generally used only in crackers, pretzels, and pastry. All-purpose flour is a combination of the two. There are also innumerable other types of white flour, such as self-rising and instant granulated flours, which contain additives or are designed for special uses or diets. Although bread flour is ideal for mak-

ing bread, it is difficult to find for home use. Consequently, the recipes in this chapter call for all-purpose flour when white flour is needed. Unbleached all-purpose flour is preferable; however, bleached flour can also be used.

Whole wheat flour and rye flour are also called for in some of the recipes. Whole wheat flour is made from the entire wheat kernel, including the bran and the oily germ. Rye flour is made from the rye grain. Cornmeal can also be used in breads.

Yeast comes in two forms: in compressed cakes and in powdered form. Both are equally efficient. One 2/3-ounce cake of compressed fresh yeast is equal to a single packet or 1 tablespoon of active dry (powdered) yeast. However, cake yeast spoils quickly and must be refrigerated or wrapped airtight and frozen. It will keep about a week in the refrigerator or for several weeks in a freezer. When fresh, cake yeast is uniformly gray with no discolored spots. Most powdered yeasts have an expiration date stamped on the packet. Be sure to use the yeast before this date. If you suspect that the yeast may be too old, dissolve it in the warm water called for in the recipe and stir in a tablespoon of flour and a pinch of sugar. If the yeast is still good, it will begin to foam and increase in volume in about 8 minutes. Never put yeast into water that is hotter than 38°C. Yeast is a living organism, and excessive heat will kill it. To test the temperature of the water, sprinkle a few drops of it on the inside of your wrist. If it feels warm but not hot, the temperature is correct.

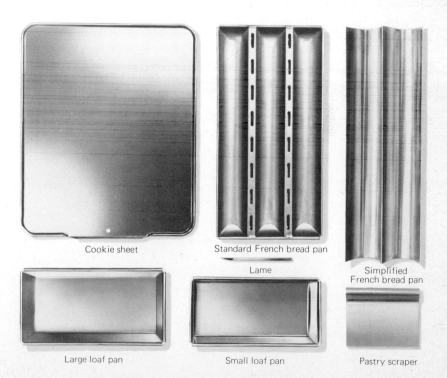

Cookie sheet

Standard French bread pan

Lame

Simplified French bread pan

Large loaf pan

Small loaf pan

Pastry scraper

Breads from around the world

French bread

French bread is made only of flour, water, salt, and yeast. French bakers are forbidden by law to use anything more. The ingredients are kneaded into a light, sticky dough and left to rise three times in a draft-free place that is around 21°C. The third rising takes place after the loaves have been shaped. It is important that this final rising take place in a fairly dry location, or the loaves may stick to the surface on which they are rising. Before the loaves are baked, they are slashed in several places to allow the dough to bulge up from underneath during baking and create a decorative pattern.

An illustrated recipe for French bread is given at right. To make three fat 15-inch-long loaves you will need: 1 cake fresh yeast or 1 packet powdered yeast, 1/3 cup warm water (it should be about 38°C), 3½ cups all-purpose flour, 2 teaspoons salt, and 1¼ cups tepid water. You will also need cornmeal for spreading under the loaves to keep them from sticking and a small supply of extra flour.

In France bread is baked in brick ovens that are shot full of steam during the first half of the baking time, giving the bread its crisp brown crust. The home baker must put a pan of boiling water into the bottom of the oven during the first half of the baking time, as described in Steps 19 and 20. Although this procedure may not produce as brown a crust as a real baker's oven, the bread will taste as good.

1. Dissolve yeast in 1/3 cup warm, but not hot, water. Put flour and salt into a mixing bowl and gradually stir in water and dissolved yeast. Mix ingredients thoroughly, stirring mixture and cutting into it with a rubber scraper.

2. Turn dough out onto a lightly floured board and let it rest about 3 min. Then lift one side of dough with pastry scraper or one hand and flip it over onto itself. Turn dough upside down, lift another side of it, and flip it over onto itself.

3. Continue this kneading process for 10 min, working quickly and vigorously. If dough is excessively sticky, sprinkle it with a little flour. After a few minutes of kneading, add a quick forward push with heel of hand to the kneading process.

8. Fold each piece in half, put aside, cover loosely with plastic wrap, and let rest 5 min. Meanwhile, prepare rising surface by sprinkling finely ground cornmeal into French bread pans or over canvas pastry cloth spread out on a tray.

9. Sprinkle the pastry board lightly with flour, and gently rub flour into surface. Also lightly flour your hands. Uncover one piece of rested dough (leave others covered), place it on the floured board, and pat it into a rough oval shape.

10. If any gas bubbles appear in dough, deflate them by pinching. Fold the oval-shaped dough in half lengthwise by grasping the far side of the oval with both hands and bringing it down to rest on the edge of the near side. Work quickly.

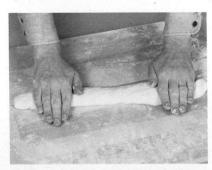

15. Move your hands away from each other as you roll the dough. Continue rolling quickly until dough is about 15 in. long. Keep thickness of dough as even as possible as you roll, and deflate any gas bubbles that appear by pinching.

16. Place loaf (with seam up if still visible) on rising surface prepared in Step 8. If you are using pastry cloth, pull it up on both sides of loaf so that loaf lies in a trough. Brace edges of cloth with something to keep them in place.

17. Cover loaf loosely with plastic wrap. Shape other loaves and place them on rising surface as you did first loaf, one at a time. If you are using pastry cloth, prop up loose edges. Loosely cover loaves with plastic wrap and a towel.

4. Put kneaded dough into bowl, cover bowl with plastic wrap, and drape a towel over it. Let dough rise at 21°C until it nearly triples in bulk—about 4 hr. (Dough should increase to about 10 cups; mark 10-cup level on bowl before adding dough.)

5. When dough is ready, plunge your fist down into the middle with one sharp blow to deflate it. Fold sides into center and turn dough upside down. Then cover it and let it rise again to nearly triple its bulk—about 1½–2 hr.

6. When dough has risen sufficiently (again it should come to the 10-cup mark), loosen sides of dough from bowl with rubber scraper and turn dough out of bowl onto a lightly floured board, being sure to scrape bowl clean.

7. If dough is sticky, sprinkle it with a little flour. Gently pat dough into a roughly rectangular shape and cut it into three equal pieces with a large, sharp knife. Hold handle of knife in one hand and steady end of blade with other hand.

11. Using the sides of your thumbs, seal the edges of the dough by pressing them firmly together. Check often during the shaping process to be sure that the pastry board is still lightly floured, or the dough may stick and tear.

12. Roll the sealed dough forward until the seal is at the top, and flatten the dough into an oval again. Then form a trench running down the full length of the center of the dough by pressing it firmly with the edge of your hand.

13. Fold dough in half lengthwise along trench, bringing two edges together. Seal edges by pressing them together with the side of your hand, moving from one end of dough to other. Roll dough toward you until seal is underneath.

14. Make sure that the work surface and your hands are still lightly floured. Place your hands, palms down and slightly overlapping, onto center of dough and begin rolling dough forward and backward to lengthen it into sausage shape.

18. Let loaves rise until more than doubled (1½–2½ hr). If you are using pastry cloth, sprinkle cookie sheet and length of cardboard with cornmeal, then gently roll each loaf onto edge of cardboard and slide it onto cookie sheet.

19. Preheat oven to 220°C 20 min before baking time. Put pan with 1½ cups boiling water into bottom of oven 15 min later. With lame or razor blade, cut three 1/2-in.-deep slashes into top of each risen loaf.

20. Spray fine mist of water over bread, and place cookie sheet or French bread pans with loaves into top third of oven. During first 15 min of baking, open oven door and spray loaves again every 3 min. Remove pan of water after 15 min.

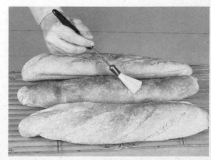

21. Bake bread 10–15 min more or until loaves are crisp and sound hollow when thumped. Remove from oven. If you want bread to shine, paint crust with cold water immediately. Let loaves cool on racks or standing on end for 2–3 hr.

Breads from around the world

Other shapes for French bread

Most people think of French bread only as long, slender loaves, but it is also commonly made into round loaves *(boules)* and dinner rolls *(petits pains)*. Even the long loaves vary; they are classified by length and thickness. The most common types are the *baguette,* which is about 24 inches long and 2 inches thick; the *bâtard,* which is about 16 inches long and 3 inches thick; and the *ficelle,* which is about 12 inches long and 3 inches thick.

Make the rolls or any of the loaves (except the baguette, which will probably not fit into your oven) by following the recipe on pages 416–417. All the long loaves are shaped in the same way. The only difference is the length to which the loaves are stretched.

Round loaves are shaped differently. Although you could simply roll the three pieces of dough into balls, you will get higher, lighter loaves by shaping them in the manner illustrated below. By doing so, you will anchor the network of coagulated gluten, creating tension on the surface of the loaf and holding the bread in shape as it rises.

Shape rolls in the same way as you would round loaves, but cut the dough into 10 or 12 pieces instead of 3 and use your fingers instead of your hands to shape the rolls. Cut only a single straight or curved slash into each roll.

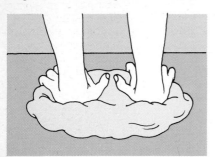

Making a round loaf. 1. Follow recipe on pages 416–417 through Step 8, let dough rest 5 min, then flatten it into a large circle. Flip left side two-thirds of way over to right and flip far side two-thirds of way over to near side.

2. Flatten the dough with the palms of your hands, then flip the left side of the flattened dough two-thirds of the way over to the right side. Flatten dough again and flip right side two-thirds of way over left side. Turn dough upside down.

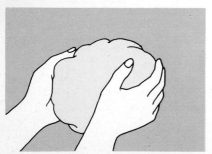

3. Pick up dough and rotate it a dozen times or so between palms of your hands, tucking a bit of dough under ball as you work. Place dough upside down on floured cloth, and pinch tucked under parts together. Cover dough and let it rise.

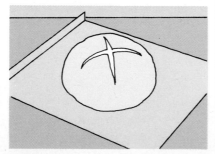

4. When dough has more than doubled in bulk, gently roll it, puckered side down, onto cookie sheet that has been sprinkled with cornmeal. Cut two slashes in shape of an X into top of loaf and bake the bread as you would a long loaf.

Bread baked in a pan

Many breads are baked in pans instead of free-form (as is French bread). The only basic difference in the techniques used in making these breads is in the shaping. Raisin bread, which is particularly popular with children throughout North America, is usually baked in pans. A recipe for two loaves of raisin bread and directions for shaping loaves for pan baking are given below.

American raisin bread

1 cup milk
1/2 cup butter
2 cakes or 2 packets yeast
1/4 cup warm water (about 38°C)
5¼ cups sifted all-purpose flour
1½ tsp salt
1/2 cup sugar
1 tbsp cinnamon
1½ cups raisins
2 beaten eggs

Heat the milk to just below the boiling point to scald it, then remove it from the stove. Cut the butter into small pieces and add it to the milk to melt it. Let the milk and butter cool to tepid.

Meanwhile, dissolve the yeast in the warm water. When the milk is ready, measure the sifted flour (sift it before measuring) into a large mixing bowl and gradually stir in the tepid milk and butter, the dissolved yeast, then the salt, sugar, cinnamon, raisins, and eggs. Keep stirring the mixture vigorously until all of the ingredients are well blended into a soft dough that leaves the sides of the bowl. (Begin mixing with a spoon and finish with your hands.)

Turn the dough out onto a lightly floured board and knead it for about 10 min, or until it is smooth and springy. Shape the kneaded dough into a ball, and put it into a large bowl. Cover the bowl with plastic wrap and a towel, and leave it in a warm place (about 27°C) until the dough has doubled in volume (about 1½–2 hr). Punch down the risen dough, turn it out onto a lightly floured board, and let it rest for about 15 min.

Cut the dough into two equal pieces, shape the pieces, and put them into pans as shown at right. Cover the pans with plastic wrap and towels, and leave them in a warm place until the loaves have doubled in volume. Make three diagonal slashes across the top of each loaf. Bake the bread in a 190°C oven for about 45 min or until the loaves are golden brown and sound hollow when thumped. Remove the loaves from the pans and let them cool on wire racks.

The baked loaf

Shaping a loaf for a pan. 1. Flatten the dough into a rough rectangle a bit longer than the pan. **2.** Roll up the rectangle lengthwise as you would a jelly roll. **3.** Pinch the seam and the ends closed, and tuck the ends under the loaf. **4.** Carefully transfer the loaf, seam down, to the pan, and push the corners of the dough down so that the loaf lies flat and touches the pan all around.

Braided breads

Most breads can be braided to give the loaves a festive appearance. Hallah, the traditional Jewish white bread, is often braided. In biblical times law required Jews to share a portion of their bread with the priests. Today when hallah is eaten, a portion of it is burned in remembrance of this law. A recipe for two hallah braids and directions for braiding are given below.

Jewish hallah braids

3 cakes or 3 packets yeast
1/3 cup warm water (about 38°C)
5 cups all-purpose flour
2 tbsp sugar
2 tsp salt
3 tbsp melted butter
3 beaten eggs
1 cup tepid water
1 egg yolk mixed with 1 tbsp cold water
Poppy seeds (optional)

Dissolve the yeast in the warm water. Put the flour into a large mixing bowl and gradually stir in the other ingredients except for the egg yolk mixture and the poppy seeds. Stir the mixture vigorously, beginning with a spoon and ending with your hands. The dough should become very stiff. If it does not, mix in more flour a little at a time until it does.

Turn the dough out onto a lightly floured board and knead it briskly for about 10 min, or until it becomes smooth and elastic. Put the kneaded dough into a large bowl, cover the bowl with plastic wrap and a towel, and leave it in a warm place (about 27°C) until the dough has doubled in volume (about 1½–2 hr).

Punch the dough down, turn it out onto a lightly floured board, pat it into a rough rectangle, and cut it into six equal pieces. Roll each of the six pieces into a rope about 1 in. thick. All six ropes should be of equal length and thickness. Place three of the six ropes side by side and braid them as shown at right, then repeat with the other three ropes. Always braid gently and loosely; do not stretch the dough.

Place the two braids 6 in. apart on a buttered cookie sheet, or form the two braids into a single wreath by curving them and pinching their ends together. Cover the braids lightly, and let them rise in a warm place until they have doubled in bulk (about 45 min–1 hr).

Brush the bread with the egg yolk and water mixture and, if you wish, sprinkle poppy seeds over the top. Bake the bread in a 205°C oven for 40 min or until it sounds hollow when thumped. Cool the bread on wire racks.

The baked loaf

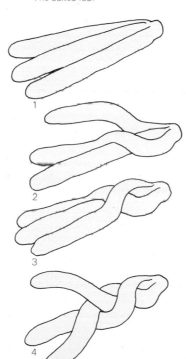

Shaping a braided loaf. 1. Place three strands of dough near each other and pinch their tops together. **2.** Bring right strand over to left side. **3.** Bring left strand over to right side so that the two outside strands cross over middle strand. **4.** Hold middle strand up and cross two side strands under it. Repeat Steps 2–4 until you reach ends of strands, then pinch ends together.

What can go wrong

Any reasonably good cook who faithfully follows the directions given in the recipes in this chapter should produce excellent breads most of the time. However, to make truly superior bread every time takes experience, for only experience can familiarize you with the many variables involved, such as how long to knead the dough, to let it rise, and to bake it.

The most important thing to learn is how the dough should feel. Although exact amounts of flour are specified in the accompanying recipes, you may have to alter the amounts to compensate for the properties of the flour or for weather conditions. In humid weather you may need more flour; in dry weather you may need less. You can judge only by the feel of the dough during kneading. If it is too sticky, add more flour by sprinkling in a little at a time until the dough feels right. If the dough is too dry, add a bit of water. If the dough feels too sticky after the first rising or while you are shaping it into loaves, sprinkle a little flour on top of it. Unfortunately, the dough for every type of bread is different. French bread has a light, sticky dough that will cling to your fingers if pressed but not otherwise. The dough for black bread is heavy and drier. Only experience with the particular type of dough will teach you how it should feel.

The temperature of the rising place and the degree of kneading and rising as well as the temperature of the oven and the length of baking time also affect the quality of the bread. If you try to rush the rising by placing the dough in too warm a place, if you fail to knead the dough enough, or if you bake it for the wrong amount of time or at the wrong temperature, you will have problems with your bread. A list of the most common breadmaking problems with suggestions on what can cause these problems follows.

Dough did not rise. The yeast was too old, or the water it was dissolved in was too hot and the yeast was killed. The other ingredients may have been too cold—they should be at room temperature or tepid to allow the yeast to grow.

Crust too dark. Too much salt, sugar, or glaze was used, or the oven was too hot. If the bread begins to get too brown, cover it with aluminum foil.

Crust too pale. Too little salt was used, the loaf was placed too low in the oven, or the oven was too cool.

Crust too thick or tough. The loaf rose in too humid a place, or it was baked in too cool an oven.

Crust cracked or blistered. The dough was not mixed enough, or it rose too long or in too hot a place.

Bread heavy, dense, or hard. Too much flour or salt or not enough yeast was used, the dough was overkneaded, the dough rose too quickly or not enough, or the oven was too hot.

Bread soggy. Too much liquid or too little flour was used, or the bread was wrapped before it was thoroughly cool.

Bread too full of air holes. Too much yeast or not enough salt was used, the dough was not thoroughly mixed, or it rose too long or in too warm a place.

Bread too chewy. The dough rose too quickly or was baked in too cool an oven or for too short a time.

Bread too crumbly. Too much liquid was used, the dough was not kneaded enough, it rose too much, or it was baked in too cool an oven.

Bread lumpy. The dough was not mixed enough, or it was left to rise for too long or in too warm a place.

Bread tastes sour or yeasty. The dough was left to rise in too warm a place. The rising temperature for bread should not exceed 30°C.

Bread staled quickly. The flour was too soft, not enough liquid or salt was used, the dough did not rise enough, or the oven was too cool.

Breads from around the world

Other bread recipes

Kulich—a Russian Easter bread

1/2 cup milk
1 cake or 1 packet yeast
1/4 cup warm water (about 38°C)
4 cups all-purpose flour
1 tsp salt
1/4 tsp saffron
1 tbsp brandy
3 egg yolks
3/4 cup sugar
3/4 cup butter, melted and cooled
1/2 cup candied fruit
2 tsp grated lemon rind
1/2 cup chopped almonds
1/2 cup raisins
1/2 tsp vanilla
1/2 tsp ground cardamom
2 stiffly beaten egg whites
1/2 cup sifted confectioner's sugar
2 tsp cream
Candied lemon rind

Scald the milk by bringing it almost to a boil, then let it cool. Dissolve the yeast in the warm water. In a mixing bowl, combine 1 cup of the flour with the salt, milk, and dissolved yeast. Stir until thoroughly mixed, then cover the bowl and leave it in a warm place (about 27°C) until the batter is light and bubbly (about 1 hr). Dry out the saffron in a 120°C oven for 10 min, grind it to a powder with a spoon, stir in the brandy, and set the mixture aside.

Beat the egg yolks with the sugar and mix this into the risen batter. Stir in the butter and remaining flour a little at a time. In a separate bowl mix the fruit, lemon rind, almonds, raisins, vanilla, cardamom, and saffron and brandy.

Turn the dough out onto a floured board and knead it for 15 min. Flatten the dough and spread the fruit mixture over it. Fold the fruit into the dough and continue kneading for 30 min more. Work the stiffly beaten egg whites into the dough. The dough will become very

sticky. Continue kneading it with the help of a pastry scraper until the egg whites are fully incorporated. Sprinkle a little flour over the dough.

Thoroughly grease a 2-lb coffee can, and fit a circle of waxed paper into the bottom. Put in the dough (it should half fill the can). Cover the can and leave it in a warm place until the dough rises to the rim (about 1½ hr). Bake the bread in a 175°C oven for 1 hr or until a knife inserted into it comes out clean. Let the can cool for 10 min, then turn the bread out onto a wire rack.

When the bread is completely cool, thoroughly blend the confectioner's sugar and cream, then spread the icing over the top of the bread. The loaf should resemble the snow-covered onion dome of a Russian church. Fashion a cross over the frosting with the candied rind. To serve the kulich while preserving its appearance, slice off the top, cut wedges out of the bottom, and replace the top.

Pita—a Greek flat bread

1 cake or 1 packet yeast
1 cup warm water (about 38°C)
3 cups all-purpose flour
1 tsp salt
1/4 cup olive oil

Dissolve the yeast in the warm water and mix it thoroughly with the other ingredients. Knead the dough for 10 min, or until it is smooth and springy, and let it rise in a covered bowl at 27°C until it doubles in volume (about 1½ hr). Punch down the risen dough and let it rest for 10 min. Cut the rested dough into four equal portions and roll each piece into a ball. Flatten the balls and roll them into thin circles 8 in. in diameter. Place the circles of dough on a greased cookie sheet, cover them, and let them rise at 27°C for 30 min. Bake them in a 260°C oven for 8 min, or until light brown and puffed. Cool the pitas on wire racks, cut them in half, and fill the natural pouch in each half with sandwich food.

Italian whole-wheat bread

1 cake or 1 packet yeast
1 cup warm water (about 38°C)
1 cup whole-wheat flour
1½ cups all-purpose flour
2 tsp salt
1 tbsp olive oil

Dissolve the yeast in the warm water and combine it with the other ingredients. Stir until thoroughly blended, then knead the dough for 10 min, or until it is smooth and springy. Let the dough rise in a covered bowl at 24°C–27°C until it has doubled in bulk (about 3 hr).

Punch down the risen dough and let it rise again to double (about 3 hr). Knead the dough briefly, shape it into a single round loaf, and place it on a cookie sheet that has been greased or sprinkled with cornmeal. Let it rest for a few minutes. When its surface has caked a bit, cut an x-shaped slash into the top, brush it lightly with water, and bake it in a 230°C oven for 12 min, then turn the heat down to 190°C and bake it for an additional 45 min, or until it is brown and sounds hollow when thumped. Cool the bread on a wire rack before serving.

Hungarian seeded bread

1 cake or 1 packet yeast
1 cup warm water (about 38°C)
3 cups all-purpose flour
1 tsp salt
4 tsp sugar
1/8 tsp crushed anise seeds
1/4 tsp crushed fennel seeds
1 tbsp vegetable oil
1 egg yolk beaten with 2 tsp milk
Whole anise seeds

Dissolve the yeast in the warm water. In a mixing bowl, blend the flour, salt, sugar, crushed seeds, and oil. Stir the mixture until all the ingredients are thoroughly

blended, then turn the dough out onto a floured board and knead it for 10 min, or until it is smooth and springy. Let it rise in a covered bowl at 27°C until it doubles in bulk (about 1 hr). Punch down the risen dough, then cover it again and let it rise for another 15 min. (It need not double in bulk this time.)

Turn the dough out onto a lightly floured board and knead it for 1 min. Shape the dough into a round loaf and place the loaf on a greased cookie sheet. Cover the loaf lightly and let it rise at 27°C until it doubles in bulk (about 45 min).

Make four slashes in the top of the loaf in a grid shape, then paint the loaf with the egg yolk and milk, and sprinkle it with the anise seeds. Bake the bread in a 205°C oven for 35 min, or until it is brown and sounds hollow when thumped. Cool the bread on a wire rack.

Ethiopian honey bread

1 cup milk
6 tbsp butter
1/2 cup honey
1 cake or 1 packet yeast
1/4 cup warm water (about 38°C)
4 cups all-purpose flour
1½ tsp salt
1 tbsp ground coriander
1/2 tsp ground cinnamon
1/4 tsp ground cloves
1 beaten egg

Scald the milk by bringing it almost to a boil, then add the butter and honey to it and let it cool to lukewarm. Dissolve the yeast in the warm water. In a mixing bowl, combine the flour, salt, spices, egg, dissolved yeast, and the milk, butter, and honey. Stir until all the ingredients are thoroughly blended, then turn the dough out onto a lightly floured board and knead it for 5–10 min, or until the dough is smooth and springy.

Let the dough rise in a covered bowl at 27°C until it doubles in bulk (about 1½ hr). Punch the dough down and knead it for about 2 min, then shape it into a circle and put it into a 3-qt soufflé dish or a round baking dish. (The dish should be at least 3 in. high.) Cover the dish and put it in a warm place until the dough doubles in bulk again (about 1½ hr).

Bake the risen dough in a 150°C oven for about 50 min, or until the top is crusty and golden. Turn the bread out of the pan and cool it on a wire rack. Serve it with butter and honey.

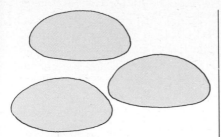

Chinese steamed bread

1 cake or 1 packet yeast
1½ cups warm water (about 38°C)
4 cups all-purpose flour
2 tbsp vegetable oil
1/4 cup sugar

Dissolve the yeast in the warm water and thoroughly blend in the flour, oil, and sugar. Knead the dough for 10 min, or until it is smooth and springy. Let it rise in a covered bowl at 27°C until it has doubled in volume (about 2 hr). Cut the dough in half and shape it into three oval loaves. Let the loaves rise for 15 min, or until they become plump.

Place the loaves on an oiled plate and put the plate on top of several small oven-proof dishes in a large pot. (There should be space between the plate and the sides of the pot.) Add water until it comes to just under the plate, cover the pot, and boil the water gently for 30 min. The resultant steam will cook the bread.

Slice the bread and serve it hot with Chinese food. Or, if you prefer, cool the bread, slice it thinly, and deep fry the slices until they are golden brown. Eat the fried bread with Chinese food, or sprinkle sugar over the slices and have them as a snack.

Broa—a Brazilian corn bread

1 cake or 1 packet yeast
1/4 cup warm water (about 38°C)
1½ cups yellow cornmeal
1½ tsp salt
1 cup boiling water
1 tbsp olive oil
1¾ cups all-purpose flour

Dissolve the yeast in the warm water. In a blender, pulverize the cornmeal a little at a time until it is a fine powder. Put 1 cup of the cornmeal into a mixing bowl and stir in the salt and boiling water. Stir

in the olive oil and let the mixture cool to lukewarm. Add the dissolved yeast to the lukewarm mixture, then gradually stir in the rest of the cornmeal and 1 cup of the flour. Work the mixture into a dough, adding more of the flour if it is too sticky. Then cover the bowl and let the dough rise in a warm place (27°C) until it has doubled in volume (about 1 hr).

Turn the risen dough out onto a lightly floured board, work in the rest of the flour, and knead the dough for 5–10 min, or until it is smooth and firm. Shape the kneaded dough into a round loaf and put it on a greased cookie sheet. Cover the loaf and let it rise at about 27°C until it doubles in bulk (about 1 hr). Bake the risen loaf in a 175°C oven for 40 min, or until it sounds hollow when tapped. Serve broa warm or cool. It is particularly good when eaten with soup.

Braided bread wreaths from Finland

1/2 cup milk
1/2 cup butter
1 cake or 1 packet yeast
1/4 cup warm water (about 38°C)
4 cups sifted all-purpose flour
2 beaten eggs
2 tbsp sugar
1 tsp salt
1½ tsp ground cardamom
1 egg yolk mixed with 1 tbsp milk

Scald the milk by bringing it almost to a boil, add the butter to it, and let it cool. Dissolve the yeast in the warm water. In a mixing bowl, combine the flour, eggs, sugar, salt, and cardamom. Add the dissolved yeast and the milk and butter, and stir until the ingredients are blended thoroughly. Turn the mixture out onto a lightly floured board and knead it for about 10 min, or until it is smooth. Put it into a bowl, cover the bowl, and leave it in a warm place (27°C) until the dough has doubled in bulk (about 2 hr).

Punch down the dough and turn it out

onto a lightly floured board. Cut it into six equal portions, and roll each piece into an 18- to 20-in.-long strand. Braid three of the strands together (see p. 419), pull the ends of the braid around into a circle, and pinch the ends together. Repeat with the other three strands. Place the wreaths a few inches apart on a greased cookie sheet, cover them lightly with plastic wrap and a towel, and let them rise in a warm place until they double in bulk (about 2 hr).

Paint the wreaths with the egg yolk and milk mixture. Bake them in a 175°C oven for 45 min, or until they are golden brown and sound hollow when thumped. Serve them warm or cool. If you are storing the wreaths for future use, cool them thoroughly on wire racks before wrapping and storing them.

English muffins

1 cake or 1 packet yeast
2 tbsp warm water (about 38°C)
1/2 cup milk
3 tbsp butter
4 cups sifted all-purpose flour
2 tsp sugar
1 tsp salt
1 cup water

Dissolve the yeast in the 2 tbsp warm water. Scald the milk by bringing it almost to a boil, then add the butter to it and let it cool. Measure the sifted flour, sugar, and salt into a bowl and gradually stir in the cup of water, the dissolved yeast, and the milk and butter. Keep stirring until all the ingredients are thoroughly mixed, then cover the bowl and let the dough rise in a warm place (about 27°C) until it doubles in bulk (about 2 hr).

Turn the risen dough out onto a lightly floured board, knead it slightly, then cut it and shape it into about a dozen 1/2-in.-thick disks. Place the shaped pieces of dough on a lightly floured board or cookie sheet and let them rise in a warm place until they double in bulk (about 1 hr). Lift the risen muffins with a pancake turner and put them on a hot, well-buttered griddle. Cook them until they are light brown on the bottom, then turn them over and cook the other side until light brown. Cool the muffins on a rack. Before eating them, split them in half and toast them. If you are not using them the same day, wrap them in plastic and freeze them—they stale quickly.

Black bread from the Black Forest

2 cups fine bread crumbs (preferably from black bread)
3 cakes or 3 packets yeast
1/2 cup warm water (about 38°C)
1 tbsp Postum
2 cups hot water
4 tbsp blackstrap molasses
3 cups rye flour
2 tsp salt
1 tsp sugar
1/4 tsp ground ginger
1/4 cup melted butter
2 cups all-purpose flour
1 tbsp Postum mixed with 2 tbsp water

Toast the black bread crumbs until they are very dark. (You can use white bread crumbs if necessary, but the darker the crumbs are, the darker the finished bread will be.) Dissolve the yeast in the warm water. Dissolve the Postum in the hot water, stir in the molasses and bread crumbs, and let the mixture stand until it is lukewarm.

Add the rye flour, salt, sugar, ginger, butter, and dissolved yeast; stir until all the ingredients are thoroughly blended. Spread the all-purpose flour over the top of the mixture and let it rest for 15 min. Then turn the mixture out of the bowl and knead it for 10 min, or until the all-purpose flour is blended in and the dough is smooth (it will be a little dry and stiff). Place the dough in a bowl, cover the bowl with plastic wrap and a towel, and leave it in a warm place (about 27°C) until the dough has risen to twice its volume (about 1½ hr).

Turn the risen dough out onto a lightly floured board, and shape it into a single round loaf. Place the loaf on a lightly greased cookie sheet, cover it, and let it rise at about 27°C until it doubles in bulk (about 45 min).

Brush the loaf with the mixture of Postum and water and bake the bread in a 205°C oven for 40 min, or until it is completely dry. Cool it on a wire rack.

421

Winemaking

Winemaking through the ages

Home winemaking has always been among the most challenging of hobbies because of the many different techniques from which to choose. The greater the home winemaker's experience, the greater his desire to improve this year's vintage over efforts of previous years. Each year he seeks to apply old, successful techniques to the new season's unique grape harvest. And every harvest tests his expertise fully, since no two are exactly alike.

In the history of civilization the cultivation of grapes is almost as old as agriculture itself. The first wines may have been produced through the accidental fermentation of stored grapes, initiated by yeasts that collect naturally on the skins of grapes while they are on the vine. But scholars tell us that wine was being produced regularly in the Near East in prebiblical times.

Wine and gods. Wine has often been thought of as a gift from the gods—the Egyptians believed it to be a gift from Osiris, while the Greeks asserted it had been given to them by Dionysus. In any case, the drinking of wine has been an integral part of religious ceremonies in widely divergent societies: the Greeks and Romans poured libations of wine to their gods; wine is mentioned often in the Old Testament and in the Babylonian Talmud; many Christians take wine in Communion services.

The art of making wine was saved from virtual extinction by Christian monastic orders after the fall of Rome. Since the monks needed to produce only enough wine for their own monasteries, they were able to dedicate their time and effort to experimentation and refinement in viticulture (the science of growing grapes). This resulted in some of the greatest advances ever made in viticulture at a time when, in the world outside monastery walls, winemaking had come to a halt.

Wines and laws. The value placed on wine in many societies resulted in its subjection to prohibitions and regulations. The Code of Hammurabi, promulgated by Hammurabi, a king of Babylonia in the 18th century B.C., makes specific mention of the sale of wine and the punishment to be inflicted upon any vendor who gave short measure to his customers. In A.D. 92 a limited prohibition was enacted in Rome by the Emperor Domitian: he felt that too much land and effort were being devoted to the production of wine and ordered that half of all the grapevines in the empire be uprooted. The command was obeyed only reluctantly, and it was repealed in A.D. 280 by the Emperor Probus. In 1936 the French passed the laws of Appelation Contrôlée to maintain the reputation of native wines and to prevent misrepresentation. The regulations, which restrict the use of well-known names, protect consumers as well as vintners.

Changing tastes. The famous wines of history might be unrecognizable today—and in many cases they would be considered undrinkable. Although the Egyptian kings drank grape wines, their subjects had only a substance fermented from palms and dates. In order to store their wines without loss, the Greeks resorted to crocks sealed with pitch, and for flavor they often added seawater or perfumes, or they exposed the wine to smoke.

Nonetheless, wine in its many variations has proved to be a drink of such universal appeal that it need only be introduced into a society in order to assume a major role in the agricultural pursuits of the people. And the home winemaker need only produce one particularly pleasing bottle to fall prey to a passion for the art.

Early Egyptian commerce in wines is recorded in this detail from a 12th century B.C. painting from the Tomb of Kha-emwése at Thebes. Painting is in collection of British Museum.

Equipment and supplies

Generally speaking, anyone in Canada is permitted to make wine at home—provided it is not for purposes of sale. Restrictions, however, do exist as to the age of the winemaker and the strength of the wine. These restrictions vary from province to province. Before making your own wine consult your provincial Liquor Licensing Board or Liquor Control Commission.

It is important to assemble all the necessary equipment before winemaking is begun. This will serve to prevent any spoilage or loss due to delays in obtaining materials and will keep an enjoyable project from becoming a series of frustrations.

When you buy equipment, remember that wine is acidic and will react with any metals it might contact. For this reason all winemaking implements should be made of wood, plastic, glass, or stainless steel.

A few specialized items must be bought from a winemaking supplier. These include fermentation locks, which are simple valves used to seal the containers in which the wine is fermented; a saccharometer (or a hydrometer), which indicates the amount of sugar present in the crushed grapes and thus the ultimate alcoholic content of the wine; a press (probably the most expensive piece of equipment), which is not essential for small amounts of grapes but is handy if significant quantities are to be crushed; and finally, a corking device, bottles, and corks. Planning ahead will allow you to save the bottles from the commercial wines you consume, but corks cannot be reused and must be purchased fresh.

The other necessary pieces of equipment can be found in either a hardware store or the housewares section of a department store. First you will need something in which the grapes can be crushed, such as a plastic (not metal) wastebasket or garbage can. This con-

tainer will also serve as a fermentation vessel. Buy plastic sheeting to stretch over the top of the container (to keep out air) and sturdy string to fasten it.

Several large glass bottles will be needed for later stages of fermentation, the process after the grapes have been fermented in the large plastic wastebasket. Those used by bottled-water suppliers are perfect. Since the bottles must be sealed with corks that hold fermentation locks, they must, whatever their size or shape, have mouths that will firmly seat the corks.

Wooden utensils, including a wooden dowel about 3 feet long, are used for any stirring or prodding of the crushed grapes. Several yards of clean cheesecloth, about 6 feet of plastic tubing to be used as a siphon hose, and a funnel complete the list of the equipment necessary for winemaking.

Some special ingredients are available only from a winemaking supplier. Potassium metabisulfite, which comes in convenient tablet form, is an absolutely essential cleaning and sterilizing agent. The sulphur dioxide it releases eliminates wild yeasts and bacteria that might harm the wine and also reduces the browning that occurs in grapes.

Wine yeast is the agent that promotes the process of fermentation. Because the wild yeasts that are present in the "bloom" on the grapes may be of unpredictable nature, they are eliminated by the addition of the potassium metabisulfite, and a specially cultured wine yeast is added. This should not be confused with ordinary baking yeast, which is not an adequate substitute. A yeast nutrient is also added to provide the wine yeast with a suitable nitrogen source for fermentation.

Tartaric acid, an acidity test kit with pH strips, and a box of confectioner's sugar complete the list of ingredients that will transform the raw grapes into wine of good quality.

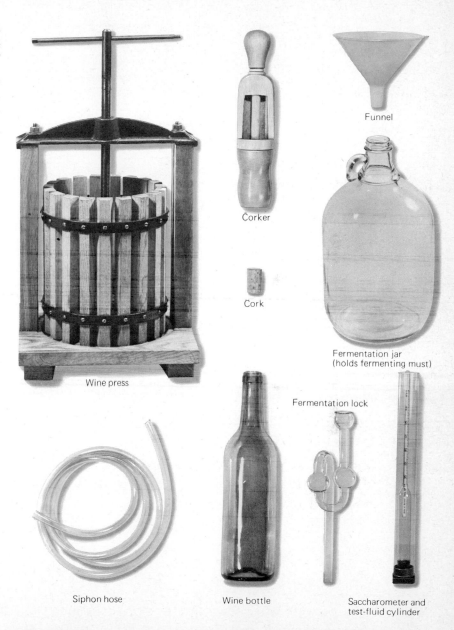

Funnel

Corker

Cork

Wine press

Fermentation jar
(holds fermenting must)

Fermentation lock

Siphon hose

Wine bottle

Saccharometer and
test-fluid cylinder

Basic equipment. Fermentation locks allow gas to escape from fermentation bottle while blocking entrance of bacteria from air. The wine press is optional; crushed grapes can be squeezed through cheesecloth. A plastic wastebasket (not shown) makes a good initial container for the must. Siphon hose, funnel are used in racking. Saccharometer tests sugar levels.

Winemaking

Grapes, concentrates, fruits, and flowers

The most important factor in obtaining a satisfactory wine is the proper selection of the raw fruits or blossoms to be used. Although corrections and adjustments can be made to the flavor of a wine (see p. 432), no truly good wine results from poor fruits or blossoms.

Wine grapes. In making a grape wine, the best results are obtained from the species *Vitis vinifera,* the staple of the wine industries of Europe and California. This grape possesses the ideal qualities for producing a wine of pleasing flavor. Its natural sugar content makes it suitable for fermentation, yielding alcohol levels of 10 percent or higher; this is essential, as a lower level of alcohol renders a wine prone to bacterial spoilage.

The acid content of *V. vinifera* is also ideal; it has less than 1 percent tartaric acid. This species also has a great range of composition, which means that the different varieties produce a strong assortment of flavors and colorings.

A grape native to eastern North America, *Vitis labrusca,* has long been used in that region's winemaking industries. It is suited to the harsher winters, but the shorter growing season results in grapes that are low in sugar content with high acidity, so large amounts of sugar must be added to provide sufficient alcoholic content. These grapes usually impart too pungent a flavor, a taste that is frequently described as "foxy."

In recent years, however, crosses of vinifera and American vines have resulted in hybrid grapes that produce elegant dry wines from vines able to withstand harsh winters. Many new vineyards are springing up in the Northeast to grow the hybrid.

In many cases you will be limited by what grapes are available in your area at the time of year you are attempting to obtain them. Grapes are harvested in the fall, and it is then that you will have the best opportunity to obtain the ones you want at their peak.

Grape properties. Whatever kinds of grapes you select, they should be reasonably firm. When crushed between the fingers, a grape should exude a slightly sticky juice. Juice that is excessively sticky indicates that the grape has been on the vine too long and is overripe. Wrinkling in the skins means that the grapes have begun to turn to raisins and are useless. Bunches of grapes that have a large number of bruises and gashes should be avoided, as the damaged pulp may have begun to rot, or to mildew; or harmful bacteria may have formed.

Yield per pound of grapes. Anticipate an average yield of about 1 gallon of wine for each 20 pounds of grapes. If you cannot find sufficient quantities of your preferred grape, experiment with mixing different kinds. Many fine wines are produced in this way, and a willingness to experiment will provide valuable experience.

Concentrates. If grapes are out of season in your region and your market is unable to obtain them from afar, commercial grape concentrates can be substituted. Do not confuse concentrate with the grape juice available at the grocery store. A concentrate is made from crushed and pressed grapes by removing the excess water, which is later added by the winemaker according to the manufacturer's directions. Once reconstituted, the liquid is treated just as if it were freshly pressed grapes.

In general, concentrates are produced from the grapes that the vineyard feels are not good enough to be used in their own wines. While they certainly give acceptable results, they should not be viewed as a primary source when you are seeking to produce the best wine of which you are capable. However, since the procedures for working with concentrates are identical to those for your own pressed juice, they can be used to develop your skills when fresh grapes are unavailable.

Other fruits and flowers. Many fine wines are made from a large variety of sources other than grapes. Apples, peaches, plums, cherries, strawberries, elderberries, apricots, blackberries, and many other fruits will produce wines that in many ways are comparable to good grape wines. While such wines will not always have a strong taste identifying the fruit used, they will have a flavor distinct from grape wine. Even dried fruits can be used, but they must contain no chemical preservatives and are most likely to be found in health-food stores.

Flowers also produce distinctly flavored wines, but their use is limited to the spring and summer months, when they are available in abundance. Rose hips (the swollen portion of the flower that appears when the petals have fallen off) or dandelion petals can be combined with raisins to make good wines. Recipes for making wines from fruits and flowers appear on pages 430 and 431 of this chapter.

Grapes   Plum   Elderberries   Strawberries   Cherries   Dandelion

Preparing the must and initial fermentation

To prepare the grapes for crushing into must (the fermentable juice), clean them thoroughly to be sure all traces of pesticides have been removed. First pour boiling water over them, then soak them in a solution of 1/2 teaspoon potassium metabisulfite to each 5 gallons water for one day. Keep more of this solution available for cleaning implements and bottles.

Remove the stems from the grapes before crushing, as the stems contain an excess of tannin, which would impart an undesirable flavor to the wine. At the same time, discard any bruised or damaged grapes. The grapes can be crushed with the hands, the feet, or by any convenient means. Just be sure that no tools used are made of metal, and rinse all tools in the potassium metabisulfite solution before using them.

Marking the container. As it will be necessary to know how much must is in the container, mark it in 1/2-gallon graduations. You can do this by pouring water into the container from quart bottles and marking the level after every 2 quarts. Each 20 pounds of grapes will yield about 1 gallon of wine. Since the container in which the grapes are crushed will also be used for the first stage of fermentation, the must

should fill it to only two-thirds of its capacity or less to allow for expansion.

Red and white wines. A red wine is made by fermenting the juice along with the skins of red grapes. A white wine can be made from either red or white grapes. If red grapes are used for white wine, the juice should be strained from the pulp, using cheesecloth, so that the wine will not have time to extract color from the skins.

Saccharometer readings. Once the grapes have been crushed, the saccharometer (or hydrometer) is used to take a reading of the sugar content of the must (see illustrations below). Saccharometers and related instruments may be marked with different scales, but all are a function of the specific gravity of the test liquid. Your scale might be specific gravity (if you are substituting a hydrometer for a saccharometer); potential alcohol; or Brix (Balling). A reading of about 1.100 specific gravity, 14 percent potential alcohol, or 25° Brix is desired.

Initial fermentation. After correcting for sugar content—by adding either sugar or water to the must as described below—add the yeast nutrient to the container of must. Use about 1/2 teaspoon of nutrient for each gallon of

must; then add 1/3 tablet of potassium metabisulfite for each gallon of must. The tablet, when it breaks down, provides sulfur dioxide, which promotes better fermentation while killing undesirable bacteria. Cover the container with plastic and fasten it.

Starter solution. This is necessary to ensure that the yeast is properly activated before adding it to the must. Begin by boiling 1/2 cup water, then allow it to cool until it is just tepid. Add 1/2 teaspoon confectioner's sugar, stir it in, then add the wine yeast, using the full amount required for the must. (Packaged wine yeast has directions as to how much to add.) Add a pinch of yeast nutrient, then let the mixture sit for an hour, or until it begins to foam and give off a characteristic "yeasty" smell. Then add this mixture to the sample of sugar-corrected must that was used for the hydrometer readings. Place the whole solution in a bottle, plug the bottle with a wad of sterilized cotton, and let it sit in a warm (21°C) area for 24 hours.

The next day the starter solution can be added to the must. (In making a white wine, the juice will be strained from the skins before the starter solution is added.) The container should be

resealed with the plastic sheeting after adding the starter.

Breaking the cap. The fermenting must should be kept in an area with a constant temperature range of 18°C–24°C. The skins and pulp will float to the surface and form a "cap." This cap is broken periodically so that heat and carbon dioxide are not trapped by it, stopping fermentation.

Two-week period. Every day or two remove the plastic sheeting and stir the cap into the must with a clean wooden dowel, then replace the sheeting. At the end of two weeks take saccharometer readings daily until the reading becomes 1.050 on a specific-gravity scale or 12.5° on the Brix scale. At this point initial fermentation is complete.

Removing skins. In the next stage of fermenting a red wine the juice is separated from the skins and fermented alone. Because the color of a wine and many elements of its flavor are derived from the skins, you will have to experiment with several batches before you know how long to let the must ferment on its skins. A rosé can be made by letting the must stay on the skins for one or two days. A red wine is left on the skins through the initial fermentation.

Testing must for sugar. Use either a saccharometer or hydrometer, which measure sugar content in terms of specific gravity. Fill measuring cup with 10 oz clear juice; pour into cylinder until saccharometer floats freely.

Alcohol potential is governed by sugar content of juice: the more sugar, the higher the saccharometer will float. The level at which it floats should read 25° on the Brix scale or 1.100 on a specific-gravity scale. Here, the reading is low.

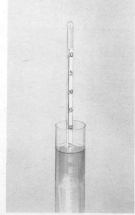

Confectioner's sugar is added to raise reading to 25°. Pour juice in cylinder back into cup. Add sugar, 1 tsp at a time, taking readings after each addition. (If the reading were high, water would be added, 1/2 oz at a time.)

Reading is now correct. Add teaspoons of sugar to main batch of must in same proportion as to the sample of juice in measuring cup by following this formula:
$$128 \times \text{no. gal of must} \times \text{no. tsp in sample} \div 10$$

Winemaking

Preparing the must and initial fermentation (continued)

With experience you can attempt to reproduce in your own wines the characteristics you find most desirable in fine vintage wines.

The wine yeast you choose can have a great effect on the finished product. The strains of yeast are usually named after the region where they were first isolated. While the use of a Burgundy yeast does not mean a true Burgundy has been produced, it does contribute to the distinctive Burgundy flavor.

Montrachet is a good all-purpose yeast. Dry wines, those with little or no sugar left at the end of fermentation, can be enhanced by the use of a Bordeaux or Zeltinger yeast. A medium-sweet wine can benefit from the use of a Rhine or Liebfraumilch yeast, and a sweet, full-bodied wine would take a Port, Sherry, Tokay, or Sauterne yeast. These yeasts must be used in conjunction with the proper fermenting techniques (the basics of which are detailed on these pages) to achieve suitable levels of alcohol in relation to unfermented sugar.

The amount of sugar remaining in a wine at the end of fermentation will affect its sweetness. But it would be a mistake to heavily dose a must with sugar so that some will remain at the completion of the fermenting—once an alcohol content of about 17 percent is obtained, the remaining yeast cells will fail to ferment; however, the sugar left over may be oddly flavored or too syrupy. It is better to sweeten the wine by the addition of confectioner's sugar after fermentation has stopped. Wait a week or two before bottling to make certain that the sugar has not restarted the fermentation.

Different wines can be blended to average out their qualities. This should be done first with a small sample to determine the correct ratios. Even a blend that seems indifferent upon mixing may improve when aged.

1. Pick grapes off stems. Discard stems and any bruised, broken, or moldy grapes. Collect grapes in container, such as a plastic wastebasket. (A glass container is used in these pictures to make all steps clearly visible.)

2. Crush the grapes by hand, foot, or any convenient implement. All the grapes should be crushed in this manner before they are put into the press (next step) or, in lieu of a press, are squeezed through cheesecloth.

3. Wrap the base of the press in plastic to contain overflow (see next picture). After turning up the crank to its highest position, remove pressure plate from bottom of press; then pour mixture of crushed grapes and juice into the press.

4. Begin to press the grapes. Give the crank half a dozen twists, then wait for the pulp to drain before cranking again. Do not try to press the pulp completely dry, as this could split the seeds, releasing unwanted substances into the must.

5. If you do not have a press, you can squeeze the hand-crushed grapes through cheesecloth; squeeze no more than a large handful at a time to ensure that you get all the juice. Save skins if you are making red or rosé wine from red grapes.

6. Test the juice for sugar content as explained in the text and captions on page 425. If reading is low, add sugar as described on page 425; if high, add water, 1/2 oz at a time. Take readings after each addition. Here, sugar is added.

7. Refer to page 425 in performing the following procedures: add sugar (or water) to the main batch of must; add potassium metabisulfite to the must; then add yeast to test sample to prepare starter solution, as seen here.

8. After one day starter solution is added to must, which has already been sugar-corrected and treated with potassium metabisulfite. For red wine, must is allowed to ferment on skins, as seen here. Next steps are on page 428.

Fermentation and bottling

After the must has gone through the initial stages of fermentation in the container, it is ready to be transferred into large fermentation bottles, which then will be sealed with fermentation locks. The siphoning process by which this is achieved is called racking; it is done as shown in the photographs on the next two pages.

Cease puncturing the cap at least one full day before racking so that the must under the cap will be as free as possible of drifting particles. Because the must will be siphoned, not poured, into the fermentation bottles, the container should at this time be placed on a surface above them.

Pressing the cap. Begin racking by scooping the cap from the surface (using only wood or plastic utensils). Place it in cheesecloth to be squeezed into the bottle. A funnel lined with cheesecloth should be placed in the bottle's neck, as it is desirable to filter out as much sediment as possible.

If a press rather than cheesecloth is used to squeeze the skins and pulp of the cap, the pressure plate should be lowered only a few turns at a time. Allow ample time for the wine to drain from the mass of pulp before exerting more pressure. Too much force could result in splitting of the pips, which would inject too much tannin and affect the flavor of the wine.

Racking the free run. The "free run," the clear wine on which the cap floated, must be racked (siphoned), not poured, into the bottle. It is essential that the dead yeast cells and other sediment covering the bottom of the container be left undisturbed. The siphon hose should be handled carefully so that it does not suck up any sediment.

Although the free run may appear to be clear, retain the cheesecloth in the funnel, as the liquid may contain fine particles that are not readily visible. The cheesecloth filter also serves as a safeguard against racking any sediment into the clean bottle.

Applying fermentation locks. After all the wine has been transferred into the large fermentation bottles, they should be capped with fermentation locks that are filled with water. These locks prevent any contaminants from entering the bottles, while they allow the carbon dioxide produced during the conversion of sugar to alcohol to escape. If you cannot obtain fermentation locks, pieces of plastic food wrap held in place by rubber bands will make adequate substitutes.

Subsequent fermentation. The wine will continue to ferment during this subsequent stage. Bubbles will be seen in the water in the locks. When the bubbles cease to appear, there may still be active fermentation; at this point a saccharometer reading gives the best indication of progress.

A saccharometer reading taken after two weeks or when the bubbling seems to have subsided should indicate a specific gravity reading of 1.000, or a Brix or potential alcohol level near 0°. This does not mean that fermentation is complete; an inaccuracy will exist at this point caused by the presence of both sugar and alcohol. What is indicated is that it is time to repeat the racking process so that the fermentation can continue. If the proper reading is not obtained, allow more time, taking a new reading every other day.

Second racking. This racking procedure is quite similar to the first racking and with the same purpose—to leave the sediment of dead yeast cells behind and to continue the fermentation. The wine is racked into other bottles that have been thoroughly cleaned. This time make a point of splashing the wine from the hose against the insides of the new bottles so that it is aerated. Aerating will give a boost to the remaining yeast cells so that they can complete the fermentation process. The new bottles should be capped with fermentation locks or plastic wrap exactly as the first ones were.

Fermentation will proceed at a slower rate from this point on, and there will be few visible indications of activity. After a month the saccharometer test should be repeated at three- or four-day intervals until a specific gravity reading of .990 to .995, or a Brix reading of 0° is obtained. At this time the wine is ready for the final adjustments before bottling.

Removing remaining impurities. *Fining* is the process by which any impurities still suspended in the wine are removed. Bentonite or isinglass can be purchased for this purpose from a winemaking supplier, or a plain gelatin can be dissolved in warm water, then added to the wine. The impurities will cling to the fining agent and settle to the bottom of the bottle, where they will be left behind during the subsequent racking. Fining is important not just for the visible clearing it performs but because any particles left suspended in the wine could adversely affect its flavor or contribute unnecessarily to spoilage.

Acidity correction. After the fining you may want to purchase a test kit to test the acidity of the wine. The acid content of a wine is one of the main factors governing its flavor and its effect on the palate. Too much acid will produce an astringent quality, and too little will leave the wine tasting flat and out of balance.

The acidity is found by immersing a pH strip in the wine and allowing it to dry. Compare the dry strip to the color-coded chart that comes with the test kit. If the reading is less than 3.5, the acidity is too high. This can be corrected by placing the wine in a refrigerator (not a freezer) for a week; the cold will cause the excess tartaric acid to precipitate out of the wine in the form of white crystals that will settle to the bottom of the bottle. If a refrigerator is not available, crumbled chalk can be added to the wine, enough to coat the bottom of the fermentation bottle. Over the course of a few days acid will be absorbed by the chalk; take repeated pH readings to determine when the acid content has been reduced to the correct level. If the pH reading is 4.5 or more, the wine is not acid enough and tartaric acid, the acid common to grapes, should be added in small amounts, rechecking with the pH strips for a reading of 3.5–4.5.

Vitamin C (ascorbic acid) can be added at this time to prevent oxidation of the wine while it is ageing in the bottle. Buy 50-milligram tablets and use one tablet per gallon of wine. Crush the tablet and add it as a powder.

Final racking. The wine is now ready to be bottled. The bottles should be cleaned with the solution of potassium metabisulfite, then plugged with clean cotton if they are not be be filled immediately. The wine can be racked directly into the bottles. Allow for a small amount of air between the level of the wine and the cork (see photograph, p. 429). After boiling the corks in water for 15 minutes, drive them into the bottle necks, using the corking device. Bottles should be stored on their sides so that the corks are kept moist by the wine at all times. This prevents the corks from drying out and shrinking, which would allow bacteria-laden air to reach the wine and spoil it.

Ageing in the bottle. Ageing the wine is necessary to allow the acids to mellow and to give all the components time to interact. Although ageing of anywhere from six months to five years might be appropriate for wine made at home, how long each bottle will remain unopened is subject to the curiosity of the winemaker.

Winemaking

Fermentation and bottling

1. Piercing of cap is done every two days with a clean wooden dowel. Gases that may inhibit fermentation are thus released, and heat that builds up is vented. The plastic sheeting should be replaced immediately after each piercing to prevent contamination.

2. Two weeks after the wine is begun, sugar level should be checked every other day. A saccharometer reading of half the initial level means the wine should be pressed and racked into a closed bottle. Reading here is 12½° on Brix scale, or half initial reading of 25° (see p. 425). The cap should not be pierced or stirred for a full day before racking.

3. Use a cup or a ladle to transfer the cap of pulp into the press. Work carefully so as not to stir things up. The object is to leave the "free run" clear of pulp so that it can be siphoned directly into the fermentation bottle. Yeast sediment should also be left at bottom of container undisturbed.

4. Using cheesecloth to line the press ensures that pulp and skins are kept from running into the bottle. If you have no press, the pulp can be squeezed through cheesecloth by hand.

5. Cheesecloth should also be used to line funnel in bottle, particularly if white wine is being made and the grapes are pressed directly into the bottle. If a lot of grapes are pressed at one time, the cloth should be replaced so that juice runs freely. Operation of press is seen on page 426.

6. The bottle is closed with a fermentation lock that permits gas to escape but keeps out bacteria and dust. Potassium metabisulfite is used to fill the two glass globes about half full, as seen here. Add more if any evaporates.

7. Wine is racked after fermentation has slowed and sediment of more dead yeast cells has accumulated in the bottle (see text, p. 427). The siphon must not suck up the dead cells during racking; knife cut being made on dowel marks level below which the siphon will pick up dead cells.

8. Siphon hose is tied to the wooden dowel with its end lined up with the cut. This acts as depth gauge to keep the siphon from reaching layer of sediment. The dowel is held firmly once it is placed in the bottle to prevent it from stirring up dead cells.

9. Because one bottle must be higher than the other to begin the siphoning, a work area should be selected in which the fermenting wine can be left on a box or table after Step 6. Then siphoning can be done without moving the bottle and stirring up dead yeast cells. Here the winemaker starts siphon action by sucking on tube.

10. Racking wine into a fresh bottle as seen here is essential to the fermenting process, and all correct procedures must be followed. The new bottle, siphon hose, and dowel used must be sanitized, as the wine is vulnerable to any bacteria in the air. Clean them carefully, using the potassium metabisulfite solution described in the text on page 425.

11. Hold siphon hose to direct the stream of wine against the upper inside wall of the bottle. The wine is splashed and allowed to mix with air. This is called aerating the wine and will promote continued fermentation.

12. Before next racking, fermentation has begun to slow and most of the sugar has turned into alcohol (see text, p. 427). During this siphoning the siphon hose should be kept near the bottom of the fresh bottle so that the wine is not aerated, causing oxidation.

13. A saccharometer reading of about 0° Brix is obtained, and fermentation is completed. Because the presence of a small amount of sugar may cause an inaccuracy at this stage, a Brix of slightly below 0° should be obtained to ensure completion.

14. Soaking bottles in potassium metabisulfite solution for a day before scrubbing and rinsing will help loosen any remaining sediment from wine previously stored in them. Detergent or soap will leave a film that can ruin the wine and must not be used. Scrub with bottle brush, as seen here.

15. A crushed tablet of vitamin C (50 mg per gal) can be added to the large bottle just before the wine is to be bottled and corked. The hose should still be tied to the dowel, as there will be some sediment; the wine should not be aerated.

16. Only about 1 in. of air space should be left between the wine and the cork. A cork can be used to measure the correct level of wine as each bottle is filled. The corks should be boiled in water for 15 min just before the corking is done.

17. The left hand should hold both the bottle and the corker so that neither slips. The boiled cork should be seated in the corker and pushed down with the thumb. A few swift blows with the mallet straight down on the plunger head are used; do not tap lightly.

18. Bottles must be stored on their sides so that the wine is against the cork. If the cork is allowed to become dry, it will crumble and allow air to get at the wine, causing wine to spoil. Bottles should be examined periodically for any leaking corks.

Winemaking

Wines from fruits and blossoms

Wines made from fruits and blossoms are often just as flavorful as those made from grapes. In this section several traditional recipes for popular fruit and blossom wines are provided, along with a few more unusual recipes. In many cases a fruit or flower that is similar to the one in the recipe can be substituted for it, requiring no more than a change in the yeast used. For example, blackberries, loganberries, or mulberries can be used instead of elderberries; plums can be substituted for peaches; and clover, mint, pansies, primroses, or marigolds can replace dandelions. Experience and experimentation will disclose other possibilities pleasing to your palate.

Most of the winemaking procedures that are used for grapes (described in the preceding pages) apply to fruits and flowers. The important differences occur in the preparation of the must. The fermentation and subsequent rackings remain much the same, with a few noted exceptions.

Flowers are often too low in the nutrients necessary for the healthy activity of wine yeasts; therefore, raisins should be added to those recipes using flowers as the main ingredient. Many fruits and flowers also lack sufficient levels of acidity to promote the growth of yeast; thus the addition of the rinds of lemons or oranges will often be called for. It should be noted that only the outer peel of the orange or lemon is used, not the white pith just below it: the pith would make the wine too bitter. Some fruits, such as apples, strawberries, plums, and peaches, contain large amounts of pectin, which can cause the finished wine to be undesirably cloudy. The use of a pectic enzyme will eliminate the haze.

The quantities specified in the following recipes are for 1-gallon batches of wine. For greater amounts the recipes can be expanded proportionally.

Strawberry wine

2 lb strawberries
8 oz raisins
confectioner's sugar as needed
1/2 tsp grape tannin
1 tsp pectic enzyme
Sauterne wine yeast (follow package directions)

Cut washed, stemmed strawberries into quarters, then place them in an open fermentation container with the raisins. Crush this mixture with a clean wooden utensil until a fine mash results. (The raisins should be chopped beforehand if the utensil will not tear them easily.) Cover mash with 1 gal of boiling water, then cover container with plastic wrap and allow mash to steep for a day. Stir mixture following day, then re-cover it.

On the third day stir the pectic enzyme and grape tannin into must, then make the sugar correction with the use of the saccharometer (see p. 425). Add the Sauterne yeast to the must in a starter solution (pp. 425–426), and allow the strawberries to begin fermenting under plastic wrap in the open container.

Because of the pulp and seeds of the strawberry, it is not possible to rack the wine with a siphon hose by the usual method. Place manageable amounts of the pulp in a double layer of cheesecloth, using a plastic cup as a scoop. Be careful not to stir up any of the sediment on the bottom of the fermentation container. Squeeze the juice from the pulp into a cheesecloth-lined funnel set in the mouth of a gallon bottle. If any seeds or pulp do get into the bottle, simply repeat the straining by holding a double layer of cheesecloth over the bottle mouth and pouring the liquid into a second bottle equipped with a cheesecloth-lined funnel (see photographs, pp. 426, 428, and 429).

At this point the wine is racked and fermented like grape wine, as described in the preceding pages of this chapter. It should be fit to drink in under a year.

Rose-hip wine

3½ lb fresh rose hips
or
2½ lb dried rose hips
8 oz raisins
confectioner's sugar as needed
2 lemons
Tokay or Riesling wine yeast (follow package directions)

Hips can be purchased dried from a winemaking supplier; these can be used alone or to supplement fresh hips. Do not obtain hips from florist's roses, as they may have been sprayed with chemicals.

Chop rose hips, put in a container along with the raisins and the skins of the lemons, and cover with 1 gal of boiling water. When cool, add juice of lemons, adjust sugar content, and add yeast in a starter solution (pp. 425–426).

In approximately two weeks press the mixture and strain it into a bottle with a fermentation lock (p. 428).

Peach wine

3 lb whole, ripe peaches
confectioner's sugar as needed
2 lemons
2 oranges
1/2 tsp grape tannin
2 tsp pectic enzyme
Montrachet wine yeast (follow package directions)

Quarter the peaches and place them in an open container. Mash them into a pulp, using a wooden implement, and cover with boiling water. Let stand for a day.

Adjust sugar content (see p. 425), add skins of lemons and oranges, and squeeze their juice into must. Then add pectic enzyme and the yeast in starter solution. Rack and ferment as for any grape wine. Canned peaches can be substituted if they contain no preservatives. Fresh plums can also be substituted. This dry wine need only be aged six months.

Banana wine

4 lb overripe bananas
8 oz banana skins
4 oz raisins
confectioner's sugar as needed
1 lemon
1 orange
Montrachet wine yeast (follow package directions)

Break bananas into small chunks and place them in a saucepan with 2 qt of water. Add 8 oz of banana skins torn into long, thin strips. Next add the skins, free of any white pith, from the lemon and orange. Simmer the mixture for 30 min, then press and strain through a double layer of cheesecloth into the primary fermentation container.

When the mixture has cooled, add the juice of the lemon and orange, adjust sugar content after taking saccharometer reading (p. 425), and add wine yeast in starter solution (pp. 425–426). Stir must daily for seven days. Replace the plastic covering over the container after each stirring of the must.

After seven days in the container, pour liquid through funnel into gallon bottle. Then cap the bottle with a fermentation lock (pp. 428–429). Racking is not necessary at this stage. If the liquid does not fill bottle, it can be topped off with a little water. Leave wine in a cool place for six weeks, during which time a thick sediment will form. (The wine will look odd at this point because it has a much larger amount of sediment than ordinary wines. Don't worry: it is supposed to look that way.)

When six weeks have passed, rack the wine into another fermentation bottle. Chop the raisins finely, add them to the wine, and replace the fermentation lock. Rack the wine again in two months. Hereafter it is treated like any wine, but it will improve with age to a greater degree than many other fruit wines. Sample bottles at intervals of several weeks.

Date wine

2 lb dates
confectioner's sugar as needed
1 lemon
1 orange
1 grapefruit
8 oz flaked barley
3/4 tsp pectic enzyme
Montrachet wine yeast (follow package directions)

The dates used to make the wine must be the unsulfured variety. They can be found in health-food stores. Cut the dates into small pieces and place them in a saucepan. Add the skins (but not the pith) and the juice of the lemon, orange, and grapefruit to the dates in saucepan. Boil the flaked barley in 2 qt water for 15 min, then strain and pour the liquid over the dates and citrus fruit.

Boil entire mixture for 10 min. After it cools, place it in primary fermentation container (see pp. 425–426). Because the pits of the dates contain tannin, which in small amounts will enhance the flavor of the wine, crack a handful of pits and add them to the must. If the dates used were already pitted, then 1/2 tsp of grape tannin can be added instead. At this point also add 3/4 tsp of pectic enzyme.

Although dates contain much natural sugar, the sugar level must be measured with the saccharometer (p. 425); add sugar as indicated. Add the wine yeast in starter solution and cover the container with plastic (p. 426). Stir mixture daily for a week (p. 428), then take a reading daily to monitor the progress of the fermentation.

Because of the must's consistency, it may be difficult to rack by the usual method. If this is so, strain it through a double layer of cheesecloth into a cheesecloth-lined funnel set in mouth of a bottle. The nature of dates is such that wine may be cloudy, in spite of the pectic enzyme. It may need additional fining with isinglass or bentonite (see text, p. 427).

Coffee wine

8 oz ground coffee
confectioner's sugar as needed
2 lemons
8 oz sultanas
Montrachet wine yeast (follow package directions)

Simmer coffee and grated lemon skins in 2 qt water for 30 min. Chop sultanas finely, place in open container. Strain coffee and lemon mixture through doubled cheesecloth over sultanas.

After the mixture has been allowed to cool, add the juice of lemon and correct sugar content of the must (p. 425). Add the wine yeast in a starter solution (pp. 425–426) and cover the container with plastic wrap. Stir must daily for a week, then strain must through cheesecloth into a bottle and cap it with fermentation lock (p. 428). Wine is racked and fermented in usual way (pp. 427–429).

Apple wine

5 6-oz cans frozen apple juice concentrate
or
1 gal bottled apple juice
confectioner's sugar as needed
1/4 tsp grape tannin
1/2 tsp pectic enzyme
Montrachet wine yeast

Although apple wine is often made from fresh apples, the hardness of the fruit makes it quite difficult to extract juice without a press. Store-bought juice gives the winemaker a simpler option.

Reconstitute the frozen concentrate following directions on the can. Check the label on the can or bottle to be sure there are no preservatives in the juice, as they would prevent yeast from growing. Adjust the sugar content (see p. 425), add the tannin and pectic enzyme, then add yeast in a starter solution. Rack and ferment as for any grape wine. Golden wine will have aroma of fresh apples.

Elderberry wine

4 lb elderberries
8 oz raisins
confectioner's sugar as needed
2 lemons
6 cloves
Bordeaux wine yeast (follow package directions)

Because of its popularity in England, the elderberry has been called the English grape. The use of a Bordeaux yeast will enhance the resulting dry red wine. Remove the stems and thoroughly wash the elderberries, then place them in the open fermentation container. Chop the raisins and add them to elderberries. (If you have difficulty in chopping raisins for larger quantities of wine, dusting the cutting implement with confectioner's sugar will help keep the raisins from sticking to and clogging the implement.)

With a sterilized wooden spoon or masher, crush elderberries and raisins until they are well-mixed pulp. Then boil just enough water to completely cover fruit and pour it into the container. Cover the container with plastic wrap and let mixture steep for one day. Then, just as with a grape wine, take a saccharometer reading of the must and make any necessary corrections of the sugar content (see p. 425).

Peel lemons, being careful to exclude the white pith below the skin, and add peels and juice of two squeezed lemons to the must. Then add the cloves.

The procedure for making a starter solution and adding the yeast is the same as for a grape wine. The elderberries are fermented under a plastic wrap in the container, then racked into a bottle closed with a fermentation lock. Because elderberries have a relatively high tannin content in comparison to other berries or blossoms, the wine will need to be aged considerably longer to allow the tannin to mellow. Up to two years should be allowed for aging, as for a wine made from red grapes.

Dandelion wine

3 qt dandelion blossoms
confectioner's sugar as needed
2 lemons
2 oranges
1/2 tsp grape tannin
Montrachet wine yeast (follow package directions)

Like elderberry wine, this is a traditional American favorite from our rural heritage. The blossoms should be gathered while petals are fresh and fully opened. The stems and leaves of the dandelion are discarded; only the blossoms are used in the wine. Flowers should not be picked from lawns or near highways unless it is known with absolute certainty that they have not been sprayed with chemicals.

Rinse the blossoms in cold water, then place them in a fermentation container (pp. 425–426). Pour 1 gal of boiling water over the flowers. There is no way to speed up the extraction of the essence from the flowers; dandelions must be allowed to steep in the water for five days. The mixture should be stirred every day, and the winemaker must be extremely careful to replace the plastic wrap over the container after each stirring.

After five days wring the dandelions through cheesecloth folded double until blossoms are completely dry. Return the pressed-out liquid to the fermentation container. Flowers can be discarded at this point. Add the skins from the lemons and oranges (but not the pith), then squeeze the juice into the must. Quarter lemons and oranges, remove their seeds, and add them to the must. Take a saccharometer reading and adjust the sugar content of the must (p. 425). Add wine yeast in a starter solution (pp. 425–426) and rack and ferment wine in the usual fashion (pp. 427–429). Some variations of recipe call for the addition of 1/4 oz of ginger root per gal of wine or for using 1 lb of raisins in place of the lemons and oranges. You can also try using only one of the citrus fruits.

Winemaking

Solving some common problems of winemaking

The novice winemaker may assume that because he uses measuring cups and calibrated instruments, good wine will inevitably result from his efforts with the predictability of laboratory chemical reactions. This is not so, as every winemaker eventually learns. So many factors contribute to the completion of a good wine that it is often too easy to overlook minor but essential details that are critical to the outcome. The day will come for every winemaker when he approaches his fermentation container to check on the progress of his wine only to discover that all activity has stopped—or worse, that he has made "vinegar." The spoiled wine is beyond salvage and goes down the drain, but almost every other problem can be corrected.

Starter solution. The first problem to become apparent is usually that fermentation has not begun within a reasonable amount of time after the addition to the must of the starter solution, which contains the yeast. If fermentation has not begun in a week, it is possible that you were impatient to get things moving and did not allow enough time for the yeast to begin working in the starter solution (24 hours) before adding it to the must. The yeast will then need more time to grow in the must before it can initiate the fermentation of the grapes. Allow another week for the yeast cells to cultivate. If fermentation does not begin then, the problem lies elsewhere.

Temperature. The temperature may not have been regulated carefully enough, so that the must is either too warm or too cool. The temperature of the must should be taken with a suitable thermometer (special thermometers are available from winemaking suppliers) to see if the temperature is right for the growth of the yeast. If the must is too cool, it should be moved to a warmer room so that it can heat up a bit. If it is too warm, it should be moved to a cooler spot. If your thermometer reading falls within the desired 18°C–24°C range, the temperature of the room may be dropping below 18°C during the night, thus preventing the must from maintaining a consistent working temperature.

Potassium metabisulfite. If too much potassium metabisulfite was added to the must, the yeast cells may have been "stunned" and their normal growth curtailed. An excess of sulfur dioxide from the potassium metabisulfite will harm the must and should not be added with the notion that the more used the better. It is meant to be a sterilizing agent with minimal side effects that disappear in 24 hours. Add only enough potassium metabisulfite to sterilize the must (see text, p. 425) and allow a full day before introducing the starter solution.

Puncturing the cap. Fermentation can halt after it has begun, a process called sticking. If the must sticks during the initial fermentation, it will be apparent from the lack of bubbling in the cap. Again, fluctuating environmental temperature conditions may be the cause of the problem. Or, if the cap has not been punctured often enough (see p. 428), the heat and gases of fermentation may be trapped within the must, and the yeast may have suffocated on the carbon dioxide that has been produced. Stir the cap vigorously, and make sure that the cap is punctured at least once a day thereafter.

Sugar, yeast, yeast nutrient. Sticking of the fermentation during the subsequent stages is usually more difficult to detect. During the final period the winemaker may think that fermentation is complete when it has really stopped short of its goal. When the bubbling in the fermentation lock diminishes, make a daily check of the sugar content with the saccharometer.

If the saccharometer reading changes less than one unit on the Brix scale in the course of a week (see pp. 425–429), then the must is stuck. At this point several questions should be asked.

Was sufficient yeast nutrient added for the amount of yeast used? A stuck fermentation will make the winemaker realize how important it is to keep a diary of all quantities used and to record any variation attempted with a formerly successful recipe.

Was enough yeast used? If it appears there might be insufficient yeast, a small amount of starter solution, containing a little additional yeast, can be prepared and added to the stuck must.

Frequently a winemaker wishes to attempt a wine with a higher alcoholic content than is customary, and he adds extra sugar to achieve his goal. Too much sugar will cause a problem with fermentation. In any case, no amount of sugar will result in an alcoholic content above 17 percent; higher concentrations of alcohol inhibit yeast growth. If too much sugar is the problem, then adding some water or fruit juice (if it has a very low sugar level) may help to correct it.

Sterilization of equipment. Fermentation might stick at the point when the must is transferred from the initial fermentation container into the large bottles. If this occurs, it is possible that some bacteria were introduced into the must during the transfer or that the siphoning equipment or the bottle was not sterilized properly. Perhaps the winemaker substituted a household cleaning agent for the potassium metabisulfite solution when cleaning the equipment.

In any case, an attempt should be made to revive the yeast. Plug the bottle with cotton and let it sit for a week. Then add a small amount of yeast in a starter solution. Wait two weeks to see if the yeast revives.

Unwanted tastes and aging. If the finished wine tastes strongly of yeast, then too much yeast was used for the amount of wine being made and the wine was not racked often enough. Racking the wine several more times is the only way to eliminate the unwanted yeast, and this means the wine is not close to being ready for bottling. The wine should be allowed to sit undisturbed for several weeks before any attempt is made to rack it again.

A strong taste of tannin in the wine—an astringent taste that makes the mouth pucker—is not necessarily a problem, because tannin will mellow with age and add to the flavor. The wine cannot be judged before it has been bottled and allowed to age for some time; red wines, which have a large amount of tannin, need at least a year to age and often longer.

Color. If a red wine seems to be turning a brownish color, then it has been given too much exposure to either light or oxygen. Care should be taken during the last few rackings (and during the bottling) not to aerate the wine. Although clear wine bottles are made, the use of green or brown glass is recommended, as its filtering properties shield the wine from light.

Exploding bottles. If bottles of wine explode after they have been corked and stored, it means that the wine was bottled before fermentation was complete. If one bottle explodes, then all the bottles from that batch should be uncorked and the wine poured into a large bottle, which is then capped with a fermentation lock. Allow the wine to complete fermentation; check it with a saccharometer (pp. 428–429) to verify the completion of fermentation before any attempt is made to rebottle it.

Dry corks. A dry cork means that the bottle has been stored improperly. Bottles should be stored on their sides so that the corks are kept moist.

Restoring furniture

What to look for when restoring old furniture

Restoring old furniture is becoming an increasingly popular craft throughout the country. Pieces that have been sitting for years in an attic or storeroom or under layers of dirt and debris in a basement can be made attractive and valuable through restoration. Furniture suitable for restoring also turns up at secondhand stores, flea markets, auctions, garage sales, and movers' storage warehouses.

Many furniture repairs, such as tightening loose joints and refinishing damaged surfaces, are quite simple. Such restoration can be done following the techniques for wood construction and finishing described in *Woodworking*, pp. 360–403. One of the most popular and enjoyable restoration crafts is reseating chairs with ash splint, rush, or cane. These three procedures are described on the following eight pages.

Repairing. All repairs and refinishing of a chair frame must be completed before the seating material is attached. Even small defects in a chair should be repaired—if left unattended, they will only get worse.

Cracks and fractures can usually be repaired by cleaning the crack out, applying white wood glue (PVA), and clamping. Loose joints can sometimes be repaired simply by injecting glue into the joint. However, most joints, such as those between rungs, legs, and rails, usually require that the parts be disassembled, sanded clean, glued, reassembled, and clamped while the glue dries. If dowels in joints have broken, the dowels should be replaced by drilling out the old ones.

Avoid disassembling good joints. If a repair to one part of the chair forces you to partly disassemble the frame, take apart the joints that are the least firm. Be sure to remove any braces or other supports that are holding the

parts together. The gluing and clamping techniques used to reassemble the chair frame are described and illustrated in detail on page 381.

If the chair still contains remnants of an old seat, they must be removed. Remove any nails or barbs, and drill through any blocked holes. Sand the rails or seat edges so that they will not cut through the seating material.

Finishing. If the finish on antique furniture is intact, do not remove it. Overrestoration, to the body as well as to the finish, may depreciate the value of an antique.

Old furniture is frequently caked with layers of dirt and grime, and it is assumed that the finish is ruined. This is often not true—the wood may simply need a good cleaning. A variety of commercial products, including benzine and furniture polish, can be used to clean and revive old finishes. The choice of cleaning products depends on the condition of the finish—inquire at a hardware or furniture store. Where you find that the old finish cannot be revived, it should be stripped.

Choosing a seating material. If you are reseating an old chair, the remnants of the old seat will indicate what material should be used. If the chair has a complete old seat, save it—it will be valuable as a guide for the new weaving. Even if the chair has no remnants of its former seat, choosing the appropriate material is quite simple. If the chair has four rounded rails, as does the Early American ladder-back chair, it can be given either an ash splint seat (pp. 434–435) or a rush seat (pp. 436–438). Chairs with holes drilled around the seat perimeter should be given woven cane seats (pp. 439–441). Chairs that have a continuous groove around the seat opening can be given seats of prewoven cane webbing (p. 439).

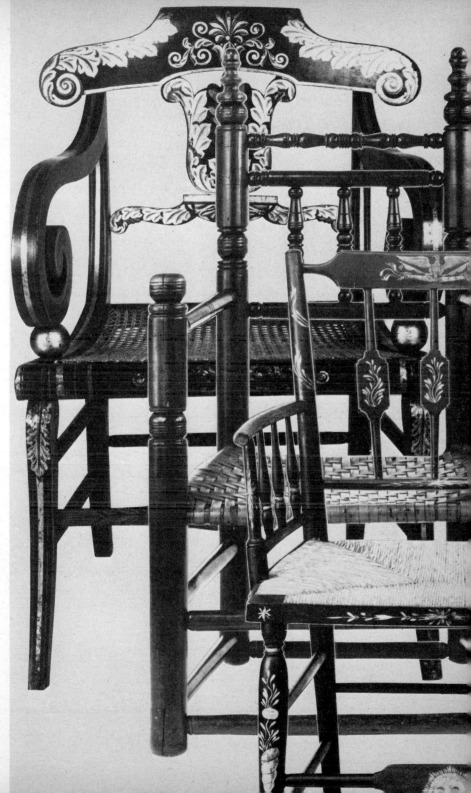

Rush, splint, and cane weaving are used in restoration. Sheraton chair (foreground), c. 1815, employs rush; Carver chair (center), c. 1650, splint; late classical chair (top), c. 1835, cane.

Restoring furniture

Ash splint seats

Ash splint chair seats are made of thin strips of wood (cut from the annual rings of ash trees) that are interwoven in a tight, regular pattern.

Tools and materials. Commercial machine-cut ash splint comes in pieces 6 feet long and 1/2, 5/8, or 3/4 inch wide. An ordinary chair requires 12 to 15 such splints, a large chair up to 20 splints, and a stool or child's chair 8 to 10 splints. Splints 5/8 inch wide are used for normal work, but narrower splints can be used if you want a smaller weave and don't mind the extra work. Wider splints should be used only on wider chairs; they can look most ungainly on very small seats.

Splints can be purchased from dealers of seat weaving supplies and from some crafts stores. For information on natural splints, see *Preparing natural ash splint and rush*, p. 441.

In addition to the splints, you will need twine; heavy short-bladed scissors, a utility knife, and a cutting block for cutting and trimming the splints; a pail for soaking the splints; and a brush and a sealant containing tung oil, such as Danish oil or boiled linseed oil, for the protective finish.

Ash splint must be soaked in warm water to make it pliable enough to weave. Soak three or four splints in a pail for about 10 minutes. As you remove one splint from the pail to weave, replace it with another.

Weaving techniques. A seat is woven in two basic stages. First, splints are passed across the seat from front to back for the entire width of the chair (except the triangular side areas if the chair is splayed—wider in front than in back). Then a second group of splints is woven across the first group. If the seat is splayed, the side areas are filled in last (see *Weaving pattern*, below).

Ash splint has a smooth and a rough side (see illustrations below). The smooth side must always face outward, on both the top and bottom of the seat. New splints are joined to the ones already woven (see below) as the work proceeds—be sure that the new piece is also turned smooth side out.

Ash splint shrinks as it dries; therefore, allow enough looseness initially so that you can depress the front-to-rear splints about 1/2 inch on a small chair and 1 inch on a large one.

When the weaving is complete, trim off any rough edges or splinters with scissors. The seat can then be stained if you choose, and it should be coated on both sides with sealant for protection.

Finding the smooth side

Ash splint has a rough and a smooth side; the smooth side is always kept to the outside during weaving. To determine the smooth side, wet the splint and bend it. The rough side has small splinters, as shown in the bottom illustration; the smooth side (top) has no splinters.

Joining splints

Splints are joined by means of a special locking configuration: Free end of splint coming from weaving is cut with scissors to shape of blunt arrowhead with a narrow neck, as seen in illustration at far left. Head will slip through a narrow slot cut with knife in end of next splint to be woven; slot is slightly longer than width of arrowhead, allowing it to pass through sideways, as in center illustration. Head is then rotated so that the splints align and the neck is caught by the slot, as at left. Head should be 3 in. long. Slot is located 3 in. from end of connecting splint. Make these joints on underside of seat, with arrowheads to inside.

Weaving pattern

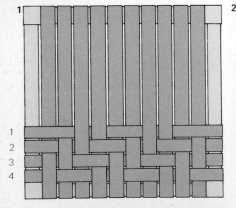

1

1
2
3
4

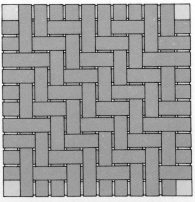

2

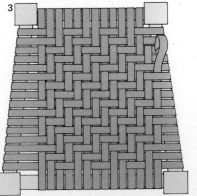

3

After the front-to-back splints are in place, the side-to-side, or cross, weaving begins. The cross strands pass under two of the front-to-back rows, then over two, under two, and so on. The diagonal pattern in the weave is created by staggering the position where the weave for each cross strand begins. For example, the first cross strand (Diagram 1) goes under the first lateral strand, then starts its pattern of over two, under two; the second starts under two, over two; the next two strands are staggered as shown. The four-strand sequence then repeats, beginning with the fifth row, until the seat is filled (Diagram 2). In a splayed seat (Diagram 3), the central rectangular area is woven, then the triangular side areas are filled by adding individual front-to-back splints, as seen in Steps 7 and 8 on opposite page. Keep pattern on side consistent with weaving in rest of seat.

Weaving an ash splint seat

1. Take the first splint from the pail of water and loop it around the front and back rails of the chair. Tie the free outside length to the side rail with twine.

2. Continue looping the splint around the rails. When you need a new splint, attach it as shown on the facing page; the joints should all be made on the underside of the seat.

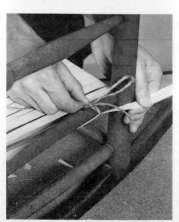

3. Loop the splints until the entire width of the chair is filled. Be sure that splints are parallel, with an even but loose tension. Tie the free end of the last splint to the side rail with twine.

4. Weave the first splint across the front-to-back rows, following the weaving pattern shown on the facing page. Weave across the top of the seat, bring the splint over the rail, and weave back across underside. Bring the loose short end over the rail and tuck it into the weave as shown in Step 8. Use a new splint for each row.

5. Continue weaving in a regular pattern, as shown on the facing page. As the weave tightens, use a short piece of splint to pry openings between lengthwise splints to facilitate passage of the cross strand.

6. Another way to ease weaving when the seat begins to tighten is to place a short piece of splint beneath the cross strand. Use this piece to help grip the strand. Pinch strand between splint and your finger and push it across.

7. When the side-to-side weaving is complete, untie the loose ends left in Steps 1 and 3 and tuck them into the weave as shown in Step 8. If your seat is splayed, now fill the triangular side areas by adding splints, as shown. Maintain a consistent weaving pattern.

8. Secure the ends of the added splints by folding them and tightly tucking them in, as shown. Use as many splints as necessary to fill the side areas created by the splay.

9. When working at the corners, it may be necessary to cut a notch in the splint to make it fit neatly against the corner post. When weaving is complete, trim off splinters with scissors. Then stain the seat, if desired, and seal it with tung oil.

Restoring furniture

Rush seats

Natural rush seats are made by weaving a tight pattern from twisted leaves of rush, or cattail, plants (see *Preparing natural ash splint and rush, p. 441*).

Tools and materials. Artificial rush—a strong kraft paper twisted into a continuous uniform strand—is easier to work, cheaper, and more readily available than natural rush. It can be purchased from dealers of seat weaving supplies or at crafts supply stores. About 3 pounds of artificial rush are required for an average dining room chair, up to 5 pounds for a large armchair or rocker, and about 2 pounds for a stool or an antique Shaker chair. Artificial rush comes in various sizes and an array of colors.

You will also need a hammer and tacks, a smooth piece of hardwood or a yardstick (called an evener), a protective sealant containing tung oil (such as Danish oil or boiled linseed oil), and sheets of corrugated cardboard (used for padding inside the seat).

Weaving techniques. A rush seat is woven from the outside corners toward the center in a regular pattern that goes over and under the seat rails (see diagrams immediately below). Because seats are rarely square, there is usually a central area left after basic weaving, which is then filled with figure-8 loops over the front and back rails. When weaving a splayed seat, the triangular side areas created by the splay are woven first; then the remaining square or rectangular area is filled using the basic weave (see diagrams, bottom of page). This sequence is the reverse of

ash splinting, in which the splayed areas are woven last (see pp. 434–435).

A taut, uniform tension must be kept on the rush cord during weaving because, unlike cane and ash splint, rush does not shrink and tighten when weaving is completed. The effort needed to maintain this tension can be minimized by using leverage on the rails and posts during weaving. The rush cords should be kept as close together as possible—every five or six rows, dress the strands with the evener, making them tightly parallel.

The illustrations on pages 437–438 show the rush weaving of a simple splayed seat. If the frame on which you are working is rectangular or square, start with the basic continuous weave (see diagram below) at Step 7.

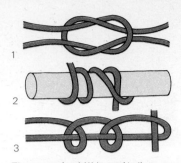

The square knot (1) is used to tie on new lengths of rush. The knots are tied on the inside of the seat. The clove hitch (2) is made by making turns around a chair rung and passing the cord under the last turn. It is used to maintain the tension during a pause in the weaving. The half-hitch (3) secures last cord to inside.

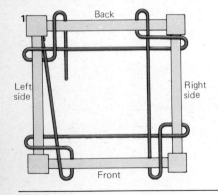

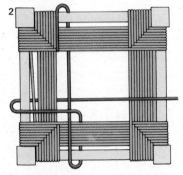

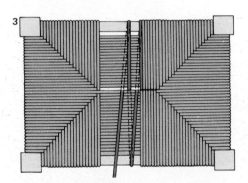

The basic weaving pattern for a rush seat (Diagram 1) is to first tack a length of rush to the back left corner of the seat. Pass the rush over and around the front rail, over and around the left side rail, across to the right side, then repeat as shown, weaving all around seat. This pattern is repeated continually to fill a square seat (Diagram 2). Rush is woven in 15- to 20-ft strands; new pieces are tied on with square knots on the inside of the seat. On a rectangular seat (Diagram 3), the weaving continues until the side rails are completed. The center space is then filled with figure-8 loops over the front and back rails; all loops pass through the same opening between the central cross rows.

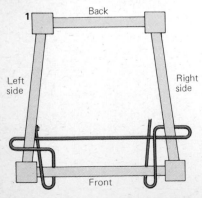

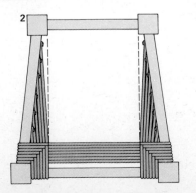

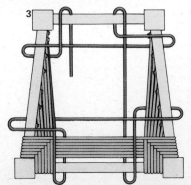

On a splayed seat the side triangular areas are filled first. Tack a 3- to 4-ft cord to the left rail near the front, pass it around both front corners, and tack it to the right rail exactly opposite the first tack (Diagram 1). Tack on a second cord, slightly behind the first, and weave it around. Continue tacking on new lengths of rush until the space between the weaving on the front rail is as wide as the back rail (Diagram 2). Once these side areas are filled, the remaining square or rectangular area is filled (Diagram 3) just as shown in basic weaving diagrams above.

Weaving a rush seat

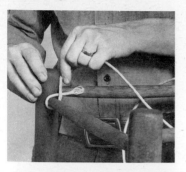

1. Cut a 3- to 4-ft length of cord. Tack one end to the left rail and loop the cord around the front rail close to the corner post, then around the side rail (see diagrams on facing page).

5. Continue adding more cords to fill the triangular side areas created by the splay. Every five or six rows compress the strands into each corner with the hardwood evener so that the rows lie parallel and close together.

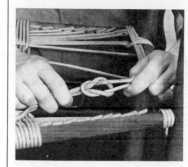

9. Bring the cord over the left rail, then around the back rail—this completes the first row of continuous weaving. Bring the cord up to the front left corner and continue weaving.

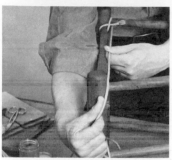

2. Bring the cord over to the right front corner. Loop the cord over the side rail, then over the front rail. Keep the cord taut and the tension uniform.

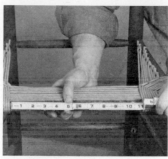

6. Measure the distance between the woven cords on the front rail. When this space is as wide as the back rail, start continuous weaving around all four corners (see facing page).

10. New rush is attached to the old with square knots (see illustration on facing page). Be sure that knots are not in the corner weaving, but rather toward the center, where they will be covered by later weaving.

3. Tack the cord to the inside of the right rail, as far from the front post as the tack on the left rail. Untwist the rush slightly to insert the tack. Trim the cord to 1/2 in. from the tack.

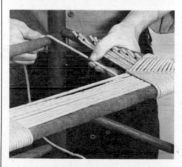

7. Cut a 15- to 20-ft length of rush. Tack one end to the left rail near the back post. Weave over the front rail, around the left rail, over to the right rail, then to the back right corner (see diagrams on facing page).

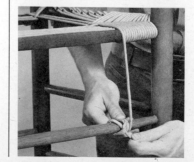

11. Use the hardwood evener to dress the cords, making them lie close together and perpendicular to the seat rails. Repeat this process in all four corners of the chair after every five or six rows.

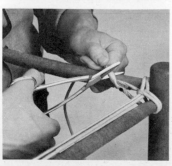

4. Tack another piece of rush behind the first, weave it around the side and front rails, then tack the other end behind the first cord. Trim the cord.

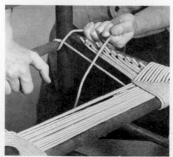

8. Bring the cord over the back rail, then around the right rail, just as was done in the front corners. Keep the cord tight, and press it closely against the corner post.

12. When you want to pause during weaving, tie off the cording around a rung of the chair, using a clove hitch (see illustration on facing page). Be sure that the cord is taut and securely tied.

437

Restoring furniture

Weaving a rush seat (continued)

13. After weaving a few rows, cut two pieces of cardboard to the shape of the corner diagonals, and push them firmly between the cords against the front rail. The pieces of cardboard should meet, not overlap.

14. After further weaving, cut pieces of cardboard to fit into the sides and back corners of the seat, and push them into place between the weave. Cardboard acts as padding to prevent excessive rubbing between the cord and rails.

15. Padding can also be inserted into the underside of the seat. The padded seat, with the cardboard in place, should be slightly greater in thickness than the diameter of the rails. Dress the cords with the evener after inserting the padding.

16. The padding is covered as the weaving progresses. The color of the cardboard should match that of the cord, because the cords may separate slightly, revealing the padding beneath.

17. To complete the last cross row, pass the cord around the side rail and up through the narrow center opening. Tie on additional cord to finish the seat.

18. The seat is completed with figure-8 loops over the front and back rails (see diagram, p. 436). All loops pass through the narrow center opening. Use the evener to keep the loops parallel and close together.

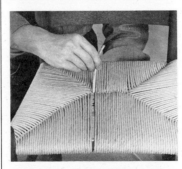

19. To complete the last figure-8 loop, bring the cord up through the center opening as shown. Then stretch it over the front rail to the underside of the seat. Turn the chair over.

20. The cord is tied off with several half-hitches (see illustration, p. 436). To make a half-hitch, first pass the last cord under the opposite strand.

21. Pull the cord taut—it is essential to maintain tension on the cord while tying the knot. Then bring the end of the cord into position to make the loop shown in the next step.

22. Make the loop and pass the cord back through it as shown. Tie two or three more half-hitches, then cut off any excess cord. Push the knots down into the center so that they are covered by the weave.

23. Dress the entire seat with the evener, forcing the cord into tight, even rows. Rub the flat surface of the evener over the loops on the rails so that no strands protrude above the others.

24. Tung oil sealant darkens and protects the finished seat. To apply it, brush it onto the underside of the seat, then onto the top of the seat. Let it stand for 15 min, then wipe off any excess. Let the chair dry overnight.

Cane seats

Cane seats are made by weaving long, thin strands of wood into a tight, open octagonal pattern (see illustration, right). Prewoven cane can be attached to certain seats in sheet form, a process called *spline caning*, as shown in the box at the bottom of the page.

Cane is cut from the bark of a tropical palm called rattan, which can grow to hundreds of feet in length but is seldom more than 1 inch in diameter. Cane can be bought from basket

Size of hole	Space between holes	Width of cane
1/8 inch	3/8 inch	Superfine
3/16 inch	1/2 inch	Fine fine
3/16 inch	5/8 inch	Fine
1/4 inch	3/4 inch	Medium
5/16 inch	7/8 inch	Common

weaving supply stores or crafts stores; it comes in hanks 1,000 feet long and in various widths. Use the chart above to determine the proper width for your chair. Sold with each hank is a wider strand, called the *binder*, which is used to form a border around the seat after

the seat has been woven. About 250 feet of cane are needed for the seat of an ordinary wooden kitchen or dining room chair.

Plastic cane is also available. It is strong, easier to weave than natural cane (it needs no soaking), and fairly inexpensive. Plastic cane is good for use on painted chairs; natural cane should be used on antique chairs.

To weave cane seats, you will need scissors, caning pegs or golf tees to temporarily secure the cane ends during weaving, an awl to clear the holes in the seat, a pail for soaking the cane, clothespins, and boiled linseed oil, Danish oil, or some other sealer containing tung oil.

Cane is soaked before it is woven to make it pliable. When it dries, it shrinks, tightening the weave. Begin by separating a few strands of cane from the hank, disposing of any defective strands. Coil the strands, fasten each coil with a clothespin, and soak the cane in a bucket of warm water for 15 minutes. As you remove one coil from the bucket, replace it with another—this will provide you with a continuous

supply of soaked splints as you weave. Periodically wet the underside of the weaving with a warm, damp towel to prevent the weave from prematurely drying and tightening.

Cane has a rough, flat side and a smooth, shiny, convex side—always weave with the shiny side facing up. The cane is run through the holes in the seat, and the ends are held in place with pegs until they are tied to other strands beneath the seat at a later stage in the weaving (see diagram below, right). Leave an extra 4 inches at each end when pegging a strand for tying off. Keep the tension uniform but loose enough so that when you push down lightly on the seat you can depress the strands 1/2 to 3/4 inch.

As you weave, hold one hand above and one below the seat; move the cane down through one space and up through the next in a continuous motion, taking care that the cane does not twist in your hands. A cane seat is woven in six stages (p. 440). At the end of each stage of weaving be sure that none of the strands has twisted and that the weaving is parallel and absolutely regular in appearance.

Weaving a splayed or irregularly shaped seat entails some special considerations, which are discussed in *Cane weaving a splayed seat, p. 441.* When the six stages of weaving are completed and all of the ends are tied, the wide strand (the binder) is attached as shown on page 440. The binder makes a neat border around the perimeter of the seat. After the binder is attached, push a peg through all of the woven octagons in the seat to even the pattern. Then singe off any frayed cane with a moving match flame while the cane is wet, or trim it off with a razor blade. Stain the cane, if you desire, and coat both sides of the seat (underside first) with the sealant. After the sealant dries, the chair is ready for use.

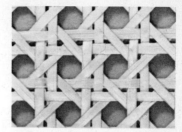

Weave pattern. Tracing path clockwise around any of the woven cane octagons, each strand should pass under the next strand.

Tying off loose ends under rail

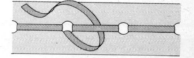

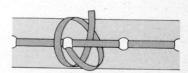

During weaving, the loose ends of the cane are held in place with pegs, which are wedged into the holes in the seat. The loose ends are tied off under the chair rails later in the weaving, when other cane lengths pass through the same holes as the loose ends. To tie the knot, first pass the loose end under the weave (top illustration). Loop the end around once again and pass it between the first loop and the weave (bottom). Then pull the end tight and trim the cane 1 in. from the knot. These views show the underside of the chair frame, where tying off is done.

Spline caning

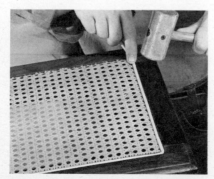

A seat with a continuous groove around the seat opening can be filled with prewoven cane webbing. The process is quite simple: the sheet of cane webbing is cut to size and soaked in warm water for about 10 min. White glue is squeezed into the groove. The cane is placed over the seat, and the edges of the cane are tucked into the groove. The spline, a thicker, tapered strip of wood that fits tightly into the groove, is also soaked. It is placed over the cane and knocked into the groove all around the seat with a mallet, wedging the cane firmly into place. Sealant is then applied.

Restoring furniture

Steps for cane weaving

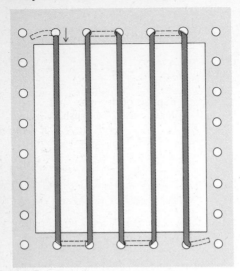

1. First run the cane from the front of the seat to the back, through all the holes in the front and back edges, filling the entire seat. (For clarity, the pegs used to hold the loose ends are not shown in these diagrams. Golf tees make suitable pegs.)

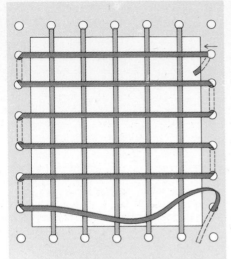

2. Next run a series of strands from one side of the seat to the other, over the tops of the front-to-back strands. Each strand advances by passing under the frame (dotted line) and up through the next nearest hole along the rail.

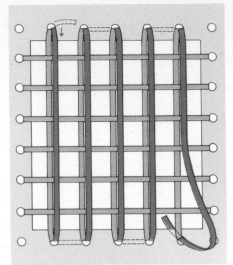

3. Run a second series of front-to-back rows through the same holes used in Step 1. Keep them consistently to one side of the first weave (in this case, to the right). These strands pass over the tops of the cross strands added in Step 2.

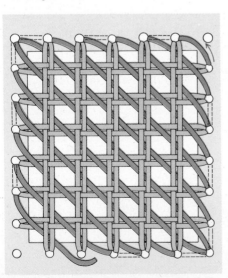

4. Begin actual weaving. Pass the cane side-to-side, under the strands woven in Step 1 and over those woven in Step 3. Maintain the same pattern whether the strand is moving from right to left or from left to right across the seat.

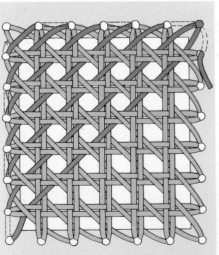

5. Pass the strands of the first diagonal weave under the front-to-back rows (Steps 1 and 3) and over the side-to-side rows (Steps 2 and 4). Weave all strands with uniform pressure. Keep the cane wet with a warm, damp towel.

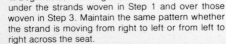

6. Weave the second diagonal strands perpendicular to the first. Pass them over the front-to-back rows and under the side-to-side rows. When weaving is finished, check the pattern, tie off the ends (p. 439), and attach the binder.

Applying the binder

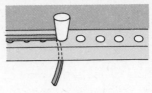

1. Cut the binder several inches longer than the perimeter of the seat. Push an awl through the holes in the seat to make room for the stitching. Peg the binder into the back center hole.

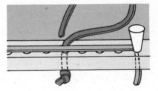

2. Knot a piece of cane. Bring it up through the fourth hole from the peg. Bring the cane up over the binder and then back into the same hole on the other side of the binder. This completes one stitch.

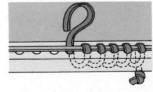

3. Bring the cane under the seat to the next hole and repeat the stitch, wrapping the cane around the binder. Move to the next hole; continue working all the way around the seat in this manner.

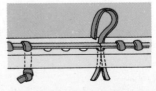

4. Remove the peg and put the loose end of the binder through the starting hole; knot it to the starting end. Stitch past this hole until the stitching is complete. Tie off, and trim the end.

440

Cane weaving a splayed seat

Though weaving a splayed seat is fundamentally similar to weaving a rectangular seat (you follow the same sequence of six steps, shown on the facing page), it does entail certain departures. Rather than beginning from the corner, the first strand starts in the center holes of the front and back, which are found by counting in from the corners of the seat. Insert the cane, secure it with a peg, and run it back to front toward one side (Diagram 1, right). When you reach the side of the chair, it will be necessary to skip holes (especially near the back of the chair) in order to keep the rows of cane parallel and equidistant. You can skip holes by simply running the cane under the seat past the skipped holes, unless by doing so you will block these holes (they will be woven at a later stage). If so, cut the cane and weave the last row(s) with a separate strand. If you skip holes on one side of the chair, do so on the other—maintain symmetry.

In weaving from side to side, it will be necessary to skip holes near the very front and back of the seat to maintain a parallel and equidistant weave (Diagram 2). As in front-to-back weaving, do not let the weave block the skipped holes from underneath, and maintain symmetry. Holes at the farthest extremities are skipped so that there is no weaving atop the wooden frame.

When weaving the diagonals, the rows will not always line up directly with holes; weave into the holes that will cause the least deviation from a straight line. Sometimes the diagonal weave will require that a strand come out of the same hole that it entered. When this happens, weave into the hole, bring the strand out of the adjacent hole, and weave the next diagonal (skipping one diagonal) across the seat. On the return weave fill in the diagonal that was skipped; then proceed with the normal sequence (Diagram 3).

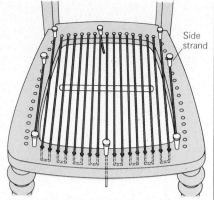

Side strand

Splayed seat requires individual side strands.

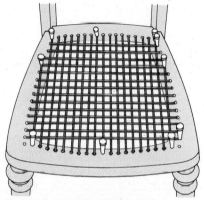

Keep weave parallel by skipping holes.

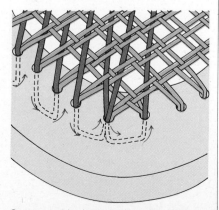

Corners require improvised weaving patterns.

Preparing natural ash splint and rush

Natural ash splints should be cut from black ash trees (also known as hoop, basket, brown, swamp, or water ash), which are found in wet areas, such as low woods or cold swamps. Splints can also be cut from white ash (also known as American, Biltmore, or Dane ash).

Splints are cut from trees that are felled and then soaked in water. Choose a tree 7 to 9 inches in diameter, with a straight trunk and no twists, knots, or limbs for a least 6 feet. Cut the tree down 8 to 10 inches from the ground, then cut the trunk into a log 6 feet long or longer.

Submerge the log by mooring it below the surface of a pond or lake for at least a month, and preferably over the entire winter. As long as the log is totally submerged, there is no danger that the wood will rot.

After the log has been soaked, shave off the outside bark with a drawknife; also remove the pithy, fibrous layer beneath it. Shave down until you reach a slick surface, which is the sapwood; do not cut into the sapwood.

The log must be struck, preferably with a thick wooden club, to break down the fibers that connect the annual rings of the tree. Start at one end of the log and move down it in a straight line. As you strike the log with crisp strokes of the club, you should see thin sheets separating from the rest of the log. Pull off the strips down the length of the log. Peel only as much wood as you will need, then return the log to the pond.

Using a mat knife, trim the wood to the width used for weaving. At this stage the splints will have two rough sides. While the splints are still wet, split each one down the middle, like a long, flat sandwich. This will expose a smooth face on each splint, which is the side that faces out during weaving. If the rough side of the splint is too rough to weave, it can be smoothed by drawing a jackknife blade over the splint while holding the blade perpendicular to the splint.

Preparing natural rush. Natural rush is made from the leaves of cattail plants, which can be found growing in wet, swampy places. Cattails are easily recognized by their cylindrical brown bobs, or spikes of flowers.

The leaves used for rush weaving should be long (about 7 feet) and thin. Cut the plant at water level late in the summer, when the stalks are green but the tips are beginning to turn brown. Select only perfect leaves, taking care not to bend or break them.

Pull the leaves from the stalks, and sort the leaves into groups by size. Run a heavy needle and twine through the thick bottom part of the leaves, and hang them upside down to dry. Rush leaves should be dried for at least 2 to 3 weeks in a dry, dark, airy room.

Unlike the artificial rush shown on pages 436–438, natural rush is soaked before it is used in a solution of equal parts water and glycerine for 8 to 12 hours. It is then put through a ringer to force out excess water and to break up air pockets.

The weaving of natural rush proceeds as shown on pages 436–438, but it is more complicated. Artificial kraft rush is made in one continuous wound strand. Natural rush leaves are flat, and several must be twisted together as they are being woven. Rush leaves must be knotted together frequently because they rarely exceed 7 feet in length. The care and attention demanded by the simultaneous tying, twisting, and weaving makes natural rush a more exacting material to work with than kraft fiber rush.

Natural rush does make an attractive and more textured and variegated seat than kraft fiber rush does. But because of the difficulties involved, it is best to master weaving with kraft rush before attempting to use natural rush.

Bookbinding

Anatomy of a book

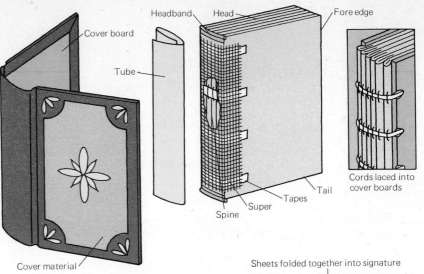

This Spanish velvet binding with silver mountings was created in Valencia in 1687.

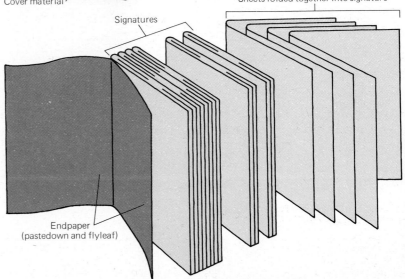

Bookbinding began in the first few centuries of the Christian Era, when it was discovered that scrolls of parchment could be folded up, accordion-like, and tied together through holes punched in the margins. Later leather strips were added to protect the stitching, and wooden boards were attached to prevent the leaves from curling.

During the Middle Ages bookbinding became a full-fledged art form, supported by Church, royalty, and private patrons. Book covers were beautifully engraved and sumptuously decorated with precious metals, ivory, and jewels. Byzantine emperors paraded their most magnificent books on golden poles in public processions. Even books covered with wood or vellum were so valuable that it was customary to chain them to the tables in libraries to prevent theft.

By the 14th century paper replaced parchment as the most common leaf material in books. Because of its superior suppleness and lower cost, the use of paper increased the speed and ease

of bookbinding and brought on the demand for cheaper bindings. The invention of movable type in the 15th century made the mass production of books possible for the first time. The introduction of cloth as a binding material 300 years later ushered in the age of the popular accessibility of books.

Creative hand bookbinding has remained an exacting and rewarding craft to the present day. However, a vast majority of books are now produced by massive computerized machines that turn out hundreds of books in a minute. Even so, the basic problems of bookbinding are the same for the modern computer and the modern hand bookbinder as they were for the artisan in the Middle Ages: how to hold together the leaves of a book; how to protect the leaves once they are together; and how to identify and/or decorate the protective cover.

Despite the profound evolution in bookbinding, the principles for solving these problems have remained much the same.

Structure of a book. The pages of a book are folded in units called signatures, each of which is made of anywhere from 1 to 16 folded sheets, yielding from 4 to 64 pages. The signatures are sewn together and to each other; the stitches pass through the folds and over tapes or cords that act to anchor the signatures. Protective cover boards are usually attached to the cords or tapes, or they are glued to a piece of coarse mesh cloth, called the super. The super is first glued to the folded edge, or spine, of the book. In some books small pieces of embroidered cloth, called headbands, are attached to the spine's top, or head, and/or to its bottom, or tail. Sometimes a hollow tube is glued to the spine to give support to the material that covers the book, usually paper, cloth, or leather. Endpapers are folded sheets that line the covers and make the flyleaves.

Equipment

Besides sewing needles and the tools seen at right, three pieces of equipment, the press, the sewing frame, and backing boards, are essential for bookbinding. If you do not care to purchase the professional models, you can make perfectly acceptable substitutes by following the directions given below. The dimensions of these pieces vary with the size of the book being made; those given are for a book that is approximately 8 by 10 inches. If your book will differ appreciably, read through this chapter and make appropriate adjustments when you make your equipment. Backing boards should be longer than your book, but they must also fit inside the press.

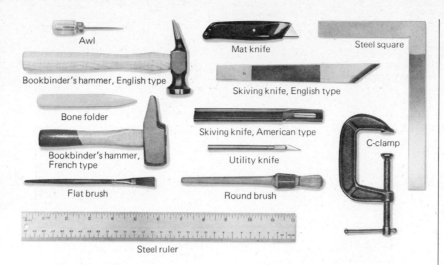

Awl

Bookbinder's hammer, English type

Bone folder

Bookbinder's hammer, French type

Flat brush

Mat knife

Skiving knife, English type

Skiving knife, American type

Utility knife

Round brush

Steel square

C-clamp

Steel ruler

Tools and materials

The tools commonly used in bookbinding are shown at left. Most of them can be purchased at a hardware store. The bone folder, used for folding, creasing, smoothing, etc., and the skiving knife, used to pare leather, are available at crafts shops.

Hammers. The two hammers shown are special bookbinder's hammers, but any flat-headed hammer will do.

Papers. Choose a durable paper for signatures. Endsheets are frequently made of patterned or marbled paper. You will also need brown kraft paper for construction of the cover, wax paper to protect the book during gluing, and sandpaper to smooth edges.

Fabrics and leathers. Standard book cloth, called buckram, can be purchased at bookbinding supply stores, but any fairly heavy fabric will do (for example, linen, burlap, or denim). If you are making a leather cover, choose a supple goatskin or calfskin.

Adhesives. Polyvinyl acetate (PVA) is right for the book's flexible joints. Library paste, used on the endpapers and cover, can easily be made. Add 6 parts water to 1 part flour and heat to a boil, stirring constantly to eliminate lumps. If you are going to use it for several days, add a little alum or thymol as a preservative.

Boards, cords, tapes, and threads. For cover boards it is best to use professional binder's board. Chipboard, strawboard, and ordinary poster board are acceptable substitutes. White cotton tape, about 1/2 in. wide, is used for books sewn on tapes. Any cord that can be easily frayed at the ends is used for sewing on cords. Size 16/2 linen thread is good for normal sewing.

Headband and super. Headbands are available at bookbinding stores. Alternatives to binder's super are cambric, muslin, and crinoline.

Wax. Beeswax is used to coat thread and to polish page edges.

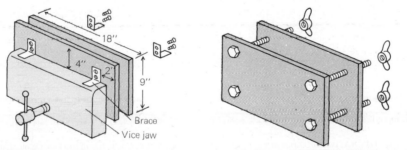

18''

4''

2''

9''

Brace

Vice jaw

A professional press is shown in the photo. If you have a large vise, you can make a press by screwing braces into each of two hard, thick boards so that the boards rest evenly on the braces within the jaws of the vise as suggested at left. A press can also be made using boards and C-clamps or long bolts, of at least 3/4 in. diameter, with washers and wingnuts.

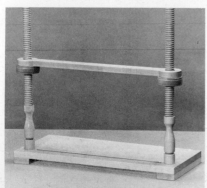

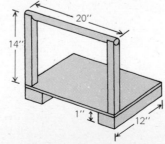

20''

14''

1''

12''

A professional sewing frame is shown in the photo. To make a homemade frame, cut scrap wood to dimensions shown. Be sure baseboard is smooth and edges of crosspiece are rounded.

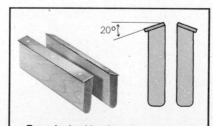

20°

To make backing boards, bevel edges angled at 20° on two pieces of wood, each at least 1 in. thick. Attach strips of metal to beveled edges with wood screws. Countersink the screws.

443

Bookbinding

Preparing signatures for the cover

The illustrations on this and the following five pages show two ways to construct the body of a book and two ways to construct a cover, starting with blank paper and raw materials.

If you want to repair a damaged book or rebind an old favorite, first turn to *Preparing a book for rebinding* (p. 449). The only convenient ways to bind existing printed or manuscript pages into book form are either to use a spring binder, available from stationery stores, or to side-sew the pages—drill holes through the margins and stitch through the holes—then glue on a super and a cover as shown beginning with Step 19 on page 446.

Creating signatures. A more complete project is to bind a book of blank signatures for use as a diary or journal, as illustrated beginning with Step 1 on page 444. If you choose to do this, you must start by creating the signatures. Cut your paper so that it has pleasing proportions when it is folded once. The fold must run parallel to the grain of the paper. You can find the grain by dampening a small piece of the paper. It will curl along the grain.

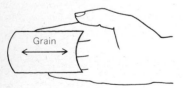

Dampened paper curls along grain (arrow).

Signatures of normal lightweight bond paper should be made of four folded sheets. (Use fewer sheets per signature for thick paper and more for very thin paper.) Folded in half, four sheets form signatures of 16 pages.

Sewing. Signatures are sewn together over either tapes or cords, which run perpendicular to the signatures on the spine. The use of tapes is shown in the photographs on this and the fol-

lowing two pages. (For cords, see *Sewing on cords,* p. 446.) Use three to five tapes, depending on the length of your book's spine. The tapes are set on the frame so that they subdivide the book at equal intervals along the spine.

When you thread your needle, run the needle back through the thread to lock it in place. You can run the thread

At start, pass needle through thread.

over beeswax to help prevent the thread from kinking. The signatures are put in the frame one at a time, and each one is sewn into place over the tapes. After the third and every succeeding signature, the *kettle stitch* (see below) is made.

Keep the thread at an even, firm tension throughout the sewing. To prevent tearing, draw the thread parallel to the back fold of the paper, rather than perpendicular to it. Press each sewn signature with the bone folder to keep the swell caused by sewing to a minimum. When you run out of

thread, knot on more so that the knot falls inside the fold of the signature.

Tipping-in, rounding, backing. When the sewing is complete, the book is cut from the frame. Endpapers are then attached to the first and last signatures of the book. This is done by applying a narrow strip of library paste near the fold of each endpaper and pressing it to the signature. This process is called *tipping-in,* and it is shown in Step 12 on page 445. If the edges of the book pages are uneven, they can be trimmed at this point. The final smoothing can be done later with sandpaper.

After the spine has been glued, it is knocked with a hammer to give it its traditional rounded shape. This use of the hammer is called *rounding.* In a process known as *backing* the rounded spine is then knocked outward to further distribute the swell caused by sewing and to make ridges that will form the hinges with the cover boards.

After smoothing the edges of the pages with sandpaper, you may want to paint the head and tail edges with watercolor and polish them with wax. You also have the option of applying headbands, as seen in Step 18 on page 446.

Finally, the super and a strip of kraft paper are glued on to support the spine and to prepare the book for its cover.

Making a kettle stitch

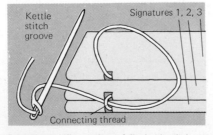
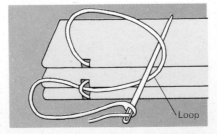

Bring the needle out through the kettle stitch groove of the third signature and draw it under the thread that connects the first two signatures, as seen at left. Pass the needle through the loop, as seen at right. When pulled tight, this forms the kettle stitch. Push the needle in the adjacent kettle stitch groove of the fourth signature and continue sewing.

1. Divide the sheets of paper into groups of four for signatures. Fold each signature with the bone folder. All the signatures, when compressed in a stack, should not be much more than 1 in. thick.

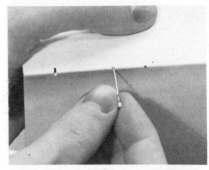

6. Before you sew each signature, hold the signature open and push a pin through the pencil marks made in the previous step. This will make the sewing much quicker and easier.

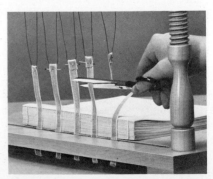

11. Cut the thread close to the last kettle stitch. Also cut off the tail of thread from the first signature. Cut the tapes 2 in. above the top signature and remove the book from the frame.

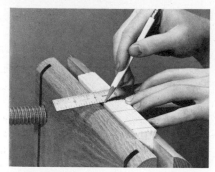

2. For placement of the tapes, clamp signatures firmly in the press and draw pencil lines at equal intervals on the spine. Also draw lines 1/2 in. from each end of the spine.

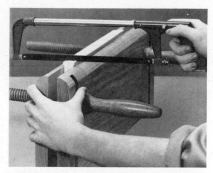

3. With a hacksaw carefully cut the two lines drawn 1/2 in. from the ends to a depth of 1/16 in. These are for the kettle stitches, the stitches that connect the signatures to each other.

4. Place signatures on sewing frame. Suspend tapes from crosspiece with string, as shown, to save tape. Center tapes on lines drawn in Step 2. Tack tapes to base of frame leaving 2-in. tails.

5. Compress signatures and draw lines next to both sides of each tape on folded edge of each signature. Lines mark points where thread will be stitched through signatures.

7. Place the first signature on the frame. Hold the signature open and push the threaded needle through the right kettle stitch groove. Leave a 2-in. tail of thread outside the signature.

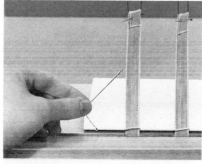

8. To sew, bring needle out through pinhole on right side of tape and back in on left side; then go behind the fold to the next tape. Sew across tapes and come out left kettle stitch groove, as shown.

9. Add next signature; insert needle through left kettle stitch groove. Sew in and out, across tapes; come out right kettle stitch groove, as shown. Tie knot with tail of thread left in Step 7.

10. Sew third signature and make kettle stitch (see diagram, p. 444). Make it after every subsequent signature. Sew remaining signatures and make two kettle stitches at end of last one.

12. Fold two sheets to serve as endpapers for top and bottom signatures. Brush library paste on 1/8-in. strip along fold of each sheet, masking with wax paper. Smooth endpapers down.

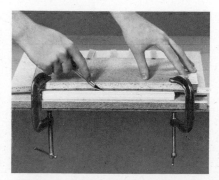

13. To trim page edges even, clamp steel ruler on signatures 1/8 in. inside edge of shortest page. Draw sharp knife or razor blade over book lightly, cutting one or two pages at a time.

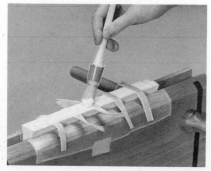

14. Screw signatures lightly into the press. Brush a thin but thorough layer of PVA glue onto spine and work it into the crevices between signatures. Take book out of press when glue starts to set.

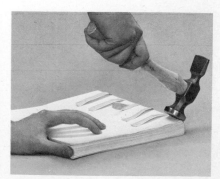

15. To round the book, lay it on a flat surface. Push on fore edge of signatures while hammering gently on spine. Turn book over and repeat. Eventual result should be a gentle, even arc.

Bookbinding

Preparing signatures for the cover *(continued)*

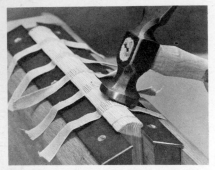

16. To back the book, place it between backing boards so that 1/4 in. of the spine is above the boards; lock tightly into press. Knock signatures outward with light glancing blows to form ridges.

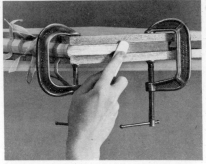

17. To tint page edges, clamp the book between two boards. Brush on a light layer of watercolor and let it dry. Rub on beeswax, then burnish with bone folder to polish and remove excess wax.

18. Cut headband a bit wider than spine. Apply PVA glue to spine and lay down headband, with ornamented side inward. When dry, cut edges of headband flush with edges of spine.

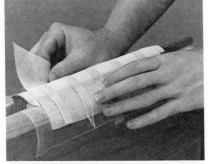

19. Cut super so it is 1 in. shorter than spine and wide enough to extend across spine and project 2 in. on either side. Apply PVA glue to spine, lay down super; rub with bone folder.

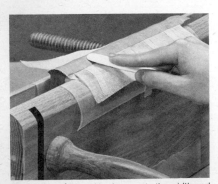

20. Cut two pieces of kraft paper to the width and a little more than the length of the spine, with paper grain parallel to spine (see p. 444). Apply glue to spine; lay down one strip and rub down.

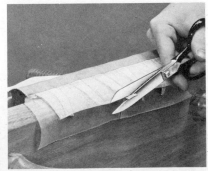

21. Cut the strip glued into place in Step 20 flush with the spine. Put the other strip aside. Cut the tapes flush with super. Leave the book in the press until the glue dries.

Sewing on cords

Signatures can be sewn over cords instead of tapes. Cords have two advantages over tapes. First, they can be laced directly into the cover boards, which gives the binder many options in choosing a cover and makes the super unnecessary. Second, the binder can choose among sinking the cords deeply into the signatures, sewing them flush with the spine, or allowing them to stand raised on the spine. Raised cords are the reason many leather-covered books have distinct ribs on the spine.

Because of their thickness, cords are a bit more difficult to work with than tapes. Follow the directions for sewing shown in the preceding section, with the following difference: cut grooves on the spine to hold three to five or more cords, depending on the length of the spine. Cords sewn into grooves are easier to work with than raised cords.

During the sewing (see below) the thread encircles each cord, rather than just crossing over it, as with tapes. It is important to keep tension in the thread between stitches, since it is impossible to take up any slack after a cord has been stitched. After the book has been sewn, it is endpapered, trimmed, glued, rounded, backed, painted, waxed, and headbanded as shown in previous pages.

Make lines for grooves so they evenly divide signatures along spine. Cut grooves deep enough so cords will lie flush. Also cut grooves 1/2 in. from each end for kettle stitches.

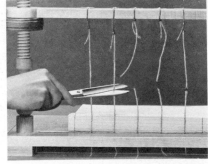

Line up the cords on the frame so that they fit into the grooves. Leave a 2-in. tail on the bottom of each cord. After finishing sewing (see below) cut the cord 2 in. above top signature.

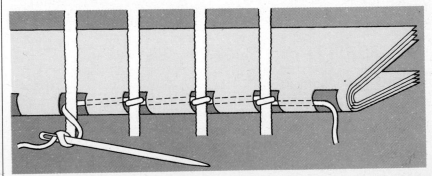

Bring the needle through the right kettle stitch groove of the first signature. Draw the needle out on the left side of first cord and then come back across the cord; push the needle back in on the right side of the cord. Continue behind the fold to the next cord. Stitch each cord to the signatures in this way. Make kettle stitches as in a book sewn on tapes (see diagram, p. 444).

Attaching a cloth or paper cover to a book sewn on tapes

The illustrations on this page show how a book sewn on tapes is covered with paper or cloth by a process called *case binding*. Using leather to cover a book sewn on cords is illustrated on pages 448 and 449.

There is one major difference between the two techniques illustrated, aside from the difference in materials: in case binding (below) the boards are first glued to the cover, and the cover is then attached to the book; in the other type of binding (see pp. 448–449) the cords are sewn directly into the boards before the cover is attached. A book sewn on tapes can have a leather cover, but the boards must be attached to the book before the leather is put on. Though it is not shown here, this can be done using the *split-board* technique, in which the super is glued between a pair of thin boards for each cover.

Case binding offers the creative binder a vehicle for all sorts of improvisation. Many kinds of cloth and thick paper can be used. Different materials can be mixed; for example, decorative paper can be pasted over the outer three-quarters of the front and back covers, leaving a contrasting cover cloth showing around the spine.

To start your case binding, cut the cover boards (see illustrations, p. 442; *Tools and materials*, p. 443). When they lie against the backing ridge on the spine (see Step 16, p. 446), the boards should extend 1/8 inch over the other three edges. Trace the book, with the boards temporarily in place, on the cover material. Roll the book over, being careful not to move the spine, and trace the other side. Cut the cover material 3/4 inch outside this line all around.

1. After cutting cover material (see text, above), spread PVA adhesive over entire inside from a spot near middle. Move cover to a clean surface.

2. Hold cover boards on book (they should overhang on three sides by 1/8 in.). Lay book on glued cover 3/4 in. from each edge.

3. Cut second kraft strip (see Step 20, p. 446) to length of the boards. Lay it on the cover so its edge touches the edge of the spine.

4. Draw the covering material tightly around the back of the book and lay it on the top cover board. Smooth the cover with your hands.

5. Pull cover back. The boards will adhere to the cover. Make an identifying mark on the front board and its facing endpaper. Put book aside.

6. Carefully cut each corner of the cover at a 45° angle. Leave about 3/16 in. of material between the cut edge and each corner of the boards.

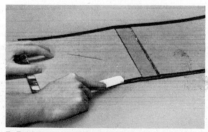

7. Fold the material over the boards on the head and tail edges, and smooth it down with the bone folder. Wipe away any excess glue.

8. As you fold the material over the fore edges, tuck in the excess left at the corners. Smooth edges with the bone folder.

9. Turn the cover over and rub the face side with the bone folder through a piece of paper. Accentuate the hinges, as shown.

10. Place the book inside the case to check the fit. Then remove the book and lay the cover flat, under a weight, until the glue dries.

11. To attach cover to book, glue tapes, super, and outside of front endpaper. Protect flyleaf with wax paper. Close cover firmly. Repeat on back.

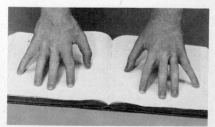

12. After pressing glued book overnight with its spine protruding, open it carefully—a few pages at a time from the outside in.

Bookbinding

Attaching a leather cover to a book sewn on cords

A leather cover's construction is a demanding task. Cut the cover boards (see illustrations, p. 442; *Tools and materials,* p. 443) so that they extend 1/8 inch over the other three edges when they are flush with the ridges of the spine (see Step 16, p. 446). First the cords are laced into the cover boards and glued; then the tube (see illustra-tions, p. 442) is made and attached.

After the leather is cut, its margins are skived, or shaved down on the wrong side. When the skiving is done, the leather cover is pasted to the book with library paste. After the cover is trimmed, you have the option of either using the endpapers already attached to the signatures or tearing them out and putting in new decorative ones. The book is then put in the press until it is completely dry.

Adhesive-backed gold leaf or gold vinyl letters, available from art supply stores, can be applied to the leather cover. The cover can also be given its title or decoration by hand tooling (see *Leatherworking,* pp. 14–27).

Putting on the covers

1. Trace the full outline for the book's cover on the wrong side of the leather, rolling the book over on its spine to do so. Draw lines 3/4 in. outside tracing; cut the leather along these lines.

Attaching the cover boards

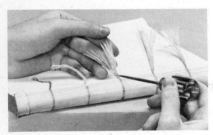

1. Remove any glue that seeped onto the cords of your freshly sewn signatures (see pp. 444–446). Unwind and fray each cord until it is limp.

2. With cover boards in place against spine ridge, overlapping other edges by 1/8 in., mark position of each cord on boards.

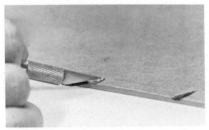

3. Cut a V-shaped groove at each mark made in Step 2; grooves are 1/2 in. long and about 1/16 in. deep. Be careful not to cut through board.

4. Place the spine of the book carefully on the pasted leather. Pull one side of the leather up gently and smooth it to the board with your hand. Repeat with the other half of the cover.

4. Punch a hole at the apex of each groove with the awl. Do not remove the material that is pushed out on the other side of the board.

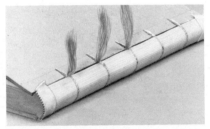

5. The grooved side of the board is the outside. Thread the cords through the holes and to the inside of the boards as seen at top right of photo.

6. Brush PVA glue over the cords. Hammer board to close holes and flatten cords. Put wax paper inside boards, close book, and let glue dry.

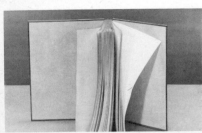

7. Paste a piece of paper inside each board, leaving a 1/8-in. border all around. This will help prevent the boards from warping later on.

8. Cut a slot 1/16 in. wide and 5/8 in. long at the head and tail of each board. Here, a piece of a tin can protects the signatures from the knife.

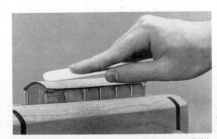

9. Mark dimensions of spine on kraft paper. Fold, cut, and glue to make tube (see illustrations, p. 442). Glue tube to spine and rub down.

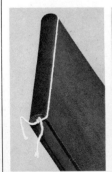

7. Tie string tightly around book in hinge groove. Work head and tail of spine into a pleasing shape. With wax paper inside boards, put book, up to and including string, into press overnight.

2. Use the skiving knife to pare down leather out from and including the tracing line, so that the edges will fold over easily. Pare two extra-thin semicircles, for head and tail of spine.

3. Wet the right side of the leather thoroughly. Brush a layer of library paste onto the wrong side. Wait 5 min and brush on another layer. Put the leather on a clean surface.

5. Work the leather under the spine and through the slots made in the boards in Step 8 on page 448. Use the bone folder to flatten the folded leather so it does not make a ridge on the spine.

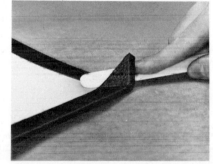

6. Turn the leather over the boards and smooth with the bone folder. Bring each corner to a 45° angle and cut the leather 1/4 in. above the board. Fold the fore edge over the top edge.

8. On the inside of each board, find the narrowest point of turned-over leather; cut all the leather to this width. Cut a piece of thin cardboard to fit the space exactly and paste it in.

9. If you prefer, tear out the endpapers and tip in decorative replacements. Apply paste and work new sheets in. Trim endpapers even. Paste down; rub with bone folder through scrap paper.

Preparing a book for rebinding

There are generally two reasons to rebind a book: either because it is worn and requires rebinding, or because you wish to give it a more distinguished cover. If you are considering rebinding a book, there are several judgments you should make first: Is the book worth the time and effort? Can a few minor repairs suffice and make rebinding unnecessary? Is it too valuable to risk rebinding it yourself?

The process of rebinding is very similar to the process of binding. Once the extent of disrepair is determined, the book can be broken down as far as necessary; then it can be bound as if it were new, following the steps illustrated in the preceding pages.

If a cover is loose, it can often be repaired without being removed. Pull the covers straight back and apply PVA glue to the inside of the cover hinges. Should you decide to remove the cover, refer to the top diagram below. If the sewing is in good shape, don't disturb the signatures; simply put on a new cover.

There is a type of binding, called a *perfect binding,* in which the pages are held together by glue at the spine; there are no sheets, signatures, or sewing. Most paperbacks and some modern hardcovers are bound this way. If your book is perfect bound, you can put on a new cover, but you cannot redo the binding of the pages.

If your book is sewn and the sewing is in disrepair, the book should be resewn. Take the signatures apart, referring to the middle diagram below. Pile the signatures in groups of four and gently hammer out the backing ridges. If any pages are damaged in the fold, put on a reinforcement, as shown in the bottom diagram. Use discretion—too many reinforcements will swell the signatures and make them all the more difficult to bind.

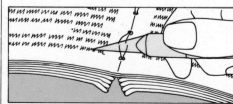

To remove an old cover, pull the cover board back. With a utility knife, cut through the endpaper, the super, and the tapes, if there are any.

To separate signatures, first remove the tube or kraft strip and glue from the spine. Cut threads with utility knife and pull signatures out one at a time.

To reinforce damaged sheets before resewing signatures, cut strip of tissue or onionskin paper, grain parallel to sheet. Paste in; put under weight.

Index

XYZ

Photo Credits

Special Credits

Metric Conversion Tables

Metrication in Canada is in a state of flux: some industries have "gone metric," others will do so in a few years. The projects in *Crafts & Hobbies* draw from a variety of industries. Although most of the materials mentioned will be available in imperial measure (inches, pounds, gallons, etc.) for the foreseeable future, it is wise to become familiar now with metric equivalents.

The following tables have been prepared with this in mind. Use them where you require metric conversions—but remember that metric sizes are not always *direct* counterparts of imperial measurements. When in doubt, determine the nearest equivalent and consult your local crafts shop or supplier. Where possible, avoid mixing the two systems—work either in metric or in imperial.

TEMPERATURE

Celsius	−30	−20	−10	0	10	20	30	40	50	60	70	80	90	100
Fahrenheit	−22	−4	14	32	50	68	86	104	122	140	158	176	194	212

To convert Celsius to Fahrenheit, multiply the °C reading by 9/5 and add 32. To convert Fahrenheit to Celsius, subtract 32 from the °F reading and multiply the result by 5/9.

LINEAR MEASURE

in. (64ths)	cm	in. (64ths)	cm
1	0.04	33	1.31
2	0.08	34	1.35
3	0.12	35	1.39
4	0.16	36	1.43
5	0.20	37	1.47
6	0.24	38	1.51
7	0.28	39	1.55
8 (1/8")	0.32	40 (5/8")	1.59
9	0.36	41	1.63
10	0.40	42	1.67
11	0.44	43	1.71
12	0.48	44	1.75
13	0.52	45	1.79
14	0.56	46	1.83
15	0.60	47	1.87
16 (1/4")	0.64	48 (3/4")	1.91
17	0.67	49	1.95
18	0.71	50	1.98
19	0.75	51	2.02
20	0.79	52	2.06
21	0.83	53	2.10
22	0.87	54	2.14
23	0.91	55	2.18
24 (3/8")	0.95	56 (7/8")	2.22
25	0.99	57	2.26
26	1.03	58	2.30
27	1.07	59	2.34
28	1.11	60	2.38
29	1.15	61	2.42
30	1.19	62	2.46
31	1.23	63	2.50
32 (1/2")	1.27	64 (1")	2.54

AREA

sq in.	cm²	sq ft	m²
1	6.45	1	0.09
2	12.90	2	0.19
3	19.35	3	0.28
4	25.81	4	0.37
5	32.26	5	0.46
		9 (1 sq. yd.)	0.84

WEIGHT

ounces	grams	pounds	kilograms
1	28.35	1	0.45
2	56.70	2	0.91
3	85.05	3	1.36
4	113.40	4	1.81
5	141.75	5	2.27
6	170.10	6	2.72
7	198.45	7	3.18
8	226.80	8	3.63
9	255.15	9	4.08
10	283.50	10	4.54
11	311.84	15	6.80
12	340.19	20	9.07
13	368.54	25	11.30
14	396.89	30	13.60
15	425.24	50	22.70
16 (1 lb.)	453.59		

VOLUME (Liquids)

pints	litres	gallons	litres
1	0.57	1	4.55
2 (1 quart)	1.14	2	9.09
3	1.70	3	13.64
4	2.27	4	18.18
5	2.84	5	22.73
6	3.41	6	27.28
7	3.98	7	31.32
8 (1 gallon)	4.55	8	36.37

Units used in recipes are translated into metric as follows:

1 cup	125 ml	½ teaspoon	2 ml
1 tablespoon	15 ml	¼ teaspoon	1 ml
1 teaspoon	5 ml		

MULTIPLES

prefix	means
mega	one million times
kilo	one thousand times
hecto	one hundred times
deca	ten times

DIVISIONS

prefix	means
deci	one-tenth
centi	one-hundredth
milli	one-thousandth
micro	one-millionth

When buying lumber, look at these figures:

inches*	millimetres	inches*	millimetres
1 x 2	19 x 38	2 x 6	38 x 140
1 x 3	19 x 64	2 x 8	38 x 184
1 x 4	19 x 89	2 x 10	38 x 235
1 x 5	19 x 114	2 x 12	38 x 286
1 x 6	19 x 140		
1 x 8	19 x 184	3 x 4	64 x 89
1 x 10	19 x 235	4 x 4	89 x 89
1 x 12	19 x 286	4 x 6	89 x 140
2 x 2	38 x 38		
2 x 3	38 x 64	6 x 6	140 x 140
2 x 4	38 x 89	8 x 8	191 x 191

*Keep in mind that these measurements are commercially standardized. Actual dimensions are slightly smaller.

For hardboard, use this:

feet	millimetres*	feet	millimetres*
4	1,200	10	3,000
8	2,400	12	3,600

*Keep in mind that these measurements are commercially standardized. Actual dimensions are slightly bigger.

Plywood thicknesses:

Sanded hardwood. Available in 3-, 4-, 5-, 6-, 7-, 8-, 9-, and 10-mm sizes.*

Sanded softwood. Available in 6-, 8-, 11-, 14-, 17-, and 19-mm sizes.*

*These are not direct equivalents of imperial thicknesses but new sizes created by the industry.

Unsanded softwood.

inches	millimetres**	inches	millimetres**
¼	6	½	12.5
5/16	7.5	¾	18.5
3/8	9.5		

**These measurements are commercial equivalents, not exact conversions.